T0114057

POLICING THE WOMB

Policing the Womb brings to life the chilling ways in which women have become the targets of secretive state surveillance of their pregnancies. Michele Goodwin expands the reproductive health and rights debate beyond abortion to include how legislators increasingly turn to criminalizing women for miscarriages, stillbirths, and threatening the health of their pregnancies. The horrific results include women giving birth while shackled in leg irons, in solitary confinement, and even delivering in prison toilets. In some states, pregnancy has become a bargaining chip, with prosecutors offering reduced sentences in exchange for women agreeing to be sterilized. The author shows how prosecutors may abuse laws and infringe women's rights in the process, sometimes with the complicity of medical providers who disclose private patient information to law enforcement. Often the women most affected are poor and of color. Goodwin warns, however, poor women are simply the canaries in the coal mine, as some legislators now claim that women's constitutional rights equal those of embryos and fetuses. In this timely book, Michele Goodwin brings to light how the unrestrained efforts to punish and police women's reproduction has led to the United States being the deadliest country in the developed world for pregnant women.

Michele Goodwin is an Executive Committee member of the American Civil Liberties Union and elected member of the American Law Institute. She is also a Chancellor's Professor at the University of California, Irvine, where she teaches torts, constitutional law, and directs the Center for Biotechnology and Global Health Policy. She is an internationally recognized voice on women's rights, reproductive health, health policy, and constitutional law and lectures worldwide on matters relating to the exploitation of women and girls and the rising regulation of pregnancy and criminalization of women.

Policing the Womb

INVISIBLE WOMEN AND THE CRIMINALIZATION OF MOTHERHOOD

MICHELE GOODWIN

University of California, Irvine

CAMBRIDGE
UNIVERSITY PRESS

CAMBRIDGE
UNIVERSITY PRESS

University Printing House, Cambridge CB2 8BS, United Kingdom

One Liberty Plaza, 20th Floor, New York, NY 10006, USA

477 Williamstown Road, Port Melbourne, VIC 3207, Australia

314-321, 3rd Floor, Plot 3, Splendor Forum, Jasola District Centre, New Delhi - 110025, India

103 Penang Road, #05-06/07, Visioncrest Commercial, Singapore 238467

Cambridge University Press is part of the University of Cambridge.

It furthers the University's mission by disseminating knowledge in the pursuit of
education, learning and research at the highest international levels of excellence.

www.cambridge.org
Information on this title: www.cambridge.org/9781108747592
DOI: 10.1017/9781139343244

© Michele Goodwin 2020

First published 2020
First paperback edition 2022

A catalogue record for this publication is available from the British Library

ISBN 978-1-107-03017-6 Hardback
ISBN 978-1-108-74759-2 Paperback

For the Triplets and the Nieces

Contents

Preface

Making child abuse laws applicable to pregnant women and fetuses would, by definition, make every woman who is low-income, uninsured, has health problems, and/or is battered who becomes pregnant a felony child abuser.

National Advocates for Pregnant Women[1]

In the twenty-first century reproduction translates differently across class and race lines. On inspection, examples abound in this context, but assisted reproductive technology (ART) provides a particularly provocative illustration of my point. In that sphere, liberty and risk translate into a multi-billion-dollar industry, where a woman's reproductive possibilities resemble a candy store of options: freedom to purchase ova and sperm in her local community or across the country and world, in vitro fertilization, preimplantation genetic diagnosis, intracytoplasmic sperm injection (ICSI) of ova, embryo grading, cryopreservation of ova, assisted hatching, embryo transfer, day-five blast transfers, and more. This dizzying array of options is mostly unchecked by federal and state regulations, leaving physicians and their wealthier patients to coordinate pregnancies according to personal choices.

Technology facilitates a degree of leisure associated with some of these practices, as a few options described above are easily coordinated from the comfort and privacy of home. Functionally, then, with the click of a computer button, an intended parent may purchase sperm, rent a womb, buy ova, and select a clinic to assist in the harvesting, implantation, or embryo development processes. For wealthy women (infertile or not), reproductive privacy and freedom are tangible concepts in uninterrupted operation. Noticeably, there is little, if any, state regulation or interference in this domain, despite considerable risks, poor health outcomes, and miscarriages associated with some of these medicines.

By contrast, recent criminal prosecutions targeting destitute pregnant women illuminate another reproductive space, where the threat of state intervention through punishment and extralegal retribution overarch pregnancies and compromise the physician-patient relationship. In this alternate reproductive realm, public regulation trumps expectations of privacy. Undeniably, in the United States a poor pregnant woman's reproductive options are deeply constrained and contested. For example, a woman's poverty and drug dependence or use during pregnancy might result in heightened legal consequences, including the threat of life imprisonment, birthing while in jail, and even shackling during labor, depending on the state in which the pregnant woman resides.

A poor woman determined to carry a pregnancy to term often unwittingly exposes herself to nefarious interagency collaborations between police and physicians, quite possibly leading to criminal prosecution, incarceration, and giving birth while in highly unsanitary prison conditions, sometimes without the appropriate aid of hospital physicians and staff. But make no mistake, all women should be wary of the political mobilization against reproductive health, rights, and justice.

Today, it is not uncommon for a headline to feature a tragic story about a woman giving birth alone in a jail, without the aid of anyone, let alone medical staff. This is what happened to Diana Sanchez as she screamed and "writhed on the small bed inside her cell . . . gripping the thin mattress with one hand," as she tried frantically to free a leg as the baby was crowning. A *Washington Post* headline captured her experience this way: *"Nobody Cared": A Woman Gave Birth Alone in a Jail Cell After Her Cries for Help Were Ignored, Lawsuit Says.*

Sadly, these are not outlier incidents, but rather what has bled into the soil of reproductive politics in the United States, which now uses pregnancy as a proxy for punishment, particularly against poor women. The depth of state-sanctioned cruelty targeted toward poor pregnant women seemingly has no boundaries in contemporary American politics. Gone are the days when Prescott Bush, the father of George H.W. Bush, served as treasurer of Planned Parenthood or Richard Nixon signed Title X into law, which provided reproductive healthcare for the poorest Americans.

A range of laws now police and criminalize behavior during pregnancy. These include fetal protection laws (FPLs); laws that criminalize illicit drug use during pregnancy – fetal drug laws (FDLs); child abuse laws pertaining to fetuses – maternal conduct laws (MCLs), which seek to criminalize otherwise legal conduct that may cause risk to pregnancies, including cigarette smoking, alcohol consumption, falling down steps, and refusing bed rest. The emergence of such legislation offers an important opportunity to present a counternarrative to the provocative accounts offered by legislators advocating the use of "sticks" to discourage certain prenatal conduct.

Importantly, as this book shows, what legislators seek to reduce – the incidence of babies born with low birth weight in their states – is tangled in race and class profiling, which detracts from an evidence-based approach to reducing fetal health harm. On inspection, prescription drug use, domestic violence, and assisted reproductive technology measure significantly (and more so) in the incidence of fetal health harm and the rise in neonatology treatments and costs. Building on prior work, this book deliberates on an important social policy matter – the policing of women's reproductive conduct and the absurdity of lawmaking in this regard. The book weighs the social, economic, and health costs associated with punitive state policies that effectively harm all pregnant women and their interests.

This book tells a public policy story by elevating the narratives and experiences of pregnant women and girls, investigating how the state tracks pregnant women, and reporting the consequences of punitive state actions. It exposes the irrationality of laws that suppress sex education, force brain-dead pregnant women to gestate fetuses while their bodies rot and decompose, and threaten pregnant women with life imprisonment for endangering their fetuses. It reflects on the history of pernicious state legislating of women's reproductive rights dating back to eugenics and slavery.

The book comes about because rarely are the voices of those caught under the state's gaze afforded a legal venue. Legal casebooks carefully edit out what facts may be available to the authors, and because appellate decisions focus on the legal questions, students, scholars, and those who read legal cases and legal scholarship bypass the personal accounts that humanize litigants, victims, or defendants. As described in this book, an emerging jurisprudence stands replete with instances of women giving birth in handcuffs and shackles, on metal prison benches, and being dragged away from hospitals in bloodied gowns. Yet, their chilling experiences rarely become an elemental or integral component of legal reflection.

The origins of this book emerged as I studied assisted reproductive technology. The glaringly high failure rates often resulted in miscarriages and stillbirths after Herculean efforts by some couples and individuals to become pregnant, often involving hyperstimulation of ovaries, drug injections, and repeated cycles of this. Yet, the failures resulted in enormous personal losses and tragedies for the individuals and their seeking to conceive. The public responses were nearly universal with sympathy and support. When such tragic cases made the news, financial support and prayers often followed.

With success rates hovering at only 35 percent in the best cases, inevitably the practice is something of a lottery, which is why, prior to Nadia Suleman's birth of eight babies, doctors often implanted multiple embryos in the intended mother or surrogate, trying to game the odds of a pregnancy resulting. When the cycles failed, or miscarriage resulted, criminal punishment was surely not the answer.

However, the media and legal responses were startlingly different for poor women struggling through their pregnancies. Early on, I began to notice arrests and the promulgation of laws that, when enforced, targeted poor, pregnant Black women. Even then, I thought these women would ultimately become the euphemistic canaries in the coalmine. At the time, they were condemned as pariahs in their states – girls like Rennie Gibbs, at sixteen years old charged by a Mississippi prosecutor with depraved heart murder for having a stillbirth; or Regina McKnight, a South Carolinian woman, who at twenty-three years old was criminally charged for her stillbirth and was sentenced to twenty years in prison. This book unpacks these stories and more, examining the long arc of women's efforts to achieve reproductive justice.

The journey to tell this story has been long and winding. In 2000, I began conceptualizing the ideas in this book, but anticipated that someone else would write it. A few years before, I read Professor Dorothy Roberts' *Killing the Black Body* with great enthusiasm, shortly after its publication. Groundbreaking in its depth and scope, it affirmed the experiences of so many Black women and told the story that needed airing about systemic harms to Black women's bodies from slavery through the last century. Her work remains deeply influential for me. Dorothy's work was an invitation to consider exploring the meaning of liberty in the reproductive context that included women of color generally, and Black women specifically. I took that invitation to extend to matters of assisted reproduction and emerging strategies deployed in the service of policing women's bodies.

In part, the journey of writing this book is the story of the book. The more one looked, the more there was to find – harmful laws restricting women's reproductive health rights, criminalization and arrests of poor women, absurd state interventions in women's reproductive lives – and the graver became the consequences of the failed drug war and its sticky tentacles. The drug war reached into the lives of poor women, making collateral damage of them and their children. However, too frequently, their arrests were rendered invisible while activists and politicians skeptical about the drug war focused on justice for male, nonviolent drug offenders. For me, steeped in this research for nearly two decades, the more obvious was the impending opioid crisis, but also the resistance of legal scholars to credit that the struggles of poor Black women during pregnancy could one day be reflected in white women's addictions to prescribed opioids.

This research involved extensive interviewing, visiting women's prisons and girls' juvenile detention centers, and compiling a data set of legal cases and prosecutions from many primary sources. I reviewed pleadings and briefs and interviewed attorneys involved in these cases, including state prosecutors and lawyers who represent these women. My research also involved participant observation. I served as an expert witness in Bei Bei Shuai's case, conceptualized and chaired Amnesty International's first engagement with this issue (Taskforce on Criminalizing Pregnancy, which gave rise to the 2017 Criminalizing Pregnancy Report), consulted with the Obama White House on the criminalization of women, and joined the boards of organizations focusing on women's incarceration, reproductive rights, and civil liberties. In these various roles, my research benefited from being at the center of articulating policies and interventions. My aim is to humanize the women who are the subjects of these cases and prosecutions so as to illuminate what is at stake when state power is used against them.

Acknowledgments

I am grateful to John Berger, my editor at Cambridge University Press and friend. He saw the value in this project many years ago and waited patiently for the story to emerge in this form. This book is among the final manuscripts that John will shepherd through Cambridge University Press. For so many of his authors, John has provided a platform for us to engage and enlighten, to broaden perspectives and revisit our own preconceptions, and meaningfully contribute to discourse. I am proud of the work we have done together and thankful for our friendship.

One of the most meaningful aspects of being a professor is teaching and working with outstanding law students. I have been fortunate to teach, mentor, and work with dynamic women and men who served as my research assistants at different points along this journey. They are familiar with my encouragement – *"blossom where you are planted."* This book and many articles represent the evolution from seeds planted over the years, and I am thankful to them for sowing and tilling with me. I am grateful for the excellent research assistance provided by students who cared deeply about my work and the future of reproductive health, rights, and justice. Those who contributed in some part to this research include John Roberts, Ana Bosch, Cathy Sons, Joni Holder, Stephanie Jean-Jacques, Sarah Malkerson, Nicole Elasser, Oleg Shik, Robert Crist, Shiveta Vaid, Meigan Thompson, Haley Penan, Mariah Lindsay, Sabrina Ly, and Allison Whelan. This work was further aided by Garret Stallins, whose sharp eye is deeply appreciated.

My gratitude also extends to law librarians at the University of Minnesota Law School, the University of Virginia Law School, and the University of California, Irvine School of Law. With them, I was able to access obscure archives – including treatises from the 1600s that demarcated women as property or that clarified the historical status of the fetus – and obtain police records, mug shots, sentencing briefs, and more.

This book gained further context through conversations and interviews with lawyers, judges, nurses, doctors, researchers, activists, prosecutors, women and girls impacted by state prosecutions, and families affected by maternal deaths, as well as colleagues who take a different view than I do. Among the many, I am thankful to retired Chief Judge Pamela Alexander; Sue Ellen Allen, Founder and Executive Director of Reinventing ReEntry; Jack Cole, Cofounder and former Executive Director of Law Enforcement Against Prohibition; Dr. Claire Coles, Professor and Director of the Maternal Substance Abuse and Child Development Program at Emory University; Carol Gilligan, University Professor at New York University; retired Chief Judge Glenda Hatchett; Dr. Hallum Hurt, Medical Director of the Neonatal Follow-up Program and Attending Neonatologist at CHOP Newborn Care at the Hospital of the University of Pennsylvania; Charles Johnson, Founder of 4Kira4Mom, an organization founded in the wake of his wife's death shortly after she gave birth; Louise Melling, Deputy Legal Director and Director of the Center for Liberty at the American Civil Liberties Union (ACLU); Aryeh Neier, President Emeritus of the Open Society Foundations and former Director of the ACLU; Professor David Orentlicher, former Director of the American Medical Association's Division of Medical Ethics and drafter of the AMA's first patients' bill of rights; Lynn Paltrow, Executive Director of National Advocates for Pregnant Women; Linda Pence, who courageously defended Bei Bei Shuai; Anthony Romero, Executive Director of the ACLU; and Loretta Ross, Cofounder and former National Coordinator of SisterSong Women of Color Reproductive Justice Collective.

Filmmakers also offered the means to further express the urgency behind this book. Among them, I am grateful for the collaborations with Rebecca Haimowitz, Marion Lipschutz, Rose Rosenblatt, and Civia Tamarkin.

This book tells a story about the ways in which law enforcement intervene in pregnant women's lives. Interviews with prosecutors, especially in Alabama, including Lyn Head, Kyle Brown, Angela Hulsey, and Steve Marshall, current Attorney General of the state of Alabama, were essential to helping me understand their motivations, the manner in which they interpret law, and even how prosecutors' personal and even religious beliefs sometimes spill over into their work for the state. My research gained further clarity and urgency based on my interviews with them. I provide a special salute to my colleagues within the ACLU, an organization committed to protecting the civil liberties of the marginalized and disenfranchised, including for many women who recognized the organization as their only point of hope.

Finally, my deep appreciation and special recognition go to the organizations that have long recognized the human dignity of the most vulnerable women and advocate on their collective behalf.

To the Triplets and Nieces. May you be able to shape your own paths and destinies.

1

Introduction

This is not a work of fiction, although I wish it were. Some of the cases described here could recall the imagery evoked by Mary Shelly, author of *Frankenstein; or, The Modern Prometheus*, who tells a horror story about a young rogue scientist who creates an unsightly monster through clandestine, aberrant experimentation. Although Frankenstein is the name of the monster's creator, Dr. Victor Frankenstein, readers would be forgiven for debating who the real monster happens to be. In *Policing the Womb*, the story of Marlise Muñoz comes to mind – brain-dead, decomposing in a Texas hospital, forced by state legislation to gestate a barely developing fetus while her body decays and the anomalies in the fetus mount. Eventually, it is reported that the fetus is hydrocephalic, which means severe brain damage in this case and water or fluid developing on its brain. Medical reports also show that the fetus is not developing its lower extremities. The state knows brain death is irreversible.

The hospital forces Marlise's dead body to shake, placing it on a bed that constantly, violently moves, which makes the dead woman's eyes flap open and shut. Likely frightening to some hospital staff, they decide to tape Marlise's eyes shut. Even if Marlise could see anything, which is unlikely, because she is dead, now no one needs to look into her eyes to search for any signs of life. If the state believes, despite well-accepted medical science, that she is alive, it has now taken away her sight and forced her into a state of blindness, while her body is poked and prodded. Marlise's shaking corpse stays hydrated through tubes that bring fluids into the body. Somehow, the hospital finds a way to pipe away the waste. Everyone – including even the state – agrees that really she is an incubator. This is why the Texas law exists.

This is not the novel *The Handmaid's Tale*, a dystopian opus written by Margaret Atwood, made exceedingly relevant today. The shaking bed is not in the totalitarian fictional state of Gilead. No, this is Texas. This is why the state forces machines to be attached to Marlise's body – to keep her organs functioning until they give out. The machines are not keeping her alive; they are simply keeping her organs viable. This is why the hospital cleaves into her body with slicing, lacerating, and stitching tools, tapes her eyes shut, pumps her with fluids, and then drains other liquids from what remains of her. Her decaying has nothing to do with senescence or aging. Rather, it is the typical decomposition characteristic of brain-death cases.

Hoses, pipes, and cylinders serve as the conduits between the state and Marlise's decaying body. This is known as mechanical support. The hospital cuts a hole into Marlise's neck to create an opening in the trachea. She will receive a tracheotomy. The widower, Erick, objects. This is a desecration of Marlise's body. The hospital must be used to ignoring Erick's objections. He said no and objected to the second resuscitation attempt; the hospital did it anyway. He sits there daily as her light brown skin transitions from supple to hard – like a mannequin, Marlise's father said. Her body loses muscle tone and begins to smell. Erick comments on the smell. That smell lingers. It is not the smell of Marlise's favorite perfume or flowers from the tidy hospital gift shop. No, the smell that fills the room and Erick's nostrils – and those of anyone who visits the room – is that of a rotting body.

No one, except perhaps the select group of antiabortion protesters outside, is confused about this: Marlise is dead. Outside, someone tells a filmmaker, Rebecca Haimowitz, just give Marlise a week. You'll see, he says. A week or two will turn this all around, he says. This particular protester, captured in Haimowitz's documentary *62 Days*, travels to cases like this. She told me he's like a professional at this. A thought comes to my mind – *Sleeping Beauty*, the 1959 animated musical produced by Walt Disney. It is based on the seventeenth-century French fairy tale *La belle au bois dormant*, by Charles Perrault. In the fairy tale, a beautiful princess is forced into hypnotic slumber; the spell she is under will only be broken by the magical kiss of the prince. The prince will awaken her.

However, Marlise's real-life prince, Erick, does not harness this magic. Or perhaps the state has dethroned Erick. But if that is the case, who is the new prince? The Texas legislature? In any case, Erick Muñoz lacks any special powers to rouse Marlise, despite what the protesters outside the hospital claim. In fact, Erick no longer has rights over his wife's body until the state is satisfied with Marlise's gestation and cuts open her body to remove the fetus. It turns out that marriage and the rights of next of kin mean very little when the state takes control of a pregnant woman's body in order to protect the fetus. The state refers to this as fetal protection. In this case, the state is protecting the fetus from Marlise's husband and her parents, who say let her rest in peace.

The hospital serves as a surrogate or agent of the state. This is not a role its staff have asked for, but some may fear the consequences if they do not follow the state's legislation. The medical staff know that she is dead, but they must follow the Texas law, which ignores death, do-not-resuscitate orders, medical directives, and living wills only if the patient is pregnant.

***

On Tuesday, November 8, 2016, Donald Trump secured the presidency of the United States. In a startling victory, Mr. Trump soundly defeated Secretary Hillary Clinton by securing the most Electoral College votes in that election, a feat accomplished in part by breaking through the so-called blue wall of the Upper Midwest, which consistently voted Democratic for decades. The political fabric that held the blue wall together proved too porous and fragile. It disintegrated in a tide of fear associated with the economy, immigration, and job loss.

As the blue wall dissolved, the vulnerability of reproductive rights in the United States became more glaringly apparent. As time would tell – but anyone paying close attention at the time could predict – a Trump administration would bring about a serious threat to the preservation of reproductive healthcare rights such as abortion and possibly contraceptive healthcare access. More optimistic views cautioned against such concerns. However, in light of Mr. Trump's campaign promises to fill the Supreme Court with justices committed to overturning *Roe v. Wade*, the decision upon which abortion rights are founded, the safeguarding of women's fundamental rights to reproductive autonomy and constitutional equality takes on new meaning and urgency. However, the President alone cannot end abortion rights; courts and legislatures matter too. That's why the Republican Party platform, which explicitly references opposition to abortion thirty-five times, should also cause concern. The tragic result of these strategic moves, as well as efforts at the state level to strip away reproductive health options, is not only to cripple access to safe, legal abortions but also to undermine women's constitutional rights and ultimately their basic health.

Prior to the 2016 presidential election, scholars imagined the possibility of a Hyde Amendment repeal. The fortieth anniversary of that law, which prohibited the use of federal dollars to terminate a pregnancy, coincided with the possible election of the first female President of the United States. Arguments that discriminatory distribution of government benefits produces coercive interference with the exercise of a fundamental right and that government cannot be discriminatory in how it distributes benefits were eager to be unpacked and remain so.

On deeper reflection, however, the fundamental threat to reproductive healthcare was already under way, even before Donald Trump's election and the elevation of two conservative, antiabortion judges to the Supreme Court, Justices Brett Kavanaugh and Neil Gorsuch. That is, the fundamental right to an abortion was already more illusory than real for poor women in light of robust antichoice legislating in the shadows of *Roe*. Financing abortion was only one significant obstacle in their way. Other barriers to reproductive rights that have emerged in recent years prove as intractable and cumbersome as the inability to finance an abortion. For example, the ability to carry a pregnancy to term without dying in the process or being arrested for "endangering" the fetus are shocking new norms. Fetal protection and personhood efforts are not only on the rise in the United States but, like prior "tough on crime" rhetoric, they serve as the bases on which to justify myriad unconstitutional and unethical interventions in women's lives.

In Utah, for example, Governor Gary Herbert recently signed into law the Criminal Homicide and Abortion Revisions Act,[1] which specifically applies to miscarriages and other fetal harms that result from "knowing acts" committed by women and girls. A prior version of the bill drafted by state representative Carl Wimmer (Utah) sought to authorize life imprisonment for pregnant women who, during pregnancy, engage in reckless behavior that could result in miscarriage and stillbirth. Representative Wimmer informed reporters that he was crafting similar "model legislation" for other states. Interestingly, Wimmer's original bill advanced through both the Utah Senate and House before the American Civil Liberties Union intervened and drew attention to the legislation and its consequences for girls and women in the state of Utah. Could a woman's unhealthy eating habits be considered reckless during pregnancy? Or continuing to work or serve in the military?

Wimmer sponsored the legislation after Jane Doe, a minor, offered Aaron Harrison, a twenty-one-year-old, $150 to beat her up in order to induce a miscarriage. Jane Doe's boyfriend threatened to leave her if she did not terminate the pregnancy. Ultimately, both Jane Doe and Harrison were criminally punished, although the baby survived and was later adopted. Harrison pleaded guilty to second-degree felony attempted murder and was sentenced to five years. Jane Doe pleaded no contest to second-degree felony and was ordered to be placed in Utah's Juvenile Justice Services.

Unsatisfied with these outcomes, Representative Wimmer claimed, "the judge is absolutely stretching ... there's no way the judge believes the Utah Legislature left open this loophole. I guarantee it will be closed this next session." With very little debate, his bills advanced. To understand just how severe Representative Wimmer's bill is, a teenage girl like Jane Doe could face from fifteen years to life in prison for a similar act if the fetus does not survive.

Even while Representative Wimmer claimed that his legislation was about protecting the health and safety of women and girls, and the Utah legislature seemingly concurred, their inaction in relation to sex education revealed something far more problematic and troubling. As one journalist reported, "ironically, just three days after Utah's House and Senate overwhelmingly passed Rep. Wimmer's Criminal Homicide and Abortion Amendments bill," which could criminally punish girls with up to life imprisonment for trying to induce an abortion, "the Senate refused to even debate legislation that would have allowed teachers to provide comprehensive sex education to students who had their parent's permission."[2] In Utah, "current state law says teachers can't advocate or endorse the use of contraceptive methods or devices," notwithstanding the fact that in Utah twelve teenage girls become pregnant every day.[3]

However, Utah is not alone. Across the nation, attacks on women and surveillance of their bodies, although rarely making the news, result in arrests of pregnant women for falling down steps, charges of first-degree murder for attempted suicide, prosecutions for stillbirths, and plea deals that include sterilization. And that is not all: the tale of horrors is both wide and deep. There are the threats of arrests for refusing cesarean sections, denial of lifesaving care in order to enhance the possibility of fetal survival (even if it kills the pregnant woman), court-ordered bed rest, and legislation in some states that grant gametes and embryos personhood and legal rights, among others.

This policing also affects girls, with male-led state legislatures enacting policies that remove sex education from schools. A number of states now shift toward abstinence-only teaching, making it an offense to actually teach children about their bodies, intercourse, contraception, and pregnancy. The results have been deadly. The United States has the highest rates of sexual disease and infection transmission in the developed world. Young people in the United States are more likely to contract chlamydia, gonorrhea, human immunodeficiency virus (HIV), and other sexual diseases than their peers in England, France, Germany, Italy, Portugal, Spain, Switzerland, and other nations. They are also more likely to experience unintended and unwanted pregnancies.

For all the handwringing and legislating in the United States – restricting information and rights available to girls and women and claiming moral authority over pregnancies – the results are devastating for women, their families, and the economy. According to research conducted at the Guttmacher Institute, a research clearinghouse on reproductive health, the unintended pregnancy rate "is significantly higher in the United States than in many other developed countries."[4] Nearly half of the pregnancies in the United States are unintended. The highest rates of unintended pregnancies are among the poor, adolescents, and women with the least education. For example, among teenagers between fifteen and nineteen years old, 75 percent of their pregnancies are unintended.[5] Not all of the pregnancies will result in childbirth, but a significant percentage will, often interrupting education and employment. Overwhelmingly, unintended pregnancies are publicly funded and the public funding naturally extends to children of poor mothers.

Yet, the state also punishes, stigmatizes, and stereotypes these mothers for becoming pregnant and relying on public welfare like Temporary Assistance for Needy Families, otherwise known as TANF. The Trump administration has proposed eliminating food assistance for millions of Americans and restricting food choice for those fortunate enough to retain their benefits. In what some pundits are calling a "major shake-up" of perhaps the nation's most important safety net program – the Supplemental Nutrition Assistant Program (SNAP), commonly referred to as "food stamps" – the Trump administration proposes limiting the purchases families can make with their food subsidies, which are already heavily monitored and restricted. Already, families that receive SNAP cannot purchase soap, paper products, household supplies, hot foods, or vitamins with their benefits.[6] The federal government lists "hot food" as a luxury item along with "grooming items" as well as food that can be eaten at the store. And while a woman could purchase a birthday cake for her child using SNAP benefits, the state monitors if the "value of the non-edible decorations" exceeds 50 percent of the "purchase price of the cake." If it does, the cake cannot be purchased with SNAP benefits.

The Trump administration's proposal would gut the food program by $213 billion dollars – almost 30 percent of its current budget. For families that receive $90 per month or more, roughly half of their benefits would be in the form of a USDA food package. This package would consist of "shelf-stable milk, ready to eat cereals, pasta, peanut butter, and beans." There would be fruit and vegetables, but none fresh, only canned. How could legislators and policymakers possibly believe such policymaking is good for mothers and their babies?

Individual states are also sometimes punitive toward poor single mothers, monitoring how they spend their aid, including surveilling what foods they purchase, monitoring their bank accounts, and enforcing drug testing as a condition for receiving aid. So few women test positive for illegal substances that the testing is economically inefficient and cruel. As Professor Joan Maya Mazelis wrote in *The Hill*, "Florida taxpayers, for example, spent $118,140 to reimburse people who tested negative for the cost of testing, which was $45,780 more than the state saved by denying benefits to the 2.6 percent of applicants who tested positive. And other states are doing the same thing over and over and expecting different results."[7]

As Lauren Gellman predicted twenty years ago in *Poverty & Prejudice: Social Security at the Crossroads*, "The fact that individuals will be forced to find employment within two years is not the crux of the problem. The uncertainty and skepticism comes when one considers that there are not enough jobs that pay a high enough wage to support a mother and her children. As a result, in the long run, instead of seeing a greater number of people on their feet, supporting themselves, we may see a larger number of individuals living in poverty, especially children."[8] She was right. The state's tough love on welfare shows disdain and disregard for the dignity of poor people as well as their children.

The devastating and demoralizing consequences of the state's policing of women's reproduction results not only in the prurient surveilling of what food they purchase and whether decorations happen to be on their child's birthday cake or a non-edible gourd is purchased at Halloween, but also their conduct during pregnancy. Disturbingly, some state and federal officials have also begun secretly monitoring the menstrual cycles of women and girls. The most devastating consequence of the precarious double bind in which the state handcuffs women and girls with the potential to become pregnant is America's alarming maternal mortality rate.

This of course belies the punditry of legislators who claim their policing of women and girls reflects care and concern about keeping women safe and healthy. The paternalistic argument that antisex education, anticontraception, and antiabortion measures benefit women and girls simply does not bear that out, leading instead to high rates of unintended pregnancies, maternal mortality, and infant mortality. Even so, legislators seek to justify their attacks on reproductive rights as a means of safeguarding women and, sadly, courts often defer to this sophistry. However, federal data shows how dire birthing in the United States happens to be.

Simply put, women in the United States now die during pregnancy at unprecedented rates.[9] According to Central Intelligence Agency (CIA) data, the United States ranks about fiftieth in the world for maternal safety, behind blighted, war-torn nations struck by civil wars and genocide like Serbia and Bosnia. As the data shows, Saudi Arabia, Kazakhstan, and Libya are some of the nations where the maternal mortality rate is lower than in the United States. For those who have paid attention, this does not come as a surprise.

In 2000, nations throughout the world agreed to participate in the United Nations Millennium Development Goals (MDGs), one of the key objectives of which specifically targeted reducing pregnancy-related deaths.[10] Nearly two dozen international organizations and 191 member state nations publicly committed to achieve eight goals, among them reducing maternal mortality. All but a few nations showed demonstrable progress. The United States was among the few nations to fail or regress. Maternal mortality rates actually increased in the United States at a rate of nearly 140 percent. As one reporter noted, "Just as the world turned its attention to this matter with marked success, the United States stopped offering data and began moving backward."[11]

What accounts for this? Texas holds some clues. Texas has the regrettable distinction of the deadliest state in the developed world in which to birth a child.[12] As one commentator explained, "the Texas maternal mortality rate 'now exceeds that of anywhere else in the developed world.'" It is also a state with an overwhelmingly male legislature, which prides itself on enacting the most restrictive abortion laws in the nation.[13] As *The Texas Tribune* wrote in 2017, "Once again, the Texas Legislature is mostly, white, male, middle-aged."[14] At that time, men held nearly "80 percent of the Legislature's seats." And that legislative body filed nearly twenty antiabortion bills in 2017 alone. This is not surprising, however, because the Texas legislature prides itself on legislative efforts to criminalize and suppress reproductive rights and, despite a recent defeat in the U.S. Supreme Court in *Whole Woman's Health v. Hellerstedt*, the legislature successfully closed down clinics that perform abortions. What they failed to account for is that so many of those clinics provided care for the overlooked and underserved poor women in their state.

Sadly, Texas is not alone. Other states follow a similar destructive path, including Mississippi[15] and Louisiana.[16] In these states, legislators have left, respectively, 1.5 and 2.4 million female residents with only one abortion clinic remaining in their states. Alabama, Kentucky, Georgia, and others similarly show efforts to eviscerate reproductive rights on the one hand and staggering rates of maternal mortality on the other. A common thread in these abusive practices is the impact they have on Black women.

For example, Louisiana exceeds the nation's maternal mortality rate by a dramatic proportion. In particular, while maternal mortality is dire among Black women in the United States generally, in Louisiana the incidences of death are far greater. The average maternal mortality for white women is 18.1 in the United States and 27.3 in Louisiana. For Black women, the U.S. incidence of maternal mortality is 47.2 and in Louisiana 72.6. Overall in the United States, Black women are nearly four times more likely than white women to die due to a pregnancy-related cause. This is why thinking about these matters requires more than a reproductive rights framework, but rather one of reproductive justice.

The intergenerational suffering of Black women in these former slave states remains visceral and part of the horrific legacies of institutionalized chattel bondage. For Black women in Texas, Louisiana, Alabama, Georgia, West Virginia, and elsewhere, not only is their reproductive freedom illusory, but staying alive during pregnancy is not a guaranteed, foregone conclusion. Private reproductive bondage in these former slave states is now public. That is, where planters once controlled Black women's reproduction on their plantations and elsewhere, now the state controls what Black women (and others) may do with their bodies during pregnancy. In neither case has the regard for Black women resulted in the autonomy, independence, or privacy deserved.

Staggering maternal mortality rates in these states and others come as little surprise considering that dozens of clinics that provided contraceptive care, breast, ovarian, and cervical cancer screenings, and testing for sexually transmitted diseases shuttered in the wake of antiabortion lawmaking. When clinics closed, many women in those regions had no other health providers, but only crisis pregnancy centers.

The erosion of reproductive healthcare rights and access, as well as the criminalization of women's conduct during pregnancy, underscore the importance of scrutinizing the legislature, Supreme Court, and lower judicial branches. Even while *Planned Parenthood v. Casey* and the basic principles of the Supreme Court's decision in *Roe v. Wade* still stand, these cases are increasingly vulnerable and regularly under attack. A study published by the American Civil Liberties Union reports that 35 states proposed over 300 abortion rights restrictions in 2013 alone.[17] What explains this? In part, this can be linked to the rise of the Tea Party, an evangelical, conservative movement that swept into American legislatures shortly after the election of Barack Obama, the nation's first Black President. Along with efforts to gut reproductive rights, voting rights became vulnerable and gerrymandering ensued, and the flames of anti-immigration stirred to successful effect. During the period 2010–15, state legislatures proposed and succeeded in enacting more regulations to restrict abortion and contraceptive access than in the prior three decades combined.[18]

In 2015, the Guttmacher Institute published a report placing this legislative movement in context. It explained, "The goal of antiabortion advocates is to make abortion impossible to obtain by layering multiple restrictions, even though many claim that their motivation is only to protect women's health."[19] These efforts to derail women's privacy rights are well funded and coordinated in legislatures throughout the nation. Seventy antiabortion restrictions were enacted in twenty-one states[20] – the second highest number of restrictions passed in one legislative session. In fact, "[n]o year from 1985 through 2010 saw more than 40 new abortion restrictions; however, every year since 2011 has topped that number."[21]

Despite Texas, and increasingly other states, urging women and teens to engage in abstinence-only intimacy, unmarried and unprotected sexual activity and unintended pregnancies have remained at the same level or increased and not declined. This is true in other Republican strongholds. At the same time, legislatures in traditionally Republican states have sought to restrict abortion access, causing a threat not only to the fundamental right to terminate a pregnancy but also to women's health. As one woman told a Texas healthcare worker, "I will terminate this pregnancy. . . . So how about I tell you what I have in my cupboards, under my sink and in my medicine cabinet, and you tell me what to use and how to use it in order to do my own abortion."[22] In that case, the pregnant woman was pleading with a healthcare worker whose clinic (along with dozens of others) abruptly closed in the wake of a newly enacted and restrictive Texas statute targeting the provider – a circuitous legislative way of defeating a fundamental right.

In Texas, lawmakers believed that "[t]he fight for the future of [the state] is just beginning."[23] In the summer of 2013, Texas state Senator Wendy Davis urged lawmakers to vote down a bill that, if enacted, would decisively restrict women's reproductive health rights in that state. Warring factions of reproductive rights advocates and antichoice advocacy groups assembled in the state's capitol to monitor the progress of the omnibus abortion bill – arguably containing the most restrictive abortion regulations enacted in Texas since *Roe v. Wade*.[24] As lawmakers shepherded the bill through special sessions of the legislative process, impassioned floor speeches that professed either the sanctity of fetuses or the fundamental nature of woman's reproductive healthcare rights echoed throughout the halls of the Texas State Capitol.[25] In the end, however, abortion rights proponents lost.

Despite robust efforts to thwart the passage of legislation referred to as H.B. 2 (the legislation deceptively lacked any outward reference to abortion or reproductive healthcare in its title) and to weaken its substantive provisions,[26] the Texas legislature voted to enact the law. In the first special session, Texas Democrats proposed twenty different H.B. 2 amendments aimed at lessening the severity of restrictions by creating specific exemptions for teen mothers or victims of rape and incest in different provisions of the law. None of these amendments advanced; all were rejected along partisan party-line votes, demonstrating the highly partisan nature of the abortion rights issue in Texas. Texas lawmakers celebrated the legislation as one of the most restrictive laws to limit women's access to abortion in the country. Legislators boasted that they were pioneering "some of the toughest restrictions on abortion in the country."[27] Women's rights advocates argued that the Texas legislature delivered a knockout blow to women's healthcare rights.[28] In the end, strategic lawmaking at the state level – what could be called strategic federalism – successfully intervened against precedents established in *Roe v. Wade*[29] and *Planned Parenthood v. Casey*[30] to undermine women's reproductive healthcare rights and ultimately the authority of the Supreme Court.

In recent years, scholars and activists have described this type of lawmaking as part of the "war on women." The war metaphor signifies the battles fought in state houses, the death threats aimed at abortion clinic staff, and even the violent campaigns to deter and block women from entering abortion clinics. Professor Johanna Schoen explains that antiabortion activists became confrontational when they sensed in the 1970s and 1980s that legislative action might not render the victories they desired.[31] Copiously documented evidence details the harsh impacts produced by laws targeting women's reproductive healthcare rights, including serious hurdles to access abortion rights, criminalization of certain conduct during pregnancy, and even restrictions on pregnant women's medical autonomy at the end of life.[32]

Lawmakers refer to the latter as "pregnancy exclusion laws," because that type of legislation functions to literally exclude or prevent pregnant women from autonomous decision-making at the end of life. This turn to policing the womb is so dramatic that Civia Tamarkin, an award-winning journalist, came out of retirement to make a film, *Birthright*, chronicling such cases. Others have done the same, including Rebecca Haimowitz, whose film *62 Days* tells the story of a decomposing, brain-dead pregnant woman in Texas, forced to stay on life support in order to gestate her fetus over her family's objections. In the film, the husband tearfully recounts that one of the most painful things to bear was the smell of his dead wife, hooked up to feeding tubes and various machines, rotting away as the state of Texas forced her to gestate their fourteen-week-old fetus.

Why this type of lawmaking? Some commentators and scholars point to conservative values surreptitiously influencing legislatures or pressure from the alt-right in the political and legislative processes.[33] Professor Caitlin Borgmann says that when conservatives portray fetuses as persons, it influences and ultimately pervades how the public understands and talks about abortion. She and other scholars believe that conservatives have successfully shaped public discourse on abortion such as "to have the embryo or fetus treated as a legal person in many contexts outside abortion." She explains that "[v]iewed in this light, abortion restrictions are transformed into measures that promote women's health and well-being and that protect women from the exploitation and deception of abortion providers."[34]

Some scholars argue that antiabortion efforts reflect religious fundamentalism creeping into the legislative space.[35] Still others maintain that implicit and explicit biases explain antichoice lawmaking; they argue that men simply do a poor job legislating on behalf of women. Catharine MacKinnon argues that because "pregnancy can be experienced only by women, and because of the unequal social predicates and consequences pregnancy has for women, any forced pregnancy will always deprive and hurt members of one sex only on the basis of gender."[36] Reva

Siegel brilliantly describes this type of legislating as resting "on traditional assumptions about women's natural obligations or instrumental uses as mothers."[37] These matters are further compounded by transgender status.

As this book shows, robust legislating that chips away at reproductive rights and encroaches on women's reproductive healthcare is about more than abortion. Rather, it is about a fundamental respect for the humanity, dignity, and citizenship of girls and women. It shows how conservative movements, combined with the rise and influence of a religious orthodoxy, successfully express themselves at the legislative level, particularly in the realms of reproductive autonomy and privacy. The book sharpens its gaze on the sex and gender asymmetries in legislatures, which more likely than not lead to the enactment of Targeted Regulation of Abortion Providers (TRAP) laws.

The book illumes *how* the recent robust lawmaking that restricts when and under what circumstances women may access reproductive healthcare rights functions not only to undermine women's constitutional rights but also leads to the surveillance of their reproduction, criminalization of their conduct during pregnancy, and ultimately the burdening of their health. In the abortion context, antiabortion lawmaking purposefully and strategically operates in the shadow of Supreme Court decision-making to intentionally thwart the spirit of the Court's guidance in *Roe v. Wade* and *Planned Parenthood v. Casey*, which articulate that "a provision of law is invalid, if its purpose or effect is to place substantial obstacles in the path of a woman seeking an abortion before the fetus attains viability."[38]

Policing the Womb considers how these strategic moves function to undermine fundamental constitutional rights. The book issues a cautionary tale to highlight the weaknesses in current Supreme Court's jurisprudence, particularly the framework articulated in *Casey*, which revived paternalistic ideologies associated with women's capacity to reason, consent, and make autonomous reproductive healthcare decisions, because historically the state and courts have been complicit in undermining women's economic capacities and liberty interests.

Policing the Womb offers a candid reflection on the personal costs associated with states policing women's pregnancies and bodies. It highlights how the state's selective interest and punishment often targets women of color and the poor. As states enact measures to prosecute women for drug dependence during pregnancy or any conduct that endangers their pregnancies, what becomes clear is that such rules are not intended to be universalized and applied to all women, but rather to profiled, vulnerable subgroups. The book challenges the provocative legislative story that locates fetal health harms at the feet of illicit drug users. As such, it analyzes what the stick approach means when the American war-on-drugs policy focuses exclusively on street-level drugs rather than drug addiction (or addictive drugs). This subtle, but important, distinction exposes arbitrary fault lines in medical- and criminal-law policy. The book concludes by focusing on the problems likely to emerge from continued reproduction policing in the United States and what we ought to do about it.

2

Pregnancy and State Power

Prosecuting Fetal Endangerment

For all the important and even urgent attention to reproductive rights, focused on preserving abortion access in an era of political and judicial backlash, far less advocacy is devoted to protecting the liberty and dignity interests of women who wish to remain pregnant. That is, abortion rights are the primary focus of reproductive privacy advocacy movements in the United States and have been for some time.[1] Arguably, abortion has become so fundamentally intertwined linguistically and conceptually with the terminology of "reproductive privacy" and "reproductive rights" that little else fits within the taxonomy. This is a mistake.

One might even argue that the right to be free from government intervention in pregnancy has been excised from the framework of reproductive rights altogether, as some feminist scholars now refer to pregnancy preference as "birth activism" rather than as a part of the bundle of rights framed within reproductive privacy.[2] Pro-choice, or even to exercise choice, within this narrow conception of reproductive rights serves only to affirm an abortion right.[3] The reductive meaning of having choice is the ability to exercise agency over pregnancy termination. Unfortunately, this approach to reproductive rights suffers significant blind spots because it ignores the spectrum of reproductive health decisions a woman is called to make and in which women can be subjected to state power.

A reproductive rights framework that anticipates pregnancy termination as the primary or exclusive legal or social obstacle a woman may encounter fundamentally misreads reproductive health and the social contexts in which women live their lives. From a legal perspective, a conspicuously narrow reading of reproductive rights limits rather than expands rights for women, because it ignores the importance of choosing when and under what circumstances to give birth, terminate a pregnancy, parent or not to parent.

The case of *Captain Susan Struck v. Secretary of Defense*[4] advances my argument. Captain Struck became pregnant during air force service in 1970, while stationed in Vietnam. The U.S. Air Force's regulation 36-12 prohibited pregnant women as well as mothers from serving in its military division at that time.[5] The

Air Force presented Captain Struck with an ultimatum: terminate the pregnancy or leave the military base within forty-eight hours.[6] In the years before *Roe v. Wade*, military bases were among the few places where a woman could legally obtain an abortion.

However, Captain Struck did not want an abortion, which the military demanded she have. Instead, her choice was to continue the pregnancy and not suffer the stigmatizing repercussions of both losing her job and livelihood for making that decision. Seeking compromise and under immense pressure, Captain Struck offered to surrender the child for adoption after its birth. The Air Force rejected this option and discharged Captain Struck.[7] She appealed the discharge seven times, including to the Secretary of the Air Force; in each instance, she lost.

Eventually, Captain Struck appealed her case to the District Court for the Western District of Washington, claiming that the Air Force regulations violated equal protection of the law. She argued that the regulation constituted an unconstitutional sex-based classification and, as applied, infringed upon her right to privacy. According to Captain Struck, this infringement interfered with the ability to conduct her personal life. Struck also argued that the regulations infringed on her right to free exercise of her religion, because she was Catholic.

The district court held that the Air Force regulation concerning pregnant officers was reasonable and constitutional.[8] The court dismissed her motion. Captain Struck's application for a stay pending appeal failed too. A team of four lawyers from the American Civil Liberties Union (ACLU), including Ruth Bader Ginsburg, appealed Struck's case to the Ninth Circuit Court of Appeals.

The Ninth Circuit Court of Appeals dismissed her claim, noting that, had there been "an attack by the enemy" at the hospital in which she served, "a not improbable consequence might have been" that Captain Struck would have become "a patient instead of a nurse."[9] According to the Ninth Circuit, "as such, instead of being a useful soldier, she would have been a liability and a burden to the Air Force."[10] The court found it "irrelevant" that "other personnel, males and non-pregnant females, might have been disabled and made useless" in the hypothetical "attack."[11] In 1972, a year before the Supreme Court decided *Roe v. Wade*, it granted *certiorari* in Captain Struck's case.[12] In response, the military waived the application of its regulation on pregnancy and rescinded Struck's discharge.[13] By that time, Captain Struck had placed her baby for adoption.[14] She never had another child.

Captain Struck's experience serves as an important reminder that any reproductive rights framework that defines or equates abortion as its chief agenda problematically excludes or ignores a broader bundle of choices and rights essential to women's health, autonomy, privacy, and equality. They include contraception, testing and treatment for sexually transmitted infections (STIs), pregnancy screenings, pre- and postnatal care, and, of course, the equally important right to maintain or terminate a pregnancy.

Contemporary fetal protectionism now includes sanctioning women for refusing cesarean surgeries.[15] It also includes forcibly confining them to administer bed rest[16] and instigating arrests and prosecutions for otherwise legal conduct.[17] Frequently, class matters as much as race, meaning that Black and Latina women no longer serve as the default targets of fetal protection prosecutions and laws.[18]

For example, in 2015, journalist Nina Martin reported that in Alabama alone, nearly 500 "new and expecting mothers" had been prosecuted in recent years for violating the state's chemical endangerment statute.[19] Most of these pregnant women were white and overwhelmingly poor.[20] A decade ago, my research began articulating these concerns, including a prediction that fetal protection prosecutions could jump the so-called color line.[21] That is, Black women were simply the euphemistic canaries in the coal mine.

One could argue that robust legislative and prosecutorial action in reproductive health might nonetheless exist even if feminists shifted the reproductive rights framework to make it more inclusive. Yet, that argument would miss an important point. Imagine if civil rights leaders, advocates, and pundits during the racially oppressive Jim Crow era had narrowed their vision of civil rights to school integration. Rather than viewing *Brown v. Board of Education*[22] as the last train stop on a path to freedom, equality, and citizenship, it was only the beginning of securing a broader bundle of rights.

The traditional reproductive rights framework operates much to the detriment of a broader set of conditions fundamental to a meaningful privacy right. It ignores or pays inadequate attention to a host of legal concerns affecting pregnancy and liberty, including pregnancy discrimination,[23] forced and coerced sterilization,[24] and the rise in threats of criminal prosecutions and sanctions against poor pregnant women.[25] Most obviously, a failure to integrate a broader perspective and framework into the reproductive rights discourse harms poor women, and among them women of color in particular.

This Chapter introduces a problem concerning overlooked victims who may be perceived as having far less noble lives compared to a military officer. It turns to the difficult cases of women who are otherwise perceived as "bad mothers" for the choices they make, including to be pregnant at all or to birth in a particular manner.

The Chapter has three goals. First, it traces a story of legal innovation – how old law has been used in new ways to punish pregnant women and how new laws emerge to do the same. From the perspective of legislators and prosecutors who seek to cabin or limit reproductive rights, they are the innovators, experimenting with new types of legislation, pushing the envelope, increasing prosecutions, expanding the type of conduct punishable under their laws, and spreading their messaging to other states. Second, it helps us see the women affected by criminal policing of pregnancy in ways that quantitative data alone cannot do. In this way, we better understand what is at stake so as to inspire action. Third, I argue that how a movement conceptualizes an issue frames what it sees. Because mainstream reproductive rights advocacy groups framed reproductive rights and choice in a narrow way regarding abortion, they failed to see what was happening in other areas of women's reproductive health.

2.1 SETTING THE STAGE: ETHNOGRAPHY AND THE LEGACY OF THE PAST

In 2012, the British publication *The Guardian* reported that there is a "creeping criminalisation of pregnancy across America."[26] Shocking yet nonetheless true, to be pregnant and poor in the United States is to play a game of roulette with one's privacy, presumed confidential relationship with medical providers, and basic constitutional and medical rights. Christine Taylor discovered this after falling down steps in her Iowa home. A trip and fall resulted in her arrest while returning home from the hospital. Taylor was jailed for attempted feticide.[27] Why? She was pregnant when the stumble occurred.

On the one hand, Taylor's arrest was alarming – a potent reminder about the recasting of laws intended to protect women from domestic violence, adapted and transformed to use in their surveillance and punishment. Ironically, some feminist organizations supported the enactment of feticide laws by state legislatures as a means of addressing the increased incidences of domestic violence during a woman's pregnancy.[28] Most did not foresee the potential reconditioning of such legal tools in the service of criminalizing pregnant women's behavior.

Currently, thirty-eight states have implemented feticide statutes – a particularly worrying species of fetal protection laws – up from zero in 1986.[29] Nearly thirty states have enacted "fetal homicide laws that apply to the earliest stages of pregnancy ('any state of gestation/development,' 'conception,' 'fertilization,' or 'post-fertilization')."[30] In 2004, President George Bush signed into law the Unborn Victims of Violence Act,[31] which recognizes an embryo or fetus in utero as a legal victim if killed or harmed during the commission of any one of over sixty federal crimes.

On the other hand, criminal prosecutions of pregnant women dated back to the late 1980s, invigorated by the nation's war on drugs. Prosecutors' creative application of child abuse statutes, anticorruption laws, and drug conveyance legislation, among others, provided a foundation for arrests and prosecutions of poor Black pregnant women.[32] These vulnerable women embodied the cautionary metaphor of the miner's canary. They served as an advanced warning for detecting dangers ahead when their physicians were complicit in their arrests, police searched their medical records, and then prosecutors mounted criminal charges against them.

This Chapter takes up the challenge presented by Professor Victoria Nourse when she argued that "we must take the ethnographer's view of experience about our most basic cultural and social concepts, whether they find their way into law cases or newspapers, diaries or Supreme Court opinions."[33] By doing so, this Chapter contributes to scholarship seeking to "dislodge even the firmest of our contemporary concepts,"[34] which includes the concept of reproductive rights and notions related to poor pregnant women's dignity and social value. Otherwise, we fail to take them into account in our framing of legal issues, including women's constitutional reproductive rights, and thus our responsiveness to their plights.

2.1.1 *Canaries in the Coal Mines*

In 1999, Regina McKnight, a poor Black farmworker, became the first woman to be prosecuted and convicted in the United States for a stillbirth.[35] A South Carolina court sentenced her to twenty years in prison, suspended to twelve years. McKnight suffered a cascade of harms and subsequent punishment by the state. She was a twenty-one-year-old rape survivor. The year before she gave birth, she suffered the loss of her mother, killed by a hit-and-run driver.[36] She was no hardened criminal; she had no prior convictions.[37] She suffered from depression and anxiety, which led to self-medication – illicit drugs purchased off the streets of South Carolina. Without her knowledge or consent, McKnight's doctors turned her medical records and tests over to the police, who, without scientific support, claimed that the stillbirth she endured must have resulted from the illicit substance.[38]

In Regina McKnight's case, the state built and rested its prosecution on the fact that she birthed a dead baby.[39] Indeed, the prosecutor claimed that he did not care whether the drugs she ingested were illegal or not: "if we determine you are medically responsible for a child's demise, we will file [homicide] charges."[40] The dogged nature of his prosecutions trickled down to the hospital level as prosecutors collaborated with nurses and doctors to catch poor pregnant women as they came for prenatal care. In 2008, the South Carolina Supreme Court unanimously overturned the conviction based on, among other things, a finding that prosecutors put forth faulty scientific evidence at trial.[41] But by that time Regina had served nearly a decade in prison.

Regina's case is illustrative of a broader pattern in South Carolina, where dozens of poor pregnant women suffered similar fates. Paula Hale, also a rape victim from South Carolina, likely did not expect that, by carrying her pregnancy to term rather than aborting, she would be "dragged out of the hospital in chains and shackles."[42] Lynn Paltrow, Executive Director of National Advocates for Pregnant Women (NAPW), compared the disturbing images of law enforcement entering hospitals, separating newborn Black babies from their mothers, and carting the women off in shackles and chains, to the cruelty embedded in antebellum slavery.[43]

In Hale's case, medical staff at the Medical University of South Carolina (MUSC) voluntarily submitted her prenatal screenings, which showed evidence of drug use, to police and prosecutors.[44] Charles Condon, the former state prosecutor in South Carolina responsible for the shackling and arrests of many poor rural women, passionately extolled in an essay that he needed more than carrots to encourage pregnant women to avoid unhealthy habits; he needed "a real and very strong stick."[45] Arrests and criminal prosecutions serve as this "strong stick" in South Carolina and elsewhere in the United States.

Many of the women prosecuted by Condon sought prenatal care at state-subsidized medical facilities. They wanted to maintain their pregnancies and give birth. Seeking prenatal care was a sign that, despite their drug dependency, they wanted help. Some had responded to public service announcements and billboards cheerfully advertising that help was available even for women with drug addictions: the only thing the women needed to do was to show up. Prior to their treatment at MUSC, little did these women know that Condon actively collaborated with administrators and medical providers at the hospital, receiving the patients' medical records, toxicology screenings, and the health records of their newborns without patient consent.[46] Nor were these women aware that race would play a central role in their care and the state's surveillance.

According to court documents from a class action lawsuit filed by some of the women,[47] during Condon's era of policing pregnancy in the 1990s most of the women to whom he applied his stick at MUSC were Black, even though the rates of illicit drug use are similar among Black and white women.[48] Of the dozens of women arrested at that facility for exposing their fetuses to illicit drugs, all were Black with one exception. Special dispensation was sought for at least one white woman who, although not arrested, otherwise met the criteria for arrest.[49] In that instance, a lead collaborator "admitted that she called the [prosecutor's] office and requested another "chance" on behalf of a white patient who should have been arrested under the Policy's terms."[50] For the only other white woman identified or targeted by MUSC medical staff, racial profiling may have contributed to her arrest, because a nurse and member of Condon's interagency task force made a point of notating the patient's chart with the following information: "patient live[s] with her boyfriend who is a Negro."[51]

While this notation did not serve a medically relevant purpose, it does reveal that an illicit extralegal consideration – race – was involved in the implementation and enforcement of Condon's interagency policing of pregnant women.[52] This particular nurse admitted at trial that she believed interracial relationships violated "God's way,"[53] and "raised the option of sterilization for Black women testing positive for cocaine, but not for White women."[54] An MUSC physician testified that, "although ingestion of heroin or alcohol poses serious risks of fetal harm, the nine criteria established by the taskforce members for searching pregnant women were drafted specifically to uncover cocaine use."[55]

Condon's search process introduced an unusual level of cruelty into the delivery of medicine, altering a common understanding about hospitals providing safety, comfort, and respite to those seeking medical help. As transcripts in the case reveal, some women subjected to arrest were "denied the opportunity to change out of their hospital gowns or to make a phone call to family members to make arrangements for the care of their children."[56] In other instances, police apprehended the new mothers "while still bleeding, weak and in pain from having just given birth."[57] Some were handcuffed and shackled, with chains circling their abdomens. Leg irons were used in some cases. For any woman who could not walk, "a blanket or sheet would be placed over the woman, and she would be wheeled out of the hospital to a waiting police car and transported to jail."[58]

Across the nation in the late 1980s, throughout the 1990s, and into the new millennium, cases like those at MUSC could be and were easily misread as poor Black women lacking concern, care, and discipline for their pregnancies – based on their arrests, prosecutions, and plea deals. Journalists could point to the records of arrests and plea deals and draw the conclusion that "a bio-underclass, a generation of physically damaged cocaine babies whose biological inferiority is stamped at birth," lurked among Americans in poor neighborhoods, born to Black mothers.[59]

The award-winning journalist Charles Krauthammer warned that this was "worse than 'brave new world.'"[60] He interviewed Douglas Besharov, the former director of the National Center on Child Abuse, who originally coined the term "bio-underclass." Besharov predicted that up to 15 percent of African American children have "permanent brain damage" due to fetal crack exposure, but this was based on no scientific or other empirical data. According to Besharov, "[t]he inner-city crack epidemic is now giving birth to the newest horror: a bio-underclass."[61] Besharov told Krauthammer that this was a particularly acute problem in the Black community. However, Professor Carl Hart, a behavioral neuroscientist at Columbia University, who investigates neuropharmacological effects of psychoactive drugs, reminds us that "the majority of crack users were white."[62]

Krauthammer's reporting fitted the widely accepted and adopted view: a consensus of narratives among journalists published in the *New York Times*, *Washington Post*, and *Rolling Stone* magazine, among others, prophesied that "crack babies" would grow up to be "joyless," their futures would be "bleak," and schools were destined to be overwhelmed by their presence in the classroom.[63] Some journalists described these babies as having smaller brains, physical abnormalities, and various physical disabilities.[64] Krauthammer wrote that infants born to mothers who used crack risked having "abnormal genitals and intestinal organs."[65] He urged that these offspring would suffer "permanent brain damage." The future he forecasted included "probable deviance ... [and] permanent inferiority."[66] At best, he predicted, their lives would be "menial." This, he claimed, was "biologically determined from birth."[67]

Similarly, journalist Ellen Hopkins wrote in the *Rolling Stone* magazine that babies born to "crack-addicted mothers are like no others." She claimed these offspring were "brain damaged in ways yet unknown, they're oblivious to any affection." She asked, "how do you care for a baby who hates to be held?" The only problem with this reporting is that it was inaccurate.

Today, Hopkins' claim that babies born to crack-addicted mothers do not want to be looked at, regarded with affection, or held would be met with serious skepticism.

This would certainly not be said of white babies born to opioid-addicted white mothers. But such reporting was largely unchallenged at the time. The strange conclusion from all of this was that these babies lacked the capacities to appreciate affection or even a parent's warm gaze and that they were biologically and mentally inferior. In this vein, Hopkins wrote that "[a]ctually any human contact can overwhelm a crack baby."[68]

By notable contrast, journalists rarely referenced two prominent researchers conducting the most empirically relevant and rigorous studies on fetal impacts from cocaine and other drug exposures – Dr. Claire Coles and Dr. Hallam Hurt. I interviewed both for this book.[69] Drs. Coles and Hurt challenged the prevailing anecdotal evidence that linked crack to genetic malformations and chronic syndromes in babies and children. Dr. Claire Coles, a professor of psychiatry and behavioral sciences, who also directs the Maternal Substance Abuse and Child Development (MSACD) program at Emory University in Atlanta, Georgia, studies the effects of teratogens on behavior and development in babies through adolescence. Specifically, her research examines social, biological, and neurological development in children prenatally exposed to cocaine, alcohol, and tobacco.

Dr. Coles recalled that when she refused to concur with the anecdotal news accounts about babies prenatally exposed to crack, journalists rebuffed her data, dropping her as a medical source or expert.[70] According to her, she was "blacklisted." There was a notable difference in the way the media portrayed Blacks and their use of cocaine compared to whites. Dr. Coles told me, "It was a complicated issue. We were studying alcohol and pregnancy. In the eighties there was the upswing in cocaine use; it was upscale [and] it was fashionable to talk about it. You could go to a party and people were talking about cocaine. People would wear silver spoons around their necks. It was fashionable [for white people]."

In fact, when she first started studying cocaine, "[w]e noticed in the eighties women beginning to use cocaine in pregnancy; it was wealthier white women." However, the media began selling a story that was race-related, which, according to Dr. Coles, "tapp[ed] into a deep fear that people have about the other. In the cocaine era, [the other] were the poor Black people. Even now there is a huge fear about more Black people." She explained that we injure those whom we fear and "then we have to find a justification for that fear." Today, she notes, "the whole thing is about reproduction now and there seems to be a terrible fear." Dr. Coles described this "fear" as an "irrational kind of thing going on ... from some deep sociological fear."

The media refused to engage with the basic science. Across several interviews and meetings with Dr. Coles, she explained that the rhetoric around babies born addicted to crack and going through withdrawal were not accurate. She explained that "withdrawal is a particular condition related to developing a resistance to drugs like Valium, alcohol, heroine, depressants ... it changes the membranes and the body builds up resistance to the drug." The result is that "you have to take more; when you take away the drug, the body pushes back and reacts to the absence of the substance it is used to." However, "gradually over time, the body adjusts to it." But what about cocaine, I wanted to know. She explained that this "does not occur with cocaine" because, as she pointed out, "cocaine is a stimulant and not a depressant." Dr. Coles told me, "This is drugs 101 and no one should be getting confused about this who knows anything about medicine."

The consequences of the fearmongering were real. Dr. Coles felt an urgency to relate what she knew, which was based on scientific evidence derived from her studies. She was concerned that "because of the way this was portrayed, children were being put in foster care, women put in jail," much of it on the basis of inaccurate information associated with crack. At one point, she told me that "legislators called the university so that I would be fired." Fortunately for her and Emory University, the chair of her department at the time – someone whom she described as "old-fashioned" – cared about scientific integrity and believed that "there is a tradition in the academic world that you don't attack people for their scientific research." However, newspapers were not "happy" with her research findings because "it was not a good story."

Equally, Dr. Hurt's groundbreaking longitudinal research on gestational drug exposure, underserved youth, and high-risk infants provided pertinent, empirically grounded counternarratives to the crack baby myth that had surfaced in the 1980s.[71] Former Chair of the Division of Neonatology at the Albert Einstein Medical Center in Philadelphia, Dr. Hurt cautioned, for example, that poverty had as significant (if not greater) an impact on a child's brain than gestational exposure to crack.[72] So why was crack so deeply racialized? Dr. Hurt believed that "it was just easier to go after the bad ones," and the "bad ones" or "bad mothers" were Black. She told me that she thinks this is still the case.

When I interviewed her on an early morning in the thick of summer in 2013, she explained, "First I need to tell you what we did. We excluded [pregnant women] pre–thirty-four weeks." This meant that she enrolled subjects who were farther along in their pregnancies to test the effects of crack use during pregnancy. By enrolling women at an advanced gestational period in their pregnancies, the women were likely to have been using crack cocaine for a longer period of time. She cautioned, "I should also tell you that I don't think cocaine is a good thing to do during pregnancy. It is deleterious in pregnancy."

That said, the women they enrolled "were heavy users." They used "up to ninety-nine days." She did not want women who "snorted one line . . . we didn't do that." Instead, she said, "we only enrolled those who used in two trimesters. That sets the scene for the relatively well child born at term or near term." For years, Dr. Hurt followed the offspring of women in her study who were heavy crack users. At the time of our interview, there were still 110 in the study (down from the 224 when enrolment was at its peak). The oldest children at the time of her study's conclusion were in their early twenties. It was planned to be a two-year study and she never planned that it would extend as long as it did. And so she followed the kids through elementary school, middle school, high school, and – for those who did attend – college. She explained that "for years we were trying to unravel the difference from the two groups, looking at play activities, responses to stress, and cognitive abilities" – that is, comparing the kids exposed to crack in utero with the average kids who grew up alongside them in poverty. Although "every now and then a blip [would appear] where there was a difference," in terms of "positive urine screens, teen parents, adjudication, and school failure [or success] there was no difference."

However, these were not the accounts that journalists and their editors published. Rather, reporters and editors invested in the crack baby myth to such a degree that reporting on the subject lacked the rigor commonly associated with their flagship news organizations.[73] Typical of this type of journalism were reporters filming babies afflicted by heroin exposure or prematurity and attributing the effects to crack.[74]

By the early 2000s, the racial stereotypes and conflations associated with so called crack babies began to give way, following publications in scientific journals. Scientific evidence mounted by the doctors Hurt, Coles, Deborah A. Frank, and others exposed the gaps and unfounded, unconfirmed claims in prior research.[75] The leading American medical journals, the *New England Journal of Medicine* and the *Journal of the American Medical Association*, announced their rejection of the term "crack baby" in future publications.[76] In 2013, the *New York Times* issued a video retraction of its reporting on this subject.[77] The newspaper acknowledged that it "ran articles and columns that went beyond the research."[78]

Yet, because of the absence of surveillance and arrests of white women for illicit drug use, illegal use of prescription medications, or abuse of prescription medications during pregnancy or otherwise, a false narrative emerged. To policymakers, pundits, and perhaps even to women's rights organizations, it appeared that drug addiction during pregnancy existed primarily, if not exclusively, among Black women. In significant part, this was due to who was targeted by medical providers and law enforcement for surveillance and arrest, rather than who illicit drug users happened to be. A study conducted by the National Center for Perinatal Addiction Research and Education found that about 15 percent of white and Black women use illicit drugs during pregnancy.[79] However, "Black women were 10 times as likely as whites to be reported to the authorities, and poor women were more likely to be reported than middle-class women."[80]

This data comports with an ACLU study in the 1990s, which found that 80 percent of the women targeted for criminal intervention for drug use during pregnancy were Black, Latina, and "members of other minorities."[81] Importantly, prosecutors and news organizations aided in this. Prosecutors claimed that the Black women whom they prosecuted manifested an extreme indifference to human life. News organizations supplied slanted accounts about drug abuse in the United States.

Prosecutors and legislators lacked interest in a more nuanced account of drug use during pregnancy. Lawmakers and prosecutors invested attention and resources in connecting illicit drugs to pregnancy, and therefore fetal harms, ignoring what would blossom and devolve into the opioid crisis. At meetings with legislators and lectures in the early 2000s, I began calling attention to these matters, but my efforts had limited effect and met with unease on both sides. In some instances, my foreshadowing of what lay ahead with opioid addiction among white women including during their pregnancies encountered strong resistance and utter disbelief. In fact, from time to time, predominantly white academic audiences seemed outraged and hostile by what I reported. Perhaps they were dumbfounded; I was presenting data on opioid addiction not yet in the public sphere and it challenged these audiences on many levels. At the root of the resistance might have been naiveté, implicit racial bias, or both.

Frequently, I was told that doctors would never prescribe anything that was not "good" or "healthy" for their (white) pregnant patients. And perhaps even more telling, scholars, prosecutors, legislators, and others seemed skeptical about comparing the pregnancies of women who were prescribed medications by doctors with the pregnancies of women who acquired their drugs "on the streets." They were different. Perhaps so, but the drugs were not as dissimilar as they wanted to believe. Today, the "National Prescription Opiate Litigation," consolidated cases in federal court, is seeking almost $50 billion to settle lawsuits related to opioid addiction.

In 2011, a groundbreaking study conducted by Dr. Allen A. Mitchell, Director of the Slone Epidemiology Center, debunked presumptions and racial stereotypes about drug use during pregnancy. The study, *Medication Use During Pregnancy, with Particular Focus on Prescription Drugs: 1976–2008*, published in the peer-reviewed *American Journal of Obstetrics and Gynecology*,[82] found that educated white women were more likely to rely on prescription medications like Xanax, Demerol, Valium, Tylenol with codeine, Oxycontin, and Ritalin during pregnancy and their use of these drugs increased with age.[83]

Moreover, more than 70 percent of women reported taking at least one medication that was not a vitamin or mineral during the first trimester of pregnancy, and that drug use increased with age and by race. The study's conclusion: white women were more likely to ingest prescription medications during pregnancy generally, and they relied on more prescription medications during pregnancy as they aged. Importantly, the cocktail of prescription drugs used more often by white women during pregnancy "affect[s] the function of the placenta ... which can affect the blood supply to the baby or cause preterm labor and birth."[84]

The seductive appeal of racialized accounts of drug addiction and pregnancy played to common, and even dangerous, stereotypes affecting not only the women involved but also their offspring, as well as women who would become its future targets. Race obscured recognition of underlying reproductive privacy discrimination against women more generally. Mainstream women's rights organizations, including those that focus on reproductive rights, such as Planned Parenthood, ignored the civil liberties concerns undergirding the pregnancy-based prosecutions poor Black women encountered during the 1990s and early 2000s.

Reproductive rights advocacy organizations paid little attention to the underlying justifications put forth by law enforcement to justify pregnancy-based surveillance and arrests, including fetal personhood. As a result, reproductive rights organizations seemed to ignore the precedents accumulating in states' courts, the evolving prosecutorial and legislative strategies to justify intervention in women's pregnancies, and the possibility that one day fetal health concerns articulated by states could implicate abortion rights. Tellingly absent from the amicus briefs filed in the landmark prosecution of Regina McKnight were any from women's reproductive rights advocacy organizations. The narrow framing of reproductive rights in terms of abortion rights would come back to haunt as new laws and jurisprudence propagated.

2.1.2 *The Past's Legacy: Preservation Through Transformation*

Like eugenics decades before, the crack baby myth conflated random health conditions with heredity and genetics. Once more, similar solutions were proposed: sterilize them.[85] The vilified, poor, addicted Black mother of the 1990s occupied a point on a longer timeline, dating back at least decades, if not centuries. What many journalists covering the crisis of addiction failed to account for was the longer arc of female marginalization and subjugation associated with pregnancy, particularly the enactment of eugenics laws in the early twentieth century. Proposals to sterilize Black women in the 1990s fitted the dynamic described by Reva Siegel as "preservation-through-transformation."[86] That is, "efforts to dismantle an entrenched system of status regulation can produce changes in its constitutive rules and rhetoric, transforming the status regime without abolishing it."[87]

The history of eugenics and its influence on the regulation of reproduction in the United States (even now) remains instructive for myriad reasons, including for developing strategies to address the current opioid crisis and for avoiding prior pitfalls. Reflecting on the similarities that link the political strategies and social sentiments of the eugenics period and the era of intensified crack addiction is valuable for women's movements – namely, an inward-facing reflection would illume not only the historical failure to include marginalized women in the enterprise of "women's rights," but more importantly, their purposeful exclusion.

In other words, the women's movements of the early twentieth century perpetuated the very stereotypes that harmed the broader reproductive rights enterprise for all women. A lengthy accounting of that history is not the work of this Chapter. However, it is worth briefly examining here that highly regarded feminists supported eugenics platforms, which, in Justice Oliver Wendell Holmes's words, explicitly sought to "cut [] the Fallopian tubes" of "unfit women."

Famously, Margaret Sanger, the founder of what is today Planned Parenthood, lectured on the importance of "reducing 'the rapid multiplication of the unfit and undesirable.'"[88] As Adam Cohen wrote, "[m]any influential feminists supported the cause" and were "particularly influential at the grassroots level."[89] Indeed, "women were among the most active lobbyists for eugenics laws of all kinds" and "legislators . . . considered eugenics, with its focus on reproductive issues, a proper realm for female guidance."[90] Their efforts bore fruit. Interestingly, the enterprise of choice, which Sanger promoted in relation to family planning (i.e., contraception access), was not intended for the women thought unworthy of childbearing, because, for those women, sterilization was perceived as the only option as it would eliminate their future choices.

In 1927, more than twenty years after the first eugenics law was enacted in Indiana, the U.S. Supreme Court issued the landmark decision of *Buck v. Bell*, upholding the constitutionality of Virginia's Eugenical Sterilization Act.[91] In an 8–1 decision, the Court ruled that the power that gives states the authority to vaccinate is broad enough to compel the forced sterilization of women and men deemed socially unfit.[92] Writing for the majority, Justice Holmes issued a haunting condemnation of vulnerable women, declaring that "three generations of imbeciles are enough."[93]

The case centered on Carrie Buck, whom Holmes described as "a feeble minded white woman."[94] He claimed that she was the "daughter of a feeble minded mother"[95] and "the mother of an illegitimate feeble minded child."[96] These statements were inaccurate. However, the state presented evidence that the Court found persuasive. One evaluation of Carrie's "fitness" came from Harry H. Laughlin, who, although not a physician (and though he never examined her), was a distinguished leader in the eugenics movement, serving as the superintendent of the Eugenics Record Office in the Department of Genetics at the Carnegie Institute and the "eugenics expert" to various congressional committees, including the Committee on Immigration and Naturalization.[97]

In Carrie Buck's case, her poverty, perceived intellectual shortcomings, teenage pregnancy (the result of a rape), and family history of alcoholism were invoked to justify the state's reprisal and her sterilization.[98] The Court found:

> It would be strange if it could not call upon those who already sap the strength of the State for these lesser sacrifices, often not felt to be such by those concerned, in order to prevent our being swamped with incompetence. It is better for all the world, if instead of waiting to execute degenerate offspring for crime, or to let them starve for their imbecility, society can prevent those who are manifestly unfit from continuing their kind.[99]

In the wake of the Supreme Court declaring the Virginia eugenics law constitutional, more than 60,000 Americans were convicted of social unfitness and surrendered to public health officials for compulsory sterilizations.[100] Aided by the enactment of eugenics legislation, the "stick" approach to poor, vulnerable women's reproductive health was operationalized. At its core, it featured surveillance, government intrusion, reprisal, and retribution to discourage not only vice but also sex, single parenting, and reproduction among the socially undesirable. At their core, these policies were rooted in social judgments about the poor. These were not platforms imposed on feminist elites.

In the United States, eugenics was practiced and perfected on the bodies of children – young girls under the age of eighteen. In North Carolina, nearly 30 percent of forced sterilizations were inflicted on children "under age 18" and Black people comprised 60 percent of all sterilization victims.[101] Two examples among the many thousands deserve mention. Elaine Riddick, raped as a little girl, did not know until many years later that the state of North Carolina sterilized her at the age of fourteen.[102] Even in the 1970s, states continued to carry out these practices. In 1974, Alabama sterilized sisters Mary Alice and Minnie Relf when aged fourteen and twelve respectively. Years later, a lawsuit filed by the Southern Poverty Law Center on behalf of the Relf sisters revealed that federally funded programs sterilized 100,000 to 150,000 people each year.[103] Clearly, some of those sterilizations may have been voluntary, but the majority were likely facilitated through coercive means.

Sixty years after *Buck v. Bell*, legislators proposed similar laws in response to crack addiction. Among the chief lobbying organizations targeting Black women was Children Requiring a Caring Kommunity (CRACK), which proposed legislation and offered payments to women who agreed to sterilization.[104] Barbara Harris, the founder of CRACK, defended its mission to a reporter in the following terms: "How many victims does this person need to have before she doesn't have the right to have children?"[105]

Harris's style of frank talk and activism impressed lawmakers and resonated with many who were deeply concerned about the health of babies born to addicted women.[106] According to her, "if they are drug addicts, they are drug addicts by choice. . . . People say it is a disease, fine. But it is a disease of choice – however they go there and whatever their background and however screwed up their life is. The babies don't have a choice." The bottom line, she said, is that "these women are literally having litters of children . . . not acting any more responsible than a dog in heat."[107] As alarming as her messaging might be viewed today, for a period of time the organization successfully cultivated its appeal among donors and legislators, with offices throughout the United States, including in Detroit, Houston, Nashville, New Orleans, Pittsburgh, San Francisco, Seattle, and Washington, D.C. The rebranded organization, now Project Prevention, based outside Charlotte, North Carolina, has shifted its mission to offering cash incentives to women and men who agree to use "long term or permanent birth control."[108] It no longer focuses solely on women using crack. Yet this type of messaging continues to resonate. Unwanted, coercive, and even illegal sterilization practices continue.

More recently, in 2009, a twenty-one-year-old mother of three agreed to a tubal ligation as a condition for probation after she pleaded guilty to possession with intent to distribute marijuana. Reports about that case emphasize that the West Virginia mother was unmarried.[109] One could argue that this type of sterilization was less coercive than the compulsory sterilizations of the early twentieth century, because women like Carrie Buck had no choice, unlike in this case. However, such arguments are inherently problematic, if not altogether flawed, particularly when anyone, let alone a mother of three, weighs incarceration against returning to her children.

In Tennessee, prosecutors now negotiate plea deals based on women agreeing to sterilization.[110] It is difficult to determine the frequency of such negotiations, particularly in instances where the woman (or man) refuses. Nevertheless, the handful of cases since 2010 in Nashville alone where women have agreed to sterilization as part of their plea deals (and an early release or probation) indicate that such negotiations are occurring.[111]

Nor are these concerns geographically dependent or limited to the south. A 2013 legislative report conducted by California's state auditor Elaine Howe found "numerous illegal surgeries and violations of the state's informed-consent law."[112] The investigator reported that nearly 150 women were sterilized while incarcerated in California prisons during the period 2006–2010.[113] In a letter to former Governor Jerry Brown, Ms. Howe wrote that in some instances women were sterilized without physicians signing the forms or certifying the competency of the women or that they understood the lasting effects of the procedure.[114] In other instances, the state's Correction Office ignored the state's waiting period before the sterilizations could take place.

At least 25 percent of the sterilizations occurred without any lawful consent and the "'true number' of illegal procedures might be higher," according to the audit, because "records were lost in a routine purging."[115] The state claimed the sterilizations occurred without its approval because in 2006 the federal receiver's office assumed jurisdiction over medical care in the state's prisons. Yet this provided little solace to incarcerated women whose illegal or coercively facilitated sterilizations were enabled by agents and employees of the state, as well as those with whom the state contracted. Coercive sterilizations epitomize the preservation of status-based interventions in women's reproductive health, even though laws and formal policies may have changed.

2.2 CONCLUSION

Poverty, addiction, homelessness, and promiscuousness chiefly represented categories of "impurity" and "unfitness." Placement into one of these categories could, and too frequently did, result in criminal incarceration or psychiatric institutionalization in state-run asylums. Carrie Buck, the unsuccessful petitioner in *Buck v. Bell*, lived in such an institution. States justified incarcerations and the forced sterilizations practiced on unfit boys, girls, and women as a means of protecting the welfare of its citizens from the so-called degeneracy rampant among the lower classes.

The vestiges of that legacy survive, or at least the moral intuitions and foundations remain. For example, *Buck v. Bell* has never been overturned. It continues to serve as a chilling example of how the pregnancy penalty endures. The case exemplifies the failure of the law and the Supreme Court to intervene on behalf of vulnerable citizens against abuses of state power.

Yet, it is not enough to make the case that women's reproduction at times has been subject to the property interest of others, including the state. For example, that alone does not satisfy my inquiry here, nor explain why contemporary wars are waged about women and their prenatal conduct. What story can be told to explain why doctors, judges, legislators, and prosecutors police women's reproduction?

Another way to view the trend toward criminal punishment of pregnant women is that it serves to punish vice and status.[116] James Fitzjames Stephen argues that society must feed its desire to scapegoat others and to generate resentment or even hatred for those who breach moral codes in society. He suggests that there is a fundamental human desire for revenge, even if one is not harmed by the act one seeks to avenge— it is enough that the act was immoral and threatens harm to the moral fabric and values of a society. This view of crime and punishment is informative in relation to the punishment of pregnant women in the United States. Stephen wrote that criminal punishment can be rationalized because "the feeling of hatred and the desire of vengeance are important elements in human nature which ought in such cases to be satisfied in a regular public and legal manner."[117]

3

Creeping Criminalization of Pregnancy across the United States

By the term "fetal protection laws," I refer to an array of legislation that purports to promote the protection of fetuses. Such legislation includes feticide laws,[1] drug policies,[2] statutes criminalizing maternal conduct,[3] and statutes authorizing the confinement of pregnant women to protect the health of fetuses.[4] In some instances, existing laws intending to protect children from physical abuse have been interpreted to apply to fetuses – and thus fall within the category of fetal protection laws.[5] Fetal protection laws are intended to promote the health and safety of fetuses by criminalizing actual or intended harm to the unborn.[6] These laws create bright-line rules that are intended to place pregnant women (who know about them) on notice.

Today, the full scope of liberty-infringing pregnancy interventions, including threats of arrest and other coercive conduct that does not necessarily lead to criminal punishment, is unknown. There is no national database, and any state-level record-keeping related to mothers prosecuted under the guise of fetal protection can be difficult to access. Reporters like Nina Martin file "multiple information requests to identify" those arrested under child endangerment laws and child abuse statutes, which now apply to fetuses in a number of states. Vigilant investigation in Alabama revealed dramatic undercounting by "more than three times the number previously identified."[7]

Evidence of arrests and prosecutions gathered by Martin, as well as national and international advocacy organizations such as National Advocates for Pregnant Women and Amnesty International, indicate that the numbers of women vulnerable to pregnancy policing are on the rise.[8] New prosecutions of pregnant women for acts of feticide and attempted feticide illustrate this shift; such prosecutions simply did not occur before.

3.1 THE HISTORIC APPROACH

Historically, the common law predicated manslaughter and murder of an infant on two elements: first, an actual birth; second, the child must have been alive at the time the criminal act occurred. Unless these factors were met, an individual could not be convicted under state law for causing injury, whether to a fetus or a child.[9] Treatises dating back to Sir Matthew Hale (echoing Sir William Stanford and Sir Edward Coke) articulate this principle, which rooted in fourteenth-century common law. Hale articulated this principle in the following manner:

> If a woman be quick or great with child, if she take, or another give her any potion to make an abortion, or if a man strike her, whereby the child within her is kild, it is not murder nor manslaughter by the law of *England*, because it is not yet *in rerum natura*, tho it be a great crime, and by the judicial law of *Moses* (g) was punishable with death, nor can it legally be known, whether it were kild or not, 22 *E*. 3. *Coron.* 263. so it is, if after such child were born alive, and baptized, and after die of the stroke given to the mother, this is not homicide. 1 *E*. 3. 23. *b. Coron.* 146.
>
> But if a man procure a woman with child to destroy her infant, when born, and the child is born, and the woman in pursuance of that procurement kill the infant, this is murder in the mother, and the procurer is accessary to murder, if absent, and this whether the child were baptized or not. 7 *Co. Rep.* 9. *Dyer* 186.[10]

As related to childbirth and criminal law, the theory of *in rerum natura* translates as "in the nature of things" or "in existence" in English law.[11] In *Regina v. Knight* (one of the earliest reported cases involving the manslaughter prosecution of a woman for failing to protect her fetus), upon hearing compelling evidence leading to the "conclusion that the child had been born alive, and had died by the hands of the mother," the English court reasoned that even under those circumstances the mother could not be guilty of manslaughter as there was no basis in law or doctrine for such a prosecution.[12]

In utero harms generally did not serve as a basis for child abuse, manslaughter, or murder convictions, particularly because proximate causation was considered too remote and indirect. In the 1904 case *Rex v. Izod*, an English court again reasoned that, although a woman may be guilty of neglect for failing to care for her fetus, the neglect "is not enough to justify a verdict of manslaughter" if the neglect is confined to the time the child is in utero, because the legal presumption of life is rooted at birth not conception.[13] In that case, a widow's failure to provide care to her fetus during labor and postbirth was evidence of negligence and serious neglect but not manslaughter, because there was no finding of "neglect of the child itself treated as a separate being."[14] The court held that "a child must be completely born before it can be the subject of an indictment for either murder or manslaughter."[15] This suggests that until a child is "completely born," it is not considered a legal entity for purposes of murder or manslaughter.

Cases like *Regina v. Knight* and *Rex v. Izod* present troubling facts: poor women who at delivery passively allow their infants to expire. In at least one case it appears that the woman may have taken affirmative steps to end the life of the infant. Yet, in each instance, the courts take great strides to clarify that criminal punishment in the form of manslaughter does not apply to a woman's failure to provide appropriate prenatal, labor, and postnatal care even when it contributes to fetal harm or infant death.

When similar cases reached courts in the United States, they followed the English approach. *Dietrich v. Northampton* is instructive on this point. In 1884, Oliver Wendell Holmes – then an associate justice of the Massachusetts Supreme Court – wrote that it would be far too remote if an action could be maintained on behalf of a fetus still dependent on the pregnant woman bearing it. Justice Holmes reasoned that any argument which suggested that a fetus "stands on the same footing as . . . an existing person" is hindered and not helped by the fact that a fetus does not have even a "quasi independent life."[16] In dicta, the court maintained that if a pregnant woman could not recover for the injury sustained by the fetus, neither would it be legally sound for the fetus to recover.

Years later, in *State v. Osmus*, the Wyoming Supreme Court established that, to convict a defendant of infanticide, it must be shown "first, that the infant was born alive, and second, if the infant was born alive that death was caused by the criminal agency of the accused."[17] In that case, the Wyoming Supreme Court overturned the manslaughter conviction of Darlene Osmus for her newborn's death.[18] Darlene Osmus was a twenty-year-old unmarried woman who claimed ignorance of her pregnancy. At some point she went into labor and gave birth in the bathroom late one night. She testified that the infant was stillborn and that three days later she left the infant's body on the side of the highway. She was accused of murder, found guilty of manslaughter, and sentenced to two-to-four years in prison until the verdict was overturned.

In rejecting the state's two central claims that (1) Osmus was guilty of nonfeasance under Wyoming's child abuse and neglect statute and (2) guilty of manslaughter for failure to obtain prenatal and delivery care, Justice Blume emphasized that the law "relates to a really living child." Justice Blume explained that "such nonfeasance must, of course, have occurred prior to the birth of the child and hence has no possible connection with [the law] so that an instruction setting out that section was error again in the light of that theory."[19] The court framed the matter as follows: "one of the questions is as to whether or not the child was born alive."[20] According to the court, the law did "not directly provide or even intimate that it applies to a child such as involved in this case."[21]

3.1.1 *Taxonomies of Legal Innovation*

By contrast, contemporary fetal protection efforts mark a troubling legal innovation and a dramatic departure from prior criminal law jurisprudence. The legal innovations may be categorized into four primary techniques: (1) old laws are applied and interpreted in new ways; (2) old laws are slightly amended to expand existing prescriptions and sanctions; (3) new laws are applied in unintended ways against pregnant women; and (4) new laws are introduced that expressly create new pre-scriptions and sanctions.

In each case, a salient aspect of these legal innovations is the shifting definition of personhood, because legislative advocates of fetal protection adopt the standard that fetuses are persons. Under this framework, a fetus is a child for purposes of criminal prosecution. Viability and the capacity to live outside the womb are neither deemed necessary nor relevant. This shift in the law is significant as it normalizes treating the unborn as if they were born and alive at the time of injury, but for the most part only against pregnant women. This implicates abortion policy, criminal law, and women's constitutional rights.

Since 1973, authorities in at least forty-five states have sought to prosecute women for exposing their unborn children to drugs. Those efforts continue under a wide variety of laws even in states where high courts have previously rejected the criminalization approach. A 2019 report published by the Guttmacher Institute shows that state policies on substance use during pregnancy are wide-reaching.[22] Think about this:

- Twenty-three states plus the District of Columbia have enacted laws establish-ing that drug use during pregnancy is child abuse.
- Twenty-five states plus the District of Columbia actually mandate that medical providers snitch on their pregnant patients if they suspect drug use.
- Eight states strong-arm medical providers to perform toxicology screens on pregnant patients if drug use is suspected. If providers fail to comply, they could be punished.

Three states – Minnesota, South Dakota, and Wisconsin – have enacted laws pursuant to which women who ingest drugs during pregnancy can be involuntarily committed to a treatment program. The Wisconsin law, recently challenged follow-ing the solitary confinement of a woman who protested her incarceration, is parti-cularly draconian. The Wisconsin Unborn Child Protection Act permits the detention of a woman against her will for the duration of her pregnancy.[23] The law entitles a fetus to its own court-appointed lawyer – even though the pregnant woman could lose custody of her baby after birth. These proceedings are purpose-fully secret, "because they are part of Wisconsin's children's code."[24]

However, legal innovation in the reproductive rights realm is not limited to states' interests in surveilling pregnancy and drug abuse for criminal and civil punishment. So far, thirty-eight states have implemented feticide statutes –a particularly worrying species of fetal protection laws.[25] Nearly three dozen states prohibit removing life support from brain-dead pregnant woman.[26]

The few selected cases described below could be substituted by other examples in Alabama,[27] Indiana,[28] Maryland,[29] Mississippi,[30] South Carolina,[31] or Tennessee,[32] among others. Sometimes, criminal cases in this domain are overturned on appeal, but not always. Lynn Paltrow and Professor Jeanne Flavin estimate the figure of 413 criminal interventions that they recently documented between 1973 and 2005 "is a substantial undercount."[33] Importantly, in each of the cases they found "a woman's pregnancy was a necessary factor leading to attempted and actual deprivations of a woman's physical liberty."[34]

3.1.2 *Old Law Applied in New Ways: First-Degree Murder*

On a chilly April morning in 2013, I stood on a small square in downtown Indianapolis with a group of people bundled in their coats, blowing puffs of moist, hot air into their hands. Many had adorned their coats and jackets with pins that read: "Free Bei Bei." Organizers had hoped for a larger crowd and that maybe the local mainstream women's rights organizations would lend their voices and support to this small crowd assembled for a rally. So far, no such luck.

Instead, with the exception of a modest showing of undergraduate students from a nearby university and a handful of women law students, the crowd consisted mostly of middle-aged, middle-class white women from a local church group that had taken an interest in Bei Bei Shuai's case. Some of these women made sure to explain to me that they were not "political" and did not "get caught up" in feminism, but this was different.

Shuai's supporters believed that the failed attempt to end her life two days before Christmas, on December 23, 2010, by eating multiple packs of rat poison pellets was a sign of her distress and depression and not premeditation to murder her fetus. They told me her case was a tragedy; a romance gone bad, compounded by stigmatization and shame. To these women, Shuai's bungled suicide effort – botched by a friend who rushed her to the hospital where doctors undertook aggressive and heroic efforts to save her life – was not a cause for criminal punishment.[35] For a few days, her baby even lived before dying.

The women I spoke to were alarmed that the local Marion County prosecutor, Terry Curry, a self-professed Democrat, brought first-degree murder and attempted feticide charges against Shuai in the wake of her failed suicide attempt while pregnant. To their point, suicide is not a crime in Indiana. Indeed, this was the first prosecution in Indiana's nearly two-hundred-year history in which the state sought to criminally punish a woman after attempting a suicide.[36]

Instead, weeks after Shuai's release from the hospital and subsequent care at a mental health facility where she was treated for severe depression, police arrested her. Denied bail, Shuai was confined to Marion County Jail, a facility described in news reports and court documents as beset by sexual coercion (where male guards demand sexual favors from female inmates), physical abuse, corruption, and medical neglect.[37] For fourteen months, while Shuai was incarcerated and awaiting trial, the women who attended the rally wrote to her. At the rally, Shuai would later say that those notes were her lifeline, as was the modest financial support the women provided.

Shuai, a soft-spoken Chinese accountant from Shanghai, legally migrated to the United States with her now estranged husband, hoping to partake in the American dream. She told a reporter, "I knew America as the best country in the world"[38] – and at the time it looked as though many dreams would be within her grasp: Shuai's husband was offered a prestigious job as a mechanical engineer and she planned to continue her education.

However, little by little the dream fragmented, splintering and unraveling in adultery, embarrassment, and shame. The first fracture in her plan involved university enrollment – Shuai could not afford to obtain the education she sought. University admission is less competitive in the United States, but obtaining a degree in this country is far more expensive than in China. Although she likely would have qualified to attend a very good Indiana university, Shuai could not afford to pay the bills. Then, the marriage "collapsed."[39]

Instead of pursuing a career in accounting, Shuai found herself working at a low-end Chinese restaurant, pregnant with a married man's child.[40] On a cold December night in 2010, that man, Zhiliang Guan, threw a wad of money at her. That represented his part in the pregnancy. Zhiliang confessed that he was still married and committed to his other children, warning Shuai to keep away.

Court records[41] document the events that rapidly unfolded, which ultimately led to Shuai's suicide attempt, the death of her baby, and charges of first-degree murder by a new district attorney who wanted to prove he was tough on crime. Rather than keeping away, Shuai ran after Zhiliang Guan, pregnant and crying in the parking lot outside the Chinese restaurant. She dropped to her knees, begging for his help and imploring him to stay.[42] Instead, he drove away, leaving behind only a plume of smoke in the frigid air and Shuai on the cold pavement.

Within days of Zhiliang's abandonment, Shuai began plotting to kill herself; the options were seemingly endless in Indiana. In the United States, women kill themselves with pills, by suffocating themselves with gas, hanging, crashing their cars, and jumping off bridges. Alcohol, prescription painkillers, antidepressants, and opiates frequently combine with suicide efforts in the United States.[43] Shuai researched the various methods to kill herself, deciding on rat poison.[44]

Rat poison and pesticides are common, low-cost ways in which women in China choose to end their lives. According to one researcher, 62 percent of deaths by suicide in that country can be attributed to the ingestion of rat poisons and pesticides.[45] A peer-reviewed article published in the *British Journal of Psychology* surmises that "easy access to pesticide and rat poison" in China "may account for the high fatality rate" among women who kill themselves by this method.[46] A number of studies offer some insights as to why women choose rat poison, but they do little to explain why the majority of female suicides worldwide are in China.[47] The former head of the World Health Organization's Division of Mental Health, Norman Sartorius, has argued that in China it is believed that "Americans have depression. The English have depression. It's their disease."[48] To place that perspective in context, a decade ago there was one psychiatrist in China for every 100,000 people, whereas "in Europe, the average ratio ranges from 1 in 3,000 to 1 in 5,000."[49] In the United States the ratio is roughly 1 to 8,600.[50]

Shuai's prosecution made her supporters worry about their daughters. If convicted, Prosecutor Curry made clear he would seek the maximum sentence – forty-five years – and would only accept a plea deal of twenty years. In fact, Curry told a reporter that even if he had to throw out the first-degree murder charge for lack of evidence, he would nevertheless continue to pursue the attempted feticide charge.[51] Some people saw this as a means for a liberal prosecutor to burnish conservative credentials at the expense of women.

Shuai described to me a cascade of embarrassments and humiliations compounding her life at the time: she was pregnant, unmarried, and essentially destitute.[52] She was ashamed and afraid. Shuai told me, "In China, women like [her]" – adulterous and pregnant – "are an embarrassment to their parents."[53] She was fearful about being an embarrassment in the United States too. An unfavorable mood regarding immigration and single motherhood was taking root across the United States. Former congressman Eugene Clay Shaw, the key architect of federal welfare reform, the Personal Responsibility and Work Opportunity Reconciliation Act of 1996 (PRWORA), put it this way, "The inscription at the base of the Statue of Liberty was written before welfare … Now the question becomes, are these handouts a magnet that is bringing people into this country?"[54]

Ultimately, Shuai's case boiled down to this: prosecutors' insistence that her real motive was to kill the fetus, and thereby humiliate and shame her married boyfriend – hence the charge of first-degree murder. They informed me that this was why she mentioned a baby in the suicide note. For the lawyers who prosecuted Shuai, the case was open and shut – all of the depression, anxiety, rat poison, and drama boiled down to a woman conspiring to harm or abort her fetus.[55]

3.1.3 *Old Law Applied in New Ways: Manslaughter and Depraved Heart Murder*

Rennie Gibbs's criminal prosecution in Mississippi for the "depraved heart murder" of her stillborn further illustrates the extent to which existing laws may be interpreted and applied in new ways. Rennie Gibbs was only fifteen years old when she became pregnant and, although a teenager, she struggled with drug dependence.[56] In December of 2006, one month after turning sixteen, Gibbs suffered a stillbirth[57] in the thirty-sixth week of her pregnancy.[58] Prosecutors concluded that her baby suffered from in utero exposure to cocaine, which caused its death.[59] As a result, the stillbirth was prosecuted as murder. Despite a rigorous defense, the Circuit Court of Lowndes County denied Gibbs's Motion to Dismiss.[60]

As in Bei Bei Shuai's case, the potential criminal sanctions were quite severe. Under state statute, Gibbs's pregnancy was by default the product of statutory rape, given her age. Prosecutors ignored that, instead charging her with a crime that has an automatic life sentence in Mississippi.[61] Gibbs's prosecution was one of first impression in Mississippi, as no previous second-degree murder charges had been instigated against a woman or girl for a case of stillbirth. According to Gibbs's legal counsel, "there ha[ve] been no reported cases and no media reports showing that the State of Mississippi ha[s] ever applied the depraved-heart homicide statute to a pregnant woman who suffered a stillbirth or miscarriage."[62] That no prior cases are reported of a pregnant woman charged with this offense is unsurprising, because the explicit language of the statute does not "encompass the death of an unborn child."[63] Nor does the legislation on its face include pregnant women within the scope of the class of persons who can be prosecuted for violating this statute.[64]

In 2014, charges related to her 2006 stillbirth were finally dismissed. Even so, Mississippi prosecutors vowed to reindict her for manslaughter.[65] Gibbs's attorneys continue to argue that the Mississippi legislature never intended the statute to apply to the unborn. They specifically cite the statutory language, highlighting that the statute underpinning Rennie Gibbs's prosecution, Mississippi Code § 97-3-37, "specifically provides that an 'unborn child' can be the victim of assault, capital murder, and certain types of manslaughter, but not depraved heart murder."[66] Moreover, they assert that, because there is "no reference to 'unborn child[ren]' in the depraved heart section of that statute, 97-3-19(1)(b)." A reasonable interpretation of the law is that the legislature never intended the law to apply against pregnant women and therefore the statute is misapplied against Miss Gibbs.[67] Yet, the risks and trauma of prosecution and incarceration remain. And legislatures amend existing laws and enact new ones to criminalize fetal endangerment.

3.1.4 *Amending Old Law to Cover the Unborn*

Legal innovation in reproductive health also includes expanding existing legislation to cover the unborn. For example, in Florida, the "killing of unborn quick child by injury to mother" law expanded criminal laws to include the unlawful killing of a fetus or an "unborn quick child" as murder in the same degree "as that which would have been committed against the mother."[68] Other provisions of the law created new crimes to include the killing of a fetus as manslaughter, and extended punishment to vehicular homicide[69] and driving under the influence (DUI) manslaughter.[70] It is worth noting that at the time of this Florida enactment the law carved out an exception for abortion and prosecuting pregnant women.

Recently, however, Florida and other state legislatures have turned to personhood legislation to expand fetal protection, even against pregnant women. For example, in Arizona, SB 1052 (enacted on April 25, 2005) amended several state statutes[71] to grant viable and nonviable fetuses the status of minors less than twelve years of age for purposes of determining criminal sentencing in murder and manslaughter cases.[72]

Such statutes and ensuing court rulings provide models that conservative activist groups mobilize legislatures to adopt and prosecutors to prosecute.[73]

3.1.5 *New Laws and Expansive Interpretations of Them*

States sometimes pass general statutes, such as drug laws, which state courts then expansively interpret to cover the endangerment of fetuses, even nonviable ones. For example, in 2006, Alabama legislators enacted § 26-15-3.2, Alabama Code 197, commonly referred to as the chemical endangerment statute. The statute provides that "a responsible person commits the crime of chemical endangerment [by] exposing a child to an *environment* in which he or she ... knowingly, recklessly, or intentionally causes or permits a child to be exposed to, to ingest or inhale, or to have contact with a control substance, chemical substance, or drug paraphernalia."[74]

State courts, however, expansively interpret these statutes to cover fetuses. In 2013, the Alabama Supreme Court did so, further expanding fetal rights in that state by interpreting the term "child" as used in this statute to include both viable and nonviable fetuses.[75] The Alabama Supreme Court upheld this ruling in *Ex parte Hope Elisabeth Ankrom* – ruling it not only illegal for a pregnant woman to ingest illicit substances, but also to enter dwellings and other locations where such substances are manufactured or sold. In that case, the court reasoned that the word "environment" includes where a person lives and can refer to "an unborn child's existence within its mother's womb."[76] Because the court held that the term "child" included unborn fetuses, now exposing a fetus to an environment where controlled substances are present could be considered child endangerment.

3.1.6 *A New Legislative Movement: Personhood for Preembryos, Embryos, and Fetuses*

Proponents of fetal personhood argue that no differences in status or rights exist between children and fetuses. They claim that no differences exist between children and fetuses whether the former are viable or not. To them, the line between child and fetus is spurious at best.[77] Representative Dick Jones (R-Topeka, Kansas) has explained the theory behind the new personhood movement this way: "The moment of conception when the finger of life is touched to that fetus, to that egg, it becomes a human being with all the inherent rights."[78] Staunch interpreters of personhood propose granting constitutional rights to preembryos and even claim those rights are on a par with pregnant women's rights.

In Georgia, embryos are now deemed to have "rights and responsibilities" under state law.[79] The bill granting embryo rights in that state, HB 388, is the nation's first embryo adoption law.[80] The legislation's sponsor, former Representative James Mills, has also sought to amend Georgia's constitution to include the "Human Life Amendment," which he described as "a peaceful and positive movement to restore respect for life, liberty and the pursuit of happiness for Americans of all ages."[81] Representative Mills issued statements comparing embryos that have not developed to fetal stage to "children" for purposes of law.[82] Relatedly, in Wisconsin, lawmakers proposed a bill that "would grant human embryos the same civil rights as people."[83]

Personhood referenda mark a significant phenomenon in legal innovation and the advancement of fetal protection efforts. Personhood legislation grants the status and rights of being born to fetuses and sometimes embryos, including in nonviable pregnancies, contradicting the framework of prevailing constitutional law. For example, the North Dakota Senate and House passed the "inalienable right to life of every human being at every stage of development" law in 2013, granting embryos and conceivably preembryos "inalienable" rights.[84]

The North Dakota law failed a popular ballot vote in 2014. Nonetheless, the legislation – the first of its kind in the United States to pass both the Senate and House – mandated that "the inalienable right to life of every human being at any stage of development must be recognized and protected." In an interview with a news magazine, Senator Margaret Sitte, sponsor of North Dakota's personhood law, admitted that undermining *Roe v. Wade* was the purpose of her legislation. She explained, "We are intending that it be a direct challenge to Roe v. Wade, since [Justice] Scalia said that the Supreme Court is waiting for states to raise a case."[85]

States and their lawmakers invoke a range of chilling arguments to support the establishment of fetal rights and impose limits on women's reproductive rights. Texas representative Michael Burgess argued in favor of fetal rights because he believes male fetuses feel sexual pleasure. According to the congressman, "male bab[ies] . . . may have their hand between their legs," because "they feel pleasure."[86] He asked colleagues, "If [male fetuses] can feel pleasure, why is it so hard to think that they could feel pain?"[87]

Representative Trent Franks (R-Arizona), a proponent of fetal rights and advocate for the position that fetuses experience pain, sponsored the Pain-Capable Unborn Child Protection Act, which aimed to preclude all women from having abortions, except in the case of impending death. When amendments were proposed permitting exceptions in cases of rape and incest, "Republicans on the [House Judiciary Committee] unanimously voted against the amendments, arguing that rape and incest exceptions were unacceptable."[88] The lawmakers believed that fetal rights superseded those of pregnant women, even pregnant victims of rape.

That these measures are gaining momentum is evidenced by the broad number of states taking up personhood legislation – even when such measures ultimately fail at the ballot. Referenda in Colorado and Mississippi and petitions in Alabama, California, Florida, Georgia, Kansas, Montana, Nevada, Ohio, Virginia, and other states to redefine "personhood" mark only the most recent manifestations of legislative fetal protection efforts. Despite the fact these personhood amendments (except in Alabama) have so far failed, arrests, prosecutions, and involuntary "maternity rest" restraining orders obtained against pregnant women under other extant state laws evidence that such fetal protection efforts are more than an isolated, fringe legislative movement.[89]

3.1.7 *Other State Interventions: Civil Incarceration*

Civil incarceration is another means by which women's pregnancies may be subject to surveillance and hostile state intervention. Civil incarcerations in Wisconsin pursuant to that state's Unborn Child Protection Act[90] demonstrate how states may prioritize the legal interests of fetuses above those of pregnant women. In 1997, when Governor Thomas Thompson signed the legislation into law, lawmakers and others euphemistically referred to it as the "crack mama law". At the time, crack was stereotyped as a drug primarily or exclusively used among Blacks, and because of this some civil rights activists perceived the law as unfairly targeting Black women.

However, many recent civil confinements have not concerned Black women alone. According to National Advocates for Pregnant Women, while the exact number of women in Wisconsin civilly confined under its laws is unknown, "through their litigation they discovered more than 3,300 cases alleging what is called unborn child abuse in Wisconsin," resulting in actions taken against nearly 500 women since 2006.[91] Nor is the Wisconsin law benign, because the statute delegates proceedings to juvenile courts where there are no public records of the proceedings and adult women have no right to counsel, although the state accords their fetuses this right.

In July 2013, Alicia Beltran, a twenty-eight-year-old white woman, was arrested, shackled, and confined by court order to a drug treatment center for seventy-eight days after she refused a doctor's order to take a potentially dangerous opiate blocker that she had decided was unnecessary.[92] She was fourteen weeks pregnant and at the time no medical threat to her fetus existed.[93] In that case, Beltran had confided to medical staff at a prenatal checkup that she battled addiction to opiates in the past but had overcome drug dependency and had recently taken only a single Vicodin tablet for pain before becoming aware of her pregnancy.[94] The state denied Beltran's request for an attorney at each of her hearings, although legal counsel was provided for her fetus. Because Beltran was incarcerated, and thus unable to return to work, she lost her job and housing. When finally released from the state's custody, Beltran lacked the means to support herself or the baby she was soon to deliver.

Within a year of Beltran's incarceration, Tamara Loertscher, a twenty-nine-year-old white woman, was forced into solitary confinement by the state of Wisconsin, also for the purpose of protecting her fetus, after she refused to submit to a pregnancy test and inpatient treatment.[95] Loertscher claimed that, in addition to subjecting her to solitary confinement, correction officials threatened "to use a taser on her."[96] Loertscher was subjected to confinement until she signed a consent decree requiring her to submit to drug treatment and monitoring by authorities.

In her case, Loertscher filed a lawsuit under 42 U.S.C. § 1983, claiming that the law violated her constitutional rights. In 2017, District Judge James Peterson agreed and blocked enforcement of Wisconsin's civil confinement law, finding the statute unconstitutionally vague. He explained that "the expert evidence here makes one thing abundantly clear: current medical science cannot tell us what level of drug or alcohol use will pose a substantial risk of serious damage to an unborn child."[97] The state appealed to the Court of Appeals for the Seventh Circuit and ultimately to the United States Supreme Court. Wisconsin argued that the injunction threatened the health and safety of unborn children. The Supreme Court lifted the injunction.[98]

3.2 EXTRALEGAL CONSEQUENCES

Who are the victims in these prosecutions? Despite the stories conveyed here, the women described in this Chapter are for the most part invisible. Concerns related to reproductive rights generally focus on abortion and not punishments for continuing pregnancies. These women are also unaccounted for in the broader discussions about criminal justice.

Women's invisibility to lawmakers, activists, and scholars studying the drug war may account for their misreading of the drug war as a problem in society generally about men and especially Black men. This misreading of the drug war and its gendered impacts neglects the unique ways in which women and children become invisible, collateral damage, and endure mass incarceration. Lawmakers overlooked or ignored the potentially harmful impacts of these policies.

3.2.1 *The Perspective of Prosecutors*

I interviewed Angela Hulsey and Kyle Brown, both Alabama prosecutors.[99] They are two of the five prosecutors I spoke to about the striking trend in Alabama of doctors surrendering patient information and medical records to law enforcement, the arrests, and plea deals. Many of the cases simply end in plea deals. A ten- or twenty-year plea deal is a bitter pill, but not unusual in these cases. Prosecutor Hulsey told me that, in her experience, "these cases settle 95 percent of the time because of the nature of the evidence that has already been presented to us against the person who has been accused."

I wondered about the quality of lawyers and they told me that for the relative few that can afford a private lawyer, they have "noticed a difference." However, "it is pretty clear to most of the attorneys with clients charged ... it is clear the law is on the side of the state."[100] Carrie Buck, the poor white girl whom the state of Virginia compulsorily sterilized, quickly flashed to my mind. I wondered about her case. Her attorney also knew the law was on the side of the state and therefore did very little to defend her against the reach of the state's law.

They let me know that one key reason their cases settle before trial is because the women are afraid. They tell me that it is obvious when the women know prosecutors will bring the case "to a jury it is going to be inflammatory particularly before a conservative Colbert County jury." This is "something that would factor into the attorney's counsel to a client – a heavy consideration."

We talk about the case of Amanda Kimbrough. I spent weeks in Alabama but never had the opportunity to meet Ms. Kimbrough, then an inmate at the "notoriously tough" Tutwiler women's prison in Wetumpka, Alabama.[101] Her mugshot is among the many my research assistants and I spent months gathering. I think about this image and the word stoic comes to mind.

In September 2008, Kimbrough was charged under the Alabama chemical endangerment statute. Her bond was set at half a million dollars. According to the indictment, she "did knowingly, recklessly, or intentionally cause or permit a child, Timmy Wayne Kimbrough, to be exposed to, to ingest or inhale, or to have contact with a controlled substance, to wit: methamphetamine."[102]

Kimbrough's mugshot (and those of other similarly situated women in Alabama) interrupts the old narrative commonly associated with drug prosecutions of pregnant women (or women who were pregnant). She is white, tall, blond, and with penetrating blue eyes. She is married and a mother to two daughters. However, through her prosecution and plea deal, she became Alabama prisoner 287089, convicted for the death of her premature baby, Timmy Wayne Kimbrough, who survived nineteen minutes after birth.

As she told others at the time, "I am against abortion, I was going to keep my baby no matter what . . . It's my baby. I'd do any and everything I could for my kids."[103] For this reason, even when she discovered at twenty weeks that the baby might be at risk of Down syndrome, she rejected a doctor's recommendation that she travel to Birmingham, Alabama for an abortion. However, these are not the concerns of prosecutors.

Kimbrough's case was unique, because she took her case to trial. Prosecutor Hulsey confidently told me, "We had put all our evidence in and she pled guilty." She did not seem surprised by Kimbrough's guilty plea. Instead, she mentioned that Kimbrough "raised an issue about how these types of cases should not be prosecuted."[104] I remain silent, as I believe the same.

She intimated that Kimbrough's case fell apart when "it was her turn to show their case before the jury." Maybe Hulsey was right: the fear of a tougher sentence motivates these women to settle. She told me, "Her last hope was maybe the judge would grant a motion for a judgment of acquittal. The only option was to go to the jury and take her chances or plead." The bottom line was this, according to the prosecutor, "had she taken it to the jury, the judge could have sentenced her to the maximum."[105] Instead, she took a ten-year plea deal. This was the first case of its kind tried through their office. She paused. Since Kimbrough, her office has prosecuted about fifteen other pregnant women or new mothers.

Prosecutor Hulsey informed me that a lot of times these cases hinge on informants – and many times the informants come from within the hospital. She told me there are motions that can be made "to protect the identity of informers." She explained, "We want to protect the identity of the reporter." Before we end the call, she informed me that "when a case is presented ... our goal is to represent the state of Alabama in the best of our ability; our goal is to represent the victims; the victims are the most vulnerable, relying on their mothers' womb[s]; they have no means to protect themselves."[106] Who, I wondered to myself, protects the pregnant women? Kyle Brown, who had not said much in this interview, closed our call by noting that the Alabama Supreme Court has now given "widespread legal recognition that unborn children have rights by law, and the only place where they do not have rights is with abortion." His final words to me were: "unborn children have rights."[107]

The prosecutors were courteous and generous with their time. When our interview ended, I still had more questions, but I was not sure if they have answers. Is Alabama's use of its chemical endangerment law to prosecute pregnant women in line with legislative intent? Did legislators really intend to use that law as a dragnet against pregnant women in its state or rather enact it to deter exposing children to noxious fumes and even fires resulting from makeshift methamphetamine laboratories and dispensaries cropping up in trailer homes? The legislation's author never intended its application against pregnant women.[108] However, at this stage, that seems not to matter to the Alabama prosecutors whom I interviewed, or to judges for that matter.

3.2.2 *Learning from McKnight's Case*

Even when prosecutors believe they vindicate the rights of fetuses and newborns, they do so at enormous costs. Significant costs are associated with surveilling pregnancy for purposes of criminal law enforcement. The rise in the incarceration of pregnant women and mothers; the chilling prenatal visits and honest disclosures to medical providers, forging distrust in the physician-patient relationship; the increasing fiscal responsibility of the state; the long-term socioeconomic consequences to women; and the psychological harms to pregnant women and their children are all significant costs. The monetary costs alone can be quite high. The range is vast: in New York nearly $70,000 per inmate per year, versus $20,000 per year in South Carolina. Even at the lower end, when multiplied by decades and number of convictions, the costs add up.[109]

Consider once more the case of Regina McKnight, sentenced to twenty years in prison for her stillbirth. Remember she was an example of why prosecutors needed to brandish a "stick" approach to monitoring pregnancy. After serving nearly a decade in prison, McKnight was released, her sentence unanimously overturned by the South Carolina Supreme Court. On the one hand, her case exemplified the criminal justice system working after all – eventually, McKnight secured her freedom.

On the other hand, by the time of her release, McKnight had suffered the shaming, stigma, and indignity of multiple trials, accusations that she was cold-hearted and indecent, and a lengthy confinement in prison. Moreover, because most states do not automatically expunge criminal records after acquittals and pardons, women like Regina McKnight often suffer lingering consequences of incarceration, including difficulty in finding employment, housing, and even volunteer work. In many states, women with criminal records are unable to qualify for seemingly innocuous jobs such as cutting or braiding hair. The economic burdens related to incarceration, especially for drug-related offenses, are long-lasting and particularly harsh for single mothers.

McKnight's prosecution should be viewed as a cautionary tale. The case highlights the increasingly dangerous zone that pregnancy occupies in American law. Criminalizing conduct during pregnancy can ultimately undermine fetal health by chilling voluntary participation in prenatal medical visits. If women stand the risk of harassment and arrest while seeking medical care, the most vulnerable amongst them may choose to go without, particularly as incarceration impacts not only their own lives but also those of their children and families.

McKnight's case set a dangerous precedent, soon followed by other courts in other jurisdictions even while her prosecution and conviction went largely unnoticed in popular media and public discourse. The case marked a watershed moment in U.S. law for several reasons. First, the case sanctioned the criminalization of pregnancy. It established the troubling precedent that a woman's pregnancy could give rise to criminal investigation, prosecution, and punishment for murder against *her*. For centuries, courts resisted this type of jurisprudence in both tort and criminal law.[110] But no longer.

Second, McKnight's prosecution established conduct during pregnancy as a site for criminal law intervention. It contributed to the normalization of police and prosecutorial involvement in women's reproductive health. In McKnight's case, the result was a prosecution for murder. In subsequent South Carolina cases, law enforcement targeted poor women of color in the wake of healthy births, premature births, and for miscarriages.[111]

Third, McKnight's prosecution advanced a seriously distressing proposition related to perfection in pregnancy. Under this ruling, women's pregnancies could be held to a standard of faultlessness in South Carolina. Prosecutors erroneously assumed (and the court did too) that, absent depraved conduct on the part of pregnant women, stillbirths do not occur and that all pregnancies produce healthy babies except if the mother's conduct threatens fetal health. To the contrary, "stillbirth is one of the most common adverse outcomes of pregnancy."[112]

Stillbirths result from any number of factors.[113] Upwards of 30 percent of pregnancies will terminate in miscarriage or stillbirth.[114] Notwithstanding rigorous efforts to identify what causes perinatal fetal mortality, researchers report that "a substantial portion of fetal deaths are still classified as unexplained intrauterine fetal demise,"[115] because stillbirths are linked to environment,[116] diabetes,[117] hypertension,[118] poverty,[119] sexually transmitted diseases,[120] and stress.[121]

Implicit in McKnight's conviction and subsequent cases involving pregnant women arrested and jailed for refusing cesarean sections, falling down steps, attempting suicide, and more, are assumptions and expectations about women's conduct during pregnancy. The message of McKnight's case was that failure to comply with the state's perceptions of healthy conduct could result in arrest and punishment. This overbroad and vague standard could logically produce extreme anxiety in any pregnant woman, because even drinking tap water in some U.S. cities and towns could produce negative impacts in fetuses and children.[122] The McKnight case demonstrated that if stillbirths could be prosecuted, then in all probability so could other pregnancy outcomes.

Finally, McKnight's conviction served to politicize pregnancies, linking gestation with federal efforts to demonstrate toughness on drug crimes. McKnight's conviction ensnared pregnancy as part of the "tough on crime" and "tough on drugs" policies of the drug war. Her prosecution opened a new avenue for police and prosecutors to advance an unsuccessful campaign to reduce the incidence of illicit drug use by arresting women at prenatal visits, dragging them into police cars shackled and handcuffed after delivery, and calling on doctors to disclose confidential medical records in the process.

3.2.3 *Children and Collateral Damage*

What happens to the children when their mothers agree to lengthy plea deals or suffer civil confinement? This questions are relevant to the concerns addressed in this Chapter and the policy solutions that follow. Emerging empirical research answers important questions regarding whether the children of incarcerated mothers are better or worse off, thus challenging some of the intuitions undergirding contemporary criminal punishment generally, and maternal policy specifically. The data illumes the myriad traumas experienced by children of incarcerated parents.

That is, the collateral consequences of policing pregnancy extend beyond pregnant women, reaching children in devastating, unintended, and frequently overlooked ways. More than two-thirds of women in prison are mothers.[123] Often, these mothers are the primary caregivers to their children (and other relatives) prior to entering the criminal justice system – by a wide margin. Incarcerated women are three times more likely than fathers to be the sole source of income and provider of basic needs for their children.

According to the Bureau of Justice Statistics:

Mothers were more likely than fathers to report living with at least one child. More than half of mothers held in state prison reported living with at least one of their children in the month before arrest, compared to 36% of fathers. More than 6 in 10 mothers reported living with their children just prior to incarceration or at either time, compared to less than half of fathers.[124]

When their mothers are removed from home to serve time in states' jails and prisons, instability and insecurity enter children's lives.[125] Sometimes their mothers are relocated to other states, making it difficult to maintain contact and facilitate visits. Research led by Professor Kristin Turney, a sociologist studying the effects of parental incarceration in the lives of children, offers disquieting insights. Her research identifies the deleterious impacts of parental incarceration on children.

Children who experience parental incarceration suffer greater harms related to attention deficit, behavior or conduct problems, language and articulation challenges, and developmental delays than children who experience parental divorce or parental death.[126] Parental incarceration is so deleterious to children that those who have a household member with a "drug or alcohol problem" are yet better off according to physical and psychological indicators than children with a parent in jail or prison.[127]

In essence, parental incarceration harms children in ways previously unreported and states' actions are implicated in the harms to children of incarcerated parents. According to Turney, these harms include both physical and psychological impacts on the children, which can be long-lasting. These are matters about which lawmakers and other stakeholders should be concerned.

Additionally, the escalation of mothers behind bars now results in babies born behind bars and children incarcerated alongside their mothers as a policy solution. This highlights another area of concern and inquiry, because mass incarceration's deeply contentious and fraught realities have direct impacts on babies and children who essentially serve time with their mothers. These incarcerations are not necessarily due to fetal protection laws; most are for drug-related offenses of some sort.[128]

In its report *Mothers, Infants and Imprisonment*, the Women's Prison Association's Institute on Women and Criminal Justice, states that because "the number of women in prison has skyrocketed over the past 30 years, states have had to consider what it means to lock up women, many of whom are pregnant or parenting."[129] In most cases, children of incarcerated mothers, whether their births occur behind bars or not, move into various forms of "other" care, which may include relatives, foster homes, shelters, group homes, and other arrangements.

For the babies and children who have the benefit of residing with their mothers in prison nursery programs, the outcomes for both mothers and their babies show significant promise: recidivism rates are lower and, so far, "children show no adverse effects" from their lives behind bars.[130] Research shows that "by keeping mothers and infants together, these programs prevent foster care placement and allow for the formation of maternal/child bonds during a critical period of infant development."[131] However, these options are complicated too. Overcrowding, medical neglect, and unsanitary conditions describe only some of the difficulties incarcerated people experience. These are also tough places, where violence is common. One reporter described the conditions of American prisons where nurseries are found: "you walk through a metal detector and a locked steel door to a courtyard surrounded by razor wire and two 20-foot fences."[132] This is what the children of the nursery cast their gaze upon when they look outside. Research has yet to address the long-term consequences of children accompanying their mothers to prison.

3.3 CONCLUSION

As this Chapter explains, choosing birth has become a political landmine and trigger for state surveillance and criminalization of poor pregnant women, with severe extralegal consequences. These penalties now include criminal and civil incarceration for miscarriage and stillbirth, as well as punishments for behaviors perceived to threaten fetal health. This political shift in reproductive politics now redefines women's responsibilities and obligations during pregnancy, the status of preembryos, embryos, and fetuses, and the power of the state vis-à-vis pregnant women.

This Chapter articulates three important themes about this shift in contemporary reproductive politics in the United States. First, it tells a story about legal innovation through the propagation of fetal protection laws. It explains how the frontlines of fetal protection strategically shifted to pregnancy. As such, existing laws were applied in new ways, such as extending child abuse statutes to fetuses and embryos, thereby redefining the terms of engagement with reproductive rights. New laws also emerged making explicit states' agendas in both surveilling pregnancy and criminalizing conduct perceived as threatening fetal health. Through this agenda, fetal rights have now emerged.

Second, the Chapter underscores the importance of ethnography in reproductive rights. That is, it emphasizes the value of hearing the stories of women targeted by these new legal innovations as a way of perceiving what is at stake in their lives. By doing so, we come to understand legal innovations that disrupt and undermine reproductive rights – frequently at the expense of the most vulnerable.

Third, the Chapter articulates a blind spot within reproductive rights discourse and advocacy. It argues that a reproductive rights framework, which perceives abortion rights as its only or primary objective, woefully misreads reproductive health and the social contexts in which women live their lives. Framing reproductive rights as abortion rights both undermines the security of an abortion right and problematically ignores the broader interests contained within reproductive privacy. Simply put, limiting reproductive rights to abortion rights undermines the importance of women's reproductive health. This framing disserves women who choose to parent even under arduous circumstances and ultimately impairs the abortion right itself.

4

Abortion Law

"I will do anything and everything to stop the unmitigated murders of fetuses. I will do anything to stop the atrocities committed by your clinic every minute of every day at your clinic. You are all pieces of shit and I will kill to stop these atrocities. I will blow you up if I have to, burn the clinic down. I will do whatever is necessary. I swear to God I will. After that you are in God's hands and He will do His thing."

Luke Daniel Wiersma (sentenced to eighteen months in federal prison)

In the late fall of 2015, three people were tragically gunned down at a Planned Parenthood clinic in Colorado Springs. The shootings were followed by hours of standstill. Businesses were evacuated. I thought of a colleague who performs abortions. She works in a conservative county and many of her patients are women who tell her that they want her care, but they do not want to call it an abortion. They tussle with words as she explains that she cannot provide the service if they do not understand what it means. They say they understand, but want to make sure that the doctor knows they are not like the other women. She wonders, who are the other women? Most of these women are white, regularly attend church, and would identify as conservative. After the doctor and her patients come to terms with the language – it is an abortion – the women have the procedure and go home.

Sometimes, the women my colleague sees have been raped. Sometimes, they are domestic violence victims, not yet survivors, trying to figure a way out. One time, a patient came with her boyfriend, but did not want the doctor to give any hint of what was happening. The boyfriend was possessive and abusive, and simply would not let the girlfriend out of his sight and reach. Sometimes I receive a call from my colleague as she is curious about a certain question of law. The thing that stays with me is that she never posts her photo at the university where she teaches. When she is the plenary or keynote speaker at an event, she refuses to have her image in the program. She reminds me that she has two children. Two little girls. She does not want anyone to find her daughters, show up at her doorstep, and gun them down.

Are the doctor's fears irrational? Should she just ease up? I think about Michael Griffin, James Kopp, Paul Jennings Hill, Peter Knight, and John Salvi – killers who stalked doctors who perform abortions. They showed up at homes, churches, and the workplace with bombs and guns. The National Abortion Federation estimates that there have been almost 400 credible death threats against medical providers or clinics that help women with their abortions. The doctors are afraid not only for themselves but also their families.

The fatal shooting in Colorado could be counted alongside a deadly history of violent attacks on abortion providers. The victims are doctors, guards, friends of patients seeking medical care at clinics. In Colorado, it was Robert L. Dear, Jr. who opened fire with a semiautomatic weapon. He told authorities that he was concerned about the "body parts." The shooting occurred after undercover, surreptitious, illegal videos were made and spliced together, seeming to suggest that abortion providers at Planned Parenthood were selling fetal remains. Planned Parenthood was investigated and cleared of allegations, but even so, that would not bring back the lives of those who were stalked and killed.

***

The battle over women's autonomy, especially their reproductive healthcare and decision-making, has always been about much more than simply women's health and safety. Rather, male power, control, and dominion over women's reproduction historically served political purposes and entrenched social and cultural norms that framed women's capacities almost exclusively as service to a husband,[1] mothering,[2] reproducing,[3] and sexual chattel.[4] For example, tort law carved out specific remedies for husbands who suffered the loss of their wives' servitude and sex under the "loss of consortium" cause of action. Historically, loss of consortium litigation provided economic remedies only for husbands. This law derives from the legal premise that the husband is the master of the wife. She is his servant. Thus, when wives suffered a physical injury, husbands could file suit against third parties for the "loss" of their wives' servitude, companionship, and sex.

Due to the widespread practice of chattel slavery in the seventeenth, eighteenth, and nineteenth centuries in the United States, most Black women, their mothers, and daughters encountered or directly suffered the physical norms and conditions of that cruel enterprise, including physical bondage, food deprivation, and physical torture (whippings, brining, and amputations of fingers and toes). They also endured reproductive coercion and terror, including sexual assaults, rapes, forced reproduction, and stripping away of offspring. Not every state tolerated the physical and sexual barbarism common to states like Mississippi, South Carolina, and Louisiana. However, even states like New York, Vermont, and Maine practiced slavery with fervor. In New York, it is estimated that 20 percent of its colonial population were slaves (over 40 percent of New York households owned slaves), meaning that Black women were no more protected from the abuses of chattel slavery there than in Alabama, Georgia, or Virginia.

Coverture laws extended an aspect of bondage and repression to white women. Coverture laws adopted by U.S. courts were unmistakably distinct in form and practice from chattel slavery, especially as white women retained many other freedoms, including the ability to own slaves. Nonetheless, coverture rendered white women the property of their husbands, and one key aspect of their servitude was obedience to their husbands. Courts legitimized coverture by upholding laws that sanctioned or imposed no punishments against husbands beating and sexually assaulting their wives.

Even after the ratification of the Fourteenth Amendment, while legislatures recognized women's citizenship, they insisted upon denying them suffrage based on the fiction that women lacked the sophistication of mind and judgment to cast a vote.[5] Legislatures debated whether a woman's vote would essentially accrue to her husband. The Supreme Court deferred to state legislatures on this sophistry and solidified women's political subordination by ruling in *Minor v. Happersett* that although the Constitution granted women citizenship, it did not confer upon them a right to vote.

These were not the norms foisted on men. White men in particular were spared the indignities of legal marginalization as legislatures and courts reserved and promoted special status for them. As the Supreme Court declared in *Ozawa v. United States* in 1922, "The provision is not that Negroes and Indians shall be *excluded* but it is, in effect, that only free white persons shall be *included*. The intention was to confer the privilege of citizenship upon that class of persons whom the fathers knew as white, and to deny it to all who could not be so classified."[6]

In that case, the Supreme Court unanimously ruled that a Japanese-American man was ineligible for citizenship because the legislature intended naturalization in the United States only for "free white persons." One year later, in *United States v. Bhagat Singh Thind*, the Justices unanimously affirmed that a person of Indian Sikh ethnicity did not fit the "common sense" definition of "free white person," despite being anthropologically Aryan and a former World War I army veteran. The Supreme Court left no room for doubt that the Naturalization Act of 1906 intended to confer citizenship and whiteness only on people who looked white. Justice Sutherland wrote the Court's opinion, stating, "it may be true that the blond Scandinavian and the brown Hindu have a common ancestor in the dim reaches of antiquity, but the average man knows perfectly well that there are unmistakable and profound differences between them today; and it is not impossible, if that common ancestor could be materialized in the flesh, we should discover that he was himself sufficiently differentiated from both of his descendants to preclude his racial classification with either."

Instead, in the United States, common law granted white men not only citizenship but also recovery for the losses associated with their wives' sexual unavailability and even for the debauchery of their daughters.[7] Women's sex and sexuality were not only the legal domains of husbands but also the preoccupations of fathers, because the law deemed wives, daughters, slaves, and field animals the property or chattel of men.[8] In other words, law serves a profound role in the making and unmaking of persons, particularly women, and especially women of color.[9]

In turn, such social norms – often enforced by statutes and court rulings – were rooted in rhetoric rather than the realities of women's autonomy, humanity, experiences, capacities, and lived lives. Courts played a profound role in conscribing women to second-class citizenship that denied them broad civic participation, including voting, participating on juries,[10] and professional employment. In *Bradwell v. Illinois*, the U.S. Supreme Court upheld a law barring women law graduates from practicing law.[11] Justice Joseph Bradley found that nature and law deemed it "repugnant" for a woman to adopt "a distinct and independent" civic life from her husband because by law she lacked fundamental capacities. A subsequent ruling by the Wisconsin State Supreme Court in *In re Goodell* further illustrates the rhetoric strategically deployed by legislatures and courts to deny women personhood and autonomy over their lives:

> We cannot but think the common law wise in excluding women from the profession of the law. . . . The law of nature destines and qualifies the female sex for the bearing and nurture of the children of our race and for the custody of the homes of the world and their maintenance in love and honor. . . . There are many employments in life not unfit for female character. The profession of the law is surely not one of these. The peculiar qualities of womanhood, its gentle graces, its quick sensibility, its tender susceptibility, its purity, its delicacy, its emotional impulses, its subordination of hard reason to sympathetic feeling, are surely not qualifications for forensic strife.[12]

Of course, such rhetoric constrained women's abilities to use their bodies in professional labor. Most importantly, by declaring that so-called laws of nature dictate that women bear children, the court served to trap women into lives of subordination and servitude to husbands, children, and ultimately the state, which commanded women to serve those roles. Ironically, promoting women's safety, virtue, and protection was the legal lark that normalized this type of misogyny. It justified the subordination of women through harsh regulations and practices. Notably, however, neither legislatures nor courts were concerned about the validity of their claims on women's capacities. That is, facts and empirical truths regarding women's lives were meaningless or irrelevant.

Justice Harry Blackmun's majority opinion in *Roe v. Wade* significantly interrupted the Supreme Court's prior jurisprudence and therefore its rhetoric related to women, their autonomy, and capacities. In that case, roughly one hundred years after the Supreme Court upheld state laws barring women from voting and entering the practice of law, the Court acknowledged the chilling impacts associated with social stereotyping and stigmatization of women. In *Roe*, which decriminalized abortion in the United States, the Court finally acknowledged the "detriment" that the state had imposed on women by denying them choices about their reproductive destinies. Justice Blackmun candidly acknowledged the "[s]pecific and direct harm medically diagnosable even in early pregnancy" that some women may endure by being forced by the state to bear children.

Roe's reliance on social science represented a sea change; Justice Blackmun consulted science, history, and sociology to dispel the notion that abortion had always been illegal in the United States.[13] For the first time, the Court clearly articulated that motherhood and childbearing could be harmful to women. Further, forcing women into those destinies violated their constitutional right to privacy. Justice Blackmun wrote:

> Maternity, or additional offspring, may force upon the woman a distressful life and future. Psychological harm may be imminent. Mental and physical health may be taxed by child care. There is also the distress, for all concerned, associated with the unwanted child, and there is the problem of bringing a child into a family already unable, psychologically and otherwise, to care for it. In other cases, as in this one, the additional difficulties and continuing stigma of unwed motherhood may be involved.[14]

The Court explained, "we are also told ... that abortion was practiced in Greek times as well as in the Roman Era, and that 'it was resorted to without scruple.'"[15]

Indeed, abortion was practiced legally in the United States for centuries prior to brutal nineteenth-century antiabortion campaigns launched by male physicians who sought to monopolize women's healthcare by driving out and criminalizing midwives and stigmatizing abortion.[16] Dr. Horatio Storer, a chief architect of the nineteenth-century antiabortion/antimidwife movement, wrote that "[midwives] frequently cause abortion openly and without disguise."[17] Even more unsettling to him, "[t]hey claim a right to use instruments, and to decide on the necessity and consequent justifiability of any operation they may perform."[18] Undoubtedly, that level of expertise, autonomy, and independence among midwives, who were predominantly Black, proved too threatening for an organized group of powerful men seeking to create the new profession called gynecology.

Referencing aspects of this history, the Court wrote: "It is undisputed that at common law, abortion performed *before* 'quickening' – the first recognizable movement of the fetus in utero, appearing usually from the 16th to the 18th week of pregnancy – was not an indictable offense."[19] Justice Blackmun canvassed Christian theology and canon law, finding that "[t]here was agreement ... that prior to [quickening] the fetus was to be regarded as part of the mother, and its destruction, therefore, was not homicide." The Court noted that prior to "the anti-abortion mood" that became prevalent in the late nineteenth century, abortions were not criminalized. In other words, "a woman enjoyed a substantially broader right to terminate a pregnancy" until the antiabortion campaigns that coincided with the abolitionist and suffrage movements in the United States.

Today, however, *Roe's* legacy remains uncertain. In 2018, the Trump administration announced that it would enact new rules barring U.S. medical providers that receive Title X funding from counseling their patients on abortion or making referrals for the medical treatment. The new rule, if successfully implemented, will impact four million poor Americans who receive reproductive health services under the Title X program.[20] In essence, the administration is proposing a gag rule on American doctors, much like that imposed on foreign providers.

Campaigns to undo the hard-fought rights gained by women to govern their bodies and reproductive health now result in the closing of clinics that perform not only abortion but also a plethora of women's reproductive health services. Millions of poor women are trapped, living in states where only one abortion clinic remains – such as Missouri, Mississippi, North Dakota, South Dakota, and Wyoming – forced to drive hours, even in life-threatening pregnancies, to arrive at the nearest clinic. Despite the promise of *Whole Woman's Health v. Hellerstedt*,[21] states continue to erect serious barriers to women's reproductive autonomy by enacting Targeted Regulation of Abortion Providers (TRAP) laws, which claim to protect and promote women's health. Empirically, however, such laws do not promote women's health. As described earlier in this book, in the United States a woman is fourteen times more likely to die in pregnancy or childbirth than during an abortion. This simple and important fact – that abortion is safer than childbirth – is obscured in the antiabortion legislating.

For example, in 2017, only months after the Supreme Court struck down ambulatory surgical center requirements as a condition for a clinic's licensure to provide abortions, Minnesota state legislators sponsored an almost identical bill before that state's legislature.[22] Notwithstanding the fact that the bill lacked constitutional muster, because statutes requiring ambulatory surgical center standards for abortion clinics are unconstitutional as a matter of law, litigating TRAP legislation exacts an enormous financial toll on women's health organizations. However, these laws are not about promoting women's health.

In Minnesota, according to data I obtained from the Minnesota Department of Health, complications associated with an abortion are less than 0.01 percent. In my written and public testimony before the Minnesota State Legislature Committee on Judiciary and Public Safety Finance and Policy, I emphasized this. My testimony informed the legislators that a woman in Minnesota is more likely to die from gun death, domestic violence, drug poisoning, homicide, and childbirth than from an abortion. Predictable deaths in Minnesota will not be from an abortion, but rather domestic violence and traumatic injuries from firearms. Firearms are the second leading cause of brain injury in Minnesota. A woman is more likely to die from a urinary tract infection during pregnancy than an abortion.

Finally, I told the nearly all-male committee that ambulatory surgical center requirements run afoul of constitutional law and Supreme Court precedent because they are medically unnecessary, create undue burdens, and offer no added health benefit to women seeking care. Increasingly, legislators opposed to abortion ignore these facts.

Those most disenfranchised by recent legislative policies that criminally target abortion providers are poor women, especially women of color nationally and internationally. Internationally, the United States now aggressively invests in depriving and divesting women and girls of reproductive privacy, autonomy, and equality.[23] Not surprisingly, the rhetoric used to justify the enactment of far-reaching antiabortion (and increasingly anticontraception) laws domestically and abroad ignores science, history, sociology, and women's lived lives. When and if the Supreme Court undertakes an abortion law challenge, will the Justices heed the path of Blackmun or ignore empirical evidence altogether?

Much of the scholarly discussion unpacking antiabortion campaigns features Anthony Comstock, an antivice crusader and U.S. postal inspector, as the main force behind the outlawing of abortion. Yet, such important accounts overlook the explicit and direct role of doctors as fellow crusaders, whose interest in elevating their professional status came at the expense of female reproductive healthcare providers and patients. By law then, women were not only the property of their husbands at home, but ruled also by men in medicine. As Dr. Storer wrote, "medical men are the physical guardians of women and their offspring," because "their position and peculiar knowledge necessitated in all obstetric matters to regulate public sentiment and to govern the tribunals of justice."[24]

Ironically, antiabortion laws root not in claims of protecting the sanctity of life but, strangely, in the blocking of women from the practice of medicine and midwifery. Historically, abortion was legal and not criminalized in the United States. Women Colonial women had practiced both the delivery of pregnancies and the termination of the same since the earliest European settlements in this nation. Indigenous women governed the same with their bodies. These matters were the domains of pregnant women and the midwives who largely and quite successfully administered their care. In southern states many of these midwives or women trained in pregnancy delivery and termination were African American.[25] It is estimated that 50 percent of births in the United States were attended by Black midwives.[26]

Historically, the ban on abortion coincided with the monopolization of women's medical care by male physicians, supported and largely directed by the American Medical Association (AMA) and the efforts of its leadership. This largely disregarded or unknown history deserves greater attention within legal literature as it helps to contextualize abortion rights, debunk the notion that antiabortion sentiment is rooted historically in care for the fetus, and illuminates the entanglement of social status, political power, and the fight over control of women's bodies.

Today, abortion is a constitutionally protected right in the United States. Nevertheless, the law governing this right could be described as a mishmash –due, in part, to its history in the United States but also, in significant part, to the subordinate status of women, which spills out in the implicit and explicit paternalistic language of the U.S. Supreme Court. Currently, abortion law is governed by constitutional and state laws, federal statutes, and executive orders. Most importantly, no Supreme Court jurisprudence provides a basis for denying a woman access to an abortion, although state laws have been enacted in Alabama and Georgia to facilitate and justify this.

4.1 ABORTION AND MEDICAL CARE GOVERNING WOMEN'S BODIES

Medicinal as well as surgical abortions were legal in the seventeenth and eighteenth centuries in the United States. In fact, not until the late nineteenth century, during the post-antebellum period, did abortions come under attack and ultimately were banned in the United States – significantly because of shifts in the *politics* of medicine – with the consolidation of medical care taking a decidedly male turn, forcefully and legally shutting out midwives of all ethnic backgrounds from the practice of gynecological care.[27] According to Sharon Robinson, author of *A Historical Development of Midwifery in the Black Community*, "by the early 19th century, the male physician had succeeded in replacing midwives among upper- and middle-class white urban American women."

The origins of gynecology – a male dominated profession at its inception – is troubling. Physicians such as Dr. Marion Simms, known for conducting brutal experiments on the Black female slaves he rented, were associated with the birth of gynecology in the United States. Simms, who notoriously tortured Black women by lacerating, suturing, cutting, and experimenting on them (often without anesthesia) became hailed as the "grandfather" of gynecology in the United States. He practiced and perfected the cesarean section on nonconsenting, enslaved Black women. His innovations earned him a statue in New York's famed Central Park. Only recently has it been removed.

The rise of gynecology replaced midwifery and also contributed to the backlash against abortion. Abortion served as a powerful political tool to justify displacing midwives. The disdain for not only midwives but women generally comes through in the writings of early male gynecologists like Storer. He claimed that no one should doubt the criminality of abortion, "least of all . . . mothers, however ignorant or degraded." He wrote with umbrage about male gynecologists not being consulted for abortions. Passages in his writings seethe with contempt, despisement, and scorn against women and midwives. For Storer, it was a problem that women are not "deterred by [gynecologists'] refusal [to perform abortion] from going elsewhere for aid, or from inducing abortion upon themselves."[28]

Someone reading Storer's writings could be forgiven for mistakenly conclud-ing that women were the legal subjects not only of their husbands, but also of their gynecologists. Or that the uterus was the exclusive domain of men from sexual pleasure to medical science. In essence, women were incidental to their own bodies, and their opinions and interests simply did not matter that much.

The AMA, then an exclusionary, segregated organization that banned African Americans from membership, spearheaded this shift toward the monopolization of gynecological care, abortion, and ultimately women's bodies. Its membership lobbied Congress and state legislatures to require licensure for midwifery and also to criminalize abortion.[29] The AMA incited racist fears, contributing to nativism and anti-immigrant sentiment. Dr. Horatio Robinson Storer played a pivotal role in this regard. He warned that too few whites inhabited "the great territories of the far West, just opening to civilization, and the fertile savannas of the South, now disenthralled" due to the abolition of slavery; he asked whether those regions of the country would "be filled by our own children or by those of aliens? This is a question our women must answer; upon their loins depends the future destiny of the nation."[30]

Not until the wake of such actions, in 1869, did the Catholic Church condemn abortion. Prior to this time, the Catholic Church espoused the view that human life did not begin before quickening. However, a newly established AMA Committee on Criminal Abortion, spearheaded by Dr. Storer, urged that quick-ening had "its commencement at the very beginning, at conception itself" and, as such, the doctors stated, "we are compelled to believe unjustifiable abortion always a crime."[31] Importantly, the impetus for legislative bans on abortion or designations of who should be able to deliver babies did not relate to health or safety.

Naturally, it was in the self-interest of gynecologists to claim that "the deliberate prevention of pregnancy ... [is] detrimental to the health" and that "occasional child-bearing is an important means of healthful self-preservation."[32] Empirically, we know the latter statement lacked scientific merit then and now, as pregnancy presents a far greater risk to a pregnant woman's health than an abortion.

Laws such as the following in Massachusetts came to represent the new move-ment toward criminalization of abortion:

> Every person who shall knowingly advertise, print, publish, distribute, or circulate, or knowingly cause to be advertised, printed, published, distributed, or circulated, any pamphlet, printed paper, book, newspaper, notice, advertisement, or reference, con-taining words, or language, giving or conveying any notice, hint, or reference to any person, or to the name of any person, real or fictitious, from whom, or to any place, house, shop, or office where any poison, drug, mixture, preparation, medicine or noxious thing, or any instrument or means whatever, or any advice, directions, information, or knowledge, may be obtained for the purpose of causing or procuring the miscarriage of any woman pregnant with child, shall be punished ....[33]

Thus, antiabortion laws reflected the consolidation of power and economic opportunity under the guise of professionalism and safety. Seemingly, these laws rooted in anti-immigrant sentiment as much as, if not more than, any concern for women's health. Tellingly, although women's bodies became a contested political site for the control of a vibrant industry where pecuniary gains were to be made, medical schools barred women from entry and elite medical organizations did the same. At a time in which transplants were not performed, enhancement surgeries did not exist, and other medical technologies were yet to burgeon, pregnancies represented a dynamic and profitable space in which to practice medicine.

However, reproductive healthcare did not claim the prestige associated with other areas of medicine. At least one significant reason for this was that female midwives – many of whom were formally uneducated (although nonetheless successful) – dominated that space. A close reading of books and pamphlets published at the time shows that male gynecologists sought to transform the stature of reproductive healthcare, but they believed they could not achieve this if such healthcare was also provided by midwives. Criminalizing abortion and urging the prosecution of women who sought abortions advanced their goal, smothering the practice of midwifery in the United States.

At the Sixth Annual Meeting of the American Association for Study and Prevention of Infant Mortality, in 1915, Dr. Joseph DeLee, a preeminent twentieth-century obstetrician, leading casebook author, and fervent opponent to midwifery, launched his remarks with the words: "I desire to state that I am fundamentally opposed to any movement designed to perpetuate the midwife."[34] He claimed that "the midwife destroys obstetric ideals." He told the audience that midwives were "not absolutely necessary at the time," and, even if they were, the "[midwife] is a drag on our progress as a science and art."[35]

The legal history of abortion and its regulation root in the quagmire created out of the racialization and sex-exclusivity of reproductive medicine in the United States. In the wake of slavery's end, skilled midwives represented both real competition for male doctors who sought to enter the practice of child delivery and also a threat to how obstetricians viewed themselves. According to Joseph DeLee, "[i]f an uneducated woman of the lowest classes may practice obstetrics, is instructed by the doctors, and licensed by the State, it certainly must require very little knowledge and skill – surely it cannot belong to the science and art of medicine."

DeLee, Storer, and others were successful in stigmatizing midwifery as a "backward" reproductive healthcare practice. Obstetricians lauded obstetrics as a *trained* profession at the cusp of innovation with tools such as forceps[36] and other technologies that offered the modern convenience of hospitals. At the time, even if midwives wanted to practice in hospitals, those institutions effectively excluded them, because hospitals barred women from practice within their institutions. As researchers note, these changes in replacing midwives with doctors and homes with hospital-based medical care were not rooted in evidence.[37]

Rather, male gynecologists explicitly revealed their motivations in undermining midwifery: they desired pecuniary gain, recognition, and a monopoly. As one leading obstetrician explained, "there is high art in obstetrics and [the public] must pay as well for *it* as for surgery. I will not admit that this is a sordid impulse. It is only common justice to labor, self-sacrifice, and skill."[38] Moreover, these shifts were also deeply racialized. American hospitals zealously and faithfully practiced segregation, barring the admission of African Americans both to practice and as patients.

Even legislation said to support women's healthcare, such as the Sheppard-Towner Maternity and Infancy Act of 1921 – also known as the "better baby" bill – curiously shut midwives out of the process of reproductive healthcare and under-girded the shift toward hospital-based care. Interestingly, the only female member of Congress at the time, Alice Mary Robertson, opposed the bill, famously stating that it would prove "harmful." Strict regulation of midwifery and licensure requirements, along with states racializing the hiring of healthcare workers who traveled to rural communities, further burdened the practice of midwifery and excluded Black women from the profession. Despite the growing numbers of African American doctors and nurses in the United States during the early twentieth century, they were rarely included in states' efforts to educate poor women about reproductive healthcare.[39]

This churning of racism and sexism in the provision of reproductive healthcare created a new class of nurses and female public health workers to provide *assistance* to doctors. Overwhelmingly, those selected for these roles (traveling healthcare nurses) were white women. And, despite the fact that historically white colleges and universities with nursing schools admitted only white women, African Americans were being educated in medicine and nursing at the new crop of schools like Tuskegee University, Spellman College, Morehouse University, Hampton University, and others. Nonetheless, the professionalization of reproductive medicine was decidedly white and exclusive.[40]

Successful smear campaigns cleverly designed for political persuasion and to achieve legal reform described midwives as unhygienic, barbarous, nonefficacious, nonscientific, dangerous, and unprofessional. At the root of these actions were the deliberate efforts to elevate men who wanted to monopolize gynecology and obstetrics. Accord to Dr. DeLee:

> The midwife is a relic of barbarism. In civilized countries the midwife is wrong, has always been wrong. ...
>
>   ... The midwife has been a drag on the progress of the science and art of obstetrics. Her existence stunts the one and degrades the other. For many centuries she perverted obstetrics from obtaining any standing at all among the science of medicine.
>
>   Even after midwifery was practiced by some of the most brilliant men in the profession such practice was held opprobrious and degraded. Less than 100 years

ago, in 1825, the great English accoucheur Ramsbotham complained of the low esteem in which he was held by his brother surgeons. He was denied admittance to the Royal College and his colleagues would not dare to be seen talking to him on the street![41]

The power of such potent rhetoric manifested itself in laws and practices that ultimately outlawed midwifery or imposed such onerous and expensive licensing requirements that many who practiced midwifery could not afford them. The ultimate result was the male monopolization of women's reproductive healthcare. Today about 1 percent of reproductive healthcare is performed by midwives.

Yet, even under deeply constrained conditions while helping poor women complete their pregnancies, midwives achieved better birth outcomes than male doctors did. Contemporary studies dispel the myths and stereotypes that for decades demeaned and stigmatized midwife care.[42] Robust empirical evidence points to the efficacy of midwife-based care.[43]

The professionalization of reproductive medicine represented a new era in the treatment of women, promising better outcomes and minimized risks. However, it also promised to be almost exclusively male and white. By shutting out midwifery altogether, male gynecologists solidified male domination and control of reproductive health in medical school obstetrics and gynecology training, systems of practice and licensure, and membership of professional medical organizations.

4.2 THE SUPREME COURT AND ABORTION CASES

I mean, I was on one of those crappy ass yellow tiled dining room tables, with my legs up in the air, and blood in the kitchen sink right there next to me.

Cathy, 69, Ormond Beach, Florida (1962 abortion)[44]

In her landmark work, *When Abortion Was a Crime*, author Leslie J. Reagan copiously details the deaths and infections that overwhelmed hospitals in New York and Chicago in the years before *Roe*. Reagan writes that by the "early 1960s, [illegal] abortion-related deaths accounted for nearly half, or 42.1 percent, of the total maternal mortality in New York City."[45] She explains that in Chicago, "[p]hysicians and nurses at Cook County Hospital," one of the busiest hospitals in the nation, "saw nearly one hundred women come in every week for emergency treatment following their abortions."[46] Sadly, "[s]ome barely survived the bleeding, injuries, and burns; others did not."[47]

In the years before *Roe*, hospital emergency wards in major cities across the nation were so completely overwhelmed by girls and women who sought care for "abortion related complications" that they created special secret wards in which to treat them for the burns, infections, uterine tears, poisonings, and the myriad near-death conditions resulting from trying to end a pregnancy. These abortion-related complications, including deaths, were not isolated. Rather, they affected "[t]ens of thousands of women every year."[48] Deaths were particularly acute among women of color.[49] Sadly, all the deaths, infections, and complications were preventable, because legal abortions are far safer than even childbirth.

Exact numbers are unclear, but reports from hospitals and other sources estimate that nearly one million illegal abortions occurred each year in the United States prior to *Roe v. Wade*, which decriminalized the procedure. Rachel Benson Gold, Vice President for Public Policy at the Guttmacher Institute, explained that "[t]he toll the nation's abortion laws took on women's lives and health in the years before *Roe* was substantial."[50] She was right. In 1967, Dr. Alan Guttmacher founded the organization that bears his name out of concern for women dying in the most horrific, but preventable, ways due to so-called back-alley abortions that annually resulted in the deaths of women and teenage girls throughout the United States, and even more staggering infections, infertility, and emergency hospital interventions.[51]

Over the years, researchers and women's health organizations collected the harrowing narratives of women who sought and survived illegal abortions during that devastating pre-*Roe* era. Sometimes their friends, sisters, and mothers provided the stories, because the women themselves – like Geraldine "Gerri" Santoro – died during the procedure or shortly thereafter. In Gerri's case, a photo captured in black and white memorializes her death as the twenty-eight-year-old mother of two died alone, hemorrhaging on a motel floor at the Norwich Motel in Connecticut. Her boyfriend fled in a panic. The next day, the motel's maid discovered Gerri's naked body, collapsed on her knees, blood saturating the once white sheet and the carpet beneath her. Years later, *Ms.* magazine would publish the photo with the headline "Never Again."

Gerri's death and similar stories provide a narrative backdrop to the haunting images of women, bloodied and dead in bathtubs, with coat hangers or some other common household appliance refashioned into an instrument to gut the uterus nearby. They provide context for the terms kitchen-table and back-alley abortions and serve as a potent reminder that the demand for abortion is not a new manifestation and that the risks associated with criminalized abortions are predictable.

The National Association for the Repeal of Abortion Laws (also known as NARAL Pro-Choice America) published *Choices: Women Speak Out About Abortion* to encourage women to tell their abortion stories to remove the stigma and shaming.[52] Their stories illume the indignities and humiliation pregnant women experienced, as well as traumas and health risks. Polly Bergen shared this account of her experiences:

> A greasy looking man came to the door and asked for the money as soon as I walked in. He told me to take off all my clothes except my blouse; there was a towel to wrap around myself. I got up on a cold metal kitchen table. He performed a procedure, using something sharp. He didn't give me anything for pain – he just did it. He said

that he had packed me with gauze, that I should expect some cramping, and that I would be fine. I left.[53]

Her experience was typical of the many chilling experiences encountered by girls and women who wanted to end their pregnancies pre-*Roe*. Simply put, Polly's experience was not unusual. Barbara S. told *Vice News* that in her case, at eighteen years old, she did not know if the man to perform her abortion "was a fry cook, a doctor, a plumber . . . or what he did."[54] He was simply the guy who opened the door for the desperate girl. Sometimes the pregnancies resulted from rape, as in the case of Judi M., who was molested by her parents' friend in 1968, when she was sixteen years old, and became pregnant. She was desperate, so she did not turn away when a man wearing an apron opened the door to the apartment where she was to have her abortion. She wrote that "this was my only choice."[55] She did not flee when he demanded, "Give me the money." Perhaps she might have been spared what followed, including being punched in the face, blacking out, waking up where she "was lying in a pool of blood, and the guy wasn't there anymore."[56]

Sometimes the abortionists were sexual predators. Cathy, from Ormond Beach, Florida, recalls that she was sixteen years old when her abortion took place and the "doctor" told her, "You have a tight pussy."[57] At other times, abortionists chastised their clients, telling them they deserved punishment for their sins.

However, the verbal cruelty did not compare to the risks associated with incompetently performed abortions. As one woman wrote to *Ms.* magazine:

> "My submission is very short. It is about my Mother, b. 1924, d. 1971.
> She was found in a pool of blood on her cold white tile bathroom floor. Her mother found her. She was discovered, [she] did not die. Later, she had my sister and me. After her suicide at age 46, her mother told [me] about finding her daughter unconscious in a pool of blood." – Carol F.[58]

Frequently, the most devastating accounts came from girls and teenagers who sought to end their pregnancies. Evelyn H. recounted the memory of her friend who died after a botched abortion:

> "In 9th grade a good friend became pregnant by our AAU coach. He threatened to kill her if she told how she became pregnant. Her parents were divorced and her mother had committed suicide a few weeks prior. She borrowed money from everyone and wrote a check on [her] dad's account to go to [the] local abortionist. She died in [the] girls bathroom a week later. . . . She was a very talented artist and composed music. I had known her since third grade and even now, at 62, can hear her laughter and have a caricature of myself she drew. She had to be buried in a different cementary [sic] as [she] was Catholic raised, as did her mom. After her death a group told the coach to quit or we would tell. We were 14-year-old kids doing the best we could for our friend. . . . She was just a baby herself." – Evelyn H.[59]

In another testimony, William P. tells the story of his mother, who "had an illegal abortion in her teens" before he was born. He discloses that the procedure nearly killed her. His mother simply could not stop bleeding. Bleeding to death following botched abortions was not unusual. In his mother's case, she could not risk seeking medical care "without facing criminal charges." So she bled on the newspapers her boyfriend collected. As William shares, "All she could do was wait it out in her hotel room," sitting on the stack of newspapers "to collect the blood."[60]

The best chance that a woman had in obtaining an abortion was to be in danger of death if she carried the pregnancy to term or if deemed suicidal, schizophrenic, or so psychologically fragile that the abortion was necessary to spare her mental health. With the aid of sympathetic doctors, some women feigned these conditions in order to spare themselves an unwanted pregnancy or an unsafe abortion. Others might have been fortunate enough to find an underground member of the Jane Collective or the Abortion Counseling Service of Women's Liberation, an underground railroad of sorts for women and girls who sought to safely end their pregnancies. The Jane Collective operated out of Chicago, mostly helping poor women who could not afford to travel to states where abortion services were legal. However, they took enormous risks in carrying out their efforts. In 1972, Chicago police raided the Jane Collective and seven members of the organization were arrested and each charged with eleven counts of committing abortion and conspiracy to commit abortion. The maximum prison sentence was 110 years per woman. The Court's ruling in *Roe* effectively ended their prosecution, and the group disbanded shortly thereafter.

Inaccessibility to contraception exacerbated these problems. Even access to contraception for single women was illegal in many states until *Eisenstadt v. Baird*, the 1972 Supreme Court decision that held that denying single persons the right to contraception, while allowing it for married couples, violated the Fourteenth Amendment's Equal Protection Clause. Justice Brennan wrote, "If the right of privacy means anything it is the right of the individual, married or single, to be free from unwarranted governmental intrusion into matters so fundamentally affecting a person as the decision whether to bear or beget a child." In that case, the state of Massachusetts made it a felony for any unmarried person to receive birth control – and even married couples had to receive their contraceptives from a registered doctor or pharmacist.

The Massachusetts law was not unusual; other states enacted similar laws, making it a felony to obtain birth control. Such laws served as enduring legacies of Comstock's nefarious antivice movement. These laws ultimately conferred state control over the most intimate aspects and acts in a woman's life. However, the groundwork for a constitutional challenge to abortion criminalization was being laid in states like New York, where the sobering volume of deaths and injuries resulting from kitchen-table and back-alley abortions left hospitals without sufficient space to treat the affected women.

Aryeh Neier, who was the national executive director of the American Civil Liberties Union during that period, said to me there was "no question that . . . back-alley abortions" played a pivotal role in the legislative decriminalization of abortion.[61] But even then, as Neier explained, decriminalizing abortion "was not originally portrayed as a women's rights issue." Instead, it was about sparing male doctors criminal punishment for performing abortions.

Although Neier disagreed with the approach adopted to end the criminalization of abortion, because it situates reproductive rights "from the physician's standpoint," the strategy was successful. Women's deaths remained secondary to the criminal punishment of doctors who helped women safely terminate their pregnancies. The basic concept of a "woman's right" had yet to take shape, at least in the reproductive health context. That would soon change.

Neier hired a young lawyer, Ruth Bader Ginsburg, in 1971 to direct a women's rights program after he became national director of the organization. Neier told me, "to some extent I share [Ruth Bader Ginsburg's] perspective." That is, "she always wanted to deal with abortion from a women's rights standpoint, whereas *Roe* deals with it from a physician's standpoint." When asked about the ACLU's pivotal leadership on women's reproductive rights, he responded, "I was fortunate to get [Ruth Bader Ginsburg] to direct the women's rights project. She wanted to push a litigation campaign on women's equality in a step-by-step way. It was remarkably well planned."

4.2.1 *Roe v. Wade: Strict Scrutiny and the Trimester Framework*

In 1973, the U.S. Supreme Court overturned Texas criminal laws that prohibited abortion except in cases where the pregnancy endangered the woman's life.[62] In a resounding 7–2 decision, the Court held that, "as a unit," all of the Texas abortion statutes "must fall." The Court advised that its "task [wa]s to resolve the issue by constitutional measurement, free of emotion and of predilection."

That opinion, *Roe v. Wade*, established that the constitutional right to privacy included a woman's decision to terminate her pregnancy. Justice Blackmun opined that the right of personal privacy is "fundamental . . . in the concept of ordered liberty." The Court reasoned that "where certain fundamental rights are involved, the Court has held that regulation limiting these rights may be justified only by a 'compelling state interest' and that legislative enactments must be narrowly drawn to express only the legitimate state interests at stake."

The Court held that criminal abortion statutes such as those in Texas (and throughout the nation), which criminalized pregnancy terminations without consideration of the pregnant woman's interests, the stage of pregnancy, or recognition of other considerations involved, "violate the Due Process Clause of the Fourteenth Amendment." Blackmun summarized:

A state criminal abortion statute of the current Texas type, that excepts from criminality only a lifesaving procedure on behalf of the mother, without regard to pregnancy stage and without recognition of the other interests involved, is violative of the Due Process Clause of the Fourteenth Amendment.

The Court established a trimester framework, which foregrounded and later gave way to the undue burden standard found in *Casey*.

According to the Court, Roe sought to terminate her pregnancy and desired that the abortion be "performed by a competent, licensed physician, under safe clinical conditions."[63] Yet, section 2A of the Texas Penal Code (1961) permitted the criminal punishment and incarceration of physicians who administered abortions.[64] The law sanctioned punishment "in the penitentiary not less than two nor more than five years; if it be done without her consent, the punishment shall be doubled."[65] A doctor who violated the law could be fined "not less than one hundred nor more than one thousand dollars" if she attempted but did not complete the abortion.[66] If the pregnant woman died as a result of the abortion, or any attempt at it, the law treated that as murder.

Norma Leah Nelson, a single pregnant woman, challenged the Texas prohibitions, describing to the Court how severe economic hardships and social stigma unduly injured her and "all other women similarly situated."[67] Nelson, later known by the pseudonym Jane Roe, and her lawyers claimed that the Texas statutes amounted to "unconstitutionally vague" abridgments of personal privacy rights "protected by the First, Fourth, Fifth, Ninth, and Fourteenth Amendments."[68] The Court referenced the brief, which describes Nelson as having attained a tenth-grade education but no matriculation beyond that point. A string of low-paying jobs, including bartending and carnival barking, barely allowed Nelson to support herself.[69]

The Court ruled that a state's imposition of motherhood onto women who would not otherwise choose that for themselves is a severe injury.[70] Blackmun wrote, that "[m]aternity, or additional offspring, may force upon the woman a distressful life and future," burdened by potentially imminent psychological trauma. The Court stated that "there is also the distress, for all concerned, associated with the unwanted child, and there is the problem of bringing a child into a family already unable, psychologically, and otherwise to care for it."[71]

Justice Blackmun observed that the movement to criminalize abortion was of a "relatively recent vintage." For example, "[t]hose laws, generally proscribing abortion or its attempt at any time during pregnancy except when necessary to preserve the pregnant woman's life, are not of ancient or even of common law origin," he wrote. Rather, as he described, the laws derived from "statutory changes effected, for the most part, in the latter half of the 19th century," when Anthony Comstock launched his notorious antivice campaigns against contraception, abortion, naked images – even in medical books – and vice generally, which ultimately resulted in federal bans on contraception and twenty-four states enacting similar prohibitions on contraception and abortion.[72]

In *Roe*, the Court ruled that a right to terminate a pregnancy is rooted in the right to privacy, "whether it be founded in the Fourteenth Amendment's concept of personal liberty and restrictions upon state action, as we feel it is, or, as the District Court determined, in the Ninth Amendment's reservation of rights to the people." This privacy right, according to the Court, "is broad enough to encompass a woman's decision whether or not to terminate her pregnancy."

The Court concluded that the state has a dual interest and that it includes protecting fetal life and ensuring the health of the pregnant woman. To capture these competing interests of a woman's right to privacy and state protection of life, the Court created a trimester framework to govern the constitutionality of abortion regulations: During the first trimester of a woman's pregnancy, when the fetus was not medically viable, the woman's right to privacy outweighed state interests. In the second trimester, however, a state could, "if it chooses," regulate abortion where such regulations were "reasonably related to maternal health." In the third trimester, according to the Court, the state could, "if it chooses," regulate abortion "and even proscribe" it, "except where it is necessary in appropriate medical judgment, for the preservation of the life or health of the mother."

Today, advocates for women's rights, health, and equality and reproductive justice struggle with the meaning of *Roe*. On the one hand, it decriminalized abortion and recognized women's lived lives – how early and out-of-wedlock motherhood stigmatized women and destined them to lives of hardship and "additional difficulties." Previously, the Supreme Court had been complicit in regulating women's reproduction (upholding forced sterilization laws) and decisive in relegating women to destinies of motherhood and subordination. *Roe* did not overturn prior Supreme Court precedents in this regard, but it did begin to chip away at that dark mark on the Court's record by recognizing a woman's fundamental right to privacy. And "this right of privacy, whether it be founded in the Fourteenth Amendment's concept of personal liberty and restrictions upon state action ... or ... in the Ninth Amendment's reservation of rights to the people, is broad enough to encompass a woman's decision whether or not to terminate her pregnancy."

On the other hand, as Aryeh Neier, who was at the forefront of New York's decriminalization of abortion told me, *Roe* and the decriminalization movement was ultimately framed around doctors and women's relationships *or consultations* with their doctors. Women's control over their reproduction may have been freed from the grasps of husbands and the clutches of the state, but *Roe* situated a woman's right to privacy alongside her doctor's evaluation of her decision. As then Judge Ruth Bader Ginsburg explained to Senator Metzenbaum in her nomination hearing to become a Supreme Court justice, "[t]he *Roe* decision is a highly medically oriented decision, not just in the three-trimester division," because it "features, along with the

right of the woman, the right of the doctor to freely exercise his profession."
Reflecting on this, Ginsburg noted that "[t]he woman appears together with her
consulting physician, and that pairing comes up two or three times in the opinion,
the woman, together with her consulting physician."[73] Ginsburg's criticism was that,
ironically, although *Roe* liberalized abortion and recognized a woman's right to
privacy and bodily autonomy, women were not the sole focal point of the decision.

The Court and its decisions that followed in the 1970s further complicated *Roe*'s
legacy, including whether abortion would be accessible to the poor women that
Justice Blackmun evoked in the decision.

4.2.2 *Poverty and Abortion: Maher, Beal, and Harris*

Mary Poe and Susan Roe, like Jane Doe, were poor. At age sixteen, Mary sought and
received an elective abortion at a Bridgeport, Connecticut hospital. The state of
Connecticut refused to reimburse the hospital because Mary had not obtained the
required physician certification of medical necessity under Connecticut law. Susan
Roe was a twenty-six-year-old unmarried mother of three young children. Both Mary
and Susan sought abortions in their first trimesters of pregnancy. The problem was
that they could not afford the costs of their abortions. In each case, the state would
have paid for the more costly prenatal and postnatal expenses if Mary and Susan had
maintained their pregnancies. Connecticut would also have underwritten the costs
of a "therapeutic" abortion – to save the life of a pregnant woman.

If you are poor and cannot pay for an abortion, *Roe v. Wade* may provide little
solace. That was the case in 1977 (and continues to be for many poor women), when
the Supreme Court issued an opinion in *Maher v. Roe*. Funding restrictions tethered
poor women to the fraught conditions that characterized the pre-*Roe* era. That is, if
a woman sought to exercise her constitutional right to terminate a pregnancy, as
granted by *Roe*, because she did not wish to remain pregnant or because it would
result in further economic hardship, interfere with her education, cause imminent
psychological distress, or any of the conditions described in *Roe*, Connecticut
required that she pay the costs. By this time, Justice Blackmun was in the minority –
the losing side, joining with Justices Brennan and Marshall, dissenting in a case
where the Supreme Court disingenuously held that Connecticut did not interfere
with an indigent woman's right to *seek* an abortion. Whether a poor woman could
actually obtain an abortion was not a question the Court considered.

Rather, the Court ruled that indigent girls and women were free to find other,
private means to pay for the procedure. Justice Powell wrote that "[a]n indigent
woman who desires an abortion suffers no disadvantage as a consequence of
Connecticut's decision to fund childbirth; she continues as before to be dependent
on private sources for the service she desires."[74] An indigent woman who desired an
abortion simply did "not come within" the category of disadvantage that the Court
had ever recognized – and the Court was not inclined to consider poor women's

poverty in relation to their reproductive rights. The Court condescendingly noted that the state of Connecticut was not responsible for the indigency of Poe and Roe and, as such, not required to remedy it. In reality, for most poor pregnant women, not just some "indigency makes access to a competent licensed physician not merely 'difficult' but 'impossible.'"[75]

Even though the Court expressly stated that its decision was not a "retreat from *Roe*," in effect it was. By refusing to fund abortion services – a procedure less expensive and safer than childbirth – the state served to coerce women into continuing pregnancies. Justice Brennan wrote in his dissent that "many indigent women will feel they have no choice but to carry their pregnancies to term because the State will pay for the associated medical services, even though they would have chosen to have abortions."[76] Most importantly, this coercion worked only on poor women, "who are uniquely the victims of this form of financial pressure."[77]

The Court's distressing insensitivity and hostility toward the lives of poor women revealed itself soon after. Like Gerri Santoro pre-*Roe*, Rosaura "Rosie" Jimenez's post-*Roe* death epitomized the hardship borne by women who wanted to end their pregnancies. Jimenez was a single mother attending college to provide better opportunities for her daughter than she had as a child with nearly a dozen siblings. She was already receiving welfare benefits and knew that she could not afford to have another child. She cleaned houses on weekends to supplement her income and worked part-time jobs. When she discovered that she was pregnant, she learned that Medicaid would not pay for her abortion, even though it would pay for a pregnancy, which costed thousands more. Much like the women before *Roe*, Rosie received her unsafe, trailer-park abortion from someone unskilled. Within a day she was hospitalized and dead a week later after all the organs in her body shut down. She was twenty-seven years old.

The lives of these pregnant women and their stories are important to recognize, because they inform us about the pragmatic realities of abortion rights after *Roe*. On the one hand, *Roe* spared middle-class white women from the horrific conditions and indignities of abortions obtained in back alleys, on kitchen tables, in seedy motel rooms, inside filthy buildings, and in bathtubs. On the other hand, poor women struggled to access abortion care. By 1977, the sex disparities in pay, education, work opportunities, and social mobility persisted, and states along with private industries ardently resisted women's efforts to demand equality.[78] In fact, companies devised coercive strategies and adopted fetal protection policies as strategic means to use women's pregnancies as a reason to discriminate against them.[79]

Meanwhile, states enacted laws prohibiting government funding for abortion services. *Maher v. Roe*,[80] *Beal v. Doe*,[81] and *Harris v. McRae*[82] – a spate of alarming Supreme Court decisions affecting abortion access and rights for indigent women – mark the Court's substantive departure from a commitment to allowing all women to participate in the broader reproductive privacy right articulated in *Roe*. Reviewed as companion cases, *Maher* and *Beal* established that states are not required to fund abortions.[83] Moreover, states may economically prioritize childbirth over abortion, even if doing so undermines the state fisc and denies poor women their medical choices. In *Harris*, the Court upheld the Hyde Amendment's denial of public funds even in the case of medically necessary pregnancy terminations, such as when an abortion is "necessary to avert severe and permanent damage to the health of the mother."[84]

Of the three cases, all of which upheld laws that placed abortion out of reach for poor women, *Harris v. McRae*, decided 5–4, broached a level of high immorality toward the lives of poor pregnant women hitherto not present in the Court's highly contentious, punitive post-*Roe* jurisprudence. Congress adopted a rider known as the Hyde Amendment, which effectively bans federal funds in abortion care by blocking federal Medicaid funding for pregnancy termination except in cases of rape, incest, and "where the life of the mother would be endangered if the fetus were carried to term."[85] The Hyde Amendment is particularly distressing constitutionally, because it not only excludes indigent pregnant women in dangerous pregnancies from Medicaid benefits, even when recommended by a doctor, but also demands the expenditure of millions of federal dollars in order to impede the exercise of a constitutional right. As Justice Stevens expressed in his dissent, this inflicts serious, enduring harm on indigent pregnant women who need to end their pregnancies for urgent medical reasons. In upholding the Hyde Amendment, the Court sanctioned "a blatant violation" of the government's "duty to govern impartially."[86]

Representative Hyde, sponsor of the rider that bears his name, sought to ban abortion access altogether, but could not curry sufficient legislative support for a constitutional amendment to do so. However, limiting poor women's access was within reach. Notably, he said, "I certainly would like to prevent, if I could legally, anybody having an abortion, a rich woman, a middle-class woman, or a poor woman. Unfortunately, the only vehicle available is the ... Medicaid bill."[87] The results continue to be devastating. Rosie Jimenez was the Hyde Amendment's first known victim.

Specifically, in *Harris*, the Court found that "Title XIX does not obligate a participating State to pay for those medically necessary abortions for which Congress has withheld federal funding."[88] Carving out an exception for those that require an abortion to pay privately for it, while the state pays for other pregnancy-related medical treatments, disserves the social welfare goals on which Medicaid is founded. The Court stated:

> [R]egardless of whether the freedom of a woman to choose to terminate her pregnancy for health reasons lies at the core or the periphery of the due process liberty recognized in *Wade*, it simply does not follow that a woman's freedom of choice carries with it a constitutional entitlement to the financial resources to avail herself of the full range of protected choices.[89]

When authorizing Medicaid, Congress decided to fund *all* medically necessary procedures, however. In part, this is why singling out poor pregnant women who choose not to remain pregnant as disqualified from this government benefit amounts to an illogical and economically irresponsible government scheme. Notice that in such instance the government does not deny coverage because treatment is medically unsound, too costly, experimental, or dangerous to the woman. The government denies poor pregnant women this treatment because it chooses her to remain pregnant and wields its resources to achieve that affect. Congress could very well have decided that it would not fund any pregnancy-related care, whether prenatal care, labor and delivery, postnatal care, or abortion. Congress acted not only irrationally but also unconstitutionally when it decided to fund one outcome of a pregnancy and not another, because doing so is impermissibly coercive, nonneutral, and a strong-arm tactic to discourage indigent women from exercising a constitutionally protected right. The Hyde Amendment effectively conditions indigent pregnant women's care on them remaining pregnant.

Unlike *Maher*, which involved nontherapeutic abortions, *Harris* established that even if the life of the mother were at risk, the government does not place an "obstacle in the path of a woman who chooses to terminate her pregnancy, but rather, by means of unequal subsidization of abortion and other medical services, encourages alternative activity deemed in the public interest."[90] Yet, how could the significant suffering or injury to a pregnant woman be in the public's interest, or serve a defensible legislative interest? How could it be a rational, important, or compelling state interest for pregnant women to suffer grave injury during pregnancy? Justice Stevens concluded that the Court's tolerance of the Hyde Amendment's exclusion of abortion in the case of life endangerment was tantamount to severe, unconstitutional "punishment." Wasn't this what *Roe* was intended to prevent?

Again, the Court reasoned that "although government may not place obstacles in the path of a woman's exercise of her freedom of choice, it need not remove those not of its own creation."[91] According to the Court, "indigency falls in the latter category."[92] Still, had not states, their judiciaries, and even the Supreme Court cultivated and nurtured the types of conditions that subordinated, oppressed, and limited the rights of women – including basic freedoms and rights to an equal and unsegregated education and employment – and were particularly and aggressively maintained during Jim Crow, immediately preceding the civil rights advancements of the 1960s and 1970s?

In his dissenting opinion Justice Brennan wrote that "[t]he Hyde Amendment's denial of public funds for medically necessary abortions plainly intrudes upon [the] constitutionally protected decision" in *Roe*. He was right. The Court "studiously avoid[ed] recognizing the undeniable fact that for women eligible for Medicaid ... denial of a Medicaid-funded abortion is equivalent to denial of legal abortion altogether," especially for poor women of color.[93] Given this, Justice Marshall predicted that poor women would resort to "back-alley butchers" or attempt to "induce an abortion themselves by crude and dangerous methods, or suffer the serious medical consequences of attempting to carry the fetus to term." The incredibly high maternal mortality rates in states where only one abortion clinic remains highlights the prescience of Justice Marshall's dissent.

The majority's opinion in *Harris* manifested the Court's profound, lingering failure to recognize the intersectional nature of sex, race, and economic oppression.[94] In 1980, the year in which *Harris* was decided, state legislatures sanctioned and courts upheld sexual assault, rape, and domestic violence in marital relationships, reinforcing the antiquated ideals of women as sexual property of their husbands. One could read *Harris* as reifying the notion that pregnant, indigent women were not deserving of basic human rights and fundamental constitutional protections of privacy, autonomy, or a right to life.[95] Sadly, the Court's blind spot to its own distressing record on women's rights and sex equality has yet to be fully acknowledged and remedied, particularly in relation to reproductive health.[96]

In a line of cases stretching from more than a century ago up to today,[97] the Supreme Court and lower courts failed, at important times, to protect women and their interests. In this, the Court has not only failed women per se. In upholding sexist legislation historically and now, the Court has failed to protect fundamental values of liberty and justice embedded in the Constitution – as related to women.

That is, the Court has spoken with suspect and hostile authority about the limits of women's capacities in matters of work, contracting, voting, and more. The Court's derisive framing of women and their capacities, which ultimately creates the very double standards it is charged with dismantling, manifests itself across cases that involve women seeking the better fruits of full citizenship and economic independence. Lurking in plain sight is the Court's jurisprudence that anchored women to marginalized status, leaving little wonder why and how states seek strategically to slide legislation within the gaps of constitutional jurisprudence to further stymie women's equality. In its 1948 opinion in *Goesaert v. Cleary*, the Court upheld a draconian Michigan law that stated that "no female may be … licensed [to bar tend] unless she be 'the wife or daughter of the male owner' of a licensed liquor establishment."[98] The Court held that "[t]he Fourteenth Amendment did not tear history up by the roots," and venerated the regulation of liquor as "one of the oldest and most untrammeled of legislative powers," before concluding that "Michigan could, beyond question, forbid all women from working behind a bar."[99] The Court seemed unfazed by what it described as "the vast changes in the social and legal position of women."[100]

Thus, in 1961, when the Court upheld a Florida law distinguishing women from men in the jury selection (women had to opt in, whereas men were simply drawn from the local pool of citizens), it reasoned that "woman is still regarded as the center of home and family life."[101] Arguably, this signaled that women still remained in service to their husbands. Neither the state of Florida nor the Supreme Court would grant women freedom from the status the former created by law and that the latter upheld. In reality, opting into such service, which is fundamental to United States' democracy, might not have been easy for many women who desired to serve on juries, because of social forces that further entrenched women's compromised status in home and society. In that light, signing up for jury duty was made an act of social rebellion with all the stigma attached, rather than a normal civic obligation for women. Once again, the Court failed not only women, but the very purpose and cause of a democracy: "We cannot say that it is constitutionally impermissible for a State, acting in pursuit of the general welfare, to conclude that a woman should be relieved from the civic duty of jury service ...."[102] Then and more recently, the Court has upheld legislation that implicitly and explicitly reinforces the exclusion of women from opportunity.[103]

When the Court reasons that poor women are responsible for or the cause of their poverty, it not only assumes innocence on the part of the state in shaping the status of women, but absolves states' odious records of discrimination against women across decades and centuries. First, in such instances the Court misreads its weak, inconsistent, and sometimes appalling record, too, such as in *Buck v. Bell* upholding forced sterilization of indigent women. Second, contraceptive and abortion access matter to women's economic equality and independence. Thus, when states curtail women's access to economic opportunity and family planning, and courts sanction this, these institutions ultimately contribute to women's second-class citizenship.

4.2.3 *Planned Parenthood of Southeastern Pennsylvania v. Casey*

In reality, reproductive healthcare rights hinge not on *Roe v. Wade* but on a later case, *Planned Parenthood of Southeastern Pennsylvania v. Casey*, where the Supreme Court abandoned the trimester approach.[104] In that case, the Court upheld the central holding of *Roe v. Wade*, which it defined as "the right of the woman to choose to have an abortion before viability and to obtain it without undue interference from the State."[105] However, *Casey* also represented a new era in antiabortion legislating, which found expression in TRAP laws. This new strategy sought to undermine the abortion right by creating myriad hurdles for medical providers, clinics, and patients – effectively chipping away at the abortion right by making it burdensome for providers to offer medical treatments and difficult for patients to access that care.

At issue in this case were five provisions of the Pennsylvania Abortion Control Act of 1982 section 3205 of which "require[d] that a woman seeking an abortion give her informed consent prior to the abortion procedure, and specifie[d] that she be provided with certain information at least 24 hours before the abortion is performed," and section 3209 of which "require[d] that, unless certain exceptions apply, a married woman seeking an abortion must sign a statement indicating that she has notified her husband."[106] Prior to any of the provisions taking effect, petitioners challenged the law.

The Court ruled that the state's power to restrict abortions is limited, both temporally and by the mode of restriction. That is, states may not restrict abortion during the period of nonviability. Further, the Court made it clear that any regulations burdening abortion rights after fetal viability must create exceptions to preserve women's health. *Casey* established that the state may regulate abortion prior to viability only so long as the regulations do not establish an "undue burden" on a woman's ability to have an abortion. And while the Court did not define the contours of what would amount to an undue burden, it upheld several provisions of the Pennsylvania law, including the twenty-four-hour waiting period, its so-called informed consent requirements, and regulations imposed on minors seeking abortions. The Court struck down the provisions requiring that married women notify their husbands.

The antiabortion movement interpreted *Casey* as a victory and reproductive rights advocates recognized it as a lifeline protecting the fundamental principle in *Roe*. In the former case, *Casey* legitimized the TRAP law strategy, perversely grounding it in preserving and furthering the health interests of pregnant women. It wedged a boot in the door. Prior to *Casey*, the Court did not permit a state to second-guess a woman's readiness to schedule and receive a medical procedure that would relieve her of stigma, shame, pain, and physical threats to her health and safety. After *Casey*, that changed. A state could force a pregnant woman seeking treatment to end her pregnancy, to wait twenty-four, forty-eight, or even seventy-two hours (not including weekends and holidays) before she receives an abortion, under the guise of promoting informed consent. A state could claim – as some do now – that its waiting period policy furthers a woman's right to be informed, and as such is not deployed as a measure to interfere with a woman's right to end a pregnancy. *Casey* also legitimized infringements on physicians' free speech by ruling that states could require doctors to be conduits for its messaging, even if the messages are inaccurate and not based on evidence. Again, this too was justified as protecting a woman's health. *Casey* tolerated these intrusions.

Some reproductive health proponents view *Casey* as more than life support for abortion rights. In her nomination hearing to the Supreme Court, Justice Ginsburg remarked that the "*Casey* decision, at least the opinion of three of the Justices in that case, makes it very clear that the woman is central to this." In other words, the woman stands independently, not reliant on a doctor's consultation and not needing permission from a doctor. Justice Ginsburg stated that "this is her right," in contrast to *Roe*, where her decision had to be "in consultation with her physician."[107]

Nevertheless, TRAP legislation highlights and underscores the weaknesses in current Supreme Court jurisprudence, particularly the framework articulated in *Casey*. Sadly, the Court revived paternalistic ideologies associated with women's capacity to reason, consent, and make autonomous reproductive healthcare decisions, because historically the state and courts have been complicit in undermining women's economic capacities and liberty interests. That is, while functionally,

TRAP laws impose onerous constraints on abortion providers, substantively the laws challenge the underlying principles of women's reproductive rights, such as autonomy, privacy, and equality. In many states, legislatures have been quite successful in using this tactic, even though Supreme Court precedent does not provide a right for legislatures to unduly burden or interfere with women's reproductive healthcare rights. Yet, this is exactly what some states are doing.

4.2.4 *Gonzales v. Carhart*

In one of the most disturbing opinions addressing abortion, the Supreme Court ruled 5–4 that the Partial-Birth Abortion Ban Act of 2003 did not unconstitutionally violate personal liberty protected by the Fifth Amendment, despite the fact that the law lacked an exception for the procedures when necessary to protect the health of a pregnant woman.[108] Writing for the majority, which included Justices Roberts, Scalia, Thomas, and Alito, Justice Kennedy concluded that imposing a medical exception for whenever "medical uncertainty" existed would impose "too exacting a standard . . . on the legislative power [. . .] to regulate the medical profession."[109]

In that case, doctors sued to bar the law from going into effect, given that it was not only misleading by its title and inference but would apply to common abortion procedures such as dilation and evacuation ("D&E"), as well as intact dilation and extraction (referred to as "intact D&E" or "D&X").[110] Abortion providers argued that the law was unconstitutional and that it would violate the spirit of *Casey* by imposing an undue burden on abortion access rights, especially as the law would essentially ban most late-term abortions. Such procedures rarely take place, and when they do, in most instances it is to protect the health of the pregnant woman or for other medical reasons.

In fact, abortion providers made a profoundly strong case, because the federal law provided no safeguards for the protection of the pregnant woman's health, thus making it unconstitutional under the Court's precedent in *Stenberg v. Carhart*. Abortion providers argued that even if Congress believed that late-term abortions are never medically necessary, such findings would be immaterial given that abortion regulations that could impose harms on women's health establish an undue burden on the right to terminate a pregnancy. Government lawyers argued that a health exception is not required when Congress decides that a banned procedure is never necessary to promote the health of the pregnant woman.

Not only did the Court uphold the law, but Justice Kennedy introduced into the Court's abortion jurisprudence the erroneous notion that abortion taxes a pregnant woman's mental health. He wrote, "While we find no reliable data to measure the phenomenon, it seems unexceptionable to conclude some women come to regret their choice to abort . . . . Severe depression and loss of esteem can follow."[111]

To the contrary, research demonstrates that "there is no increased risk of low self-esteem or life dissatisfaction following an abortion relative to being denied one."[112]

Justice Kennedy made no mention of women who experience severe depression and emotional anxiety in pregnancy, childbirth, and parenting – though empirical evidence on these matters is readily available. As researchers and medical providers in the U.S. Department of Health and Human Services and National Institute of Mental Health explain, "with postpartum depression, feelings of sadness and anxiety can be extreme and might interfere with a woman's ability to care for herself or her family."[113]

The U.S. Department of Health and Human Services further explains that "without treatment, postpartum depression can last for months or years . . . affecting the mother's health, it can interfere with her ability to connect with and care for her baby and may cause the baby to have problems with sleeping, eating, and behavior as he or she grows."[114] A multidisciplinary group of Canadian researchers, composed of women's health experts in psychiatry, psychology, sociology, public health, and nursing, recently reported as follows:

> Postpartum depression (PPD) is a significant public health problem which affects approximately 13% of women within a year of childbirth. Although rates of depression do not appear to be higher in women in the period after childbirth compared to age matched control women (10–15%), the rates of first onset and severe depression are elevated by at least three-fold."[115]

My point here is not to stigmatize women for the mental health stress that may attend pregnancy, but rather to point out the Court's coercive use of rhetoric in cases addressing abortion. For example, Justice Kennedy avoids acknowledging the enormous physical and psychological relief experienced by some women who terminate their pregnancies.[116] A research team led by gynecologists at the University of California San Francisco reported that "the overwhelming majority of women felt that termination was the right decision for them over three years."[117] They explained, "In particular, research has found that the positive sentiments women report over time post-abortion included maturity, deeper self-knowledge, and strengthened self-esteem."[118] In other words, a woman's life satisfaction trajectory after abortion did not receive acknowledgment or mention from the Court.

In a study of 35,000 adult identical twins, findings "showed that more children make mothers less happy." Furthermore, it does not seem that "additional children beyond the first child" have a positive effect for females in relation to happiness.[119] Professor Hans-Peter Kohler's research sheds greater light on the problematic assumption built into Justice Kennedy's opinion. Kohler explains, "in contrast to the large positive effect of the first child on well-being, additional children beyond the first child are not associated with higher levels of happiness; instead, the within-[monozygotic] results reveal that additional children beyond the first tend to be associated with *lower* levels of happiness for females."[120] In fact, "[e]ach child beyond the first decreases the happiness indicator by 13% of one standard deviation for females, and three additional children almost completely compensate for the positive effect resulting from the first child."[121]

There are significant costs to women when the Court perpetuates stereotypic attitudes toward their sex, particularly in abortion cases, because, problematically, "the notion that abortion lowers women's self-esteem has been the basis, in part, for legislation to restrict abortion access."[122] Perhaps no other institution has been more steadfast than the Court in anchoring women's identity to home, pregnancy and child-rearing. The Court's jurisprudence on abortion reflects this. In addition to this, the *Carhart* decision also problematically contributed to a moral panic about the rarely performed abortions in the third trimester of pregnancy.

There are many reasons to criticize the Court's decision. Here, I will point out three problematic features of the Court's decision. First, it violates the spirit of *Roe* and *Casey*, and shows disregard and even contempt for pregnant women's health. Second, Kennedy grants medical authority to Congress to fulfill an unconstitutional agenda. In the wake of the Court's decision, "legislatures in thirty-one states exploited the loopholes by enacting misnamed, but carefully worded, 'partial-birth' abortion laws precisely to create doubt as to whether they 'outlaw standard methods of terminating a pregnancy before fetal viability.'"[123] Third, the Court stereotypes and patronizes women who seek abortion.

4.2.5 *Whole Woman's Health v. Hellerstedt*

The battle over reproductive healthcare rights has moved significantly to states, where strategic TRAP legislation functions to circumvent and undermine women's fundamental constitutional rights at the state level. As a result, recent encroachments on women's reproductive healthcare rights raise important questions about reproductive rights and federalism or states' rights.

In 2013, after heated debate and an ambitious, but unsuccessful, filibuster by Wendy Davis, the Texas legislature enacted House Bill 2 (H.B. 2). The law contained two provisions at issue in the 2016 U.S. Supreme Court case *Whole Woman's Health v. Hellerstedt*.[124] The legislation represented another tool in the antiabortion arsenal built and primarily cultivated by male lawmakers. Ironically, Texas lawmakers claimed H.B. 2 and similar laws protected women, preserved their health, and enhanced patient safety. Governor Rick Perry signed the legislation, heralding it as part of the "culture of Texas" and destined to make abortion "a thing of the past."[125] Indeed, Perry and Texas legislators cleverly erected so many barriers in the paths of women seeking abortions in Texas that the right to terminate a pregnancy became more illusory than real. Their goal – to hobble abortion access (while not actually banning the procedure) – proved successful in the short term. Lawmakers celebrated the deceptively framed law as a hopeful strike against *Roe v. Wade*.

Problematically, Governor Perry's legislative victory in the name of women's health and safety also perpetuated a profoundly misleading medical narrative.

Despite unambiguous scientific research[126] and empirical outcomes from abortion clinics[127] proving that legal abortions are as safe as penicillin shots,[128] antiabortion legislators and activists steadfastly campaigned that TRAP laws constitute "sensible women's health legislation." Antiabortionists have proven successful, shaping the narrative about abortion to such a chilling degree that only one abortion clinic remains in each of these states: Kentucky, Mississippi, Missouri, North Dakota, South Dakota, West Virginia, and Wyoming. In reality, pregnant women in Texas were no safer after the enactment of H.B. 2 than before, because women are fourteen times more likely to die during pregnancy and childbirth than by terminating a pregnancy.[129] Moreover, the United States ranks behind all other elite (and many developing) nations on maternal and infant mortality matrixes, including England, France, and Germany, but also Belarus, Cuba, Guam, Hungary, Poland, and Taiwan.

The two provisions at issue in *Whole Woman's Health* concerned the constitutionality of two Texas Health and Safety Codes. Section 171.0031, or the "admitting privileges" requirement, mandated that "[a] physician performing or inducing an abortion must, on the date the abortion is performed or induced, have active admitting privileges at a hospital that is located not further than 30 miles from the location at which the abortion is performed or induced."[130] The second provision, related to Texas Health and Safety Code section 245.010, required that "an abortion facility must be equivalent to the minimum standards adopted under Section 243.010 for ambulatory surgical centers."[131]

According to the Texas Policy Evaluation Project, within months of the law's enactment the number of abortion clinics in Texas dramatically declined by 56 percent from forty-one licensed clinics to eighteen.[132] After the bill's passage, researchers recorded a dramatic uptick in the number of women who sought to self-induce abortions. They estimated that between 100,000 and as many as 250,000 women in Texas attempted self-induced abortions. On the one hand, the number of legal abortions in Texas immediately declined, due to the reduced number of clinics in the state. On the other hand, waiting periods for an abortion increased by nearly three weeks.[133] Longer waiting periods produced serious barriers and harsh consequences, particularly for poor women, because Texas also enacted a ban on abortions after twenty weeks. Many women reported that the Texas restrictions placed an undue burden on their constitutionally protected right to an abortion by constructing barriers to access. One such example could be found in the Rio Grande of Texas, where only one abortion clinic operated. With its closure, the nearest clinic to perform abortion services would have been 230 miles away, a twelve-hour round-trip car ride.[134]

The weeks leading up to the Supreme Court's announcement of the ruling were intense. A defeat in this case would mean clinics that perform abortions could effectively be regulated out of business. The Supreme Court's 5–3 decision struck down both provisions.[135] The Court overturned the Fifth Circuit Court of Appeals' decision, finding that both the admitting privileges requirement and the surgical center requirement were undue burdens on a woman's right to terminate a – pregnancy.[136] The Court found that the legislature's rationale for enacting H.B. 2 was inconsistent with the effects produced by the law.

Writing for the majority, Justice Breyer pointed out the dubiousness of the law, because abortion was "extremely" safe prior to the law's enactment.[137] In fact, an abortion is one of the safest medical procedures that a woman could receive. It is safer than childbirth and carrying a pregnancy to term and safer than common outpatient procedures such as colonoscopies.

Citing an amicus brief from the Society of Hospital Medicine, the Court noted the "undisputed" fact that "hospitals often condition admitting privileges on reaching a certain number of admissions per year."[138] As such:

> [I]t would be difficult for doctors regularly performing abortions at the El Paso clinic to obtain admitting privileges at nearby hospitals because "[d]uring the past 10 years, over 17,000 abortion procedures were performed at the El Paso clinic [and n]ot a single one of those patients had to be transferred to a hospital for emergency treatment, much less admitted to the hospital."[139]

Justice Breyer explained that "[i]n a word, doctors would be unable to maintain admitting privileges or obtain those privileges for the future, because the fact that abortions are so safe" means abortion providers were unlikely to treat patients whom they could admit.[140] Moreover, amicus briefs filed by Medical Staff Professionals and the American College of Obstetricians and Gynecologists (ACOG), clarifying that "admitting privileges . . . have nothing to do with the ability to perform medical procedures,"[141] provided a persuasive factual foundation for the Court. In the latter brief, ACOG specifically related that "some academic hospitals will only allow medical staff membership for clinicians who also accept faculty appointments."[142]

Justice Breyer took special note of a particular gynecologist with nearly forty years of practice experience, who, despite experience in delivering over 15,000 babies, was yet unable to obtain hospital admitting privileges at the seven hospitals within a thirty-mile radius of his office. The Court cited a letter from one of the nearby hospitals, which explained that the refusal to provide the doctor admitting privileges was "not based on clinical competence considerations."[143] To that end, the Court concluded that "[t]he admitting privileges requirement does not serve any relevant credentialing function." Instead, the law resulted in numerous clinic closures throughout the state of Texas and inordinate, unjustifiable burdens placed on pregnant women.

The second issue the Court turned to was whether H.B. 2's surgical center requirement violated the constitutional standards set forth in *Casey*. Prior to the enactment of H.B. 2 and the surgical center requirements, "Texas . . . required abortion facilities to meet a host of health and safety requirements."[144] Specifically, Justice Breyer stated that Texas law already required clinics that perform abortions to develop, complete, and maintain: environmental and physical requirements; annual reporting; infection control; record keeping; patients' rights standards; quality assurance mechanisms; disclosure requirements; and anesthesia standards, among others. Moreover, clinics performing abortions in Texas were subject to random and unannounced inspections as a means of monitoring compliance with nearly a dozen separate standards. The Court struck down this provision.

4.3 CONCLUSION

As this book goes to press, the United States Supreme Court has decided to take up *June Medical Services v. Gee*, a case that challenges its authority and prior ruling in *Whole Woman's Health*, which was decided barely three years before. The case involves a Louisiana admitting privileges law virtually identical to the Texas law the Supreme Court struck down as unconstitutional in 2016. This type of challenge to the Court's authority and precedent is virtually unheard-of and thus highlights the unique and brazen disregard for Supreme Court precedent as related to women's reproductive rights.

Clearly, antiabortion laws are not about protecting the health or safety of women and girls or people who can become pregnant. Safety serves as an expedient, duplicitous proxy in these instances. For the most part, male legislators control women's reproductive healthcare access in the United States, and in the context of abortion some cling to their power over women's bodies with an ironclad grip. Overwhelmingly, these policymakers have no history of providing medical care and no experience in the sciences. Yet, they legislate against reproductive health with an outsized authority relative to their knowledge and in ways that are both condescending to women and dangerous. Some in this cohort champion legislation that denies abortion even in cases of rape and incest. Even saving or preserving the life of the pregnant woman does not matter. Women's health and safety are only incidental to what really matters: preserving power.

Brie Shea spells out how their power was strategically executed in 2019 to hollow out abortion rights.[145] Nearly four hundred antiabortion laws were proposed in the first half of 2019 and more than a dozen states debated legislation that would give constitutional rights to fetuses. Those same laws would prioritize the "rights" of fetuses over pregnant women. State legislatures introduced a spree of laws criminalizing abortion during the first and second trimesters, claiming to protect fetuses after a heartbeat is detected, notwithstanding the fact that those early pulsations they legislate about have nothing to do with a developed, beating heart.

Nevertheless, sixteen states introduced legislation seeking to ban abortion after the so-called detection of a fetal "heartbeat." Mississippi's governor signed a law banning abortion after six weeks. The Arkansas legislature enacted the "Cherish Act," which makes it a felony to perform an abortion after eighteen weeks of fetal gestation. Violating this law could result in six years imprisonment. Lawmakers in Utah enacted a similar law. Ohio's governor signed antiabortion legislation that provides no exception for rape or incest. Beyond a doubt, the ability to terminate a pregnancy is under serious threat and the future of abortion rights secured under *Roe, Planned Parenthood v. Casey*, and *Whole Woman's Health* rests with a deeply divided, partisan, and politicized Supreme Court.

Yet, also contributing to the mishmash of state statutes, federal law, and cases are little-known executive orders and amendments that restrict the use of federal funds for abortion, domestically and abroad. For example, even former President Obama added to the list of antiabortion executive orders. In 2010, he signed one into law. Executive Order 13535 – Patient Protection and Affordable Care Act's Consistency with Longstanding Restrictions on the Use of Federal Funds for Abortion – ensures the enforcement and implementation of abortion restrictions in the Affordable Care Act (ACA).[146] The executive order emerged from negotiations and a compromise struck with Democratic congressman Bart Stupak, who refused to support the passage of the ACA unless the legislation included strong language prohibiting the use of federal funds for abortion.[147]

The compromise allowed the ACA to move forward in Congress with the support of Stupak and others.[148] In the process, it further entrenched a problematic notion, however – namely, that Congress may unconstitutionally impose reproductive preferences on women, violating their privacy rights. The executive order "maintains current Hyde Amendment restrictions governing abortion policy and extends those restrictions to the newly created health insurance exchanges."[149] The executive order also extends to other federal laws. For example, it seeks to "protect conscience" by upholding the Church Amendment[150] as well as the Weldon Amendment.[151] President Obama's executive order also shields entities that discriminate against women based on conscience, by allowing preexisting federal laws to apply.[152]

President Obama's executive order not only applies Hyde to the ACA, it also expands protections by "prohibit[ing] discrimination against healthcare facilities and healthcare providers because of an unwillingness to provide, pay for, provide coverage of, or refer for abortions."[153] Ironically, entities that discriminate against and harm women based on religious views are now permitted to do so under an executive order without repercussion. Further, the executive order includes strict guidelines prohibiting the "use of tax credits and cost-sharing reduction payments to pay for abortion services (except in cases of rape or incest, or when the life of the woman would be endangered)."[154] Ironically, the Act forces upon state health insurance commissioners the responsibility of ensuring that exchange plan funds, which were intended to provide greater access to healthcare, comply with the expanded restrictions meant to deny women reproductive healthcare.

However, President Obama's little-known executive order stands alongside other executive orders and amendments, such as the Mexico City Policy, otherwise known as the "global gag rule," which is discussed in Chapter 9.

5

Changing Roles of Doctors and Nurses: Hospital Snitches and Police Informants

On July 4, 2017, I presented a paper in Paris, France, entitled *When Bioethics and Law Collide: Considerations in Tort and Criminal Law*. Back at home, this date is a holiday, marked by fireworks, parades, family gatherings, and closed businesses. The "Fourth," as Americans call it, is a day of celebration. It represents the importance of fighting for liberty and freedom. In Paris, it was simply another day.

The audience of bioethicists, philosophers, and doctors from Germany, the Netherlands, Poland, the United Kingdom, and other points around the world gathered for an annual meeting sponsored by the Cambridge Consortium for Bioethics Education. The thrust of the meeting focused on innovation and teaching bioethics. For example, there were brilliant talks on uses of visual arts and nifty ways of incorporating technology into teaching strategies for medical students.

From a technological point of view, my talk was far more mundane; there was no snappy app or video to pitch to the audience. In fact, the one video that I had of Barbara Dawson begging a police officer, John Tadlock, not to remove her oxygen mask would not play. So I described how Ms. Dawson, a fifty-seven-year-old Black woman, died, pleading and gasping, right outside the Calhoun Liberty Hospital in Blountstown, Florida, shortly before Christmas in 2015. She pleaded to keep the oxygen mask that allowed her to breathe.

In some sense, there is nothing extraordinary about the image of Ms. Dawson or the interactions of the hospital and officer, which further complicates their deadly interaction. It was far too normal – poor people at the behest and mercy of nurses and doctors; Black women fearing for their health and safety when they do not seek care and, troublingly, even when they do.[1] When I first saw a photo of Ms. Dawson, cloaked in her red church hat and Sunday clothes, it reminded me of the sepia-hued images of southern, Black grandmothers lined up for church. The hat perfectly crests on her head and her eyes directly meet the camera with that look of "no time for foolishness." All that seemed normal – just as ordinary as being transported to a hospital in an ambulance, complaining of severe pain, and expecting to receive care, but also, sadly, just as common as the fear and risk of being denied the appropriate medical services and turned away in the United States if you are poor and a woman of color.

Numerous studies confirm unequal healthcare treatment in the United States – chief among them the federal Institute of Medicine's voluminous treatise on the subject, *Unequal Treatment: Confronting Racial and Ethnic Disparities in Health Care.*[2] However, the personal accounts shed attention in ways that raw numbers and important statistics simply do not.

Police dashcam and other audio recordings, as well as the Blountstown Police Department transcripts, capture the interactions.[3] Officer Tadlock says, "You can either walk out of here peacefully or I can take you out of here." Ms. Dawson, panting while the officer calmly informs her of those terribly constrained options (notably, neither includes giving her the oxygen she needs), fitfully calls on God. Tadlock then reaches to remove her oxygen mask. "Let's take this off," he says. Dawson responds, "You can't take that off." My students are sometimes confused by how they should relate to this. Officer Tadlock speaks in a calm, almost entreating voice. For many of them, this is not what racism sounds like. Ms. Dawson, some of them say, "is loud."

When Ms. Dawson refuses to surrender the mask, hospital staff gesture to the wall, informing Officer Tadlock that the oxygen supply hose could be disconnected from a port located there. He does so, he disconnects the hose. Afterward, Ms. Dawson wails, "Leave me alone, leave me alone . . . I can't even breathe . . . I beg you." Her options were limited; there was not much the grandmother could do but to beg – in essence, for her life. Within a short while, she would be dead.

In his police report, Officer Tadlock describes his efforts to handcuff and arrest Ms. Dawson for disorderly conduct and trespass for refusing to leave Calhoun Liberty Hospital. He writes that she was nonviolent, but also noncompliant. "At this time I placed handcuffs on Dawsons [sic] left hand and attempted to place it behind her back. After a brief struggle and multiple verbal attempts to get Dawson to place her hand behind her back, I was able to get her left hand behind her back." Because she was able to plead for oxygen, Tadlock and hospital staff deduced that Ms. Dawson was not "having trouble breathing." The report details the use of a male hospital staff member to pull Ms. Dawson's right arm behind her back in order to complete cuffing her. It explains Ms. Dawson's forcible removal from the hospital, including Tadlock "push[ing] her from behind to get her to go with me" to the patrol car, and the cuts and bruises on her feet and knees as she collapsed by the back door of the police car.

Officer Tadlock reprimands Ms. Dawson: "Falling down like this and laying down, that's not going to stop you from going to jail." Someone, maybe the officer, assures one of Ms. Dawson's family members that "she's ok." One voice on the recording says, "Come on now. There ain't nothing wrong with you," and another, "You are going to go to jail one way or the other."[4] Photographs show Ms. Dawson slumped next to the police car. Her life ended on the pavement, feet away from the entrance of the hospital that phoned the police on their patient – because she refused to leave. She lay there nearly twenty minutes before being pronounced dead. Calhoun Liberty Hospital concedes that she died from a blood clot in her lungs. According to records obtained by the *New York Times*, the hospital phoned police regarding their patients more than a dozen times in 2015.[5]

The audience of bioethicists was stunned, perplexed by Dawson's death in circumstances where medical providers phoned police to remove a Black woman complaining of breathing, who was in need of medical services. I spoke about implicit and explicit bias in the medical setting and how negative stereotypes may influence medical decision-making, particularly when vulnerable patients are involved. To this, a physician from the United States, who had grown up in the American South, urged me to consider that nothing is implicit about racial discrimination; it is simply "explicit bigotry." A bioethicist from Australia asked, "People are turned away from hospitals in the United States?" A doctor from Germany demanded that "this cannot happen!" I wondered which part the doctor meant – being turned away from medical care or the criminalization of women seeking care. I pointed to how breaches of fiduciary responsibilities can lead to the criminalization of women like Ms. Dawson, and even more pointedly, pregnant women.

Ms. Dawson's story, which all in the audience could relate to (or feel some sense of empathy about), opened the door for a conversation about race, class, and the criminalization of pregnant women and, more specifically, the shifting roles of doctors, nurses, and hospital staff. As outrageous as Ms. Dawson's arrest for trespassing at the hospital in which she sought care (and later died) is, it is an illustration of the cases I have closely followed for nearly fifteen years of women being shackled while giving birth, threatened with arrest for refusing cesarean sections, or their medical providers surreptitiously collaborating with law enforcement to secretly share private patient information.

A key link in the numerous arrests and prosecutions of pregnant women throughout the United States is their medical providers, whose roles as undercover informants and modern day "snitches" belie their sacred fiduciary obligations. From their once revered roles as fiduciaries, duty-bound with the tasks of protecting and promoting the interests of their female patients, some medical providers now police their pregnant patients' conduct and even serve as quasi law enforcers for the state. For my European colleagues, physicians entreating law enforcement against their pregnant patients was simply unimaginable. Once upon a time, it might have been unthinkable in the United States, too. However, that period is long gone. Indeed, even race can no longer spare white women some of the indignities suffered by Black women.

For example, when Lisa Epsteen indicated that she wanted to wait two additional days for a vaginal delivery rather than undergo the cesarean section recommended by Dr. Jerry Yankowitz, chairman of the University of South Florida's (USF) department of obstetrics and gynecology, he sent the mother of five a threatening email. It stated: "I would hate to move to the most extreme option, which is having law enforcement pick you up at your home and bring you in, but you are leaving the providers of USF/TGH no choice."[6] Mrs. Epsteen knew she had a complicated, high-risk pregnancy,[7] but did not expect intimidation from her medical providers or involvement of law enforcement in giving birth.

She recounted to a *Tampa Bay Times* reporter fears about "cops on my doorstep taking me away from home – in front of my children – to force me into having surgery."[8] Lisa told reporters she felt betrayed, bullied, and abandoned by her doctor. Eventually, medical staff at USF accommodated Epsteen's request after receiving a letter from National Advocates for Pregnant Women (NAPW) demanding that Dr. Yankowitz cease and desist from "any further threats or actions against Ms. Epsteen."[9]

Epsteen's traumatic encounter with her medical providers highlights concerns central to this book, including the fact that fetal protection efforts and laws embolden some doctors to threaten criminal punishment even when no crime has been committed. After all, it is not a crime to want or have a vaginal delivery in childbirth or to wait until labor for birthing. For millennia, women gave birth, frequently without the aid or involvement of men. Threats to include criminal punishment in the process is a newer manifestation.

In their politicized roles as deputized interpreters of the law, physicians and nurses may misinterpret the law or, even worse, prioritize the exercise of their legal judgment over that of their medical judgment. In this context, physicians and nurses are called upon to wear two hats: those of health care provider and law enforcer. However, significant conflicts arise when medical personnel act as both.

First, patients' interests in their health and privacy may become subordinate to physicians' desires to accommodate or promote state interests. Indeed, physicians and nurses may fear civil or criminal punishment for failing to inform on their patients. Second, physicians' legal duties to comply with law enforcement protocols may conflict with their ethical duties to the patient, including maintaining confidentiality and avoiding malfeasance. Third, law enforcement obligations may conflict with physicians' obligations to the profession by interfering with their independent medical judgment to "do no harm" to their patients. Importantly, in addition to any conflicts of interest that may arise in this context, medical professionals' legal decisions may also be at odds with patients' constitutional rights. As Lynn Paltrow, Executive Director of NAPW, explains, Epsteen's experience "raises serious concerns about the misuse of state authority to deprive pregnant women of their constitutional personhood and to endanger the health of women and babies."[10]

5.1 STATES INCREASINGLY RELY ON MEDICAL PROVIDERS TO INTERPRET STATE LAW

Cases across the United States illustrate how physicians and hospital staff operate not only as caretakers to their patients, but also interpreters of state statutes. States increasingly seek physicians' appraisal of pregnant women's behavior under the guise of promoting fetal health. Their interventions in women's pregnancies seem far more related to evaluating women's compliance and obedience. Indeed, fetal protection efforts expose legislative antagonism to the interests of low-income pregnant women. Many fetal protection laws are intended to measure women's obedience and not actual fetal risk, since these laws do very little to promote fetal health. The cases described in this Chapter, and more widely within this book, could be substituted by other examples in Alabama,[11] Maryland,[12] Mississippi,[13] South Carolina,[14] and other states. Although the number of cases resulting in law enforcement is unknown, Lynn Paltrow estimates that the hundreds of cases her organization has documented – in some of which they have also provided legal counsel – represent "a substantial undercount."[15] She is right because, apart from her work, nearly 500 women have been arrested in Alabama alone in recent years for "endangering" their pregnancies.

The accounts below call our attention to hard realities: obtaining appropriate prenatal care can be subject to state (political) rather than medical (patient-centered) considerations. Moreover, the cases are particularly illustrative of a trend that extends beyond specific geographic regions in the United States.

5.1.1 *Samantha Burton's Involuntary Bed Rest*

In 2010, during a routine prenatal medical visit at Tallahassee Memorial Hospital (TMH), Samantha Burton's physician ordered bed rest at the hospital for the duration of her pregnancy – when she was only twenty-five weeks pregnant.[16] The doctors cited the need to manage her pregnancy. Burton was a smoker and struggled with cessation. Recommending bed rest to a patient is not particularly unusual;[17] seeking a court order to enforce it is another matter. Yet, officials at the hospital did just that, setting into motion a plan to obtain a court order allowing the involuntary confinement of Ms. Burton by the hospital against her will.[18] In the process, her medical providers refused to consider Ms. Burton's protestations for a second opinion, her expressed desire to return home to her two children, or her pleas to switch to a different hospital.[19] Hospital staff denied her requests and appealed to the courts.

Based on the medical staff's recommendation, the Leon County Circuit Court issued a stunning ruling that ordered Burton's indefinite confinement.[20] The court stated that, "as between parent and child, the ultimate welfare of the child is the controlling factor,"[21] and found that Florida's interests in the fetus "override Ms. Burton's privacy interests at this time."[22] The circuit court judge, John Cooper, authorized the hospital to take any action "necessary to preserve the life and health of Samantha Burton's unborn child." The court order clarified that this included "but [was] not limited to restricting Samantha Burton to bed rest, administering appropriate medication, postponing labor, taking appropriate steps to prevent and/or treat infection, and/or eventually performing a cesarean section delivery of the child at the appropriate time."[23]

Simply put, the court granted Burton's physicians the authority to take whatever medical course of action they desired, even if it violated her privacy, autonomy, and bodily integrity.[24] The court did not require a second opinion. On appeal, the District Court of Appeal of Florida explained that there was no case precedent to this. Nor were there any Florida laws governing or authorizing compulsory medical confinement for pregnancy management. There was no Florida legislation authorizing compulsory cesarean sections to benefit fetal health.[25] Despite a lack of legal authority to justify Ms. Burton's confinement, the county court granted the hospital's request.

The trauma of state-compelled confinement can be deleterious for anyone. This case was no different. Alone in a dreary hospital room, Ms. Burton endured forced "rest" until her fetus died and was surgically removed three days later. If that were not enough, Samantha's distress was compounded by the fact that the court also ordered TMH to notify the Florida Department of Children and Families "and/or other appropriate agencies of Samantha Burton's [forced bedrest]" and to intervene as necessary in the monitoring of her children.[26] Such a process usually leads to a file alleging some form of parental absence, neglect, or abuse, which triggers mothers temporarily and in some cases permanently losing custody of their children.[27]

Forced medical solitary confinement, while distinct from prison solitary confinement, shares relevant parallels that trigger human and constitutional rights concerns pertaining to the deprivation of liberty, forced institutional restraint, and isolation from the general population and community. By constraining someone in solitary confinement, the state is necessarily denying them contact and the confined person loses freedom to move within a facility. Studies show that this can lead to mental health deterioration and result in stigma.

Individually and collectively, conditions such as these raise serious concerns related to human dignity, so much so that Senator Dick Durban cautioned that only when "absolutely necessary" should solitary confinement be used in the prison context.[28] Similarly, the late Senator John McCain recounted from personal experience that "it's an awful thing, solitary." He explained, "it crushes your spirit and weakens your resistance more effectively than any other form of mistreatment."[29]

More than a century ago, the U.S. Supreme Court recounted the devastating effects of solitary confinement on prisoners:

A considerable number of the prisoners fell, after even a short confinement, into a semi-fatuous condition, from which it was next to impossible to arouse them, and others became violently insane, others still, committed suicide . . . and in most cases did not recover sufficient mental activity to be of any subsequent service to the community.[30]

Given this, why would medical professionals subject any pregnant woman to such circumstances? In 2012, the Senate Judiciary Committee's Subcommittee on the Constitution, Civil Rights and Human Rights took up similar concerns in a hearing entitled "Reassessing Solitary Confinement: The Human Rights, Fiscal, and Public Safety Consequences."[31] Senator Patrick Leahy issued a statement acknowledging that, "[a]lthough solitary confinement was developed as a method for handling highly dangerous prisoners, it is increasingly being used with inmates who do not pose a threat to staff or other inmates."[32] Among those forced into confinement are many "who don't really need to be there" from "vulnerable groups like immigrants, children, [and] LGBT inmates supposedly there for their own protection."[33]

Relevantly, confinement is not simply deleterious because of forced isolation; it often represents misuse of state-sanctioned authority by individuals in charge of vulnerable populations.[34] In this case, Samantha Burton had not committed a crime, nor had she signed up for combat; she was simply a mom and pregnant patient. Yet, her experience points to a different type of war – one in which some pregnant women find themselves unarmored and lacking the resources to fight back. After three days of state-compelled confinement, "doctors performed an emergency cesarean section on Ms. Burton and discovered that her fetus had already died in utero."[35] Hospitals, like prisons, "are psychologically powerful places, ones that are capable of shaping and transforming the thoughts and actions of the persons who enter them."[36] Often, patients benefit from their hospital experiences, but sometimes medical stays are counterproductive and adverse, as in Samantha Burton's experience.

In this case, law and medicine intersected in pernicious ways, extending even beyond the physician's decision to seek an order to confine Samantha Burton against her will. For example, Burton was not provided with any legal representation at the civil commitment hearing, despite the significant liberty and privacy interests at stake.[37] Over fifty years ago, in its landmark ruling *Gideon v. Wainwright* (a case that originated in Florida courts), the U.S. Supreme Court affirmed that the Sixth Amendment establishes a constitutional right to appointed counsel in criminal cases.[38] In that case, the Court found that "[f]rom the very beginning, our state and national constitutions and laws have laid great emphasis on procedural and substantive safeguards designed to assure fair trials before impartial tribunals in which every defendant stands equal before the law. This noble ideal cannot be realized if the poor man charged with crime has to face his accusers without a lawyer to assist him."[39]

This well-established principle is no less salient in civil cases. For example, in *Lassiter v. Department of Social Services*, the Supreme Court ruled that the Due Process Clause of the Fourteenth Amendment establishes a right to counsel when the state risks depriving an individual of her physical liberty.[40] The Court stressed an interest balancing test, weighing government interest against private interest, "and the risk that the procedures used will lead to erroneous decisions."[41] The Court established that there is a presumption to a right to appointed counsel in adjudications where the indigent, "if he is unsuccessful, may lose his personal freedom."[42] A decade earlier, *In re Gault* reached a similar conclusion, establishing a right to counsel for civil delinquency proceedings "which may result in commitment to an institution in which the juvenile's freedom is curtailed."[43]

As acknowledged on appeal, Burton's physical and liberty interests were no less paramount than the interests at stake in *Lassiter* and *In re Gault*. She was involuntarily hospitalized and mandated to undergo an invasive medical procedure that required anesthesia and the insertion of a broad incision in the abdomen and a second in the uterus. These procedures are painful postoperatively and can render the patient vulnerable to infection at the point of incision in the abdomen or uterus, blood clots in the legs or lungs, heavy blood loss, and drug side effects such as migraines, nausea, and vomiting.[44] Some women die after the procedure. Cesarean surgeries can leave weak spots in the uterus, making subsequent efforts for a vaginal delivery risky. Yet, no counsel appeared to address these concerns (or any others) on behalf of Ms. Burton until after the forced cesarean section occurred. As Judge William Van Nortwick admonished in a concurring opinion, appointment of counsel subsequent to the hearing and after such a significant invasion of privacy cannot satisfy the clear due process requirement established by the Constitution.

This case represents a glaring example of pregnancy serving as a proxy for involuntary confinement, physical deprivation of liberty, and the denial of legal assistance. Even the Florida Constitution spells out a fundamental right to privacy and autonomy: "to be let alone and free from governmental intrusion into the person's private life."[45] So what went wrong here? Let's understand Burton's case in context and not as an isolated instance of a state policing a woman's pregnancy with the aid of medical intervention or a random act of medical professionals threatening a pregnant woman and using courts to do so.

Ms. Burton's experience is an alarming illustration of the unconstitutional constraints imposed on pregnant women's right to security in their bodies. Were it not for a troubling pattern of states unconstitutionally depriving pregnant women of their bodily integrity, privacy, and civil liberties, with doctors as overseers to that politicized agenda, this case could be read as unfortunate, but isolated and uncommon. If this case were isolated and random, it could be characterized as very rare – an unusual example of medical providers appealing to law enforcement or courts against the constitutional interests of their pregnant patients. But that is not the story this book tells. Increasingly, that is not the story of reproductive healthcare in the United States.

5.1.2 *Christine Taylor's Arrest for Tripping While Pregnant*

Fetal protection cases like Samantha Burton's illuminate the vulnerabilities of pregnant women to civil law constraints. Her case highlights how medical staff sometimes interfere with and undermine their pregnant patients' constitutional rights, thereby making the medical setting hostile to medical care and legal interests. These types of problems are well documented within the criminal law. That is, the medical setting has also served as a place of criminal law intervention in pregnant women's lives. Unbeknownst to many women, hospitals and medical clinics have perversely become places where some pregnant women risk the disclosure of their confidential medical information to law enforcement, which can lead to arrest and criminal punishment.

Like Samantha Burton, Christine Taylor, a twenty-two-year-old pregnant mother of two living in Iowa, did not anticipate that a medical visit could result in her incarceration. Christine's "crime" was to trip and fall down the stairs during the second trimester of her pregnancy in Iowa.[46] In her case, after a troubling phone call related to her dissolving marriage, she became "upset and frantic," so much so that she "almost blacked out" and "tripped and fell."[47]

She immediately sought care and received treatment from emergency medical technicians, who confirmed that she and the fetus were fine. She voluntarily sought further care at a hospital. During interviews with a nurse and a doctor, Taylor, a Maryland native, confided that she felt ambivalence about her pregnancy during its early stages. She informed medical staff about feeling vulnerable in the early stages of her pregnancy. Christine shared intimate details about her estranged husband's threat that he was leaving her; he had already moved back to Maryland. Taylor explained her anxiety to an Iowa reporter: "And here I was alone, pregnant with two young kids, with no family around or support."[48]

The prospect of raising three children as a single parent was daunting. Christine confided that upon confirmation of her pregnancy she contemplated different options, including having an abortion, carrying the pregnancy to term and then placing the child for adoption, or simply welcoming one more child into her life. This was a challenging decision – as it can be for anyone assessing whether to have another child. Yet, little did Christine Taylor know that as a result of her confiding in medical staff about her marital relationship and the stress of pregnancy, they would contact law enforcement. The medical team's response was clandestine; they alerted local police, because they interpreted Taylor's case to fit within Iowa's criminal feticide statute, which prohibits "intentionally terminat[ing] a human pregnancy after the end of the second trimester of the pregnancy."[49]

Police stopped Christine Taylor shortly after she left the hospital, while on her way home to her children. Two squad cars intercepted her taxi and officers arrested her. Police incarcerated her at the local jail for two days, while they launched an investigation to determine whether she meant to kill her fetus by tripping in her home. For three weeks, local prosecutors pursued their attempted feticide investigation against Ms. Taylor until the case was finally dropped. According to the prosecutor, Taylor was lucky to be in the second trimester of her pregnancy, and not the third, when she fell. Had the fall been a few weeks later, it might have implicated her under the criminal feticide statute.[50]

It is difficult to know what exactly triggered the medical staff's call to the police, other than their belief that Christine Taylor had attempted to kill her fetus. Did they think considering an abortion during the first trimester of a pregnancy violated the Iowa law? Maybe they believed a physically harmless fall during pregnancy was by default probative of motivation to harm a fetus and triggered the state's feticide law.

According to a reporter who interviewed Ms. Taylor, "she believes the personal views of medical workers . . . played a part in a decision to accuse her last month of attempted feticide."[51] Perhaps Christine Taylor simply lacked credibility in the eyes of the medical staff who treated her, leading them to assume that, given her earlier ambivalence about the pregnancy, the fall was a surreptitious attempt to abort her fetus. Or might this case simply be about a perceived medical duty to report? In other words, given the pressure and anxiety experienced by medical providers to serve not only as interpreters of state fetal protection laws but also as informants on their patients, perhaps they believed the Iowa law required physicians to report any and all medical visits indicating an intentional or negligent threat of harm to a fetus. It may be that the medical staff believed they were simply doing what was legally expected of them and that failure to report would put their licenses at risk. Even so, under any of these circumstances, the call to the police and Taylor's subsequent ordeal serve as chilling examples of misuse and misapplication of fetal protection laws and of medical providers trampling the legal interests of their pregnant patients.

In both cases described above, physicians erred in their interpretation of the law: there was no legal foundation for the forced confinement and cesarean section ordered in Samantha Burton's case, and Christine Taylor's medical providers lacked sufficient legal grounds to alert law enforcement against her. Notably, in both cases, subsequent legal actors (a judge in one and police officers in the other) relied on statements made by physicians and nurses in determining that confinement or arrest were the next appropriate courses of action. Tripping down steps while pregnant may cause injury to a woman and even her fetus, but it is not a crime. Even if the nurse and doctor treating Taylor disbelieved her version of events, that still does not make falling down steps a crime. It appears the medical staff misread Iowa's feticide law, the statute on which they based their call.

5.1.3 *Rennie Gibbs's Charge of Depraved Heart Murder in Stillbirth Case*

Rennie Gibbs's criminal prosecution in Mississippi for depraved heart murder of her dead fetus[52] further illustrates the extent to which physicians and medical staff may misconstrue and misinterpret fetal protection laws and, in the process, undermine their pregnant patients' constitutional rights and trigger criminal prosecutions. As with Christine Taylor's encounter at a hospital in Iowa, which resulted in her arrest, the prosecution of Rennie Gibbs, an African American teen, hinged on how a doctor construed her conduct during pregnancy.[53] In Gibbs's case, the medical examiner claimed that her drug addiction, which did not abate during pregnancy, demonstrated indifference toward the life of her fetus and that its death was the direct result of her depraved heart. Rennie's arrest and prosecution following a traumatic perinatal outcome is yet another example of the misuse and misapplication of medical information for politicized reproductive purposes. Unlike Taylor's traumatic ordeal, Gibbs's prosecution, which began in 2006, endured for many years – with a lingering threat: if ever convicted of depraved heart murder for birthing a stillborn baby, Rennie Gibbs will face a mandatory life sentence.

Gibbs was only fifteen years old when she became pregnant and, although a teenager, she struggled with drug dependence on crystallized cocaine (crack).[54] In December of 2006, one month after turning sixteen, Gibbs suffered a stillbirth[55] in the thirty-sixth week of her pregnancy.[56] Dr. Steven Hayne performed an autopsy on the dead baby and concluded that it suffered from in utero exposure to cocaine, which caused its death.[57] He ruled the stillbirth a murder, noting that Rennie had admitted to using crack during her pregnancy.

Research now discredits this longstanding misperception of pregnancy demise being associated with crystalized cocaine. Crack use became a particularly targeted offense during the U.S. war on drugs, earning its convicted users grossly disparate, tougher sentences than those for powder cocaine sellers and users. The sentencing disparity, only recently addressed in 2013 by U.S. Attorney General Eric Holder,[58] was 100 to 1, because politicians speciously claimed crack caused more socially deleterious behavior than powder cocaine, such as violence, crime, and the birth of "crack babies" (supposed biologically inferior children permanently hampered by physical and cognitive disabilities).[59]

According to the legal documents that I obtained in Gibbs's case, "[u]nder the statutory interpretation advanced by the prosecution, Ms. Gibbs faces life in prison because of her combined status as a pregnant woman and drug user."[60] The statute at issue reads: "The killing of a human being without the authority of law by any means or in any manner shall be murder in the following cases: . . . (b)When done in the commission of an act eminently dangerous to others and evincing a depraved heart, regardless of human life, although without premeditated design to effect the death of any particularly individual, shall be second-degree murder."[61] This Mississippi law provides that "every person who shall be convicted of second-degree murder shall be imprisoned for life . . . if the punishment is so fixed by the jury."[62]

Because of the drug war, which spawned legislation and criminal prosecutions that applied old laws in new ways, pregnant drug users in the 1980s and 1990s endured a particularly intense and unique attack, not only as intensified targets of the drug war but also as "bad mothers." Back then, the targets of enforcement, arrests, and prosecutions were mostly Black pregnant women. Law enforcement ignored drug addiction among pregnant white women, whether associated with opioids, methamphetamines, cocaine, or prescribed drugs.

However, pundits and politicians stereotyped poor Black women as on the path toward swamping the United States with crack babies, who develop into uneducable, disabled, and malformed children.[63] States responded by prosecuting Black women under existing child abuse statutes for drug dependence occurring during pregnancy. Meanwhile, meticulous empirical studies debunking politicized and inaccurate science on crack were published in leading peer review journals years before Rennie Gibbs's arrest and in the years since her prosecution began.

Dr. Hallam Hurt, former chairwoman of the Division of Neonatology at the Albert Einstein Medical Center, conducted the most extensive longitudinal study on fetal cocaine exposure. In a 2009 study published in the peer-reviewed journal *Neurotoxicology and Teratology*, she reported:

> [In] middle school-aged children, we found no evidence of impaired [neurocognitive] function caused by gestational cocaine exposure, despite the fact that our sample size was adequate to detect a statistically and clinically significant difference (effect size of 0.5) and we used a [neurocognitive] battery shown to be sensitive to age and IQ. . . . [W]e found no difference between groups even with isolation of specific cognitive systems for evaluation of cocaine effects.[64]

Across numerous peer-reviewed articles, published in leading medical journals, Hurt's conclusions were consistently the same: there was no significant difference between the children exposed in utero to crystallized cocaine and those who were not. Poverty played a more significant role in children's lives. Other scholars who seriously studied the matter reached a similar conclusion.

For example, in 2001, Deborah Frank and her coinvestigators reported in *JAMA*, the journal of the American Medical Association, that "there is no convincing evidence that prenatal cocaine exposure is associated with developmental toxicity effects different in severity, scope or kind from the sequelae of multiple other risk factors."[65] The researchers based their conclusions on the review of thirty-six studies related to maternal-fetal cocaine exposure and subsequent outcomes with children. Hallum Hurt's 1997 study reported that children with in utero cocaine exposure did not differ from control subjects on intelligence testing.[66] Both Hurt and Frank attribute poverty as a cofounding factor for poor outcomes in children exposed to cocaine.

Even though compelling evidence discrediting the crack baby myth, its lore lingers. Based on faulty, limited studies, journalists and even medical providers concluded that "a generation of children would be damaged for life."[67] These predictions gained mileage through media sensationalism in the 1980s and 1990s, likely fueled through implicit and perhaps even explicit biases in some cases. The result was an escalation of public fear, resentment, and blatant misinformation.

Politicians capitalized on public anxiety, urging a "crack down" on pregnant drug users as part of the so-called war on drugs. However, they were wrong.

Despite rigorous scientific evidence discrediting unreliable medical and political accounts about fetal cocaine exposure, and without evidence that Rennie Gibbs's stillbirth was caused by an illicit drug, prosecutors charged her with "depraved heart murder." On the basis of Dr. Hayne's autopsy report, Gibbs was arrested on February 4, 2007 for "kill[ing] her unborn child, a human being, while engaged in the commission of an act eminently dangerous to others and evincing a depraved heart, by using cocaine while pregnant with her unborn child … in violation of MCA § 97-3-19."[68] And, although she was barely sixteen at the time, Rennie Gibbs was charged as an adult.

That Gibbs's fetus was stillborn is undisputed. However, the factors that ultimately contributed to its death are not as clear-cut as prosecutors suggest, because "stillbirth is one of the most common adverse outcomes of pregnancy,"[69] and it results from any number of factors.[70] More than 30 percent of pregnancies terminate in miscarriage or stillbirth.[71] Notwithstanding rigorous efforts to identify what causes perinatal fetal mortality, researchers report that "a substantial portion of fetal deaths are still classified as unexplained intrauterine fetal demise"[72] because stillbirths are linked to the environment,[73] poverty,[74] stress,[75] diabetes,[76] hypertension,[77] and sexually transmitted diseases.[78] A comprehensive study on stillbirth published in *The Lancet* posited that "women from disadvantaged populations in high-income countries continue to have stillbirth rates far in excess of those living without such disadvantage," leading the authors to believe that "poverty could be the overriding factor preventing access to care" and thereby increasing risk of stillbirth.[79]

The American Congress of Obstetricians and Gynecologists (ACOG) warns that race may be a risk factor in stillbirths, because Black women are nearly twice as likely to suffer a stillbirth as compared to all other women.[80] My only clarification here is that racism, rather than race itself, may be the cause of such stress in the lives of Black pregnant women that the results can be fatal. For example, Black women's stillbirth rate lies at 11.25 per 1,000 births, compared to Asian, white, and Native American women, all of whom experience stillbirth at rates less than 6 per 1,000.[81] This disparity persists even among Black women who receive "adequate" prenatal care, because stress, hypertension, and other medical, psychological, social, and economic factors uniquely prey on the lives of pregnant Black women. As such, this may explain the gross disparity in stillbirths occurring in their pregnancies.

Gibbs's prosecution is one of first impression in Mississippi, as no woman or girl prior to her was ever charged for having a miscarriage or stillbirth. According to Gibbs's legal counsel, "there ha[ve] been no reported cases and no media reports showing that the State of Mississippi ha[s] ever applied the depraved-heart homicide statute to a pregnant woman who suffered a stillbirth or miscarriage."[82] That no prior cases are reported of a pregnant woman charged with this offense is unsurprising, because the explicit language of the statute does not "encompass the death of an unborn child."[83] Nor does the legislation on its face include pregnant women within the scope of the class of persons who can be prosecuted for violating this statute.[84]

For these reasons, Gibbs's attorneys argued that the Mississippi legislature never intended the statute to apply to the unborn. They specifically cited the statutory language, highlighting that the statute underpinning Rennie Gibbs's prosecution, Mississippi Code § 97-3-37, "specifically provides that an 'unborn child' can be the victim of assault, capital murder, and certain types of manslaughter, but not depraved heart murder." Despite a rigorous defense, on April 23, 2010 the Circuit Court of Lowndes County denied Gibbs's Motion to Dismiss.[85] Not until 2014 were the murder charges against her finally dismissed.

5.2 THE PREGNANCY PENALTY AT THE END OF LIFE

5.2.1 *Marlise Muñoz: Brain Dead and Tethered to Life Support to Incubate Fetus*

In Texas, hospital officials refused to remove thirty-three-year-old Marlise Muñoz, a brain-dead woman, from life support for sixty-two days because she was pregnant.[86] In November 2013, fourteen weeks into her pregnancy, Muñoz collapsed at her Texas home, possibly from a blood clot that entered her lungs.[87] Shortly after receiving medical attention at the John Peter Smith Hospital in Fort Worth, Texas, doctors informed Muñoz's family that she suffered brain death and would not recover. However, instead of preparing to remove Munoz's body from life support, as requested by her husband, Erick Muñoz, and her parents, Lynne and Ernest Machado, hospital officials refused. The medical staff cited a Texas law that prohibits healthcare providers from complying with patient medical directives to terminate life support when the patient is pregnant.

Texas is one of more than two dozen states that prohibit removing life support from a pregnant woman. However, the Texas law is among the strictest in the nation. A dozen state statutes, including those of Kentucky, South Carolina, Texas, Utah, and Wisconsin, "automatically invalidate a woman's advance directive if she is pregnant."[88] A study published by the Center for Women Policy explains that these laws "are the most restrictive of pregnancy exclusion" legislation because, regardless of fetal viability or the length of pregnancy, these laws require that a pregnant woman must "remain on life sustaining treatment until she gives birth."[89]

These laws also reflect a pattern of politically targeted legislation that misuses pregnant women's medical crises as opportunities to legislate about reproduction. This type of legislation conflicts with pregnant women's fundamental constitutional interests, most obviously their autonomy, liberty, and privacy. In such instances, the state quite literally enslaves a woman's body for its political purposes and benefits – not for hers.

The Muñoz case differs from those discussed above as it sheds light on reproductive justice at the end of life. For the most part, Americans may take end-of-life decision-making for granted. Most people assume that their medical directives carry substantive weight in the law. Well, in fact, medical directives are an essential part of one's healthcare planning, and hospitals and the medical providers that care for patients generally take them very seriously. After all, these are legal documents. The problem, however, is that medical directives may not be taken seriously *if the patient is pregnant.*

One problem, as pointed out in the *Center for Women Policy Studies*, is the public's lack of awareness that such fetal protection laws exist. When there is no public awareness and limited disclosure about a law, the public has no way to either shape or contest its implementation. Furthermore, there is virtually no uniformity in pregnancy exclusion laws. The statutes are often written and enacted under unrelated or confusing titles – whether intentionally or not. In some states, legislators align fetal protection laws such as these with statutes directly addressing advance directives. In other states, pregnancy exclusion legislation might be located with trust and estate legislation.[90] Given this, even the most perceptive women and their advocates may not be on notice about pregnancy exclusion legislation in their states or aware that their advance directives and explicit instructions about end-of-life care could mean nothing.

The application of fetal protection law to brain-dead pregnant women borders on the absurd. Ernest Machado lamented that the hospital and Texas legislature reduced his daughter to "a host for a fetus."[91] Until ordered to do otherwise, hospital officials apparently planned to keep Munoz's body on life support until her fetus became viable, against the express wishes of her family members.[92] As Lynne Machado explained to a *New York Times* reporter, "It's not a matter of pro-choice and pro-life," rather, "It's about a matter of our daughter's wishes not being honored by the state of Texas."[93]

5.2.2 *Angela Carder: Denying a Pregnant Patient Chemotherapy*

As with Marlise Muñoz's end-of-life tragedy, the deaths of Angela Carder, aged twenty-seven, and her fetus starkly illustrate how doctors' authority and power relative to their pregnant patients may undermine the exercise of their medical judgment in treating those women.[94] Carder, a former cancer patient, bravely battled Ewing's sarcoma in childhood and survived. Ewing's sarcoma is a rare and deadly disease, afflicting connective tissues. In most instances patients lose their battles with this aggressive form of cancer.

Angela received experimental treatment through the National Institutes of Health (NIH) at the National Cancer Institute (NCI). At thirteen, doctors removed her left leg and part of her pelvis, but this targeted and aggressive treatment saved her life. Angela survived when nearly all other children who suffered from this disease died.

After thirteen years and, as court records note, "free of all evidence of cancer," she married and later became pregnant.

Angela sought medical care at the George Washington University Hospital, in a unit for higher-risk pregnancies given her prior medical history with cancer.[95] The early stages of her pregnancy progressed smoothly. However, Angela soon developed shortness of breath and back pains. After conducting medical tests, specialists at the NIH consulted with the National Institute of Cancer and determined that she suffered a reoccurrence of cancer. There seemed little doubt on their part that Angela needed radiation and chemotherapy.

In fact, a specialist at the NIH most familiar with Angela's prior cancer treatment determined that radiation and chemotherapy were necessary and could be facilitated without risking fetal health. In his affidavit the specialist explained that "[t]he consensus of [NIH] physicians was that the risk of chemotherapy to the fetus was not nearly as great as the risk of not treating the tumor."[96] Chemotherapy was a key part of the treatment Angela also wanted, particularly because it was virtually impossible to remove the tumor.

Unfortunately, Ms. Carder's cancer specialist did not have hospital admission privileges at George Washington Hospital. Nevertheless, he spoke to Angela's medical team at the hospital at least six times between June 10, 1988 and June 16, 1988, advising on her medical care. It is important to note that not one of the doctors on Carder's medical team at the hospital specialized in cancer treatment. Again according to legal documents in the case, "hospital personnel never took the diagnostic and treatment steps apparently agreed upon, nor did they contact the cancer specialist to advise him that Ms. Carder had been given no treatment."[97] Even though the cancer specialist "asked . . . that lung fluid and tissue be taken from Ms. Carder for essential diagnostic purposes, the Hospital never did so."[98]

Days later, the specialist "discussed such a biopsy again and Ms. Carder's deteriorating condition with her doctors . . . at the Hospital, at which time her doctors apparently agreed that Ms. Carder needed radiation and chemotherapy."[99] However, the doctors did not take a biopsy. Nor did they provide radiation or chemotherapy. Angela was also concerned about this. She confided in her cancer specialist that "nothing was being done to figure out what was wrong and to start treatment."[100] As days went by without any treatment, Angela and her mother, Nettie Stoner, were understandably frightened. They had confronted cancer before, during Angela's childhood, and they were prepared to battle it again. However, the doctors at George Washington did not provide any ammunition that they could use in this battle. The treatments recommended by the NIH cancer specialist, which might have offered Angela a fighting chance, never came. In the absence of treatment, "the tumor in her lungs grew uncontrolled."[101]

Angela and her family were not alone in fighting for her to receive treatment. Her cancer specialist traveled to George Washington Hospital to advocate on her behalf and to see Angela. He met with Drs. Lessin and Hamner and again thought that they agreed to provide the care recommended. The specialist recounted that experience in an affidavit entered into court records:

> We went back to the ward and met Dr. Hamner outside Ms. C's room. First we went into her room, and Dr. Lessin examined Ms. C. Then we stepped out and talked in the hallway outside her room. Dr. Lessin agreed that Ms. C. was in significant respiratory distress. I again advocated therapy for Ms. C., although at this point I felt we had fewer options than we had had on Friday, June 12. It was clear that any therapy at this point carried a higher risk now that Ms. C. was more ill. Specifically, I recommended:
>
> a) moving Ms. C. to an intensive care unit;
> b) emergency radiation therapy, with adequate shielding for the fetus;
> c) chemotherapy with etoposide and ifosfamide;
> d) the biopsy should be foregone in light of Ms. C's deteriorating condition.
>
> I believed that Drs. Hamner and Lessin agreed with this plan . . .. I again told Dr. Hamner I felt that Ms. C. had hours to days to live if therapy was not promptly initiated. I wrote a note in the chart documenting the discussion with Ms. C. and my understanding that treatment was to be quickly initiated.[102]

Despite agreeing to this course of action, the hospital did not follow through with the treatments recommended. Indeed, the hospital never provided the radiation or chemotherapy Ms. Carder sought and that a specialist recommended. Instead, the hospital contacted its lawyers and initiated a court hearing that would grant them the legal authority to remove the fetus, even over Ms. Carder's objections, and the possibility that the procedure might hasten her death.

Physicians informed Ms. Carder that chemotherapy posed medical risk to her twenty-six-week-old fetus and that they were reluctant to provide the chemotherapy care that Carder needed while she was pregnant.[103] There were no guarantees that Angela would survive if she did receive chemotherapy but, for certain, without the treatment she would die. The physicians proposed a cesarean section, which would not benefit Ms. Carder but might in the most remote chance enhance the potential survival of her fetus.

Angela refused; she did not want a cesarean operation; she wanted chemotherapy. She wanted to live for as long as she could. In fact, according to the D.C. Court of Appeals, "there was no evidence ... showing that A.C. consented to, or even contemplated, a caesarean section before her twenty-eighth week of pregnancy."[104] Further, testimony from Dr. Alan Weingold makes clear that Carder opposed the surgery:

THE COURT:	You could hear what the parties were saying to one another?
DR. WEINGOLD:	She does not make sound because of the tube in her windpipe. She nods and she mouths words. One can see what she's saying rather readily. She asked whether she would

> survive the operation. She asked [Dr.] Hamner if he would perform the operation. He told her he would only perform it if she authorized it but it would be done in any case. She understood that. She then seemed to pause for a few moments and then very clearly mouthed words several times, "I don't want it done. I don't want it done." Quite clear to me.[105]

Dr. Weingold explained to the court: "I would obviously state the obvious and that is this is an environment in which, from my perspective as a physician, this would not be an informed consent one way or the other. . . . I'm satisfied that I heard clearly what she said."[106]

Over Ms. Carder's objections and despite her family's opposition, medical providers at George Washington Hospital petitioned the Superior Court of the District of Columbia to authorize an immediate cesarean operation.[107] Mrs. Stoner, her mother, explained to reporters: "The hospital staff told us we were needed at a 'short meeting.' They did not tell us it was a court hearing."[108] She told reporters that the hearing took the family away from Angela, and it lasted hours. The hospital did not inform the cancer specialist about the rushed hearing or call him to testify.

Mrs. Stoner recounted, "Poor Angie, first she's told she's dying and the next thing everybody abandons her and leaves her alone in her room. . . . Then even before the hearing was over they started prepping her for surgery – she was already in so much pain."[109] The court appointed an attorney to represent Angela's fetus. That attorney, along with counsel for the hospital, argued that it was in the best interest of the fetus that it be removed from Angela's body. Over objections made by Angela, her family, and their lawyer, the "court ordered that a caesarean section be performed to deliver A.C.'s child."[110] The family protested: "We told the judge she didn't want the surgery, that we didn't want her to suffer anymore, that we didn't think the baby would live. But they didn't listen."[111] According to the amicus brief submitted by NOW Legal Defense and Education Fund, "the court heard only the expert testimony that the Hospital arranged for it to hear."[112] The District of Columbia Superior Court judge who issued the ruling never visited Angela prior to permitting the course of action that ultimately hastened her death.

Angela's court-appointed lawyer immediately requested a stay, which would at least temporarily bar the procedure from taking place. However, a "hastily assembled" panel consisting of three D.C. Court of Appeals judges denied the proposed injunction.[113] In its subsequent written opinion the panel wrote: "We well know that we may have shortened A.C.'s life span by a few hours."[114] By all accounts, the operation was performed against Angela Carder's will. Two hours after the court-ordered cesarean operation, Angela's baby, Lindsay Marie Carder, died. She was too fragile and premature to survive. According to Angela's mother, "After the surgery and after they told her the baby was dead, I think Angie just gave up."[115] Angela died two days later without receiving the cancer treatment she sought.

Another legal case mounted after Angela's death, brought by the American Civil Liberties Union (ACLU). They appealed the panel's ruling, arguing that the cesarean operation, which hastened Angela's death, violated her constitutional rights. They argued that even though Angela was dead, the issues were not moot. The hospital was not opposed to this litigation and had previously filed a Memorandum in Support of Petition for Declaratory Relief. In that memorandum the hospital asserted that pregnant women could be forced to undergo invasive cesarean operations even absent their consent and acknowledged that in some instances "such an operation would most likely be fatal."[116]

As a legal matter, Angela's experience was ripe for repetition, because other pregnant women would seek medical care at hospitals, some of those pregnancies might be complicated, and, based on the court's decision, forced cesareans – even when they risked pregnant patients' lives – would be permissible. The attorneys pointed to a case only a year or two before Angela's death, *In the Matter of Madyun Fetus*, where a panel of the same court, the D.C. Court of Appeals, affirmed an order for a forced cesarean on a competent, nonconsenting adult woman. The court did not issue a written opinion in that case.

In this case, however, the ACLU scored a victory on appeal. The D.C. Court of Appeals held that "in virtually all cases the question of what is to be done is to be decided by the patient . . . on behalf of herself and the fetus."[117] Sadly, Angela was already dead.

5.3 CONCLUSION

Angela Carder's forced cesarean is not unique. In 2004, Pennsylvania doctors obtained a court order to force Amber Marlowe to deliver by cesarean section because ultrasound imaging indicated that her baby might weigh as much as thirteen pounds.[118] Despite the chilling lessons from *In re A.C.*, a Pennsylvania court order granted Marlowe's doctors and the hospital the authority to perform a nonconsensual cesarean operation.[119] Marlowe, the mother of six children, who were all big babies, fled the hospital and later delivered a healthy eleven-pound baby girl at another medical facility. In a subsequent interview, she confided: "When I found out about the court order, I couldn't believe the hospital would do something like that. It was scary and very shocking."[120]

The scope of the problems identified here – physicians prioritizing fetal health over maternal health, rights, and decision-making based on legislative, law enforcement, and political pressure – are difficult to track. Not all cases of compelled caesarean operations, confinement, or arrest are afforded judicial review or a written opinion when, and if, a court is involved. Nevertheless, the collateral consequences that flow from even this small sample of cases cause serious alarm. Indeed, each of these cases is "capable of repetition." Furthermore, this phenomenon illumes a serious corruption of the physician-patient relationship.

What these cases and many others demonstrate are the troubling ways in which medical staff implicate themselves in the civil and criminal punishments of pregnant women. Sometimes, as discussed, medical staff initiate these matters by calling state attention to the women they serve and disclosing confidential patient information. These pregnant women are overwhelmingly poor and often women of color. On close examination, it becomes clear that nurses and doctors serve as more than just the eyes and ears of the state. Rather, as a formal matter, these cases illustrate that medical staff are the primary detectives and enforcers of state fetal protection statutes, often with the support of police, prosecutors, and even judges.

Are medical providers qualified to make legal judgments about their patients' legal rights? I am not convinced that they are, or that those roles of informant or "snitch," as some might say, are best suited to them. Certainly, patients receive no warnings, as they would with actual police and prosecutors, that the information they share may be used against them. Moreover, it is also apparent that pregnant patients are rarely, if at all, informed about the dual roles increasingly played by their medical providers in those instances. This matters, because non-legally trained medical staff participate in the front-end enforcement of fetal protection laws. Now, as thirty-eight states have adopted some form of feticide legislation, pregnant women may be under intensified criminal and civil scrutiny during their prenatal medical visits.[121]

As these cases demonstrate, in applying fetal protection laws, medical staff may subordinate good medical judgment to criminal law enforcement objectives, which introduces problematic norms into the physician-patient relationship. Specifically, medical staff may prioritize criminal punishment over fiduciary responsibilities to patients. Thus, in some instances, pregnant women's medical treatment becomes not merely subordinate but extraneous and peripheral.

6

Revisiting the Fiduciary Relationship

Is it ethical when doctors breach their pregnant patients' confidentiality? Is it legal? What about HIPAA (properly known as the Health Insurance Portability and Accountability Act of 1996)?[1] Are there different rules for pregnant women than for men? These are some of the questions women ask me after I give a talk. I understand this bewilderment and, for many, fear. At the heart of their questions resides this chilling thought: Could this happen to me or my daughter? Depending on where they live, the answer may be yes. And, increasingly, wealth will not save them. This Chapter focuses on the physician-patient relationship, although I am mindful that nurses wield enormous power and can also be complicit in undermining pregnant women's privacy and breaching confidentiality.

In 2015, I received an invitation to give a talk to a conservative women's group in Laguna Niguel, a suburban community in Orange County, California. I agreed and the date was set months off. Orange County, often described as a Republican stronghold dating back to Presidents Richard Nixon and Ronald Reagan, was reliably "red." Former congressman Dana Tyrone Rohbacher, considered one of the most conservative members of Congress, represented the district for thirty years. And, within Orange County, Laguna Niguel was regarded as one of the more conservative communities.

The organizers scheduled the talk at a beautiful local country club. Despite the enduring drought, the gardens and golf course were lush. In Orange County, where an annual income of $84,000 per year now qualifies as low-income,[2] the grounds of the country club gave no hint of the grave need for water in the state. The community was gated, which is not unusual in Southern California, where many people live in such communities. This tends to signify that something inside the gates is worthy of protection from outsiders. The audience largely reflected the town's demographics – 80 percent white, with a clustering of women of Persian and Asian descent. The women gathered for the talk in a beautifully appointed room. They were smart, elegant, and wealthy. I was the academic who had recently relocated to Southern California from the Midwest.

I came with a story to tell. It was a time in our nation's political history when the fight to upend women's reproductive healthcare and rights had been led by Republicans at the state and federal levels. In the few years leading up to the talk, more antiabortion and anticontraceptive legislation had been proposed and enacted than in the three prior decades combined. Just the year before, the United States Supreme Court's conservative majority ruled in *Burwell v. Hobby Lobby* that corporations with religious objections could circumvent federal law requiring that contraceptives be covered in insurance plans.

I pondered, How would my audience receive the talk I planned to give? Would this turn into what pundits on the Left and Right were calling "gotcha" moments, designed not to illicit information and nuanced debate but political or ideological attack? Admittedly, I was concerned. After fumbling and failing with technology and the projector refusing to project, I settled into a conversation about women's reproductive health, rights, and the myriad injustices cropping up around the country. The crux of the talk was that pregnancies were being policed in clandestine and nefarious ways and often at the center of poor decision-making were medical professionals.

This was not a new set of issues or talk for me; I had shared aspects of my research at law schools, universities, and in other settings. More often than not, those audiences would likely self-identify as liberal, feminist, or progressive. Yet, even in those settings, I encountered doubters or those who, deep down, believed that women arrested and convicted for "endangering" their fetuses somehow deserved the criminal punishment they received. In fact, at one elite law school the reception to this work was so jarring that probably they and I could not wait for it to be over.

In that case, a member of the faculty whose wife had recently given birth seemed very offended by the subject of my work – or maybe the work itself. He took umbrage at the notion that doctors could be irresponsible in prescribing opioids for their patients, particularly pregnant women. He scoffed at this and behaved as if the notion was absurd. He challenged my comparison of poor pregnant women to wealthier women (as I suggested pregnancy could be challenging, no matter the socioeconomic distinctions).

Perhaps he was thinking that his wife and her pregnancy were very different from those of the women I wrote about. After all, he taught at a top law school, with an elite academic background. And possibly his wife was of a similar background. My point was that the same traumas and ailments that would lead privileged white women to seek medical relief such as prescription medications from their doctors was really not that much different than poor women also seeking help. Albeit, for pregnant women, their drugs were not negotiated in clinics and hospitals. The professor claimed one real difference was that "prescription medications do not harm patients." His colleagues nodded. I was baffled. I had an endowed chair in health law, he did not.

During the question and answer period, the professor announced to me and his colleagues that "doctors would never prescribe anything that would harm patients." Again, his colleagues nodded. He chuckled at the notion that white women could become addicted to prescription medications like OxyContin. That was in 2012. As I finish this book, the *New York Times*, *Wall Street Journal*, *Washington Post*, and virtually every other major and local news media in the United States have announced that Purdue Pharma and the Sackler family have reached a multibillion-dollar settlement to dismiss lawsuits related to the thousands of deaths and overdoses related to OxyContin.

However, my talk in Laguna Niguel was different, particularly for me. By the end of the talk, several women raised their hands almost as in a confessional. They understood the challenges of pregnancy and that doctors were offering cocktails of potent drugs to wealthy pregnant women. The news media in 2015 was just beginning to scratch the surface of the opioid crisis. Yet there were other issues they wished to raise with regard to the physician-patient relationships and the problems related to the authority physicians wield over their female patients.

They began telling their stories. One began crying, recalling how her doctor refused to provide medical care, even though she was miscarrying, because it would mean terminating the pregnancy. She recounted how she almost died. Another woman told the story of her doctor threatening to call the police if she refused to be compliant with his recommendations for the pregnancy. Another woman recounted switching doctors, because she felt uncomfortable by her medical provider's demands that she schedule and undergo a cesarean delivery rather than vaginal delivery. Despite their affluence, wealth did not spare the women. They recalled various indignities and threats, religious objections and interventions, and other harms carried out by their medical providers. Only one woman stated that she decided to fight back and threatened to sue her doctor – while she was pregnant.

As hands were raised and stories told, it became clear to each of us that any woman could potentially be vulnerable to surveillance, policing, and criminalization during pregnancy, even in California, a state that embedded a woman's right to reproductive privacy in its constitution. One woman asked, "Where can women turn to?" Another woman, looking at the audience and directing her question at them as much as at me, asked, "Are women wrong to trust their doctors? And if women can't trust their doctors during pregnancy, what are they to do?" Some of the women expressed feeling vulnerable rather than confident with their doctors. For years, I warned that poor women, particularly those who are Black, were simply the canaries in the coalmines and that a medical and political culture that devalues women's reproductive autonomy, privacy, and basic dignity could potentially respond unjustly to all women regardless of race and class. That message resonated with the women gathered at my talk. I stayed an extra two hours before saying goodbye.

6.1 THE FIDUCIARY RELATIONSHIP

As this Chapter explains, physicians owe their patients care, confidentiality, loyalty, and trust, and the principle that undergirds all of this – the fiduciary relationship – is not contingent on the sex of the patient. However, with increased pressure from state legislatures and prosecutors, some doctors and nurses have abrogated their responsibilities to their patients. Among them, some are genuinely fearful that unless they adhere to whatever law enforcement demands of them, they may lose their licenses to practice medicine. Some of these doctors are genuinely ambivalent about their duties. In child abuse cases, they are mandatory reporters, meaning they must inform state authorities of suspected abuse. Does the same hold true with a pregnancy, where there is a fetus, but not a living child? Some prosecutors make such claims, stating there is no difference between a five-year-old child and a five-week-old fetus. In light of such rhetoric, these doctors tell me they feel powerless. Others claim that their religious values inform and direct their decision-making regarding pregnant patients' reproductive health. Among these doctors and nurses are some who also refuse to provide emergency contraceptives, such as Plan B, to patients even after rape, which would protect the woman from becoming pregnant. To them, the life worth defending and healing is that of the "unborn."

Others, however, may be confused about their ethical and legal duties, even though medical organizations have articulated clear opposition to doctors serving as deputized law enforcement, snitching on their pregnant patients, and releasing confidential medical information to police and prosecutors. The reasons for this opposition are not new but long-standing in law and medical ethics, because physicians (like lawyers) have a fiduciary relationship with the individuals whom they serve. The textbook definition of a fiduciary is one who owes a legal obligation to another. However, this is no ordinary duty, but rather, in the words of Professor Kenneth Rosen, one of "extreme fidelity."[3]

The late, defining voice on fiduciary law, Professor Austin Scott, wrote, "A fiduciary is a person who undertakes to act in the interest of another person. It is immaterial whether the undertaking is in the form of a contract. It is immaterial that the undertaking is gratuitous."[4] Indeed, perhaps the worst breaches of all are when a fiduciary commits acts without the consent of the principle (beneficiary), engages in conduct intended to undermine the beneficiary, or when the fiduciary self-deals – meaning commits acts that benefit himself.

Fiduciaries are explicitly obligated to act in their client's best interests and to subordinate their personal and professional interests to the benefit of the client. In law, we refer to this as the "fiduciary obligation" or "fiduciary duty," and it applies to doctors and nurses (as well as lawyers and others who by their position owe a very special duty to others). Simply put, fiduciaries must be undivided in their loyalty to their beneficiaries. Legal philosophers and courts describe the fiduciary's duty of loyalty as being rooted in moral law.[5]

Justice Benjamin Cardozo – one of the most revered legal jurists of the twentieth century – described the fiduciary duty as "the duty of the finest loyalty."[6] In a landmark decision, *Meinhard v. Salmon*, which dealt with fiduciary duties among business partners, the famous judge emphasized that fiduciaries are "held to something stricter than the morals of the market place."[7] In fact, not their honesty, but rather "the punctilio of an honor the most sensitive, is … the standard of behavior." This, he said is "unbending and inveterate."[8] Plainly stated, the fiduciary duty requires, "uncompromising rigidity."[9] Make no mistake, the benefits of the fiduciary relationship are to inure to the patient or client – and solely him or her – and not the fiduciary. Nor is the fiduciary relationship contingent on special considerations of others.

An elementary exercise for law students on this point goes something like this: Brad, a college freshman, is arrested in state X for driving under the influence. His frantic parents consult, hire, and pay for a lawyer to represent him. Who is the client – Brad or the parents? Even though it might appear that the parents are the client, because they found the lawyer and pay to retain her, the answer is that the son, Brad, is the client and, as such, the lawyer owes her loyalty to Brad, despite his parents paying the legal fees.

Years ago when teaching legal ethics, I would add additional facts – imagine Brad informs the lawyer that while driving under the influence he injured a pedestrian on the night of his arrest and, since that time, has learned that the person died. Can the lawyer disclose this to law enforcement? What if the lawyer learns that another person, Kelly, was arrested for killing the pedestrian struck by Brad? May the lawyer disclose this information to law enforcement and prosecutors? The answers to the above questions are all no. The lawyer is obligated to keep Brad's confidence to herself, even if he is not paying her legal fees. The duties of loyalty, care, and confidentiality prohibit the lawyer from disclosing Brad's secrets. The lawyer is even obligated to make efforts so that the "inadvertent or unauthorized disclosure of, or unauthorized access to" this information does not occur.[10] Importantly, these types of hypotheticals derive from actual legal cases – and not simply the lofty musings of a law professor.[11]

Briefly, consider the case of Robert Garrow and his attorneys Frank Armani and Francis Belge. The lawyers were appointed to represent Garrow in the brutal murder case of Phillip Domblewski, an eighteen-year-old college freshman. Domblewski was camping with three friends when Garrow attacked and tied them to trees. Domblewski's friends were able to escape, but sadly he was not. Garrow disclosed this and more to the attorneys. He told them about other murders, abductions, and rapes that he had committed, including where he had disposed of the bodies. He relayed in gruesome detail the defilement of two female victims. The lawyers confirmed this information – one took photos of the disclosed remains. However, the lawyers did not reveal what they knew. Eventually, Garrow confessed (while on direct examination by Belge at trial). He was sentenced to life in prison. Of Garrow, one newspaper wrote that he was "a malignant cancer on the society that fostered him." The paper said he was "less than useless to the human race."

However, it was only after Garrow confessed at trial that the lawyers acknowledged what they knew. Lawyers commended Armani and Belge for maintaining client confidentiality – even under such aggravating and vexing circumstances. After all, Armani's daughter was the classmate of one of the victims. Nonetheless, the lawyers were ridiculed in the local paper and among lay people in their town. They lost business and one of them stopped practicing law. They were the subjects of a grand jury investigation where Belge was convicted. In dismissing those charges, a judge lauded Belge for zealously protecting his client's rights. When parents of one victim filed an ethics complaint against the lawyers, that too was dismissed. Citing ethical cannons and codes, the Committee on Professional Ethics of the New York State Bar Association stated:

> Both the fiduciary relationship existing between lawyer and client and the proper functioning of the legal system require the preservation by the lawyer of confidences and secrets of one who has employed or sought to employ him. A client must feel free to discuss whatever he wishes with his lawyer and a lawyer must be equally free to obtain information beyond that volunteered by his client. A lawyer should be fully informed of all the facts of the matter he is handling in order for his client to obtain the full advantage of our legal system. It is for the lawyer in the exercise of his independent professional judgment to separate the relevant and important from the irrelevant and unimportant. The observance of the ethical obligation of a lawyer to hold inviolate the confidences and secrets of his client not only facilitates the full development of facts essential to proper representation of the client but also encourages laymen to seek early legal assistance.[12]

This duty of confidentiality is no more nor less stringent in relation to other fiduciary matters: trusts and estates, financial dealings, or medicine.

So, if the patient is the sole beneficiary of the medical relationship – not relatives or police officers, prosecutors, judges, or legislators – why is it that in states like Alabama doctors are reporting poor pregnant women to law enforcement? Confidentiality and loyalty are not new concepts in medicine. Most patients intuitively know and understand this – even if they cannot explain how they know or became aware that their physicians owe them undivided loyalty, confidentiality, and a commitment to "do no harm or injustice to them."

Some patients might point to the Hippocratic Oath, which dates back to 460–370 BC, as their source of knowledge about what their medical personnel owe them, including privacy. This makes sense – after all, the oldest surviving fragments of the Hippocratic Oath date back to AD 275. For millennia, patients have understood their physicians' duties of confidentiality and loyalty to be inviolable and sacrosanct. They believe this important bond of confidentiality to be unbreakable under nearly all circumstances – much like a lawyer's obligation to a client.

As the next section illustrates, contemporary fetal protection cases illustrate how doctors who snitch on their patients or who threaten them with arrest because they refuse cesarean sections, or who prioritize serving prosecutors over their pregnant patients, ignore fiduciary standards embedded not only in ethics but also in law. The institutional shifts that embed doctors as criminal law gatekeepers have led to the abdication of their legal fiduciary duties to their pregnant patients, perhaps to protect their medical licenses, despite the fact that trust and loyalty remain vital to the physician-patient relationship.

6.2 ETHICS AND MEDICINE

The principles that undergird the fiduciary relationship between lawyer and client are no less important and venerated in the medical context. Nonetheless, when law enforcement tracks and arrests a pregnant woman, usually this is the result of a medical provider surreptitiously disclosing private, confidential medical statements and records of their female patients – without informed consent. The cruelty of this clandestine behavior must be understood in the contexts of medical providers' obligations to the women they surrender to the police. Medical providers' ethical duties are to the patients – not to law enforcement. These obligations to the patients are not contingent on whether the pregnant patients have medical insurance or can pay for the care provided, or on whether the doctors believe the pregnant women who seek their care will be lousy mothers.

The fiduciary obligation of doctors is rooted not only in law but also in an internationally recognized code of ethics imposed on doctors, derived from the trials at Nuremberg.[13] As medical providers cast a punitive gaze on pregnant women, often overlooked or simply ignored are these foundational, internationally agreed upon bioethics principles: informed consent, autonomy, social justice, and voluntary participation. The earliest collective iteration of these principles dates from the adjudicative process in the criminal trials of Nazi doctors at Nuremberg, whose deliberate disregard for the health and safety of nonconsenting human subjects in their research studies on sterilization, serology, and human survival under distressing conditions resulted in deaths and severe disabilities among survivors.[14] Nazi doctors disregarded the humanity of the children, women, and men they subjected to this horrific research and their aggressive eugenics practices.

American and international medical ethics are rooted in the collapse of Nazi Germany and the subsequent trials at Nuremberg, where Third Reich physicians and researchers revealed the mass horrors of their human experimentation and broader brutality in the quest for scientific knowledge. The Nuremberg Doctors' Trial (one of thirteen criminal trials at Nuremberg) was conducted by the International Military Tribunal at Nuremberg and presided over by an international panel of judges. It began in 1946 and concluded in 1947.

The Nuremberg Doctors' Trials contributed to the articulation and establishment of universally recognized human rights principles in law and medicine that specify doctors' fiduciary duties and form the ethical framework for the physician-patient relationship. Originally, these principles defined the general standard in medical experimentation on human subjects. However, as described in this Chapter, they now cohere to form the basis for physician fiduciary obligations to patients – namely, that voluntary consent is an essential component of any medical treatment; that confidentiality is essential to the physician-patient relationship and medical providers should not violate this principle; that medical providers should avoid subjecting patients to unnecessary suffering, including, but not limited to, unnecessary reproductive surgeries; and that patients must be at liberty to withdraw from medical treatment, even if rejecting medical assistances might result in their deaths.

The principle of preserving patient confidence is enshrined in law and ethics. The American Medical Association offers this clear statement on the issue: "The physician should not reveal confidential information without the express consent of the patient," and in limited cases where an exception is enforced by law or court order, the Association cautions that the physician should notify her patient and only "disclose the minimal information required by law, advocate for the protection of confidential information."[15] Equally, the Privacy Rule established by HIPAA protects against medical providers' disclosure of individuals' health information.[16]

In fact, the bases for some of these principles predate Nuremberg. Some of the principles were already rooted in law. For example, informed consent for medical treatment, particularly surgery, was already founded in American law and affirmed by courts. Dating back more than a century, U.S. courts established that express or implied consent must be granted by patients prior to surgery. Justice Cardozo's famous dictum – "Every human being of adult years and sound mind has a right to determine what shall be done with his own body; and a surgeon who performs an operation without his patient's consent commits an assault for which he is liable in damages" – highlights the standard for informed consent in a case where a female patient claimed that doctors removed a tumor from her uterus against her will and without regard to her specific instructions prohibiting them from doing so.[17]

Decades later, courts throughout the United States would repeatedly chastise doctors for causing women's suffering by removing their uteruses without their consent. This strange and horrific pillaging of women's most intimate organs resulted in rulings like *Hundley v. St. Francis Hospital*, where a court held that a "jury could find that it is not accepted surgical practice to remove [the uterus] when there are no pathological abnormalities."[18] Similarly, in *Steele v. St. Paul Fire & Marine Ins. Co.*, a Louisiana court held that a woman unnecessarily suffered the "removal of a healthy organ of her body, i.e., her uterus and the unnecessary loss of her childbearing potential."[19] In Maryland, a court affirmed a jury award of $1,200,000 in a case involving a nonconsensual hysterectomy.[20] More recently, courts have awarded significant settlements in cases where plaintiffs successfully alleged unnecessary hysterectomies.[21]

Courts have also recognized the right to confidentiality as distinct from, but complimentary to, the privacy right to control one's information. In reproductive rights cases, the U.S. Supreme Court has explained that privacy rights encompass two distinct spheres: an individual's interest in independent decision-making and in avoiding or refusing disclosure of intimate information, including medical records.[22] In *Eisenstadt v. Baird*, which addressed single women's access to contraception, the Court ruled that "if the right of privacy means anything, it is the right of the individual ... to be free from unwanted governmental intrusions into matters so fundamentally affecting a person as the decision whether to bear or beget a child."[23]

Not only does a woman possess a right to control her reproductive healthcare, and a right to the privacy associated with it, she also possesses the right to refuse a doctor's care. In *Norma Wons v. Public Health Trust of Dade County*, the Florida Court of Appeals held that a competent adult woman possesses the lawful right to refuse blood transfusions even when she might die and leave behind minor children. In that case, the court ruled that "the state has no compelling interest under the circumstances of this case sufficient to override the patient's constitutional right (a) to practice her religion according to her conscience, and (b) to lead her private life free from unreasonable government interference."[24]

6.3 LAW AND MEDICINE

The modern fiduciary relationship between healthcare providers and their patients represents a complex set of physician obligations that flow to their patients as a bundle of rights. Courts explain that the fiduciary relationship demands an important level of care, confidence, and loyalty across a broad sphere of physician-patient interactions.[25] For example, the Kansas Supreme Court stated decades ago that "[t]he courts frequently state that the relationship between the physician and his patient is a fiduciary one," placing upon the physician "an obligation to make a full and frank disclosure to the patient of all pertinent facts related to his illness."[26] The court stated that "each man is considered to be master of his own body" even if he expressly rejects "the performance of life-saving surgery, or other medical treatment."[27]

This was not an unusual or rare position for the court to take. Rather, it was consistent. For example, the California Court of Appeals, likely the first court to adopt the legal criterion of "informed consent" (replacing a general consent standard), clarified that "[a] physician violates his duty to his patient and subjects himself to liability if he withholds any facts which are necessary to form the basis of an intelligent consent by the patient to the proposed treatment."[28] The Minnesota Supreme Court issued a similar rule in 1958. That court explained that while it did not wish to burden the medical profession and its progress, physicians were nevertheless obligated to inform patients about their medical treatment, including less invasive surgical alternatives, in order to allow the patient to decide whether to live with the "serious consequences" of refusing medical care.[29] In other words, a doctor's fiduciary obligations to her patients is expansive; it includes confidentiality, providing clear information, obtaining informed consent before proceeding with medical interventions, maintaining trust, and more. The legal obligations of physicians in relation to their patients impose duties on the provider and give legal rights to the patient. These legal rights provide a sanctuary for patients.

My point here is that the legal rights owed to a patient and the obligations of a physician or any other medical provider, including nurses, are no less salient when the patient is pregnant. American law begins with the premise of self-determination and that each patient is the master of her own body, vested with the authority to grant a physician the license to treat a condition or to expressly refuse medical interventions and therapies.[30] From this muscular legal principle spring forth other patient rights as well as constraints on healthcare providers. Notably, a physician's multiple duties to inform pregnant patients about the risks and benefits of a given medical treatment, recognize potential physicians' conflicts of interests, safeguard confidence, and perform medical duties with competence and care give rise to enforceable legal obligations vital to the interests of her patients. Among this bundle of rights is the basic "natural right" to be left alone.

The Supreme Court underscored the magnitude of the physician-patient relationship and the significance of loyalty, trust, and confidence in *Jaffee v. Redmond*, explaining that "the mere possibility of a therapist's disclosure may impede development of the confidential relationship necessary for successful treatment."[31] The Court also recognized that the privilege should extend to social workers. Justice Stevens, writing for the majority, stated that "protecting confidential communications between a psychotherapist and her patient" sufficiently promoted important interests.[32] Justice Stevens compared the patient's private communications with her therapist to the protected speech between spouses and between attorneys and their clients, ruling that the conversations and notes exchanged between a police officer who shot and killed a man during the course of responding to a "fight in progress" and her therapist were protected from compelled disclosure.

It is not only courts that have reinforced the importance of medical professionals maintaining confidentiality, so too have federal and state laws. Federal law further clarifies and codifies confidentiality requirements among some medical professionals, including those working on federally funded drug treatment programs, prohibiting the organizations involved from divulging patient records. For example, federal law prohibits the disclosure of:

> Records of the identity, diagnosis, prognosis, or treatment of any patient which are maintained in connection with the performance of any program or activity relating to substance abuse education, prevention, training, treatment, rehabilitation, or research, which is conducted, regulated, or directly or indirectly assisted by any department or agency of the United States.[33]

In a special section on criminal proceedings, the federal law further emphasizes that "no record . . . may be used to initiate or substantiate any criminal charges against a patient or to conduct any investigation of a patient."[34] Courts and Congress are not alone in having issued clear pronouncements about the legally enforceable fiduciary duties placed on doctors, so too have all fifty state legislatures and the District of Columbia, medical boards, and professional organizations. For example, in 2013 the North Dakota State Board of Medical Examiners issued a stinging censure against a doctor for breaching patient confidence to an insurer, referring to the physician's actions as "engaging in conduct that is dishonorable, unethical . . . and that is likely to deceive, defraud, or harm the public," and noting that "breaching the confidentiality between physician and patient is proscribed" by North Dakota statutes.[35] In another 2013 case (decided on the very same day), that Board of Medical Examiners suspended the license of a physician who accessed the medical records of an individual who was not her patient, which it found to have violated that individual's physician-patient confidentiality.[36]

In addition to state oversight boards disciplining, suspending, and terminating the licenses of doctors who have trampled their patients' privacy, national medical organizations have warned their membership against abusing their patients' trust. The American Medical Association (AMA) and the American Public Health Association (APHA) offer unequivocal statements that the role of doctors and nurses must be first and primarily to serve patients' needs and not law enforcement goals. These medical organizations justifiably caution against states' efforts to conscript physicians and nurses into serving as informants, because it confuses the role of health care providers, misleads patients without providing any notice, and potentially chills the physician-patient relationship.

Taking fiduciary duties seriously, what then explains, let alone justifies, the dilution, if not abandonment, of legal and ethical obligations by doctors in cases involving pregnant patients – to the point that doctors threaten their pregnant patients with arrests for refusing cesarean sections, alert law enforcement when their pregnant patients confide about drug use or addiction, or seek to civilly confine their patients either by imposing bed rest or for the purported benefit of the fetus? Why have long-standing principles of the medical fiduciary relationship been abrogated in cases of pregnancy?

Professor Michelle Oberman explains that a double standard has emerged in the context of pregnancy, whereby doctors see not one but "two lives involved."[37] She wisely warns that doctors who embrace this view in the name of pregnancy ultimately advance the view that "women should have fewer rights than do their male counterparts," which Oberman argues is a "legally and ethically obsolete premise."[38] I agree. However, the fetal protection cases described in this book, many of which were not envisaged even fifteen years ago, now challenge whether these assumptions are obsolete. They are outmoded for sure, but sadly present.

6.4 THE CORRUPT PHYSICIAN-PATIENT RELATIONSHIP

Ferguson v. City of Charleston[39] represents such a shift in the role of medical staff from serving the needs of patients to gathering medical evidence for the state to use against them. In that case, ten women initiated section 1983 litigation[40] against the Medical University of South Carolina (MUSC) and local government officials, claiming that they were the victims of warrantless and nonconsensual searches initiated and performed by medical staff. Medical officials at MUSC had volunteered to serve as informants against their patients, initiating contact with a local prosecutor, Charles Condon, upon learning that he campaigned to extend child abuse laws to the use of drugs by pregnant women. Condon then established an interagency task force, which included police, the local prosecutor's office, and hospital staff. Together, they created what plaintiffs called the "Search Policy."

In a series of memoranda and meetings, Condon and his team informed medical personnel how to collect urine samples for use in criminal investigations and protect the samples' chain of custody, and also devised the method by which MUSC staff would report to police. Law enforcement staff trained the doctors and nurses, and Condon provided written guidance "listing criminal charges that could apply to women coming under the Search Policy."

According to court records, medical staff at MUSC, along with police and prosecutors, "disproportionately targeted indigent, African-American women for search and arrest."[41] In their search program, of the thirty women arrested twenty-nine were African American. Special dispensation was sought for at least one white woman who, although not arrested, otherwise met the criteria for arrest. In that instance, "Nurse Brown admitted that she called the Solicitor's office and requested another 'chance' on behalf of a white patient who should have been arrested under the Policy's terms."[42]

For the one other white woman ensnared by the Search Policy, racial profiling may have contributed to her arrest as well, because a nurse and member of the interagency task force made a point of notating the patient's chart with the following information: "patient live[s] with her boyfriend who is a Negro."[43] While this notation did not serve a medically relevant purpose, it revealed that an illicit extralegal consideration – race – was involved in the implementation and enforcement of South Carolina's fetal protection law.[44]

In fact, this particular nurse admitted at trial that she believed interracial relationships violated "God's way"[45] and "raised the option of sterilization for black women testing positive for cocaine, but not for white women."[46] This search process introduced a level of unusual cruelty into the delivery of medicine, altering a common understanding about hospitals providing safety, comfort, and respite to those seeking medical help. As transcripts in the case reveal, some women subject to arrest were "denied the opportunity to change out of their hospital gowns or to make a phone call to family members to make arrangements for the care of their children."[47] In other instances, police apprehended the new mothers "while still bleeding, weak and in pain from having just given birth."[48] Some were handcuffed and shackled, with chains circling their abdomens. Leg irons were used in some cases. For any woman who could not walk, "a blanket or sheet would be placed over the woman, and she would be wheeled out of the hospital to a waiting police car and transported to jail."[49]

The collaboration between MUSC medical staff and law enforcement to obtain incriminating evidence against pregnant women seeking prenatal care exposes a provocative and dangerous example of physicians wielding significant discretion in the furtherance of a criminal law purpose rather than serving patients' medical interests. In fact, the medical director of the Neonatal Intensive Care Unit testified that the drug screens and medical tests conducted on the poor, Black pregnant women were solely for law enforcement purposes and not for medical reasons.[50]

The discretionary power described above, much like that prosecutors or police officers are afforded, can be corruptible and vulnerable to selective, but largely unchecked, enforcement, social bias, political ideology, and prejudice. This is particularly worrisome in physician-patient contexts because doctors and nurses enjoy unique and limitless access to patients' medical, social, and personal histories. Yet, unlike police and prosecutors, doctors do not receive legal training to understand patients' constitutional rights. There is no detached scrutiny by a neutral authority or judge to assess the permissibility of doctors gaining access to patient information for law enforcement purposes. No legal authority supervises the subjective dealings of doctors who may use the veil of medicine to obtain information for nonmedical purposes. By contrast, police cannot sign their own search warrants, and for good reason. Justice Brandeis explained that the "greatest dangers to liberty lurk in the insidious encroachment by men of zeal, well-meaning, but without understanding."[51]

Entangling doctors into quasi agent roles circumvents legal process and deceives patients, because pregnant women lack notice and warning that, while in the physical care of their physicians, a prenatal visit may also serve as a potential criminal investigation. Famously, in *Miranda v. Arizona* the Supreme Court ruled that in criminal investigations suspects in police custody must be warned of their right not to self-incriminate lest their constitutional rights be violated.[52] From this, "Miranda rights" emerged, resulting in the following warning becoming ubiquitous with law enforcement: "You have the right to remain silent. Anything you say can and will be used against you in a court of law. You have the right to an attorney. If you cannot afford an attorney, one will be provided for you. Do you understand the rights I have just read to you? With these rights in mind, do you wish to speak to me?" A corollary principle does not exist in medicine; there is no medical Miranda warning, although there should be, especially to avoid law enforcement circumventing legal process by using medical providers as proxies.

The *Ferguson* case is also about deception. Alarmingly, in *Ferguson* medical staff lured women into a legal trap under the pretense of providing medical services. For example, the lead nurse searched Darlene Nicholson's urine under the guise of medical treatment for hydration and threatened arrest after a positive urinalysis. Ms. Nicholson testified:

> They said I was dehydrated and I needed to be hooked up to glucose. . . . They told me to drink lots of water. . . . I asked them if I was to be hooked up to the glucose machine. . . . They just told me to keep drinking water . . . and told me to use the bathroom in a cup. . . . And I asked what for and they said to see if I had enough fluid in my system so they could send me home.[53]

Court documents further expose the extent of the hospital's deception, threats, and entrapment. Sandra Powell arrived at MUSC in labor. There, she was informed that because of a positive urine toxicology screen for cocaine, she would be arrested immediately. When Ms. Powell begged for medical help – "Please, what could I do to stop this or could you help me?" – the nurse "responded simply that she would 'be locked up.'"[54] Ms. Powell was arrested, "still in pain and bleeding from childbirth." To cover her body, she was given only a thin hospital gown on her transport to jail.[55] The nature of the arrests belies claims that the program had a medical emphasis.[56] In fact, patients arrested during the Search Policy's early months did not receive any drug treatment referral and "no opportunity to obtain treatment as an 'alternative' to arrest." Instead, "each aspect of the Search Policy was designed to assist law enforcement personnel in performing their duties."[57]

From the very start of MUSC's campaign to lure drug-dependent women to the hospital, the hospital staff's efforts took on a criminal focus. Mr. Good, MUSC's general counsel, even penned a letter to the local prosecutor indicating this. He wrote, "I read with great interest in Saturday's newspaper accounts of our good friend, the Solicitor for the Thirteenth Judicial Circuit, prosecuting mothers who gave birth to children who tested positive for drugs." On behalf of the hospital, Mr. Good asked that the prosecutor inform him "if your office is anticipating future criminal action" and inquired as to "what if anything our Medical Center needs to do to assist you in this matter."[58] *Ferguson* court documents, including memoranda, briefs, court transcripts, plaintiff exhibits, joint exhibits, and the briefs' appendices illuminate that the program's primary goal was to facilitate the arrests and criminal prosecutions of patients who used crack cocaine during their pregnancies by selectively targeting them for drug screenings rather than women who used other illicit substances generally.

For example, an MUSC physician testified that "although ingestion of heroin or alcohol poses serious risks of fetal harm, the nine criteria established by the taskforce members for searching pregnant women were drafted specifically to uncover cocaine use."[59] The Supreme Court's ruling that the MUSC program violated the *Ferguson* plaintiffs' Fourth Amendment rights, because the program authorized nonconsensual searches and seizures without a valid warrant, holds promise for future pregnant women who are tracked and arrested under similar circumstances. However, as a practical matter, such legal victories may obscure the immediate costs associated with this type of racial profiling and arrests. Nor did the plaintiffs' victory in *Ferguson* signify an end to the very conduct at issue in that case. It should have done so, but it did not. More typical of the current efforts to upend reproductive rights is the tendency for legislators and prosecutors to seek to relitigate their losses.

Moreover, the problems extend beyond the physician's office, clinic, and hospital. Consider the following. Pregnant patients may not know that they risk the termination of parental rights after two years of incarceration. This matters, because legal appeals may take years after conviction. Even waiting for trial can take years. Pregnant women caught in the criminal justice system often experience pressure to accept corrosive plea deals – sometimes under threat of life sentences. Sadly, in today's political climate a poor pregnant woman takes these risks – when she simply wants prenatal care.

In assessing fetal protectionism, medical personnel may – and frequently do – make wrong calls. To comply with state statutes that encroach on and burden pregnant women's constitutional rights, doctors increasingly subordinate ethical obligations to their pregnant patients, while prioritizing punitive legal redress over medical treatment. It is not surprising that medical personnel are poor interpreters of state law. They are neither elected nor appointed. They are not trained or studied in the law or legislative processes. Worst of all, fetal protection laws' coercive effects and absurd outcomes harm not only pregnant women and their children but also the medical profession.

6.5 CONCLUSION

Most doctors seek to provide the best care possible for their pregnant patients and to keep them healthy and safe. However, the increased politicization of pregnancy and reproductive health catch doctors in ideological crosshairs, shifting reproductive health to a deeply political space that has very little to do with the provisions of healthcare. Instead, the politicization of reproductive healthcare generally, and pregnancy specifically now implicate criminal and civil law with significant consequences for women caught within that web.

For pregnant women, regardless of income, detecting and defending against the pitfalls of reproductive healthcare in the United States is a serious matter. Spotting when and whether medical providers might engage in conflicting behaviors, conflating their roles as medical providers with that of criminal informants can be virtually impossible. Lab coats and stethoscopes do not give this away. Nor is it likely that a doctor will reveal his or her conflicted interests to patients before taking on the role of their medical provider. Patients assume that voluntary interactions with physicians pave the path toward promoting their health and that confidentially sharing their social and medical histories serve to achieve that goal.[60] Unfortunately, a culture where doctors breach confidentiality and share private patient information caution against that presumption, which is not good for society.

7

Creating Criminals: Race, Stereotypes, and Collateral Damage

The state finds many ways of making criminals out of its citizens. Sure, there are people who commit heinous crimes that imperil the safety of others. However, as it turns out, most of America's incarcerated population are nonviolent offenders. They are like Shanesha Taylor. The painful costs of motherhood became strikingly clear during the spring and summer months of 2014, when Ms. Taylor, a single, homeless mother, was arrested for leaving her two children in a parked car while at a job interview for a Scottsdale, Arizona, insurance agency.[1] Shanesha did not think she had many options. She was homeless. Where and how would she find childcare? In Arizona, one organization estimates that for one child, childcare can cost around $6,000 per year. How could she afford it?

However, Shanesha wanted to uplift her family. She was desperate for options. That new job would have provided more opportunities for her children. Advocates pointed out that she had left the car fan on, windows cracked open, and that it was seventy-one degrees outside – even though they acknowledged that leaving children alone in cars can be dangerous. Taylor was promptly arrested after completing the interview. A *Washington Post* reporter remarked that her "mugshot image was a painfully heartbreaking one: a mother, struggling not to cry, tears running down her cheeks."[2] The image is indelibly etched in my memory.

Shanesha Taylor's mugshot spread across the United States, like water rolling downhill, becoming morning and nightly news. What mother leaves her kids in a car? Likely to some, the shaming she endured was deserved. Strangely, people take pleasure in such things with the rise of websites devoted only to mugshots. Yet, I must admit, the image of Shanesha Taylor caused a different response in me. In her mugshot, I witnessed the pain of a parent caught in a legal and socioeconomic quagmire, a cruel double bind. Was she to take the children into the interview? Was she to cancel the interview because she had no childcare? Without the interview, she was unlikely to be considered for the job (let alone receive a job offer) and would remain unemployed. If she remained unemployed, homelessness would also persist for Shanesha and her children.

Being caught in the criminal justice system brings about other pressures, problems, and pains for incarcerated parents (and those under court supervision), especially mothers who disproportionately are primary parents. Months after her arrest Shanesha was finally granted limited visitation with her children. Arizona prosecutors refused to drop the charges. Eventually, a judge sentenced her to eighteen years of supervised probation. For her children, their mother will endure this and the legal stigmas attached to it for the entirety of their childhood. For people under supervised probation, they must always appeal to law enforcement anytime they wish to leave the state – in all circumstances. They must regularly meet with a probation officer, and in most states they must pay fees to the state – as a means of reimbursing the state for the supervision they must endure. Of course, someone unable to pay their fees could be arrested again and sent to jail.

Rather than an anomaly, Taylor's case reflects the broader realities of single motherhood in the United States. Childcare is expensive; in many states, payments for one year of childcare equals or exceeds that of college tuition. Some might even argue that Shanesha Taylor's experiences represent the broader policing of parents in the United States – such that even middle-class white Americans have come to the attention of child protective services simply for allowing their children to walk to nearby parks in their neighbourhoods. In those instances, the parents are perceived as "negligent" in the supervision of their children. As terrible as that is, the difference, however, is that middle-class white parents are far less likely to end up in the criminal justice system, even though investigation by the state for being considered negligent is scarring for the parents and children.

During the summer of 2014, Debra Harrell, a South Carolina forty-eight-year-old single mother, was arrested for "abandoning" her nine-year-old daughter, whom she allowed to play at a nearby park while she worked at McDonald's.[3] In that case, she fitfully tried various options to manage childcare. However, childcare is expensive, even in South Carolina. So Ms. Harrell tried allowing her daughter to spend the day with her at the McDonald's restaurant, providing a laptop for her daughter to use. The laptop was stolen. After that, Harrell gave her daughter a cellphone and permitted her to play in a popular nearby park. There were other adults at the park, as well as other children. It was the best she thought that she could do.

However, another parent called the police. Debra Harrell was charged with a felony and her daughter removed from their home.[4] Taylor and Harrell share the realities of poverty, motherhood, and race: both are African American. The outcomes of their experiences are very different from cases of dads who have accidentally left their kids locked in cars. Sometimes, those dads' names are not even mentioned when the cases are reported in the news. I understand the effort to protect their privacy. One thing is clear: the state often turns to criminal punishment when it has failed in its responsibilities in some way. In these cases, despite the rising costs of childcare, states are incredibly slow to respond.

The cost of giving birth is only an initial economic factor – a small one – in comparison with the cost of raising a child. A few years ago a young law professor, who is married to a doctor, informed me that he and his wife were not sure if they could afford to have children. I asked why. With a straight face, he informed me that "the cost of childcare in San Francisco," where they live, "is simply too high." If a law professor and doctor believe they cannot afford the costs of childcare, who can?

The costs associated with rearing a child in the United States have risen dramatically in recent decades. According to the United States Department of Agriculture, an average middle-income family spends over $233,000 to raise a child from birth to age seventeen.[5] These expenses include, but are not limited to, food, housing, transportation, healthcare, clothing, education, and childcare. Further, the Economic Policy Institute (EPI) reports that infant care can cost between $4,822 and $22,631 annually, depending on the state.[6] Take Alabama, for example, a state that has imposed many restrictions on reproductive rights while at the same time inflicting cruel criminal punishments on pregnant women who seek to carry their pregnancies to term. Whether restricting abortion access or punishing pregnant women, that state's power is punitively inflicted on poor women.

Despite Alabama's pronatalist stances, the state does a poor job supporting parents, finding solutions for the rising costs of childcare, or assisting poor and working-class parents with childcare costs. This matters, because childcare expenses are high in that state when reconciled against income. EPI's research shows that average annual cost for infant care in Alabama is $5,637, and the cost for a four-year-old's care is $4,871. In Alabama, infant care costs almost 70 percent of average rent! That is astounding, especially given costs that exceed 10 percent of rent are considered unaffordable according to the United States Department of Health and Human Services (HHS). Alabama is hardly alone. For example, the most expensive place to raise a child in the United States is Washington, D.C. There, the annual average cost of childcare is $22,631 per infant. In thirty-three states, the cost of childcare exceeds that of public university tuition.[7] The United States is the only developed country that does not offer paid maternity leave as a federal mandate, and when it comes to choosing childcare, most mothers (and families) are on their own.

As in the cases of Shanesha Taylor and Debra Harrell, failure to secure what the state considers "proper" childcare may result in civil and criminal punishments, despite compelling mitigating circumstances. Those punishments include arrests, prosecution, and jail time for the mothers. These criminal penalties are meant to be severe, and they are. And the civil punishments are no less frightening given that children may be removed from the home and placed in foster care until the state determines the mother is "fit."

***

The questions and concerns addressed in this book cannot be evaluated in isolation from race and class. Racial disparities dominate all forms of policing in the United States, regardless of sex and income. However, the shocking toll of male incarceration crowds out research and more nuanced understandings of women's engagement with the penal system. After all, 1 in every 106 white males (eighteen years or older) is incarcerated, compared to 1 in every 15 Black males,[8] and "[i]f current trends continue, one of every three black American males born today can expect to go to prison in his lifetime."[9]

Given these deeply troubling statistics, researchers and policymakers tend to view incarceration through a male lens. However, they are missing a very grave, rapidly emerging social problem: the mass incarceration of women. Simply put, marginalized women are funnelled in and out of the American criminal justice system at alarming rates. They are invisible. As such, their experiences with mass incarceration, police brutality, sexual violence, shackling while pregnant (if in the penal system), birthing behind bars, medical neglect, restrictions on housing access after release, and other pernicious encroachments on their daily lives are rarely rendered visible in news media or by policymakers.

Consequently, male accounts about mass incarceration, while troubling and certainly not inaccurate, fail to problematize and offer a detailed reading of prisons and penal systems. And male-focused narratives about mass incarceration ignore the myriad ways in which women are policed and ensnared in the penal system. Importantly, these depictions fall short of informing the American public about women and children as the casualties of the nation's terribly flawed criminal justice system.

This broken system includes the nation's overpriced and unsuccessful drug war, which targets not only men but women, too. Thus, reform agendas focusing primarily on men neglect to account for children raised in prison alongside their mothers.[10] Such efforts ignore how and why states target women, particularly during their pregnancies, and fail to notice grave racial disparities in women's mass incarceration. For Black women, 1 in 18 will experience incarceration in her lifetime.[11]

***

FIGURE 1: One in eighteen Black women will be incarcerated in her lifetime

In 2013, Eric Holder, the former United States Attorney General, issued an urgent call for drug-law reform.[12] Indeed, drug reform, decreasing mass incarceration, and reducing overcrowded conditions in jails and prisons can no longer be ignored, even by ardent proponents of toughness toward crime, without acknowledging the economic and human costs of such policies. As Holder explained to an audience of lawyers, judges, and academics at the 2013 annual meeting of the American Bar Association (ABA), American jails are overcrowded and unsustainable, packed with nonviolent drug offenders, who frequently serve disparate sentences based on a strange confluence of race, class, and lack of privilege.[13] With more than 1.5 million people incarcerated in the United States, which accounts for 25 percent of all prisoners in the world, the failure of the U.S. drug war and sentencing policies is apparent, particularly as the United States "has only 5% of the world's population."[14]

One year later, at the national meeting of the National Association for the Advancement of Colored People (NAACP), President Barack Obama made similar claims about the urgency of penal reform.[15] He, too, decried the conditions of prisons and jails in the United States (following up his speech by visiting a prison). President Obama acknowledged the disparate impacts of policing and jailing. He urged that it was time to act. Like Mr. Holder, President Obama made a plea for men of color locked behind bars. They both forgot about women.

The President and his former Attorney General, both men of color, articulated their concerns about the broader harms of the American criminal justice system through a male-focused lens. This could have much to do with the fact that the United States incarcerates so many men. After all, the United States experiences the highest rate of incarceration of any country in the world – more than England (153 in 100,000), France (96 in 100,000), Germany (85 in 100,000), Italy (111 in 100,000), and Spain (159 in 100,000) combined, because the United States incarcerates about 743 per 100,000.[16] More than half of U.S. incarcerations relate to drug offenses.[17] And this is terribly expensive.

In 2010, the U.S. federal government planned to expend $15 billion dollars in its war on drugs, at a rate of $30,000 per minute and $1,800,000 per hour.[18] By 2012, the White House had revised its drug budget structure, increasing its National Drug Control Budget to $26.2 billion – a significant increase from two years previously.[19] Expenditures to fight the drug war dramatically increase each year. Before he left office, President Obama requested an additional $415.3 million over the level of spending enacted earlier in his administration, expanding federal efforts by establishing "two new bureaus to the National Drug Control Budget."[20] This system and its subsystems rely on the brokenness of individuals in order to fuel its economy, which pays its police, prosecutors, judges, guards, wardens, parole officers, and less visible players who arguably have a stake in mass incarceration.

In 2019, the Center for American Progress highlighted the problem like this: about every half minute someone is arrested for drug possession in the United States. However, the organization reports, incarceration is not linked to a reduction in drug use or misuse. Rather, incarceration is associated with increased mortality, because within the first two weeks after incarceration individuals are nearly thirteen times more likely to die – and this is associated with overdose.

However, as with any war, collateral damages accumulate, expanding the risks of battle and the suffering of those intimately involved and at the periphery. In this context, the price of war extends to "lost productivity, healthcare, and criminal justice costs,"[21] burdening the federal government to the tune of $193 billion in the mid-2000s alone. A report published by the CATO Institute, a conservative think tank based in Washington, DC, noted that the drug war exacts a toll on state and local governments as well, costing them an estimated $25 billion in 2010.[22] What accounts for such significant spending in light of illicit drug use remaining constant and prescription drug abuse on the rise? As Holder reflected to a reporter in 2014, Congress "put in place some pretty draconian sentencing measures … [w]here people who were not engaged in the violent distribution of drugs ended up with ten, twenty, thirty [years] – lifetime sentences."[23] Ironically, many of those serving stiff prison and jail sentences are nonviolent offenders, including women who "possessed" drugs during their pregnancies but were not drug distributors.

The drug war drafts police, prosecutors, and judges to carry out its mission and metaphorically casts some of America's most vulnerable as enemy combatants to be tracked, policed, and – if caught – jailed. Reports of U.S. military equipment populating the artillery in America's police departments further underscore the salience of the war metaphor. According to the *New York Times*, "[a]s the nation's wars abroad wind down, many of the military's surplus tools of combat have ended up in the hands of state and local law enforcement," including armored vehicles, aircrafts, machine guns, and even mine-resistant, ambush-protected armored vehicles.[24] The militarization of U.S. police captured the nation's attention in the wake of law enforcement responses to community outrage to the police killings of unarmed African American men in Ferguson, Missouri, in 2014 and Baltimore, Maryland, in 2015.

Yet, so often overlooked is the fact that Black women are overpoliced and over-incarcerated relative to the crimes with which they are charged. For example, when former Attorney General Eric Holder offered a broad and bold new agenda during the summer of 2013, he cast the drug war and mass incarceration as male problems.[25] In the dozens of articles featuring the Attorney General's remarks I have read, no commentator observed that women were virtually absent from Holder's powerful commentary. In fact, Holder mentioned women only once – as middle-class, educated victims of sexual violence, but not as the drug war's casualties. Politicians and pundits celebrated the Justice Department's effort and proclaimed it as long overdue, emphasizing the staggering expansions of U.S. prisons to detain drug offenders and the racial impacts on African American men.[26]

To realize what scholars, policymakers, and media pundits overlook, consider the stunning data collected by the Women's Prison Association, the leading national policy center quantitatively and qualitatively researching women in prison.[27] The population of women in prison grew by 832 percent in the period from 1977 to 2007 – twice the rate of men during that same period. More conservative estimates suggest that the rate of incarceration of women has grown by over 750 percent during the past three decades.[28] This staggering increase now results in more than one million women incarcerated in prison, jail, or tethered to the criminal justice system as a parolee or probationer in the United States. The Bureau of Justice Statistics underscores the problem, explaining in a special report that "[s]ince 1991, the number of children with a mother in prison has more than doubled, up 131%," while "[t]he number of children with a father in prison has grown [only] by 77%."[29]

7.1 AN EMPIRICAL ACCOUNT: THE SCALE AND SCOPE OF WOMEN'S MASS INCARCERATION

To better comprehend the scale and scope of incarceration in the United States, consider that it confines more women than any other country in the world.[30] To place this in context, the United States jails more women than Russia, China, Thailand, and India combined.[31] Nearly a third of the world's women inmates are incarcerated in the United States.[32]

Predictably, in the United States mass incarceration of women suffers from features similar to male criminal institutionalization, namely race and class disparities. One in 118 white women stands a likelihood of imprisonment in her lifetime.[33] However, Latinas can expect that, within their demographic, 1 in 45 will be imprisoned at some point in her lifetime; for African American women the numbers are worse: 1 in 18 will likely experience incarceration.[34]

These stark figures frame the raw numbers of mass incarceration, but do little to explain and account for its broader social implications, which extend to children, family, and communities. Much of the nation's current incarcerated population, including women, are drug offenders – many of them first-time offenders – caught in the powerful, punitive grip of the war on drugs policy. Significantly, what accounts for the 800 percent increase in the rate of female incarceration over the past three decades is drug offenses.[35] Importantly, women's drug use has not increased in the last thirty years – only their rate of incarceration.[36] In fact, the proportion of incarcerated women who are in prison for drug offenses now surpasses that of men.[37] At the state level, 25 percent of women prisoners were serving time for drug offenses in 2012, compared to 15 percent of male prisoners.[38]

Women suffer the collateral damage of federal and state drug war policy; they and their children are the drug war's casualties.[39] According to the Women's Prison

Association, "[o]ver 2.5 million women were arrested in 2008."[40] This accounted for nearly a quarter of arrests that year and an increase of nearly 12 percent from ten years earlier. To appreciate the increase in women's incarceration, consider that the "female prison population grew by 832% from 1977 to 2007," while male prison incarceration grew by "416% during the same time period."[41] Equally disproportionate during that period were women's arrests for drug violations: up 19 percent compared to 10 percent for men.

Further disaggregation of this data reveals significant racial disparities. For example, the U.S. Department of Justice reports that the rate of imprisonment for Black women is 113 per 100,000, more than twice that of white females (51 per 100,000).[42] Even more troubling are the new trends in mass incarceration among young women.

Black women caught at the end of their teen years are almost five times more likely to be imprisoned than their white counterparts: 33 inmates per 100,000 versus 7 inmates per 100,000.[43] And despite comprising roughly 6 percent of the U.S. population, Black women make up 22 percent of the prisoner population in the United States, and Latinas represent 17 percent of the prison population.[44] At every phase within their life span, Black women's incarceration dramatically outpaces that of white and Latina women. Sadly, federal data-keeping neglects to further disentangle certain racial categories, lumping ethnic populations such as Native American women with Asians and Pacific Islanders.

Despite the power of these statistics to highlight women's incarceration, missing are narratives that help us to understand who these women are, why they are behind bars, who benefits from their incarceration, and who is harmed. Missing is an account that informs scholars, policymakers, and an interested lay public about why women's incarceration rate outpaces that of men – even if the raw numbers are much lower.

In *The Eternal Criminal Record*, Professor James B. Jacobs argues: "One reason that the United States has such an immense population of persons with criminal records is the overuse of criminal law."[45] He lists drug offenses as one such area, where 1,552,432 arrests were made in 2012 alone.[46] Of the drug arrests, Jacobs casts particular attention on the 42.4 percent involving marijuana possession.[47] Jacobs further emphasizes this point, explaining that in the past few decades "millions of people have been convicted of selling and possessing illicit mood and mind-altering drugs, especially marijuana."[48]

Jacobs urges us to imagine the possession of cannabis not being illegal or criminal; in such a scenario, "all those people ... would not have a criminal record."[49] He does not unpack how such laws and criminal policing particularly impact women. However, federal data gives some indication. Nearly 60 percent of the "most serious offense[s]" committed by "women in federal prisons and 25.1% of women in state prisons [are for] violations of drug laws."[50]

A considerable percentage of women arrested, convicted, and serving prison sentences suffer either from drug addiction or from the causes of their addiction, which motivated the crimes that ultimately resulted in their arrests.[51] For example, in its *Prisoners Report* the Bureau of Justice Statistics calculates, without further detail, that nearly 10 percent of women's prison sentences relate to "commercialized vice, morals, and decency offenses" and liquor law violations.[52] Vice crimes, along with petty property thefts, fraud (writing "bad checks"), and stealing cars, account for over a third of women's prison sentences.[53] Importantly, these crimes often relate to and mask drug addiction. Unlike their male counterparts, where over half serve time for violent offences, two-thirds of women's offenses were nonviolent. Among these women – especially those serving time for drug-related offenses – incredibly high percentages are mothers.

Moreover, while the Bureau of Justice Statistics clarifies some racial disparities and highlights room for more research regarding others, it does not include women caught within the revolving door of criminal justice – out on probation or parole, living in a halfway house, suspended in the limbo of confinement before or after adjudication, or in a court-ordered rehabilitation program. Nor does it offer a better sense about motherhood and incarceration.

7.2 MOTHERHOOD AND THE CRIMINAL JUSTICE SYSTEM

The problem of mass incarceration is also the problem of parents behind bars and children suffering the loss, support, and relationship with their mothers and fathers. Indeed, the rate of parental incarceration raises important public policy concerns, particularly as a third of children who have parents in prison will reach adulthood while that parent is behind bars.[54] Between the early 1990s and 2007, mothers and fathers detained in state and federal prisons increased by 79 percent.[55] The number and rate of children whose parents are incarcerated increased, too.[56] From 1991 to 2007, the number of children whose parents were incarcerated nearly doubled from 860,300 to 1,427,500.[57] And while the number of incarcerated fathers increased by 77 percent, it more than doubled for mothers – up by 131 percent.[58] To further disentangle this data, let us consider what accounts for this and what the mothers were convicted for.

According to federal research data available at the time of this book's publication, 63 percent of women held in state prisons for drug-related offenses report being a mother; equally, more than half of women in federal prisons for drug-related crimes acknowledged being mothers.[59] Thus, not only do drug offenses significantly account for women's incarceration, but also drug policies, and particularly the drug war, directly impact the lives of children in the United States. This latter point deserves further explanation, because illicit drug use can often be perceived as a "bad choice" made by "bad mothers" and thus the convictions and punishment of these women are not only justified through this rationalization but also are deemed necessary.

By default, illicit drug users are perceived as uncaring, selfish mothers, who risk not only their own health but also the well-being of their families. Frequently and erroneously, policymakers and the general public perceive female drug abusers as Black and Latina, despite the fact that white and African American women use illicit drugs at about the same rate (white women a scant higher).[60] However, African American women are ten times more likely to be reported to Child Protective Services (arguably another branch of law enforcement) than white women.[61] Equally, when accounting for legal but potentially addicting drugs, such as alcohol and prescription medications (like opioids), white women's use outpaces that of their African American counterparts.[62] However, illicit drugs often carry the stigma and shame of poverty, dereliction, irresponsibility, disorderliness, and violence. Arguably, these perceptions significantly shaped federal drug policies that erroneously designated crystallized cocaine as substantially distinct from powder cocaine (the former viewed as dangerous and the latter recreational).

The trope of the bad mother perversely extends to the criminal justice system. In part, this pattern continues due to erroneous distinctions between illicit drugs and prescription "medications." As discussed in Chapter 2, a longitudinal study conducted by Dr. Allen A. Mitchell, director of the Slone Epidemiology Center at Boston University, debunks misperceptions about drug use, particularly during pregnancy.[63] Reflecting on Dr. Mitchell's research is relevant here too, because the study revealed that educated white women were more likely to rely on prescription medications during pregnancy and their reliance increased with age.[64] Importantly, the prescription drugs most likely to be relied upon during pregnancy include powerful narcotics such as Demerol, Tylenol with codeine, Xanax, Oxycontin, and Ritalin.[65] My point here is to suggest that drug policies and trends that fuel mass incarceration disparately and erroneously police women and mothers through stereotype and bias.

More than two-thirds of women in prison are mothers,[66] and the collateral impacts of their incarceration reach beyond the criminal justice system into the lives of their children. For example, these women are more likely to be the primary caretakers of their children – three times more likely than fathers (77 percent).[67] A relatively small percentage of incarcerated mothers had any support in caring for their kids prior to incarceration – unlike dads, who overwhelmingly acknowledge that mothers were the primary caregivers to their children.[68] According to research conducted by the Bureau of Justice Statistics:

> Mothers were more likely than fathers to report living with at least one child. More than half of mothers held in state prison reported living with at least one of their children in the month before arrest, compared to 36% of fathers. More than 6 in 10 mothers reported living with their children just prior to incarceration or at either time, compared to less than half of fathers.[69]

For example, the collateral costs of the drug war and mass incarceration include burdens on parental rights. When lawmakers enacted the Adoption and Safe Families Act of 1997, which requires states to file petitions to terminate parental rights on behalf of any child who has been in foster care for fifteen of the most recent twenty-two months, they did not provide any special provisions for incarceration.[70] The typical time served for a drug-related offense far exceeds fifteen months,[71] meaning that after being convicted of a drug-related offense, most women risk the permanent loss of parental rights.

No group is more impacted by this than African American children. Black children are more than seven times more likely to experience a parent in prison compared to white children.[72] For Latino children, they are more than twice as likely as white children to experience a parent's incarceration.[73] And, at least when interviewed, incarcerated women claim more children than men.[74] Often, these women are the primary caregivers prior to entering the criminal justice system. Furthermore, the psychological impacts of parental incarceration can be quite severe.

Professor Kristin Turney's research argues that the impacts of incarceration on children are worse than experiencing a parent's death or suffering through divorce.[75] The growing impact of mothers behind bars now extends to babies being born behind bars and children being incarcerated alongside their mothers as a policy solution, which highlights the deeply contentious and fraught impacts of mass incarceration. In its report *Mothers, Infants, and Imprisonment*, the Women's Prison Association's Institute on Women and Criminal Justice explains that because "the number of women in prison has skyrocketed over the past 30 years, states have had to consider what it means to lock up women, many of whom are pregnant or parenting."[76] In most cases, children of incarcerated mothers, whether their births occur behind bars or not, move into various forms of "other" care, which may include relatives, foster homes, shelters, group homes, and other arrangements.

For the babies and children who have the benefit of residing alongside their mothers in prison nursery programs, the outcomes for both mothers and their babies show significant promise: recidivism rates are lower and, so far, "children show no adverse effects" of their lives behind bars.[77] So far ... as one reporter explains, the conditions in these prisons where nurseries are found are so dire that "you walk through a metal detector and a locked steel door to a courtyard surrounded by razor wire and two 20-foot fences."[78]

Years ago, when conducting field research in the Philippines, I interviewed an NGO staffer who was incarcerated for political activities. As part of her punishment, her children were placed behind bars, too. At the time I thought, How cruel! What government does such a thing? Today, the U.S. does such a thing. Even having the privilege of raising a child behind bars is a fraught option. For example, the conditions in prisons and jails in the United States suffer from blight and neglect, and not just overcrowding. As such, at some the water may be contaminated and the facilities may be rat- and roach-infested.

Male-centered accounts about mass incarceration fail to paint a more vivid and illuminating tapestry about children forced into foster care due to their mother's incarceration[79] or the dramatic increase in the number of women incarcerated for drug-related offenses.[80] Pregnant women who are nonviolent, low-level drug users experience similar penalties to black-market drug traffickers with ties to cartels, large-scale organizations, and gangs.

Women's invisibility to lawmakers, activists, and scholars studying the drug war may account for their distressing misreading of the drug war as a problem in society for and about men generally and Black men especially. This misunderstanding of the drug war and who it impacts neglects the unique ways in which women and children endure mass incarceration and the drug war. Rendering women invisible disserves lawmaking because it ignores the potentially harmful impacts of some policies, muddying and muddling how to better shape law to address poverty, drug abuse, and other social concerns. Misreading women and mass incarceration also ignores the long-term impact and consequences of a woman's criminal record.

7.3 COLLATERAL CONSEQUENCES AND COLLATERAL DAMAGE

According to James Jacobs, "[t]he criminal record is a kind of negative curriculum vitae or resumé."[81] It contains only "disreputable" information, and the longer the "rap sheet," the more a woman will endure the stigma of a career criminal. The longer a woman's criminal record, the more difficult for her to plea-bargain within the criminal justice system or to convince judges of her contrition. It likely also impacts relationships with defense attorneys (the longer the criminal record, the more pressure to plea-bargain even when a woman may be innocent of the charges alleged). Jacobs warns that the criminal record, originally a bookkeeping mechanism, has morphed to "drive decision making at every step of the criminal justice process."[82]

As a practical matter, the criminal record also impacts every step and opportunity that a woman may seek outside the criminal justice system, rendering civilian life a different form of punishment from which she cannot exit. Criminal records are traded like any commodity, commercially sold and acquired for tenant screening, employment, eligibility to serve as a volunteer, or even to become a student. The criminal record now creates what Jacobs refers to as an enhanced pathway into the public domain. These enhanced pathways no longer serve the criminal justice system alone, but now link to the commercialized reach of private information vendors.

Criminal record vendors promote and sell criminal background checks to anyone willing to pay a fee, including for noncriminal justice purposes. These policy choices coincided with drug war policies of the 1970s.[83] Congress chipped away the FBI's policy that prevented criminal records from being shared with non-law enforcement agencies, including "certain industries, businesses, and voluntary associations."[84] Congress has now extended the privilege of obtaining criminal background information from the FBI to the securities industry, banks, child and eldercare organizations, housing authorities, and many more. Even if obtaining some criminal background information could be reasonable for some industries, that hardly justifies the use of this information by commercial enterprises that "download court and other publicly accessible criminal record information to their own proprietary databases,"[85] essentially privatizing public information, claiming the same types of rights to this information as government.

Thus, the very pathways to a restored and rehabilitated life may be cut off to women and men when they leave government incarceration, because this seemingly private (and certainly personal) record not only becomes public but also follows them. And the impacts are corrosive and far-extending. Further, for those who fall back into the clutches of criminal conduct, such as drug possession, they are "subject to heavy sentence enhancements" because "the defendant's prior record has a significant impact on the sentence."[86] Jacobs argues that these policies are deliberate, but unexamined.

7.3.1 Housing

Consider the Housing Opportunity Program Extension Act of 1996.[87] This law provides that the housing authority may request criminal conviction information as a screening device for housing applicants, to filter out those who have been convicted.[88] Even when low-income women stay clear of law enforcement, the convictions of the men in their lives also become their problems, because "[u]nder HUD's one-strike policy, any drug offense may lead to eviction from public housing, even offenses of which the tenants themselves are unaware and even if the offenses were committed off-site."[89] This policy came under significant scrutiny in the wake of Shelly Anderson's eviction from low-income housing in Alexandria, Virginia.

Anderson, a mother of three, only weeks away from a kidney transplant, was found to be in violation of the one-strike policy enforced by Alexandria public housing officials, because her boyfriend pleaded guilty to cocaine possession charges. In turn, Anderson's home was searched. Ms. Anderson, diagnosed with stage 5 renal failure, knew the only possibility of curing her disease was a kidney transplant. She was desperate and prepared for her transplant. However, authorities had what they call a "hit" when her townhome was searched.

The search did not turn up drugs, but it surfaced paraphernalia inside her mother's purse. For Anderson, this meant she was out of housing. Despite not having a history of drug use, Anderson now had a record within the government's housing system associated with a drug violation. And for many women, this is a powerful form of disenfranchisement, especially as primary caretakers.

7.3.2 Education

Housing aside, the criminal record now serves as a gate-keeping function for many other purposes. In 1998, Congress passed a law that bars any student with a drug conviction from obtaining federal loans to fund her education.[90] Prospective students most impacted by this law will not be wealthy young adults from educated families but low-income persons. Journalist Clarence Page refers to such laws as creating a "[w]ar on our children."[91] However, this too may be a war on mothers who seek to return to school as a new pathway in their lives, because such policies cut off the pathway.

7.3.3 *Employment Opportunities*

In most states individuals convicted of felonies are prohibited from many opportunities, even though they are tethered to legal fees associated with their conviction and subsequent probation. These women are forced to work to pay off their fines and fees. And, they want to work to feed, shelter, and clothe their families. For many who have children, they must prove to the state that they can be responsible, law-abiding parents. But first, they must get a job. Almost any job will show the state that a mother who was convicted is on the path to repair. Except that reentry and obtaining jobs is very difficult – some would say, nearly impossible.

Most will be denied jobs that require a license, even if the license has little or nothing to do with their crime. Thus, in many states a woman with a felony conviction cannot work in childcare, healthcare, or acupuncture, and cannot become a dietician, barber, cosmetologist, speech or language pathologist, architect, accountant, dentist, doctor, pharmacist, psychologist, realtor, nurse, and more. To many of you, some of these restrictions will seem severe, overly punitive, and perhaps nonsensical, such as banning a mother with a felony conviction from becoming a chiropractor, physical therapist, or even funeral director. All of these restrictions restrict what limited options a woman might have as she attempts to reclaim her life. These restrictions also harm her children and community.

7.3.4 *Other*

Women convicted of felonies also lose other rights that matter to the core of citizenship, such as the ability to vote, to join the military, and to travel. Some states have restored voting rights to the formerly incarcerated, but not every state has. And, while a felony conviction may not bar a woman from applying for a passport and possibly receiving one, it may affect where and when she may travel. And, if she is on probation, she cannot travel out of town, let alone to another country, without permission from the probation officer supervising her release.

7.4 CONCLUSION

For lawmakers, activists, and scholars who care about mass incarceration, education reform, safe housing, and related social issues, urging policy solutions that filter out women and concentrate primarily on the lives of men is to ignore women's interactions within the broader criminal justice system. In such circumstances, not only are women invisible, but the sometimes abusive interactions they have with police who exploit their drug dependence, the selective prosecutions of women – particularly those who are pregnant – for drug offenses, and the long-term problems associated with their criminal records are also imperceptible.

8

The Pregnancy Penalty: When the State Gets It Wrong

We sat at a Minneapolis restaurant to talk about her case – one that upended retired judge Pamela Alexander's trajectory.[1] By the time of the case that hindered her career, she had celebrated many firsts. She was the first Black judge in the state of Minnesota. Around the time of the case she was being considered for an appointment by President William Clinton for a nomination to the Eighth Circuit Court of Appeals. It made sense; she was highly respected, spoken of, and well-qualified. Judge Alexander's awards and recognitions are countless. She was a credible pick. Often, Presidents then select judges from the courts of appeal to serve on the Supreme Court. Her star was in the right place and it was rising.

But then the case came.

Judge Alexander decided *State v. Russell* in 1990 – thirty years ago, and maybe that is what also makes her and the case extraordinary. The case involved disparate sentencing in drug offenses. At the federal level, the sentencing for offenses involving crystalized cocaine compared to those involving the powdered substance was 100 to 1. In Minnesota, it was 25 to 1. The racial implications were hard to miss and ignore. Politicians claimed it needed to be that way; that people who used crystalized cocaine or "crack," as opposed to powdered cocaine, became violent and deadly. According to police and prosecutors, they become like rabid animals: unpredictable, unmanageable, and unreachable. This is why women needed to be punished, too. After all, they were birthing this "bio underclass" that would be uneducable and, really, unsalvageable.

According to Judge Alexander, further aggravating sentencing in those cases were gun possessions. She told me, if a person was caught with "one rock of crack cocaine with a gun anywhere near, it is a mandatory minimum sentence." In Judge Alexander's view, guns were driving up the prison population.

Judge Alexander consulted scientists and learned that what was being touted in the popular media was simply not accurate. As the judge put it, on a practical level someone who sold crack in Minnesota to an undercover agent suffered the same penalty as someone who "goes into a restaurant and draws a gun and robs everybody."

She told me, "The penalties should not have been the same." So, in 1990, this is what she decided. The disparate sentencing was simply unconstitutional.

· She told me, "We were not ready for the hailstorm that came after that." She was "shocked at the vehemence" that came from the community and likely colleagues, too. She told me that the "day I made the decision, I had ten or twelve death threats. Just terrible stuff." She wondered, "Why is it logical to me and no one else is seeing it?" News stories now use the word "vindicated" when they profile her.

At the time, however, the case stalled a very bright career. The case was appealed to the Minnesota Supreme Court. It took them nearly a year before they returned a judgment affirming her decision, 6–1. The sentencing guidelines for the state were also changed. These were victories, no? Yes, for all the men and women who would otherwise have been subjected to very heavy sentences, amounting to ten, twenty, thirty years behind bars for drug possessions and transactions involving crack. However, in that year, her life changed. The process had begun for her nomination to the Eighth Circuit Court of Appeals, but now it would be a complicated pick for that high post. She told me that people ask her whether, if she had to do it all over again, she would have made such a big sacrifice. She could not imagine doing anything differently.

So, we talked about the racialization of drugs and women. Judge Alexander was concerned about the racialization of drug use and did not think sufficient attention was being paid to how disparities are addressed. In her court, she noticed that Black female defendants were usually under forty, with kids to care for. These women get separated from their children and often end up losing custody. This was a very different reality from the white women who appeared before her on prescription drug charges. She told me that the latter group of women "present well" and in court this often means they will not be sent to prison – unlike the indigent mothers of color, who end up "broken down, beat down . . . they have nothing left." She told me:

> I think the racialization of drugs and drug use across the country has made the average American anesthetized against the overall racial impact and making this an "us and them" kind of thing. The problem [is] . . . it is so easy to blind yourself if you think it is not you, not your community. We have to take this out of "us and them." At this juncture, it should be easier to do. Heroin and meth are used by white Americans and there is a dramatic difference in how those cases are perceived. Once we start seeing whites in jails in droves, we will have to do something about it. But even now, we are separating meth users from cocaine users and that is racialized [and based on class]. Look at heroin; its resurgence is among young white kids. But we have to look at people who are drug addicts in the same. How are we going to handle this? We need to talk about this globally, to . . . have an honest conversation about why we are nation of drug use.

What about the mothers? The women who appear in her court? What does the law have to say about them? The message from Judge Alexander is that a defendant's race or ethnicity can play a significant role in how she is perceived in the criminal justice system and this will often relate to whether she is sentenced or her sentencing is diverted, such that she does not go to jail but to a treatment program. Motherhood is no exception. Poor women do not catch a break because they are pregnant or mothers. In fact, an arrest might result in a hidden, unspoken penalty if one is pregnant, poor, and in the criminal justice system. Race only exacerbates this if the defendant is a woman of color. For the most part, many of the new laws criminalizing pregnant women's conduct derive from the assumption that state interventions in pregnancies promote the health of fertilized embryos and fetuses. Lawmakers express frustration with the women and the systems they have helped to create. They tell me their hands are tied to come up with better solutions. They believe that the women who end up in the criminal justice system and in front of judges like Pamela Alexander had many chances to do better and simply refused to live healthier lives – for themselves and their fetuses. Or they tell me that these women simply lack the capacity for self-control needed to stay off drugs. Some prosecutors agree. They believe criminal punishment is the only way to help poor pregnant women who are making "poor life choices."

Prosecutors in Alabama and other parts of the country indicate that their priorities are to "save the babies" and "get these women the help they need." Admittedly, these are powerful expressions of concern. After all, who doesn't want to save babies? Who doesn't want to help women? These messages are reinforced in the religious communities of some of the prosecutors. Steve Marshall, the current Attorney General of Alabama confided to me that he is opposed to abortion and that he enjoys helping children. He has even given his time to organizations where adults mentor children. Taken at their word, legislators and prosecutors feel helpless. Their arguments are convincing to judges, especially in Alabama, where courts regard even nonviable fetal life with the same reverence and legal rights as children.

But are these civil and criminal interventions that result in incarceration or the removal of children from the home safe and helpful for policed women and girls? Do they really promote fetal health? Are the interventions described in this book the least constitutionally burdensome means of promoting those interests? Much of this thinking presumes a life and rights for embryos and fetuses apart and distinct from that of the pregnant women who bear them.

However, as shown throughout this book, neither fetal nor maternal health outcomes are necessarily improved by punitive state interventions in women's pregnancies. In fact, according to the American Public Health Association (APHA) and other medical organizations, fetal protection efforts may result in worse health outcomes for pregnant women and their fetuses.[2]

Studies reveal that in the years since the aggressive involvement of states in women's pregnancies, maternal mortality has nearly doubled and only slight decreases in fetal mortality have been observed.[3] Globally, the United States ranks fiftieth among nations reporting maternal morbidity to the World Health

Organization. The rate of maternal death has doubled since 1987, while other nations' rates of maternal morbidity declined during the same period. There is no explicit correlation between maternal and fetal mortality and fetal protection interventions. However, the data provides a broader view of maternal health at a time when states have enacted extreme criminal interventionist strategies in the name of promoting health.

Despite the intuitive pull that fetal health benefits result from punitive state intervention in women's pregnancies, the empirical literature on maternal-fetal health suggests otherwise. When states introduce punitive norms into childbearing, including interference in the physician-patient relationship and threats of arrests and incarceration, women may forego care. Furthermore, there are no guarantees that women who come under the supervision of the state necessarily give birth in a hospital or under dignified circumstances. Babies are sometimes born in prison in exceedingly unsanitary conditions.[4] That is what happened to Tara Keil and Ambrett Spencer, women whose experiences are partially captured below. The extracts provided here barely offer a glimpse of the lives and communities altered, probed, and turned upside down by criminal law intervention of the cruelest kind. Not surprisingly, inflicting inhumane conditions on a woman during her pregnancy does not make her better off in terms of health, safety, or drug addiction.

This Chapter highlights how legislators, prosecutors, and judges sympathetic to a tough-on-crime or "using the stick" approach to pregnant women and their bodies miscalculate the human and financial costs of their decision-making. Simply put, their approaches do not improve health outcomes for women or their children. Rather, legislators, prosecutors, and judges are misguided to believe that harsh criminal punishments and invasive civil sanctions reduce the incidents of miscarriage, stillbirth, low birth weight, genetic abnormalities, childhood asthma, obesity, diabetes, and more. Yet these conditions are not improved, let alone cured, through criminal punishment or civil confinement of pregnant women.

8.1 TREATING DRUG ADDICTION

South Carolina senator and former prosecutor Charles Condon has stated: "Nothing could be more heart-breaking than the sight of a baby born with an addiction to cocaine. There is very little doctors and nurses can do to ease the pain of these innocent newborns, whose mothers' use of hard, illegal drugs during pregnancy constitutes nothing less than blatant child abuse."[5] Similarly, Chief Reuben of the Charleston, South Carolina, Police Department said, in regard to drug-addicted pregnant women, that "[u]nless you have sanctions in place, unless you understand the basic irresponsibility of these drug-addicted women, it won't work." However, it is hard to imagine a medical benefit to the pregnant patient or the fetus that would otherwise not be realized without the imposition of civil commitment, forced caesarean operations, or criminal sanctions. In other words, empirical data examining rehabilitation versus incarceration for drug use provides more reliable answers than tough-on-crime anecdotes from political campaigns and law enforcement.

In fact, research provides compelling evidence that rehabilitation may be more successful than incarcerating pregnant drug offenders. In the spring of 2018, at a Ninth Circuit judicial conference on reentry, I had the opportunity to speak with Sandra Burton, a soft-spoken, formerly incarcerated woman, whose world was upended when her five-year-old son was killed by a police officer driving an unmarked van on the block where the family lived. The officer took off and did not stop.

Sandra acknowledged that this was an accident; her son had run across the street, likely not seeing the van and possibly the officer not seeing her son in time to properly stop. Even so, she never received an acknowledgment from the officer, the police department, or the city of Los Angeles.

To cope with her grief, Sandra, who had never been incarcerated and had no criminal record, began self-medicating. Her drug dependency eventually resulted in her arrest and cycling in and out of prison for over fifteen years. She cycled in and out of the system six times – each time for possession of a controlled substance. She lamented, "You'd think someone in the system might have gotten the bright idea that I needed drug treatment, that I needed therapy."[6] She was not offered help and did not know how to ask for it. She explained, "People with my color skin, and who grew up where I did, didn't know concepts like rehab. I was always remanded to prison."[7]

So, not once during her incarceration did she receive the drug rehabilitation she needed. Had she tried, particularly with a doctor rather than a support group led by other prisoners, she might have been required to make a co-pay of $5 per visit in California. This may seem nominal but, for women making only pennies per hour in prison wages, paying for medical-related visits was often out of reach. In Texas, female inmates must contribute $100 in copays for their medical visits, and "in Alabama, prisoners were responsible for *actual medical* costs, and the balance – what could be tens of thousands of dollars – would follow you after your release."[8] For those who did not or could not pay their medical bills, "the state could issue a warrant for [their] arrests," bringing them back into the system.[9]

Eventually, Sandra acquired the rehabilitation services she needed. She found them on her own. Since then, she has devoted her life to helping other women who face similar struggles. She now shares a credible message: rehabilitation works much better than incarcerating pregnant women and mothers who are drug dependent.

To measure the success rates of treatment versus incarceration, studies track recidivism, arrest rates, and the reduction of illicit drug and alcohol use.[10] Few studies comprehensively measure each of these factors collectively. However, tracking multiple studies provides sturdy evidence that drug treatment programs are far more health-and cost-effective than prison. Maryland's alcohol and drug abuse administration reports that patients in treatment were less likely to be rearrested and more likely to maintain employment.[11] Patients who completed treatment were less likely to be readmitted to treatment. Some of the findings include:

- Among a sample of patients attending treatment in Baltimore City, treatment completion was associated with a 54 percent decrease in the likelihood of being arrested postdischarge, after adjustment for individual characteristics.
- In Baltimore City, treatment completion was associated with both increased wages following treatment and a 28 percent increase in the likelihood of becoming employed postdischarge, after adjustment for individual characteristics.

In Oregon, treatment completion "is associated with substantially fewer incarcerations in the state prison system and with fewer days of incarceration."[12] A study sponsored by the Oregon Office of Alcohol and Drug Abuse Programs, which examined data from that state, discovered "residential treatment completers were incarcerated at a rate of 70% lower than the matched group."[13] In the period following treatment, patients who completed the treatment, "received 65% higher wages than those who didn't complete treatment."[14] In addition, "the use of food stamps was reduced significantly for clients who completed treatment compared with those who were non-completers."[15] The study also found that patients who completed treatment programs were much less likely to use medical emergency rooms, indicating that preventative services were more likely to be utilized and perhaps that less risky activities became the norm among the population completing treatment.

In another study, researchers report positive correlations associated with drug treatment.[16] This multistate empirical study found "completers were 22% to 49% more likely than non-completers to be employed and to earn higher wages in the year following treatment, holding other variables constant."[17] Authors of this study confirmed that patients who remained in treatment for more than ninety days were more likely to be employed in the year following treatment. The findings were "consistent across the three state project with different client populations, treatment delivery systems, and labor markets."

Key to patients' success are doctors focusing on reducing their patients' addiction to illegal drugs and alcohol, along with providing mental health services. The success of rehabilitation programs is in stark contrast to the outcomes associated with incarceration, including negative outcomes for children of incarcerated parents,[18] recidivism,[19] and sexual and physical abuse while in prison.[20]

For example, the Beckley Foundation reports that "there is little evidence that large scale imprisonment of drug offenders has had the desired results in deterring drug use or reducing drug problems."[21] In a very sophisticated research study, engaging analysis across multiple countries, including the United States, researchers found that incarcerated drug users are likely to continue drug use while in prison. Moreover, those who previously were not drug users are more likely to begin using drugs during their incarceration. Not surprisingly, prison is a high-risk, low-social-benefit environment for pregnant patients.

Not all prosecutors or law enforcement believe criminal punishment is the answer for addressing drug addiction in women or men. Some realize that prison may only feed into vulnerable drug users' addictions and dependencies. They want to find solutions to the distressing problems of drug disease but realize that mass incarceration is a losing battle. They are not naïve; they know the incarcerated have access to drugs in prison.

In 2014, I interviewed Lyn Head, then District Attorney for Tuscaloosa County, Alabama. Alabama has become notorious for arresting pregnant women on drug charges.[22] In a special investigative report published by Politico, Nina Martin found over 500 cases in recent years. Likely there are more. Some of the women take plea deals of twenty years, because a conviction could result in an even more severe sentence. So the women hedge their bets, pleading with prosecutors for mercy and leniency.

Lyn grew up in Montgomery, Alabama, and has been involved in groups that seek to feed, clothe, and provide basic needs for people struggling to make ends meet. Unlike many in law enforcement, she has also been deeply concerned about reentry. What happens when the incarcerated leave prisons and jails? Today, she is the chairwoman of the Board of Pardons and Paroles in Alabama – an appointment she received in 2018 from Governor Kay Ivey.

Here's what Lyn told me, "I know for sure there is access to drugs in prison. I tried a case last year, a plot to kill a law enforcement person in one of our prisons. Soap in a sock. I wanted people to see how dangerous that could be. One of the inmates who had been in the initial plan . . . gave a full statement. I sat down with him for a long time. If I had to guess, he had 70 or 72 IQ; too dumb to lie. No need to lie." Lynn told me that he asked a question and answered it for himself. "He said, 'Are we done; I'm ready to go.'" She wondered why and he responded, "I love prison, I can get anything I want. . . . You name it; I can get it. We get these Walmart cards and I could sex here . . . marijuana, meth, pills, cocaine." She concluded, "Yes they can get everything they want."

When I asked her about the availability of rehabilitation programs in prisons, she acknowledged that the resources simply are not there. And because of that, "it is not being addressed." As Lyn explained, "My firm opinion is that to address that we have to put more money in corrections. No one on either side of the aisle wants to give money to that." And prosecutors like Lyn know that more prison begets more prison. She told me, "Crime is not down; we are having to find alternative ways to deal with it."

And at least in 2014 when we spoke, correction officers in the state of Alabama were not "required to have a high school diploma." Given the lack of educational attainment, what special skills and capacities could correction officials in her state bring to addressing the unique circumstances of incarcerated pregnant women? Given my talk with Lyn, it was hard to believe that fetal health in Alabama is improved by exposing pregnant women to prison.

8.2 MISREADING PREGNANCY AND MISREADING POVERTY

Locating children's risks from these conditions and others at the site of pregnancy misreads poverty altogether and often serves to scapegoat poor women for the state's failure to protect the environment, provide equitable schools in the most blighted communities, and generate opportunities for all Americans. Therefore, states' efforts to concentrate criminal attention on maternal conduct as a means to promote fetal health are destined to fail, not only on moral grounds but also as a matter of medical efficacy. For poor women, pregnancy is a penalty.

Many factors influence pregnancy outcomes beyond maternal conduct and control. They include secondhand smoke, living in pesticide-ridden environments, housing near toxic waste sites, and more. These are the conditions of poverty. This should not be surprising to lawmakers. Any number of the common realities of womanhood and poverty pose risks of harm to fetuses, even under a pregnant woman's most vigilant efforts to protect herself and her pregnancy.

8.2.1 Domestic Violence and Low-Birth-Weight Babies

Domestic violence is one of the leading threats to fetal health and development in developed as well as developing nations. According to the World Health Organization (WHO), pregnant women are "60% more likely to be beaten than women who are not pregnant."[23] Intimate partner abuse during pregnancy injures not only the health of the pregnant woman but also that of the fetus, causing "threat to health and risk of death" from trauma.[24] Jacquelyn Campbell, the study's author, concluded that intimate partner abuse at the time of pregnancy causes not only physical trauma but also the type of psychological distress that results in severe depression and anxiety.

The types of mental and physical health traumas associated with domestic violence include physical injury, gastrointestinal harms, sexually transmitted diseases, depression, chronic pain, and post-traumatic stress disorder. These conditions result in insufficient weight gain, vaginal/cervical/kidney infections, abdominal trauma, hemorrhage, miscarriage, placental abruption, fetal bruising, fractures, and hematomas, as well as death of the pregnant woman and fetus. Professor Campbell's research and that of others suggest that the frequency of domestic violence during pregnancy is as high as 20 percent.[25] However, women who experience domestic violence during pregnancy may be less likely to report the abuse for fear of reprisal from their partners and the threat of child welfare services removing children from the home and/or the baby after its birth.

From a fetal health perspective, reducing intimate partner violence should be a far more urgent social and legal policy priority than the problematic and fallible fetal endangerment efforts directed at pregnant women, because "violence is cited as a pregnancy complication more often than diabetes, hypertension, or any other serious complication."[26] Physical violence during pregnancy can account for some percentage of drug use during pregnancy,[27] whether legal, illegal, or over the counter. More research would help disentangle the impacts of maternal drug use during pregnancy and its association with domestic violence. Nevertheless, available research provides sturdy indications that domestic violence is neither an isolated phenomenon nor a contained occurrence during pregnancy.[28]

According to Professor Campbell, the primary health effects associated with domestic violence at the time of pregnancy include substance abuse, sexually transmitted diseases, including HIV-1, depression, urinary tract infections, and other harms. A number of studies associate fetal distress, pre-eclampsia, antepartum hemorrhage, preterm delivery, and fetal distress with domestic partner abuse of pregnant women.[29] However, the issue most relevant to states in their effort to promote child welfare and healthy births is birth weight. Children born with low birth weight are at risk of greater health traumas.

Conservative estimates, "using all or most appropriate control variables, or well matched case-control studies," demonstrate a link between domestic violence and low birth weight in infants.[30] A meta-analysis of more than a dozen peer-reviewed research studies in Europe and the United States indicates a measurable connection between low birth weight and domestic violence during pregnancy.[31]

8.2.2 *Environment, Poverty and Racism*

In their important study, researchers at the University of Pennsylvania found that African American women are three times more likely to suffer death in pregnancy than white women in the United States.[32] Their research also confirmed that African American women are two times more likely to experience a premature birth. In fact, African American women may be up to four times more likely to suffer a "very early" preterm delivery than all other ethnic groups. The researchers attributed possible lower numbers of prenatal visits among poor women to the "inability to pay for otherwise available services, and failure to seek services, because of prior negative experiences."

A pregnant person's poverty may expose her to negative environmental factors that simply are not present in the pregnancies of wealthier women, including pesticides,[33] carcinogens,[34] and lead.[35] In fact, in their study researching environmental toxin exposure, maternal health, and adverse pregnancy outcomes, Professor Elizabeth Harrison and colleagues found that "[a]ir pollutants and pesticides also are linked to poor pregnancy outcomes ... PCBs and DDT, increase[] the risk of preterm birth, low birth weight, and miscarriage." Lead exposure through inhalation or consumption can result from lead paint, contaminated soil, and dust. The effects include a risk of miscarriage and stillbirth, as well as preterm birth, low birth weight and neurological developmental effects. Professor Harrison and colleagues report that environmental toxins are an emerging public health challenge.

Sometimes, these factors perniciously combine in relentless cycles; poor women suffering the awful hardships of poverty are more likely to be exposed to lead in their homes, inhale pesticides intended to control pest infestations, and live near toxic waste facilities[36] due to housing stratification, proximity to a military base, or the affordability of hazard-intense neighborhoods.[37]

Since the 1980s, a series of environmental studies have revealed that private industries, as well as local, state, and federal governments, were systematically placing chemical plants, oil refineries, garbage dumps, and other hazardous waste sites in poor and African American communities. A *New York Times* reporter noted that in some of the worst-hit communities, "the air can be thick enough to make you gag, and you find that the rates of cancer, heart disease, stroke and the like are off the chart."[38] Some of these states are the very ones where African American women have been prosecuted for fetal endangerment, miscarriages, or stillbirths. However, this carnage is often hidden, invisible to lawmakers and law enforcement, whose interests in criminalization locate at the individual rather than the systemic, institutional level.[39]

For example, the largest hazardous waste landfill in the United States is located in Emelle, Alabama, a part of Sumter County.[40] Recall Alabama's fetal endangerment law? This is a community where 90 percent of the population is African American. In the county as a whole, African Americans account for 70 percent of the population. In this Alabama community residents absorb hazardous waste from forty-eight states and some foreign nations. The disparities associated with where hazards are dumped and what communities are left to suffer the consequences are devastating penalties of poverty and racism. Further, when communities fight back, they usually suffer huge disadvantages, with environmental lawyers sometimes simply not addressing the environmental challenges in poor communities. Also, as Professor Michael Healy notes, the U.S. Supreme Court's interpretation of the commerce clause to apply to the disposal of waste across state lines prevents states from imposing higher fees for out-of-state waste imported into the state.[41]

The Government Accountability Office's (GAO) report on the correlation between hazardous waste dumping and racial and economic status further underscores the tragic circumstances in which low-income women of color live.[42] In a study based on census data from 1980, the GAO examined four hazard sites in the United States. It reported that with three of the four sites – Chemical Waste Management, Industrial Chemical Company, and the Warren County PCB Landfill – "the majority of the population ... where the landfills are located is

Black." The GAO also noted that at each of the four sites, the African American population had a lower mean income than the mean income of all other racial and ethnic populations within those towns and represented the majority of those living below poverty for families of four. The mean income for a family in poverty was roughly $7,400 per year. The income of the African Americans living near hazardous waste was lower than even the nation's poverty level.

These are not narratives of intent. No polluter intends to harm communities and threaten the health and well-being of future generations. Equally, no local municipality that negotiates for the location of toxic waste landfills amongst their neighborhoods wants their constituents' health to suffer. Clearly, no legislature intends for its poorest to suffer in the ways described here. Nor is it reasonable to think that pregnant women want such outcomes for themselves or their pregnancies. In fact, they have virtually no control over who gets to release waste in their communities, but sadly may suffer the blame for the health outcomes that result. While legislators generally absolve themselves from responsibility toward poor communities and their health, it seems poor women cannot. Yet, so much in legislative accounts about pregnant women's conduct toward fetuses wrongly assumes that a woman's pregnancy is the only determinant of fetal health.

In its study involving 2,000 women, the California Birth Defect Monitoring Program found that women who lived within a quarter of a mile of a hazardous waste site were twice as likely to birth babies with neural tube disabilities. They also found that this cohort was four times as likely to birth children with serious heart conditions.[43] Following the environmental trail matters. Researchers studying other fetal anomalies associated with environmental hazards in Texas report that mothers of babies experiencing Down syndrome were also more likely to live within one mile of a hazardous waste site than the control-group mothers.[44] The study revealed that living in close proximity to hazardous waste was also associated with spina bifida and anencephaly. The authors noted common characteristics among the women who lived in closer proximity to the hazardous waste sites they researched in Texas: they were more often Latina and with modest education.

What this research tells us is that the conditions of abject poverty compound everything else. There are myriad harms associated with poverty. What legislators perceive as the results of maternal harms may also be caused by environmental conditions associated with indigence and destitution. It would be absurd to attach punitive reproductive standards to these women's pregnancies in the name of promoting fetal health when the state has failed these women.

Fetal protection efforts largely ignore many of the intractable socioeconomic conditions experienced by low-income pregnant women. And though these conditions could also motivate state action on behalf of fetuses, states choose not to impose constraints on industries, manufacturers, municipalities, or themselves to reduce the environmental factors that may cause fetal harm. Dr. Hallum Hurt's decades of research into the factors that cause poor academic performance, stress, and violence concludes that "poverty is a more powerful influence on the outcome of inner-city children than gestational exposure to cocaine."[45]

8.2.3 *The Business of Fetal Health*

As doctors began complying with fetal protection regulations by informing on their patients and as courts swelled with the prosecutions of pregnant women for "delivering" crack to their fetuses, fetal impacts from alcohol consumption[46] and cigarette smoking[47] fell precipitously under the radar. It is worth thinking about why this occurred. After all, experts consider exposure to alcohol in utero the leading cause of developmental disabilities in children, affecting brain and organ development, growth delays, and central nervous system disabilities. The literature on smoking's contribution to negative health outcomes is now well settled. According to the CDC, women who smoke during pregnancy are more likely to experience miscarriage than women who do not. The organization also cautions that smoking can cause difficulties with the placenta, such as premature separation from the womb, putting fetal and maternal health at risk. It also links smoking during pregnancy to premature birth, low birth weight, cleft lip or cleft palate, death, and sudden infant death syndrome.

The point of such an inquiry here is not to add one more category of concern to the growing list of issues that states find relevant to justify punitive interventions in women's lives. To the contrary. Rather, it is worth thinking about why politicians carve out fetal protection exceptions for alcohol or tobacco use or addiction, particularly in light of the fact that U.S. women "are almost 20 times more likely to drink alcohol or smoke cigarettes than to use cocaine during pregnancy."[48]

Beyond matters of race, which explicitly and implicitly influenced policy and rhetoric regarding pregnancy in the 1980s, my hunch is that business interests matter in the national debate about fetal health. In 1996, Justice Breyer explained that "unregulated tobacco use causes '[m]ore than 400,000 people [to] die each year from tobacco-related illnesses, such as cancer, respiratory illnesses, and heart disease.'"[49] Breyer emphasized that "tobacco products kill more people in this country every year 'than ... AIDS ... car accidents, alcohol, homicides, illegal drugs, suicides, and fires, *combined*.'"[50] However, the majority in *Food and Drug Administration v. Brown & Williamson Tobacco Corporation* reasoned that, although the FDA "amply demonstrated that tobacco use, particularly among children and adolescents, poses perhaps the single most significant threat to public health in the United States," banning smoking would impose significant costs on a vital U.S. business interest.[51]

For example, while Congress recognizes the detrimental health risks associated with cigarette smoking (and secondhand smoke), as demonstrated by at least six congressional hearings since 1965, it has "[n]onetheless ... stopped well short of ordering a ban." Instead, the Supreme Court explained that Congress "has generally regulated the labeling and advertisement of tobacco products, expressly providing that it is the policy of Congress that 'commerce and the national economy may be ... protected to the maximum extent consistent with' consumers 'be[ing] adequately informed about any adverse health effects.'" Despite known health risks, "Congress, however, has foreclosed the removal of tobacco products from the market. A provision of the United States Code currently in force states that '[t]he marketing of tobacco constitutes one of the greatest basic industries of the United States with ramifying activities which directly affect interstate and foreign commerce at every point, and stable conditions therein are necessary to the general welfare.'" At the same time as members of Congress struggled with how best to handle the impoverished Americans' increasing use of and dependency on crystalized cocaine, – the answer was clear regarding tobacco. That is, while they were wringing their hands, determining punitive criminal policies as their preferred response to the disease of crack dependency, they were making an economic calculation with regard to Americans' dependency on cigarettes.[52]

Nevertheless, a copiously detailed 978-page report on smoking, issued by the surgeon general in 2014, explains that its effects extend from fertility through gestation and beyond, resulting in cases of fetal growth restriction, preterm delivery, placenta previa, placental abruption, some congenital abnormalities, and impacts on lung development.[53] Because over 400,000 infants experience in utero exposure to tobacco from maternal smoking, it would be unwise to ignore the consequences. From a health perspective, the question remains one of providing care and support for the pregnant women. The reproductive repercussions associated with smoking, however, affect not only women's reproductive health but also that of men. According to the Dr. Boris Lushniak, the acting surgeon general, "cigarette use before and/or during pregnancy remains a major cause of reduced fertility as well as a maternal, fetal, and infant morbidity and mortality in the United States."[54]

Notwithstanding smoking's well-documented health risks, federal legislators chose to exempt it from more aggressive government intervention measures that could protect fetal health. Two clear reasons why emerge from the Supreme Court. First, smoking is a matter of consumer choice and the exercise of autonomous decision-making. As long as consumers receive adequate information about the health risks associated with smoking, Congress finds no reason to ban the activity. Second, federal legislators prioritized economic considerations in the case of smoking. The Supreme Court understood "Congress' decisions to regulate labeling and advertising and to adopt the express policy of protecting 'commerce and the national economy ... to the maximum extent'" to "reveal its intent that tobacco products remain on the market."[55]

In their article on legislative efforts to protect children from tobacco, Professor Joseph DiFranza, a medical doctor at the University of Massachusetts Medical School, and his colleagues observed that despite the passage of public health laws to reduce the incidence of child smoking, legislative efficacy was so lax that an eleven-year-old was able to purchase cigarettes on seventy-five attempts out of a hundred.[56] The Court's ruling in *Food and Drug Administration v. Brown & Williamson Tobacco Corporation* makes clear that, despite known health risks and costs associated with smoking,[57] those concerns did not trump federal lawmakers' market considerations and national financial interests.

The foregoing demonstrates that lawmakers express and enforce their concerns about fetal protection along inconsistent, arbitrary lines. In the 1980s and 1990s lawmakers lacked urgency and attention to some well-documented fetal-injurious activities, such as smoking and alcohol use during pregnancy, not because those activities were legal but perhaps because those industries are profitable and have considerable political influence. The absence of fetal protection guidance, let alone regulation, in those areas exposes the insincere commitment to promoting and protecting fetal well-being. Meanwhile, poor Black women became the subjects of deeply injurious criminal campaigns based on claims that their behavior posed a risk of harm to fetal development and future offspring, without any attempt being made to help them recover from their dependence on crystalized cocaine (or the underlying causes of their dependency). Much of this suggests that fetal protection laws cannot justifiably be only about a commitment to fetal health. My concern here is to distinguish known fetal health risks from nonhealth risks and highlight the arbitrariness of fetal protection regulation, because the ways in which selective punishment manifests though arbitrary rulemaking undermines the legitimacy of criminal and civil law interventions in this domain.

8.2.4 *If Dignity of the Fetus and Babies Mattered*

In some states, like Maryland, prisons force pregnant women in their third trimesters into twenty-four-hours-a-day confinement. This type of involuntary isolation could hardly promote psychological well-being. Victoria Law, author of *Resistance Behind Bars: The Struggles of Incarcerated Women*, writes about sex, race, and incarceration. Her work sheds light on this practice and how it harms incarcerated women. She also helps incarcerated women tell their stories. Her work, like that of Carolyn Sufrin, examines issues like pregnancy in prison.

In an illuminating article published in *ReWire News*, Law tells the story of Angela, who was eight months pregnant when she entered a correctional facility in Jessup, Maryland. Shortly after arrival, Angela was "locked behind a steel door nearly 24 hours each day."[58] According to Law, this is what prison officials referred to as "restrictive housing," but most people know it as solitary confinement – or at least that is how reproductive justice advocates would likely describe it. When Angela was locked up in restrictive housing, there was no recreational time or time to go outside. In the thirty minutes she was permitted to leave her cell, she could either wait to use the telephone (there were only two in her cell block) to call her three children or take a shower.

Some of those who are tough on crime are less sympathetic to women like Angela. They say, "Do the crime, pay the time." However, in Maryland, even pregnant women who have not yet been convicted – who are waiting for trial – are subjected to the same types of conditions – cell-isolation in an infirmary unit until they give birth. In such instances, these women have not been proven to have committed a crime. Law enforcement makes the argument that isolation programs like the one in Maryland promote pregnant women's health and are intended to maximize the potential for a healthy delivery. This way, there is no need to escort and transport a woman from some other housing unit to this particular area where medical support is supposedly nearby.

However, as Victoria Law describes, Angela's "cell had no emergency call button," and "while her cell was close to the nurses' enclosed desk area," they were "rarely at their post."[59] According to Angela, the nurses spent most of their time near where the officers were posted, beyond earshot. When the pregnant women needed their attention, they would "have to scream and bang on [their] cell door repeatedly." Together, the women would join in making noise, in order for one to "catch the nurses' attention." One woman at the prison in which Angela was housed gave birth in her cell. No one came until it was too late.

In my prior scholarship I questioned policies like this. What legislative intent justifies such practices? Rarely are the victims of such policies afforded a legal forum. Their chilling experiences rarely become an elemental or integral component of legal reflection.

Tara

In May 2009, Tara Keil screamed for help from her jail cell. She told a reporter, "I was screaming I needed help, and I even pounded on the door a few times, but nobody came . . . [a]nd that's when it hit me – I'm going to have this baby on my own."[60] The nineteen-year-old inmate's contractions indicated the imminence of her son's birth. Blood covered her hands and thighs. Amniotic fluid was on the floor of her cell. Despite her screams and pleas for help, no one came to render aid. The day before, Miss Keil was pulled over while walking to a friend's home. Within minutes the nine-months pregnant teenager was arrested and whisked to the Dubuke County Jail, charged with violating parole conditions for a prior drug charge. A warrant had been issued for Keil after she stopped meeting regularly with her parole officer.

Despite Tara Keil indicating the nearness of her delivery in her answer to question 53 of her intake medical questionnaire, staff paid no particular attention to the pregnant girl. According to Tara, after pleading to one of the guards that a call be placed to a nurse, the officer's response was to ask whether she wanted breakfast or not. With no other options, she sat on the metal toilet located in her cell and gave birth to her son. By the time of the nurse's arrival, the cell, sink, toilet, and other areas were covered in Keil's blood and, according to reports, the new mother was visibly shaking and crying. Two days later the baby was placed in foster care, and Tara received a three-month jail sentence.

Ambrett

In Ambrett Spencer's case, she recounted, "I kept praying that she would just open her eyes because she looked like she was alive."[61] Studies indicate that African American women's pain is usually misdiagnosed or treated with some skepticism on the part of doctors.[62] Ambrett Spencer's story fits that paradigm. In April 2006, Ambrett, a pregnant inmate at the Maricopa County Estrella Jail in Phoenix, called for assistance at three o'clock in the morning, indicating a pain level of ten on a scale from one to ten. She alerted jail staff that her medical condition was painful and urgent.

In her case, the nurse ordered immediate action, but the sergeant on duty declined to follow the nurse's order. Instead, Ms. Spencer was shuttled to the infirmary an hour later. But there Ambrett, who was incarcerated for driving while intoxicated, was ignored. Her pain was not treated, nor was she taken to a hospital. Her blood pressure decreased, the pain intensified, she grew pale. An hour passed before the nurse on duty decided to call an ambulance. By that time Ambrett had collapsed, and the nurse was unable to insert an intravenous drip into her arm. On arrival, the emergency medical technician noted, "If you are turning that color, you're not getting enough blood to your organs and skin."[63] He was right. Ambrett's baby, Ambria, was born dead.

Ambrett suffered from placental abruption, a condition in which fetuses have a promising rate of survival, but only if the patient receives timely treatment. The nearly four-hour wait for appropriate medical attention may have caused the baby's death. According to John Dickerson, a reporter for an Arizona newspaper, while the number of women in Maricopa jails is relatively low, the complaints made by these women about jail conditions, including water contamination and other matters, should not be dismissed; the local environmental agency found the fecal matter of mice in the drinking water.

Paula

Paula Hale's nightmare began with being raped, which precipitated both her pregnancy and illicit drug use. She informed hospital officials about the rape and its traumatic physical and emotional consequences. However, Ms. Hale never received rape counseling for the trauma and, like other women and girls with sexual violence histories, she treated the subsequent depression and anxiety with illegal drugs.[64] By deciding to carry her pregnancy to term, she ruled out an abortion and pursued prenatal care for the baby she was carrying. For her, it was a rational decision to seek treatment at the Medical University of South Carolina (MUSC), the only hospital she knew to serve poor Black women like her. However, she received no drug treatment there.

Paula Hale encountered something other than what she expected; she did receive prenatal care, but she did not anticipate how dramatically her life and that of her baby would change by making that decision. Hale did not realize that, by seeking prenatal treatment, she would surrender privacy and provide presumptive consent for medical staff at MUSC to disclose her medical data to local law enforcement. More specifically, Paula Hale did not anticipate that MUSC nurses and doctors would investigate and test her and the baby for the presence of illicit drugs. Nor did she foresee that the medical test would become "evidence" in a criminal investigation initiated by medical staff, or that the tests to which she did not consent would be turned over to police and prosecutors. Like the twenty-eight other Black women also using the MUSC prenatal services, Hale was dragged from the hospital, shackled and chained. To Lynn Paltrow, Executive Director of National Advocates for Pregnant Women, Hale's haunting experience conjures up images of slavery.[65] Indeed, race seemed to dominate every aspect of pregnant patients' treatment at MUSC.[66]

Shawanna

Ms. Nelson was a nonviolent offender. Unlike the other pregnant women described above, she did not come to the attention of law enforcement for harming her fetus. Rather, she wrote "hot checks." However, like the women described above, she committed a crime during her pregnancy. The state used a very strong stick to send Ms. Nelson a message. Shawanna endured labor while handcuffed and shackled to a medical gurney. When finally freed from the shackles, she delivered and was then immediately restored to her shackled position. It was in this position that she pleaded for relief from the shackles as the pain was intense. It was also from this position that Shawanna soiled herself, surely causing her to experience embarrassment, humiliation, and degradation.

The matter of shackling pregnant women during delivery is alarming. It raises basic questions about what justifies this breach of human rights. Even though the federal government has now banned this practice in its prisons, shackling pregnant women during labor and birth still occurs. Here is the sophistry the state wishes people to take seriously: poor pregnant women, while in the deep and agonizing pangs of delivery, will overtake medical staff and guards; it is probable that poor pregnant women in labor will make Herculean attempts to escape delivery rooms and hospitals with guards posted and orderlies in full attendance (and could plausibly succeed in doing so); and women in labor can masterfully will themselves to disappear. Why otherwise do states enforce, and courts permit, the shackling of pregnant women? What purposes do such extralegal measures serve? And at what cost?

8.2.5 The Scapegoat: Retribution and Punishment

If fetal protection efforts are not about the health of fetuses, what function(s) do they serve? Increasingly, fetal interventions are asserted to vindicate the supposed criminal interests of embryos, fetuses, and the state. This is embodied in the metaphoric "stick" used to describe how noncompliant poor pregnant women must be responded to and handled by the state.[67] Viewed in this context, the laws are at least as much, if not more, about formal retribution and punishment as the alleged goals of protecting fetal health. In this way, states seek to protect the purported dignity interests of embryos and fetuses against the perceived reckless, lazy, and negligent conduct of "bad mothers."

Research suggests that Americans imagine and depict the bad mother in racialized ways. Media and even legislators, courts, and law enforcement contribute to this. And media has an outsized influence on public opinion. Research suggests that how media bring issues to the public can influence how the public responds to a particular issue. Professor Franklin Gilliam, Jr., refers to this as "agenda setting"; when the public make their mind up about a thing, they have been "primed" to view it in a certain way. This is how he introduces readers to The "Welfare Queen" Experiment: How Viewers React to Images of African-American Mothers on Welfare.[68]

In the article, Professor Gilliam reports on his social welfare policy research, noting that the near unanimity half a century ago has given way to "discord and dissonance." Adopting a novel experimental design, he investigated the impact of "media portrayals of the 'welfare queen' . . . on white people's attitudes about welfare policy, race and gender." What he learned was that "among white subjects, exposure to these script elements reduced support for various welfare programs, increased stereotyping of African-Americans, and heightened support for maintaining traditional gender roles." Professor Gilliam reported his findings as having important implications for the practice of journalism – and I would agree.

However, his findings also have substantive significance for how policies and social attitudes are shaped as a result. The crack scare provides one disturbing example. Another is the notorious welfare queen.[69] The welfare queen mythology came to be associated with African American women. Throughout the second half of the twentieth century, depictions of welfare recipients were often women of color. Sometimes, these images were quite exaggerated and focused on the neediest indigent women as the most depraved and irresponsible: single with multiple children. As Ronald Reagan ran for the office of President, he frequently warned audiences about the greedy welfare queens usurping government resources. On reflection, this played to powerful effect, especially with working-class white Americans, who perceived their hard work as being unrewarded while the fictionalized Black welfare queens reaped unearned benefits and luxuries derived from their tax dollars.

Fetal protection laws play into faulty cultural constructs about race and responsibility, likely because they derive from racialized values and conceptions. That is, states seek to intervene in women's pregnancies on health grounds rooted in historic racial and class stereotyping and bias, as the grossly selective prosecutions in *Ferguson v. Charleston* demonstrated.[70] In other words, promoting health and safety is simply a pretext or proxy for class and racial discrimination. In *Ferguson*, prosecutors never implemented their drug scheme in the private obstetrics practice of the Medical University of South Carolina – only in the public care practice, thereby not only implicitly associating low-income women with "bad motherhood," but also shielding wealthier, white women from any possibility of such characterization.

A rich scholarship in law and motherhood provides a sturdy foundation for understanding the intersections of race, class and "bad motherhood" in the United States. While no one trait defines "bad motherhood" in the sociopolitical contexts, several recurring themes emerge in a review of scholarship. Historically, motherhood has concerned race and class. It has also included the explicit exclusion of certain classes of women from ever attaining a legal or social status of being good mothers or mothers at all. Eugenics laws introduced in the early twentieth century deprived tens of thousands of poor women in the United States from ever acquiring the status of motherhood. In *Buck v. Bell*, Justice Oliver Wendell Holmes opined that "three generations of imbeciles are enough" to justify the state depriving socially "unfit" women from "continuing their kind." Viewed in that light, America's poorest women were doomed to be this nation's "bad mothers," because they were indigent, lacked property, often could not vote, and sometimes reared their children as single parents.[71]

For centuries, African American women have been the selective targets of prurient state interest, alongside stereotyping as oversexualized, incompetent, incapable, neglectful mothers.[72] Some scholars refer to this by an acronym: BBM – Bad Black Mothers. In her iconic work, *Black Sexual Politics*, Professor Patricia Hill Collins describes how poor, working-class Black women are historically represented as individuals who "neglect their children either in utero or afterward." She explains that "these Bad Black Mothers are stigmatized as being hypersexualized" or "inappropriately feminine," and "they allegedly pass on their bad values to their children who in turn are more likely to become criminals and unwed teen mothers."[73] This stereotype suggests that implicit in the nature of Black women is the primitive animal instinct described centuries ago in the writings of Thomas Jefferson and others, who believed the proper place for Black women was the status of a field animal, or "chattel," because it suited their character and stature as "dull, tasteless, and anomalous," lacking "reason and imagination."[74] Jefferson subscribed to firm beliefs in the genetic differences between Blacks and whites. Jefferson also thought that Blacks sweat more and required less sleep – likely the misunderstanding of what it meant to force his slaves, including his Black children, into unpaid labor, where they had to till his fields in the hot Virginia sun of summer, without the luxury of adequate sleep afforded to his white family and guests at Monticello.

Thirty years ago, Dr. Ira Chasnoff explained to a *New York Times* reporter that significant racial disparities in fetal interventions persisted despite evidence of "equal rates of drug use" among white women and women of color, because "our perception of who a drug abuser is" influences who is reported to law enforcement.[75] In other words, there was no empirical foundation that justified disparate arrest rates, because African Americans' use of illicit drugs was no greater than that of their white counterparts. Nevertheless, as Chasnoff explained, "there is a perception that the people using drugs are mostly minority, inner-city people."[76]

States make an example of "bad mothers" by subjecting them to punitive state measures ranging from civil confinement to criminal incarceration. Meanwhile, states ignore the extralegal punishment[77] of pregnant women, precisely because the extralegal humiliations and stigmatization serve an implicit retributive purpose connected with purported fetal protection goals. What else realistically justifies the barbarity of shackling pregnant women during labor and birth? For example, Minnesota law permitted the "use of full restraints – waist, chain, black box over handcuffs and leg irons – during transportation of an inmate for the purpose of giving birth."[78]

8.3 CONCLUSION

Importantly, neither the health interests nor the retribution justifications for state intervention in women's pregnancy are satisfactory. While promoting fetal health is an important and achievable goal, the impermissible exercise of state authority, which infringes privacy and autonomy and inflicts cruel and unusual punishment, violates fundamental principles of the Constitution. Equally, to the extent that states articulate a sincere desire to promote fetal health, appreciating that maternal conduct and health alone do not control fetal health outcomes is crucial. States' unyielding gaze on low-income, pregnant women as "maternal environments" or "containers"[79] ignores the myriad ways in which fetal health may be shaped by stress, unemployment, environmental harms, and poverty, which pregnant women encounter but do not control.

9

Policing Beyond the Border

9.1 THE HELMS AMENDMENT: LIMITING USE OF FUNDS
FOR ABORTIONS

In 1973, by a 52–42 vote, the U.S. Senate adopted the Helms amendment, a law that prohibits the use of federal foreign assistance funding for abortion research and procedures.[1] Congress did not hold a single hearing related to the legislation, despite the seriousness of family planning access and the fact that women's reproductive healthcare was at stake. Only months before, the U.S. Supreme Court ruled in *Roe v. Wade* that the right to terminate a pregnancy was a fundamental constitutional right rooted in privacy and protected under the Fourteenth Amendment's Due Process Clause.

In dramatic contrast, the Helms amendment effectively conditioned U.S. foreign aid policy on the antiabortion platform long advocated by the legislation's author, "the late, stridently antiabortion Sen. Jesse Helms (R-NC)."[2] Senator Helms, a former journalist, was a master of rhetoric. He claimed, "My amendment would ... stop the use of U.S. Government funds to promote and develop ways of killing unborn children."[3]

Senator Helms harangued colleagues to vote for the amendment, and then did not vote for it himself, likely because of his hostility toward foreign aid altogether.[4] In fact, during his career in the United States legislature, Senator Helms repeatedly and aggressively asserted an unwillingness to promote or endorse legislation to advance women's reproductive and safety rights internationally.[5] According to Helms, treaties to protect women's rights were being "negotiated by radical feminists with the intent of enshrining their radical anti-family agenda into international law."[6]

Helms, a proud segregationist and widely described and known as racist, excelled at race-baiting and politicking on the bases of Southern white fear and resentment. Racism served as the foundation for his rise in politics from a radio newsman to working on the Senate campaign for another unapologetic segregationist, Willis

Smith. According to a *Wall Street Journal* commentary written by Chuck Smith,[7] "Mr. Helms is credited with inventing the description of UNC, the University of North Carolina, as the 'University of Negroes and Communists.'" Smith's campaign ran inflammatory advertisements with wording such as: Do you want Negroes working beside you and your wife and daughter, eating beside you, sleeping in the same hotels, teaching and disciplining your children in school, occupying the same hospital rooms, using your toilet facilities?

Helms frequently pandered to racial and sexual fears, biases, stereotypes, and tensions. Chuck Smith writes about another political campaign advertisement that "featured a doctored photo of the incumbent's wife dancing with a black man," and although Helms denied involvement, "a newspaper advertising manager told Helms biographer Ernest Furgurson that Mr. Helms personally cut up the photos." Helms was surely well aware that at the time such incendiary images and innuendoes could lead to the harm of others. The violation or perceived violation of sexual mores in the South, such as interracial intimacy, could result in racial terrorism directed at Black communities, ranging from harassment and threats of physical violence to the bombings of churches, homes, and businesses and lynchings. Emmett Till's heinous murder serves as a powerful example. In his case, the fourteen year old allegedly whistled at a white woman in a rural Mississippi store. Days later, his body was discovered in a river with a cotton gin tied around his neck.

Senator Helms was unabashed in exploiting white resentment and triggering violence. Indeed, it is what made Senator Helms dangerous. Helms once said, "The Negro cannot count forever on the kind of restraint that's thus far left him free to clog the streets, disrupt traffic, and interfere with other men's rights."

Helms grew up in a North Carolina household where his father, Jesse Helms, Sr., served as the local police chief, a position with considerable local power in a racially segregated community in the thick of Jim Crow. In the widely hailed biography of civil rights leader Robert Williams, the historian and biographer Timothy Tyson[8] writes that, as a young child, Williams saw Helms, Sr., punish a Black woman by unmercifully beating and dragging her along concrete to jail with "her dress up over her head." This image and her tortured screams haunted Mr. Williams for the rest of his life.

Senator Helms would come to wield enormous power in Washington, D.C., much like his father had in their small, Southern town of Monroe, North Carolina. However, he held little political regard for women of any race, regardless of their rank. Upon seeing Senator Carol Mosley-Braun (an African American) in an elevator, he commented to fellow Republican senator Orrin Hatch of Utah, "Watch me make her cry. I'm going to make her cry. I'm going to sing 'Dixie' until she cries." According to Chuck Smith, "He then proceeded to sing the song about the good life during slavery."

He expressed a particularly potent disregard for gays and lesbians, once announcing that "homosexuals, lesbians, [are] disgusting people, marching in the streets, demanding all sorts of things, including the right to marry each other." Yet Helms's power and influence went beyond juvenile taunts. He used his political power and influence to block funding for AIDS research. And, as chair of the Senate Foreign Relations Committee, on International Women's Day he once again announced his opposition to the Convention on the Elimination of All Forms of Discrimination Against Women (CEDAW) and effectively stalled its ratification. To this day, the United States is one of only eight nations that has not ratified the CEDAW.

For all of the senator's racism, sexism, and homophobia, he was also a master maneuverer and effective strategist. The Helms amendment bears this out. In the 1970s, just as now, the Senate did not reflect population demographics in the United States; it was overwhelmingly male. It was nearly all white. At the time, no women were among its membership and only two nonwhite members served in the Senate: Senators Edward Brooke of Massachusetts and Joseph M. Montoya of New Mexico. Representative Bella Abzug of New York, one of the few women in Congress at the time, expressed serious concerns regarding inclusion of a restriction on abortion in USAID funding, warning that "[t]he emotional prohibition of abortion is a misuse of the legislative process and of the aid program."[9] She stated, "I regret that the section does seem to place us in the questionable position of imposing on women abroad a restriction recently overturned by our Supreme Court and constitutes a serious interference with the internal affairs of other countries."[10] She was right.

Even the Nixon administration opposed the Helms amendment. Nixon's "U.S. Agency for International Development (USAID) issued a statement to Congress expressing its strong opposition" to the amendment.[11] According to the Guttmacher Institute, "USAID protested that following an era of decolonization, this new restriction was at odds with the fundamental philosophy of U.S. population assistance policy, because of its seemingly imperialistic and hypocritical overtones."[12] USAID officials urged Congress to consider the urgency and value of reproductive healthcare services for poor women and reject the Helms amendment. USAID staffers logically feared that the policy "could amount to a form of coercion" in developing countries.[13] After all, the United States was forging a duplicitous double standard. For women in the United States, abortion was at that time, and continues to be, constitutional and private. This was not the case for poor women living in developing nations – many of which continued to struggle with repugnant vestiges of colonialism, slavery, and imperialism.

The Helms amendment represented a fundamental shift in the Foreign Assistance Act. Helms knew that nations desperate to relieve poverty would likely concede to the coercive demands of the United States. He said, "Foreign countries already understand that assistance is received only if they adhere to reasonable conditions,"[14] which include "social reform" mandated by "the host country."[15] And while the United States typically engaged in soft law practices (economic incentives or sanctions) to advance the rule of law or forge constitutional standards similar to those adopted in the United States, the Helms amendment and its progeny directly broke with that practice.

The new law undermined the foundational principle of foreign aid legislation – namely, to relieve endemic conditions of poverty and aid in the promotion of the rule of law. USAID officials amplified these concerns, explaining that the law "explicitly acknowledges that every nation is and should be free to determine its own policies and procedures with respect to population growth and family planning."[16] They said, "the amendment would place U.S. restrictions on both developing country governments and individuals in the matter of free choice among the means of fertility control . . . that are legal in the U.S."[17]

In an attempt to win votes, Senator Helms claimed that his amendment would benefit poor women in developing nations, because that is what foreign aid does. He denounced skeptics who predicted that the amendment would negatively affect U.S. relationships abroad.[18] As Senator Helms put it, the amendment was a limited proposal,[19] because the United States could be even more aggressive about ending access to abortion in developing countries. He said, "We could, in fact, go far beyond the present amendment and require all abortion activities, from whatever funds, to be stopped before our assistance could be received."[20] Eventually, the United States adopted that approach with the Mexico City Policy (MCP) during the Reagan administration.[21] Given its broad expansion under the Trump administration, the MCP now represents the most regressive foreign aid policy tied to reproductive healthcare of any developed nation.

9.2 THE HELMS AMENDMENT AND ITS PROGENY: HOBBLING RESEARCH

The birth control pill revolutionized family planning, just as long-acting contraceptives – medications to halt ovulation and prevent pregnancies – and even safe hysterectomies did. In reality, research plays a vital role in expanding women's reproductive healthcare options and promoting safety. Without medical research many of the advancements in women's healthcare would not exist. For example, the very existence of Plan B – one of the few medications now available in the United States that inhibit pregnancies after sex, including rape – is the result of medical research. Similarly, medication-based abortion, which can be safely performed at home through the administration of pills, reflects the progress of medical research in recent decades. Imagine, however, if these advancements did not exist due to bans on research. The Helms amendment and its progeny now extend antiabortion restrictions beyond the procedures to include hobbling research, which ultimately negatively impacts women's health and safety.

More than forty years ago, Senator Helms's proposed halt to abortion-related research (as a condition for receiving aid from the U.S. government) failed. That provision failed to garner sufficient votes in 1973, but years later resurfaced in

Senator Joe Biden's amendment to the Foreign Assistance Act of 1961 (FAA). Like the Helms amendment, Senator Biden's legislation also called for bans related to abortion and appears to have been added to the law for "emphasis."[22] Enacted in 1981, the Biden amendment states:

> None of the funds made available to carry out this part may be used to pay for any biomedical research which relates, in whole or in part, to methods of, or the performance of, abortions or involuntary sterilization as a means of family planning.[23]

The Biden amendment extends beyond the FAA and "has also been included in foreign operations appropriations acts."[24] In 2016, during the Obama administration, it was included in the Department of State, Foreign Operations, and Related Programs Appropriations Act and, as such, "applies to all foreign assistance activities authorized by ... [the] FAA," particularly development assistance.[25] Moreover, the language is broad and could be interpreted to ban research related to abortion procedures, fetal tissue research, and technologies associated with ending a pregnancy. Not only do these bans target women, they also undermine the work of the scientific and medical communities.

The Biden amendment's protective aims related to involuntary sterilizations could be lauded, because the history of forced sterilizations under U.S. policies is quite shameful, albeit instructive. On close inspection, this amendment also hurts women, medical research, and ultimately society. Why? Restricting research on abortion essentially means precluding the advancement and enhancement of the medical technologies associated with the procedure, including making it the safest, least invasive, and most efficient and accessible procedure available to women.

Other subsequent amendments further constrain reproductive rights abroad. Like the Helms and Biden amendments, Representative Mark Siljander's amendment bans the use of any federal funds for lobbying "for abortion."[26] Representative Siljander identified himself as part of the so-called silent majority, supported by "morally concerned citizens who are sick of the situation" in the United States.[27] According to *Time* magazine, Siljander championed "the Christian's role in American government."[28] True to his opposition on women's rights, he even publicly criticized President Reagan's nomination of Sandra Day O'Connor to the U.S. Supreme Court, telling reporters that he was "very angry" about her nomination because she lacked a track record on ultraconservative values.[29] Subsequent amendments to the FAA include the Tiahrt amendment (1998) and the Livingston amendment (1986).[30]

The efficacy and goals of these amendments remain an important point of discussion and deserve clarification. For example, the amendments did not stop pregnancy terminations, but dangerously drove abortions underground. Data shows that women who experience violence, including in developing countries, are nearly twice as likely to have an abortion, regardless of the availability of safe abortions.[31]

Adolescent girls in disaster or conflict zones face heightened risks of sexual violence because of increased exposure to coerced sex, early marriage, and forced childbearing.[32] Moreover, while legal abortions, particularly in the West, are very safe, roughly 55 percent of abortions in developing nations are unsafe, and data suggests that, despite a decline in the overall abortion rate, "the proportion of unsafe abortions is on the rise, especially in developing nations."[33]

Mexico City Policy: Undermining Structural Developments in Women's Health

Another setback to women's reproductive rights abroad came in the form of a presidential executive order issued by the Reagan administration in 1984: the Mexico City Policy (MCP), also known as the "global gag rule." This section argues that the MCP is more than a mere temporary financial mandate or mild financial incentive invoked during Republican administrations. To the contrary, the MCP operates in deeply coercive ways that condition speech on cooperation with U.S. financial mandates, ultimately stripping NGOs (working on behalf of women) of speech. Second, it articulates the MCP's longer-term and more devastating effects in undermining women's advancement, including by erecting barriers to building infrastructures that address women's health.

In August 1984, President Reagan announced the MCP at the Second United Nations International Conference on Population in Mexico City.[34] The MCP is referred to as the global gag rule because, in addition to prohibiting NGOs operating in poor countries from using U.S. funds for voluntary abortion services, it prevents those organizations from using their own funds to provide advice or information on a public or private basis.

In this way, the MCP expanded reproductive health restrictions beyond the constraints previously established and policed by the Helms amendment. Under Helms and its progeny, no federal dollars could be used to promote, educate about, provide information on, or fund abortions. The MCP imposes additional restrictions, tethering U.S. funds to other foreign dollars. "While the Helms amendment limits the use of U.S. foreign aid dollars directly, the gag rule went far beyond that by disqualifying foreign NGOs from eligibility for U.S. family planning aid entirely by virtue of their support for abortion-related activities subsidized by non-U.S. funds."[35] The current policy "denie[s] grants to international family-planning organizations for any purpose if they also perform[] abortions or promote[] abortion rights."[36] It mandates that NGOs certify that they will not "perform or actively promote abortion as a method of family planning" using funds from any source, as a condition for receiving funding from the U.S. government.

The MCP asserts that "[a]ttempts to use abortion, involuntary sterilization, or other coercive measures in family planning must be shunned, whether exercised against families within a society or against nations within the family of man ... [and that] the United States does not consider abortion an acceptable element of family planning programs."[37] Further, the policy restricts NGOs' use of funding that relates to:

> 1) procurement or distribution of equipment intended to be used for inducing abortions as a method of family planning; 2) special fees or incentives to women to coerce or motivate them to have abortions; 3) payments to persons to perform abortions or to solicit persons to undergo abortions; 4) information, education, training, or communication programs that seek to promote abortion as a method of family planning; and 5) lobbying for abortion.[38]

An analogy may help to illustrate what this means. Imagine if the federal government conditioned foreign aid to reduce or eliminate HIV/AIDS on NGOs not mentioning the words "sex," "intercourse," "homosexuality," "prostitution," or "sex work." It would be all the more coercive and repugnant if the government went further and prohibited the use of the words "male latex contraceptives," "vaccines," "circumcision," or "antiretroviral therapy (ART)," all of which demonstrably reduce or prevent the spread of HIV/AIDS. And it would be deadly if the government forbade NGOs from using resources from other nations to provide ARTs or condoms. Or imagine if the federal government in its contracts involving de-escalation of terrorism abroad insisted that NGOs, organizations, governments, and subcontractors never mention the words "war," "missiles," "terrorism," "weapons of mass destruction," "refugees," "peace and reconciliation," and the like. It would be impossible for such organizations to effectively carry out their missions. It would be even worse if the United States barred such organizations from using funds from other allied nations to advance antiterrorism efforts.

Ironically, President Reagan cited the United Nations Declaration of the Rights of the Child as the foundation for the law. He claimed that because the Declaration of the Rights of the Child "calls for legal protection for children before birth as well as after birth ... the United States does not consider abortion an acceptable element of family planning programs and will no longer contribute to those of which it is a part." Ironically, the United States has never ratified the Convention on the Rights of the Child.[39] Today, it remains the only nation to reject even the symbolic value of embracing a doctrine that establishes rights for living, born children. As one commentator recently wrote, "The United States can learn from other member nations on how to reduce poverty, ensure women's rights, improve education and educational access, and healthy living conditions, for starters."[40]

After the Reagan presidency, each Republican President has implemented the MCP through executive action, while every Democratic President, including Presidents Clinton and Obama, rescinded the policy.[41] President Clinton repealed the MCP on his first day in office. In a memorandum, he wrote that the MCP "undermined efforts to promote safe and efficacious family planning programs in foreign nations."[42] President Clinton directed USAID to remove all conditions "not explicitly mandated by the Foreign Assistance Act or any other law" from current and future grants.[43]

Arguably, to a significant degree, women's reproductive health in developing countries has been determined by a stroke of a pen – in the United States. The consequence is a dramatic and arbitrary contraction and diminution of access to and provision of healthcare at the turn of an administration. As healthcare options diminish for poor women in Africa, Asia, Central America, and South America, harmful impacts expand – not only for pregnant women but also their children, especially with regard to rape, incest, and miscarriages.[44]

Indeed, U.S. policy has undermined the creation of vital reproductive health infrastructures and resulted in the full-scale ban of abortion and, sometimes, difficulties in obtaining contraception. In some developing countries that receive U.S. foreign aid, abortion is simply illegal and criminalized even in cases of rape and incest. Not surprisingly, then, in countries like El Salvador and Nicaragua, miscarriages are treated with suspicion and can lead to arrest and incarceration.[45]

The devastating report published by the Los Angeles Times in 2015 highlighted cases of rape victims jailed in El Salvador after miscarriages and stillbirths, cruelly handcuffed to hospital beds, and then carted off to jail.[46] The journalist investigating the story also uncovered a particularly disturbing case of a teenager sentenced to thirty years in prison after experiencing a miscarriage.[47] In that case, like many others, she was a rape victim.[48]

As antiabortion politics play out strategically in the United States through policies like the MCP and the Helms amendment, nations come to adjust to those economic conditions by curtailing reproductive access and failing to build vital and safe infrastructures for reproductive health. The MCP is particularly pernicious as it applies to the application of non-U.S. aid. At the structural level, it imposes significant disincentives to build reproductive healthcare infrastructure. Thus, even with the revocation of the MCP, during democratic administrations, reproductive healthcare facilities in some nations that receive U.S. foreign assistance remain woefully underdeveloped, contributing to the notion that women's healthcare rights are more illusory than real under Republican administrations.

To better understand why women's rights organizations strongly oppose U.S. foreign policy on reproductive healthcare, consider the inconstant nature of that policy. The global gag rule was first revoked by President Clinton and then reinstated by President George W. Bush. President Bush expanded the scope of the MCP from USAID funding to all population planning assistance by any agency, bureau, or office President Barack Obama[49] rescinded the policy, and it was later reinstated by President Donald J. Trump almost immediately after his inauguration.[50]

Furthermore, when President Trump reinstated the global gag rule, his administration expanded its scope to include "global health assistance furnished by all departments or agencies."[51] Trump wrote, "I further direct the Secretary of State to take all necessary actions" to carry out the order.[52] This means that the global gag rule "will apply to assistance provided by USAID, the Department of State, and the Department of Health and Human Services (principally the National Institutes of Health and the Centers for Disease Control and Prevention)."[53] As one human rights organization advocating on behalf of girls and women describes:

> Foreign NGOs receiving U.S. government health assistance for family planning, maternal and child health, nutrition, HIV/AIDS (including PEPFAR), infectious diseases, malaria, tuberculosis, and neglected tropical diseases, will now be required to certify that the organization does not provide abortion services, counsel or refer for abortion, or advocate for the liberalization of abortion laws with non-U.S. funds as a condition of receiving assistance from the U.S. government.[54]

The monetary impact of the MCP under the Trump administration "means that more than 16 times the amount of funding may be impacted than if [the global gag rule] was applied only to bilateral family planning assistance."[55] In raw numbers, groups estimate that previous levels of aid amounting to roughly $575 million could be exponentially multiplied to $9.5 billion "for global health assistance, government-wide."[56]

And, while neither President Clinton nor President Obama made any substantive changes to the MCP other than rescinding it during their terms in office, the cast was set. During both administrations, women in developing countries where U.S. aid is distributed experienced high rates of unintended pregnancies. Some suffered and died from abortions performed under perilous and often unsanitary conditions and others endured significant rates of infant mortality. Sadly, maternal mortality remains a glaring problem, both domestically and abroad.

By imposing broad restrictions on funding for foreign NGOs, the MCP effectively forces organizations to choose to accept funding to provide essential health services with restrictions that can jeopardize the health of their patients, or reject the policy and lose a major source of financial support. The Helms amendment and the global gag rule belie the foundational principles and values on which the rule of law is founded. In essence, the funding exacerbates inequalities, distributing and suppressing rights according to social status. Ultimately, the U.S. antiabortion campaigns abroad undermine women's autonomy, as well as that of the governments and NGOs impacted by its policies.

In fact, the Center for Health and Gender Equity reports that

> [d]ocumentation and analysis of the impact of the global gag rule has shown that the policy restricts a basic right to speech and the right to make informed health decisions, as well as harms the health and lives of poor women by making it more difficult to access family planning services. It has also been found that the policy does not reduce abortion.[57]

Given its scope and scale, the Trump version of the MCP threatens women's health in far deeper and broader ways than previous versions. Under Trump, agencies and departments that receive direct appropriations for global health include:

1) the Department of State (including the Office of the Global AIDS Coordinator, which oversees and coordinates U.S. global HIV funding under the President's Emergency Plan for AIDS Relief (PEPFAR));

2) two operating divisions of the Department of Health and Human Services: Centers for Disease Control ("CDC"), the Food and Drug Administration ("FDA") and the National Institutes of Health ("NIH"); and

3) the Department of Defense ("DoD").[58]

Arguably, the restrictions on funding applied to subrecipients of USAID and others effectively impose similar restrictions on U.S. NGOs.[59] Some advocates stress that loopholes exist in the law to permit some limited consultations on abortion.[60] For example, they stress that where legal abortions were available pre-MCP, USAID's funding restrictions allow foreign NGOs to passively respond to a question about where a safe and legal abortion may be obtained.[61] Even so, there are conditions relating to the manner of the question and the status of the women.[62] That is, an NGO may "passively" respond if the question is asked by a woman meeting the following criteria: (a) the woman is already pregnant; (b) she clearly states she has already decided to have a legal abortion; and (c) the family planning counselor reasonably believes that the medical ethics of the country requires a response to where an abortion may be safely obtained.[63] In reality, however, U.S. foreign policy has contributed to nations having a negative view of abortion and, at worst, criminalizing the procedure.

Decades after the Helms amendment and MCP became law, unsafe, illegal abortions continue to be performed in developing countries receiving U.S. aid. In other words, the laws failed to reduce the incidence of abortion. After all, women continue to have abortions and some NGOs refuse to receive U.S. government aid in order to provide urgent care to girls and women who need it most, including in cases of rape, incest, and to save women's lives.

In many ways, however, the Helms amendment and the MCP also represent five enormous victories for antiabortion forces in the United States. First, Congress and a succession of Republican Presidents successfully politicized abortion to the degree that some nations continue to outlaw the practice, despite the safety of legal abortions. Second, abortion continues to be stigmatized in developing countries (and the United States) to such a degree that even where it may be legal, women are discouraged from seeking or obtaining them, even in life-threatening situations. Third, NGOs that receive U.S. government funds do not offer any information, counseling, or abortion-related services. Moreover, many of the NGOs that rejected U.S. aid have been shuttered and disbanded, unable to meet the needs of women who so desperately require their services. Fourth, the United States has effectively restricted the speech of poor women of color in developing countries, even though domestically such restraints would not be acceptable under U.S. law. Fifth, the United States has succeeded in creating a culture of punishment, fear, and shame for pregnant girls and women who seek abortions. Given these effects, it is not surprising that abortion services in developing countries are primarily underground, often illegal, and frequently unsafe.

Earlier parts of this Chapter addressed the laws that govern foreign aid policy and that determine rules on the ground concerning information about and access to women's reproductive healthcare. next section addresses the costs of this policy abroad, including maternal mortality due to unsafe, illegal abortions, criminalization of abortion, and the real-life tragedies of women and girls. It also casts light on the discriminatory effects of seemingly neutral policies.

9.3 AGGRAVATING THE EFFECTS OF RAPE, WAR, AND DISASTER

Forced sex is one key contributing factor to high rates of unwanted pregnancies in developing countries. In some nations, rape does not exist in the vocabulary. And even where rape exists in the local nomenclature, it may apply only between strangers, but not between husband and wife. In Afghanistan, for example, the word rape lacks the significance and meaning attributed to it in many other parts of the world:

> There are no words for "rape" either in Dari or in Pashto. The phrase "sexual attack" (*tajawuz-e jensi*) is used but not in the context of marital rape. To an Afghan raping one's wife is nonsense. Men do "it" whenever they feel like. It does not matter whether she likes it or not. If a wife went to court and complained, the judge would laugh and tell her not to make a fool of herself. For the same reason, Pashto and Dari have no word for "foreplay." This is because females are perceived as property and sex objects for the pleasure of men.[64]

Ironically, sometimes states' efforts to address ending violence against women and girls further undermine their sexual and reproductive security. Consider a 2009 Afghan law on the elimination of violence against women. The law does not clearly differentiate between rape and adultery, both of which the government considers crimes. As an unfortunate result, rape victims have actually been accused of and criminally charged for committing adultery, which is a punishable offense. Activists and civil society organizations strive to "remove the concept of 'adultery' from the definition of rape;" however, these notions of female (victims') culpability in sexual violence remain deeply entrenched in cultural, and now legal, understandings.[65]

The consequences of such policies speak for themselves. According to one news account, authorities in Afghanistan charged a sixteen-year-old rape victim with "'adultery by force' – a 'crime' that carried a 12-year jail sentence."[66] Subsequently, the girl became pregnant and gave birth in prison. According to a prominent NGO in the region, Women for Afghan Women (WAW), 90 percent of their clients were survivors of violence. Their "clients have been raped, sold, beaten, starved and mutilated – primarily at the hands of a family member, or in some cases, multiple family members." Afghanistan receives significant USAID resources, but the American government has been notoriously silent about child rape and pregnancies in Afghanistan.[67]

The problem for marginalized women and girls in developing nations is that local laws may not address their suffering, even when they encounter extreme sexual victimization. Women and girls may be subject to sexual violence at home and in society. Sexual violence and rapes are exacerbated during conflict; rape is a horrific spoil of war – which governments do too little to change.

Although accurate information about the incidences of rape is especially difficult to obtain in conflict zones, researchers and aid workers confirm high occurrences. Compelling research exists that documents the use of rape as a weapon and tactic of war in at least thirty-six different conflicts.[68] Researchers and NGOs estimate that between 250,000 and 500,000 girls and women suffered rapes during the 100-day Rwandan genocide.[69] They report that the West Pakistan army raped 200,000 Bangladeshi women in 1971.[70] Approximately 20,000 children in Rwanda and 25,000 children in Bangladesh were born as a result of the aforementioned rapes.[71] In the conflict between Bosnians, Croatians, and Serbs in the former Yugoslavia, the Trial Chamber of the International Criminal Tribunal for the Former Yugoslavia found camps "specially devoted to rape, with the aim of forcing the birth of Serbian offspring."[72]

In the abstract, the concerns over foreign women and girls articulated in this Chapter may be more difficult to grasp in the United States or even in the developing nations. For example, the local government's response to a recent case in Paraguay is not atypical: "We're totally against interrupting the pregnancy . . .. The girl is getting assistance permanently in a shelter and the pregnancy is progressing normally without a problem."[73] In that case, government officials ordered the eleven-year-old to undergo a cesarean section and then placed her in a shelter for troubled and difficult youths. The victim's stepfather had raped her. However, such cases, particularly involving rape and incest of little girls and teenagers, occur with far greater frequency than described in legal scholarship.

Ultimately, the consequences of restrictive health services can be deadly. In Latin America, girls under sixteen suffer maternal death at a rate that is "four times higher" than that of older women.[74] According to the United Nations, annually "an estimated 70,000 adolescents in developing countries [die] from complications related to pregnancy and childbirth."[75] The European Parliament, which commissioned a study on this issue, reports that "[s]exual violence against minors is a major problem in Latin America."[76] The study's authors concluded that girls are at risk not only at home but also at school and within the larger community.[77] High rates of physical and sexual violence against girls can (and often does) continue into adulthood: "46.3% of Ecuadorian and 70% of Peruvian women experience physical, sexual and/or emotional violence in their lifetime."[78]

Data shows that women living through such conditions are nearly twice as likely as other women to obtain abortions, regardless of the availability of safe abortions. Data also shows that adolescent girls in disaster or conflict zones faced a heightened risk of sexual violence because of their increased exposure to coerced sex, as well as early and forced marriage and childbearing. However, these conditions of war, including rape and sexual assault of girls and women, occur with such frequency that they should not escape lawmakers' attention. If the poor women who suffer such fates abroad lived in the United States, federal dollars would pay for their abortions as they arise in cases of rape. Thus, what does the United States' silence on these issues signify to governments abroad?

According to the WHO, a legal abortion is as safe as a penicillin shot.[79] Clearly, the same is not true of illegal, criminal abortions, which the organization considers "unsafe." That is, an "unsafe abortion" occurs when "terminat[ion] [of] an unintended pregnancy [is] carried out either by persons lacking the necessary skills or in an environment that does not conform to minimal medical standards, or both."[80] Obtaining accurate data for abortions is challenging, even more so for unsafe abortions, and many abortions are undocumented. However, researchers attribute 13 percent of worldwide maternal mortality to unsafe abortions.

In raw numbers, each year nearly 20 million unsafe abortions take place.[81] And while nearly 3 percent of abortions in Western nations are unsafe, 55 percent of abortions in developing nations are unsafe. Further, empirical research shows that, despite a decline in the overall abortion rate, the proportion of unsafe abortions is rising, especially in developing nations. At the very least, the impact of the Helms amendment is the loss of opportunity for the United States – the largest bilateral donor for family planning and reproductive health programs globally – to save millions of lives.

On the one hand, the Helms amendment and the MCP result in less accessible legal abortions in developing countries that receive foreign aid from the United States. On the other hand, women in developing countries continue to terminate their pregnancies – albeit under unsafe conditions and mostly illegal circumstances, driven underground by these policies. Very likely, these policies will never end abortions, but their being driven underground puts women's lives at greater risk.

For example, a study of reproductive outcomes for women in Ghana between 1972 and 2007 showed that while the MCP was in effect, there was no reduction in the use of abortions in urban areas, but there was a substantially larger reduction in rural areas.[82] Similarly, a 2011 study of twenty countries by Bendavid, Avila, and Miller showed that in the period between 1994 and 2008 the induced abortion rate *rose* while the MCP was in effect.[83] Countries with high exposure to the MCP experienced sharp increases in abortions after the MCP was reinstated in 2001 during the Bush administration. Very likely, this is because NGOs that provide holistic women's healthcare, including counseling and contraception, are negatively impacted by Helms and the MCP, resulting in closures.

Furthermore, women living in countries with high exposure to the MCP were more than three times likely to have an induced abortion after the MCP was reinstated than during the period from 1994 to 2000 (when the MCP was not in effect) or than women living in less exposed countries.[84]

These policies also impact contraceptive use. The Bendavid, Avila, and Miller study also showed that the use of contraceptives declined in high-exposure countries while the MCP was in effect.[85] Consistently, the data reported lower prevalence of contraceptives usage in high-exposure countries than in low-exposure countries. In other words, the research revealed that U.S. policies produced perverse effects on reproductive health. Similarly, a 2015 study conducted by the International Food Policy Institute (IFPI) demonstrated an overall reduction in the availability of contraceptives in Ghana while the MCP was in effect.[86] Likewise, Population Action International (PAI) reported that by 2002 family planning associations in sixteen developing countries no longer received USAID-donated contraceptives because they declined to sign the policy.[87]

Taken together, the Helms amendment and the MCP place NGOs and nations in a difficult position. If they forego U.S. funding, they risk crippling access to and development of urgent resources. Yet, by accepting U.S. foreign aid funding, including the attendant conditions, they could contribute to the unnecessary and preventable deaths of girls and women in the country.

9.4 CONCLUSION

Some of the most dangerous international reproductive health policies can be tied to Senator Helms, a Southern segregationist notorious for his lifelong racism, sexism, and homophobia. Of course, he alone is not responsible for the amendment that bears his name, which conditions foreign aid on abortion policies. He was one man, with one vote. Rather, the complicity and duplicity of an overwhelmingly male, nearly all-white senate was persuaded by his coercive agenda.

Senator Helms feigned an interest in the lives of poor women abroad, cautioning that USAID funding practices potentially targeted them as abortion research subjects. Yet, as history demonstrates, Senator Helms theatrically and vehemently opposed legislation and international protocols of all kinds to advance women's equality and safety domestically and abroad. He was not a sympathizer of women's health, rights, or safety.

Senator Helms claimed foreign aid for abortion research abroad was a ruse and underhanded strategy for abortion proponents in the United States to perfect the technology abroad and then make it domestically available. According to him,

USAID funds were simply "the guise" for an "alleged" benefit to foreign nations. Helms claimed that after effective and safe abortion techniques were developed abroad, those technologies would come to the United States. And while that might have been true, abortion was already legal in the United States. If anything, Helms undermined research efforts to make contraception and abortion safer and more effective.

In this context, Senator Helms was likely less concerned with women abroad serving as research subjects for American interests than he was focused on denying women throughout the world the right to govern their bodies. As Nina Crimm writes, "having failed domestically to legislatively reverse the impact of *Roe v. Wade*, pro-life groups took a path of lesser resistance and partially derailed the momentum of U.S.-supported international population assistance," by enlisting the help of Senator Jesse Helms, a staunch, "ultra-conservative," Southern Baptist.[88]

The Helms amendment catalyzed the promulgation of federal antiabortion policy directed at developing countries and nongovernmental organizations (NGOs) serving those nations. It was simply the first in a wave of problematic U.S. foreign policies related to abortion. Helms demonstrated that legislation could be a powerful weapon against reproductive rights. By 1974, "despite President Nixon's strong support for global population programs, USAID created policy ... against providing U.S. funding for 'information, education, training, or communication programs that seek to promote abortion as a method of family planning.'"[89]

10

Lessons for Law and Society: A Reproductive Justice New Deal or Bill of Rights

Throughout the process of writing this book, I struggled to understand what accounts for this period of policing the womb, the vileness directed at women, and the various indignities cast upon indigent women by the state. I filled notepad after notepad with names and stories. Among the many disturbing narratives was that of twelve women sodomized and raped by police officer Daniel Holtzclaw, who literally policed and terrorized their bodies. He raped one of his victims while she was handcuffed to a hospital bed. She testified that she had to think about survival while he raped her. Another victim was underage.

According to the lawsuits, "Holtzclaw's actions were part of a common pattern and practice of sexually assaulting middle-age African-American females whom he identified as vulnerable to his sexual abuse and whom he believed would either be reluctant or unwilling to come forward or who would not be believed if they did come forward."[1] These women were not policed because of pregnancy or the potential to become pregnant, but because of their race, poverty, and sex. It is these very biases – poverty, sex, and race – that motivate reproductive policing.

On the one hand, this is nothing new; Black women experienced reproductive horrors during chattel slavery, and in many cases their reproductive rights barely improved during Jim Crow, when eugenics policies resulted in coercive state sterilizations. Dr. Marion Sims notoriously lacerated, punctured, and then sutured the uteruses of the enslaved women he kept at his home. He regularly tortured Black women he rented as human research subjects, nightly lacerating their wombs and conducting experiments, denying them anesthesia in the process. He was doubtful of their ability to experience pain. Today he is hailed for his research. Until recently a statue of him adorned Central Park in New York City.

Black women continued to endure humiliating policing into the 1980s and 1990s, during the height of the crack phase of the drug war. So, was this new, or simply a newer iteration of something old, amorphous, and malleable, which had simply taken another shape? Is there something different about the robust lawmaking at the state level to both eviscerate abortion access and punish women if they endanger their pregnancies? Anthony Romero, the executive director of the American Civil Liberties Union, sees it like this: "Politicians are smart political animals; they gain political points by being hostile to abortion and win elections. . . . [Whether] conservative Republicans or moderate Democrats, [politicians] can curry political favor by being antichoice."[2]

For all the thoughtful first and second wave feminist legal theory, robust attention to constitutional doctrine, and refinement of legal theory related to pornography, work, capacity, assisted reproduction, domestic labor, and marriage, few legal scholars explored the early emergence of this new wave of hostility toward women's reproductive health and rights, which took the form of states' policing the womb through fetal protection laws. Dorothy Roberts, April Cherry, and Linda Fentiman were among the exceptions. They wrote brilliant works, building a platform for legal thought related to criminalization, confinement, illicit drug use, privacy, and equality. Their works and the scholarship of Lori Andrews have been foundational to my thinking about these issues over the past two decades.[3]

In this Chapter, I consider what lessons can be learned and pathways forward. The reproductive battleground was once in the courts, where incremental advancements through landmark decisions were achieved. *Skinner v. Oklahoma* (overturning a compulsory sterilization law that treated similar crimes differently), *Griswold v. Connecticut* (overturning a Connecticut law that barred married couples from accessing contraceptives), *Eisenstadt v. Baird* (striking down a Massachusetts law that restricted nonmarried persons from accessing contraceptives), and *Roe v. Wade* (decriminalizing doctors' performing abortions) formed the foundation for the reproductive rights discourse, advancing concepts such as privacy and autonomy in the reproductive health space.

However, recent retreats from the primacy of those holdings by the United States Supreme Court suggest that, at least for the present time, the Court may gerrymander reproductive rights and weaponize the First Amendment to advance the personal views of five conservative male Justices of the Court. Drawing on the brilliant contributions of scholars, civil society, activists, a bold new cohort of female legislators at the state and federal levels, and the intuitions of judges committed to the equality of women, this Chapter concludes that a Reproductive Justice Bill of Rights is needed and that new pathways in litigation must involve an equal protection analysis.

10.1 A REPRODUCTIVE JUSTICE BILL OF RIGHTS

The concerns addressed in this book were occupying not only my thoughts but also the thoughts of others, and I needed to speak with them, too. In the late fall of 2013, I had tea with Carol Gilligan in her top-floor office off a narrow corridor in the New York University Law School. Best known for her groundbreaking book, *In a Different Voice*, Gilligan is credited with forging new ways of understanding the psychology of girls, women, boys, and men. Her work was so influential that *Time* magazine named her as one of the twenty-five most influential Americans in 1996. By the time we met she had left Harvard, where she taught for thirty years, and was a university professor at NYU, with an appointment at the law school.

I wondered how she understood the hyperintensive work – legislating really – taking place in male-dominated legislatures throughout the country. Sure, Barack Obama was the President at the time and just the year before had been reelected for a second term. However, in state houses across the country a new group, known as the "Tea Party," swept into office. They were catalyzing their own movement. They protested healthcare mandates, arguing that the government should not force individuals to maintain health coverage. They ushered in new laws that undermined voting rights and committed themselves to platforms of gerrymandering. In the reproductive health space, they proposed and enacted more antiabortion laws than had ever been seen at any time. They were also pushing back against federal legislators concerned about gun control and climate change. By the power of their surge into office, they carried significant influence among white voters. Gilligan's response was that much of this amounted to an effort "to restore patriarchal order."[4] She explained that it was simply "crazy-making" and that the new crop of legislators "should be hysterical about education, equality, climate" but instead were preoccupied with gay marriage and women's progress.

To that end, she described this period as a "last gasp of patriarchy." In her view, these are "dangerous" times, and the reproductive policing tactics described here and elsewhere are simply "desperate attempts" to hold on to power and white women are key to that, because married white women are more likely to feel pressured to accommodate their husbands' interests. In her view, married "women became disassociated from their bodies." Single women, however, are a threat to patriarchy, because of their independence. The patriarchy fights back through "control of women's sexuality." This, Gilligan predicted, "would be their move." On the one hand, the move was already taking shape. On the other, in the few years since my time with Carol Gilligan, states have introduced legislation seeking to ban abortion before a woman would even know that she is pregnant, and state courts have issued rulings granting fetuses rights. Seemingly, more is yet to come.

A connection can be made between this modern maternal policing, aimed at "perfecting" women's conduct during pregnancy so that they deliver "perfected" offspring to the state and their families, and the old reproductive policing of eugenics. Legislatures in Georgia, California, and North Carolina are now revisiting their legislative complicity in the legalized terror of forced sterilizations carried out in their states years ago in the name of promoting racial purity and intellectual "fitness." Feminist jurisprudence urgently needs a robust narrative that, bridging the gap between sex, race, and status, will provide a more dynamic and accurate account of the implementation of fetal protection law and the exercise of state violence against pregnant women. This gap filling has long been called for and is the foundational commitment of reproductive justice.

When I interviewed Loretta Ross shortly before Thanksgiving, during the late fall in 2014, she warned that "obviously the womb and reproduction are central, but [they are] not the only [pathway] to eugenics, particularly in the twenty-first century. There are so many diverse ways of manipulating and controlling populations. This is where the reproductive justice analysis comes in."[5] Ms. Ross is one of the original framers of "reproductive justice," both as a term and a movement. Although her formal credentials include cofounder and former national coordinator of the SisterSong Women of Color Reproductive Justice Collective from 2005 to 2012, she was a key pilot in the reproductive justice arena long before. As she explained, these are deeply troubling times.

To her, the reproductive policing occurring throughout the United States is not just about the state attempting to control the reproductive health of individual women. She said it is part of "a continual ideology of white supremacy and patriarchy" and that "[women of color] are the roadkill on the pathway to policing white women's pregnancies." People who are not aware of the hundreds of women in Alabama arrested for endangering their fetuses and the many other cases and stories documented in this book might find her comments alarming or alarmist. Ms. Ross explained though that the criminalization policies and practices on the upswing in the United States are not about increasing the number of Black babies.

Maybe she is right. Legislators, however, claim that their only purpose is promoting a safe and healthy environment for the "unborn" in their states. "I will take a dystopian view," Ms. Ross admitted. "I bridge the feminist world and the science fiction world . . .. *The Handmaids Tale* was like a gift to me." In her view, "rather than 'fitter families' being voluntary, it is going to become compulsory." In saying this, she evokes the horrid, largely forgotten practices of eugenics in the United States, where over 60,000 people were forcibly sterilized, including little girls. In the South, when Black girls were forcibly sterilized, doctors referred to the practice as "Mississippi appendectomies." Only years later did the women understand the extent of the grave injustices carried out on their bodies.

The points Loretta Ross make are worth close attention, even if they might seem unimaginable. After all, the United States now leads the developed world in maternal and infant mortality – while promoting criminal polices and interventions that claim to support women's health. On multiple reproductive health matrixes, the United States currently fails its women and girls. More girls in the United States will become infected with sexually transmitted diseases than in any other so-called first world nation. American girls are also the least likely among their cohorts to be educated about their bodies and sex, particularly in the aftermath of states gutting their sex education programs in recent years. These young women are also more likely than their peers in Europe (and some developing nations) to experience unintended and unwanted pregnancies. So, I asked Ms. Ross, Why did she believe that a reproductive justice framework matters?

Without pause, she explained that reproductive justice matters "because in reproductive justice we believe that the ability of any individual to make any decision about their reproduction or bodies is directly tied to the communities in which they are embedded." That is, if you are in a community that is experiencing immigration raids, that will influence whether you should be pregnant at a certain time; or if you are in a community that lacks healthcare, that will influence whether you choose to keep the baby or not."

And the future? Ross and others believe it involves resistance. What form that resistance takes matters, because these are not issues in the abstract or lofty considerations for the purpose of legal study. In fact, the questions related to what comes next and future legal strategies are not abstract. Even one day in prison can be cruel and unusual punishment for the person who should not be there.[6] But what is the platform for resistance? How should it take shape?

An important aspect of my thinking builds on a framework offered by Professor Monica McLemore, whose leadership in the reproductive health and justice discourse is unmatched in productivity, creative vision, and concern for the underserved.[7] Professor McLemore strikes an important chord in urging for a new deal; in addressing maternal mortality and reproductive health concerns, she argues that pathways forward "require a bold approach similar to the New Deal." She asks what might that look like and offers important suggestions such as universal health coverage, a basic minimum income, paid family leave, mandated maternity coverage, full funding of Title X, and more.

Professor McLemore's important interventions complement the on-the-ground movement building and care being provided by organizations that attempt to educate the most vulnerable as well as the legislators who hold the keys to their futures – organizations like SisterSong, Black Mamas Matter Alliance, the Black Women's Health Imperative, and National Latina Institute for Reproductive Health, to name but a few. Unlike the ACLU or National Advocates for Pregnant Women, these organizations do not litigate per se, but they do work toward providing vulnerable women with access to basic and reproductive healthcare. They defend the interests of indigent and immigrant women before legislators and the broader public. At the heart of their work is their embrace of the reproductive justice model, which demands looking beyond rights and abortion discourse to underscore the value and relevance of a "whole woman" or "whole person" reproductive health framework.

In other words, women are more than the children they decide to have or the pregnancies they experience. This would of course include thinking about the right of immigrant women not to be separated from their babies and children at the borders when seeking asylum in the United States. Addressing the full spectrum of a woman's life and decision-making includes taking serious account of women's lived lives. It is with this understanding that a Reproductive Justice Bill of Rights is overdue.

A Reproductive Justice Bill of Rights begs considerations of baselines, floors, and ceilings. When conservatives criticized Franklin Roosevelt's New Deal policies, so too did progressive Louisiana senator Huey Long. Conservatives claimed that the New Deal amounted to excessive interventionism and that it was time to "dismantle the machinery" and end or dramatically scale back the welfare state, while Long argued that the New Deal did not go far enough in advancing equality for all citizens. He recommended a "Share Our Wealth" program, which would "provide a decent standard of living to all Americans by spreading the nation's wealth among the people."[8]

A Reproductive Justice Bill of Rights takes into account that policing of this sort does not happen in isolation from social, political, cultural, and economic institutions. To that end, a few key platforms should include certain key tenets. Here is what I imagine to address the vulnerability of women's personhood – the state's recognition of her right of self-determination. The Reproductive Justice Bill of Rights does not use the universal "person" because it lacks emphasis on the specific subordination of women. Despite guarantees of "equality for all," women remain locked out. Importantly, this platform includes concern for transgender women as well. What might such a platform contain?

Article I: The personhood of all women shall not be denied or abridged by the United States or by any state on account of sex; the personhood of a woman shall at all times take priority in all matters, including concerns related to her health and dignity.

Article II: A woman's right to bodily autonomy, privacy, and equality under law shall not be denied or abridged by the United States or by any state on account of sex; the right to bodily autonomy shall include the right to decide if, when, how, or not to procreate.

Article III: Reproductive self-determination shall not be denied or abridged by the United States or by any state on account of sex.

Article IV: Equality of rights under the law shall not be denied or abridged by the United States or by any state on account of sex.

Article V: A woman's right to speech shall not be denied or abridged by the United States or by any state on the basis of sex; speech shall not be imposed by the United States or any state on the basis of sex; the right to assemble peaceably shall not be denied or abridged by the United States or any state on account of sex.

Article VI: In all criminal and civil prosecutions, the accused shall enjoy the right to a speedy and public trial, by an impartial jury of the state and district wherein the offense has been committed, and to be informed of the nature and cause of the accusation; to be confronted with the witnesses against her; to have compulsory process for obtaining witnesses in her favor, and to have the assistance of counsel for her defense.

Article VII: Excessive bail shall not be required, nor excessive fines imposed, nor cruel and unusual punishments on account of sex.

Article VIII: Drug rehabilitation services shall be provided and not denied or abridged by the United States or by any state.

A Reproductive Justice Bill of Rights is at least conceptually necessary, if not an actual federal or model document to safeguard reproductive civil liberties and protect vulnerable persons from encroachments and discrimination carried out by the state. It might actually save lives.

10.2 THE COURTS

How exactly might reproductive rights meet an end? This was not a plausible question in 1973, when the U.S. Supreme Court, in a 7–2 decision, decriminalized abortion and articulated that the constitutional right to privacy and autonomy extended to a woman's right to decide whether to end a pregnancy. Justice Blackmun wrote: "Our task, of course, is to resolve the issue by constitutional measurement, free of emotion and of predilection." Because of this, the Court "inquired into, and ... place[d] some emphasis upon, medical and medical-legal history," to uncover public opinion about abortion over time. In canvassing that history, Justice Blackmun surmised that restrictive criminal abortion laws in effect at the time, like today, were mostly of "relatively recent vintage." These laws, prohibiting abortion outright or at particular times during a pregnancy (except to preserve a pregnant woman's life) were "not of ancient or even common law origin." Instead, like now, those laws derived from legislative platforms expressly rooted in dogmas on vice or morality, primarily articulated by men.

However, *Roe* represents more than the establishment of an abortion right. The Court reaffirmed the principle that "a right of personal privacy, or a guarantee of certain areas or zones of privacy ... exist under the Constitution." This was not a new concept. Rather, the roots of this principle, had been located by the Court or individual Justices in the First, Fourth, and Fifth Amendments, as well as in the penumbras of the Bill of Rights, in the Ninth Amendment, and as a concept of liberty guaranteed by the Fourteenth Amendment. Justice Blackmun concluded that a line of Supreme Court cases offered clarity that "only personal rights that can be deemed 'fundamental'" are included in the Constitution's guarantee of personal privacy. The Court compared this fundamental right with the privacy rights articulated in *Skinner v. Oklahoma* in relation to procreation, *Eisenstadt v. Baird* in relation to access to contraception, and *Loving* in relation to activities regarding marriage.

And yet, since his inauguration, President Trump has nominated and the United States Senate has confirmed 152 federal judges, including 43 judges to the United States Courts of Appeals and two to the United States Supreme Court. That's one in four federal courts of appeals judges appointed by President Trump. Beyond any doubt, women's reproductive healthcare is in serious jeopardy domestically and abroad due to federal and state policies promulgated by lawmakers in the United States. Shortly after taking office, President Donald Trump issued an executive order reinstating and expanding the Mexico City Policy, which literally silences medical providers abroad from speaking about certain reproductive healthcare options, including abortion, for women and girls in nations receiving USAID funds.[9] Activists refer to the Mexico City Policy as the "global gag rule" because, in addition to prohibiting nongovernmental organizations from utilizing U.S. funds for voluntary abortion services, it prevents organizations from using their own funds to provide advice or information on both a public and a private basis.

A more optimistic view might caution against such concerns, urging that a President can wield only so much power and noting that Mr. Trump has vacillated on a number of issues. Who knows exactly what he will do? What can he do? After all, what role will Congress play? The President alone cannot undue constitutional protections for reproductive healthcare, right? What about state legislatures? Surely reproductive healthcare access is safe at the state level, where the costs of unintended pregnancies, HIV transmission, and Medicaid-funded births are the types of public health and fiscal concerns that should forge greater reproductive healthcare access, no?

However, Mr. Trump's campaign promises to shape a Supreme Court that will overturn *Roe v. Wade*, the decision upon which abortion rights are founded, and his commitment to appointing only Justices hostile to reproductive rights should be taken seriously. The President wields enormous power in appointing Justices to the Supreme Court and the federal bench more broadly. Indeed, Mr. Trump's appointment of Justices Brett Kavanaugh and Neil Gorsuch, staunch reproductive rights opponents, to replace Justices Anthony Kennedy and Antonin Scalia, respectively, underscore the strength of Mr. Trump's antiabortion commitments and the vulnerability of reproductive healthcare rights in the United States.

First, in Justice Gorsuch, President Trump added to the Supreme Court a member with a judicial record replete with hostility toward women's contraceptive access, the funding of Planned Parenthood, women's privacy rights, and pregnancy rights.[10] Justice Gorsuch's record on women's rights as a judge on the Tenth Circuit Court of Appeals causes deep alarm and likely foreshadows his Supreme Court jurisprudence.[11] With Justice Kavanaugh's appointment, the Court adds a jurist who shortly before his appointment supported the government in its unconstitutional effort to block an immigrant girl from terminating her pregnancy in *Garza v. Hargan*.[12]

In that case, Justice Kavanaugh – then a judge of the District of Columbia Court of Appeals – dissented from the majority opinion, erroneously claiming that the court was expanding constitutional principles by permitting "immediate abortion on demand" for "unlawful immigrant minors." Kavanaugh's sweeping dissent was both disingenuous and alarming. As Judge Millet, who wrote for the majority, pointed out, Jane Doe, the minor in question, had already satisfied each of the state's preapproval procedures and "under binding Supreme Court precedent [could] choose to terminate her pregnancy."[3] In 1979, the Supreme Court expressly affirmed a minor's right to terminate a pregnancy in *Bellotti v. Baird*. Simply put, Jane Doe's status as an immigrant surely could not signify that her body was no longer her own. Perhaps most troubling about Justice Kavanaugh's lower court dissent was its erring toward punishment. After all, there was no question as to whether the constitutional right extended to Jane Doe, and she had fulfilled all of the requirements imposed by the government.

With these appointments, and the possible need to fill other Supreme Court vacancies arising from the potential, if not likely, retirements of Justices Stephen Breyer and Ruth Bader Ginsburg,[14] Mr. Trump could reshape the philosophy of the Supreme Court.

Further, the Court's recent 5–4 decisions in *Burwell v. Hobby Lobby* (2014) and *NIFLA v. Becerra* (2018) demonstrate the breadth and depth of conservative Supreme Court Justices' hostility to reproductive rights. Their contempt manifests itself beyond questions of abortion rights, encompassing also poor women's access to contraception, testing for sexually transmitted diseases, and basic information. In *Burwell*, the Court held that the Religious Freedom Restoration Act of 1993 permits a private, for-profit company to deny its female employees contraception, which the workers would otherwise be entitled to under the Patient Protection and Affordable Care Act (PPACA), commonly known as the Affordable Care Act (ACA) or Obamacare. The case is widely regarded as a landmark ruling because, for the first time, the Court held that a private, for-profit company with thousands of employees could have religious views and religious rights. So, compliance with the ACA mandate could infringe on the religious rights held by the employers. Justice Alito, who wrote for the majority, clarified that the Court's ruling applied only to the contraceptives mandate of the ACA and not to other religious objections that any other company might have – such as refusing to fund blood transfusions or vaccines.

Burwell opened the door to further strategized use of religious argumentation to defeat reproductive health access. More recently, in *NIFLA*, the Supreme Court further weaponized the First Amendment in a case where the Court struck down a California law requiring crisis pregnancy centers (CPCs) to inform their clients whether they are licensed medical facilities and to post information related to California's Reproductive Freedom, Accountability, Comprehensive Care, and Transparency Act (FACT Act). Investigative reports commissioned by the California legislature revealed that CPCs operating in that state misled clients, claiming that abortions cause cancer. Sixty percent of CPCs in California told clients that condoms are ineffective in reducing the transmission of sexual diseases and reducing pregnancy. Forty percent warned that infertility was increased by the use of hormonal birth control. Eighty-five percent of the CPCs investigated in California led women to believe that abortions cause mental trauma. Most CPCs are religiously affiliated and do not provide actual medical care, even though they convincingly portray what they offer as reproductive healthcare or even abortion.

Again, in a 5–4 decision with all the conservative, male Justices in the majority, the Court split along familiar ideological lines to strike down the California law. The decision is particularly worrying, because CPCs specifically target indigent teenagers and women in poor communities. They present themselves online and in person as medical facilities (with employees wearing lab coats and carrying stethoscopes). Despite their costuming, which to a reasonable person would give the appearance of a licensed medical provider, their employees are in many instances neither medically trained nor college educated. They may wear lab coats but lack the legal and medical capacities to administer tests, treat sexually transmitted diseases, or prescribe medicines. What they do – and what appears to be their chief strategy – is to persuade pregnant teens and women against abortion (and even contraception) and steer them toward receiving an ultrasound – one of the few services CPCs provide.

Justice Thomas's condescension toward the lives of the women most impacted by the CPCs operating in California is apparent. Writing for the majority, Justice Thomas suggested there were other, less burdensome means for California to reach indigent women, such as placing its messages on billboards or public service announcements. Can you imagine poor pregnant women or scared teenage girls trying to clarify their healthcare options by roaming the streets of Los Angeles or San Francisco looking for billboards? The Court also selectively departed from its prior jurisprudence. In *Planned Parenthood of Southeastern Pennsylvania v. Casey*, the Court upheld a law that mandated doctors to provide information to women who were considering whether to terminate a pregnancy.

In both *Burwell* and *NIFLA*, the Court went to great lengths to contort the rule of law – in the former by expanding constitutional protections for businesses that seek exemption from federal law in order to discriminate against their female employees; in the latter by ignoring fairly recent precedent. In the process, the Justices gerrymandered women's constitutional rights. In *Burwell*, the Court crafted a bold, new right for private corporations: they too could now possess and exercise religious rights, just like individuals. However, Justice Alito articulated limits on this new rule; the Court's decision would not extend to other classes of medical objections, such as blood transfusions (a well-documented and well-known objection within the Jehovah's Witness religious community) or vaccines (which are opposed by practitioners of Scientology). The ruling applied only to employers who oppose women's reproductive health rights such as contraception or abortion.

Despite episodic victories, such as *Whole Woman's Health v. Hellerstedt* in 2016, which struck down two antiabortion laws in Texas, the cases cited above and others suggest that effective, innovative strategies to stave off further trampling and advance reproductive health, rights, and justice must engage important legal arguments, but also reach beyond litigation and petitions to the Supreme Court. This Court's recalcitrance on settled principles of constitutional law, such as personal privacy, should cause alarm. It indicates this Court's willingness to ignore *stare decisis* (or precedent) when it suits an ideological objective. And, while advancing the goals of equality, privacy, and autonomy sometimes calls upon courts to dispense with precedent, such as denouncing state-sanctioned racial discrimination and segregation in public schools and housing, or overturning centuries of case law barring African Americans from voting, this is not the case in the reproductive health realm. The majority's approach in *NIFLA* and *Burwell* does not advance principles of equality and privacy for women, it undermines them.

The rule of law necessitates equality before the law, fairness in the application of law, legal certainty or predictability, accountability to the law, procedural transparency, and the avoidance of arbitrariness. Adherence to these principles indicates the legitimacy and credibility of a branch of government, such as courts or the legislature. When the Supreme Court selectively suspends its neutrality and its commitment to these principles, it begins to lack legitimacy and coherence. It reveals dysfunctionality and a lack of independence from the tides of political pandering and persuasion that seek to withhold civil liberties from the most vulnerable. *Dred Scott v. Sandford* (denying free and enslaved Blacks citizenship),[15] *Plessy v. Ferguson* (legalizing state-sanctioned racial segregation policies),[16] *Buck v. Bell* (instantiating eugenics in American law by upholding compulsory sterilization laws),[17] *and Korematsu v. United States* (affirming the constitutionality of an executive order forcing Japanese Americans into internment camps regardless of their citizenship),[18] all bear this out.

In *Dred Scott*, the Supreme Court issued an edict proclaiming that all persons of African descent, whether born free or enslaved, could never be counted as citizens in the United States. Chief Justice Taney's opinion in that case is a potent reminder of the social castes, legal barriers, and political obstacles for Blacks forged by a slave economy:

> [Black slaves] had for more than a century before been regarded as beings of an inferior order, and altogether unfit to associate with the white race, either in social or political relations; and so far inferior, that they had no rights which the white man was bound to respect; and that the negro might justly and lawfully be reduced to slavery for his benefit. He was bought and sold, and treated as an ordinary article of merchandise and traffic, whenever a profit could be made by it.[19]

Taney explained that no one found it morally or politically repugnant to subject Blacks to the conditions of slavery. As he opined, these were not "matters of public concern" and, according to him, no one for a moment doubted the "correctness of this opinion." It is not surprising that Taney himself had a voracious appetite for the tastes of slavery and profited from the human bondage of Africans, as did his family. Similarly, of the nine Justices, proslavery Presidents appointed seven of them. More than half of the Justices were from slave-owning families. History marks Justice

Taney's opinion as uncharitable and regrettable, but it did not tarnish his reputation. His bust sits in the halls of Congress.

Now is an important time to consider these matters in order to develop a more robust jurisprudence in exile.[20] To answer Stephen Saks's question – "If law is a matter of social practice, as most seem to agree, can there be social practices that hardly anybody in society knows about?"[21] – yes, forcing women to undergo cesarean sections under threat of criminal punishment; denying youth sex education based on religious beliefs rather than best public health practices; denying pregnant women urgent medical care, such as chemotherapy, because of pregnancy; criminally punishing pregnant a woman for falling down steps, attempting suicide, or "endangering her fetus" are among such little-known societal practices. For pregnant, incarcerated women, the state's punitive practices include shackling during labor and delivery; permitting only one hour (if any time at all) with the newborn; and enforced isolation and solitary confinement for the sake of "protecting" the pregnancy, despite the fact that forcing someone into solitary confinement is known to produce serious psychiatric consequences in the individual, ranging from sensory deprivation and severe depression to feelings of isolation. According to Dr. Stuart Grassian, these symptoms form a major psychiatric syndrome.

Apart from that, incarceration postpregnancy triggers a litany of humiliating state practices that translate into extralegal punishments ranging from transfers to facilities in other states, making it difficult to maintain connections with family and children; exorbitant fees to make brief phone calls home; rampant medical neglect; and even the tactless practice of denying women adequate monthly menstrual hygienic care. States' practices that deny appropriate monthly sanitary care count among the shameful legal tactics designed to induce compliance and obedience that hardly anyone knows about, except the legislators and law enforcement that sanction and apply them.

Speaking from the floor of the Colorado legislature on March 19, 2019, Colorado state representative Leslie Herod had this to say: "We had a conversation about the Department of Corrections denying women tampons within their facilities. We then found out that tampons were being used to barter, to trade, and to sanction."

What Representative Herod, an African American legislator elected in 2016, was referring to is the fact that in jails and prisons across the United States, and Colorado too, "[w]omen were having to trade sex for access to tampons." Herod exclaimed before her colleagues, "How humiliating that must be! I could only imagine what it must be like for a woman to be denied access to feminine hygiene products that she needs because she cannot afford to pay for them." Furthermore, she learned, "that women who soiled their clothes because they didn't have access to the right products ... were being sanctioned and were denied access to the commissary, in some places." In other words, "you bleed through your clothes because you cannot afford to pay for a tampon, and then you get sanctioned and can't use a commissary to buy a tampon."

I agree with Representative Herod; it must be humiliating for incarcerated women to endure this type of extralegal punishment or at least obliviousness and disregard for their basic human needs. What's more, in Colorado, some women will be allowed a tampon, but the state subjects them to another cruelty. According to Representative Herod, "there's one more piece, because in the department of corrections, you were allowed to have a tampon if you could prove medical need to a male guard, typically. That's not only humiliating for the woman, it's humiliating for the male guard who has to say, 'Yes, I saw that she needed a tampon.'" Herod has sponsored a bill to provide free menstrual hygiene products to women in custody who need them.

These social practices, largely hidden from view, result in constitutionally problematic extralegal criminal and civil punishments that deny pregnant women privacy, autonomy, dignity, and equality after criminalization related to their pregnancies. For women forced to endure a pregnancy to term, even when it may threaten their health, mothering is their punishment for having sex.

10.3 JURISPRUDENCE IN EXILE

There is no tacit agreement that sex should produce punishments for women.

Scholarly responses to attacks on reproductive liberty most often turn to arguments rooted in autonomy and privacy found in the Fourteenth Amendment's Due Process Clause. The principle arguments that ground liberal substantive due process analysis in reproductive health relate to the infringement on women's individual autonomy and personhood as well as the invidious force imposed by the government on women's childbearing, which unconstitutionally burdens a fundamental right. These concerns are rooted quite simply in the right to be "let alone" and "left alone" with respect to both decisional autonomy and matters of flesh – to be free from the physical impositions of others.

Much reproductive health scholarship borrows from the individual liberty framework established by the Supreme Court in *Roe*, which situates constitutional protections for the right to procreate, as well as to terminate a pregnancy, in the Due Process Clause. In *Roe*, the Court reasoned that the right to privacy applies across a set of intimate life decisions, including "activities relating to marriage ... procreation ... contraception ... family relationships ... and child rearing and education."[22]

However, the challenge for those committed to forging a jurisprudence in exile will be to look beyond the prior descriptive and normative accounts of privacy and autonomy. Instead, I urge reasserting an equality framework in women's reproductive health generally, and specifically to apply to fetal protection cases in pregnancy such as those described in this book. A sex equality argument in fetal protection would ask whether state interventions are really about promoting fetal health, or whether fetal protection laws might also manifest constitutionally repugnant judgments about women, particularly pregnant women.[23]

A sex equality framework would build on principle arguments articulated by Dr. Anna Pauline "Pauli" Murray, a foundational voice in constitutional law, reproductive rights, and social policy. Dr. Murray's research, activism, and scholarship were essential to the early civil rights work of the National Association for the Advancement of Colored People (NAACP) and the civil liberties work on sex and sex equality of the American Civil Liberties Union (ACLU). Thurgood Marshall referred to her landmark 1951 publication, *States' Laws on Race and Color*, as "the bible," as it helped him and the organization challenge racially discriminatory, unequal laws throughout the United States and particularly in the American South.[24] If lost to mainstream feminist and race discourse, it is likely due to her race, sex, and sexual orientation.

Dr. Murray's advocacy for, and perceptive articulation of, an equality framework to address sex-based discrimination predated[25] the keen arguments made by Ruth Bader Ginsburg and ACLU colleagues decades later, even though Ginsburg is largely credited with framing this legal approach.[26] Murray was profoundly impacted by the racial discrimination she encountered as a Black woman. Dating back to the early 1940s, she had challenged sex-based discrimination prior to serving on a committee of the President's Commission on the Status of Women (PCSW), which was launched in 1961 under John Kennedy. Murray's leadership on the Committee on Civil and Political Rights resulted in a pivotal 1962 report, *A Proposal to Reexamine the Applicability of the Fourteenth Amendment to State Laws and Practices Which Discriminate on the Basis of Sex Per Se*, which "presented comprehensive analysis of judicial decisions on cases involving legal distinctions on the basis of sex, and it stressed the need for reexamination by the courts, in light of present-day knowledge and conditions, of state laws and practices that discriminated solely on the basis of sex."[27] Murray recognized parallels between the race-based doctrines of "separate but equal" and the sex-based discriminatory doctrine "sex as a basis for legislative classification."[28] She suggested that this latter doctrine had become as invidious as the former. Murray's proposal on the constitutional position of women resulted in the PCSW's adoption of language she drafted in 1963 with Mary Eastwood, an attorney from the Department of Justice:

> Equality of right under the law for all persons, male or female, is so basic to democracy and its commitment to the ultimate value of the individual that it must be reflected in the fundamental law of the land. The Commission believes that this principle of equality is embodied in the 5th and 14th amendments to the Constitution of the United States . . ..[29]

Murray's legal analysis and relationships in Washington, D.C., would also play a crucial role in keeping the word "sex" in Title VII of the 1964 Civil Rights Act – again on the basis of sex equality – when Senator Dirksen announced opposition to adding sex to the civil rights legislation. Murray's *Memorandum in Support of Retaining the Amendment to H.R. 7152 (Equal Employment Opportunity) to Prohibit Discrimination in Employment Because of Sex*, pointed to the "historical interrelatedness of the movements for civil rights and women's rights and the tragic consequences in United States history of ignoring the interrelatedness of all human rights." She wrote: "A strong argument can be made for the proposition that Title VII without the 'sex' amendment would benefit Negro males primarily and thus offer genuine equality of opportunity to only *half* of the potential Negro work force." Furthermore, she stated: "The 'uniqueness' of the nature of the discrimination on the basis of sex is largely fictitious and cloaks both timidity and paternalism."

The application of an equality lens to answer punitive fetal health interventions in women's pregnancies reflects a concern that states uniquely enlist law enforcement (including doctors acting in a quasi-state agent capacity) to deploy their interests in gendered ways. If states deploy their fetal health interests in gendered ways, might that sex-selective approach indicate constitutionally suspect motivations? When states manifest their interest in fetal health, they express these concerns almost exclusively among indigent women, who lack the social and economic capacities that protect wealthier, educated women from similar punitive encroachments by the state.

For example, when states pressure physicians to subject poor African American pregnant patients to invasive protocols as a means of determining illicit drug use in furtherance of fetal health, but significantly exclude white female patients from similar interventions, that action indicates a suspect motivation not explained by health or law rationales. A clear example of an impermissible standard of equality would be if states were to discriminate against those persons legally entitled to have access to abortion services, limiting the right to only one ethnic group, for example, or differentiating between married and unmarried women when granting the right.

Equally, when punitive fetal protection efforts operate exclusively in indigent communities (or where the indigent seek care) and not universally, such actions reflect decision-making that carves out unjustifiable, discriminatory distinctions between classes of citizens that bear no relationship to a permissible governmental purpose. Such distinctions might reasonably be explained by constitutionally impermissible stereotypes about good motherhood, maternal responsibility, and citizenship guiding legislative action. Such stereotypes might be argued to resemble caste legislation or caste enforcement. When this type of legislating cannot be shown to further its purported governmental interest, it reveals itself to be arbitrary.

Traditionally, equal protection granted states broad latitude in enacting legislation. That is, courts required that the challenged legislation be rationally related to a permissible governmental interest. States needed only to show that the classification set forth in the legislation rationally related to a legitimate government interest and that such state action was not arbitrary. Modern Supreme Court application has involved three tiers of review: strict scrutiny of racial classifications (requiring the state's regulation to further a compelling governmental interest); heightened intermediate scrutiny of sex discrimination (requiring that the legislation serve important governmental objectives and be substantially related to achieving those goals); and a rational relationship level of review (requiring only a rational relationship to legitimate governmental ends).

A sex equality framework is concerned not only about distinctions among women; distinctions between sexes are no more permissible than distinctions within sexual classifications. In *Skinner*, the Court unanimously held that where Oklahoma's Criminal Sterilization Act provided for the sterilization of habitual criminals convicted three times or more of felonious crimes of moral turpitude, but provided exemptions for white collar criminals, such regulations violated the Equal Protection Clause of the Fourteenth Amendment. In *Kirchberg v. Feenstra*, the Court struck down a Louisiana law where the state failed to demonstrate an important interest in permitting husbands the authority to unilaterally dispose of joint property, but not wives. Similarly, in *Wengler v. Druggists Mutual Insurance*, the Court found a provision of the Missouri workers' compensation law unconstitutional because it denied a widower benefits on his wife's work-related death unless he could show mental or physical incapacity or prove dependence on his wife's earnings. This law was particularly odious, because it granted a widow death benefits without her having to prove dependence on her husband's earnings. The Court ruled that the Missouri law violated the Equal Protection Clause of the Fourteenth Amendment. In *Califano v. Goldfarb*, the Court reached a plurality decision, pointing out that where "female insureds received less protection for their spouses solely because of their sex," such circumstances were a discriminatory violation of the Fifth Amendment's equal protection guarantee. Finally, as between fathers and mothers, the Court has evaluated the reaches of the equal protection principle, extending it in *Caban v. Mohammed*, where the Court found that a state law violates the Equal Protection Clause when it permits the mother, but not the father, of a child born out of wedlock to intervene in the child's adoption.[30]

Distinctions between sexes to advance fetal health reifies stereotypes and ignores medical facts. For example, when the state uniquely and exclusively burdens women in the advancement of fetal health, but not men, it does so under the flawed theory that women alone determine fetal health. Such regulations thereby reduce women to symbolic wombs and human incubators for the state. When states selectively express and enforce fetal health interests, distinguishing between the sexes and among the sexes, such considerations belie an interest in protecting fetal health. Instead, states' selective interest in protecting fetal health reflects adverse stereotypes about women and pregnancy. The Supreme Court has ruled that such arbitrary rules about pregnancy cannot stand.[31]

10.3.1 Geduldig v. Aiello: *An Equality Hurdle?*

Scholars hesitant over this line of argumentation point to *Geduldig v. Aiello* as feminism's lost battle on equal protection and pregnancy.[32] In that case, California's disability insurance program, which mandated participation by all workers, exempted work loss due to normal pregnancies from insurable coverage. It is worth noting that the original language exempted all pregnancies from coverage, even those requiring medicalization and lengthy hospital stays. The original statute read:

> 'Disability' or 'disabled' includes both mental or physical illness and mental or physical injury. An individual shall be deemed disabled in any day in which, because of his physical or mental condition, he is unable to perform his regular or customary work. In no case shall the term 'disability' or 'disabled' include any injury or illness caused by or arising in connection with pregnancy up to the termination of such pregnancy and for a period of 28 days thereafter.[33]

In the lawsuit, four petitioners (three of whom experienced abnormal pregnancies resulting in terminations and miscarriages and one who experienced a normal pregnancy) argued that the program violated the Equal Protection Clause because it precluded the payment of benefits for any disability resulting from pregnancy. This particular issue was moot on hearing, because California changed its law shortly before the case reached the Supreme Court. The new law would cover the pregnancy concerns for three of the four petitioners. The Court rejected the equal protection explaining that excluding normal pregnancies did not constitute invidious discrimination. Applying a rational basis standard, the majority held that (1) California has a legitimate interest in maintaining the self-supporting nature of its insurance program; (2) the state has an interest in "distributing the available resources in such a way as to keep benefit payments at an adequate level for the conditions covered"; and (3) California "has a legitimate concern in maintaining the contribution rate at a level that will not unduly burden participating employees, particularly low-income employees who may be most in need of the disability insurance."[34]

In the 1970s and 1980s, feminist scholars read the opinion as closing the door on equal protection claims brought by pregnant women. They roundly criticized the opinion. In fact, the decision was met with such reprobation that, in the words of Sylvia Law, "[c]riticizing *Geduldig* has since become a cottage industry."[35] Katharine Bartlett pointed out that the Court had fashioned a "uniqueness trap" and joined other scholars in condemning the Court's "failed logic" and picking it apart. Others took the case to mean that not all classifications that discriminate against women or disadvantage them as a class or a sub-class are necessarily based on sex.

It appears that many scholars read Justice Potter Stewart's majority opinion as saying either that equal protection analysis does not apply to pregnancy or that conditions of pregnancy do not qualifying for equal protection analysis. In a much-criticized footnote Justice Stewart wrote that "the California insurance program does not exclude anyone from benefit eligibility because of gender but merely removes one physical condition – pregnancy – from the list of compensable disabilities." However, as Reva Siegel and Neil Siegel pointed out, there is more to be said contextually about the *Geduldig* decision and subsequent sex-based equality analysis argued before the Supreme Court. They cautioned that the case "should be read to say what it actually says, not what most commentators and courts have assumed it to say."[36] I agree.

First, it is important to understand what the case actually does and does not say. For example, the Court does not dismiss pregnancy as never qualifying for protection under the equality standard guaranteed by the Fourteenth Amendment. Nor does the Court reject the principle that pregnancy regulation can be sex regulation and, as such, can be discriminatory. The Court did not hold that discrimination based on pregnancy deserves a lower level of review and classification than cases that involve sex. The Court held that state regulations affecting pregnancy are not always suspect of sex discrimination. When a regulation is not suspect of sex, as when it is not suspect of race, a rational basis analysis will be used. Instead, Justice Stewart recognized that "distinctions involving pregnancy" can be "mere pretexts designed to effect an invidious discrimination."

Second, despite divergent readings of the case, the Court's language is unambiguous. Selective actions by a state involving pregnancy, based purely on pretext for other causes or concerns, can be invidious. It is not among the objectives of this Chapter, or the book, to explain this misreading of *Geduldig*. However, Justice Brennan's powerful dissent holds relevant insights. Brennan's methodic push for the application of a strict level of scrutiny to sex discrimination cases resurfaces in his dissent in *Geduldig*, just as it had in prior Supreme Court jurisprudence.[37] Brennan articulated a vision for strict scrutiny jurisprudence in sex cases in *Frontiero*, decided just one year prior to *Geduldig*, and in that case he achieved a plurality decision. In this case, he issued a bristling warning to fend off a rollback on gains secured in prior cases and to hold tight the fragile plurality built on sex classification and strict scrutiny:

> Yet, by its decision today, the Court appears willing to abandon that higher standard of review without satisfactorily explaining what differentiates the gender-based classification employed in this case from those found unconstitutional in *Reed* and *Frontiero*. The Court's decision threatens to return men and women to a time when "traditional" equal protection analysis sustained legislative classifications that treated differently members of a particular sex solely because of their sex.[38]

Over time, a misreading of Brennan's dissent has resulted in a general misevaluation of *Geduldig*. Be this as it may, Brennan's dissent serves as an evolved framework for equality analyses based on sex and ultimately developed in a line of cases that expanded the contours of sex equality.[39] It is an important example of jurisprudence in exile.

Finally, the temporal and jurisprudential gap that separates *Plessy* from *Brown* provides instructive lessons for sex equality's journey. That is, in 1896 when Homer Plessy challenged the Louisiana Separate Car Act's requirement of separate accommodation for African Americans and whites on the basis that it violated his rights under the Thirteenth and Fourteenth Amendments of the U.S. Constitution, a civil rights movement had yet to take shape. The Court's equality jurisprudence had yet to evolve. Likely, the Court felt no urgency for the people who suffered unequal living, working, school, and accommodation conditions in the United States. The Court rejected Plessy's claims, declaring that Louisiana had not implied any inferior status for African Americans in violation of a Fourteenth Amendment interest. Justice Brown declared, "We consider the underlying fallacy of the plaintiff's argument to consist in the assumption that the enforced separation of the two races stamps the colored race with a badge of inferiority. If this be so, it is not by reason of anything found in the act, but solely because the colored race chooses to put that construction upon it."[40] The Court dismantled its "separate, but equal" citizenship doctrine with *Brown v. Board of Education*.

Sex equality now awaits its *"Brown"* to close the gap in equality jurisprudence. In the meantime, while *Geduldig* offers an important spotlight on the Court's jurisprudence on pregnancy equality, another spotlight focuses on fetal health protection in the workplace, as discussed below.

10.3.2 *Fetal Protection and the Workplace*

In *International Union v. Johnson Controls*, the Supreme Court opined that male health may have as much bearing on fetal outcomes as women's health.[41] In the decade leading up to *International Union*, prominent manufacturing companies, including American Cyanamid, Allied Chemicals, General Motors, B.F. Goodrich, St. Joseph Zinc, Gulf Oil, Dow Chemical, DuPont, BASF Wyandotte, Bunker Hill Smelting, Eastman Kodak, Firestone Tire & Rubber, Globe Union, Olin Corporation, Union Carbide and Monsanto adopted fetal protection laws framed as "medical regulations" or "medical policies" that prohibited fertile women from employment in certain jobs.[42] Some policies excluded women from most jobs based on the presumption that female employees might become pregnant at some point. The policies did not take into account women's sexual orientation, desire to bear children, or marital status.[43]

For example, American Cyanamid introduced a fetal protection policy in 1978. Its plant, located in the valley of economically depressed West Virginia, provided a competitive income for its 500 employees, approximately 5 percent of whom were women. The plant was located on Willow Island, later known for one of the most devastating construction accidents in the United States, which killed fifty-one people. Senior management met with its twenty-five female employees to inform them that the new policy barred all women between the ages of fifteen and forty from working in most positions at the plant. Other companies adopted similar fetal protection regulations, effectively prohibiting women from employment in some of the better paying jobs at manufacturing plants. At least five women then voluntarily had themselves sterilized, hoping they would not lose their jobs.

Fetal protectionist rules in the workplace served not only to exclude women from meaningful, gainful employment but also to secure a monopoly for men in coveted factory jobs. Fetal protection rules provided a persuasive proxy for sex discrimination. In *International Union*, the company had established a fetal protection rule much like that of American Cyanide.[44] The company's manufacturing operation involved lead elements, which can pose fetal health risks. This had not been a concern for the company in the years prior to the Civil Rights Act of 1964, because the company did not employ any woman in its battery-manufacturing factory. However, in June of 1977 the company issued "its first official policy concerning its employment of women in lead-exposure work."[45] The policy read:

> Protection of the health of the unborn child is the immediate and direct responsibility of the prospective parents. While the medical profession and the company can support them in the exercise of this responsibility, it cannot assume it for them without simultaneously infringing their rights as persons.
> . . . Since not all women who can become mothers wish to become mothers (or will become mothers), it would appear to be illegal discrimination to treat all who are capable of pregnancy as though they will become pregnant.[46]

When Johnson Controls issued its official policy statement, it stopped short of preventing women of childbearing capacity from working within lead-exposed areas. However, the company issued stern warnings to its female employees about lead risks. It also instituted a policy that "required a woman who wished to be considered for employment to sign a statement that she had been advised of the [pregnancy] risk."[47] The statement indicated "that women exposed to lead have a higher rate of abortion" and although this risk was "not as clear . . . as the relationship between cigarette smoking and cancer," it was, "medically speaking, just good sense not to run that risk if you want children and do not want to expose the unborn child to risk, however small."[48]

Several years later, Johnson Controls shifted its policy again, from one that cautioned female employees about the risks of lead exposure to fetal development, to a policy that excluded women's employment in manufacturing jobs that could expose them to lead. The company barred all women, except those who could prove infertility, from holding certain jobs that could expose them to lead. The new fetal protection policy stated: "It is Johnson Controls policy that women who are pregnant or who are capable of bearing children will not be placed into jobs involving lead exposure or which could expose them to lead through the exercise of job bidding, bumping, transfer or promotion rights."[49]

Johnson Controls initiated the new fetal protection policy after learning that eight of its female employees who became pregnant continued to test high for lead exposure. The new company policy defined women who are "capable of bearing children" as "all women except" the infertile. The female employees were required to medically prove their infertility.[50] Like other companies at the time, Johnson Controls justified its policy based on concerns for fetal health, which the Court flatly rejected.

Writing for the majority, Justice Blackmun found the fetal protection policy "obvious" in its "bias" against women. For example, fertile men were not subjected to the burdensome employment restrictions placed on fertile women. Fertile men were afforded the "choice as to whether they wish to risk their reproductive health for a particular job."[51] Section 703(a) of the Civil Rights Act of 1964 does not tolerate this type of discrimination, however, because it "prohibits sex-based classifications in terms and conditions of employment, in hiring and discharging decisions, and in other employment decisions that adversely affect an employee's status."[52]

Blackmun reasoned that a sex-based policy expressed as "protecting women's unconceived offspring" was not benign. To the contrary, such policies constitute sex-based discrimination. Any assumptions otherwise are "incorrect." Simply put, the policy constituted facially impermissible discrimination. For example, the fetal protection policy classified its employees on the basis of gender and childbearing capacity rather than just fertility. Moreover, the company did not care to protect its male employee's future offspring from possible risk of lead exposure, despite, as the record showed, "the debilitating effect of lead exposure on the male reproductive system"; only Johnson Control's female employees were targeted.[53] In other words, it was sex and not fetal health that ultimately proved important to the company for the purpose of its regulation. As Blackmun stated, the company was "concerned only with the harms that may befall the unborn offspring of its female employees."[54] In this case, the company "chose[] to treat all its female employees as potentially pregnant," and that policy evinces a form of unjustifiable sex discrimination.

Johnson Control responded that its policy involved third-party safety – an argument that the Court rightly rejected because the female employee's unconceived fetuses were not third parties.[55] According to the Court, even if they were third parties, their safety was not essential. As Blackmun wrote, "[n]o one can disregard the possibility of injury to future children," but the business exception claimed by Johnson Controls was not deserving of the special solicitude it demanded of the Court. According to Blackmun, battery making was not so essential as to overcome the Court's suspicion of regulations that discriminate on the basis of sex, even if to theoretically protect third-party unborn.

10.3.3 *Means, Ends, and Chilling Prenatal Conduct*

This Chapter proceeds by turning to its normative argument that fetal protection laws violate the Equal Protection Clause of the U.S. Constitution. This advances an analysis based on how *Geduldig* should be read in light of both the Court's full opinion in that case and *International Union*, which serves as a reasonable guidepost. Finally, even a conservative reading of *Geduldig* needs to be reconciled with the evolved equal protection jurisprudence that has been articulated by the Court in the years since 1974, as evidenced through *International Union* as well as *Nevada Department of Human Services v. Hibbs.*[56]

In *Hibbs*, the Court noted that pregnancy discrimination had become intractable and pervasive. According to the Court, "[m]any States offered women extended 'maternity' leave that far exceeded the typical 4- to 8-week period of physical disability due to pregnancy and childbirth, but very few States granted men a parallel benefit: Fifteen States provided women up to one year of extended maternity leave, while only four provided men with the same." In that case, the Supreme Court ruled that Nevada family leave policies discriminated against men by providing reduced time compared to that granted to women to care for a family member. This constituted sex discrimination. The Court relied on expert documents and legislative history associated with the Family Medical Leave Act to point out how discriminatory stereotypes about pregnancy and sex roles influenced the construction and implementation of state pregnancy and family leave policies. The court found that discriminatory implementation of family leave policies based on sex violated the Equal Protection Clause.

Thus, to understand invidious pregnancy discrimination as "never" evincing impermissible sex discrimination risks ignoring the expansive equal protection landscape cultivated by the Court. By modest analogy, it would be similar to grounding race equality analysis on *Plessy v. Ferguson*. I will not repeat the arguments made earlier rejecting the conventional reading of *Geduldig* that pregnancy discrimination can never be sex discrimination. As Professors Neil Siegel and Reva Siegel explained, that reading is plainly inaccurate. If the conventional interpretation of *Geduldig* offers an inexact understanding of the case, how should this be addressed in light of the important interests at stake?

The clearest approach is to adopt the standard flagged in the majority's footnote 20. In that footnote, Justice Stewart explained that "distinctions involving pregnancy" may impose "an invidious discrimination against the members of one sex or the other."[57] Given that, the following arguments proceed on the basis that invidious pregnancy discrimination should be analyzed as sex discrimination under the Equal Protection Clause.

Prosecuting women for violating fetal protection statutes discriminates against women because men are not prosecuted for engaging in the same conduct as women. Simply stated, the means and ends do not fit. At best, locating fetal harms as under the exclusive control of women "must be considered an unduly tenuous 'fit.'"[58] Dating back to *Reed v. Reed*, the Court has invalidated laws permitting preferences for men over women in the appointment of estate administrators.[59] In *Frontiero*, it struck down laws that granted male members of the armed forces an automatic dependency allowance for their wives while denying the same for women and their husbands. The Court held such rules violated the Equal Protection Clause.[60] The Court has found that statutory classifications that distinguish between males and females are "subject to scrutiny under the Equal Protection Clause."[61] To withstand constitutional scrutiny, discrimination based on gender must serve important government objectives and be substantially related to achieving those objectives.

In *Craig v. Boren*, the Supreme Court carved out an intermediary level of scrutiny for sex-based discrimination.[62] In that case, the Court struck down an Oklahoma law prohibiting alcohol sales to adult males. The Court held that the law discriminated against young males, but not females, because it prohibited sales of a nonintoxicating beer to males under twenty-one and to females under the age of eighteen. The Court found that the means – discriminating against young men by denying them the right to purchase beer – was not substantially related to Oklahoma's purported ends – promoting traffic safety. The Court acknowledged the importance of traffic safety, although perhaps not to the degree advocated by Justice Rehnquist in his dissent. The majority reasoned that even though "arrest statistics assembled in 1973 indicated that males in the 18–20 age group were arrested for 'driving under the influence' almost 18 times as often as their female counterparts, and for 'drunkenness' in a ratio of almost 10 to 1,"[63] singling out one sex for gender discrimination was impermissible where the means of reducing traffic deaths and injuries was specious and only tenuously connected to the ends – even if the ends were socially important. Justice Brennan cautioned that "social stereotypes" that make their way into legislation "are likely substantially to distort the accuracy of … comparative statistics." As an example, Brennan pointed to common social stereotypes as possibly influencing law enforcement. For example, if police perceive young men as "reckless" drinkers who drive, that presumption may lead to or be "transformed into arrest statistics." On the other hand, young women may slide under the radar, including those who are "reckless" or "drunk drivers," based on other stereotypes and entrenched views about women's femininity and temperance. As to the latter, Brennan cautioned that law enforcement might be undersurveilling young women, or might not be policing them at all for driving under the influence. Brennan surmised that, rather than ticketing or arresting young women, officers "chivalrously escorted [them] home" for the same type of offenses that might have landed young men in jail.

When states single out one sex for discriminatory purposes, they should provide "an exceedingly persuasive justification," as articulated in *U.S. v. Virginia*.[64] This is a demanding burden to meet, because states must show that singling out women for punitive action serves "important governmental objectives and that the discriminatory means employed [are] substantially related to the achievement of those objectives."[65] Moreover, as the laws described in this book claim to relate to fetal health, states should be made to demonstrate how such policies actually promote fetal health.

For example, the best fetal protection efforts undertaken by pregnant women will involve seeking prenatal services.[66] Prenatal care provides the opportunity for information sharing between doctors and patients and affords patients the opportunity to address health and emotional concerns about the pregnancy, receive advice regarding diet management, and monitor fetal health and development. Healthcare providers consider prenatal care to be an essential component of gestation.

Yet, a series of cases documented by the National Advocates for Pregnant Women reveals that the overwhelming majority of intrusive state interventions, including arrests and confinement, are initiated as a result of prenatal or medical visits at hospitals and clinics. Sometimes the women are arrested at the clinics or hospitals. Ultimately, intervening in women's pregnancies at prenatal appointments may chill the very behavior that government desires to promote. When states chill medically helpful prenatal conduct, they erode the best avenue for achieving the healthiest outcomes for babies.[67] One researcher warned that the "[u]ncomfortable relationships with health care providers and fear of reprisal on the part of pregnant women who are addicted make women four times less likely to receive adequate care, thereby creating health risks for women who are addicted, their unborn fetuses, and their other children."[68] The National Women's Law Center echoes these concerns, as have – to name but a few – the American Medical Association, the Center for Reproductive Rights, and the National Partnership for Women & Families, as well as professional organizations such as the American Public Health Association and the American College of Obstetrics and Gynecology.

If using prenatal services is one of the best ways to promote fetal health, chilling that conduct will not achieve government interests, except if the objectives are actually to punish women for either having sex, becoming pregnant, being indigent and pregnant, or some combination of the foregoing. Instead, it may very well undermine child and maternal welfare by creating an "unsafe" harbor around clinics and hospitals. Some scholars predict that women who can afford to end their pregnancies may seek abortions to avoid hospital "dragnets" altogether. Others suggest that pregnant women will simply avoid medical screenings. In either case, state encroachments of the type described in this book reflect a failure to credibly engage in the means and ends analysis established as part of the Supreme Court's equal protection jurisprudence.

10.3.4 *State Action and Stereotypes*

Finally, selective, punitive interventions in pregnant women's lives evince motivations other than protecting fetal health. According to Reva Siegel and Neil Siegel, selective state action that singles out indigent pregnant women to create healthier babies while not imposing similar conditions and constraints on all others capable of fertility "reflect[s] constitutionally suspect judgments" about that class of pregnant women. In *International Union*, Justice Blackmun warned that discriminatory fetal protection policies that impose special conditions on fertile women are virtually impossible to justify, because the Equal Protection Clause is intolerant of sex discrimination, even when it is motivated by beneficence. However, the Court has found that policies that discriminate based on sex may be influenced by stereotypes about sex as well as about gender roles.

One stereotype reflected in fetal protectionist measures is that women alone control fetal health. Even though women play an undeniably vital role in the care and gestation of fetuses, they do not exclusively control fetal health. Presumptions that women alone control fetal health are grounded in stereotypes, because fetal health is not controlled exclusively by pregnant women; environment, poverty, medical resources, and other factors significantly influence and may even determine fetal health. Scholars have acknowledged this much for some time, but so too have courts.[69]

In *Ambrosini v. Labarraque*, the United States Court of Appeals for the District of Columbia found a causal connection between medroxyprogesterone exposure and fetal birth defects. In *Mahon v. Pfizer*, the Supreme Court of New York rejected a motion to dismiss a lawsuit filed to recover damages for birth defect injuries against a drug manufacturer that allegedly exposed the mother, during her pregnancy, to materials it knew to be a "High Reproductive Hazard," but which were labeled a "Least Hazardous" substance. In *Enright v. Eli Lilly*, the court evaluated whether a granddaughter who suffered third-generation birth defects allegedly caused by diethylstilbestrol (DES) could establish a cause of action against manufacturers of the drug. In that case, the grandmother, who used DES to prevent miscarriage, suffered significant reproductive health harms, as did her daughter, who gave birth prematurely, causing the plaintiff's many health challenges and physical disabilities. Even though the Court rejected the granddaughter's claim (or "third generation claim"), the decision was not based on the substance of the injury, but rather to confine liability.

My point here is that generations of legally and socially permissible sex discrimination result in legislation harboring invidious, stereotyped judgments about men and women, which presume that women exclusively control fetal health. The cases highlighted above show that women alone do not control fetal health. Nevertheless, indigent pregnant women and women of color are criminally hyperpoliced during pregnancy to reduce the incidence of low birth weight and miscarriage in ways that neither men nor wealthier, white women experience.

Again, Dr. Allen A. Mitchell's research on prescription drug dependency during pregnancy provides empirical support to buttress intuitions that stereotyping occurs in the drafting and enforcement of fetal protection policies.[70] Mitchell debunks commonly held assumptions about drug use during pregnancy, which likely drive the enactment and enforcement of fetal endangerment laws. Longitudinal studies conducted by Mitchell and other scientists find that educated white women are more likely to rely on prescription medications during pregnancy and their dependency on these medications increases with age. His research findings reveal that during the first trimester of pregnancy more than 70 percent of women reported taking at least one medication that was not a vitamin or mineral and that drug use increased with age, and also by race.

Given this, it is hard to believe that states do not police pregnant women on the basis of stereotype and class. In fact, states do police on the basis of stereotype. Stereotypes in these contexts include the assumption that pregnant women hold exclusive control over fetal health outcomes and that women of color are more likely than other pregnant women to engage in fetal-risky behavior during gestation – hence the persistent policing. If there are fetal risks associated with drug use, presuming that only illicit drugs – and not prescription medications – will cause fetal health harms is absurd. In other words, despite the dramatic rise in prescription pain relief during pregnancy, which is directly linked to wealth and race, states rely on stereotypes, primarily targeting poor women.[71] Finally, states may not create laws that allow some members of the class to be spared indignities while subjecting others to surreptitious law enforcement when they seek prenatal care.

10.4 CONCLUSION

The work of social justice – creating equitable, dignified, respectful ways of engaging with women's health generally, and reproductive health specifically – necessitates innovative approaches, which involve turning to the legislature, petitioning courts, as well as engaging with civil society to build and incorporate a reproductive justice platform. A jurisprudence developed in exile must not be the only means of resisting infringements on civil liberties and civil rights. In recent years, activists, scholars, and civil society organizations have significantly contributed to platforms that reach the most vulnerable women. Their work has also contributed to legislative action. However, much of it has been on the ground.

This book offers attention to these issues. It does not answer all the questions related to reproductive health, rights, and justice in the United States, as that is not its aim. There are other important contributions on sex, society, and the law that have yet to be authored and which should take up a range of concerns related to religion, LGBTQ concerns, childhood sexual abuse, transgender rights, reproductive healthcare in prison, and more. Some of this scholarship is underway now and much more is needed.

11

Conclusion

Still shackled, I climb up on the table, where nurses begin the very painful search for my small veins. As I begin to go under, the shackles are finally removed from my ankles. The guards will stay in the corner to watch as my breast comes off.

S.E. Allen

Understanding and addressing the enigmatic policing of pregnant women requires grappling with broader, troubling social and political issues, including mass incarceration, the U.S. drug war, welfare reform, and even our nation's notorious, but largely hidden, history of eugenics. Any of these topics would rightly deserve its own book and brilliant scholars and others have taken to writing them. These policy landmines set the stage for regarding pregnant women as objects of the state, deploying criminal punishment as a viable means of regulating their behavior, and, in essence and substance, criminalizing pregnancy. This book makes a close study of those issues and reveals that fetal protection efforts, which are often purported to justify states' persistent intrusions in poor women's lives, serve to mask other politically expedient interests: controlling women and demanding their obedience, gerrymandering, pandering to tough-on-crime strategies, achieving electoral victories, and heightening moral panic. Rarely are the well-being and dignity of babies and children a persistent concern of those politicians who most favor punitive interventions in the lives of their mothers.

In the process of writing this book, I have come to conclude that criminal threats and prosecution are measuring pregnant women's obedience, and far more than fetal risk. After all, how are shackling, birthing in prison toilets, and rearing children behind bars demonstrative of the state's respect or care for fetal or child life? Does shackling pregnant women during childbirth, which is legalized in dozens of states, amount to treating human life with dignity? Does it recognize the dignity of pregnant women?

11.1 POLICING THE WOMB: DIGNITY AND MOTHERHOOD

As this book explains, the broader turn to mass incarceration ensnares women too, creating invisible casualties, exacting unaccounted-for collateral damage in their children's lives, and instantiating troubling social norms. The costs of mass incarceration extend far beyond strained economic considerations, perversely incentivized contracts with private prisons, and states' budget shortfalls because they cannot afford to incarcerate so many Americans. The cost of relentless policing produces horrific externalities for children and the broader society, which becomes accustomed to legislative policy being shaped by politically motivated moral panic. That is, when politicians deploy the rhetoric of welfare queens bleeding the nation's economy by fraud, of needing to save babies, or claiming, as they did in the 1980s, that crack babies would overwhelm hospitals, schools, and even prisons, they trigger national hysteria, which gives way to aggressive civil and criminal interventions in the mothers' pregnancies.

However, amid the coercive incitement of moral panic by politicians and law enforcement, who demand that civil and criminal punishments be exacted upon low-income and working-class mothers, the well-being of children is often an afterthought. As Chapter 2 describes, crack baby hysteria and prosecutions were born of a myth now discredited by medical organizations.

It is a matter of great concern when a society abrogates or abandons its moral compass, loses sight of the dignity of others, and renders half of its population invisible. For example, if sentenced while pregnant, women may give birth in prison toilets or on rat-infested floors – like Tara Keil in Iowa[1] or Ambrett Spencer in Arizona.[2] Birthing in a toilet or on a rodent-infested floor demonstrates cruelty – not dignity, care, and fetal or child interest. Birthing under such conditions is an affront to the dignity of the U.S. criminal justice system – or should be. As one judge told me, prison is no resort. And while that is true, one reporter's description of Arizona's women prisons evokes nothing less than the imagery of cruel and unusual punishment: the local environmental agency found mice's fecal matter in the women's drinking water in one of Sheriff Joseph Arpaio's Maricopa County jails. Even the most hardened, ardent criminal deserves sanitary drinking water, let alone the two-thirds who are non-violent offenders.

Children suffer too from the United States' insatiable appetite for criminal punishment. The repercussion of states' policing and incarcerating pregnant women is that they give birth under arduous conditions. For the babies, this may mean coming into the world while their mothers' legs and wrists are shackled to metal gurneys through leg cuffs and chains, tethered to purportedly "prevent the women from running away" or to keep the armed guards "safe" (if the mothers are afforded hospital delivery). Callously, years ago, a male professor chuckled to me that there was no need to shackle women during delivery, because "police could just shoot the bitch if she ran." I was horrified and told him so. He apologized, but his comment was all too revealing. Poor pregnant women are perceived as expendable and deserving of punishment.

Mass incarceration exacts an enormous toll on children. Professor Kristin Turney empirically details the profound emotional and psychological health harms experienced by children of incarcerated parents. Her research reveals that the impacts of incarceration on children are far worse than previously realized. Indeed, the health harms exceed experiencing a parent's death or suffering through divorce.[3] In other words, the emotional and physical health of children of incarcerated parents deteriorates to such a degree that it becomes credibly and quantifiably measurable by researchers. The problem of mass incarceration is so extreme that even Sesame Street, the children's television program, introduced a puppet, Alex, to help the children in their viewing audience cope with the anxiety of parental incarceration. Alex is the muppet child of an incarcerated parent.

What is the solution? For some lawmakers, prison nurseries – allowing children to live alongside their incarcerated mothers – promote family unity and reduce the anxieties of estrangement and displacement. In fact, for the babies and children who reside with their mothers in prison nursery programs, the outcomes for both mothers and their offspring show significant promise: recidivism rates are lower and, so far, some say "children show no adverse effects" from their lives behind bars.[4] However, these radically fraught options expose the disturbing consequences of a problematic criminal justice system that ignores the dignity of women and their children. The prison conditions are sometimes horrific. The nurseries leave no doubt that the women and their children are still in prison; the razor-sharp barbed wire and twenty-foot-high metal fences give that away.

In most cases, children of incarcerated mothers – whether their births occur behind bars or not – transition into various forms of other care, which may include relatives, foster homes, shelters, group homes, and other arrangements. Currently, about 500,000 children live in the limbo of U.S. foster care, and hundreds now live behind bars with their mothers. For children who remain in foster care throughout their adolescence, they can expect to endure homelessness, juvenile detention, teen pregnancy, and violence.[5] Fewer than 6 percent will graduate from college.

11.2 TELLING THE STORY

Over the past decade, I have spoken to activists, prosecutors, judges, law professors, sociologists, women's groups, thought leaders, politicians, chief executive officers, theologians, former convicts, and others about the turn to policing women's reproduction and its deeply disturbing consequences, including the challenges women subsequently face in obtaining housing and education loans, voting, and maintaining the custody of their children. Sue Ellen Allen, the cofounder and former Executive Director of Gina's Team, and I placed these issues front and center at President Clinton's 2015 Clinton Global Initiative (CGI), held in Denver, Colorado. Had these various powerful groups and individuals, including mayors, governors, and various power brokers at CGI, including President Clinton, noticed the dramatic rise in female incarceration? For Sue Ellen, this was a deeply personal question: she had served seven years behind bars, during which she suffered breast cancer, endured a mastectomy, and near solitary confinement in retaliation for demanding medical care for her twenty-five-year-old cellmate, Gina. My introduction to Sue Ellen was through her powerful autobiographical opinion editorial, describing having her breast "cut off"[6] while in prison. It dawned on me that most news media ignore women in prison as a general matter, and therefore overlook their healthcare behind bars. As Sue Ellen recalled:

> Imagine the feeling of shackles on your ankles, restricting your movements to baby steps. Even when you are very careful, you wind up with blisters from the weight of the hard, cold steel dragging you down. Now imagine handcuffs. They, too, are designed to restrict. They can chafe and cut, especially if the guard who cuffs you is having a bad day. He can clamp them on too tightly, and his bad day becomes yours.[7]

Sue Ellen wanted President Clinton and the CGI attendees to know about Gina, a mother of four, who died behind bars after prison officials neglected to provide timely medical care, despite numerous complaints, fevers, headaches, nausea, and inability to eat. Gina lapsed into a coma on the day she finally received medical attention, and died three days later. She had undiagnosed leukemia. A year after we spoke about these issues in Denver, Gina's eldest daughter committed suicide.

In preparing this book and the articles and opinion editorials preceding it, I learned more than I previously thought imaginable about the troubling overuse of criminal punishment and the mass incarceration of women that results. Michelle Alexander's powerful book, *The New Jim Crow*, astonished readers about Black males and incarceration, describing how the old Jim Crow gave way to an even more pernicious pattern of contemporary institutionalization, discrimination, and disenfranchisement. In essence, she warns that in many contexts life is worse for Black men now than after the abolition of slavery, because more are incarcerated now than then. A surprising percentage are disenfranchised from voting, denied the possibility of receiving federal loans and grants for post-secondary education – essentially cutting off another lifeline – and the felony record further disenfranchises them from housing, where they can volunteer, and even working.

However, there was and continues to be a void in thinking about women behind bars. Through this research, I have come to know that the turn to mass incarceration spares not even teen mothers from what at times can only be described as undignified, cruel, and inhumane treatment. Beyond mass incarceration, had the individuals I have spoken to over the past decade considered that women who desire to become mothers may be subjected to the most inhumane and undignified treatment by the state? This includes shackling, court-ordered bed rest, involuntary civil confinement, solitary confinement, and threats of criminal punishment if they fail to meet the prosecutorial and legislative expectations of healthy pregnancy as inscribed in fetal protection laws. Why are these women the subjects of such intensified state scrutiny? Why have doctors taken up the mantel of deputized law enforcement when treating pregnant women? Ultimately, why are these women, even those who suffer from drug addiction, in prison?

Chapters in this book were the subject of talks across the country at law schools, medical schools, and with various civil society organizations. Many of the people with whom I spoke were very thoughtful on the subject, offering fascinating insights honed from their personal and professional experiences. However, most of the incredibly talented individuals with whom I had the pleasure to speak about this research – especially law professors – were unaware, startled by the cases, narratives, and costs (social and financial) associated with incarcerating women.

To gain an even sharper understanding for my research, I interviewed some of the men and women on the front line – from prosecutors in Alabama to activists in New York. I wanted to learn from them and to understand their perspectives on this alarming turn to policing women's pregnancies – namely, what accounts for this assiduous, but impalpable movement.

Steve Marshall, now Attorney General of Alabama, generously offered his time, speaking to me by phone and in person in Tuscaloosa and Birmingham when he was District Attorney in Marshall County, Alabama. Steve met with me to shed light on Alabama's prosecutions and help me understand these matters from a law enforcement perspective. He spoke about his personal and professional commitments and frustrations with combatting drug use and dependence among pregnant women. He explained that he wanted to "save the babies," and "stop abortions."[8] Steve seemed sincere; he struggled with finding the right balance and approach to address illegal methamphetamine use in his county and, more broadly, the state. Like prosecutors in other states, he strategically uses child abuse or endangerment statutes to prosecute cases involving fetuses. And while some courts strike down such prosecutions, the Alabama Supreme Court handed Steve and other Alabama prosecutors a victory: that court recognizes no difference between a fetus (even nonviable) and a child.

Sadly, contemporary fetal protection efforts often reveal hostility to the concerns of low-income pregnant women, because they counterproductively emphasize prosecution, incarceration, shaming, and stigmatization over healthy physician-patient relationships, medical treatment, and patient autonomy. Even in Alabama, very arbitrary lines are drawn between pregnant women who depend on prescription medications prescribed by their doctors to ease anxieties and pains during pregnancies and their counterparts who use methamphetamines, belying claims that states want to stamp out *all* drug use during pregnancy. I raised this with Steve Marshall. It was not something he had considered.

Rather, despite the purported aims of fetal protection prosecutions, targeted action against poor women's illicit drug use seems to be a priority – not *all* harmful drug use. Not surprisingly, significant problems and consequences flow from this approach, because it not only singles out one class of pregnant women for using drugs to treat their anxieties and pains, but also fails to recognize that prison is the worst place to promote fetal health.

This book takes up the largely ignored legislative and law enforcement turn to criminally policing pregnancy in the United States, providing a historical account of state intervention and control of women's pregnancy, while also offering theories to explain these legal and social shifts. The rising tide of criminal law enforcement in women's pregnancies coincides with deep shifts in the United States' cultural climate.

For example, the shifting cultural and political norms framing women's reproduction in the United States are marked by a troubling departure from civil, constitutional, and medical rights across a set of spheres that include rape, abortion, and pregnancy generally. As retired Republican senator Olympia Snowe informed me and a rapt audience at a summer 2013 luncheon in Minneapolis, Minnesota, when she was recruited to run for national office in the 1970s, the Republican Party leadership did not care that she was "pro-choice." Perhaps it did not matter, because George H.W. Bush shepherded Title X, which provides reproductive healthcare for the poorest women, through Congress. That legislation was signed into law by Richard Nixon. For her, it was a justice issue and at the time many within her party felt similarly, or at least believed these issues, such as abortion, rape, and pregnancy, were personal matters better left to women and their healthcare providers.

However, times have changed. Beginning in the 1980s and 1990s, special interest groups and strategic electoral campaigns used crime and unwed motherhood as the targets of animus, literally bringing pregnant women under attack. These attacks bring into question the very personhood of pregnant women. In fact, antiabortion legislators across the United States now claim that embryos and fetuses share the same constitutional status and rights as the pregnant women who gestate them. Antiabortion legislators are also shifting their tone and sympathies about rape and incest. Where, previously, even conservative lawmakers made clear that abortions should be permitted to save the life of the pregnant person as well as in cases of rape and incest, now that too is shifting. During the summer of 2019, Representative Steve King of Iowa told a crowd gathered at the Westside Conservative Club in Urbandale, Iowa, "I know that I can't certify that I'm not a part of a product of that." He pondered whether there would be "any population of the world left" if abortion exceptions existed for rape and incest. Of course, the very essence of rape and incest is an abuse of power and disregard for the humanity of the person sexually subjugated.

According to Lynn Paltrow, executive director of the National Advocates for Pregnant Women, "laws that seek to treat fertilized eggs, embryos, and fetuses as entirely separate legal persons provides the basis for creating a system of separate and unequal law for women."[9] In other words, claims to protect and promote fetal health and rights are sophisticated proxies for preserving patriarchy and the subordination of women.

In this new and seemingly neglected era of pregnancy policing, the roles of nurses and doctors are compromised as legislatures increasingly instantiate them as detectives and informants for the state, compromising well-established fiduciary roles, responsibilities, and obligations. For example, unbeknownst to pregnant patients, nurses and doctors increasingly don the roles of police informant during prenatal visits, disclosing confidential information to law enforcement, including medical tests and confidential communications, all without patient consent.[10] That law enforcement now plays a key role in American reproduction may come as a surprise, given strides gained and legal victories secured by women in employment, politics, education, and even reproduction. Yet, well over five hundred cases in recent years – in Alabama alone – bear out the aggressive turn to criminal policing of women's pregnancies. That most of these cases suffer the fates of obscurity and disregard may have to do with indifference and antipathy toward the poor.

The new reproductive politics are shaped by significant shifts to criminal law interventions in women's pregnancies and the establishment of legal rights in the fetuses. Such shifts raise important social questions and cast shadows on well-established constitutional, contract, property, and tort law norms, creating both concerns and tensions between federal and state law. For example, fetal protection laws, which now exist in thirty-eight states, impose criminal law interventions and sanctions on women's pregnancies. These laws were largely intended to protect women from domestic violence, but now serve as powerful tools used by legislatures and law enforcement officials to punish pregnant women. Child abuse statutes originally intended to protect against the neglect and abuse of children provide enforcement leverage as revamped tools in the arsenals of legislators and prosecutors seeking to criminalize behavior that potentially harms fetuses.

States such as Utah have taken up the call to use a "very strong stick" in policing women's pregnancies by enacting aggressive fetal endangerment legislation, which applies to pregnant women who harm their pregnancies. Texas representative Doug Miller authored a bill aimed at criminalizing the ingestion of any controlled substances during pregnancy, making violation of the proposed law a felony. Other legislative efforts include establishing personhood in embryos and fetuses, which broadly criminalizes any conduct that interferes with perfecting the health of a fetus. Some scholars see these attacks as being abortion-related and they build a persuasive case, pointing to legislative attempts to bar the procedure after the first sound of a fetal heartbeat (approximately six weeks) rather than viability and, in Wisconsin, Alabama, Mississippi, and North Carolina, attempting to restrict abortions based on doctors' admitting privileges at nearby hospitals.[11]

Nevertheless, these legislative turns reflect not only the reflexive and often ineffective use of criminal law to address tough social issues, such as endemic poverty, lack of employment, drug addiction, depression, homelessness, and hopelessness; they also serve political purposes and expediency that may offer limited benefit to society. On close inspection, the passage and criminal enforcement of fetal protection laws may evince motives and implicit biases beyond abortion and even fetal health protection. For example, the new reproductive politics reveal pernicious practices connected to race and class bias, moral panic, selective prosecutions, and the extralegal desire to punish and shame vulnerable women. This book takes a critical look at those issues.

11.2.1 *The Gender Box*

Several clear problems emerge in the rush to police women's pregnancies. For example, the new reproductive policing focuses exclusively on women – their lifestyles, dependencies, associations, conduct, mistakes, and behaviors during pregnancy. By taking this approach, legislators invite false scientific assumptions, stereotypes, and misconceptions into how the public comes to understand reproduction. Legislators frame pregnancy as being controlled and conditioned by women. However, women alone do not create pregnancies, nor can they account for all the conditions that might benefit or harm a gestation, including environment, paternal health and age, and access (or lack of access) to medical services.

By focusing primarily on pregnant women in enacting new fetal protection laws, legislators send a very strong signal implying that pregnant women alone determine fetal health outcomes. Empirical studies expose the inaccuracy and deceptiveness in such claims.[12] Nevertheless, like recent controversial political accounts of "legitimate rape" as a type of sexual violence that cannot lead to pregnancy,[13] erroneous reproductive claims can carry significant traction, particularly when afforded political spotlight in electoral campaigns. Framing fetal harms as exclusively and directly linked to women is scientifically invalid and only serves to exacerbate stereotypes and unconstitutionally burden the interests of pregnant women.

11.2.2 *"A Very Strong Stick"*

In recent years, the revision of child abuse statutes to include harms to fetuses, feticide laws, and the enactment of new personhood legislation represent unbridled and unchecked intrusions into women's pregnancies. Texas defines personhood as beginning at conception. In 2018, Alabama voters approved "Amendment 2," which makes it state policy to amend the Alabama Constitution and to "declare and otherwise affirm that it is the public policy of this state to recognize and support the sanctity of unborn life and the rights of unborn children, most importantly the right to life in all manners and measures appropriate and lawful; and to provide that the constitution of this state does not protect the right to abortion or require the funding of abortion."

Within months of the ballot initiative, Ryan Magers, an Alabama resident, filed a wrongful death lawsuit against an abortion provider, the Alabama Women's Center for Reproductive Alternatives, its employees, and a pharmaceutical company, claiming that an abortion received by his girlfriend in 2017 was effectively murder of his future offspring, giving rise to a civil claim. His lawsuit claimed that "under Alabama law, an unborn child is a legal person" and relied on the new Amendment 2 provision in the Alabama Constitution. Madison County probate judge Frank Barger allowed the case to advance, deciding that Baby Roe was a person with legal rights. Magers represented Baby Roe's estate. Eventually, Madison County Circuit judge Chris Comer dismissed the claim.

Fetal protection laws, including new personhood measures, broadly sweep all potential reproductive harms into the gaze of criminal law enforcement and render them liable to punishment. As a result, newly enacted fetal protection laws (and amended child protection statutes) across the United States ensnare pregnant women for a broad range of activities, including falling down steps, suffering drug addiction, refusing cesarean sections, or attempting suicide. And prosecutors now speak openly about needing to punish pregnant women – for their own good. Some, like Charles Condon, claim that a strong "stick" is needed to keep pregnant women in line.

The passionate urging that "a very strong stick" be applied against pregnant women evokes troubling symbolism and imagery. The imagery casts metaphors of violence like whippings. This symbolism is consistent with the use of metal shackles on pregnant women during pregnancy and harsh punishments meted out by prosecutors.[14] Importantly, the desire to inflict "very strong sticks" against pregnant women exposes extralegal interests beyond promoting fetal health, such as shaming, stigmatization, and retribution. Michel Foucault refers to this as the "spectacle" process.[15]

Well, does it work? Will inflicting "strong sticks" against pregnant patients reduce the incidences of low birth weight, premature births, and the other mental and physical conditions legislators seek to prevent? This is unlikely, because the conditions that contribute to the fetal outcomes legislators and prosecutors target may be caused by various factors, including domestic violence, poverty, living within close proximity to a toxic environment, poor nutrition, stress, depression, and the father (his biology, including his age). For example, as many as one-third of autism cases – a disease in which legislators have taken significant interest – result from the father's older age. Additionally, schizophrenia and numerous other mental health diseases are linked directly to paternity. Therefore, focusing criminal law interventions on pregnant women will at best achieve false security – a political placebo effect.

11.2.3 *Pregnancy Hierarchies: Implicit Class Bias*

Like the old reproductive policing during America's notorious, but significantly overlooked, eugenics' period, the new era of reproductive policing creates reproductive hierarchies that distinguish between women's pregnancies based on socioeconomic or class status. Overwhelmingly, those targeted, arrested, and incarcerated in the United States for attempting to injure their fetuses are poor pregnant women. The gross disparities in arrests might be explained by the profoundly inaccurate assumption that poor women behave in riskier ways during their pregnancies than their middle-class or wealthy counterparts.

Clearly, most doctors respect their legal and ethical duties to their patients, and they desire to treat them with dignity and respect. However, class bias likely interferes, to some degree, with medical care. Ultimately, doctors more often extend greater deference to middle-class patients, and are more inclined to preserve and protect their confidentiality. Some doctors may share class status, similar educational attainment, and comparable professional status with their middle-class and more affluential patients. Moreover, the behaviors engaged in more frequently by middle-class women (that may expose fetuses to health risks) may be perceived as morally neutral and legally permissible. Take, for example, the use of highly addictive prescription medications to treat depression and anxiety,[16] or the use of assisted reproductive technologies that increase the incidences of cerebral palsy, hearing impairment, multiple births, premature births, and cognitive delays in offspring.

Reproductive hierarchies illume double standards in the rule and enforcement of law, whereby interest in the "socially fit" or the social fitness of a pregnancy is contingent on the pregnant patient's socioeconomic status. In other words, as in the eugenics era, those most vulnerable to contemporary reproductive policing are the poor and destitute. For example, a century ago the nation's first eugenics laws declared who could reproduce in the United States and who could not. The laws forbade women and men considered socially, morally, and intellectually unfit to reproduce. Forced sterilizations rendered girls from poor families – those as young as ten and eleven – forever unable to bear children. Legislatures found safe havens and constitutional legitimacy for these laws in American courts. In one of its most alarming decisions of the twentieth century, *Buck v. Bell*, the United States Supreme Court affirmed that forced sterilizations, carried out ubiquitously against the poor, did not violate their constitutional rights.

11.2.4 *Racial Discrimination and Selective Application of Feticide Measures*

Racial biases contribute to the significant disparities in who comes under the force of police scrutiny and control during pregnancy. Frequently, the cases brought to police and judicial attention may involve thorny legal and social issues, such as the patient who desires chemotherapy but also happens to be pregnant, or the patient who ingests illicit substances during pregnancy but nonetheless desires a healthy child. Law enforcement officials view these cases as cut-and-dry fetal abuses that they are authorized to pursue. Nevertheless, profoundly apparent hierarchies frame when, how, and whether state intervention takes place at all.

For example, a slightly higher proportion of white women ingest illicit substances during pregnancy compared to Black women – 15.4 percent and 14.1 percent, respectively.[17] Yet, according to a peer-reviewed study published in the *New England Journal of Medicine*, medical professionals are ten times more likely to report African American pregnant women to state disciplinary authorities if they test positive for illicit substances.[18] These disparities offer disquieting points of reference and highlight deeply embedded implicit biases. Researchers found that only 1.1 percent of pregnant white women testing positive for illicit drug ingestion are reported, compared to 10.7 percent of Black women.[19] To explain the disparity, some commentators claim that women of color serve as the convenient political scapegoats in legislative battles on drugs, welfare, and abortion. Lynn Paltrow surmises that "pregnant women became an appealing target for law enforcement officials who were losing the war on drugs and for the anti-choice forces whose goal has been to develop 'fetal rights' superior to and in conflict with the rights of women."[20]

Legislators, prosecutors, and doctors claim their interventions are about saving babies and preventing disabilities. Yet, pregnant women caught in the criminal grips and gaze of the state are almost exclusively poor and of color, like Bei Bei Shuai, Paula Hale, Regina McKnight, Parvi Patel, and many others. Frequently, women of color are the selectively targeted victims of intense state scrutiny. For example, in an infamous South Carolina criminal dragnet involving the collaboration of Medical University of South Carolina hospital staff, prosecutors, and local police, the self-described "task force" targeted only Black women for special drug testing, shackling, and arrest during and after prenatal visits, with the exception of one white pregnant patient.[21] And in her case, the attending nurse who spearheaded the collaboration wrote on the patient's chart: "lives with her boyfriend who is a Negro."[22] Such racial biases have negative social consequences and are constitutionally unjustifiable.

11.2.5 *Deputizing Doctors as Law Enforcement and Informants for the State*

Two major shifts in the roles and functions of nurses and doctors mark this era of policing women's reproduction. The new reproductive policing involves the instantiation of medical personnel as interpreters of fetal drug laws and their assuming the function of informants for the state. Both of these shifts pervert the delivery of medicine and the roles of medical personnel. Indeed, these shifts create legal problems that unconstitutionally burden the interests of pregnant patients. The former demands legal capacities that medical staff do not possess, which exposes their judgments to discretion, fallibility, bias, and wrong calls. The latter imposes significant costs on the provider-patient relationship, as doctors and nurses risk violating fiduciary duties in order to aid law enforcement. Furthermore, patients might withhold relevant information needed to treat their conditions or entirely forego medical care during pregnancy.

Importantly, these institutional shifts that embed doctors as criminal law gate-keepers cannot be described as rare or minimal invasions of patient privacy. These shifts represent the institutionalization of realigning ideologies and the reprioritization of legal values, particularly fiduciary duties. By demanding that doctors and nurses don the hats of law enforcement and informants, fissures in the provider-patient relationship emerge and mistakes surface. For example, some medical providers might consider their fiduciary obligation to their patient as secondary to their duty to disclose their patient's medical information, including interviews, medical tests, and other records, to the state. They may mistakenly believe that law enforcement interests trump patient interests and their medical obligations to privacy, informed consent, and confidentiality.

In Christine Taylor's case, it was a nurse who interpreted her patient's fall down steps as meeting the legal standards of attempted feticide. Taylor's subsequent arrest and incarceration serve as a potent example of not only the risks associated with instantiating medical providers as interpreters of feticide laws but also the fallibility of their legal interpretations and judgments. Taylor was later released from jail as prosecutors could not substantiate an attempted fetal murder case against her. Nevertheless, the harm and stigma that resulted from that "mistake" persists, as evidenced by one national news outlet continuing to post an online article entitled *Did Christine Taylor Take Abortion into Her Own Hands?*[23]

11.2.6 *Benefiting and Harming Children*

Prosecutors claim that strict criminal punishments against pregnant women achieve justice and serve the interests of harmed fetuses and society. Such claims are seductive, but are they credible? Are they correct? In other words, are children of incarcerated mothers better off? Is there a social benefit from mass incarceration of poor, pregnant women? It turns out that children of mothers in prison are actually worse off. In a thought-provoking study published in the peer-reviewed *Journal of Child and Family Studies*, researchers discovered a high prevalence of posttraumatic stress disorder in children of incarcerated parents.[24] Other studies confirm significant incidences of anxiety, depression, and fear in children of incarcerated parents.[25]

Shay Bilchik, author of a study focusing on the children of incarcerated parents, offers important insights into the status of children affected by "the call for more punitive and accountability-based approaches to stem the rising tide of crime."[26] She emphasizes that "there seems to be little controversy over the fact that this trend has caused … collateral damage."[27] She explains that the damage is not to the community, but rather "to the children of those offenders, negatively impacted by the incarceration of their parents."[28] Indeed, the National Council on Crime and Delinquency reports that children of incarcerated mothers are one of the most at-risk groups in American society[29] and that a mother's incarceration may be particularly "destructive" for her children.[30]

Thus, while legislators express the intention "to save the babies," incarcerating mothers may lead to their children being worse off and more likely to eventually enter the criminal justice system. A mother's incarceration neither reduces the potential long-term harms to the child nor does it enrich a child's life. This type of reproductive regulation may exacerbate rather than reduce harms to children[31] and society – children with parents in prison are six times more likely to "go to prison."[32]

11.2.7 *Turning Domestic Violence Laws Against Women*

In the shadow of the relentless, high-profile abortion wars during the last three decades, state legislatures adopted feticide statutes that at the time of their enactment promised to protect pregnant women against battery and domestic violence, which tend to increase during pregnancy. The Centers for Disease Control and Prevention (CDC), the lead United States agency devoted to monitoring public health and disease, reports that domestic violence is one of the leading threats to fetal health and development in developed as well as developing nations. The United States is no exception. The CDC defines domestic violence as "physical, sexual, or psychological/emotional violence or threats of physical or sexual violence that are inflicted on a pregnant woman."

The data is startling and horrific. According to the World Health Organization, pregnant women are "60% more likely to be beaten than women who are not pregnant."[33] Intimate partner abuse during pregnancy injures not only the mother's health but also that of the fetus, causing "threats to health and risk of death" from trauma.[34] Jacquelyn Campbell's extensive research on domestic violence during pregnancy confirms that intimate partner abuse at the time of pregnancy causes physical trauma and psychological distress that can result in severe depression and anxiety.[35] The mental and physical health consequences of domestic violence include physical injury, gastrointestinal harms, sexually transmitted diseases, depression, chronic pain, and post-traumatic stress disorder.[36] And the frequency of domestic violence during pregnancy is as high as 20 percent.[37] However, women who are domestically abused may be less likely to report the abuse for fear of reprisals from their partners and the threat of child welfare services removing children from the home and/or the baby after its birth.

Professor Deborah Epstein, in her invaluable research, documents the tireless efforts of feminists to bring about legal reform in the sphere of domestic violence, which until the 1980s and early 1990s drew a tepid response from law enforcement and legislatures, who viewed physical violence against women as "private" family matters.[38] Extreme brutality, including strangulations, kicking women down steps, marital rape, sexual assaults, breaking noses, and even kidnappings, fell within the categories of "private" and "family matters." Feticide laws were intended to fill this gap and provide protections for pregnant women, whose lives were more likely to be threatened than those of nonpregnant women.

It is ironic, then, that such laws, intended to protect pregnant women against domestic violence, have gained momentum as tools for legislatures and prosecutors to perfect pregnancies and treat women's reproduction as matters of the state. Suzanne Goldberg, the director of the Center for Gender and Sexuality Law at Columbia Law School, explained it thusly: "Pregnant women are winding up victims of these laws instead of being protected by them."[39] She is right.

Consider once more the case of Bei Bei Shuai. Prosecutorial efforts to convict Shuai revealed significant disparities in the application of feticide laws in Indiana. Prosecutors desired an all-or-nothing verdict against Shuai; if their prosecution was successful, she could have served forty-five years in prison. Prosecutors claimed that their interests were the interests of the fetus and society. They argued that the state had convicted others under this law and that it must apply the law neutrally. Indeed, a prosecutor proudly informed me that she had prosecuted a man for violating the law and that he had received a forty-five-year sentence.

However, prior to Shuai's prosecution, the most recent feticide case on record was *Kendrick v. State*, where a bank robber shot the teller in the stomach, killing her twins. The defendant received a sentence of four years for each fetus. Similarly, in *Shane v. State* the defendant received eight years for the charge of killing a fetus. Finally, in *Perigo v. State* the defendant was convicted of a Class C felony feticide charge at trial and was sentenced to five years for killing a fetus. The backdrop of these cases involved torture, stabbing, shooting, and unparalleled violence against pregnant women. Most revealing are the minimal sentences sought for killing the fetuses.

11.2.8 *Extralegal Punishment: Shaming*

In prior works, I have suggested that stigma, shame, and contrition are the intended byproducts of criminal law punishment.[40] These emotion-driven aspects of criminal law seek to promote public welfare and achieve utility when applied to universally condemned crimes or when guilt is not enough. For example, the public nature of the court appearance, the subordination that attaches to incarceration, the psychological trauma resulting from institutionalization, limited access to the outside world, and being confronted with those injured by the defendant's conduct are all part of the criminal law punishment process.

In relation to pregnant women, however, criminal condemnation takes on powerful, extralegal force. It extends retribution to spheres where some scholars suggest the law should not tread.[41] These extralegal punishments bear on an ex-offender's ability to fully rehabilitate, including restoration of voting rights, the ability to become gainfully employed, and whether one can reintegrate into society. Nearly a decade ago, Martha Nussbaum provided a powerful counternarrative to the utility of shaming in the criminal law context.[42] As Nussbaum pointed out, extralegal shaming manifests negative externalities that extend beyond the reach of the type of punishment administered by the criminal justice system. In other words, shaming is enduring and applied in unanticipated ways by unanticipated actors and institutions separate from the criminal justice system. These issues are particularly relevant in the reproductive context.

11.2.9 *Curing Addiction Through Criminal Law Intervention*

Legislators turn to the criminal law to cure social and now medical ills. However, for all the efforts to rein in women's conduct during pregnancy or to promote the health and welfare of future fetuses and babies, turning to the criminal law may undermine those policy and health goals. Precisely for this reason, the American Medical Association,[43] the American Public Health Association,[44] and dozens of other medical organizations[45] emphatically oppose criminal prosecutions of pregnant women in response to their drug and alcohol addiction. Among their reasons for opposing fetal drug law policy is a concern that "the threat of criminal prosecution prevents many women from seeking prenatal care and early intervention for their drug dependence."[46]

The fear of arrest and prosecution may serve as powerful deterrents to seeking prenatal care. Studies indicate that, at least in cases involving drug addiction and illicit substance abuse, the "stick" approach is ineffective as it does not deter drug use and may exacerbate addictions and lead to the unnecessary fragmentation of the family.[47] Moreover, studies conducted by the Oregon Office of Alcohol and Drug Abuse Programs and Maryland's Alcohol and Drug Abuse Administration provide compelling, but not surprising, evidence that drug treatment programs are far more health- and cost-effective than incarceration due to their strong correlations with gainful employment, increased wages, reduced welfare use, and substantially less recidivism.[48] Given this, can incarceration of pregnant women be justified as fulfilling the state's interest in protecting children?

11.2.10 *Assisted Reproduction, Crack Babies, and Misjudging Harms*

Legislators likely understand that neonatology costs are rising; medical insurance lobbyists emphasize this phenomenon as a cause of rising healthcare costs.[49] However, politicians assume that those costs, particularly when they exceed insurance coverage and individual payment, result from the preventable or punishable choices made by indigent drug addicts.[50] Consider Representative Doug Miller's urgent warning once more: "The Texas Legislature can no longer sit idly by while its next generation is born ... with physical and mental abnormalities ... destined to be on Social Security benefits."[51] Miller is right: the potential to care for extremely low birth weight and premature babies has expanded. Medical technology now ensures the survival of fetuses and infants previously considered unviable, including "those with severe congenital malformations, those born as early as 22 weeks' gestation and those with profound asphyxia."[52] However, these babies are not so-called crack babies.

Representative Miller's fear of Texas becoming "swamped" with drug-addicted babies siphoning off state resources misjudges why neonatal medical costs are rising and what is contributing to childhood disabilities. Rigorously conducted scientific research published in the *Journal of the American Medical Association* and the *New England Journal of Medicine* reveals that medical providers and scientists rushed to judgment in the 1980s, purporting that major cities would become "swamped" by children born addicted to crack, exposed in utero by addicted mothers. This mythology spread, carried by the force of antidrug campaigns. However, a decade ago doctors courageously disavowed their earlier predictions.[53] Leading medical publications will no longer publish articles that use the term "crack baby," because researchers now find that such a baby or child does not exist. Instead, poverty is a better indicator of child health and well-being. If crack babies are not driving up healthcare costs, what is?

Recent legislative interest in fetal health has often involved more than a call to aid the development and future well-being of fetuses. As this book shows, government actors selectively deploy this interest, calling attention to some pregnancies where the state demands perfection and not others. Increasingly, those who rely on the sophisticated medical technologies found in American neonatology wards are older, educated parents who, through aggressive hormone therapies and in vitro fertilization, give birth to premature, underweight twins, triplets, quadruplets, and even higher order births.[54]

For example, assisted reproductive technologies (ART) – very expensive technologies used almost exclusively by upper-income couples – have a 65 percent failure rate, resulting in miscarriages and other traumas. According to researchers, children born via ART have an increased risk of cerebral palsy, cognitive delays, hearing and visual impairment, and premature births, among other conditions. To date, however, there are no federal laws that regulate the practice or industry despite more than two decades of robust empirical literature pointing to ART risks. Therefore, there are no ART-related prosecutions for fetal harms.

A report issued by the CDC framed the matter in this way: "ART-related multiple births are an increasingly important public health problem nationally and in many states."[55] Dr. Michael Kornhauser and Dr. Roy Schneiderman warn that "increases in maternal age and greater use of in vitro fertilization, combined with remarkable medical advances, are leading not only to increases in preterm births, but also to medical complications and associated costs."[56] The average medical costs associated with those births are one thousand percent more than for a full-term infant.

11.2.11 Abortion

Forceful state oversight increasingly dominates women's reproduction. Legislators, who adamantly argue for smaller, less involved government, nonetheless seek to deploy the government's mighty arsenal against pregnant women. This landscape is dominated by legislative appeals to grant fetuses the rights of living persons. It looks like this: rules requiring doctors to report any behaviors exhibited by their pregnant patients that might pose a threat of harm to fetuses; unscientific assessments about rape and pregnancy; the removal of children from women deemed to be unfit based on prenatal conduct; and intensified, selective arrests and prosecutions. But what accounts for this legislative trend? Some scholars claim that all of this – the war on women or at least the war on women's reproduction – is really about abortion.

This book recognizes the need to bring the use of child abuse statutes, feticide laws, and other fetal protection laws into view and out of the shadows of abortion and the discourses that dominate how scholars, activists, and politicians think about reproduction. So much has already been said about *Roe v. Wade* and abortion more generally: mandatory waiting periods; required distribution of information prior to pregnancy termination; limiting the period in which an abortion can be sought; parental and judicial approval.

Yet, there is an important gap to fill in the reproductive policing story that specifically relates to criminalizing abortion, race, and class. Indeed, legislation promulgated as this book goes to press makes clear that the criminal policing of women's pregnancies now extends to abortion in cleverly strategized and disguised ways that bear directly on access to and the affordability of the medical procedures. A slew of so-called heartbeat bills make it a crime to obtain an abortion after detection of a fetal heartbeat. Other states, such as Alabama, Iowa, Kentucky, Mississippi, Ohio, Georgia, and North Dakota have enacted similar laws. All have been challenged. Some struck down. Others have been enjoined from going into effect.

Politicians have erected legislative barriers that effectively close most clinics in some states, such as Mississippi, Arkansas, Wisconsin and North Dakota. Such laws mean that women must travel long, burdensome distances or to other states to obtain this legal medical procedure. Some of the legislation provides no exceptions for cases of rape or incest. For wealthier women, these obstacles may be burdensome, but not proscriptive.

However, there is more to be said about abortion, particularly the deployment of criminal law to undermine constitutional access to abortion. In the spring of 2019, Mississippi, a state with one abortion clinic, enacted a law banning abortions before some women would know they are pregnant – at about six weeks. For some legislators, despite U.S. Supreme Court precedent, a previability abortion is not only an act of moral turpitude but also a crime. For example, New Mexico representative Cathrynn Brown proposed legislation in 2013 that would criminally punish rape and incest victims who terminated their pregnancies. Brown's bill permitted the prosecution of pregnant women for "tampering with evidence." As Brown explained, an abortion after rape is a criminal act, because it tampers with evidence. A woman's punishment for violating Brown's law? A felony conviction, mandating up to three years' incarceration. It is no surprise, then, that reproductive rights activists claim that the antiabortion movement epitomizes a war on women.

11.3 THE WAR ON WOMEN'S REPRODUCTION

In the twenty-first century, public criminal regulation trumps expectations of privacy. This book analyzes who benefits from and who is harmed by the contemporary legislative turn to policing women's reproduction. Recent criminal prosecutions targeting destitute pregnant women illuminate another reproductive space, where the threat of state intervention through punishment and extralegal retribution overarch pregnancies and compromise the physician-patient relationship.

This book explains that poor pregnant women's reproductive options are deeply constrained and contested in the United States. A woman's poverty and drug consumption during pregnancy might result in heightened legal consequences, including threat of life imprisonment, giving birth while in jail, and even being shackled during labor, depending on the state in which the pregnant woman resides. In the United States, a woman determined to carry a pregnancy to term often unwittingly exposes herself to nefarious interagency collaborations between police and physicians, possibly leading to criminal prosecution, incarceration, and giving birth in highly unsanitary prison conditions, sometimes without the appropriate aid of hospital physicians and staff.

Policing the Womb argues that what legislators seek to reduce – the incidence of low-birth-weight babies – is tangled in racial and class profiling, which detracts from an evidence-based approach to reduce fetal health harm. On inspection, prescription drug use, domestic violence, and ART all play a role in fetal health outcomes and the rise in neonatology treatments and costs. This book deliberates on one of the most urgent social policy issues of our time – the rationality of the turn to criminally policing women's conduct during pregnancy.

Epilogue

Retain Judge Persky -- No Recall

Hon. Aaron Persky
800 W. El Camino Real, Suite 180
Mountain View, CA 94040
www.RetainJudgePersky.com

September 6, 2016

Professor Michele Goodwin
UC Irvine School of Law
401 E. Petason Dr., Suite 1000
Irvine, CA 92697

Dear Professor Goodwin,

As you probably know, I am the subject of a recall effort over one of my sentencing decisions. I am prohibited by the Canons of Judicial Ethics from discussing the case, but I am not prohibited from opposing the recall. If judges allow public opinion to influence our decisions, we corrupt the decision-making process and erode the rule of law.

Recall proponents are soliciting support and collecting money to promote the recall. They claim to have raised over $250,000 to date, with an ultimate goal of $1 million. Opposing the recall will require funding to educate voters about the need for an independent judiciary. Many members of the legal community have asked me how they can help. I would appreciate any financial support you can give as well as your endorsement. I would be honored if you would join the many law professors who have publicly opposed the recall. I am enclosing a contribution envelope, but you can also contribute online at www.RetainJudgePersky.com. Contributions may be made in any amount and are not tax-deductible.

Please feel free to contact me at my campaign email (RetainJudgePersky@gmail.com). Thank you for considering this request.

Best regards,

Aaron Persky
Judge of the Superior Court, County of Santa Clara

Paid for by Retain Judge Persky - No Recall, FPPC ID#1387571. Contributions from foreign nationals may not be accepted unless they have permanent residency status in the United States.

WHEN YOU'RE A STAR, THEY LET YOU DO IT

One week after the 2016 presidential election, I landed at Lindenberg Airport in Minneapolis, Minnesota, at the break of dawn, after flying across the country through the middle of the night. The air was crisp, but due to become even more frigid and bone chilling. After that, as meteorologists predicted, it would rain and then snow, ending what was a surprising, lingering dry period in a state known for its damp springs and snowy winters. It did not take long for the weather predictions to materialize. The snow fell heavily and quickly, causing havoc on the highways and streets; accidents were already accumulating. I felt concerned about renting a car that quite possibly was insufficiently equipped to handle the impending brunt of the storm. State officials warned people to stay off roads and highways. I understood why.

After a quick breakfast at an old diner known as "The Bad Waitress," I proceeded in my compact rental car to the University of Minnesota Law School. Early morning arrivals in cities around the country is the price some academics and others pay for living or working in California. We take overnight flights (the so-called red-eyes), arrive at five or six o'clock in the morning, and hope there is time to check into our hotels. Today, there would not be that chance; I was attending a conference honoring Professor Catharine MacKinnon, the legal scholar who pioneered the legal claim that sexual harassment is sex discrimination. That seems so logical today, but years ago that was not so obvious for judges. My talk was the first of the day.

My talk was not about sexual harassment in the workplace or pornography, two areas of legal discourse in which Professor MacKinnon made groundbreaking, hotly debated contributions. Rather, my talk was about power and the political, and the normalization of sexual violence. That is, I planned to query how sexual violence had become something that society failed to reject as repugnant and impermissible. I wondered if Americans were becoming numb to women's claims regarding sexual violence. Was indifference supplanting outrage over girls' and women's complaints about being groped publicly and privately, kissed without permission, and raped within their homes, the military, in prisons and jails, and on college campuses?[1]

***

In the fall of 2016, I received an unexpected letter from Judge Aaron Persky. In an infamous act of judicial discretion, he sentenced Brock Allen Turner, a twenty-year-old former Stanford University student and varsity swimmer convicted of three felony counts of sexual assault on an unconscious woman, to six months in the local county jail. Eyewitness testimony of two students who observed the assault (and phoned the police) and jarring medical reports offered chilling accounts of the sexual violence Mr. Turner inflicted on his victim. Jane Doe wrote about how she woke up in a hospital, disoriented, with dried blood and abrasions on her body, no panties, and pine needles in her hair, which it took three people to comb out. She wrote of feeling everything within her being "silenced." Brock Turner, the man who assaulted her, was convicted and prosecutors recommended that he be sentenced to six years in state prison, given his crimes.

However, at sentencing, Judge Persky ruled that a lengthier sentence for the Stanford swimmer would be too severe and unjust. Judge Persky even read from Jane Doe's Victim Impact Statement[2] to emphasize why a lengthier sentence would harm Turner more than help. Instead, Brock Turner's six-month sentence would mean three months of actual incarceration in a minimum security facility. Advocates for victims of sexual assault criticized the ruling as a slap in the face to victims everywhere. They argued that in this case there should be little handwringing about the victim's credibility, because witnesses saw Brock Turner atop of Jane Doe, moving his body. A national uproar ensued, resulting in a rare judicial recall effort.

Several months later, Judge Persky, a Stanford alumnus and former men's lacrosse team coach, wrote to me, asking for help (and likely appealing to many others). He needed money fast and wanted to defeat the judicial recall effort led by Michele Dauber, a professor at Stanford Law School. He was concerned that public influence could "corrupt the decision-making process and erode the rule of law." I recalled how only two months before, Judge Persky had asked, "Is incarceration in state prison the right answer for the poisoning of [Jane Doe's] life?" and had answered his own question in the negative.[3] Seemingly, for poisoning a young woman's life by sexual assault, time in the local jail outside of Stanford University is sufficient.

Today, the survivor, Chanel Miller, has come forward to give a public accounting of what happened to her. As part of her healing and reclaiming her power, she is using her name, rather than Jane or Emily Doe. By her coming forward, we now know she is a woman of color. She was unconscious when the violation occurred, learning about the violence her body had endured through friends, medical examinations, and medical reports. The reports detailed and documented her deep bruising, soreness, and pain. However, unlike many cases, eyewitnesses confirmed the assault. Two Swedish foreign exchange students recounted how they caught Mr. Turner – still on top of Chanel's mostly naked, unconscious body – "thrusting" when they demanded he stop.[4] Mr. Turner fled; one of the men tripped him up and held him until police came.

Turner's friends and family appealed to Judge Persky for leniency. They asserted that the facts were confusing and muddled by the fact that Chanel was unconscious throughout the sexual encounter. How could the judge trust her account more than Brock's? According to them, this case epitomized "he said" versus "she said." One character letter written by a female friend of Brock Turner's suggested that this case simply represented the state of affairs for college sex: too much drinking and confusion over consent. In the end, Brock Turner's friends and family members urged Judge Persky to impose probation or simply drop the charges. In a highly provocative and controversial letter to the court, Brock Turner's father, Dan, pleaded that prison would be "a steep price to pay for 20 minutes of action." Brock's father related that his son could no longer enjoy his life, including eating his favorite steaks – the ribeye cut – and he hoped that the judge would agree that Brock "has never been violent to anyone including his actions on the night of Jan 17th."[5]

Judge Persky's now infamous ruling sparked protests and dramatic headlines, in part because it reflected how social and political status may privilege men while burdening women. I obtained the June 2, 2016 sentencing transcript.[6] Judge Persky quoted from Chanel's Victim Impact Statement. Yet, he did so not to emphasize the impact of the crime on her life. Ironically, his quoting from Chanel's moving statement was not to refer to her pain and enduring suffering, nor to opine on the gravity of sexual assault. Rather, it was to mitigate Mr. Turner's punishment. He stated, "the damage is done," ostensibly surmising that a prison sentence would undermine Chanel's interests and therefore was unnecessary. Ultimately, Mr. Turner served three months in the local jail. I gave no money to the judge.

Despite the widespread media attention, the case begged for deeper inspection. Chanel did not attend Stanford; she was not an elite athlete; and she had no claims to the bright future Judge Persky wished to preserve for Brock Turner at all costs, even at the expense of a young woman sexually assaulted near a pile of trash at his alma mater. Chanel Miller interrupted Brock Turner's American dream that relatives claimed included the Olympics, national championships, and graduating from a university ranked first in the nation by *Forbes* magazine.[7] There was material value in Brock's life and liberty in a manner that did not exist for Chanel Miller. Somehow, Brock's freedom symbolically mapped onto a better America. In that better America, society was somehow better off with Brock serving what amounted to a summer boot camp in the aftermath of his sexual violence.

Even more troubling was the underlying assumption in the ruling: elite white men who commit sexual assaults do not pose risks to society or the women they presumably will encounter in the future. In fact, any incarceration may be too punitive and victimizing for these men. Yet, studies conducted by researchers at Brown University and the University of Massachusetts paint a different picture.

David Lisak and Paul Miller pooled data in which almost 1,900 men were evaluated for acts of interpersonal violence. Their study reported on 120 of the men who "self-reported acts [that] met the definitions of rape or attempted rape, but who were never prosecuted by criminal justice authorities." Their findings revealed that "a majority of these undetected rapists were repeat rapists."[8] According to these researchers, the repeat rapists in their study averaged nearly six rapes each. On the whole, these men were responsible for over 1,200 separate acts of intimate violence, including rape, but also battery, child abuse, and domestic violence.

Although alarming, Lisak and Miller's research findings are consistent with prior peer-reviewed research.[9] In a study where the majority of participants were well-educated white men, Abel and colleagues found that "the frequency of self-reported crimes was vastly greater than the number of crimes for which the subjects had been arrested."[10] In other words, "the ratio of arrest to commission of the more violent crimes such as rape and child molestation was approximately 1:30."[11] Abel and colleagues reported that rapists who were assured of confidentiality confessed to committing multiple additional rapes and sexual assaults – on average, 7.2 rapes each.[12] Abel reported that, "contrary to the stereotypic view of the paraphiliac as uneducated, the majority of the participants had received a moderate amount of education, 40% finishing at least one year of college" and "64.6% of subjects were fully employed."[13]

The outcome of Turner's case was not inconsistent with researchers' findings generally: date rapes on campuses generally go unpunished, even if reported. Embedded in Judge Persky's opinion was an old, familiar logic: incarceration illegitimately robs white men who commit sexual assault of their dignity and inherent worth to and in society. Thus, punishing them for sexual assault and rape affronts law and the legal system.

As much as many women were outraged, the outcome was not entirely unfamiliar or unusual. Disparate sentencing by race and sex historically pervades cases of sexual assault. Empirical research demonstrates that while white men are just as likely to rape as males belonging to any other ethnic group in the United States, they are the least likely to be prosecuted and punished for such crimes.[14] On indigenous lands, white men (or any other Americans) can commit crimes with almost no repercussions.[15] Sierra Crane-Murdoch wrote: "One in three Native American women are raped during their lifetimes—two-and-a-half times the likelihood for an average American woman—and in 86 percent of these cases, the assailant is non-Indian."[16]

In Professor Donald Dripps's study of 3,000 rape cases, he and colleagues reported that Black men were seven times more likely to receive the death penalty for rape. Similarly, studies published in the peer-reviewed journals *Law and Human Behavior*, *Victimology*, and *Applied Psychology*, among others, report similar findings. For instance, Black offenders receive dramatically different sentences from their white counterparts. Professor E.J. Kanin's groundbreaking study on date rapes on college campuses highlighted that while seventy-one white male undergraduates admitted having raped a woman, only six were reported to police, and none prosecuted.[17]

***

As the snow began to fall on that cold Minneapolis morning, blanketing the signposts, buildings, streets, and highways, I thought of the other recent cases where judges imposed lenient sentences on men who had committed heinous sexual assaults. The perpetrators happened to be white, and the cases were alarming. There was the case of a father in Montana who serially raped his daughter and whose sentence was only sixty days in jail[18] – even less time than Brock Turner served. I doubted whether that case would attract sustained attention or even social and legal critique by the time of this book's publication. After all, Americans had just elected Donald Trump to be the country's next President in the wake of numerous allegations and lawsuits claiming he sexually assaulted women in various public and private settings. A leaked tape, where listeners hear the President derogatively boasting about grabbing women by the "pussy,"[19] caused a momentary stir. However, a majority of white women supported Mr. Trump's candidacy (despite expressing some misgivings about the crudity of his speech).

The Montana case involved the rape of a twelve-year-old by her forty-year-old father, Martin Blake. It appeared in the news just weeks after Brock Turner's release from jail. Prosecutors claimed that Mr. Blake habitually raped his little girl – a crime he later admitted having committed.[20] Facing a potential sentence where he would surely die in prison, Mr. Blake negotiated and accepted a plea deal offered by prosecutors. Prosecutors recommended a sentence of one hundred years, with seventy-five years suspended, which would result in twenty-five years' incarceration.[21] They told Judge John McKeon that such a sentence was what Montana law called for. After taking the prosecutors' recommendation under advisement, Judge McKeon sentenced Mr. Blake to sixty days.

Like Persky, McKeon voiced doubts about the appropriateness of the recommended punishment, noting that Mr. Blake had already suffered separation from his family and was remorseful. In an expression of leniency and good faith, Judge McKeon gave the father credit for the seventeen days he had already served in jail, thereby reducing his sentence to only an additional forty-three days. Here too, the legal system served to affirm the "potential good" in a man found guilty of committing rape, setting aside the perpetrator's culpability and guilt, and minimizing the victimization, humiliation, stigma, pain, shame, and embarrassment experienced by female sexual assault victims.

Cases of incest are troubling and, unlike sexual assaults involving strangers, families struggle to determine whether reconciliation is ever possible. In the case of minors, the law generally aspires to create safety for the child, separating her from an abusive parent. Yet, even if rare, rulings such as McKeon's are a punishment for all victims. Such a lenient sentence for a serial rapist with intimate and unfettered access to the victim undoubtedly places the child at risk. Such lenient sentences send a traumatizing message to other young rape victims who experience similar crimes against their dignity, leaving them emotionally and mentally vulnerable. Who would risk telling her story and confronting an abuser if the legal system returns him to the neighborhood, let alone the family home, in a few weeks? In this case, the father was expected to relocate to his parents' home.

***

Likely, Judge McKeon's ruling will be forgotten, swallowed up in the many legal transactions of a tiny district court, quite possibly without even a lasting record of the judge's opinion. Many trial court transactions do not result in published opinions, even though there may be a transcript of the trial. I thought about a daunting statistic from the Rape, Abuse & Incest National Network (RAINN): out of 1,000 allegations of rape, "994 perpetrators will walk free." In fact, the scattered "old news" pile of cases my law students and I had tracked were only weeks or months old at the time, but seemingly no longer newsworthy.

For example, in May 2016, Judge Patrick Butler sentenced a University of Colorado student, Austin Wilkerson, to community service for the sexual assault of an incapacitated freshman.[22] In June 2016, a former Indiana University student, John Enoch, spent one day in jail after being charged with two rapes.[23] In July 2016, Judge Barry Steelman accepted a plea deal and suspended sentence of a school bus driver in Tennessee who had raped a student at a local motel.[24] In August 2016, Judge William Estes sentenced David Becker, also a student athlete, to suspended probation, rather than the two years recommended by prosecutors, after he was found guilty of sexual battery against two women.[25] In September 2016, Hadi Nabulsi was sentenced to serve one year in jail for raping a child in Massachusetts.[26] And in October 2016, Judge Michael Hensley of Madison, Indiana, refused to issue an arrest warrant for Anthony Russell, who had a history of brutally battering his wife. Hours later, Anthony Russell murdered his estranged wife.[27]

In most of the cases cited above, the perpetrators were educated white men, which presents a troubling double bind for academics, advocates, and even some policy makers who are sympathetic to rape victims, yet also desire criminal law reform. They argue that if judges succumb to pressure for tougher sentencing, the people most harmed will be men of color. And they believe some of the sentences will be flawed, that there will be admissions of guilt resulting from threat and coercion, and sentencing driven by bias bearing slim relation to the crimes. They are skeptical about a criminal justice system that has long protected affluent white men from the consequences of domestic violence, sexual assaults, harassment, rape, and even murder, while disparately criminalizing and jailing Blacks and Latinos. The historic racialized cruelty of the American criminal justice system warns against ignoring such concerns.

Rogue policing and corruption plague the criminal justice system and were disturbingly manifested in the lynching and murder of fourteen-year-old Emmett Till, who supposedly whistled at a white woman in a Mississippi convenience store.[28] In that case, the cruel vigilante punishment for transgressing social norms in Mississippi resulted in the child's death and no punishment for the men who killed him. Till's murderers (who later confessed to their crime) were acquitted in less than an hour by an all-white male jury.[29] Years later, Carolyn Bryant, the alleged victim of Till's whistle, confessed to Timothy B. Tyson, a Duke University historian, that she lied.

Similarly, a malfunctioning, rickety electric chair, euphemistically referred to as "Old Sparky," held the fate of many Black boys and men. It would be the last seat of a tiny Black boy, George Stinney – the youngest person to be executed in the United States in the last century – for the alleged rape and murder of two white girls.[30] He too was fourteen years old. Despite the fact that no evidence linked Stinney to the rapes and murders, an all-white male jury convicted him in less than ten minutes.[31]

Stinney had no legal assistance or a lawyer at any point – His swift conviction conformed to a troubling historic pattern of the state killing Black boys and men alleged to have violated white girls and women. In Donald Partington's landmark law review article on the history of the death penalty for rape in Virginia between 1908 ("when the electric chair was installed in the Virginia State Penitentiary") and 1963, he wrote: "[F]orty-one men [were] executed for rape, thirteen for attempted rape, one for rape and robbery, and one for attempted rape and highway robbery. All of these men were Negroes."[32] During that same period, the state of Virginia spared from execution 1,238 white men convicted of rape, attempted rape, statutory rape, and attempt to commit statutory rape.[33] One way to interpret the glaring disparity is that the criminal justice system regarded white men's lives as inherently more worthy and valuable, and thus worth sparing.

It would be a mistake to relegate such cases to the dusty confines of history, ignoring the current patterns of privilege and punishment that pervade the manner in which Americans (and our legal system) think about sex, rape, and guilt. More recently, the convictions of Genarlow Wilson and Marcus Dixon further highlight the concerns of disparate racial policing, prosecuting, and sentencing related to sex and sexual assault. Both were high school students at the time of their prosecutions. Both young men were academic and athletic stars whose sex with their respective fifteen-year-old white girlfriends resulted in statutory rape charges and severe criminal punishments.[34]

A court in Georgia sentenced the seventeen-year-old Wilson to ten years in prison, denying him bail and bond, notwithstanding his girlfriend's statements that the two consensually engaged in oral sex. In that case, neither the prosecutor nor the judge peered into the future and saw anything in Genarlow's life worth protecting or saving. In a bizarre twist to the case, on the night in question, Wilson's white classmates, who also engaged in sex, including vaginal penetration (at the same party) and were captured on video doing so, did not receive similar criminal sanctions.[35] Prosecutors interpreted a newly enacted Romeo and Juliet law, which permits leniency in cases of underage sex between teens, as applying to vaginal penetration but not oral sex.[36]

One powerful critique of statutory rape prosecutions is that the cases are subject to police and prosecutorial discretion, which often disfavors Black males, and judges may be less sympathetic to Black male defendants accused of sexually violating white girls and women.[37] In that context, Wilson's prosecution highlights not only the potential for sex, race, and class bias to seep into how sex is policed; it also sheds light on the broad and unfettered discretion of prosecutors in the criminal justice system. Undeniably, "[n]o government official in America has as much unreviewable power and discretion as the prosecutor."[38]

Prosecutorial discretion remains a crucial and foundational element of the American criminal justice system. And yet, "prosecutors' 'power to be lenient [also] is the power to discriminate.'"[39] That is, "[p]rosecutors have great leeway to abuse their powers and indulge their self-interest, biases, or arbitrariness."[40] In addition, unrestrained and unchecked discretion leaves room for even unintentional or what scholars now call "implicit racial bias"[41] to embed in prosecutorial decision-making, influencing (1) whether to charge an individual and what to charge her or him with; (2) whether to allow or oppose bail; (3) and whether to offer a plea bargain, among other things.[42] The most important part of the prosecutor's discretion in statutory rape cases is likely the decision on whether to institute proceedings against the juvenile.

Ultimately, these cases – from Brock Turner's to Genarlow Wilson's – raise important questions for law and society. What is the role of the state in the maintenance and production of violence against women and girls? How does the state contribute to, or serve as a primary force in, normalizing the social and legal statuses of women? Does law influence not only how courts and legislatures view men and women, but also how the sexes see themselves? How does misogyny fit into American and even global ideals of masculinity? Was Catharine MacKinnon right when she argued that the state gives birth to "the conditions that produce men who systemically express themselves violently toward women [and] women whose resistance is disabled"?[43] As she wrote in 1983, "criminal enforcement in these areas . . . punishes men for expressing the images of masculinity that mean their identity, for which they are otherwise trained, elevated, venerated, and paid."[44]

Over the years, through my research on sexual violence, it becomes clearer that these problems of disparate sentencing, lenient sentences for some rapists, the stigmatization of female and transgendered victims, and the punishment of women – both as victims and perpetrators – occupy a global space not confined to the United States. That is, judges globally are making poor decisions regarding rape and incest.

Recently, in Canada, a district court judge, Robin Camp, was elevated to the federal judiciary even after he berated a rape victim for failing to "keep [her] knees together" and suggested that she could have avoided "penetration" had she simply contorted her body into a bathroom sink.[45] In that case, Judge Camp acquitted the defendant while admonishing the complainant that "some sex and pain sometimes go together ... that's not necessarily a bad thing."[46] Similarly, in the United Kingdom, Judge David Farrell granted an incredibly lenient sentence to two men who had gang-raped an eleven-year-old, stating that she looked fourteen and had sought the men's attention.[47] In Afghanistan, reporters have chronicled how men trade girls like "commodities" to relieve families of debts.[48] In cases of rape, too frequently girls and women suffer the punishment and incarceration, as rape is not a well-established legal concept, unlike adultery and sex without marriage. A BBC reporter described one case like this:

> She is entirely hidden in a blue burka. Hundreds of men from the village are gathered as two mullahs pass sentence. As Taliban fighters look on, the sentence is passed and she is found guilty of adultery.
> The stoning lasts two minutes. Hundreds of rocks – some larger than a man's fist – are thrown at her head and body. She tries to crawl out of the hole, but is beaten back by the stones. A boulder is then thrown at her head, her burka is soaked in blood, and she collapses inside the hole.[49]

***

As I plowed through the damp snow, nearing the University of Minnesota Law School, my attention turned from Brock Turner, Judge Persky, and the various cases I had spent that summer and fall researching. Newscasters were reporting about Russian interference in the 2016 presidential election in the United States. I turned the volume up.

Barely ten days before, the United States' deep divide on matters of race, reproductive health, sexual assault, immigration policy, and perhaps history itself manifested in an election that remained raw and divisive for many Americans. Protestors gathered in Los Angeles, San Francisco, Chicago, New York, and other major cities, expressing outrage, disbelief, and frustration, claiming President-elect Donald Trump was not *their* President.[50]

On Tuesday, November 8, 2016, Donald Trump won the presidency of the United States. In a startling victory, Mr. Trump soundly defeated Secretary Hillary Clinton by securing the most Electoral College votes in that election – a feat accomplished in part by breaking through the so-called blue wall of the Upper-Midwest, which had consistently voted Democratic for decades. The political fabric that held the blue wall together proved too porous and fragile. It disintegrated in a tide of fear associated with the economy, immigration, and job loss.

However, just weeks before the election, *Washington Post* journalist David A. Fahrenthold broke a now infamous story[51] about a recording of Mr. Trump and former NBC morning show host Billy Bush speaking casually about groping women and sexual assault. The President's casual boasting, taped by *Access Hollywood* in 2005, includes audio as well as some video footage. In the candid recording Mr. Trump boasts that "when you're a star," women let you "grab them by the pussy."[52] In response to Mr. Bush's apparent surprise, "Whatever you want?" Mr. Trump assures him, "they let you do it . . . you can do anything." In the weeks that followed the release of the audiotape, various women obtained lawyers, called reporters, wrote editorials; all claimed that he inappropriately and unlawfully touched them. Lawyers offered to provide free legal services to these women and any others who had similar experiences, but were afraid in light of Mr. Trump's denials about the alleged sexual harassment and threats to sue.[53]

According to the *New York Times, Washington Post, Los Angeles Times, Chicago Tribune,* and *Wall Street Journal,* this type of verbosity and misogyny in Mr. Trump's public commentary was nothing new.[54] These various newspapers and other media covered Mr. Trump's campaign and reported on derogatory comments and accusations he made about women before and during his run to become the Republican nominee for the President, as well as after he secured that victory. For example, in the *Wall Street Journal,* Alexandra Berzon, Joe Palazzolo, and Charles Passy wrote that recordings of Mr. Trump, "talking about how he groped women has put a new spotlight on a decades long history of lewd comments . . . as well as lawsuits against him by women who allege he sexually abused them."[55] According to *Forbes,* "it's no secret that Donald Trump has made many sexist and misogynistic comments both before and during his campaign."[56]

The *Washington Post* published an article, *Trump's History of Flippant Misogyny,*[57] months before the leaked *Access Hollywood* video and tape recordings, referencing Mr. Trump's sexualized verbal attacks and noting that President Trump "has a history . . . of inflammatory statements about women – both as a sex, and with reference to his antagonists and subordinates."[58] That article mentioned Mr. Trump's sending "*New York Times* columnist Gail Collins a copy of something she had written about him with her picture circled and 'The face of a dog!' written over it." The article also referred to tweets about Arianna Huffington's husband's "good decision" for supposedly divorcing her "for a man," as well as Mr. Trump's highly publicized attack on former Fox News anchor, Megyn Kelly, who on August 6, 2015, at the first Republican presidential debate, asked him the following:

> You've called women you don't like fat pigs, dogs, slobs, and disgusting animals. . . . You once told a contestant on *Celebrity Apprentice* it would be a pretty picture to see her on her knees. Does that sound to you like the temperament of a man we should elect as President, and how will you answer the charge from Hillary Clinton, who [is] likely to be the Democratic nominee, that you are part of the war on women?

Mr. Trump dismissed Ms. Kelly's question, explaining that his comments were in jest; he was "kidding," having "fun," and enjoying "a good time." However, some pundits also took note of his ominous warning: "Honestly Megyn, if you don't like it, I'm sorry. I've been very nice to you, although I could probably maybe not be, based on the way you have treated me. But I wouldn't do that."[59] Disturbingly, months later Ms. Kelly would release her own book, claiming that not only had her question to Mr. Trump been leaked prior to the debate, but that quite possibly someone – and she does not allege who – had tried to poison her.[60] For his part, Mr. Trump concluded his scrap with Ms. Kelly on Twitter and a day later on CNN, asserting that the news anchor "had blood coming out of her eyes, blood coming out of her wherever."[61]

The 2016 election was historic and pivotal. For the first time a woman earned the nomination of a major party and, in addition, managed to win the popular vote by a margin of nearly three million votes.[62] However, it was a monumental defeat. Through the Electoral College system (a remnant of antebellum political power disputes), Hillary Clinton lost the election to a reality television host and real estate developer.[63]

As the blue wall dissolved, the vulnerability of reproductive rights in the United States became more glaringly apparent. Donald Trump's administration poses serious threats to the preservation of reproductive healthcare rights such as abortion and contraceptive healthcare access. In the past, the President has said there should be some form of punishment for women who seek abortions,[64] raising serious constitutional law questions. What types of punishment? How would the state carry out such punishment? Whom would the state choose to punish? And, despite the fact that President Trump later retreated from those comments, his anti-reproductive-rights stance manifests itself in numerous ways.

Within days of taking office in 2017, Mr. Trump reinstated the notorious global gag rule.[65] This law disqualifies foreign NGOs from receiving U.S. family planning aid if they engage in any abortion-related activity. Essentially, to qualify for U.S. aid, NGOs that serve desperate, poor women abroad are prohibited from mentioning the word "abortion" even in cases of rape and incest – hence the "gag rule."[66] Mr. Trump has proposed a similar law affecting women and medical clinics in the United States.

Mr. Trump vowed to fill the Supreme Court with Justices who would overturn *Roe v. Wade*,[67] the landmark decision establishing reproductive privacy and autonomy as fundamental constitutional rights, and with the appointments of Justice Brett Kavanaugh and Neil Gorsuch he is advancing that mission. Mr. Trump and Republican congressional leaders promised to repeal the Patient Protection and Affordable Care Act (also known as Obamacare), which mandated maternal healthcare coverage and preventative healthcare services for women, including contraception. At the time of publication of this book, legislation to replace that healthcare law offers no similar protections for women.[68] For these reasons and more, safeguarding women's fundamental rights to reproductive autonomy takes on new meaning and urgency for reproductive healthcare advocates.

For many Americans, Mr. Trump's presidency brings to light the confounding, routine nature of inequality and sexual violence in the United States, in families, politics, social settings, the workplace, and beyond. With the election, sexual violence took on a new meaning in the political landscape, arguably due to its normalization. More than a dozen women came forward, painfully recalling instances where they say Mr. Trump assaulted them – on airplanes, in his office, outside the U.S. Open tennis stadium in Flushing, New York, and various other cities and states.[69] They are mothers, instructors, businesswomen, and former beauty pageant participants.[70]

***

As I made my way into the law school that frigid morning, a question posed over thirty years ago by MacKinnon in her often cited work, *Feminism, Marxism, Method, and the State: Toward Feminist Jurisprudence*,[71] came to mind. She wondered, How does male power become state power? Had the election of Donald Trump answered the question? If so, what had scholars learned?

That morning, I spoke about history, the foundations of court-sanctioned abuse of girls and women, and the legal opinions produced by judges pertaining to it. History provides a clarifying way to understand and unpack why too many Americans have become conditioned to think that violating women and girls is normal or a condition of life and not needing law's attention, intervention, or remedy. After all, why have relatively few social commentators, political scholars, and social policy analysts invested in writing about how law, legal institutions, and legal actors create and reify the conditions that permit discrimination and violence against women to flourish?

Despite a gold mine of legal cases involving private and public law disputes (the kind young academics hunger for), most scholars bypass thinking about how formal rules of law burden women's everyday lives and police them in unimaginable ways. For example, some male scholars who teach criminal law do not teach rape. Marital rape was a legal reality during my law school matriculation, but I learned about it on my own. Across the country, students who study constitutional law – a mandatory law school course – are lucky if, out of the dozens of cases their professors teach, there are four or five cases that address women's rights. In fact, the United States Supreme Court continues to permit states to discriminate against women so long as the government demonstrates an important interest. This dramatically contrasts with the standard adopted for race, where the government must meet a heightened standard of strict scrutiny and the government's interest must be compelling.

As this book demonstrates, too frequently law itself is responsible for the oppression of women and the suppression of their capacities. The institutions charged with protecting the vulnerable also sometimes fail women. Sometimes judges claim that women bring certain conditions and traumas onto themselves. From rape and incest to ignoring cases of domestic violence, law has not always been a friend to women or the issues that concern them.

Notes

PREFACE

1. Press Release, Nat'l Advocates for Pregnant Women, Supreme Court of New Mexico Strikes Down State's Attempt to Convict Woman Struggling with Addiction During Pregnancy (May 11, 2007) (quoting Tiloma Jayasinghe, staff attorney, responding to felony child abuse charges brought against Cynthia Martinez by New Mexico prosecutors), http://www.advocatesforpregnantwomen.org/whats_new/victory_in_the_new_mexico_su preme_court_1.php.

1 INTRODUCTION

1. UTAH CODE ANN. § 76-5-201(4) (2010).
2. Rose Aguilar, *Utah Governor Signs Controversial Law Charging Women and Girls with Murder for Miscarriages*, ALTERNET (Mar. 9, 2010), http://www.alternet.org/rights/145956/utah_governor_signs_controversial_law_charging_women_and_girls_with_murder_for_miscarriages.
3. *Id.*
4. *Unintended Pregnancy in the United States*, GUTTMACHER INST. (Jan. 2019), https://www.guttmacher.org/fact-sheet/unintended-pregnancy-united-states (citing Susheela Singh et al., *Unintended Pregnancy: Worldwide Levels, Trends, and Outcomes*, 41 STUD. FAM. PLAN. 241 (2010)).
5. *Teen Pregnancy*, GUTTMACHER INST., https://www.guttmacher.org/united-states/teens/teen-pregnancy?gclid=CjwKCAjwnrjrBRAMEiwAXsCc44JXs5qtl64ErzQ28pbSpZROcL_R30I 2eZgFNoCtxZOlc3808BIZ8xoCom4QAvD_BwE.
6. *What Can SNAPS Buy?*, USDA FOOD AND NUTRITION SERVICE, https://www.fns.usda.gov/snap/eligible-food-items.
7. Joan Maya Mazelis, *Punishing the Poor Isn't Just Bad Policy, It's Wasting Taxpayer Money*, THE HILL (Feb. 20, 2018), https://thehill.com/opinion/civil-rights/374700-punishing-the-poor-isnt-just-bad-policy-its-wasting-taxpayer-money.
8. Lauren Gellman, *Female-Headed Households and the Welfare System*, POVERTY & PREJUDICE: SOCIAL SECURITY AT THE CROSSROADS (June 4, 1999), https://web.stanford.edu/class/e297c/poverty_prejudice/soc_sec/hfemale.htm.
9. *See, e.g.*, Marian F. MacDorman et al., *Recent Increases in the U.S. Maternal Mortality Rate: Disentangling Trends from Measurement Issues*, 128 OBSTETRICS & GYNECOLOGY 447

(2016); INDEP. EVALUATION GRP., DELIVERING THE MILLENNIUM DEVELOPMENT GOALS TO REDUCE MATERNAL AND CHILD MORTALITY: A SYSTEMATIC REVIEW OF IMPACT EVALUATION EVIDENCE (2016), https://www.oecd.org/derec/norway/WORLDBANKDeliveringthe MDGtoreducematernalandchildmortality.pdf. [hereinafter IMPACT EVALUATION]; The World Factbook, *Country Comparison: Maternal Mortality Rate*, CENT. INTELLIGENCE AGENCY, https://www.cia.gov/library/publications/the-world-factbook/rankorder/2223rank .html; *U.S. "Most Dangerous" Place to Give Birth in Developed World*, USA *Today Investigation Finds*, CBS NEWS (July 26, 2018, 6:14 AM), https://www.cbsnews.com/news/us-most-dangerous-place-to-give-birth-in-developed-world-usa-today-investigation-finds/.

10. IMPACT EVALUATION, *supra* note 9.

11. Jessica Ravitz, *Maternal Deaths Fall Across Globe but Rise in US, Doubling in Texas*, CNN (Apr. 17, 2018), https://www.cnn.com/2016/08/24/health/maternal-mortality-trends-double-texas/index.html.

12. Sophie Novack, *Texas' Maternal Mortality Rate: Worst in Developed World, Shrugged Off by Lawmakers*, TEX. OBSERVER (June 5, 2017), http://www.texasobserver.org/texas-worst-maternal-mortality-rate-developed-world-lawmakers-priorities.

13. Alex Zielinski, *The Growing List of Anti-abortion Bills Texas Conservative Lawmakers Hope to Pass This Year*, SAN ANTONIO CURRENT (Jan. 25, 2017), https://www.sacurrent .com/the-daily/archives/2017/01/25/the-growing-list-of-anti-abortion-bills-texas-conserva tive-lawmakers-hope-to-pass-this-year ("In the past few months, state lawmakers have filed no less than 17 anti-abortion bills (and judging by past legislative sessions, more are on the horizon).").

14. Alexa Ura & Jolie McCullogh, *Once Again, the Texas Legislature Is Mostly White, Male, Middle-Aged*, TEXAS TRIBUNE (Jan. 9, 2017), https://www.texastribune.org/2017/01/09/texas-legislature-mostly-white-male-middle-aged/ ("The members of the Texas Legislature may be elected to represent all corners of the state, but they're not necessarily reflective of it.").

15. *See* Danielle Paquette, *Why Pregnant Women in Mississippi Keep Dying*, WASH. POST: WONKBLOG (Apr. 24, 2015), https://www.washingtonpost.com/news/wonk/wp/2015/04/24/ why-pregnant-women-in-mississippi-keep-dying/.

16. *See, e.g.*, America's Health Rankings, *Maternal Mortality in Louisiana in 2018*, UNITED HEALTH FOUND., https://www.americashealthrankings.org/explore/health-of-women-and-children/measure/maternal_mortality/state/LA.

17. *States Where They Think We're Stupid: Abortion Access Under Attack in 2013*, AM. CIVIL LIBERTIES UNION, http://www.aclu.org/maps/states-where-they-think-were-stupid-abortion -access-under-attack-2013.

18. Laura Bassett, *More Abortion Laws Enacted in Past Three Years than in Entire Previous Decade*, HUFFINGTON POST (Jan. 3, 2014, 12:21 PM), http://www.huffingtonpost.com/2014/ 01/03/states-abortion-laws_n_4536752.html.

19. Andrea Rowan, *Prosecuting Women for Self-Inducing Abortion: Counterproductive and Lacking Compassion*, 18 GUTTMACHER POL'Y REV. 70, 70 (2015).

20. Those twenty-one states were: Alabama, Arkansas, Indiana, Iowa, Kansas, Louisiana, Maryland, Michigan, Mississippi, Missouri, Montana, North Carolina, North Dakota, Ohio, Oklahoma, Pennsylvania, South Carolina, South Dakota, Texas, Virginia, Wisconsin. For the specific provisions passed by each, see addendum. Heather D. Boonstra & Elizabeth Nash, *A Surge of State Abortion Restrictions Puts Providers – and the Women They Serve – in the Crosshairs*, 17 GUTTMACHER POL'Y REV. 9, 11 (2014).

21. *Id.* at 9 (explaining that states enacted ninety-two abortion restrictions in 2011, forty-three restrictions in 2012, and seventy restrictions in 2014).

22. Mary Tuma, Roe's End? Supreme Court Case Will Decide the Future of Abortion Access in the U.S., AUSTIN CHRON. (Jan. 29, 2016), http://www.austinchronicle.com/news/2016-01-29/roes-end/.

23. Morgan Smith et al., Abortion Bill Finally Bound for Perry's Desk, TEX. TRIB. (July 13, 2013, 12:17 AM), http://www.texastribune.org/2013/07/13/texas-abortion-regulations-debate-nears-climax/.

24. Act of July 18, 2013, ch. 1, §§ 1–12, 2013 Tex. Sess. Law Serv. 4795–802 (West) (codified at TEX. HEALTH & SAFETY CODE ANN. §§ 171.0031, 171.041–.048, 171.061–.064, & amending §§ 245.010–.011; amending TEX. OCC. CODE ANN. §§ 164.052, 164.055). There is no official title for this omnibus abortion bill. However, it is commonly referred to as "House Bill 2" or by its abbreviated form "H.B. 2." See Whole Woman's Health v. Cole, 790 F.3d 563, 566 (5th Cir. 2015) (the Court naming "Texas's law regulating abortions" the Texas House Bill No. 2 ("H.B. 2")).

25. For a description of events leading up to the passage of H.B. 2, see generally Becca Aaronson, House Approves Abortion Restrictions, TEX. TRIB. (July 10, 2013, 11:23 AM), http://www.texastribune.org/2013/07/10/take-two-house-debates-proposed-abortion-regulatio/; Manny Fernandez, Abortion Restrictions Become Law in Texas, but Opponents Will Press Fight, N.Y. TIMES (July 18, 2013), http://www.nytimes.com/2013/07/19/us/perry-signs-texas-abortion-restrictions-into-law.html; Smith et al., supra note 23; Jordan Smith, Updated: Senate Passes House Bill 2: Rejected Amendments, Dramatic Speeches, and Finally a Vote, AUSTIN CHRON. (July 12, 2013, 11:48 PM), http://www.austinchronicle.com/daily/news/2013-07-12/senate-considers-house-bill-2/.

26. See H.B. 2, 83d Leg., 2d Called Sess. (Tex. 2013).

27. See, e.g., Fernandez, supra note 25 (describing H.B. 2 as "some of the toughest restrictions on abortion in the country"); John Schwartz, Texas Senate Approves Strict Abortion Measure, N.Y. TIMES (July 13, 2013), http://www.nytimes.com/2013/07/14/us/texas-abortion-bill.html (characterizing H.B. 2 as "one of the strictest anti-abortion measures in the country").

28. See, e.g., Maria L. La Ganga, Most Abortion Clinics in Texas Will Be Forced to Close Under Court Ruling, L.A. TIMES (Oct. 2, 2014, 9:38 PM), http://www.latimes.com/nation/la-na-texas-abortion-20141002-story.html; Mary Tuma, HB 2 Oral Arguments: Justices Press Both Sides of Texas Abortion Law, AUSTIN CHRON. (Mar. 2, 2016), http://www.austinchronicle.com/daily/news/2016–03-02/hb-2-oral-arguments/.

29. 410 U.S. 113 (1973).

30. 505 U.S. 833 (1992).

31. JOHANNA SCHOEN, ABORTION AFTER ROE 170–71 (2015).

32. Michele Goodwin, Fetal Protection Laws: Moral Panic and the New Constitutional Battlefront, 102 CAL. L. REV. 781, 785–88, 790, 792–93, 796, 799–812 (2014).

33. See, e.g., Caitlin E. Borgmann, The Meaning of "Life": Belief and Reason in the Abortion Debate, 18 COLUM. J. GENDER & L. 551, 558–63 (2009); Hannah Fingerhut, On Abortion, Persistent Divides Between – and Within – the Two Parties, PEW RES. CTR. (Apr. 8, 2016), http://www.pewresearch.org/fact-tank/2016/04/08/on-abortion-persistent-divides-between-and-within-the-two-parties-2/.

34. Borgmann, supra note 33, at 561.

35. See, e.g., PEW RES. CTR., ISSUE RANKS LOWER ON THE AGENDA: SUPPORT FOR ABORTION SLIPS 21–23 (2009), http://www.pewforum.org/files/2009/10/abortion091.pdf (explaining that "[r]eligious beliefs hold much stronger sway over those who oppose abortion than over those on the pro-choice side of the abortion issue"); Diane di Mauro & Carole Joffe, The Religious Right and the Reshaping of Sexual Policy: An

Examination of Reproductive Rights and Sexuality Education, 4 Sexuality Res. and Soc. Pol'y: J. Nat'l Sexuality Res. Ctr. 67, 73 (2007) (noting that "[t]he Religious Right has [so] skillfully capitalized on the power of ultrasounds" that the result has included shifts in legislation and millions diverted to pregnancy crisis centers); Karen F.B. Gray, *An Establishment Clause Analysis of* Webster v. Reproductive Health Services, 24 Ga. L. Rev. 399, 418 (1990) (arguing that government-enacted abortion statutes reflect pressure from the "groups aligned with religiously motivated, anti-abortion beliefs").

36. Catharine A. MacKinnon, Women's Lives, Men's Laws 143 (2005).
37. Reva Siegel, *Reasoning from the Body: A Historical Perspective on Abortion Regulation and Questions of Equal Protection*, 44 Stan. L. Rev. 261, 341, 366 (1992).
38. 505 U.S. 833, 837–78 (1992).

2 PREGNANCY AND STATE POWER: PROSECUTING FETAL ENDANGERMENT

1. Abortion rights may include the liberty to receive or have access to pregnancy termination during the first trimester, second trimester, or third trimester. The legal minefields shaping debates on abortion include whether the right to an abortion shifts or should exist at all depending on the stage in a woman's pregnancy, such as the first, second, or third trimester. Legislation pending in states would ban abortion after ten or twelve weeks, preserving the right only in the first trimester, which arguably burdens the abortion right to such a degree that it becomes more illusory than real for many women.
2. *See* Katherine Becket, *Choosing Cesarean: Feminism and the Politics of Childbirth in the United States*, 6 Feminist Theory 251 (2005); Jessica Shaw, *Full-Spectrum Reproductive Justice: The Affinity of Abortion Rights and Birth Activism*, 7 Stud. in Soc. Just. 143 (2013); Robbie Davis-Floyd, *Anthropology and Birth Activism: What Do We Know?*, Anthropology News 37 (May 2005); Madeleine Akrich et al., *Practising Childbirth Activism: A Politics of Evidence*, Papiers de Recherche du CSI/CSI Working Paper Series, No. 023 (2012) (on file with author).
3. *See* Loretta Ross, *Understanding Reproductive Justice: Transforming the Pro-Choice Movement*, 36 Off Our Backs 14 (2004).
4. *See also* Neil S. Siegel & Reva B. Siegel, *Struck by Stereotype: Ruth Bader Ginsburg on Pregnancy Discrimination*, 59 Duke L.J. 771 (2010); *Court Backs Air Force's Ouster of an Unwed Pregnant Officer*, N.Y. Times, Nov. 16, 1971, at L33.
5. 460 F.2d 1372 (9th Cir. 1971).
6. *See* Jessica Weisberg, *This Woman's Little-Known 1972 Case Could Have Reframed Abortion History*, Elle Mag. (Oct. 21, 2014), https://www.elle.com/culture/career-politics/a14816/susans-choice/ ("a supervisor ordered her to leave Vietnam within 48 hours"); *see also Nomination of Ruth Bader Ginsburg, To Be Associate Justice of the Supreme Court of the United States*, 103d Cong. 150, 205–07 (1993) (testimony of Judge Ginsburg).
7. Brief for the Petitioner at 12–13, Struck v. Sec'y of Def., 460 F.2d 1372 (9th Cir. 1971) (No. 72-178).
8. 460 F.2d 1372.
9. *Id.* at 1375.
10. *Id.*
11. *Id.*

12. Struck v. Sec'y of Def., 409 U.S. 1071 (1972).
13. A few years after *Roe v. Wade* was decided, the Department of Defense officially changed its policy, permitting pregnant women (and those who adopted children) the option to elect remaining on active duty or discharge. *See, e.g.*, JUDITH HICKS STIEHM, ARMS AND THE ENLISTED WOMAN 117 (1989); MARSHA S. OLSON & SUSAN S. STUMPF, PREGNANCY IN THE NAVY: IMPACT ON ABSENTEEISM, ATTRITION, AND WORKGROUP MORALE 2 (1978). *See also* Crawford v. Cushman, 531 F.2d 1114 (2d Cir. 1976)(holding that the Marine Corps regulation requiring immediate discharge of a pregnant marine violated the Fifth Amendment).
14. *See* KARA DIXON VUIC, OFFICER, NURSE, WOMAN: THE ARMY NURSE CORPS IN THE VIETNAM WAR 126 (2010).
15. Letitia Stein, *USF Obstetrician Threatens to Call Police if Patient Doesn't Report for C-Section*, TAMPA BAY TIMES (Mar. 6, 2013), http://www.tampabay.com/news/health/usf-obstetrician -threatens-to-call-police-if-patient-doesnt-report-for/2107387.
16. *In re* Unborn Child of Samantha Burton, No. 2009 CA 1167, 2009 WL 8628562 (Fla. Cir. Ct. Mar. 27, 2009). The court order authorized the hospital to take action "necessary to preserve the life and health of Samantha Burton's unborn child, including but not limited to restricting [her] to bed rest, administering appropriate medication, postponing labor, taking appropriate steps to prevent and/or treat infection, and/or eventually performing a cesarean section delivery of the child at the appropriate time." *See also* Brief of Amici Curiae American Civil Liberties Union, American Civil Liberties Union of Florida, and American Medical Women's Association in Support of Appellant at 2, Burton v. Florida, 49 So.3d 263 (Fla. Dist. Ct. App. Aug. 12, 2010) (No. 1D09-1958), https://www.aclu.org/files/pdfs/reproductiverights/burton_v_florida_acluamicus.pdf.
17. *See* Kontji Anthony, *Police: Woman Earns DUI for Endangering Fetus*, WMCTV (June 30, 2013), http://www.wmcactionnews5.com/story/20525700/police-pregnant-woman-earns-dui-for-endangering-fetus/ ("A Memphis woman is behind bars on a DUI and child endangerment charge even though she did not have a child in the car with her, and blood alcohol level was under the legal limit.").
18. LYNN PALTROW, CRIMINAL PROSECUTION AGAINST PREGNANT WOMEN NATIONAL UPDATE AND OVERVIEW (1992) (listing the racial identification of pregnant women subjected to state intervention, the majority of whom were African American); Gina Kolata, *Bias Seen Against Pregnant Addicts*, N.Y. TIMES, July 20, 1990, at A13 (citing an ACLU study that found that 80 percent of the women targeted for criminal intervention for drug use during pregnancy were African American, Latina, and "members of other minorities"); Dorothy Roberts, *Punishing Drug Addicts Who Have Babies: Women of Color, Equality, and the Right of Privacy*, 104 HARV. L. REV. 1419, 1421 n.6 (1991) (noting that the majority of women targeted for state criminal prosecution because of drug use during pregnancy "are poor and Black").
19. Nina Martin, *The State That Turns Pregnant Women into Felons*, ALTERNET (Sept. 23, 2015), https://www.alternet.org/drugs/when-womb-crime-scene.
20. AMNESTY INT'L, CRIMINALIZING PREGNANCY: POLICING PREGNANT WOMEN WHO USE DRUGS IN THE USA 23 (2017), https://www.amnesty.org/download/Documents/AMR516203 2017ENGLISH.pdf.
21. *See, e.g.*, Michele Goodwin, *Prosecuting the Womb*, 76 GEO. WASH. L. REV. 1411 (2008).
22. 347 U.S. 483 (1954).
23. *See, e.g.*, Jessica Silver-Greenberg & Natalie Kitroeff, *Miscarrying at Work: The Physical Toll of Pregnancy Discrimination*, N.Y. TIMES, Oct. 21, 2018; Natalie Kitroeff & Jessica Silver-Greenberg, *Pregnancy Discrimination Is Rampant Inside America's*

Biggest Companies, N.Y. TIMES, June 15, 2018. *See also* Young v. United Parcel Serv., 135 S. Ct. 1338 (2015) (holding that a plaintiff alleging the denial of accommodation under the Pregnancy Discrimination Act may show that she sought accommodation, that the employer refused to accommodate her, and that the employer did accommodate others similar in their inability or ability at work; the employer may seek to justify its refusal to accommodate).

24. *See, e.g.*, Jorge Rivas, *California Prisons Caught Sterilizing Female Inmates Without Approval*, ABC NEWS (July 8, 2013), https://abcnews.go.com/ABC_Univision/doctors-california-prisons-sterilized-female-inmates-authorizations/story?id=19610110; Derek Hawkins, *Tennessee Judge, Under Fire, Pulls Offer to Trade Shorter Jail Sentences for Vasectomies*, WASH. POST (July 28, 2017), https://www.washingtonpost.com/news/morn ing-mix/wp/2017/07/28/tennessee-judge-under-fire-pulls-offer-to-trade-shorter-jail-sen tences-for-vasectomies/?noredirect=on&utm_term=.c4782cfa4d21; Andy Sher, *Tennessee Judge Ends Controversial Sentence Reduction Program for Inmates Choosing Birth Control*, TIMES FREE PRESS (July 28, 2017), https://www.timesfreepress.com/news/local/story/2017/jul/28/tennessee-judge-ends-sentence-reductiprogram/440713/.

25. *See, e.g.*, AMNESTY INT'L., *supra* note 20.

26. Ed Pilkington, *Indiana Prosecuting Chinese Woman for Suicide Attempt That Killed Her Foetus*, GUARDIAN (May 30, 2012, 1:36 PM), http://www.guardian.co.uk/world/2012/may/30/indiana-prosecuting-chinese-woman-suicide-foetus.

27. Kevin Hayes, *Did Christine Taylor Take Abortion into Her Own Hands*, CBS NEWS (Mar. 2, 2010, 6:55 AM), http://www.cbsnews.com/8301-504083_162-6255683-504083.html.

28. Eleanor J. Bader, *Criminalizing Pregnancy: How Feticide Laws Made Common Ground for Pro- and Anti-Choice Groups*, TRUTHOUT (June 14, 2012), https://truthout.org/articles/criminalizing-pregnancy-how-feticide-laws-made-common-ground-for-pro-and-anti-choice-groups/; *see also* PAN-AM. HEALTH ORG., DOMESTIC PARTNER VIOLENCE DURING PREGNANCY (2011), http://www.paho.org/english/ad/ge/vawpregnancy.pdf (pregnant women are "60% more likely to be beaten than women who are not pregnant"); Julie A. Gazmararian et al., *Prevalence of Violence Against Pregnant Women: A Review of the Literature*, 275 JAMA 1915, 1915–20 (1996).

29. *See State Laws on Fetal Homicide and Penalty-Enhancement for Crimes Against Pregnant Women*, NAT'L CONFERENCE OF STATE LEGISLATURES (last updated May 1, 2018), http://www.ncsl.org/issues-research/health/fetal-homicide-state-laws.aspx.

30. *Id.*

31. 18 U.S.C. § 1841, 10 U.S.C. § 919a (2004) ("Whoever engages in conduct that violates any of the provisions of law listed in subsection (b) and thereby causes the death of, or bodily injury (as defined in section 1365) to, a child, who is in utero at the time the conduct takes place, is guilty of a separate offense under this section.").

32. Roberts, *supra* note 18, at 1421; Michele Goodwin, *Fetal Protection Laws: Moral Panic and the New Constitutional Battlefront*, 102 CALIF. L. REV. 781 (2014).

33. *See* Victoria Nourse, *History, Pragmatism, and the New Legal Realism* (Nov. 2005) (on file with the author).

34. *Id.*; *see also* Victoria Nourse & Gregory Shaffer, *Varieties of New Legal Realism: Can a New World Order Prompt a New Legal Theory*, 95 CORNELL L. REV. 61, 64 (2009) (on varieties of methods and the need to focus on "real life problems" and the use of methods).

35. State v. McKnight, 576 S.E.2d 168, 171 (S.C. 2003); *see also* Shalini Bhargava, *Challenging Punishment and Privatization: A Response to the Conviction of Regina McKnight*, 39 HARV. C.R.-C.L. L. REV. 513, 517 (2004).

36. Media Advisory, Nat'l Advocates for Pregnant Women, Petition Filed Today Seeking U.S. Supreme Court Review of Unprecedented South Carolina Decision Treating a Woman Who Suffered a Stillbirth as a Murderer (May 27, 2003), http://www .advocatesforpregnantwomen.org/issues/prmcknight.htm.
37. *Id.*
38. *See* McKnight v. State, 661 S.E.2d 354, 361 (S.C. 2008) (finding that the jury may have improperly used "outdated scientific studies" provided by the state's witnesses).
39. Goodwin, *supra* note 21, at 1658.
40. E. Gaston, *Conway Homicide Case Sets Precedent*, Sun News, May 18, 2001, at A1.
41. McKnight v. State, 661 S.E.2d. 354.
42. Briefing Paper from S.C. Advocates for Pregnant Women, Nat'l Advocates for Pregnant Women, to Democratic Presidential Candidates, *South Carolina: First in the Nation for Arresting African-American Pregnant Women; Last in the Nation for Funding Drug and Alcohol Treatment* (Jan. 8, 2003), http://advocatesforpregnantwomen.org/issues/briefing paper.htm.
43. Interview with Lynn Paltrow, Executive Director, National Advocates for Pregnant Women (July 10, 2013).
44. Briefing Paper, *supra* note 42.
45. Charles Condon, *Clinton's Cocaine Babies*, 72 Pol'y Rev. (Apr. 1, 1995), https://www .hoover.org/research/clintons-cocaine-babies.
46. Ferguson v. City of Charleston, 532 U.S. 67 (2001).
47. Ferguson v. City of Charleston, 532 U.S. 67 (2001); Brief for Petitioners at 12, Ferguson v. City of Charleston, 532 U.S. 67 (2001) (No. 99-936); Transcript of Oral Argument, Ferguson v. City of Charleston, 532 U.S. 67 (2001) (No. 99-936); Brief of Respondents, Ferguson, 532 U.S. 67 (2001) (No. 99-936).
48. *See Table 50. Use of Selected Substances in the Past Month Among Persons Aged 12 and Over, by Age, Sex, Race, and Hispanic Origin: United States, Selected Years 2002–2016* Nat'l Ctr. for Health Stat. (2017), https://www.cdc.gov/nchs/data/hus/ 2017/050.pdf. (data shows Black women slightly more likely to use "any" illicit drug, whereas white women are more likely to misuse prescription or psychotherapeutic drugs, use alcohol, binge alcohol, engage in heavy alcohol use, use tobacco and cigars).
49. Brief for Petitioners, *supra* note 47 at 12 (citing Brown transcript, Brown Tr. 12/10/96 at 81:17–82:5 (JA 265-66).
50. *Id.*
51. *Id.* at 13 n.10.
52. *Id.* ("The record demonstrates that Nurse Brown, who helped establish the Search Policy and was integral to its everyday implementation, held racist views.").
53. *Id.* at 12 (citing Brown Tr. 12/10/96 at 5:18–21, 64:4–66:25, 71:6–74:9 (JA 209, 250–57); M. Williams Tr. at 132:7–133:1 (JA 1195–96); PX 119).
54. *Id.* (citing M. Williams Tr. at 128:9–129:5 (JA 1192–93)).
55. Brief for Petitioners, *supra* note 47, at 11.
56. *Id.* at 17 (citing Singleton Tr. at 61:11–14, 68:22–24, 69:5–8 (JA 1135–36, 1143); Powell Tr. at 152:2–11; 157:4 (JA 1014–15, 1020); Knight Tr. at124:20–125:17 (JA 777–78); Griffin Tr. 11:9–12:4 (JA 551–52)).
57. *Id.* (citing Singleton Tr. 68:1–69:8 (JA 1142–43); Powell Tr. 153:7–20, 155:8–16).
58. *Id.* (citing Singleton Tr. 62–64 (JA [**34] 1136–39); Powell Tr. at 154:2–156:24 (JA 1017–19); Griffin Tr. 10 (JA 549–50); Knight Tr. 126 at (JA 778–79)).

59. Charles Krauthammer, *Worse than "Brave New World": Newborns Permanently Damaged by Cocaine*, Phila. Inquirer (Aug. 1, 1989), http://articles.philly.com/1989-08-01/news/26148256_1_cocaine-babies-crack-babies-damage1.

60. *Id.*

61. Douglas Besharov, *Crack Babies: The Worst Threat Is Mom Herself*, Wash. Post, Aug. 6, 1989, http://www.welfareacademy.org/pubs/childwelfare/crackbabies-0889.shtml; Krauthammer, *supra* note 59.

62. *See* Carl Hart, *The Real Opioid Emergency*, N.Y. Times (Aug. 18, 2017), https://www.nytimes.com/2017/08/18/opinion/sunday/opioids-drugs-race-treatment.html.

63. Priscilla Van Tassel, *Schools Trying to Cope with "Crack Babies,"* N.Y. Times, Jan. 05, 1992 (quoting Dan Griffith, a developmental psychologist, "This is just the tip of the iceberg"); Sandra Blakeslee, *Crack's Toll Among Babies: A Joyless View, Even of Toys*, N.Y. Times, Sept. 17, 1989, at A1.

64. Krauthammer, *supra* note 59.

65. Charles Krauthammer, Children of Cocaine, Congressional Record, Proceedings and Debates of the 101st Congress, Aug. 1, 1989.

66. *Id.*

67. *Id.*

68. *See, e.g.*, Ellen Hopkins, *Childhood's End: What Life Is Like for Crack Babies*, Rolling Stone, Oct. 18, 1990.

69. Telephone interviews with Dr. Claire Coles (July 28, 2013) and Dr. Hallam Hurt (Aug. 13, 2013).

70. Telephone interview with Dr. Claire Coles (July 28, 2013).

71. Hallam Hurt et al., *Children With and Without Gestational Cocaine Exposure: A Neurocognitive System Analysis*, 31 Neurotoxicology & Teratology 334, 339 (2009). *See also* Hallam Hurt et al., *A Prospective Comparison of Developmental Outcome of Children with In Utero Cocaine Exposure and Controls Using the Battelle Developmental Inventory*, 22 J. Developmental & Behav. Pediatrics 21 (2001) [hereinafter *Developmental Outcome*]; Hallam Hurt et. al., *Children with In Utero Cocaine Exposure Do Not Differ from Control Subjects on Intelligence Testing*, 151 Archives Of Pediatric & Adolescent Med. 1237, 1241 (1997); Hallam Hurt et al., *School Performance of Children with Gestational Cocaine Exposure*, 27 Neurotoxicology & Teratology 203, 207 (2011) (finding no statistically significant difference between successful grade progression in grades one through four between children with gestational cocaine exposure and a control group).

72. Hurt et al., *Developmental Outcome, supra* note 71.

73. Michael Winerip, *Revisiting the "Crack Babies" Epidemic That Was Not*, N.Y. Times, May 20, 2013; Peter Lyons & Barbara Rittner, *The Construction of the Crack Babies Phenomenon as a Social Problem*, 68 Am. J. Orthopsychiatry 313 (1998).

74. Dan Baum, Smoke and Mirrors: The War on Drugs and the Politics of Failure 217–18 (1996).

75. *See, e.g.*, Deborah A. Frank et al., *Growth, Development, and Behavior in Early Childhood Following Prenatal Cocaine Exposure*, 285 J. Am. Med. Ass'n 1613, 1613, 1622–24 (2001) (finding "no convincing evidence that prenatal cocaine exposure is associated with developmental toxic effects that differ in severity, scope, or kind from the sequel of multiple other risk factors," such as alcohol or the quality of the child's environment).

76. David Brown, *"Crack Baby" Theory Doubted*, Wash. Post, Mar. 28, 2001.

77. Winerip, *supra* note 73.

78. *Id.*
79. Ira J. Chasnoff et al., *The Prevalence of Illicit-Drug or Alcohol Use During Pregnancy and Discrepancies in Mandatory Reporting in Pinellas County, Florida,* 322 New Eng. J. Med. 1202, 1202 (1990).
80. *Id.*
81. Gina Kolata, *Bias Seen Against Pregnant Addicts,* N.Y. Times, July 20, 1990 at A13.
82. *See, e.g.,* Allen A. Mitchell et al., *Medication Use During Pregnancy, with Particular Focus on Prescription Drugs: 1976–2008,* 250 Am. J. Obstetrics Gynecology 50 (2011).
83. *Id.*
84. *Abusing Prescription Drugs During Pregnancy,* Am. Pregnancy Ass'n (July 2015), http://www.americanpregnancy.org/pregnancyhealth/abusingprescriptiondrugs.html.
85. Barry Yeoman, *Surgical Strike: Is a Group That Pays Addicts to Be Sterilized Defending Children or Exploiting the Vulnerable?,* Mother Jones, Nov./Dec. 2001.
86. Reva Siegel, *Why Equal Protection No Longer Protects: The Evolving Forms of Status-Enforcing State Action,* 49 Stan. L. Rev. 1111, 1119–20 (1996–7) ("White Americans who emphatically opposed slavery regularly disagreed about what it would mean to emancipate African-Americans. Some defined freedom from slavery as equality in civil rights; others insisted that emancipating African-Americans from slavery entailed equality in civil and political rights; but most white Americans who opposed slavery did not think its abolition required giving African-Americans equality in 'social rights.'").
87. *Id.* at 1111, 1116.
88. *See* Adam Cohen, Imbeciles: The Supreme Court, American Eugenics, and the Sterilization of Carrie Buck 57 (2016).
89. *Id.*
90. *Id.*
91. Buck v. Bell, 274 U.S. 200, 207 (1927).
92. *See id.* (upholding a Virginia law that required the sterilization of incompetent persons). Carrie Buck, a victim of rape at age sixteen, bore a child out of wedlock. The state of Virginia claimed that Buck possessed low social character and intelligence; it predicted that were she to have more children they would be born of inferior intelligence. She and others like her were collected by public health officials to be sterilized. However, years after the case, Holmes and public health officials in Virginia were proven wrong: Buck's daughter, Vivian, was a successful student – well above average.
93. *Buck,* 274 U.S. at 207.
94. *Id.*
95. *Id.*
96. *Id.*
97. *Biography of Harry H. Laughlin,* Truman State University Pickler Memorial Library, http://library.truman.edu/manuscripts/laughlinbio.asp.
98. *See, e.g.,* Paul A. Lombardo, *Three Generations, No Imbeciles: New Light on Buck v. Bell,* 60 N.Y.U. L. Rev. 30 (1985).
99. *Buck,* 274 U.S. at 207 ("the principle that sustains compulsory vaccination is broad enough to cover cutting the Fallopian tubes").
100. Kim Severson, *Thousands Sterilized, a State Weighs Restitution,* N.Y. Times, Dec. 9, 2011, at A1.
101. Valerie Bauerlein, *North Carolina to Compensate Sterilization Victims,* Wall St. J. (July 26, 2013), http://www.wsj.com/articles/SB10001424127887323971204578629943220881914 ("About 2,000 of the 7,600 who were sterilized were under age 18").

102. *Id.*; David Zucchino, *Sterilized by North Carolina, She Felt Raped Once More*, L.A. TIMES (Jan. 25, 2012), http://articles.latimes.com/2012/jan/25/nation/la-na-forced-sterilization-20120126 [http://perma.cc/7BPR-3UCM].
103. *Sterilization Abuse*, SPLC, http://www.splcenter.org/seeking-justice/case-docket/relf-v-weinberger [http://perma.cc/RL7M-WWP7].
104. Yeoman, *supra* note 85.
105. *Id.*
106. Jeff Stryker, *Cracking Down*, SALON (July 10, 1998, 3:25AM), http://www.salon.com/1998/07/10/cov_10feature/.
107. *Id.*
108. *Our Mission*, PROJECT PREVENTION, http://www.projectprevention.org/.
109. *Tennessee Sterilisations in Plea Deal for Women Evoke Dark Time in America*, GUARDIAN (Mar. 28, 2015), https://www.theguardian.com/us-news/2015/mar/28/tennessee-forced-sterilizations-plea-deals-women.
110. *Id.*
111. *Id.*
112. Corey G. Johnson, *Female Prison Inmates Sterilized Illegally, California Audit Confirms, Center for Investigative Reporting*, REVEAL NEWS (June 19, 2014), https://www.revealnews.org/article/female-prison-inmates-sterilized-illegally-california-audit-confirms/.
113. CALIFORNIA STATE AUDITOR, ELAINE M. HOWLE, STERILIZATION OF FEMALE INMATES REPORT: SOME INMATES WERE STERILIZED UNLAWFULLY, AND SAFEGUARDS DESIGNED TO LIMIT OCCURRENCES OF THE PROCEDURE FAILED (JUNE 2014), https://www.auditor.ca.gov/pdfs/reports/2013-120.pdf.
114. *Id.* at iii.
115. *See* Johnson, *supra* note 112.
116. *See* JAMES FITZJAMES STEPHEN, LIBERTY, EQUALITY, FRATERNITY 99 (Stuart D. Warner, ed., Liberty Fund 1993) (1874).
117. *Id.* at 98.

3 CREEPING CRIMINALIZATION OF PREGNANCY ACROSS THE UNITED STATES

1. *See, e.g.*, ALA. CODE § 13A-6-1 (2006); ARIZ. REV. STAT. ANN. § 13-1102-05; FLA. STAT. ANN. 782.09 (West 2005); MISS. CODE ANN. § 97-3-19 (2013).
2. *See, e.g.*, ALA. CODE § 26-15-3.2 (West 2006). The term "child" as used in this statute has been interpreted to encompass fetuses. *Ex parte* Ankrom, 2013 WL 135748, at *11 (Ala. Jan. 13, 2013).
3. Utah's House and Senate passed a "criminal miscarriage" law, presumptively exposing pregnant women to criminal prosecution for miscarrying. *See* H.B. 12, 58th Gen. Sess. (Utah 2010).
4. WISC. STAT. ANN. § 48.133 (West 2013) (granting the court "exclusive original jurisdiction" over an unborn child in need of protection when the expectant mother "habitually lacks self-control in the use of alcohol beverages, controlled substances"). The Wisconsin law allowed state authorities to incarcerate Alicia Beltran at fourteen weeks pregnant after she told a healthcare provider about a past (but not current) pill addiction. Erik Eckholm, *Case Explores Rights of Fetus Versus Mother*, N.Y. TIMES, Oct. 24, 2013, at A1.

5. *See, e.g.*, Whitner v. State, 492 S.E.2d 777, 780 (S.C. 1997) (holding that a viable fetus is a "child" within the meaning of the state's child abuse and endangerment laws).
6. For a discussion of the underlying legal theories behind these laws, *see* Lynn M. Paltrow & Jeanne Flavin, *Arrests of and Forced Interventions on Pregnant Women in the United States, 1973–2005: Implications for Women's Legal Status and Public Health*, 38 J. HEALTH POL. POL'Y & L. 299, 322–26 (2013). *See also* Kenneth A. De Ville & Loretta M. Kopelman, *Fetal Protection in Wisconsin's Revised Child Abuse Law: Right Goal, Wrong Remedy*, J.L. MED. & ETHICS 332, 332 (1999) (discussing laws in Wisconsin and South Dakota that allow confinement of pregnant women who abuse drugs or alcohol and how they are motivated by "the state's interest in promoting the health of future citizens").
7. Nina Martin, *The State That Turns Pregnant Women into Felons*, ALTERNET (Sept. 23, 2015), https://www.alternet.org/drugs/when-womb-crime-scene.
8. Paltrow & Flavin, *supra* note 6, at 300.
9. *See, e.g.*, EDWARD COKE, THE THIRD PART OF THE INSTITUTES OF THE LAWS OF ENGLAND: CONCERNING HIGH TREASON, AND OTHER PLEAS OF THE CROWN, AND CRIMINAL CAUSES 50 (1680); WILLIAM STANFORD, LES PLEES DEL CORON bk. 1, ch. 13 (1557); Twinslayer's Case, 1E3 23.P. Coron. 146 (1327); Abortionist's Case, 22E.3.P. Coron. 263 (1348).
10. 1 MATTHEW HALE, HISTORIA PLACITORUM CORONÆ: THE HISTORY OF THE PLEAS OF THE CROWN 433 (London, E. & R. Nutt & R. Gosling 1736).
11. Twinslayer's Case, 1E3 23.P. Coron. 146 (1327); Abortionist's Case, 22E.3.P. Coron. 263 (1348).
12. Regina v. Knight, 2 F. & F. 46 (1860). Strangely, the court found it more repugnant that the pregnancy was concealed, and for that the defendant was found guilty and sentenced to hard labor.
13. Rex v. Izod, 20 Cox's Criminal Law Cases 690, 691 (1904).
14. *Id.*
15. *Id.*
16. Dietrich v. Northampton, 138 Mass. 14, 16–17 (1884) (fetus "was a part of the mother at the time of the injury"). For over sixty years, this opinion served as the basis for common law jurisprudence regarding the legal standing of a fetus. Courts consistently ruled that a fetus had no legal status apart from the pregnant woman bearing it. *See also* Stallman v. Youngquist, 531 N.E.2d 335 (Ill. 1988) (denying recovery against a mother for unintentional injuries sustained in utero to a child born alive); Bonbrest v. Kotz, 65 F. Supp. 138 (D.D.C. 1946).
17. State v. Osmus, 276 P.2d 469, 476 (Wyo. 1954).
18. *Id.* at 470–71.
19. *Id.* at 475; *see also* WYO. STAT. ANN. § 58-101 (1945). The statute in question reads: "It shall be unlawful for any person having or being charged by law with the care or custody or control of any child under the age of nineteen (19) years knowingly to cause or permit the life of such child to be endangered or the health or morals or welfare of such child to be endangered or injured, or knowingly to cause or permit such child to be in any situation or environment such that the life, health, morals, or welfare of such child will or may be injured or endangered, or willfully or unnecessarily to expose to the inclemency of the weather, or negligently or knowingly abandon or fail to provide the necessities of life for such child, or to ill-treat, abuse, overwork, torture, torment, cruelly punish such a child, or to negligently or knowingly deprive or fail to furnish necessary food, clothing or shelter for such child, or in any other manner injure said child."
20. *Id.*

21. *Id.* at 472. *But see* People v. Chavez, 176 P.2d 92, 94 (Cal. Dist. Ct. App. 1947) (holding that a viable fetus in the process of birth is a human being within the meaning of homicide statutes even when the birth is not fully complete).

22. *Substance Use During Pregnancy*, Guttmacher Inst. (Oct. 1, 2019), https://www .guttmacher.org/state-policy/explore/substance-use-during-pregnancy.

23. 1995 Wisc. Act 292 (1997).

24. Shamane Mills, *Opponents of Wisconsin's "Cocaine Mom" Law Continue Fight*, Wisconsin Public Radio (Aug. 1, 2018), https://www.wpr.org/opponents-wisconsins-cocaine-mom-law-continue-fight.

25. *See State Laws on Fetal Homicide and Penalty-Enhancement for Crimes Against Pregnant Women*, Nat'l Conference of State Legislatures (last updated May 1, 2018), http:// www.ncsl.org/research/health/fetal-homicide-state-laws.aspx.

26. Manny Fernandez & Erik Eckholm, *Pregnant, and Forced to Stay on Life Support*, N.Y. Times, Jan. 8, 2014, at A1.

27. *See, e.g., Ex parte* Ankrom, 2013 WL 135748, at *11 (Ala. Jan. 13, 2013) (interpreting the term "child" in a child endangerment law to include fetuses); Adam Nositer, *In Alabama, a Crackdown on Pregnant Drug Users*, N.Y. Times (Mar. 15, 2008), http://www .nytimes.com/2008/03/15/us/15mothers.html?pagewanted=all&_r=0 (relating stories of women in Alabama prosecuted for using drugs while pregnant).

28. Emily Bazelon, *Purvi Patel Could Be Just the Beginning*, N.Y. Times (Apr. 1, 2015), https:// www.nytimes.com/2015/04/01/magazine/purvi-patel-could-be-just-the-beginning.html? action=click&module=RelatedCoverage&pgtype=Article&region=Footer ("The facts supporting each count are murky, but a jury convicted Patel in February, and on Monday she was sentenced to 20 years in prison.").

29. Kilmon v. State, 905 A.2d 306 (Md. 2006) (reversing a circuit court's finding of reckless endangerment based on use of controlled substances while pregnant).

30. *See, e.g.,* State v. Buckhalter, 119 So. 3d 1015, 1017, 1019 (Miss. 2013) (affirming the trial court's dismissal of Nina Buckhalter's indictment for manslaughter, which alleged she "willfully" caused her child's death by using drugs during pregnancy, and concluding that the indictment was "fatally flawed"); Ada Calhoun, *The Criminalization of Bad Mothers*, N.Y. Times (Apr. 25, 2012), http://www.nytimes.com/2012/04/29/magazine/the-criminalization-of-bad-mothers.html?pagewanted=all (relating the story of Rennie Gibbs, who was charged with "depraved heart murder" after her baby was stillborn and tested positive for cocaine); Emily Le Coz, *Mississippi Stillborn Manslaughter Charge Raising Fears*, USA Today (May 29, 2013, 1:01PM), http://www.usatoday.com /story/news/nation/2013/05/29/mississippi-stillborn-manslaughter-charge-raising-fears /2369523/ (discussing Buckhalter's manslaughter trial for the loss of her fetus, which prosecutors claimed was caused by her illegal drug use).

31. *See, e.g.,* Ferguson v. City of Charleston, 532 U.S. 67 (2001) (concluding that a state hospital's policy requiring diagnostic tests to obtain evidence of a pregnant woman's drug use for law enforcement purposes constitutes an "unreasonable search" if the patient has not provided consent to the procedure).

32. *See* Kontji Anthony, *Police: Woman Earns DUI for Endangering Fetus*, WMCTV (June 30, 2013), http://www.wmcactionnews5.com/story/20525700/police-pregnant-woman-earns-dui-for-endangering-fetus/.

33. Paltrow & Flavin, *supra* note 6, at 300.

34. *Id.* (noting that their study may be an undercount of the instances where pregnant women's liberty has been subjected to liberty deprivations).

35. Shuai v. State, 966 N.E.2d 619, 622 (Ind. Ct. App. 2012).

36. *See* Carrie Ritchie, *Murder Charge Raises Women's Rights Questions*, USA TODAY (Jan. 6, 2013, 12:18 AM), https://www.usatoday.com/story/news/nation/2013/01/05/infants-death-raises-womens-rights-questions/1566070/.

37. Kara Kenney, *Inmates Sleeping on Floor at Marion County Jail*, RTV6, THE INDYCHANNEL (Oct. 17, 2017), https://www.theindychannel.com/news/call-6-investigators/inmates-sleeping-on-floor-at-marion-county-jail (the spokesperson for the Marion County Sheriff's Office describes the conditions as an ongoing "crisis"); Mark Alesia, *Lawsuit: Former Marion County Jail Inmate Denied His Cancer Treatment*, INDYSTAR (June 18, 2018), https://www.indystar.com/story/news/2018/06/18/prison-medical-care-marion-county-jail-correct-care-solutions/637068002/; Robin Y. Richardson, *Marion County Inmates Sue over Jail Conditions*, LONGVIEW NEWS JOURNAL (Oct. 1, 2016), https://www.news-journal.com/news/police/marion-county-inmates-sue-over-jail-conditions/article_8ead079c-60dc-5670-9e9b-bce899224238.html (highlighting litigation brought by inmates over black mold at the facility).

38. Ed Pilkington, *Indiana Prosecuting Chinese Woman for Suicide Attempt That Killed Her Foetus*, GUARDIAN (May 30, 2012, 1:36 PM), http://www.guardian.co.uk/world/2012/may/30/indiana-prosecuting-chinese-woman-suicide-foetus.

39. *Id.*

40. Ritchie, *supra* note 36.

41. Shuai v. State, 966 N.E.2d 618, 622 (Ind. Ct. App. 2012).

42. Pilkington, *supra* note 38.

43. Debra L. Karch et al., *Surveillance for Violent Deaths – National Violent Death Reporting System, 16 States, 2009*, MORBIDITY & MORTALITY WKLY. REP., SURVEILLANCE SUMMARIES 61(6), Sept. 14, 2013, at 1, http://www.cdc.gov/mmwr/pdf/ss/ss6106.pdf; CTRS. DISEASE CONTROL, *Suicide: Facts at a Glance* (2012), http://www.cdc.gov/violenceprevention/pdf/suicide-datasheet-a.PDF.

44. *Shuai*, 966 N.E.2d at 622.

45. Michael R. Phillips et al., *Risk Factors for Suicide in China: A National Case-Control Psychological Autopsy Study*, 360 LANCET 1728, 1734 (2002).

46. Paul S. F. Yip & Ka Y. Liu, *The Ecological Fallacy and the Gender Ratio of Suicide in China*, 189 BRIT. J. PSYCHIATRY 465, 465–66 (2006).

47. Lakshmi Vijayakumar et al., *Socio-Economic, Cultural and Religious Factors Affecting Suicide Prevention in Asia*, in SUICIDE AND SUICIDE PREVENTION IN ASIA 19 (Herbert Hendin et al. eds., 2008); Kenneth R. Conner et al., *Low-Planned Suicides in China*, 35 PSYCHOLOGICAL MED. 1197 (2005); Veronica Pearson, *Ling's Death: An Ethnography of a Chinese Woman's Suicide*, 32 SUICIDE & LIFE-THREATENING BEHAV. 347 (2002); Veronica Pearson, *Goods on Which One Loses: Women and Mental Health in China*, 41 SOC. SCI. & MED. 1159 (1995); Yip & Liu, *supra* note 46, at 465.

48. Bruce Einhorn, *Suicide: China's Great Wall of Silence*, BLOOMBERG BUS. WK. (Nov. 1, 2004, 9:00 PM), http://www.businessweek.com/stories/2004-11-01/suicide-chinas-great-wall-of-silence (quoting Sartorius).

49. *Id.*

50. *New Study Shows 60 Percent of U.S. Counties Without a Single Psychiatrist*, NEW AM. ECON. (Oct. 23, 2017), https://www.newamericaneconomy.org/press-release/new-study-shows-60-percent-of-u-s-counties-without-a-single-psychiatrist/.

51. *Terry Curry Discusses the Bei Bei Shuai Case*, USA TODAY, http://usatoday30.usatoday.com/video/terry-curry-discusses-the-bei-bei-shuai-case/2119743594001.

52. Interview with Bei Bei Shuai (Apr. 6, 2013).

53. *Id.*

54. Richard Lacayo, *Down on the Downtrodden*, Time, Dec. 18, 1994, at 30.
55. Brief of Appellee at 6, Shuai v. State, 966 N.E.2d 619 (Ind. Ct. App. 2012), (No. 49A02-1106-CR-486).
56. Brief of Appellant, Oral Argument Requested, Gibbs v. State at 1, No. 2010-M-819-SCT (Miss. Nov. 12, 2010).
57. *Id.*
58. Brief of Amicus Curiae of the National Association of Social Workers et al. in support of Petitioner, Gibbs v. State at 1–2, No. 2010-M-819 (Miss. May 19, 2010) [hereinafter NASW Amicus Brief], http://www.socialworkers.org/assets/secured/documents/ldf/briefDocuments/Gibbs%20v%20State%20MS%20Sup.Ct.Amicus%20Brief.pdf.
59. Brief of Appellant, Gibbs v. State, *supra* note 56, at 1.
60. Subsequently, the Mississippi Supreme Court granted Gibbs's petition for interlocutory review. *Id.* at 2. Under Mississippi's Rules of Appellate Procedure, an interlocutory appeal may be sought if a substantial basis exists for a difference of opinion on a question of law as to which appellate resolution may:(1) Materially advance the termination of the litigation and avoid exceptional expense to the parties; or(2) Protect a party from substantial and irreparable injury; or(3) Resolve an issue of general importance in the administration of justice. Miss. R. App. Proc. 5(a) (2008).
61. Brief of Appellant, Gibbs v. State, *supra* note 56, at 36 ("Under the statutory interpretation advanced by the prosecution, Ms. Gibbs faces life in prison because of her combined status as a pregnant woman and drug user." The statute at issue reads: "The killing of a human being with the authority of law by any means or in any manner shall be murder in the following cases: ... (b)When done in the commission of an act eminently dangerous to others and evincing a depraved heart, regardless of human life, although without premeditated design to effect the death of any particularly individual, shall be second-degree murder." Miss. Code Ann. § 97-3-19(B) (West 2013). Miss. Code Ann. § 97-3-21(2) (West 2013) provides that "a person who shall be convicted of second-degree murder shall be imprisoned for life ... if the punishment is so fixed by the jury.")
62. Brief of the Appellant, Gibbs v. State, *supra* note 56, at 2.
63. *Id.*
64. *Id.*
65. Jessica Mason Pieklo, *Murder Charges Dismissed in Mississippi Stillbirth Case*, Rewire News (Apr. 4, 2014), https://rewire.news/article/2014/04/04/murder-charges-dismissed-mississippi-stillbirth-case/.
66. Miss. Code Ann. § 97-3-19(B) (West 2013). Miss. Code Ann. § 97-3-21(2) (West 2013).
67. *Id.* at 2.
68. Fla. Stat. Ann. § 782.09 (West 2005). Other provisions of the law created new crimes to include the killing of a fetus as manslaughter and extended punishment to vehicular homicide (Fla. Stat. Ann. § 782.071 (West 2001)).
69. Fla. Stat. Ann. § 782.071 (West 2001).
70. Fla. Stat. Ann. § 316.192 (West 2010).
71. Ariz. Rev. Stat. Ann. §§ 13-604, 13-604.01, 13-703, 13-1102, 13-1103, 13-1104, 13-1105, 13-4062, 31-412, 41-1604.11 and 41-1604.13.
72. *See* statutes cited *supra* note 71.
73. Ala. Code § 26-15-3.2 (2006).
74. *Id.* (emphasis added).
75. *Ex parte* Ankrom, 2013 WL 135748, at *22 (Ala. Jan. 13, 2013) (Parker, J., concurring) (concluding that "the decision of this Court today is in keeping with the widespread legal

recognition that unborn children are persons with rights that should be protected by law").

76. *Id.* at *15. A LA. C ODE § 26-15-3.2 (2006).
77. Associated Press, *Kansas Law Maker Compares Abortion to Holocaust,* W ICHITA E AGLE (Mar. 9, 2015), http://www.kansas.com/news/politics-government/article13112999.html.
78. *Id.*
79. Daniel Becker, *Georgia Legislature Passes Nation's First Embryo Adoption Law,* C HRISTIAN N EWS W IRE (Apr. 3, 2009), http://www.christiannewswire.com/news/630359951 .html.
80. HB 388, 2009 Gen. Assemb., Reg. Sess. (Ga.), codified at G A. C ODE A NN. §§ 19-8-40 to 19-8-43.
81. *Georgia's "Defender of Life,"* G EORGIA R IGHT T O L IFE (date omitted), http://www.grtl.org/? q=node/174.
82. Becker, *supra* note 79.
83. Grace Wyler, *Personhood Movement Continues to Divide Pro-Life Activists,* T IME (July 24, 2013), http://nation.time.com/2013/07/24/personhood-movement-continues-to-divide-pro -life-activists/.
84. S. Con. Res. 4009, 63d Leg. Assemb. (N.D. 2013).
85. Laura Bassett, *North Dakota Personhood Measure Passes State Senate,* H UFFINGTON P OST (Feb. 7, 2013, 5:24 PM), http://www.huffingtonpost.com/2013/02/07/north-dakota- personhood_n_2640380.html; https://www.propublica.org/article/north-dakota-abortion- amendment-fails.
86. Jennifer Bendery, *Michael Burgess: I Oppose Abortion Because Male Fetuses Masturbate,* H UFFINGTON P OST (May 18, 2013), http://www.huffingtonpost.com/2013/06/18/michael- burgess-abortion_n_3459108.html.
87. *Id.*
88. Laura Bassett, *Trent Franks: "The Incidence of Rape Resulting in Pregnancy Are Very Low,"* H UFFINGTON P OST (June 12, 2013), http://www.huffingtonpost.com/2013/06/12/trent- franks-rape-pregnancy_n_3428846.html.
89. *See* Jessica Ravitz, *Two States Passed Abortion Amendments to Their Constitutions in the Midterm: What Does That Mean?,* CNN (Nov. 7, 2018, 5:25PM), https://www.cnn.com /2018/11/07/health/abortion-ballot-measures-amendments/index.html; Marcia Angell & Michael Greene, Opinion, *Where Are the Doctors?,* USA T ODAY (last updated May 15, 2012, 6:36 PM), http://www.usatoday.com/news/opinion/forum/story/2012-05-15/women- contraception-abortion-reproductive-rights-doctors/54979766/1; *see also 2011 Ballot Measures: Election Results,* N AT'L C ONF. S TATE L EG. (last updated Nov. 9, 2011, 7:45 AM), http://www.ncsl.org/legislatures-elections/elections/ballot-measure-election- results.aspx; Keith Ashley, *Voters in the Georgia GOP Primary Will Vote on Personhood,* P ERSONHOOD USA (May 22, 2012), http://cm.personhoodusa.com/voters- georgia-gop-primary-will-vote-personhood; Eckholm, *supra* note 4, at A1; Lindsay Love, *A Dangerous Initiative: "Personhood" Measure Being Pushed in Montana,* W OMEN A RE W ATCHING B LOG (June 5, 2012), http://www.womenarewatching.org/article/a-dangerous- initiative-personhood-measure-being-pushed-in-montana; Julie Rovner, *Abortion Foes Push to Redefine Personhood,* N AT'L. P UB. R ADIO (June 1, 2011) http://www.npr.org/2011/ 06/01/136850622/abortion-foes-push-to-redefine-personhood; Wyler, *supra* note 83 (discussing efforts by Wisconsin Republicans to enact a personhood amendment granting human embryos the same civil rights as people).
90. 1995 W ISC. A CT 292 (1997). The legislation's constitutionality is currently under review, *see* Andrew Chung, *Supreme Court Lifts Ban on Wisconsin's "Cocaine Mom" Law During*

Appeal, REUTERS (July 7, 2017, 5:10 PM), https://www.reuters.com/article/us-usa-court-cocaine/supreme-court-lifts-block-on-wisconsin-cocaine-mom-law-during-appeal-idUSKBN19S2YX [https://perma.cc/BSB6-HHRZ].

91. Mills, *supra* note 24 (quoting Nancy Rosenbloom, an attorney with National Advocates for Pregnant Women); *see also* Nina Liss-Schultz, *A Judge Struck Down the "Cocaine Mom" Law That Put Pregnant Women in Jail*, MOTHER JONES (May 1, 2017), https://www.motherjones.com/politics/2017/05/tamara-loertscher-unborn-child-protection-wisconsin-pregnant-jail/3/.

92. *See* Eckholm, *supra* note 4.

93. Daniella Silva, *Shackled and Pregnant: Wis. Case Challenges "Fetal Protection" Law*, NBC NEWS (Oct. 24, 2013, 9:32 AM), http://usnews.nbcnews.com/_news/2013/10/24/21117142-shackled-and-pregnant-wis-case-challenges-fetal-protection-law?lite [https://perma.cc/8594-RVHR].

94. *Id.*

95. Liss-Schultz, *supra* note 95.

96. Pieklo, *supra* note 65.

97. Loertscher v. Anderson, 259 F. Supp. 3d 902 (W.D. Wis.), *stay granted*, 137 S. Ct. 2328 (2017).

98. Loertscher v. Anderson, 259 F. Supp. 3d 902 (W.D. Wis.), *stay granted*, 137 S. Ct. 2328 (2017), *vacated as moot*, 893 F.3d 386 (7th Cir. 2018).

99. Telephone interview with Angela Hulsey and Kyle Brown (Mar. 5, 2014).

100. *Id.*

101. Ed Pilkington, *Alone in Alabama: Dispatches from an Inmate Jailed for Her Son's Stillbirth*, GUARDIAN (Oct. 7, 2015), https://www.theguardian.com/us-news/2015/oct/07/alabama-chemical-endangerment-pregnancy-amanda-kimbrough.

102. *Id.*

103. Telephone interview with Angela Hulsey and Kyle Brown (Mar. 5, 2014).

104. *Id.*

105. *Id.*

106. *Id.*

107. *Id.*

108. Ada Calhoun, *The Criminalization of Bad Mothers*, N.Y. TIMES MAG., Apr. 29, 2012, at MM30.

109. *Prison Spending in 2015*, VERA INST., https://www.vera.org/publications/price-of-prisons-2015-state-spending-trends/price-of-prisons-2015-state-spending-trends/price-of-prisons-2015-state-spending-trends-prison-spending.

110. Dietrich v. Northampton, 138 Mass. 14 (1884). *See also* Magnolia Coca Cola Bottling Co. v. Jordan, 124 Tex. 347, 359–60 (1935); Allaire v. St. Luke's Hosp., 184 Ill. 359, 368 (1900); Newman v. City of Detroit, 281 Mich. 60, 62–63 (1937); Stanford v. St. Louis-San Francisco Ry. Co., 214 Ala. 611, 612 (1926); Buel v. United Rys. Co., 248 Mo. 126, 132–33 (1913); Lipps v. Milwaukee Elec. Ry. & Light Co., 164 Wis. 272, 276 (1916); Gorman v. Budlong, 23 R.I. 169, 176–77 (1901).

111. *See* Ferguson v. City of Charleston, 532 U.S. 67, 70–73 (2001).

112. R. L. Goldenberg et al., *Stillbirth: A Review*, 16 J. MATERNAL-FETAL & NEONATAL MED. 79, 79 (2004).

113. Robert M. Silver et al., *Work-up of Stillbirth: A Review of the Evidence*, 196 AM. J. OBSTETRICS & GYNECOLOGY 433, 440 (2007) (noting that multiple factors may contribute to a stillbirth, but not cause it).

114. Brief of Appellant, Gibbs v. State, *supra* note 56, at 30; NASW Amicus Brief, *supra* note 58; Claudia Malacrida, *Complicated Mourning: The Social Economy of Perinatal Death*, 9 QUALITATIVE HEALTH RES. 504, 505 (1999).

115. Melissa A. Sims & Kim A Collins, *Fetal Death: A 10-Year Retrospective Study*, 22 AM. J. FORENSIC MED. & PATHOLOGY 261, 261 (2001).

116. "Environment" could include both the physical, natural environment (such as exposure to toxins) as well as social environment (income, education, etc.). *See, e.g.*, Carol J. Rowland Hogue, *Demographics & Exposures*, in STILLBIRTH: PREDICTION, PREVENTION AND MANAGEMENT 57, 69–70 (Catherine Y. Spong ed. 2011) (discussing various social environment factors' impact on stillbirth risk); Marc Edwards, *Fetal Death and Reduced Birth Rates Associated with Exposure to Lead-Contaminated Drinking Water*, 48 ENVIRON. SCI. & TECH. 730 (2014).

117. Stillbirth Collaborative Research Network Writing Group, *Association Between Stillbirth and Risk Factors Known at Pregnancy Confirmation*, 306 J. AM. MED. ASS'N 2470, 2471 (2011).

118. John C. Smulian et al., *Fetal Deaths in the United States: Influence of High-Risk Conditions and Implications for Management*, 100 OBSTETRICS & GYNECOLOGY 1183, 1183 (2002).

119. Victoria Flenady et al., *Major Risk Factors for Stillbirth in High-Income Countries: A Systemic Review and Meta-Analysis*, 337 LANCET 1331, 1337 (2011) (explaining that "women from disadvantaged populations in high-income countries continue to have stillbirth rates far in excess of those living without such disadvantage. ... poverty could be the overriding factor preventing access to care" and thereby increasing risk of stillbirth).

120. Goldenberg et al., *supra* note 112, at 79, 85 (2004) ("in areas where syphilis is prevalent, up to half of all stillbirths may be caused by this infection alone").

121. *See, e.g.*, Rowland Hogue, *supra* note 116. *See also* K. Wisborg et al., *Psychological Stress During Pregnancy and Stillbirth: Prospective Study*, 115 BJOG 882 (2008) (finding an association between psychological stress during pregnancy and an increased risk of stillbirth).

122. *See* Abby Goodnough, *Flint Weights Scope of Harm to Children Caused by Lead in Water*, N.Y TIMES, Jan. 29, 2016 (as many as 8,000 children under six years old have been added to a database of kids "exposed to lead in Flint's water").

123. Natasha Frost et al., *HARD HIT: The Growth in the Imprisonment of Women, 1977–2004*, INST. ON WOMEN & CRIMINAL JUSTICE 1, 26 (May 2006), http://csdp.org /research/HardHitReport4.pdf; WOMEN'S PRISON ASS'N, QUICK FACTS: WOMEN & CRIMINAL JUSTICE – 2009 (2009), http://www.wpaonline.org/wpaassets/ Quick_Facts_Women_and_CJ_2009_rebrand.pdf [http://perma.cc/XW5Y-HX8F].

124. Lauren E. Glaze & Laura M. Maruschak, *Parents in Prison and Their Minor Children*, U.S. DEP'T OF JUSTICE, OFFICE OF JUSTICE PROGRAMS, BUREAU OF JUSTICE STATISTICS 1, 2, 4 (Aug. 2008), http://www.bjs.gov/content/pub/pdf/pptmc.pdf.

125. THE SENTENCING PROJECT, PARENTS IN PRISON, 1, 4 (revised Sept. 2012), http://www .sentencingproject.org/doc/publications/cc_Parents%20in%20Prison_Factsheet_9 .24sp.pdf; *see also* Dorothy Roberts, *Prison, Foster Care, and the Systemic Punishment of Black Mothers*, 59 UCLA L. REV. 1474 (2012).

126. Kristin Turney, *Stress Proliferation Across Generations? Examining the Relationship Between Parental Incarceration and Childhood Health*, 55 J. HEALTH & SOC. BEHAV. 302, 311–14 (2014).

127. *Id.*

128. Tammerlin Drummond, *Mothers in Prison,* TIME (Oct. 29, 2000), http://www.time.com/time/magazine/article/0,9171,58996,00.html (noting that "Florida is attempting to address a disturbing national phenomenon: the explosion in the number of mothers in prison").

129. CHANDRA KRING VILLANUEVA, INST. ON WOMEN & CRIMINAL JUSTICE, WOMEN'S PRISON ASSOCIATION, MOTHERS, INFANTS AND IMPRISONMENT: A NATIONAL LOOK AT PRISON NURSERIES AND COMMUNITY-BASED ALTERNATIVES 1, 4 ((Sarah B. From & Georgia Lerner eds., 2009).

130. *Id.* at 5 ("by keeping mothers and infants together, these programs prevent foster care placement and allow for the formation of maternal/child bonds during a critical period of infant development").

131. *Id.*

132. Suzanne Smalley, *Should Female Inmates Raise Their Babies in Prison?,* NEWSWEEK (May 13, 2009), http://www.newsweek.com/should-female-inmates-raise-their-babies-prison-80247.

4 ABORTION LAW

1. *See, e.g.,* Hyde v. Scyssor (1620) 79 Eng. Rep. 462, Cro. Jac. 538; Ohio & Miss. Ry. v. Cosby, 107 Ind. 32, 34–35 (1886); Birmingham S. Ry. v. Lintner, 141 Ala. 420, 427–28 (1904). *See generally* Jo-Anne M. Baio, *Loss of Consortium: A Derivative Injury Giving Rise to a Separate Cause of Action,* 50 FORDHAM L. REV. 1344 (1982).

2. *See, e.g.,* Bradwell v. Illinois, 83 U.S. (16 Wall.) 130, 141 (1872) (affirming an Illinois statute that denied female law graduates admission to the bar because "civil law, as well as nature herself, has always recognized a wide difference in the respective spheres and destinies of man and woman. . . . The natural and proper timidity and delicacy which belongs to the female sex evidently unfits it for many of the occupations of civil life.").

3. *See* DOROTHY ROBERTS, KILLING THE BLACK BODY 29–31 (1997).

4. *See, e.g.,* Jill Elaine Hasday, *Contest and Consent: A Legal History of Marital Rape,* 88 CALIF. L. REV. 1373 (2000); Michele Goodwin, *Marital Rape: The Long Arch of Sexual Violence Against Women and Girls,* 109 AM. J. INT'L L. 326, 328 (2016). Moreover, states typically vindicated the legitimacy of marital rape and courts followed suit. *See, e.g.,* State v. Paolella, 554 A.2d 702 (1989) (finding that CONN. GEN. STAT. § 53a-70a and § 53a-70a(a) exonerates a married man from the crime of rape if the victim is his wife); *see also* Michael G. Walsh, Annotation, *Criminal Responsibility of Husband for Rape, or Assault to Commit Rape, on Wife,* 24 A.L.R. 4th 105 (1983).

5. Minor v. Happersett, 53 Mo. 58, 64–65 (1873).

6. *See, e.g.,* Ozawa v. United States, 260 U.S. 178, 195 (1922); *see also* United States v. Bhagat Singh Thind, 261 U.S. 204, 209 (1923) (emphasis added) (denying citizenship to an Indian man who claimed that his Aryan lineage entitled him to the status of a white man in the United States).

7. *See, e.g.,* Parker v. Elliott, 20 Va. (6 Munf.) 587 (1820).

8. *See, e.g.,* Hasday, *supra* note 4; Claudia Zaher, *When a Woman's Marital Status Determined Her Legal Status: A Research Guide on the Common Law Doctrine of Coverture,* 94 LAW LIBR. J. 459 (2002); Damian Corless, *When a Wife Was Her Man's Chattel,* INDEPENDENT (Jan. 4, 2015, 2:30 AM), https://www.independent.ie/life/when-a-wife-was-her-mans-chattel-30871468.html.

9. *See generally* Colin Dayan, The Law Is a White Dog: How Legal Rituals Make and Unmake Persons (2013).

10. Hoyt v. Florida, 368 U.S. 57, 61–62 (1961) ("woman is still regarded as the center of home and family life"); *see also* Strauder v. West Virginia, 100 U.S. 303, 310 (1880), *abrogated by* Taylor v. Louisiana, 419 U.S. 522 (1975).

11. *See* Bradwell v. Illinois, 83 U.S. (16 Wall.) 130, 140–42 (1873).

12. 39 Wis. 232, 244–45 (1875) ("Nature has tempered woman as little for the juridical conflicts of the court room, as for the physical conflicts of the battle field. Womanhood is moulded for gentler and better things.").

13. Roe v. Wade, 410 U.S. 113, 130–34 (1973) (referencing Christian theology).

14. *Id.* at 153.

15. *Id.* at 130 (footnote omitted) (stating that even Soranos, the "greatest of the ancient gynecologists," who personally opposed abortion, "found it necessary to think first of the life of the mother").

16. *See generally* Gertrude Jacinta Fraser, African American Midwifery in the South (1998); Sharon A. Robinson, A *Historical Development of Midwifery in the Black Community: 1600–1940*, 29 J. Nurse-Midwifery 247, 247 (1984) ("By the early 19th century, the male physician had succeeded in replacing midwives among upper- and middle-class white urban American women."); Keisha La'Nesha Goode, *Birthing, Blackness, and the Body: Black Midwives and Experiential Continuities of Institutional Racism* (Oct. 1, 2014) (unpublished PhD dissertation, City University of New York) (on file with author).

17. *See* Horatio R. Storer, On Criminal Abortion in America 56 (1860).

18. *Id.*

19. Roe v. Wade, 410 U.S. at 132 (emphasis added) (citation omitted).

20. Marie Solis, *Here's What the Trump Administration's Proposed Title X Rule Would Do to Abortion Access in America*, Newsweek (May 2, 2018, 12:22 PM), http://www.newsweek.com/heres-what-trump-administrations-proposed-title-x-rule-would-do-abortion-908474 [https://perma.cc/XN9A-UVNF].

21. 136 S. Ct. 2292 (2016) (holding that the state of Texas cannot impose restrictions on abortion services that substantially burden women seeking an abortion).

22. S.F. 704, 90th Sess. (Minn. 2017).

23. Policy Statement of the United States of America at the United Nations International Conference on Population, 2d Sess., Mexico City (Aug. 6–14, 1984), *reprinted in* 10 Population & Dev. Rev. 574 (1984).

24. Storer, *supra* note 17, at 7.

25. *See* Fraser, *supra* note 16; Robinson, *supra* note 16; Goode, *supra* note 16.

26. *See* Goode, *supra* note 16.

27. Robinson, *supra* note 16; Goode, *supra* note 16.

28. Horatio R. Storer, On Criminal Abortion in America 7 (1860), *see also* Horatio R. Storer, "Why Not?" A Book For Every Woman 16 (1868) (arguing that women who terminate their pregnancies have "deplorable tendencies of unbridled desire, of selfishness and extravagance . . . [and] an absence of true conjugal affection . . .").

29. *See, e.g., id.* at 13.

30. Horatio Robinson Storer, Why Not?: A Book For Every Woman 85 (1868) (also quoted in Leslie Reagan, *When Abortion Was a Crime: Women, Medicine, and Law in the United States, 1867–1973, in* The Reproductive Rights Reader 82 (Nancy Ehrenreich ed., 2008)).

31. *See* Storer, *supra* note 17, at 13.

32. *Id.* at 80.
33. STORER, *supra* note 17, at 57–58.
34. Joseph B. DeLee, *Progress Toward Ideal Obstetrics*, Speech at Sixth Annual Meeting of the American Association for Study and Prevention of Infant Mortality (Nov. 11, 1915), *in* 73 AM. J. OF OBSTETRICS & DISEASES OF WOMEN & CHILDREN 407–15 (1916).
35. *Id.*
36. Robinson, *supra* note 16, at 247 (noting that, with the advent of medical tools such as forceps, gynecology became male-dominated in Europe and the United States).
37. A. de Jonge et al., *Perinatal Mortality and Morbidity in a Nationwide Cohort of 529,688 Low-Risk Planned Home and Hospital Births*, 116 BJOG 1177, 1177 (2009) ("However, this move from home to hospital birth for most women was not based on evidence . . . ."). In this study, researchers noted that prior conflicting studies on the efficacy of midwives in homebirths "could not exclude high risk unplanned, unassisted home births from planned home birth group." *Id.* at 1178.
38. DeLee, *supra* note 34, at 410.
39. *See* Liana Aghajanian, *Los Angeles Midwives Aim to End Racial Disparities at Birth*, ALJAZEERA AM. (Sept. 5, 2015), http://america.aljazeera.com/articles/2015/9/5/to-los-angeles-midwives-racial-disparities-birth.html (reporting that the Sheppard-Towner Maternity and Infancy Act "forced midwives to become licensed and receive training from nurses. As medical professionals established relationships in communities that midwives once served, the use of midwives diminished in much of the country.").
40. Emily Friedman, *U.S. Hospitals and the Civil Rights Act of 1964*, HOSPS. & HEALTH NETWORKS DAILY (June 3, 2014), http://www.hhnmag.com/articles/4179-u-s-hospitals-and-the-civil-rights-act-of-1964 ("Only 10 percent of Northern hospitals accepted African-American interns or residents; only 20 percent had them on staff. Only 6 percent of Southern hospitals accepted them as interns or residents, and only 25 percent granted them staff privileges.").
41. DeLee, *supra* note 34, at 407–08.
42. *See generally* Melissa Cheyney et al., *Development and Validation of National Data Registry for Midwife-Led Births: The Midwives Alliance of North America Statistics Project 2.0*, 59 J. MIDWIFERY & WOMEN'S HEALTH 8 (2014); Melissa Cheyney et al., *Outcomes of Care for 16,484 Planned Home Births in the United States: The Midwives Alliance of North America Statistics Project, 2004–2009*, 59 J. MIDWIFERY & WOMEN'S HEALTH 17 (2014); de Jonge et al., *supra* note 37; J.T. Fullerton et al., *Outcomes of Planned Home Birth: An Integrative Review*, 52 J. MIDWIFERY & WOMEN'S HEALTH 323 (2007); E. Hutton et al., *Outcomes Associated with Planned Home and Hospital Births in Low-Risk Women Attended by Midwives in Ontario, Canada, 2003–2006: A Retrospective Cohort Study*, 36 BIRTH 180 (2009); P. Janssen, *Outcomes of Planned Home Birth with Registered Midwife Versus Planned Hospital Birth with Midwife or Physician*, 181 CANADIAN MED. ASS. J. 377 (2009).
43. Jane Sandall et al., *Midwife-Led Continuity Models Versus Other Models of Care for Childbearing Women*, COCHRANE DATABASE OF SYSTEMATIC REVIEWS, No. 4, 2016, at 1 ("We identified 15 studies involving 17,674 mothers and babies . . . . We included women at low risk of complications as well as women at increased risk, but not currently experiencing problems. . . . The main benefits were that women who received midwife-led continuity of care were less likely to have an epidural. In addition, fewer women had episiotomies or instrumental births. Women's chances of a spontaneous vaginal birth were also increased and there was no difference in the number of caesarean births. Women were less likely to experience preterm birth, and they were also at a lower risk

of losing their babies. In addition, women were more likely to be cared for in labour by midwives they already knew." *Id.* at 3.).

44. Melissa Madera, *6 women Share Their Harrowing Stories of Illegal Abortion Before* Roe v. Wade, Vice News (Jan. 22, 2018, 11:23 AM), https://broadly.vice.com/en_us/article/43qm5d/6-women-share-their-harrowing-stories-of-illegal-abortion-before-roe-v-wade.

45. Reagan, *supra* note 30, at 214.

46. *Id.* at 210.

47. *Id.*

48. *Id.* at 210–11.

49. *Id.* at 212–13 (explaining that "[t]he racial differences in abortion-related deaths and access to safe therapeutic abortions mirrored the racial inequities in health services in general and in overall health" and noting that "[m]aternal mortality rates of black women were three to four times higher than those of white women").

50. Rachel Benson Gold, *Lessons from Before Roe: Will Past Be Prologue?*, 6 Guttmacher Pol.'y Rev. 8, 8 (2003).

51. Alan F. Guttmacher, *Law, Morality, and Abortion*, 22 Rutgers L. Rev. 415, 420–21 (1967).

52. *See, e.g.*, NARAL Found., Choices: Women Speak Out About Abortion 11 (1997).

53. *Id.*

54. Madera, *supra* note 44.

55. *Id.*

56. *Id.*

57. *Id.*

58. Stephanie Hallett, *Eight Stories That Show What Abortion Was Like Before Roe v. Wade*, Ms. Magazine Blog (Jan. 19, 2016), https://msmagazine.com/blog/2016/01/19/8-stories-that-show-what-abortion-was-like-before-roe-v-wade/.

59. *Id.* For accounts that further capture women's painful, coercive experiences, *see* When Abortion Was Illegal: Untold Stories (Concentric Media 1992), http://concentric.org/films/when_abortion_was_illegal.html [https://perma.cc/VVP6-BPQQ]; Lisa Woods, *9 Older Women Share Their Harrowing Back Alley Abortion Stories*, Thought Catalog (Dec. 30, 2015), http://thoughtcatalog.com/lisa-woods/2015/12/9-older-women-share-their-harrowing-back-alley-abortion-stories/ [https://perma.cc/HW5V-MLJQ].

60. *Id.*

61. Telephone interview with Aryeh Neier (Apr. 13, 2015).

62. Roe v. Wade, 410 U.S. 113 (1973).

63. *Id.* at 121.

64. Tex. Penal Code Ann. §§ 1191–94, 1196 (1961) (historical).

65. *Roe*, 410 U.S. at 117 n.1.

66. *Id.*

67. *See* Alex Witchel, *At Home With: Norma McCorvey; Of Roe, Dreams and Choices*, N.Y. Times (July 28, 1994), http://www.nytimes.com/1994/07/28/garden/at-home-with-norma-mccorvey-of-roe-dreams-and-choices.html.

68. *Roe*, 410 U.S. at 120.

69. *See* Witchel, *supra* note 67.

70. *Roe*, 410 U.S. at 153.

71. *Id.*

72. The Pill, *Anthony Comstock's "Chastity" Laws*, PBS, http://www.pbs.org/wgbh/amex/pill/peopleevents/e_comstock.html ("The driving force behind the original anti-birth control statutes was a New Yorker named Anthony Comstock. A devout Christian . . . offended by

explicit advertisements for birth control devices, he soon identified the contraceptive industry as one of his targets.").

73. *Nomination of Ruth Bader Ginsburg, to Be Associate Justice of the Supreme Court of the United States*, 103d Cong. 150 (1993).

74. Maher v. Roe, 432 U.S. 468, 469–70 (1977).

75. *Id.* at 483–84 (Brennan, J., dissenting).

76. *Id.*

77. *Id.*

78. *See* International Union v. Johnson Controls, 499 U.S. 187, 188 (1991).

79. *Id.*

80. 432 U.S. 464 (1977).

81. 432 U.S. 438 (1977).

82. 448 U.S. 297 (1980).

83. *Id.* at 309; *Maher*, 432 U.S. at 465, 479–80; *Beal*, 432 U.S. at 444.

84. *Harris*, 448 U.S. at 338 (Marshall, J., dissenting).

85. Amendment No. 68. H.R. Rep. No. 94-1555, at 3 (1976) (Conf. Rep.).

86. *Harris*, 448 U.S. at 356–57 (Stevens, J., dissenting).

87. Heather D. Boonstra, *The Heart of the Matter: Public Funding of Abortion for Poor Women in the United States*, Guttmacher Inst., (Mar. 5, 2007), https://www .guttmacher.org/about/gpr/2007/03/heart-matter-public-funding-abortion-poor-women-united-states; *see also* 122 Cong. Rec. 20410 (1976) (statement of Rep. Hyde).

88. *Harris*, 448 U.S. at 311. *See generally id.* at 331–32 (Brennan, J., dissenting).

89. *Id.* at 316 (majority opinion).

90. *Id.* at 315.

91. *Id.*

92. *Id.*

93. *Id.* at 338 (Marshall, J., dissenting).

94. *See, e.g.*, Pauli Murray, *The Liberation of Black Women*, in Women: A Feminist Perspective 351–62 (Jo Freeman ed., 1975); Roberts, *supra* note 3; Kimberlé Crenshaw, *Demarginalizing the Intersection of Race and Sex: A Black Feminist Critique of Antidiscrimination Doctrine, Feminist Theory and Antiracist Politics*, 1989 U. Chicago Legal F. 139, 166 (urging that "[i]f any real efforts are to be made to free Black people of the constraints and conditions that characterize racial subordination, then theories and strategies purporting to reflect the Black community's needs must include an analysis of sexism and patriarchy").

95. *See, e.g.*, State v. Paolella, 210 Conn. 110 (1989) (ruling that under Conn. Gen. Stat. § 53a-70a and 53a-70a(a) a finding by a trier that the alleged offender and the victim were married exonerates the alleged offender, regardless of the proof of forcible sexual intercourse); *see also* Goodwin, *supra* note 4; Hasday, *supra* note 4; Jane E. Larson, *"Even a Worm Will Turn at Last": Rape Reform in Late Nineteenth-Century America*, 9 Yale J.L. & Human. 1, 8–9, 18–19 (1997); Walsh, *supra* note 4; Robin West, *Equality Theory, Marital Rape, and the Promise of the Fourteenth Amendment*, 42 Fla. L. Rev. 45, 64–65 (1990).

96. *See* Buck v. Bell, 274 U.S. 200 (1927) (affirming the constitutionality of forced sterilization performed on an indigent female victim of rape). Sir Matthew Hale's acclaimed 1736 treatise, *Historia Placitorum Coronae, The History of the Pleas of the Crown*, proclaimed that a "husband cannot be guilty of rape" because marriage conveys unconditional consent, whereby the wife has entered a binding contract and "hath given up herself in this kind unto her husband, which she cannot retract." Matthew Hale, The History of the Pleas of the Crown 628 (1736).

97. See Bradwell v. Illinois, 83 U.S. 130 (1872) (upholding Illinois law that denied women the right to become members of the state bar and therefore lawyers); Minor v. Happersett, 88 U.S. 162 (1875) (Court reasoning that while the Constitution granted women citizenship, it did not confer upon them a right to vote); Miller v. Wilson, 236 U.S. 373 (1915) (upholding California statute limiting women's working hours in certain jobs); Bosley v. McLaughlin, 236 U.S. 385 (1915) (extending the range of employment sectors where women could be barred from evening work hours that could secure them higher wages); Radice v. New York, 264 U.S. 292 (1924) (upholding New York law that forbade women waitresses from working nightshifts); Buck v. Bell, 274 U.S. 200 (1927) (denying poor women reproductive autonomy by upholding Virginia sterilization law against raped teenage girl). State courts too have arbitrarily denied women a range of basic rights over time: *In re* Paquet's Estate, 101 Or. 393, 200 P. 911 (1921) (wife not allowed to administer her deceased husband's estate); *In re* Goodell, 39 Wis. 232, 233 (1875) ("So we find no statutory authority for the admission of females to the bar of any court of this state. And, with all the respect and sympathy for this lady which all men owe to all good women, we cannot regret that we do not. We cannot but think the common law wise in excluding women from the profession of the law."); Cooper v. Doyal, 205 So. 2d 59 (La. Ct. App. 1967), *writ refused*, 251 La. 755, 206 So. 2d 97 (1968) (upholding employment contract provision that forced stewardesses to resign upon marriage); Forbush v. Wallace, 341 F. Supp. 217 (M.D. Ala. 1971), *aff'd*, 405 U.S. 970 (1972) (upholding state's unwritten regulation denying women the right to obtain drivers' licenses in their own names); Vorchheimer v. Sch. Dist. of Philadelphia, 532 F.2d 880 (3d Cir. 1976), *aff'd*, 430 U.S. 703 (1977) (upholding lower court decision to deny girls the right to attend an academic school that was all-male); Lanigan v. Bartlett & Co. Grain, 466 F. Supp. 1388 (W.D. Mo. 1979) (upholding sanctions against a female employee for wearing pants to work); Chambers v. Omaha Girls Club, Inc., 834 F.2d 697 (8th Cir. 1987) (dismissing suit alleging that the "negative role model rule" permitting single pregnant women to be fired violated law).
98. 335 U.S. 464, 465 (1948).
99. *Id.* at 465.
100. *Id.* at 455–56.
101. Hoyt v. Florida, 368 U.S. 57, 61–62 (1961); *see also* Strauder v. West Virginia, 100 U.S. 303, 310 (1879), *abrogated by* Taylor v. Louisiana, 419 U.S. 522 (1975).
102. *Hoyt*, 368 U.S. 57 at 62.
103. *See* Pers. Admin. of Mass. v. Feeney, 442 U.S. 256, 270, 281 (1979) (upholding a Massachusetts law that prioritized employment opportunities for veterans for civil service jobs that did not require military skills and which operated to overwhelmingly advantage men); Rostker v. Goldberg, 453 U.S. 57, 78–79 (1981) (affirming the rejection of women in military registration, reasoning that excluding women is not like exempting blacks or Lutherans, because "Congress' decision to authorize the registration of only men … does not violate the Due Process Clause. The exemption of women from registration is not only sufficiently but also closely related to Congress' purpose in authorizing registration.").
104. 505 U.S. 833 (1992).
105. *Id.* at 846.
106. *Id.* at 844.
107. *Nomination of Ruth Bader Ginsburg, supra* note 73, at 150.
108. Gonzales v. Carhart, 550 U.S. 124, 161–67 (2007).
109. *Id.* at 166 (majority opinion).
110. *Id.* at 147.

111. *Id.* at 159.
112. M.A. Biggs, *Does Abortion Reduce Self-Esteem and Life Satisfaction?*, 23 QUALITY LIFE RES. 2505, 2509 (2014) (finding "no evidence to support [Justice Kennedy's] assumption").
113. U.S. DEP'T OF HEALTH AND HUMAN SERVICES., POSTPARTUM DEPRESSION FACTS 2, https://www.nimh.nih.gov/health/publications/postpartum-depression-facts/postpartum-depression-brochure_146657.pdf.
114. *Id.* at 7; DONNA E. STEWART ET AL., POSTPARTUM DEPRESSION: LITERATURE REVIEW OF RISK FACTORS AND INTERVENTIONS 4 (2003), http://www.who.int/mental_health/prevention/suicide/lit_review_postpartum_depression.pdf.
115. STEWART ET AL., *supra* note 114, at 4.
116. *See* Corinne H. Rocca et al., *Decision Rightness and Emotional Responses to Abortion in the United States: A Longitudinal Study*, 10 PLoS ONE 1 (July 8, 2015), https://journals.plos.org/plosone/article/file?id=10.1371/journal.pone.0128832&type=printable.
117. *Id.* at 2.
118. *Id.* at 12.
119. Susan Newman, *Mothers With One Child Are Happiest*, PSYCHOL. TODAY (Feb. 5, 2010), https://www.psychologytoday.com/blog/singletons/201002/mothers-one-child-are-happiest.
120. HANS-PETER KOHLER, DO CHILDREN BRING HAPPINESS AND PURPOSE IN LIFE? 13 (Dec. 10, 2010), http://www.ssc.upenn.edu/~hpkohler/working-papers/kohl11dw.pdf.
121. *Id.* (noting also that "[m]ales ... do not suffer the same declines in happiness with additional children that do females," *id.* at 15).
122. Biggs, *supra* note 112, at 2505.
123. Jeffrey A. Van Detta, *Constitutionalizing Roe, Casey and Carhart: A Legislative Due-Process Anti-Discrimination Principle That Gives Constitutional Content to the "Undue Burden" Standard of Review Applied to Abortion Control Legislation*, 10 S. CAL. REV. L. & WOMEN'S STUD. 211, 213 (2001).
124. Whole Woman's Health v. Hellerstedt, 136 S. Ct. 2292 (2016).
125. Manny Fernandez, *Abortion Restrictions Become Law in Texas, but Opponents Will Press Fight*, N.Y. TIMES (July 18, 2013), http://www.nytimes.com/2013/07/19/us/perry-signs-texas-abortion-restrictions-into-law.html.
126. Elizabeth Raymond & David Grimes, *The Comparative Safety of Legal Induced Abortion and Childbirth in the United States*, 119 J. OBSTETRICS & GYNECOLOGY 215, 217 (2012); D.A. Grimes, *Estimation of Pregnancy-Related Mortality Risk By Pregnancy Outcome, United States, 1991 to 1999*, 194 AM. J. OBSTETRICS & GYNECOLOGY 92 (2006); S. A. LeBolt, D.A. Grimes & W. Cates, Jr., *Mortality from Abortion and Childbirth: Are the Populations Comparable?*, 248 JAMA 188 (1982).
127. *Whole Woman's Health*, 136 S. Ct. at 2302, 2311.
128. WORLD HEALTH ORGANIZATION, SAFE ABORTION: TECHNICAL AND POLICY GUIDANCE FOR HEALTH SYSTEMS 49 (2d ed. 2012).
129. *See* Raymond & Grimes, *supra* note 126.
130. TEX. HEALTH & SAFETY CODE ANN. § 171.0031(a) (West Cum. Supp. 2015).
131. TEX. HEALTH & SAFETY CODE ANN. § 245.010(a).
132. *See* Texas Pol'y Evaluation Project, *Access to Abortion Care in the Wake of HB2* (July 1, 2014), http://www.utexas.edu/cola/txpep/_files/pdf/AbortionAccessafterHB2.pdf; *see also* Manny Fernandez & Erik Eckholm, *Court Upholds Texas Limits on Abortions*, N.Y. TIMES (June 9, 2015), https://www.nytimes.com/2015/06/10/us/court-upholds-texas-law-criticized-as-blocking-access-to-abortions.html; *Fewer Abortion Clinics in Texas*, N.Y.

TIMES (June 10, 2015), http://www.nytimes.com/interactive/2014/08/04/us/shrinking-number-of-abortion-clinics-in-texas.html.

133. This impact was also attributable to fewer clinics being legally permitted to operate in Texas. Stephen Young, *Texas Women Face Long Abortion Waits in HB2's Wake*, DALLAS OBSERVER (Oct. 6, 2015), http://www.dallasobserver.com/news/texas-women-face-long-abortion-waits-in-hb2s-wake-7658610; Mark Reagan, *HB2 Increasing Wait Times for Women Seeking Abortion Services*, SAN ANTONIO CURRENT (Oct. 6, 2015), http://www.sacurrent.com/Blogs/archives/2015/10/06/hb2-increasing-wait-times-for-women-seeking-abortion-services.

134. *About Us*, WHOLE WOMAN'S HEALTH, https://wholewomanshealth.com/about-us/.

135. Whole Woman's Health v. Hellerstedt, 136 U.S. 2292, 2292 (2016).

136. *See id.* at 2300.

137. *Id.* at 2311 (citing Whole Woman's Health v. Lakey, 46 F. Supp. 3d 673, 684 (2014)).

138. *Whole Woman's Health*, 136 U.S. at 2311(citation omitted).

139. *Id.* at 2312.

140. *Id.*

141. *Id.*

142. *Id.*

143. *Id.* at 2313.

144. *Id.* at 2314.

145. Brie Shea, *Here Are All the Anti-Abortion Laws Going into Effect Next Month*, REWIRE NEWS (June 28, 2019), https://rewire.news/article/2019/06/28/here-are-all-the-anti-abortion-laws-going-into-effect-next-month/.

146. Exec. Order No. 13535, 75 Fed. Reg. 15,599 (Mar. 29, 2010).

147. *See* Emily Bazelon, *Obama's Executive Order on Abortion*, SLATE (Mar. 21, 2010, 5:37 P.M.), http://www.slate.com/blogs/xx_factor/2010/03/21/the_executive_order_about_abortion_for_health_care_reform.html.

148. *Id.*

149. 75 Fed. Reg. at 15,599.

150. Public Health and Welfare Act, 42 U.S.C. § 300a-7 (West, Westlaw current through Pub. L. No. 114-316) (prohibiting public officials from requiring an individual receiving federal funding "to perform or assist in the performance of any sterilization procedure or abortion if his performance or assistance in the performance of such procedure or abortion would be contrary to his religious beliefs or moral convictions" or an entity receiving federal funding "to make its facilities available" or "provide any personnel for the performance or assistance in the performance of any sterilization procedure or abortion if the performance or assistance in the performance of such procedure or abortion" if it "would be contrary to the religious beliefs or moral convictions" of such entity or personnel.").

151. Pub. L. No. 111-17, § 508(d)(1), 123 Stat. 3034, 3280 (2009) ("None of the funds made available in this Act may be made available to a Federal agency or program, or to a State or local government, if such agency, program, or government subjects any institutional or individual health care entity to discrimination on the basis that the health care entity does not provide, pay for, provide coverage of, or refer for abortions.").

152. 75 Fed. Reg. at 15,599.

153. *Id.*

154. *Id.*

5 CHANGING ROLES OF DOCTORS AND NURSES: HOSPITAL SNITCHES AND POLICE INFORMANTS

1. Linda Villarosa, *Why America's Black Mothers and Babies Are in a Life-or-Death Crisis,* N.Y. TIMES, Apr. 11, 2018; Nina Martin, *Black Mothers Keep Dying After Giving Birth: Shalon Irving's Story Explains Why,* NPR (Dec. 7, 2017), https://www.npr.org/2017/12/07/568948782/black-mothers-keep-dying-after-giving-birth-shalon-irvings-story-explains-why; Erika Stallings, *This Is How the American Healthcare System Is Failing Black Women,* OPRAH MAGAZINE, Oct. 2018.

2. UNEQUAL TREATMENT: CONFRONTING RACIAL AND ETHNIC DISPARITIES IN HEALTH CARE (Smedley et al. eds., 2003).

3. Report of Officer John Tadlock, Blountstown Police Department Services Event Report, Dec. 21, 2015, https://bloximages.newyork1.vip.townnews.com/wtxl.com/content/tncms/assets/v3/editorial/2/bf/2bfe2a58-ad8c-11e5-a93a-7fcf5fb02d1d/568177c748993.pdf.pdf; Christine Hauser, *Recordings Add Detail in Death of Woman Forced from Florida Hospital,* N.Y. TIMES (Jan. 7, 2016), https://www.nytimes.com/2016/01/08/us/recordings-add-detail-in-death-of-woman-forced-from-florida-hospital.html; *Florida Officer Resigns Months After Handcuffed Woman at Hospital Dies,* CBS NEWS (June 1, 2016), https://www.cbsnews.com/news/florida-officer-resigns-months-after-handcuffed-woman-at-hospital-dies-barbara-dawson/.

4. Hauser, *supra* note 3.

5. *Id.*

6. Letitia Stein, *USF Obstetrician Threatens to Call Police if Patient Doesn't Report for C-Section,* TAMPA BAY TIMES (Mar. 6, 2013), http://www.tampabay.com/news/health/usf-obstetrician-threatens-to-call-police-if-patient-doesnt-report-for/2107387.

7. In fact, her high-risk pregnancy was what led her to Dr. Yankowitz in the first place, because he was one of only a few doctors willing to try a vaginal birth after a cesarean. *Id.*

8. *Id.*

9. *Id.*

10. Press Release, Nat'l Advocates for Pregnant Women, Florida Doctor Threat of Arrest of Pregnant Woman Dangerous and Without Legal Authority (Mar. 6, 2013), http://advocatesforpregnantwomen.org/blog/2013/03/press_statement_doctor_threat.php.

11. *See, e.g., ex parte* Ankrom, 2013 WL 135748, at *11 (Ala. Jan. 11, 2013) (interpreting the term "child" in a child endangerment law as including fetuses); Adam Nossiter, *In Alabama, a Crackdown on Pregnant Drug Users,* N.Y. TIMES (Mar. 15, 2008), http://www.nytimes.com/2008/03/15/us/15mothers.html (relating stories of women in Alabama prosecuted for using drugs while pregnant).

12. Kilmon v. State, 905 A.2d 306 (Md. 2006) (reversing a circuit court's finding of reckless endangerment based on use of controlled substances while pregnant).

13. *See, e.g.,* State v. Buckhalter, 119 So. 3d 1015, 1017, 1019 (Miss. 2013) (affirming the trial court's dismissal of Nina Buckhalter's indictment for manslaughter, which alleged she "willfully" caused her child's death by using drugs during pregnancy, and concluding that the indictment was "fatally flawed"); Ada Calhoun, *The Criminalization of Bad Mothers,* N.Y. TIMES (Apr. 25, 2012), http://www.nytimes.com/2012/04/29/magazine/the-criminalization-of-bad-mothers.html?pagewanted=all (relating the story of Rennie Gibbs, who was charged with "depraved heart murder" after her baby was stillborn and tested positive for cocaine); Emily Le Coz, *Mississippi Stillborn Manslaughter Charge Raising Fears,* USA TODAY (May 29, 2013, 1:01PM), http://www.usatoday.com/story/news/nation/2013/05/29/mississippi-stillborn-manslaughter-charge-raising-fears/2369523/

(discussing Buckhalter's manslaughter trial for the loss of her fetus, which prosecutors claimed was caused by her illegal drug use).

14. *See, e.g.*, Ferguson v. City of Charleston, 532 U.S. 67 (2001) (concluding that a state hospital's policy requiring diagnostic tests to obtain evidence of a pregnant woman's drug use for law enforcement purposes constitutes an "unreasonable search" if the patient has not provided consent to the procedure); State v. McKnight, 576 S.E.2d 168, 178–79 (S.C. 2003) (holding that a urine sample taken from Regina McKnight while in the hospital, which was used in her conviction for homicide by child abuse, did not violate her Fourth Amendment rights). Fortunately for McKnight, her petition for postconviction relief was granted and she was released from prison. McKnight v. State, 661 S.E.2d 354, 356 (S.C. 2008); Sharon Greene, *Regina McKnight Released from Prison*, CAROLINALIVE.COM (June 19, 2008, 6:23PM), http://www.carolinalive.com/news/story.aspx?id=149364# .UswdqfRDu4I.

15. Lynn M. Paltrow & Jeanne Flavin, *Arrests of and Forced Interventions on Pregnant Women in the United States, 1973–2005: Implications for Women's Legal Status and Public Health*, 38 J. HEALTH POL., POL'Y & L. 299, 303 (2013).

16. *See* Brief of Amici Curiae American Civil Liberties Union, American Civil Liberties Union of Florida, and American Medical Women's Association in Support of Appellant at 3, Burton v. Florida, 49 So. 3d 263 (Fla. Dist. Ct. App. Aug. 12, 2010) (No. ID09-1958) [hereinafter ACLU Brief], https://www.aclu.org/files/pdfs/reproductiverights/burton_v_ florida_acluamicus.pdf.

17. According to the Cleveland Clinic, nearly 20 percent of pregnant women are prescribed some form of bed rest each year. *Pregnancy Bed Rest*, CLEVELAND CLINIC, http://my .clevelandclinic.org/healthy_living/pregnancy/hic_pregnancy_bed_rest.aspx.

18. *See* Susan Donaldson James, *Pregnant Woman Fights Court-Ordered Best Rest*, ABC NEWS (Jan. 14, 2010), http://abcnews.go.com/Health/florida-court-orders-pregnant-woman-bed-rest-medical/story?id=9561460.

19. *See* Lisa Belkin, *Is Refusing Bed Rest a Crime?*, N.Y. TIMES (Jan. 12, 2010, 12:50 PM), http:// parenting.blogs.nytimes.com/2010/01/12/is-refusing-bed-rest-a-crime/ ("Burton asked to switch hospitals and the request was denied by the court."). Burton's attorney argued that there were a number of more appropriate treatment options for Burton, including bed rest at home, that would have allowed her to take care of her two daughters. *See* Martha Neil, *Pregnant Pro Se Mom Argued Treatment Case from Hospital Bed & Lost; Will Lawyer Win Appeal?*, ABA J. (Jan. 26, 2010, 3:22 PM), http://www.abajournal.com /news/article/observers_await_appellate_ruling_in_suit_over_court-ordered_treatmen t_of_pr/.

20. *In re* Unborn Child of Samantha Burton, No. 2009 CA 1167, 2009 WL 8628562 (Fla. Cir. Ct. Mar. 27, 2009).

21. Burton v. State, 49 So. 3d 263, 265 (Fla. Dist. Ct. App. 2010).

22. *Id.*

23. On petition by the state attorney, the order was granted. *In re* Unborn Child of Samantha Burton, No. 2009 CA 1167, 2009 WL 8628562 (Fla. Cir. Ct. Mar. 27, 2009).

24. *Id.*

25. *Id.*

26. *Id.*

27. As a "mandatory reporter" under Florida law, TMH must report "known or suspected child abuse, abandonment, or neglect by a parent" to allow the Florida Department of Children and Families to undertake "protective investigation." FLA. STAT. ANN. § 39.201(2)(a) (West 2013).

28. *Reassessing Solitary Confinement: The Human Rights, Fiscal and Public Safety Consequences: Hearing Before the Subcomm. on the Constitution, Civil Rights and Human Rights, S. Judiciary Comm.* (June 19, 2012) [hereinafter *Reassessing Solitary Confinement Hearing*] (opening statement of Dick Durban).

29. U.S. Senator John McCain, on his treatment as a prisoner of war. JOHN MCCAIN & MARK SALTER, FAITH OF MY FATHERS 206 (1999).

30. *In re* Medley, 134 U.S. 160, 168 (1890).

31. *Reassessing Solitary Confinement Hearing, supra* note 28.

32. *Reassessing Solitary Confinement Hearing, supra* note 28 (statement of Hon. Patrick Leahy,http://www.judiciary.senate.gov/imo/media/doc/leahy_statement_06_19_12.pdf).

33. Durban, *supra* note 28.

34. Leahy, *supra* note 32 (noting that, "far too often, prisoners today are placed in solitary confinement for minor violations that are disruptive but not violent").

35. *See* ACLU Brief, *supra* note 16, at 3.

36. *Reassessing Solitary Confinement Hearing, supra* note 28 (testimony of Craig Haney, http://www.judiciary.senate.gov/pdf/12–6-19HaneyTestimony.pdf).

37. Burton v. Florida, 49 So. 3d 263, 266–67 (Fla. Dist. Ct. App. 2010) (Van Nortwick, J., concurring).

38. Gideon v. Wainwright, 372 U.S. 335 (1963).

39. *Id.* at 344.

40. Lassiter v. Dep't of Soc. Servs., 452 U.S. 18, 26–27 (1981).

41. *Id.* at 27.

42. *Id.*

43. *In re* Gault, 387 U.S. 1, 36 (1967).

44. *FAQ: Cesarean Birth*, AM. COLL. OBSTETRICIANS & GYNECOLOGISTS, http://www.acog.org /~/media/For%20Patients/faq006.pdf?dmc=1&ts=20140107T1622543905; Mayo Clinic Staff, *C-Section*, MAYO CLINIC, http://www.mayoclinic.org/tests-procedures/c-section/ basics/risks/PRC-20014571.

45. FLA. CONST. art. I, § 23.

46. *See* Bryan Nichols, *Burlington Woman Will Not Be Charged with Feticide*, RADIO IOWA (Feb. 10, 2010), http://www.radioiowa.com/2010/02/10/burlington-woman-will-not-be-charged-with-feticide/.

47. *Id.*

48. Lee Rood, *"I Never Said I Didn't Want My Baby": Mom Won't Be Prosecuted*, DES MOINES REGISTER, Feb. 10, 2010, at 1A, 8A.

49. IOWA CODE ANN. § 707.7 (West 2011).

50. *Id.*

51. Rood, *supra* note 48.

52. *See* Associated Press, *Court to Hear Case of Woman Accused in Stillbirth*, JACKSON FREE PRESS (Apr. 1, 2013 10:39AM), http://www.jacksonfreepress.com/news/2013/apr/01/court-hear-case-woman-accused-stillbirth/ (discussing two pending cases in Mississippi prosecuting Rennie Gibbs and Nina Buckwalter for their stillborns' deaths); Calhoun, *supra* note 13.

53. Associated Press, *supra* note 52; Calhoun, *supra* note 13.

54. Brief of Appellant at 1, Oral Argument Requested, Gibbs v. State, No. 2010-M-819-SCT (Miss. Nov. 12, 2010) [hereinafter Brief of Appellant, Gibbs v. State], http://judicial .mc.edu/briefs/2010-IA-00819-SCTT.PDF.

55. *Id.*

56. Brief of Amicus Curiae of the National Association of Social Workers et al. in support of Petitioner at 1–2, Gibbs v. State, No. 2010-M-819 (Miss. May 19, 2010) [hereinafter NASW

Amicus Brief], http://www.socialworkers.org/assets/secured/documents/ldf/briefDocuments/Gibbs%20v%20State%20MS%20Sup.Ct.Amicus%20Brief.pdf.

57. Brief of Appellant, Gibbs v. State, *supra* note 54, at 1.
58. Eric Holder, Attorney Gen., Remarks at the Annual Meeting of the American Bar Association's House of Delegates (Aug. 12, 2013), http://www.justice.gov/iso/opa/ag/speeches/2013/ag-speech-130812.html.
59. Charles Krauthammer, *Worse Than "Brave New World": Newborns Permanently Damaged by Cocaine*, PHILA. INQUIRER, Aug. 1, 1989, http://articles.philly.com/1989-08-01/news/26148256_1_cocaine-babies-crack-babies-damage).
60. Brief of Appellant, Gibbs v. State, *supra* note 54, at 36; MISS. CODE ANN. § 97-3-19(1)(b) (West 2013).
61. MISS. CODE ANN. § 97-3-19(1) (West 2017).
62. *Id.*
63. Krauthammer, *supra* note 59 ("The inner-city crack epidemic is now giving birth to the newest horror: a bio-underclass, a generation of physically damaged cocaine babies whose biological inferiority is stamped at birth.").
64. Hallam Hurt et al., *Children With and Without Gestational Cocaine Exposure: A Neurocognitive System Analysis*, 31 NEUROTOXICOLOGY & TERATOLOGY 334, 339 (2009). *See also* Hallam Hurt et al., *A Prospective Comparison of Developmental Outcome of Children with In Utero Cocaine Exposure and Controls Using the Battelle Developmental Inventory*, 22 J. DEVELOPMENTAL & BEHAV. PEDIATRICS 21 (2001); Hallam Hurt et. al., *Children with In Utero Cocaine Exposure Do Not Differ from Control Subjects on Intelligence Testing*, 151 ARCHIVES OF PEDIATRIC ADOLESCENT MEDICINE, 1237 (1997) [hereinafter *Intelligence Testing*]; Hallam Hurt et al., *School Performance of Children with Gestational Cocaine Exposure*, 27 NEUROTOXICOLOGY & TERATOLOGY 203 (2011) (concluding: "In this inner-city cohort, cocaine-exposed and control children had similar poor school performance. Better home environment and higher Intelligence Quotient conferred an advantage for successful grade progression, regardless of gestational cocaine exposure."); Susan FitzGerald, *"Crack Baby" Study Ends with Unexpected but Clear Result*, PHILA. INQUIRER (July 22, 2013), http://articles.philly.com/2013-07-22/news/40709969_1_hallam-hurt-so-called-crack-babies-funded-study; Janine Jackson, *The Myth of the "Crack Baby," Despite Research, Media Won't Give Up Idea of "Bio-Underclass,"* FAIRNESS & ACCURACY IN REPORTING, Sept. 1, 1998, http://fair.org/extra-online-articles/the-myth-of-the-crack-baby/.
65. Deborah A. Frank et al., *Growth, Development, and Behavior in Early Childhood Following Prenatal Cocaine Exposure*, 285 J. AM. MED. ASS'N, 1613, 1622–24 (2001).
66. *See* Hurt et al., *Intelligence Testing*, *supra* note 64.
67. Michael Winerip, *Revisiting the "Crack Babies" Epidemic that Was Not*, N.Y. TIMES (May 20, 2013), http://www.nytimes.com/2013/05/20/booming/revisiting-the-crack-babies-epidemic-that-was-not.html.
68. Brief of Appellant, Gibbs v. State, *supra* note 54, at 1.
69. R.L. Goldenberg et al., *Stillbirth: A Review*, 16 J. MATERNAL-FETAL & NEONATAL MED. 79, 79 (2004).
70. Robert M. Silver et al., *Work-up of Stillbirth: A Review of the Evidence*, 196 AM. J. OBSTETRICS & GYNECOLOGY 433, 440 (2007) (noting that multiple factors may contribute to a stillbirth, but not cause it).
71. Brief of Appellant, Gibbs v. State, *supra* note 54, at 30; NASW Amicus Brief, *supra* note 56, at 4; Claudia Malacrida, *Complicated Mourning: The Social Economy of Perinatal Death*, 9 QUALITATIVE HEALTH RES. 504, 505 (1999).

72. Melissa A. Sims & Kim A Collins, *Fetal Death: A 10-Year Retrospective Study*, 22 Am. J. Forensic Med. & Pathology 261, 261 (2001).

73. "Environment" could include both the physical, natural environment (such as exposure to toxins) and the social environment (income, education, etc.). *See, e.g.,* Carol J. Rowland Hogue, *Demographics & Exposures, in* Stillbirth: Prediction, Prevention and Management 57, 69–70 (Catherine Y. Spong ed., 2011) (discussing various social environment factors' impact on stillbirth risk); Marc Edwards, *Fetal Death and Reduced Birth Rates Associated with Exposure to Lead-Contaminated Drinking Water*, 48 Environ. Sci. & Tech. 730 (2014).

74. Victoria Flenady et al., *Major Risk Factors for Stillbirth in High-Income Countries: A Systemic Review and Meta-Analysis*, 337 Lancet 1331, 1337 (2011).

75. Hogue, *supra* note 73, at 71 (discussing a growing body of evidence showing that stress may affect stillbirth risk). *See also* K. Wisborg et al., *Psychological Stress During Pregnancy and Stillbirth: Prospective Study*, 115 BJOG 882 (2008) (finding an association between psychological stress during pregnancy and an increased risk of stillbirth).

76. Stillbirth Collaborative Research Network Writing Group, *Association Between Stillbirth and Risk Factors Known at Pregnancy Confirmation*, 306 J. Am. Med. Ass'n 2470, 2471 (2011).

77. John C. Smulian et al., *Fetal Deaths in the United States: Influence of High-Risk Conditions and Implications for Management*, 100 Obstetrics & Gynecology 1183, 1183 (2002).

78. Goldenberg et al., *supra* note 69, at 85 ("In areas where syphilis is prevalent, up to half of all stillbirths may be caused by this infection alone.").

79. Flenady et al., *supra* note 74, at 1337.

80. According to the American Congress of Obstetricians and Gynecologists, "the most prevalent risk factors associated with stillbirth are non-Hispanic black race, nulliparity [no previous births], advanced maternal age, and obesity." ACOG, *Management of Stillbirth*, 113 Obstetrics & Gynecology 748, 749 (2009).

81. *Id.* at 749.

82. Brief of Appellant, Gibbs v. State, *supra* note 54, at 2.

83. *Id.*

84. *Id.*

85. Subsequently, the Mississippi Supreme Court granted Gibbs's petition for interlocutory review. *Id.* at 2. Under Mississippi's Rules of Appellate Procedure, an interlocutory appeal may be sought if a substantial basis exists for a difference of opinion on a question of law as to which appellate resolution may:

    (1) Materially advance the termination of the litigation and avoid exceptional expense to the parties; or
    (2) Protect a party from substantial and irreparable injury; or
    (3) Resolve an issue of general importance in the administration of justice. Miss. R. App. Proc. 5(a) (2008).

86. Manny Fernandez, *Texas Woman Is Taken Off Life Support After Order*, N.Y. Times (Jan. 26, 2014), https://www.nytimes.com/2014/01/27/us/texas-hospital-to-end-life-support-for-pregnant-brain-dead-woman.html; Manny Fernandez & Erik Eckholm, *Pregnant, and Forced to Stay on Life Support*, N.Y. Times (Jan. 8, 2014), https://www.nytimes.com/2014/01/08/us/pregnant-and-forced-to-stay-on-life-support.html.

87. Fernandez & Eckholm, *supra* note 86.

88. Megan Greene & Leslie R. Wolfe, *Pregnancy Exclusions in State Living Will and Medical Proxy Statutes*, CTR. FOR WOMEN POL'Y STUDS. 3 (Aug. 2012), http://www.centerwomenpolicy.org/programs/health/statepolicy/documents/REPRO_PregnancyExclusionsinStateLivingWillandMedicalProxyStatutesMeganGreeneandLeslieR.Wolfe.pdf.

89. *Id.*

90. *Id.* at 6.

91. Fernandez & Eckholm, *supra* note 86.

92. *Id.*

93. *Id.*

94. *See In re* A.C., 573 A.2d 1235, 1237 (D.C. Ct. App. 1990) (holding that when a pregnant patient is near death and her fetus is viable, the decision of what is to be done is to be decided by the patient, unless incompetent).

95. *See id.* at 1238. *See also* Terry E. Thornton & Lynn Paltrow, *The Rights of Pregnant Patients Carder Case Brings Bold Policy Initiatives*, 8 HEALTHSPAN 10 (1991) (noting that "Angela ... decided to institute aggressive treatment of her cancer").

96. Affidavit of Ms. Carder's Cancer Specialist at 6, dated Nov. 5, 1987, filed Nov. 10, 1987, *In re* A.C., Misc. No. 199-87 (D.C. Super. Ct. 1987).

97. Amicus Brief at 3–4, NOW Legal Defense and Education Fund, National Abortion Rights Action League et.al., *In re* A.C., Rehearing En Banc, Sept. 6, 1988 [hereinafter "NOW Brief"].

98. *Id.* at 4.

99. *Id.*

100. *Id.*

101. *Id.* at 5.

102. NOW Brief, *supra* note 97, at 5.

103. *In re* A.C., 573 A.2d 1235, 1238–39 (D.C. Ct. App. 1990).

104. *See id.* at 1239.

105. *Id.* at 1240–41.

106. *Id.* at 1241.

107. *Id.* at 1257.

108. NOW Brief, *supra* note 97, at 6.

109. *Id.*

110. *In re* A.C., 573 A.2d 1235, 1240 (D.C. Ct. App. 1990).

111. NOW Brief, *supra* note 97, at 6.

112. *In re* A.C., 573 A.2d at 1240.

113. *Id.* at 1238.

114. *In re* A.C., 533 A.2d at 613–14.

115. NOW Brief, *supra* note 97, at 6.

116. *Id.* at 8–9.

117. *In re* A.C., 573 A.2d at 1237.

118. David Weiss, *Court Delivers Controversy*, TIMES LEADER (Wilkes-Barre, Pa.) (Jan. 16. 2004), at 1A, http://archives.timesleader.com/2004/2004_01/2004_01_16_COURT_DELIVERS_CONTROVERSY_MOM_REJECTS_C_SECTIONS_GIVES_BIRTH_O.html.

119. *Id.*

120. Lisa Collier Cool, *Could You Be Forced to Have a C-Section*, ADVOCATES FOR PREGNANT WOMEN (May 2005), http://advocatesforpregnantwomen.org/articles/forced_c-section.htm.

121. *Fetal Homicide Laws*, Nat'l. Conf. State Legs., http://www.ncsl.org/research/health/fetal-homicide-state-laws.aspx (last updated Feb. 2012).

6 REVISITING THE FIDUCIARY RELATIONSHIP

1. The Health Insurance Portability and Accountability Act of 1996 is a law enacted by Congress, which protects patients' medical records from nonconsensual disclosure.
2. Jeff Collins, *$84,000 a Year Now Qualifies as Low Income in High-Cost Orange County*, Orange County Reg. (May 3, 2017, updated Oct. 30, 2018), https://www.ocregister.com/2017/05/03/84000-a-year-now-qualifies-as-low-income-in-high-cost-orange-county/.
3. Kenneth M. Rosen, *Fiduciaries*, 58 Ala. L. Rev. 1041 (2005).
4. Austin W. Scott, *The Fiduciary Principle*, 37 Cal. L. Rev. 539, 540 (1949).
5. Josiah Royce, The Philosophy of Loyalty 16 (1930); Scott, *supra* note 4, at 540.
6. Meinhard v. Salmon, 164 N.E. 545, 546 (N.Y. 1928).
7. *Id.*
8. *Id.*
9. *Id.*
10. *See* Model Code of Prof'l Responsibility r. 1.6 (a), (c) (Am. Bar Ass'n 2018).
11. People v. Belge, 372 N.Y.S.2d 798 (1975).
12. New York State Bar Ass'n Comm. on Prof'l Ethics, Op. 479 (1978).
13. *See* 2 Trials of War Criminals Before the Nuremberg Tribunals Under Control Council Law No. 10, at 189, 237 (U.S. Gov't Printing Office, 1946–1949) [hereinafter Nuremberg Code]; 18th World Medical Association General Assembly, Helsinki, Finland, June 1964, Declaration of Helsinki: Ethical Principles for Medical Research Involving Human Subjects, http://www.wma.net/en/30publications/10policies/b3/17c.pdf.
14. Nuremberg Code, *supra* note 13, at 181–82; George J. Annas et al., Nazi Doctors and the Nuremberg Code 97–100 (1992) (discussing a variety of the experiments conducted by the Nazis, which often involved "grave injury, torture, and ill-treatment"); George J. Annas, *The Legacy of the Nuremberg Doctors' Trial to American Bioethics and Human Rights*, 10 Minn. J.L. Sci. & Tech. 13, 20–21 (2009).
15. *See* AMA Code of Ethics, *Opinion 5.05: Confidentiality*, Am. Med. Ass'n (last updated June 2007), https://journalofethics.ama-assn.org/article/ama-code-medical-ethics-opinions-confidentiality-patient-information/2012-09.
16. 45 C.F.R. Part 164.
17. Schloendorff v. Soc'y of N.Y. Hosp., 105 N.E. 92, 93 (N.Y. 1914). *But see* Paul Lombardo, *Phantom Tumors and Hysterical Women: Revising Our View of the* Schloendorff *Case*, J. L. Med. & Ethics 791, 793 (2005) (noting that the *Schloendorff* case may not have represented the sea change portended by Cardozo's "ringing pronouncement" until the 1950s when New York declined to recognize charitable immunity for hospitals).
18. *See* Hundley v. St. Francis Hosp., 327 P.2d 131, 136 (Cal. Dist. Ct. App. 1958).
19. Steele v. St. Paul Fire & Marine Ins. Co., 371 So. 2d 843 (La. Ct. App. 1979).
20. Thimatariga v. Chambers, 416 A.2d 1326 (Md. Ct. Spec. App. 1980).
21. *See, e.g.*, *$5M Settlement in Hysterectomy Trial*, ABC News (Sept. 17, 2009), http://abclocal.go.com/wls/story?section=news/local&id=7019803 (reporting a significant settlement in a medical case involving an unnecessary hysterectomy).
22. *See generally* Whalen v. Roe, 429 U.S. 589, 599–600 (1977).

23. Eisenstadt v. Baird, 405 U.S. 438, 450 (1972).
24. 500 So. 2d 679, 679 (Fla. Dist. Ct. App. 1987). *See also In re* Brown, 478 So. 2d 1033, 1036 (Miss. 1985) (finding that a patient's right to reject a life-saving blood transfusion is "the individual's protection against the tyranny of the majority and against the power of the state").
25. *See, e.g.,* Canterbury v. Spence, 464 F.2d 772, 782 (D.C. Cir. 1972) ("The patient's reliance upon the physician is a trust of the kind which traditionally has exacted obligations beyond those associated with arms-length transactions."); Moore v. Regents of the Univ. of Cal., 793 P.2d 479, 483 (Cal. 1990) (holding that a research physician must disclose conflicting financial interest to a patient); Salgo v. Leland Stanford Jr. Univ. Bd. of Trs., 317 P.2d 170, 181 (Cal. Ct. App. 1957); Charity Scott, *Why Law Pervades Medicine: An Essay on Ethics in Health Care,* 14 NOTRE DAME J.L. ETHICS & PUB. POL'Y 245, 264 (2000) ("Since the early part of this century, the law has expressed society's view that it was wrong – a violation of autonomy – to treat the patient without some kind of consent.").
26. Natanson v. Kline, 350 P.2d 1093, 1101, 1104 (Kan. 1960).
27. *Id.*
28. Salgo v. Leland Stanford Jr. Univ. Bd. of Trs., 317 P.2d 170, 181 (Cal. Ct. App. 1957).
29. Bang v. Charles T. Miller Hosp., 88 N.W.2d 186, 190 (Minn. 1958).
30. Davis v. Hubbard, 506 F. Supp. 915, 930 (N.D. Ohio 1980) (explaining that "there is perhaps no right which is older than a person's right to be free from unwarranted contact"); *Natanson,* 350 P.2d at 1104 (holding that the law does not permit a physician to substitute her judgment for that of the patient). Only narrow exceptions render the patient's voice mute on the subject of autonomous decision-making, such as emergency or lack of capacity to consent to medical treatment. Cunningham v. Yankton Clinic, P.A., 262 N.W.2d 508, 511 (S.D. 1978).
31. Jaffee v. Redmond, 518 U.S. 1, 10 (1996).
32. *Id.* at 9.
33. 42 U.S.C. § 290dd-2(a) (1998).
34. 42 U.S.C. § 290dd-2(c).
35. N.D. State Bd. of Med. Examiners v. Wynkoop, OAH File No. 20130085 (Nov. 22, 2013), https://www.ndbomex.org/news/board_orders.asp.
36. N.D. State Bd. of Med. Examiners v. Albertson (Nov. 22, 2013), https://www.ndbomex.org /news/board_orders.asp. *See also In re* Sudol, OIE No. 2009.5 (Dec. 9, 2009) (South Carolina medical examiners concluding that a therapist violated statutory provisions "by engaging in unethical and unprofessional behavior when she divulged confidential information without appropriate permission").
37. Michelle Oberman, *Mothers and Doctors' Orders: Unmasking the Doctor's Fiduciary Role in Maternal-Fetal Conflicts,* 94 NW. U. L. REV. 453, 454, 469–70 (1999–2000) (citing WILLIAMS J. WHITRIDGE, WILLIAMS OBSTETRICS (Jack Pritchard & Paul MacDonald eds., 16th ed. 1980).
38. *Id.* at 471.
39. 532 U.S. 67 (2001).
40. 42 U.S.C. § 1983 (1996).
41. Brief for Petitioners at 12, Ferguson v. City of Charleston, 532 U.S. 67 (2001) (No. 99-936).
42. *Id.* at 12 (citing Brown Tr. 12/10/96 at 81:17–82:5 (JA 265–66)).
43. *Id.* at 13 n.10.
44. *Id.* ("The record demonstrates that Nurse Brown, who helped establish the Search Policy and was integral to its everyday implementation, held racist views.").

45. *Id.* at 12 (citing Brown Tr. 12/10/96 at 5:18–21, 64:4–66:25, 71:6–74:9 (JA 209, 250–57); M. Williams Tr. at 132:7–133:1 (JA 1195–96); PX 119).
46. *Id.* (citing M. Williams Tr. at 128:9–129:5 (JA 1192–93).
47. *Id.* at 17 (citing Singleton Tr. at 61:11–14, 68:22–24, 69:5–8 (JA 1135–36, 1143); Powell Tr. at 152:2–11; 157:4 (JA 1014–15, 1020); Knight Tr. at 124:20–125:17 (JA 777–78); Griffin Tr. 11:9–12:4 (JA 551–52)).
48. *Id.* (citing Singleton Tr. 68:1–69:8 (JA 1142–43); Powell Tr. 153:7–20, 155:8–16).
49. *Id.* (citing Singleton Tr. 62–64 (JA [**34] 1136–39); Powell Tr. at 154:2–156:24 (JA 1017–19); Griffin Tr. 10 (JA 549–50); Knight Tr. 126 at (JA 778–79)).
50. *See id.* at 12.
51. Olmstead v. United States, 277 U.S. 438, 479 (1928) (Brandeis, J., dissenting).
52. Miranda v. Arizona, 384 U.S. 436, 478–79 (1966).
53. Brief for Petitioners, *supra* note 41, at 11.
54. *Id.* at 8.
55. *Id.*
56. *Id.* at 6. Months after the program began, drug addiction treatment was offered as an ultimatum to avoid immediate arrest. *Id.* at 8.
57. *Id.* at 4.
58. *Id.* at 3.
59. *Id.* at 11.
60. *See, e.g.,* Cynthia M.A. Geppert & Laura Weiss Roberts, *Protecting Patient Confidentiality in Primary Care,* 3 Seminars in Med. Prac. 7, 7 (2000) ("Many patients assume that physician-patient confidentiality is an absolute.").

7 CREATING CRIMINALS: RACE, STEREOTYPES, AND COLLATERAL DAMAGE

1. S.N. McDonald, *Shanesha Taylor, Arrested for Leaving Children in Car During Job Interview, Speaks,* Wash. Post (June 23, 2014), http://www.washingtonpost.com/news/morning-mix/wp/2014/06/23/shanesha-taylor-arrested-for-leaving-children-in-car-during-job-interview-speaks/.
2. *Id.*
3. N.-M. Henderson, *Debra Harrell Back on Her Job at McDonald, Lawyer Says,* Wash. Post (July 24, 2014), http://www.washingtonpost.com/blogs/she-the-people/wp/2014/07/24/debra-harrell-back-on-her-job-at-mcdonalds-lawyer-says/.
4. C. Friedersdorf, Working Mom Arrested for Letting Her 9-Year-Old Play Alone at Park, Atlantic (July 15, 2014), http://www.theatlantic.com/national/archive/2014/07/arrested-for-letting-a-9-year-old-play-at-the-park-alone/374436.
5. *The Cost of Raising a Child:* $233,610, U.S. Dep't Agric. (USDA) (Mar. 2017), https://www.usda.gov/media/blog/2017/01/13/cost-raising-child.
6. *See The Cost of Child Care in Alabama,* Econ. Policy Inst. (Apr. 2016), https://www.epi.org/child-care-costs-in-the-united-states/#/AL.
7. Dayna M. Kurtz, *We Have a Child-Care Crisis in This Country. We Had the Solution 78 Years Ago,* Wash. Post (July 23, 2018), https://www.washingtonpost.com/news/posteverything/wp/2018/07/23/we-have-a-childcare-crisis-in-this-country-we-had-the-solution-78-years-ago/?noredirect=on&utm_term=.246c347185bf.
8. Sophia Kerby, *The Top 10 Most Startling Facts About People of Color and Criminal Justice in the United States,* Ctr. for Am. Progress (Mar. 13, 2012), https://www

.americanprogress.org/issues/race/news/2012/03/13/11351/the-top-10-most-startling-facts-about-people-of-color-and-criminal-justice-in-the-united-states [https://perma.cc/4QG7-P7RJ].

9. THE SENTENCING PROJECT, REPORT OF THE SENTENCING PROJECT TO THE UNITED NATIONS HUMAN RIGHTS COMMITTEE REGARDING RACIAL DISPARITIES IN THE UNITED STATES CRIMINAL JUSTICE SYSTEM 1 (2013).

10. *See* Melissa Luck, *Born Behind Bars: Inmates Raising Children in Prison*, KXLY (Sept. 9, 2011, 5:25 PM), http://www.kxly.com/news/Born-Behind-Bars-Inmates-Raising-Children-in-Prison/-/101270/682766/-/115bxpxz/-/index.html [http://perma.cc/3HVK-P69Q] ("Right now, at Washington's largest corrections center for women, 871 inmates are serving their sentences. Among them are 8 babies being raised right in the middle of it all."); Paula Nelson, *Raised Behind Bars*, BOS. GLOBE (Dec. 14, 2012), http://www.boston.com/bigpicture/2012/12/raised_behind_bars.html [http://perma.cc/32U3-BXV8] (noting the international institutionalization of children with their mothers); Suzanne Smalley, *Should Female Inmates Raise Their Babies in Prison?*, NEWSWEEK (May 13, 2009, 8:00 PM), http://www.newsweek.com/should-female-inmates-raise-their-babies-prison -80247 [http://perma.cc/F8H6-6AE2] (reviewing the dire conditions in U.S. prisons).

11. THOMAS P. BONCZAR, BUREAU OF JUST. STAT., PREVALENCE OF IMPRISONMENT IN THE U.S. POPULATION, 1974–2001, at 8 (2003).

12. Eric Holder, Att'y Gen., U.S. Dep't of Just., Remarks at the Annual Meeting of the American Bar Association's House of Delegates (Aug. 12, 2013), http://www.justice.gov/opa/speech/attorney-general-eric-holder-delivers-remarks-annual-meeting-american-bar-associations [http://perma.cc/2VX5-DPH3].

13. *See, e.g.*, Charles J. Ogletree Jr., Opinion, *Condemned to Die Because He's Black*, N.Y. TIMES (July 31, 2013), http://www.nytimes.com/2013/08/01/opinion/condemned-to-die-because-hes-black.html?smid=pl-share [http://perma.cc/KKV6-NYQC] (noting that race, specifically being Black, as a predictive status for "future" violence has been unconstitutionally introduced in Texas trials).

14. Dan Roberts & Karen McVeigh, *Eric Holder Unveils New Reforms Aimed at Curbing US Prison Population*, GUARDIAN (Aug. 12, 2013), http://www.theguardian.com/world/2013/aug/12/eric-holder-smart-crime-reform-us-prisons [http://perma.cc/MQ3U-GRJA].

15. President Barack Obama, Remarks at the NAACP Conference (July 14, 2015), https://www.whitehouse.gov/the-press-office/2015/07/14/remarks-president-naacp-conference [https://perma.cc/L6A7-DVES].

16. ROY WALMSLEY, INT'L CTR. FOR PRISON STUDIES, WORLD PRISON POPULATION LIST 3, 5 (9th ed. 2011). *See also* JENIFER WARREN, PEW CTR. ON THE STATES, ONE IN 31: THE LONG REACH OF AMERICAN CORRECTIONS 5 (2009).

17. *See* E. ANN CARSON, U.S. DEP'T OF JUST., PRISONERS IN 2013, at 16 (2009) (reporting that "more than half of prisoners serving sentences of more than a year in federal facilities were convicted of drug offenses").

18. EXEC. OFFICE OF THE PRESIDENT OF THE U.S., NATIONAL DRUG CONTROL STRATEGY: FY 2010 BUDGET SUMMARY 1 (2009) ("In Fiscal Year 2010, the President requests $15.1 billion in support of these key [drug] policy areas, which is an increase of $224.3 million or 1.5 percent over the FY 2009 enacted level of $14.8 billion."). In reality, President Barack Obama allocated $25.9 billion in the fiscal year 2010 for fighting the drug war. EXEC. OFFICE OF THE PRESIDENT OF THE U.S., FY 2012 BUDGET AND PERFORMANCE SUMMARY: COMPANION TO THE NATIONAL DRUG CONTROL STRATEGY 5 (2011) [hereinafter FY 2012 BUDGET AND PERFORMANCE SUMMARY].

19. FY 2012 BUDGET AND PERFORMANCE SUMMARY, *supra* note 18, at 5.

20. Exec. Office of the President of the U.S., FY 2013 Budget and Performance Summary: Companion to the National Drug Control Strategy 1 (2012).

21. A *Drug Policy for the 21st Century*, Off. Nat'l Drug Control Pol'y, https://www.whitehouse.gov/ondcp/drugpolicyreform [http://perma.cc/HW89-U35V].

22. *See* Jeffrey A. Miron & Katherine Waldcock, Cato Inst., The Budgetary Impact of Ending Drug Prohibition 1 (2010) (suggesting that legalization of drugs would result in $25.1 billion in savings for state and local governments).

23. *See* Douglas A. Blackmon, *An Interview with Eric Holder on Mass Incarceration*, Wash. Monthly: Ten Miles Square (Feb. 11, 2014, 12:01 PM), http://www.washingtonmonthly.com/ten-miles- (second alteration in original).

24. *Id.*

25. Holder, *supra* note 12.

26. James Braxton Peterson, *America's Mass Incarceration System: Freedom's Next Frontier*, Reuters: The Great Debate (July 24, 2015), http://blogs.reuters.com/great-debate/2015/07/23/americas-mass-incarceration-system-freedoms-next-frontier/ [http://perma.cc/WSN4-F8KB] (questioning why it took President Obama so long to make the "mass incarceration" speech and considering how to account for losses in the system for the past thirty years).

27. Women's Prison Ass'n, Quick Facts: Women & Criminal Justice – 2009 (2009) [hereinafter Quick Facts 2009], http://www.wpaonline.org/wpaassets/Quick_Facts_Women_and_CJ_2009_rebrand.pdf [http://perma.cc/XW5Y-HX8F].

28. *Why It Matters*, Women's Prison Ass'n, http://www.wpaonline.org/about/why-it-matters [http://perma.cc/V27P-MUGS].

29. Lauren E. Glaze & Laura M. Maruschak, Bureau of Just. Stat., Parents in Prison and Their Minor Children 1–2 (2008).

30. Roy Walmsley, Int'l Ctr. for Prison Studies, World Female Imprisonment List 1 (2d ed. 2013).

31. *Id.*

32. *Id.*

33. Thomas P. Bonczar, Bureau of Just. Stat., Prevalence of Imprisonment in the U.S. Population, 1974–2001, at 8 fig.5. (2003).

34. *Id.*

35. *Id.*

36. *See* 2 Lloyd D. Johnston et al., Monitoring the Future: National Survey Results on Drug Use 1975–2014, College Students & Adults Ages 19–55, at 176 (2015) (showing that the percentage of females between ages nineteen and twenty-eight who have used any illicit drug is relatively similar in 2014 to the late 1980s).

37. Carson, *supra* note 17, at 15 tbl.13.

38. *Id.*

39. Phyllis Goldfarb, *Counting the Drug War's Female Casualties*, 6 J. Gender Race & Just. 277, 295–96 (2002).

40. Quick Facts 2009, *supra* note 27.

41. *Id.*

42. Carson, *supra* note 17, at 1.

43. *Id.* at 8.

44. *Id.* at 9 tbl.8.

45. James B. Jacobs, The Eternal Criminal Record 94 (2015).

46. *Id.*

47. *Id.* at 94–95.

48. *Id.* at 95.
49. *Id.*
50. *Women & the Drug War*, Drug War Facts, http://www.drugwarfacts.org/cms/
Women#sthash.oRmwnfob.dpbs [http://perma.cc/3CFE-3MGK] (citing *Federal
Criminal Case Processing Statistics*, Bureau Just. Stat., http://www.bjs.gov/fjsrc/index
.cfm [http://perma.cc/2LJN-2PE8]); E. Ann Carson & William J. Sabol, Bureau of Just.
Stat., Prisoners in 2011, at 1, 9 tbl.9 (2012).
51. Natasha A. Frost et al., Inst. on Women & Criminal Just., Hard Hit: The Growth in
the Imprisonment of Women, 1977–2004, at 25 fig.15 (2006).
52. Carson & Sabol, *supra* note 50, at 9 tbl.9.
53. *Id.*
54. Glaze & Maruschak, *supra* note 29, at 3.
55. *Id.* at 1.
56. *Id.*
57. *Id.* at 2 tbl.1.
58. *Id.* at 2.
59. *Id.* at 4.
60. Kellie E.M. Barr et al., *Race, Class, and Gender Differences in Substance Abuse: Evidence
of Middle Class/Underclass Polarization Among Black Males*, 40 Soc. Probs. 314, 318 tbl.2
(1993) (showing little statistical variation in illicit drug use for African American and
white women); *cf.* Sean Esteban McCabe et al., *Race/Ethnicity and Gender Differences in
Drug Use and Abuse Among College Students*, 6 J. Ethnicity Substance Abuse, no. 2,
2008, at 75, 82 tbl.1 (showing higher rates of illicit drug use among white undergraduate
women as compared with African American undergraduate women).
61. *See* Ira J. Chasnoff et al., *The Prevalence of Illicit-Drug or Alcohol Use During Pregnancy
and Discrepancies in Mandatory Reporting in Pinellas Country, Florida*, 322 New Eng.
J. Med. 1202, 1204 (1990) ("a black woman was 9.6 times more likely than a white woman
to be reported for substance abuse during pregnancy").
62. *See* John M. Wallace, Jr, *The Social Ecology of Addiction: Race, Risk, and Resilience*, 103
Pediatrics 1122, 1123 (1999) ("Among adults, recent national data indicate that annual and
current alcohol prevalences generally are highest among whites."); Denise Kandel et al.,
*Prevalence and Demographic Correlates of Symptoms of Last Year Dependence on
Alcohol, Nicotine, Marijuana and Cocaine in the U.S. Population*, 44 Drug &
Alcohol Dependence 11, 24 (1997) (noting that when accounting for those who smoke
cigarettes, "blacks and Hispanics are significantly less likely than whites to be dependent;
however, among those who used cocaine/crack within the last year, blacks are significantly more likely than any other group to be dependent"); Stephanie J. Ventura et al.,
*Trends and Variations in Smoking During Pregnancy and Low Birth Weight: Evidence
from the Birth Certificate, 1990–2000*, 111 Pediatrics 1176, 1177 (2003) ("Prenatal smoking
rates varied substantially among racial and Hispanic-origin populations ... ranging in
2000 from ... 9.2% of non-Hispanic black women, [to] 15.6% of non-Hispanic white
women ...."); Nat'l Inst. on Drug Abuse, Drug Abuse Among Racial/Ethnic
Minorities 43 (rev. ed. 2003) ("Estimates for lifetime history of illegal drug use indicate
that use is highest among White women (51.2 percent), followed by African-American
women (36.0 percent) ....").
63. Allen A. Mitchell et al., *Medication Use During Pregnancy, with Particular Focus on
Prescription Drugs: 1976–2008*, 205 Am. J. Obstetrics & Gynecology 51.e1, 51.e1 (2011).
64. *Id.* at 51.e4–.e5.

65. *Abusing Prescription Drugs During Pregnancy*, AM. PREGNANCY ASS'N, http://www
.americanpregnancy.org/pregnancyhealth/abusingprescriptiondrugs.html [http://perma
.cc/JVV7-LMAZ].
66. FROST ET AL., *supra* note 51, at 26; QUICK FACTS 2009, *supra* note 27.
67. QUICK FACTS 2009, *supra* note 27.
68. FROST ET AL., *supra* note 51, at 22.
69. GLAZE & MARUSCHAK, *supra* note 29, at 4.
70. Adoption and Safe Families Act of 1997, Pub. L. 105-89, 111 Stat. 2115, 2118 (codified as
amended at 42 U.S.C.A. § 675(5)(E) (West 2015)).
71. *See Quick Facts: Mandatory Minimum Penalties*, U.S. SENTENCING COMM'N (2011), http://
www.ussc.gov/sites/default/files/pdf/research-and-publications/quick-facts
/Quick_Facts_Mandatory_Minimum_Penalties.pdf   [http://perma.cc/4D8X-P6G7]
(reporting that the "average sentence for drug offenders subject to the mandatory minimum penalty was 132 months" and was 61 months for offenders subject to relief from
mandatory minimum sentences).
72. GLAZE & MARUSCHAK, *supra* note 29, at 2.
73. *Id.*
74. *Id.*
75. Kristin Turney, *Stress Proliferation Across Generations? Examining the Relationship
Between Parental Incarceration and Childhood Health*, 55 J. HEALTH & SOC. BEHAV.
302, 311–14 (2014).
76. CHANDRA KRING VILLANUEVA, INST. ON WOMEN & CRIMINAL JUST., WOMEN'S PRISON
ASSOCIATION, MOTHERS, INFANTS AND IMPRISONMENT: A NATIONAL LOOK AT PRISON
NURSERIES AND COMMUNITY-BASED ALTERNATIVES 4 (Sarah B. From & Georgia Lerner
eds., 2009).
77. *Id.* at 5 ("By keeping mothers and infants together, these programs prevent foster care
placement and allow for the formation of maternal/child bonds during a critical period of
infant development.").
78. Smalley, *supra* note 10.
79. *See* PARENTS IN PRISON, THE SENTENCING PROJECT 1–3 (2012) (showing that children with
incarcerated parents are at a higher risk for particularly damaging social problems and
that federal policies pose barriers that make it difficult for incarcerated parents to provide
for their children's needs); Dorothy Roberts, *Prison, Foster Care, and the Systemic
Punishment of Black Mothers*, 59 UCLA L. REV. 1474, 1494 (2012) (depicting the "deva-
luation of incarcerated mothers" through the immediate placement of a pregnant
mother's newborn in foster care).
80. Tammerlin Drummond, *Mothers in Prison*, TIME (Oct. 29, 2000), http://www.time.com
/time/magazine/article/0,9171,58996,00.html [http://perma.cc/YPA4-TDN9] ("Florida is
attempting to address a disturbing national phenomenon: the explosion in the number of
mothers in prison.").
81. *See* JACOBS, *supra* note 45.
82. *Id.*
83. *See id.* at xiii (explaining "how the expansion of criminal law and the intensification of
law enforcement since the 1970s have resulted in the proliferation of criminal intelligence and investigative databases").
84. *Id.* at 43.
85. *Id.* at 10–11.
86. *Id.* at 3.

87. Housing Opportunity Program Extension Act of 1996, Pub. L. No. 104-120, 110 Stat. 834 (codified as amended in scattered sections of 12 U.S.C. and 42 U.S.C.).
88. 42 U.S.C. § 1437d(q)(1)(A) (2012).
89. Arin Greenwood, *"One Strike" Public Housing Policy Hits Virginia Woman Who Needs Kidney Transplant*, HUFFINGTON POST (Dec. 22, 2011, 11:45 AM), http://www .huffingtonpost.com/2011/12/22/one-strike-policy-housing-alexandria-virginia-kidney-transplant_n_1151639.html [http://perma.cc/W9BD-X4CL].
90. 20 U.S.C. § 1091(r)(1) (2012).
91. Clarence Page, *College Loans Are Casualties in Drug War*, CHI. TRIB. (Apr. 29, 2001), http://articles.chicagotribune.com/2001-04-29/news/0104290396_1_student-loans-wording-applicants [http://perma.cc/3Z76-FATT].

8 THE PREGNANCY PENALTY: WHEN THE STATE GETS IT WRONG

1. Interview with Judge Pamela Alexander (Oct. 19, 2013).
2. Brief for Am. Pub. Health Ass'n et al. as Amici Curiae Supporting Petitioner at 13, Ferguson v. City of Charleston, 532 U.S. 67 (2001) (No. 99-936), 2000 WL 33599645.
3. WORLD HEALTH ORG., TRENDS IN MATERNAL MORTALITY: 1990 TO 2008; ESTIMATES DEVELOPED BY WHO, UNICEF, UNFPA AND THE WORLD BANK, annex 1 (2010).
4. Bekah Porter, *Dubuquer Gives Birth Alone in Jail Cell*, TELEGRAPH HERALD, May 15, 2009 (describing Tara Keil's unsettling birth in a toilet after minutes of screaming for help and being offered food rather than a nurse or doctor). Similarly, Ambrett Spencer suffered the distressing effects of birthing while in prison. Her baby died after she had spent hours pleading for help. *See* John Dickerson, *Arpaio's Jail Staff Cost Ambrett Spencer Her Baby, and She's Not the Only One*, PHOENIX NEW TIMES (Oct. 30, 2008), http://www .phoenixnewtimes.com/2008-10-30/news/arpaio-s-jail-staff-cost-ambrett-spencer-her-baby-and-she-s-not-the-only-one/. Shawanna Nelson was forced to endure labor while shackled; guards finally relented for the actual delivery, but immediately shackled her right after her child's birth. Adam Liptak, *Prisons Often Shackle Pregnant Inmates in Labor*, N.Y. TIMES (Mar. 2, 2006), http://www.nytimes.com/2006/03/02/national/02shackles.html.
5. Charles Molony Condon, *Clinton's Cocaine Babies*, 72 POL'Y REV. 12 (1995), http://www .hoover.org/publications/policy-review/article/6853. *See, e.g.*, DOUG MCVAY ET AL., JUST. POL'Y INST., TREATMENT OR INCARCERATION? NATIONAL AND STATE FINDINGS ON THE EFFICACY AND COST SAVINGS OF DRUG TREATMENT VERSUS IMPRISONMENT (2004) (discussing numerous studies that have looked at the success rates of treatment versus incarceration).
6. SANDRA BURTON, BECOMING MS. BURTON: FROM PRISON TO RECOVERY TO LEADING THE FIGHT FOR INCARCERATED WOMEN 6 (2017).
7. *Id.*
8. *Id.* at 87.
9. *Id.*
10. *See, e.g.*, INST. OF MED., PATHWAYS OF ADDICTION: OPPORTUNITIES IN DRUG ABUSE RESEARCH 192–215 (1996); McVay et al., *supra* note 5; JUST. POL'Y INST., *Substance Abuse Treatment and Public Safety*, (2008), http://www.justicepolicy.org/images/upload/08_01_REP_DrugTx_AC-PS.pdf (discussing studies that have shown that drug treatment within the community is "more cost-effective than prison or other punitive measures").

11. Center for Substance Abuse Research, Long-Term Drug Treatment Outcomes in Maryland: Results of the Topps II Project 5 (2003), http://adaa.dhmh.maryland.gov /Documents/content_documents/TOPPS_II/Topp2final.pdf.

12. Michael Finigan, *Societal Outcomes and Cost Savings of Drug and Alcohol Treatment in the State of Oregon*, Nw. Prof. Consortium (1996), http://www.npcresearch.com/Files/ SOCS.pdf.

13. *Id.*

14. *Id.*

15. *Id.*

16. Amelia M. Arria et al., *Drug Treatment Completion and Post-Discharge Employment in the TOPPS-II Interstate Cooperative Study Treatment*, 25 J. Substance Abuse Treatment 9 (2003).

17. *Id.* at 13–14.

18. *See, e.g.*, Rucker C. Johnson, *Ever-Increasing Levels of Parental Incarceration and the Consequences for Children*, in Do Prisons Make Us Safer?: The Benefits and Costs of the Prison Boom 177 (Steven Raphael & Michael A. Stoll eds., 2009).

19. According to a study by the Pew Center, more than 40 percent of ex-cons commit crimes within three years of their release and end up back in prison. Greg Bluestein, *Pew Study: Prison Recidivism Rates Remain High*, CNS News (Apr. 13, 2011), http://cnsnews.com /news/article/pew-study-prison-recidivism-rates-remain-high.

20. Data examined by the Bureau of Justice Statistics found that 9.6 percent of prisoners are sexually victimized during incarceration. Terry Frieden, *Study Finds Nearly 1 in 10 State Prisoners Is Sexually Abused While Incarcerated*, CNN (May 17, 2012), http://articles .cnn.com/2012-05-17/us/us_us-state-prisons-abuse_1_sexual-abuse-staff-sexual- misconduct-prisoners?_s=PM:US.

21. Kate Dolan et al., Beckley Found. Drug Pol'y Programme, Prisons and Drugs: A Global Review of Incarceration, Drug Use and Drug Services 1 (2007), http://kar .kent.ac.uk/13324/2/Beckley_RPT12_Prisons_Drugs_EN.pdf.

22. Telephone interview with Lyn Head (Mar. 3, 2014).

23. Pan Am. Health Org., Domestic Partner Violence During Pregnancy, http://www .paho.org/english/ad/ge/vawpregnancy.pdf.

24. Jacquelyn C. Campbell, *Health Consequences of Intimate Partner Violence*, 359 Lancet 1331, 1331–36 (2002).

25. *Id.*; *see also* J.A. Gazmararian et al., *Prevalence of Violence Against Pregnant Women: A Review of the Literature*, 275 JAMA 1915, 1915–20 (1996).

26. Pan Am. Health Org., *supra* note 23.

27. Campbell, *supra* note 24.

28. *Id.*; J.A. Gazmararian et al., *Violence and Reproductive Health: Current Knowledge and Future Research Directions*, 4 Maternal Child Health J. 79, 79–84 (2000); L.F. Bullock & J. McFarlane, *Higher Prevalence of Low Birthweight Infants Born to Battered Women*, 89 Am. J. Nursing 1153, 1153–55 (1989).

29. Gazmararian et al., *supra* note 25.

30. Campbell, *supra* note 24 (noting that while some of the evidence is contradictory, the variation in subsamples and samples "could account for some of the differences in individual studies").

31. Nor are the incidences of domestic violence and low birth weight concentrated among the economically disenfranchised, as at least one peer-reviewed study "suggest[s] a stronger relationship between abuse and birthweight in women of middle socioeco- nomic status than in poor women." *Id.*; C.C. Murphy et al., *Abuse: A Risk Factor for Low*

Birth Weight? A Systematic Review and Meta-Analysis, 164 CANADIAN MED. ASS'N J. 1567, 1567–72 (2001).

32. See N. Tanya Nagahawatte and Robert. Goldenberg, *Poverty, Maternal Health, and Adverse Pregnancy Outcomes*, 1136 ANNALS OF N.Y. ACAD. SCI. 80, 81 (2008)(explaining that receiving "culturally inappropriate and unsatisfying services, reproach and sanctions for poor health habits may contribute to fewer prenatal visits among low income women").

33. See ELIZABETH HARRISON ET AL., JOHNS HOPKINS WOMEN'S & CHILDREN'S HEALTH POL'Y CTR., ENVIRONMENTAL TOXICANTS AND MATERNAL AND CHILD HEALTH: AN EMERGING PUBLIC HEALTH CHALLENGE 1, 2 (2009).

34. U.S. GOV'T ACCOUNTABILITY OFFICE, GAO/RCED-83-168, SITING OF HAZARDOUS WASTE LANDFILLS AND THEIR CORRELATION WITH RACIAL AND ECONOMIC STATUS OF SURROUNDING COMMUNITIES (1983), http://archive.gao.gov/d48t13/121648.pdf; HARRISON ET AL., *supra* note 33.

35. See Claire B. Ernhart et al., *Intrauterine Exposure to Low Levels of Lead: The Status of the Neonate*, 41 ARCHIVES ENVTL. HEALTH 287 (1986); Tom Greene & Claire B. Ernhart, *Prenatal and Preschool Age Lead Exposure: Relationship with Size*, 13 NEUROTOXICOLOGY & TERATOLOGY 417 (1991).

36. See Edward Patrick Boyle, *It's Not Easy Bein' Green: The Psychology of Racism, Environmental Discrimination, and the Argument for Modernizing Equal Protection Analysis*, 46 VAND. L. REV. 937, 967 (1993) (noting "nationwide phenomenon that minority neighborhoods bear a disproportionately large environmental burden compared to whites"); Rachel D. Godsil, *Remedying Environmental Racism*, 90 MICH. L. REV. 394, 397 (1991); Marianne Lavelle & Marcia Coyle, *The Federal Government, in Its Cleanup of Hazardous Sites and Its Pursuit of Polluters, Favors White Communities over Minority Communities Under Environmental Laws Meant to Provide Equal Protection for All Citizens, a National Law Journal Investigation Has Found*, 15 NAT'L L.J., Sept. 21, 1992, at S2; Gerald Torres, *Race, Class, and Environmental Regulation*, 63 U. COLO. L. REV. 839 (1992); Keith Schneider, *Minorities Join to Fight Polluting Neighborhoods*, N.Y. TIMES, Oct. 25, 1991, at A20.

37. See, e.g., Jane Kay & Cheryl Katz, *Pollution, Poverty, People of Color: The Factory on the Hill*, ENVTL. HEALTH NEWS, June 4, 2012, (noting that low-income residents living near hazardous sites may find affordable homes and "save money on shelter, but they pay the price in health"), http://www.environmentalhealthnews.org/ehs/news/2012/pollution-poverty-and-people-of-color-richmond-day-1.

38. Bob Herbert, *Poor Black and Dumped On*, N.Y. TIMES, Oct. 5, 2006 (writing about the environmental impacts on African American health, he warns that "the carnage – the terrible illnesses and the premature deaths – is hidden").

39. *Id.*

40. Curt Davidson, *Emelle, Alabama: Home of the Nation's Largest Hazardous Waste Landfill*, http://www.umich.edu/~snre492/Jones/emelle.htm.

41. Michael P. Healy, *The Preemption of State Hazardous and Solid Waste Regulations: The Dormant Commerce Clause Awakens Once More*, 43 WASH. U. J. URB. & CONTEMP. L. 177, 179 (1993); Richard Lazarus, *Pursuing Environmental Justice: The Distributional Effects of Environmental Justice*, 87 NW. U. L. REV. 787, 790 (1993) (noting that environmental justice has been relatively underexplored by lawyers).

42. U.S. GOV'T ACCOUNTABILITY OFFICE, *supra* note 34.

43. CAL. BIRTH DEFECTS MONITORING PROGRAM, BIRTH DEFECTS AND HAZARDOUS WASTE SITES (Apr. 1999), http://www.cdph.ca.gov/programs/CBDMP/Documents/MO-CBDMP-

HazWasteSites.pdf. In this study, the authors found that women who birthed babies with isolated oral clefts were 5.7 times more likely than control-group mothers to live within one mile of a hazardous waste site. *Id.* at 6. Close proximity to hazardous waste was also associated with spina bifida and anencephaly. *Id.* The authors also noted characteristics among the women who lived in closer proximity to hazardous waste sites: they were more often Latina and with modest education. *Id.* at 8.

44. JEAN D. BRENDER & JOHN S. GRIESENBECK, TEX. A&M SCH. RURAL PUB. HEALTH, HAZARDOUS WASTE SITES, INDUSTRIAL FACILITIES, AND ADVERSE PREGNANCY OUTCOMES IN DALLAS, DENTON, AND TARRANT COUNTIES, 1997–2000, at 1 (2008) (noting that prior studies find "an association between living near hazardous waste sites and all congenital malformations combined [with], chromosomal anomalies, neural tube and heart/circulatory defects").

45. Susan FitzGerald, *"Crack Baby" Study Ends with Unexpected but Clear Result,* PHILA. INQUIRER, July 22, 2013.

46. Blair Paley & Mary J. O'Connor, *Intervention for Individuals with Fetal Alcohol Spectrum Disorders: Treatment Approaches and Case Management,* 15 DEVELOPMENTAL DISABILITIES RES. REVS. 258, 258 (2009). *See* Phillip A. May & Phillip Goassage, *Maternal Risk Factors for Fetal Alcohol Spectrum Disorders,* 34 ALCOHOL RES. & HEALTH 16 (2011); Kenneth R. Warren et al. *Fetal Alcohol Spectrum Disorders: Research Challenges and Opportunities,* 34 ALCOHOL RES. & HEALTH 4 (2011).

47. CTR. FOR DISEASE CONTROL & PREVENTION, *Tobacco Use and Pregnancy* (last updated Sept. 23, 2013), http://www.cdc.gov/Reproductivehealth/TobaccoUsePregnancy/index.htm.

48. Emily Figdor & Lisa Kaeser, *Concerns Mount over Punitive Approaches to Substance Abuse Among Pregnant Women,* 1 GUTTMACHER REP. ON PUB. POL'Y, Oct. 1998, at 5 (citing National Institute on Drug Abuse). *See also* CTR. FOR BEHAVIORAL HEALTH STATS. & QUALITY ET AL., RESULTS FROM THE 2010 NATIONAL SURVEY ON DRUG USE AND HEALTH: SUMMARY OF NATIONAL FINDINGS (Sept. 2011), http://www.samhsa.gov/data/nsduh/2k10nsduh/2k10results.htm#4.3.

49. Food & Drug Admin. v. Brown & Williamson Tobacco Corp., 529 U.S. 120, 162 (2000) (Breyer, J., dissenting) (citing 61 Fed. Reg. 44398 (1996)).

50. *Id.*

51. *Id.* at 161.

52. *Id.* at 137 (citing 7 U.S.C. § 1311(a)).

53. U.S. DEP'T HEALTH & HUMAN SERVS., THE HEALTH CONSEQUENCES OF SMOKING – 50 YEARS OF PROGRESS: A REPORT OF THE SURGEON GENERAL 117–18, 120 (2014).

54. *Id.* at 68.

55. *Food & Drug Admin.,* 529 U.S. at 139 ("A ban of tobacco products by the FDA would therefore plainly contradict congressional policy.").

56. Joseph R. DiFranza et al., *Legislative Efforts to Protect Children from Tobacco,* 257 J. AM. MED. ASS'N 3387, 3387–89 (1987).

57. *See* Jane Brody, *Coming a Long Way on Smoking with a Long Way to Go,* N.Y. TIMES BLOG (Jan. 20, 2014), http://well.blogs.nytimes.com/2014/01/20/coming-a-long-way-on-smoking-with-a-way-to-go/?ref=smokingandtobacc; U.S. DEP'T HEALTH & HUMAN SERVS., *supra* note 53; Editorial Board, *Fitful Progress in the Antismoking Wars,* N.Y. TIMES (Jan. 9, 2014), http://www.nytimes.com/2014/01/10/opinion/fitful-progress-in-the-antismoking-wars.html?_r=0; Sabrina Tavernise, *List of Smoking-Related Illnesses Grows Significantly in U.S. Report,* N.Y. TIMES (Jan. 17, 2014) (noting, among a list of various diseases such as lung cancer, heart disease, and diabetes, that smoking is

correlated with ectopic pregnancies), http://www.nytimes.com/2014/01/17/health/list-ofsmoking-related-illnesses-grows-significantly-in-us-report.html.

58. Victoria Law, *"You Go Through It Alone": New Bill Would Keep Incarcerated Pregnant Women from Being Put in Medical Isolation*, REWIRE NEWS (Mar. 22, 2019, 1:22 PM), https://rewire.news/article/2019/03/22/you-go-through-it-alone-new-bill-would-keep-incarcerated-pregnant-women-from-being-put-in-medical-isolation/.

59. *Id.*

60. *Id.* (quoting Tara Keil).

61. John Dickerson, *Arpaio's Jail Staff Cost Ambrett Spencer Her Baby, and She's Not the Only One*, PHOENIX NEW TIMES (Oct. 30, 2008), http://www.phoenixnewtimes.com/2008-10-30/news/arpaio-s-jail-staff-cost-ambrett-spencer-her-baby-and-she-s-not-the-only-one/. Note that the following scenario is based on this source.

62. Margaret Paulson & Anthony H. Dekker, *Healthcare Disparities in Pain Management*, 105 J. AM. OSTEOPATHIC ASS'N, S14 (Supp. 3 2005).

63. Dickerson, *supra* note 61 (quoting Jarrid Ortiz).

64. *Id.*; *see also* Renae D. Duncan et al., *Childhood Physical Assault as a Risk Factor for PTSD, Depression, and Substance Abuse: Findings from a National Survey*, 66 AM. J. ORTHOPSYCH. 437, 443 (1996); Sana Loue, *Legal and Epidemiological Aspects of Child Maltreatment: Toward an Integrated Approach*, 19 J. LEGAL MED. 471, 475–76 (1998).

65. *Id.*

66. *Id.* All the women who were turned over to police for using illegal drugs during pregnancy were Black, with one exception. In the case of the lone white woman surrendered to police, hospital officials made sure to note on her chart that the white patient "lives with her boyfriend who is a Negro." *Id.*

67. Condon, *supra* note 5 (justifying his metaphoric use of the "stick" in implementing fetal protection). Condon referred to drug addiction as a "blatant" form of child abuse. *Id.*

68. Franklin D. Gilliam, Jr., *The "Welfare Queen" Experiment: How Viewers React to Images of African-American Mothers on Welfare*, NIEMAN REP. (Summer 1999).

69. *See, e.g.*, KAARYN S. GUSTAFSON, CHEATING WELFARE, PUBLIC ASSISTANCE AND THE CRIMINALIZATION OF POVERTY (2011) (discussing how the perception of fraud and decep-tion now pervades public understanding about welfare, which in turn has resulted in welfare policies becoming more punitive.); Catherine Albiston & Laura Beth Nielson, *Welfare Queens and Other Fairy Tales: Welfare Reform and Unconstitutional Reproductive Controls*, 38 HOW. L.J. 473, 475 (1995).

70. Brief for Petitioners at 13, Ferguson v. Charleston, 532 U.S. 67 (2001) (No. 99-936), 2000 WL 33599645.

71. *See* Annette Appell, *"Bad Mothers" and Spanish-Speaking Caregivers*, 7 NEVADA L.J 759 (2007) (noting that "we have in this country a long and continuing history of constructing the ideal of "mother" according to skin color, religion, culture, national origin, language, ethnicity, class, and marital status"): Kimberlé Crenshaw, *From Private Violence to Mass Incarceration: Thinking Intersectionally About Women, Race, and Social Control*, 59 UCLA L. REV. 1418 (2012) (discussing the structural and political dimensions of mass incarceration and gender bias, exposing how they are interconnected in multiple ways); Martha Fineman, *Images of Mothers in Poverty Discourses*, DUKE L.J., 1991, at 274 (explaining the role of patriarchal discourse in framing welfare recipients as "constituting the cause as well as the effect of poverty"); Robin Levi et al., *Creating The Bad Mother: How the US Approach to Pregnancy in Prisons Violates the Right to Be a Mother*, 18 UCLA WOM. L.J. 1 (2010); Jane Murphy, *Legal Images of Motherhood: Conflicting Definitions from Welfare "Reform," Family,*

and Criminal Law, 83 CORNELL L. REV. 688, 689 (1998)(analyzing that criminal law provides a lens to see who the nation values as "good mothers" and who is tossed away as "bad" mothers); Sonia Suter, *Bad Mothers or Struggling Mothers?* 42 RUTGERS L. J. 695, 701–02 (2011).

72. Albiston & Nielson, *supra* note 69, at 477 ("Neither the exclusion of black women from social welfare programs nor control of their reproductive freedom are new social policies; even the connection between these policies is old."). *See also* Dorothy Roberts, *Punishing Drug Addicts Who Have Babies: Women of Color, Equality, and the Right of Privacy*, 104 HARV. L. REV. 1419, 1437–39 (1991) (noting that "[t]he myth of the 'bad' Black woman was deliberately and systematically perpetuated after slavery.").

73. PATRICIA HILL COLLINS, BLACK SEXUAL POLITICS: AFRICAN AMERICANS GENDER AND THE NEW RACISM 131 (2005).

74. THOMAS JEFFERSON, NOTES ON THE STATE OF VIRGINIA, 107, 205 (electronic ed., 2006), https://docsouth.unc.edu/southlit/jefferson/jefferson.html.

75. Gina Kolata, *Bias Seen Against Pregnant Addicts*, N.Y. TIMES, July 20, 1990, at A13 (quoting Dr. Ira Chasnoff).

76. *Id.*

77. On the legal implications of shackling, *see* INT'L HUMAN RIGHTS CLINIC ET. AL., THE SHACKLING OF INCARCERATED PREGNANT WOMEN: A HUMAN RIGHTS VIOLATION COMMITTED REGULARLY IN THE UNITED STATES; AN ALTERNATIVE REPORT TO THE FOURTH PERIODIC REPORT OF THE UNITED STATES OF AMERICA SUBMITTED PURSUANT TO THE INTERNATIONAL COVENANT ON CIVIL AND POLITICAL RIGHTS (Aug. 2013); Geraldine Doetzer, *Hard Labor: The Legal Implications of Shackling Female Inmates During Pregnancy and Childbirth*, 14 WM. & MARY J. WOMEN & L. 365 (2008); Claire Griggs, *Birthing Barbarism: The Unconstitutionality of Shackling Pregnant Prisoners*, 20 AM U. J. GENDER SOC. POL'Y & L. 247 (2011); Priscilla A. Ocen, *Punishing Pregnancy: Race, Incarceration and the Shackling of Pregnant Prisoners*, 100 CAL. L. REV. 1239 (2012).

78. Griggs, *supra* note 77, at 266 n.261 (2011) (citing MINN. STAT. ANN. § 241.07 (West 2011)).

79. George J. Annas, *Pregnant Women as Fetal Containers*, 16 HASTINGS CTR. REP. 13 (1986); Lucinda J. Peach, *From Spiritual Descriptions to Legal Prescriptions: Religious Imagery of Woman as "Fetal Container" in the Law*, 10 J.L. & RELIGION 73 (1994).

9 POLICING BEYOND THE BORDER

1. Foreign Assistance Act of 1961 § 104(f), codified at 22 U.S.C. § 2151b(f) (2012).

2. *See, e.g.*, Sneha Barot, *Abortion Restrictions in U.S. Foreign Aid: The History and Harms of the Helms Amendment*, GUTTMACHER POL'Y REV., Summer 2013, at 9, 10.

3. 119 CONG. REC. 32,292, 32,293 (1973) (statement of Sen. Helms).

4. *See* 119 CONG. REC. 39,619, 39,632 (1973).

5. *See, e.g.*, LUISA BLANCHFIELD, CONG. RESEARCH SERV., R40750, THE U.N. CONVENTION ON THE ELIMINATION OF ALL FORMS OF DISCRIMINATION AGAINST WOMEN (CEDAW): ISSUES IN THE U.S. RATIFICATION DEBATE 7 (2011), https://fas.org/sgp/crs/row/R40750.pdf [https://perma.cc /3GBS-UARZ]; *see also* U.S. S. COMM. FOREIGN RELATIONS, CONVENTION ON THE ELIMINATION OF ALL FORMS OF DISCRIMINATION AGAINST WOMEN, S. EXEC. REP. NO. 103-38, at 53–54 (1994).

6. Nicholas D. Kristof, *Women's Rights: Why Not?*, N.Y. TIMES (June 18, 2002), http://www .nytimes.com/2002/06/18/opinion/women-s-rights-why-not.html [https://perma.cc/VY77- BSKL].

7. Chuck Smith, *The Case Against Jesse Helms*, WALL ST. J., Sept. 4, 2001.
8. TIMOTHY TYSON, RADIO FREE DIXIE: ROBERT F. WILLIAMS AND THE ROOTS OF BLACK POWER (2001).
9. *See* 119 CONG. REC. 39,316, 39,317 (1973) (statement of Rep. Abzug).
10. *Id.; see also* Lynn Lilliston, *Abortion Coalition Fighting for Right to Decide*, L.A. TIMES, June 19, 1974, at D1 ("'Whether we like it or not, abortion is the most widely used method of family planning in many underdeveloped countries,' Mrs. Stengel [associate director of the Religious Coalition for Abortion Rights] said. 'Millions of women do not have access to other methods of family planning.' Thus, she said, the amendment places a restriction on foreign women, in countries with serious overpopulation, which was overthrown by the U.S. Supreme Court.").
11. Barot, *supra* note 2, at 9.
12. *Id.*
13. *Id.*
14. 119 CONG. REC. 32,292 (1973) (statement of Sen. Helms).
15. *Id.*
16. Barot, *supra* note 2, at 9 (citation omitted).
17. *Id.* (citation omitted).
18. 119 Cong. Rec. 32,293 (1973) (statement of Sen. Helms).
19. *Id.*
20. *Id.*
21. Policy Statement of the United States of America at the United Nations International Conference on Population, 2d Sess., Mexico City (Aug. 6–14, 1984), *reprinted in* 10 POP. & DEV. REV. 574 (1984).
22. LUISA BLANCHFIELD, CONG. RESEARCH SERV., RL41360, ABORTION AND FAMILY PLANNING-RELATED PROVISIONS IN U.S. FOREIGN ASSISTANCE LAW AND POLICY 2 (2017), https://fas.org /sgp/crs/row/R41360.pdf [http://perma.cc/69M5-DJZL]; *see also* International Security and Development Cooperation Act of 1981, Pub. L. No. 97–113, § 302(b), 95 Stat. 1532 (Dec. 29, 1981) (codified as amended at 22 U.S.C. 2151(b)).
23. International Security and Development Act of 1981 § 302(b)(3).
24. BLANCHFIELD, *supra* note 22, at 5.
25. *Id.*
26. Foreign Assistance and Related Programs Appropriations Act, 1982, Pub. L. No. 97–121, § 525, 95 Stat. 1657 (1981); *see also* U.S. AGENCY FOR INT'L DEV., USAID GUIDANCE FOR IMPLEMENTING THE SILJANDER AMENDMENT (PROHIBITION ON LOBBYING FOR OR AGAINST ABORTION) 1 (May 22, 2014).
27. *True Believer*, TIME, May 4, 1981, at 37.
28. *Id.*
29. John Block, *Siljander Expresses Anger Over O'Connor Nomination*, TOLEDO BLADE, July 9, 1981, at 2.
30. Omnibus Consolidated and Emergency Supplemental Appropriations Act, 1999, Pub. L. No. 105–277, § 101, 112 Stat. 2681-154 (1998); H.R.J. Res 738, 99th Cong., Pub. L. No. 99–500, § 101(f), 100 Stat. 1783-217 (1986); KAISER FAMILY FOUND., THE U.S. GOVERNMENT AND INTERNATIONAL FAMILY PLANNING AND REPRODUCTIVE HEALTH: STATUTORY REQUIREMENTS AND POLICIES (2017), https://www.kff.org/global-health-policy/fact-sheet /the-u-s-government-and-international-family-planning-reproductive-health-statutory-requirements-and-policies [https://perma.cc/FG7N-N6EJ].

31. PAI, NO EXCEPTIONS: HOW THE HELMS AMENDMENT HURTS WOMEN AND ENDANGERS LIVES 2 (2015), https://pai.org/wp-content/uploads/2014/07/PAI-Helms-PIB.pdf [https://perma.cc/8MW5-CNZ9].

32. *See* UNITED NATIONS POPULATION FUND, ADOLESCENT GIRLS IN DISASTER & CONFLICT: INTERVENTIONS FOR IMPROVING ACCESS TO SEXUAL AND REPRODUCTIVE HEALTH SERVICES 8–10 (2016), http://www.unfpa.org/sites/default/files/pub-pdf/UNFPA-Adolescent_Girls_in_Disaster_Conflict-Web.pdf [https://perma.cc/LD4S-SAR6].

33. Lisa B. Haddad & Nawal M. Nour, *Unsafe Abortion: Unnecessary Maternal Mortality*, 2 REV. OBSTETRICS & GYNECOLOGY 122, 123 (2009).

34. Policy Statement, *supra* note 21.

35. Barot, *supra* note 2, at 10.

36. Steven Lee Myers, *A Paradox for Helms on an Abortion Issue*, N.Y. TIMES (Aug. 1, 1997), http://www.nytimes.com/1997/08/01/us/a-paradox-for-helms-on-an-abortion-issue.html [https://perma.cc/KBA8-NAHU].

37. Policy Statement, *supra* note 21, at 578.

38. LARRY NOWELS, CONG. RESEARCH SERV., RL30830, INTERNATIONAL FAMILY PLANNING: THE "MEXICO CITY" POLICY 4 n.7 (2001). USAID interpreted the MCP as prohibiting funding for foreign NGOs that perform or actively promote abortion as a method of family planning, and applied the following definitions under the MCP:

> (i) *Abortion is a method of family planning* when it is for the purpose of spacing births. This includes, but is not limited to, abortions performed for the physical or mental health of the mother but does not include abortions performed if the life of the mother would be endangered if the fetus were carried to term or abortions performed following rape or incest (since abortion under these circumstances is not a family planning act).
>
> (ii) *To perform abortions* means to operate a facility where abortions are performed as a method of family planning. Excluded from this definition are clinics or hospitals which do not include abortion in their family planning programs.
>
> (iii) *To actively promote abortion* means for an organization to commit resources, financial or other, in a substantial or continuing effort to increase the availability or use of abortion as a method of family planning.

JOHN BLANE & MATTHEW FRIEDMAN, MEXICO CITY POLICY IMPLEMENTATION STUDY, A-4 (1990) (emphasis added).

39. Sarah Mehta, *There's Only One Country That Hasn't Ratified the Convention on Children's Rights: U.S.*, ACLU (Nov. 20, 2015, 1:30 PM), https://www.aclu.org/blog/human-rights/treaty-ratification/theres-only-one-country-hasnt-ratified-convention-chil drens [https://perma.cc/Q9M5-FNFJ].

40. Karen Attiah, *Why Won't the U.S. Ratify the U.N.'s Child Rights Treaty?*, WASH. POST (Nov. 21, 2014), https://www.washingtonpost.com/blogs/post-partisan/wp/2014/11/21/why-wont-the-u-s-ratify-the-u-n-s-child-rights-treaty [https://perma.cc/ACE8-Y4Q9] (noting also that "[t]he U.S. is falling behind on a number of children's rights indicators," including poverty, maternal leave, and criminal justice).

41. The MCP was instituted through legislative action for one year between October 1999 and September 2000 as part of the Consolidated Appropriations Act for Fiscal Year 2000. Consolidated Appropriations Act, 2000, Pub. L. No. 106–113, § 518, 113 Stat. 1501 (1999); *see also* KAISER FAMILY FOUND., THE MEXICO CITY POLICY: AN EXPLAINER (2017), http://files.kff.org/attachment/Fact-Sheet-The-Mexico-City-Policy-An-Explainer [https://perma.cc/8EGB-7HWJ].

42. Memorandum from President William J. Clinton on the Mex. City Policy to the Acting Adm'r of the U.S. Agency for Int'l Dev. (Jan. 22, 1993).
43. *Id.* However, even President Clinton caved in to conservative lawmakers shortly before the end of his presidency. To secure funding for nearly a billion dollars in debt owed to the United Nations, Clinton agreed not to veto the Consolidated Appropriations Act for the Fiscal Year 2000. That law included antiabortion provisions similar to the Mexico City Policy. NOWELS, *supra* note 38, at 5–6.
44. Tracy Wilkinson, *El Salvador Jails Women for Miscarriages and Stillbirths*, L.A. TIMES (Apr. 15, 2015), http://www.latimes.com/world/great-reads/la-fg-c1-el-salvador-women -20150415-story.html [https://perma.cc/38EK-PKC8].
45. *Id.*
46. *Id.* (noting that in one case a seventeen-year-old girl was granted a brief hearing and then sentenced to thirty years in prison).
47. *Id.*
48. *Id.*
49. Memorandum from President Barack Obama on Mex. City Policy and Assistance for Voluntary Population Planning to the Sec'y of State and the Adm'r of the U.S. Agency for Int'l Dev., 74 Fed. Reg. 4903 (Jan. 28, 2009).
50. Memorandum from President Donald Trump on the Mex. City Policy to the Sec'y of State, the Sec'y of Health and Human Services, and the Adm'r of the U.S. Agency for Int'l Dev., 82 Fed. Reg. 8495 (Jan. 25, 2017).
51. *Id.*
52. *Id.*; *see also With a Stroke of the Pen – Trump's Global Gag Rule Dramatically Expands Harmful Health Impacts*, POPULATION ACTION INTERNATIONAL (last updated Jan. 26, 2017), http://pai.org/newsletters/stroke-pen-trumps-global-gag-rule-dramatically-expands-harmful-health-impacts [https://perma.cc/W5BN-M2J7] [hereinafter *Trump's Global Gag Rule*].
53. *Trumps Global Gag Rules*, *supra* note 52.
54. *Id.*
55. *Id.*
56. *Id.*
57. *Global Gag Rule*, CTR. FOR HEALTH AND GENDER EQUITY, http://www.genderhealth.org /the_issues/us_foreign_policy/global_gag_rule [https://perma.cc/X3Q2-DUFD].
58. *See* KAISER FAMILY FOUND., *supra* note 41. For an overview of programs which receive U.S. global health funding, *see* KAISER FAMILY FOUND., THE U.S. GOVERNMENT ENGAGEMENT IN GLOBAL HEALTH: A PRIMER 12–15 (Jan. 2017), http://files.kff.org/attach ment/report-the-u-s-government-engagement-in-global-health-a-primer [https://perma .cc/2FMH-W7P7] [hereinafter GLOBAL HEALTH]; KAISER FAMILY FOUND., THE U.S. GOVERNMENT AND GLOBAL HEALTH (June 2016), http://files.kff.org/attachment/fact-sheet-The-US-Government-and-Global-Health [https://perma.cc/23TC-7GG9].
59. GLOBAL HEALTH, *supra* note 58, at 12–15.
60. Pontsho Pilane, *Loophole Could Protect South African Organisations from US Gag Rule on Abortions*, BHEKISISA (Nov. 16, 2017, 12:00 AM) ("[A]ctivists say there is a loophole in the policy that may offer a lifeline of sorts to local organisations that provide family planning advice."), http://bhekisisa.org/article/2017–11-16–00-loophole-could-protect-south-african -organisations-from-us-gag-rule-on-abortions [https://perma.cc/Q4XS-6RFG].
61. *See* USAID, STANDARD PROVISIONS FOR NON-U.S. NONGOVERNMENTAL ORGANIZATIONS 87 (Oct. 4, 2017), https://www.usaid.gov/sites/default/files/documents/1868/303mab.pdf.
62. *See id.*

63. Blank & Friedman, *supra* note 38, at A-4.

64. Ehsan M. Entezar, Afghanistan 101: Understanding Afghan Culture 113 (2008).

65. Human Rights Watch, "We have the Promises of the World" – Women's Rights in Afghanistan 46–47 (2009).

66. Heather Saul, *Afghan Woman Raped, Impregnated and Jailed for "Adultery by Force" Marries Her Attacker*, The Independent (Apr. 8, 2015, 2:28 PM), https://www.indepen dent.co.uk/news/world/middle-east/afghan-woman-raped-impregnated-and-jailed-for-adultery-by-force-marries-her-attacker-10162694.html [https://perma.cc/CLY7-3LG7].

67. Joseph Goldstein, *U.S. Soldiers Told to Ignore Sexual Abuse of Boys by Afghan Allies*, N.Y. Times (Sep. 20, 2015), https://www.nytimes.com/2015/09/21/world/asia/us-soldiers-told-to-ignore-afghan-allies-abuse-of-boys.html [https://perma.cc/4YAN-SDH6].

68. Global Justice Ctr., The Right to an Abortion for Girls and Women Raped in Armed Conflict 2 (2011), http://globaljusticecenter.net/documents/LegalBrief .RightToAnAbortion.February2011.pdf.

69. *Id.* at 2–3.

70. *Id.*

71. *Id.* at 2.

72. *Id.* at 6.

73. Elahe Izadi, *Denied an Abortion, 11-Year-Old Rape Victim in Paraguay Gives Birth*, Wash. Post (Aug. 14, 2015) (quoting Health Minister Antonio Barrios) https://www.washington post.com/news/worldviews/wp/2015/08/14/denied-an-abortion-11-year-old-rape-victim-in-paraguay-gives-birth [http://perma.cc/J6P4-XCY6].

74. *Id.*

75. *Id.*

76. Directorate-Gen. for External Policies, Eur. Parliament, Sexual Violence Against Minors in Latin America 2 (2016), http://www.europarl.europa.eu/RegData/etudes/ STUD/2016/578023/EXPO_STU(2016)578023_EN.pdf [https://perma.cc/2YNC-33TW].

77. *Id.*

78. *Id.* at 3.

79. World Health Org., Unsafe Abortion: Global and Regional Estimates of the Incidence of Unsafe Abortion and Associated Mortality in 2008, at 14 (6th ed. 2011), http://apps.who.int/iris/bitstream/10665/44529/1/9789241501118_eng.pdf [https://perma.cc /42ZJ-QP27].

80. *Id.* at 2.

81. Lisa B. Haddad and Nawal M. Nour, *Unsafe Abortion: Unnecessary Maternal Mortality*, 2 Rev. Obstetrics & Gynecology 122, 122 (2009).

82. Kelly M. Jones, Int'l. Food Policy Research Inst., Evaluating the Mexico City Policy: How US Foreign Policy Affects Fertility Outcomes and Child Health in Ghana 11–12 (2011), http://cdm15738.contentdm.oclc.org/utils/getfile/collection/ p15738coll2/id/126751/filename/126962.pdf [https://perma.cc/5W2P-ZFND].

83. Eran Bendavid, Patrick Avila & Grant Miller, *United States Aid Policy and Induced Abortion in Sub-Saharan Africa*, 89 Bull. World Health Org., 873 (2011), http://www .who.int/bulletin/volumes/89/12/11-091660/en [https://perma.cc/2RTE-JTNC].

84. *Id.* at 876. Furthermore, the study reported that between 2001 and 2008, when the MCP was in effect, women living in a country with high exposure to the MCP were 1.21 times more likely to have an induced abortion than women in the study's reference groups. *Id.* at 877.

85. *Id.* at 876.

86. Kelly M. Jones, *Contraceptive Supply and Fertility Outcomes: Evidence from Ghana*, 64 ECON. DEV. & CULTURAL CHANGE 31, 46–47 (2015).
87. POPULATION ACTION INT'L, THE GLOBAL GAG RULE & CONTRACEPTIVE SUPPLIES 2 (2017), http://pai.org/wp-content/uploads/2016/12/The-Global-Gag-Rule-and-Contraceptive-Supplies.pdf [https://perma.cc/EE6B-7PDA].
88. Nina J. Crimm, *The Global Gag Rule: Undermining National Interests by Doing unto Foreign Women and NGOs What Cannot Be Done at Home*, 40 CORNELL INT'L L.J. 587, 596–97 (2007).
89. *Id.* at 597.

10 LESSONS FOR LAW AND SOCIETY: A REPRODUCTIVE JUSTICE
NEW DEAL OR BILL OF RIGHTS

1. Kyle Schwab, *Women Who Accused Fired Cop Daniel Holtzclaw of Sexual Assault Are a Long Way From Resolving Lawsuits*, NEWSOK (Nov. 5, 2018), https://newsok.com/article/5613756/women-who-accused-fired-cop-daniel-holtzclaw-of-sexual-assault-are-a-long-way-from-resolving-lawsuits.
2. Telephone interview with Anthony Romero (Apr. 6, 2015).
3. Dorothy Roberts, *Punishing Drug Addicts Who Have Babies: Women of Color, Equality, and the Right of Privacy*, 104 HARV. L. REV. 1419 (1991); LAURA GÓMEZ, MISCONCEIVING MOTHERS: LEGISLATORS, PROSECUTORS, AND THE POLITICS OF PRENATAL DRUG EXPOSURE (1997); SUSAN BOYD, MOTHERS AND ILLICIT DRUGS: TRANSCENDING THE MYTHS (1999); Linda Fentiman, *Pursuing the Perfect Mother: Why America's Criminalization of Maternal Substance Abuse Is Not the Answer – A Comparative Legal Analysis*, 15 MICH. J. GENDER & L. 389 (2009); Julie D. Cantor, *Court-Ordered Care: A Complication of Pregnancy to Avoid*, 366 NEW ENG. J. MED. 2237, 2240 (2012); April Cherry, *The Detention, Confinement, and Incarceration of Pregnant Women for the Benefit of Fetal Health*, 16 COLUM. J. GENDER & L. 147 (2007); Linda Fentiman, ": *The Wrong Answer to the Crisis of Inadequate Health Care for Women and Children*, 84 DENV. U. L. REV. 537, 540 (2006).
4. Interview with Carol Gilligan (Oct. 17, 2013).
5. Telephone interview with Loretta J. Ross (Nov. 23, 2014).
6. Robinson v. California, 370 U.S. 660, 678 (1962).
7. Monica McLemore, *What Could the Future of Reproductive Justice [Look] Like?*, 2019 Sadie T.M. Alexander Commemorative Symposium, University of Pennsylvania Law School (Feb. 9, 2019).
8. *Share Our Wealth*, HUEY LONG: THE MAN, HIS MISSION, AND LEGACY, https://www.hueylong.com/programs/share-our-wealth.php.
9. The Mexico City Policy, otherwise known as the "global gag rule" or "global gag order," was originally launched by President Ronald Reagan at the Second United Nations International Conference on Population in Mexico City, in August of 1984. U.N. Conf. on Population, 2d. Sess., Policy Statement of the United States of America (Aug. 6–13, 1984),http://www.uib.no/sites/w3.uib.no/files/attachments/mexico_city_policy_1984.pdf.
10. Hobby Lobby Stores, Inc. v. Sebelius, 723 F.3d 1114, 1152–59 (10th Cir. 2013) (Gorsuch, J., concurring); *see* Little Sisters of the Poor Home for the Aged v. Burwell, 799 F.3d 1315, 1317–18 (10th Cir. 2015) (Judge Gorsuch dissenting from a denial of en banc review, wherein a Tenth Circuit panel found that the state's "accommodation scheme relieves [nursing home owners] of their obligations under the [Affordable Care Act's contraceptive mandate] and does not substantially burden their religious exercise under RFRA

or infringe upon their First Amendment rights" (quoting Little Sisters of the Poor Home for the Aged v. Burwell, 794 F.3d 1151, 1160 (10th Cir. 2015)); Planned Parenthood Association v. Herbert, 839 F.3d 1301, 1307 (10th Cir. 2016) (Gorsuch, J., dissenting).

11. Erwin Chemerinsky & Michele Goodwin, *Abortion: A Woman's Private Choice*, 95 Tex. L. Rev. 1189 (2017).
12. Garza v. Hargan, 874 F.3d 735 (2017).
13. *Id.* at 737.
14. Erwin Chemerinsky, *Chemerinsky: What Will the Presidential Election Mean for SCOTUS?*, ABA J. (Sept. 6, 2016), http://www.abajournal.com/news/article/chemerinsky_what_will_the_coming_election_mean_for_scotus [https://perma.cc/PC47-BGQX].
15. Dred Scott v. Sandford, 60 U.S. (19 How.) 393 (1857).
16. Plessy v. Ferguson, 163 U.S. 537 (1896).
17. Buck v. Bell, 274 U.S. 200 (1927).
18. Korematsu v. United States, 323 U.S. 214 (1944).
19. Dred Scott v. Sanford, 60 U.S. 393, 407 (1857).
20. Mark A. Graber, Rethinking Equal Protection in Dark Times, 4 U. Pa. J. Const. L. 314, 314–15, 317 (2002); Richard M. Re, *The New Supreme Court and the Jurisprudence in Exile*, PrawfsBlawg (Feb. 17, 2016), http://prawfsblawg.blogs.com/prawfsblawg/2016/02/the-new-supreme-court-and-the-jurisprudence-in-exile.html ("During the past 20 or so years, the Supreme Court's more liberal justices have created a kind of jurisprudence in exile.").
21. Stephen Saks, *The "Constitution in Exile" as a Problem for Legal Theory*, 89 Notre Dame L. Rev. 2253, 2255 (2014) (citation omitted).
22. Roe v. Wade, 410 U.S. 113, 152 (1973).
23. Neil S. Siegel & Reva Siegel, *Equality Arguments for Abortion Rights*, 60 UCLA L. Rev. Discourse 160, 163 (2013).
24. Pauli Murray, States' Laws on Race and Color (1951).
25. Pauli Murray and Mary O. Eastwood, *Jane Crow and the Law: Sex Discrimination and Title VII*, 34 George Wash. L. Rev. 232 (1965).
26. *See* Ruth Bader Ginsburg, *Some Thoughts on Autonomy and Equality in Relation to* Roe v. Wade, 63 N.C. L. Rev. 375 (1985); Catharine MacKinnon, *Reflections on Sex Equality Under Law*, 100 Yale L.J. 1281 (1991).
27. Pauli Murray, The Autobiography of a Black Activist, Feminist, Lawyer, Priest, and Poet, 351 (1987).
28. *Id.*
29. *Id.* at 352.
30. Skinner v. Oklahoma, 316 U.S. 535 (1942); Kirchberg v. Feenstra, 450 U.S. 455 (1981); Wengler v. Druggists Mutual Insurance Co., 446 U.S. 142 (1980); Califano v. Goldfarg, 430 U.S. 1999 (1977); Caban v. Mohammed, 441 U.S. 380 (1979).
31. International Union v. Johnson Controls, 499 U.S. 187, 188 (1991).
32. 417 U.S. 484 (1974).
33. Cal. Unemp. Ins. Code § 2626.
34. Geduldig v. Aiello, 417 U.S. 484, 496 (1974).
35. For a catalogue of the articles criticizing the *Geduldig* opinion, *see* Sylvia A. Law, *Rethinking Sex and the Constitution*, 132 U. Pa. L. Rev. 955, 983 (1984); Katharine Bartlett, *Pregnancy and the Constitution: The Uniqueness Trap*, 62 Cal. L. Rev. 1532, 1536 (1974); Harriet Hubacker Coleman, *Barefoot and Pregnant – Still: Equal Protection for Women in Light of* Geduldig v. Aiello, 16 S. Tex. L.J 211 (1975); Phillip Cockrell, *Pregnancy Disability Benefits and Title VII: Pregnancy Does Not Involve*

Sex?, 29 Baylor L. Rev. 257 (1977); Ruth Ferrell, *The Equal Rights Amendment to the United States Constitution – Areas of Controversy*, 6 Urb. Law. 853 (1974); Ruth Bader Ginsburg, *Gender in the Supreme Court: The 1973 and 1974 Terms*, 1975 Sup. Ct. Rev. 1; Ruth Bader Ginsburg, *Gender and the Constitution*, 44 U. Cin. L. Rev. 1 (1975).

36. Siegal & Siegel, *supra* note 23, at 163, 168.
37. *Geduldig*, 417 U.S. at 496, 498 (Brennan, J., dissenting) (citations omitted).
38. *Id.* at 503.
39. *Id.* at 501.
40. Plessy v. Ferguson, 163 U.S. 537, 551 (1896).
41. 499 U.S. 187, 188 (1991).
42. *See* Joan Bertrin, *Reproductive Hazards in the Workplace*, *in* Reproductive Laws for the 1990s 277, 301 n.5 (Cohen & Taub eds., 1989).
43. *See id.* at 277.
44. Int'l Union v. Johnson Controls, 499 U.S. 187, 191 (1991).
45. *Id.*
46. *Id.*
47. *Id.*
48. *Id.*
49. *Id.* at 192.
50. *Id.*
51. *Id.*
52. *Id.* at 197; Civil Rights Act of 1964, Pub. L. No. 88-352, 78 Stat. 255 (codified as amended at 42 U.S.C. § 2000e-2(a)).
53. *Int'l Union*, 499 U.S. at 197.
54. *Id.*
55. *Id.* at 203.
56. 538 U.S. 721 (2003) (quoting M. Lord & M. King, The State Reference Guide to Work-Family Programs for State Employees 30 (1991)).
57. Geduldig v. Aiello, 417 U.S. 484, n.20.
58. Craig v. Boren, 429 U.S. 190, 202 (1976).
59. Reed v. Reed, 404 U.S. 71 (1971).
60. Frontiero v. Richardson 411 U.S. 677 (1973). According to Justice Brennan, "classifications based upon sex, like . . . race, alienage, and national origin, are inherently suspect and must therefore be subjected to close judicial scrutiny." *See id.* at 688 (Brennan, J., concurring).
61. *Reed*, 404 U.S. at 75.
62. *Craig*, 429 U.S. at 202.
63. *Id.* at 223.
64. *See, e.g.*, United States v. Virginia, 518 U.S. 515, 531 (1996).
65. *See* Wengler v. Druggists Mut. Ins. Co., 446 U.S. 142, 150 (1980).
66. *See generally What Is Prenatal Care and Why Is It Important?* Nat'l Inst. Child Health & Human Dev., http://www.nichd.nih.gov/health/topics/pregnancy/conditioninfo/Pages/prenatal-care.aspx (describing the importance of prenatal care for a healthy pregnancy and a healthy infant).
67. Ctr. Reproductive Rights, Punishing Women for their Behavior During Pregnancy 4 (Sept. 2000), http://reproductiverights.org/sites/default/files/documents/pub_bp_punishingwomen.pdf (noting that punitive measures against pregnant drug users are "counterproductive or run contrary to public policy").

68. Carolyn S. Carter, *Perinatal Care for Women Who Are Addicted: Implications for Empowerment*, 27 HEALTH & SOC. WORK 166, 167 (2002) (citations omitted).
69. *See, e.g.*, Daubert v. Merrell, 509 U.S. 579 (1993) (illustrating the difficulty of establishing whether drugs or other factors cause birth defects); Int'l Union v. Johnson Controls, 499 U.S. 187, 200 (1991)(rejecting fetal protection regulation even though work environment exposed women to lead, which has a demonstrated association with negative fetal and child health); Ambrosini v. Labarraque, 101 F.3d 129, 131–32(1996)(finding a causal connection between medroxyprogesterone exposure and fetal birth defects); Mahon v. Pfizer, Inc., 2011 N.Y. Slip Op. 33121 (denying the company's motion to dismiss the case alleging fetal harms were caused through the mother's wrongful exposure to the defendant's product); Enright v. Eli Lilly & Co., 570 N.E.2d 198 (1991).
70. *See* Allen A. Mitchell et al., *Medication Use During Pregnancy, with Particular Focus on Prescription Drugs: 1976–2008*, 205 AM. J. OBSTETRICS & GYNECOLOGY 51.e1 (2011).
71. *See also* Ferguson v. City of Charleston, 532 U.S. 67 (2001).

11 CONCLUSION

1. *See* Bekah Porter, *Dubuquer Gives Birth Alone in Jail Cell*, TELEGRAPH HERALD (May 15, 2009), http://www.thonline.com/news/feature_stories/article_c527db84-db00-514e-ab65-a7615e5490f4.html.
2. John Dickerson, *Arpaio's Jail Staff Cost Ambrett Spencer Her Baby, and She's Not the Only One*, PHOENIX NEW TIMES, (Oct. 30, 2008), http://www.phoenixnewtimes.com /2008-10-30/news/arpaio-s-jail-staff-cost-ambrett-spencer-her-baby-and-she-s-not-the-only -one/.
3. Kristin Turney, *Stress Proliferation Across Generations? Examining the Relationship Between Parental Incarceration and Childhood Health*, 55 J. HEALTH & SOC. BEHAV. 302, 311–14 (2014).
4. Inst. on Women & Criminal Justice, *Mothers, Infants, and Imprisonment: A Look at Prison Nurseries and Community-Based Alternatives*, PRISON LEGAL NEWS, May 2009, at 5 (noting that "by keeping mothers and infants together, these programs prevent foster care placement and allow for the formation of maternal/child bonds during a critical period of infant development").
5. Pam Fessler, *Report: Foster Kids Face Tough Times After Age 18*, NPR (Apr. 7, 2010, 12:01 AM), http://www.npr.org/templates/story/story.php?storyId=125594259; Mark E. Courtney et al., *Midwest Evaluation of the Adult Functioning of Former Foster Youth: Conditions of Youth Preparing to Leave State Care*, CHAPIN HALL CTR. FOR CHILD. (2004), https://www .chapinhall.org/research/midwest-evaluation-of-the-adult-functioning-of-former-foster-youth/.
6. Sue Ellen Allen, *Breast Cancer Behind Bars: One Woman's Story*, REWIRE NEWS (Oct. 24, 2014, 4:25 PM), http://rhrealitycheck.org/article/2014/10/24/breast-cancer-behind-bars-one -womans-story/.
7. *Id.*
8. Interview with Steve Marshall, Amnesty Task Force Meeting, in Birmingham, Ala. (Sept. 27, 2014).
9. Telephone Interview with Lynn Paltrow, Exec. Dir., Nat'l Advocates for Pregnant Women (Feb. 5, 2013).

10. *See, e.g.*, Ferguson v. City of Charleston, 532 U.S. 67 (2001). In this case, pregnant patients at a state hospital were arrested after their urine tested positive for cocaine and the results were communicated to the police.

11. Alabama's, Mississippi's, and Wisconsin's laws have since been suspended by judges. *See* Alan Blinder, *North Caroline House Passes New Restrictions on Abortion*, N.Y. TIMES, July 12, 2013, at A11.

12. *See, e.g.*, Augustine Kong et al., *Rate of De Novo Mutations and the Importance of Father's Age to Disease Risk*, 488 NATURE 471 (2012).

13. CNN Wire Staff, *Akin Bows out of CNN Appearance at the Last Minute*, CNN (Aug. 21, 2012, 9:33 AM), http://www.cnn.com/2012/08/20/politics/campaign-wrap/index.html.

14. *See, e.g.*, Becca Cadoff, *States Aim to Make the Grade When It Comes to Shackling Pregnant Prisoners*, ACLU (Mar. 31, 2011, 7:35 PM), http://www.aclu.org/blog/prisoners-rights-reproductive-freedom-womens-rights/states-aim-make-grade-when-it-comes.

15. MICHAEL FOUCAULT, DISCIPLINE AND PUNISH: THE BIRTH OF THE PRISON 8–9 (Alan Sheridan trans., 1977).

16. Allen A. Mitchell et al., *Medication Use During Pregnancy, with Particular Focus on Prescription Drugs: 1976–2008*, 205 AM. J. OBSTETRICS & GYNECOLOGY 51 (2011).

17. Ira J. Chasnoff, Harvey J. Landress & Mark E. Barrett, *The Prevalence of Illicit Drug or Alcohol Use During Pregnancy and Discrepancies in Mandatory Reporting in Pinellas County, Florida*, 322 NEW ENG. J. MED. 1202, 1204 (1990).

18. *Id.* at 1202.

19. *Id.* at 1204.

20. *See, e.g.*, Lynn M. Paltrow, *Pregnant Drug Users, Fetal Persons, and the Threat to Roe v. Wade*, 62 ALB. L. REV. 999, 1019 (1999).

21. Reply Brief of Appellant-Petitioner at 2, 12, Ferguson v. City of Charleston, 532 U.S. 67 (2001) (No. 99-936).

22. *Id.* at n.10.

23. Kevin Hayes, *Did Christine Taylor Take Abortion into Her Own Hands*, CBS NEWS (Mar. 2, 2010, 6:55 AM).

24. Erika London Bokneck et al., *Ambiguous Loss and Posttraumatic Stress in School Age Children*, 18 J. CHILD & FAM. STUD. 323 (2009).

25. STEPHANIE BUSH-BASKETTE & VANESSA PATINO, NAT'L COUNCIL ON CRIME & DELINQUENCY, THE NATIONAL COUNCIL ON CRIME AND DELINQUENCY'S EVALUATION OF THE PROJECT DEVELOPMENT OF NATIONAL INSTITUTE OF CORRECTIONS/CHILD WELFARE LEAGUE OF AMERICA'S PLANNING AND INTERVENTION SITES FUNDED TO ADDRESS THE NEEDS OF CHILDREN OF INCARCERATED PARENTS, (Oct. 2004), http://www.nccdglobal.org/sites/default/files/publication_pdf/needs-of-children.pdf.

26. Shay Bilchik, *Mentoring: A Promising Intervention for Children of Prisoners*, 10 RES. ACTION 1, 3 (2007), https://www.mentoring.org/new-site/wp-content/uploads/2015/09/RIA_ISSUE_10.pdf.

27. *Id.* at 6.

28. *Id.* at 3; *see also* JEREMY TRAVIS ET AL., URB. INST., FROM PRISON TO HOME: THE DIMENSIONS AND CONSEQUENCES OF PRISONER REENTRY (June 2001), http://www.urban.org/pdfs/from_prison_to_home.pdf; Background Paper, "From Prison to Home" Conference (Jan. 30–31, 2002), http://www.urban.org/UploadedPDF/410632_HHSConferenceBackground.pdf.

29. Bush-Baskette & Patino, *supra* note 25, at 6.

30. *Id.* at 5.

31. Children with parents in prison are more likely to have behavioral problems, and they are more likely to experience depression, drop out of school, and engage in the type of behavior that leads to juvenile incarceration. *See* Julia Crouse, *Initiative Seeking to Keep Inmates, Children Together*, CHAPEL HILL HERALD, Jan. 16, 2008, at 1.

32. *Id.*

33. PAN AM. HEALTH ORG., DOMESTIC PARTNER VIOLENCE DURING PREGNANCY, http://www.paho.org/english/ad/ge/vawpregnancy.pdf.

34. Jacquelyn C. Campbell, *Health Consequences of Intimate Partner Violence*, 359 LANCET 1331, 1331–36 (2002).

35. *Id.*

36. *Id.*

37. *Id.*; *see also* Julie A. Gazmararian et al., *Prevalence of Violence Against Pregnant Women: A Review of the Literature*, 275 J. AM. MED. ASS'N 1915, 1915–20 (1996).

38. Deborah Epstein & Lisa A. Goodman, *Domestic Violence Victims' Experiences in the Legal System*, in STRESS, TRAUMA, AND WELLBEING IN THE LEGAL SYSTEM 45–61 (Monica K. Miller & Brian H. Bornstein eds., 2013); Deborah Epstein & Lisa A. Goodman, *The Justice System Response to Domestic Violence*, in 2 VIOLENCE AGAINST WOMEN AND CHILDREN 215–35 (Jacquelyn W. White et al. eds., 2010).

39. Helen Coster, *Are Pregnant Women's Rights at Risk?*, MARIE CLAIRE (May 30, 2012), http://www.marieclaire.com/world-reports/news/bei-bei-shuai-pregnant-suicide-attempt (quoting Goldberg).

40. *See* Michele Goodwin, *Law's Limits: Regulating Statutory Rape Law*, 2013 WISC. L. REV. 481, 532 (2013).

41. *See, e.g.*, Dorothy E. Roberts, *Punishing Drug Addicts Who Have Babies: Women of Color, Equality, and the Right of Privacy*, 104 HARV. L. REV. 1419 (1991).

42. MARTHA C. NUSSBAUM, HIDING FROM HUMANITY: DISGUST, SHAME, AND THE LAW 128 (2004).

43. Brief of the Am. Med. Ass'n as Amicus Curiae in Support of Neither Party at 8, Ferguson v. City of Charleston, 532 U.S. 67 (2001) (No. 99-936) ("Criminal sanctions are unlikely to achieve the goal of deterring drug use among pregnant women.").

44. Brief of the Am. Pub. Health Ass'n et al. as Amici Curiae in Support of Petitioners at 3, Ferguson v. City of Charleston, 532 U.S. 67 (2001) (No. 99-936) ("government physicians and nurses should not act as agents of law enforcement, nor should they use 'routine' medical examinations to covertly gather evidence for use against patients in criminal proceedings").

45. *See id.*

46. *Id.* at 21.

47. MICHAEL FINIGAN, SOCIETAL OUTCOMES AND COST SAVINGS OF DRUG AND ALCOHOL TREATMENT IN THE STATE OF OREGON (1996).

48. *Id.*

49. Michael Kornhauser & Roy Schneiderman, *How Plans Can Improve Outcomes and Cut Costs for Preterm Infant Care*, MANAGEDCAREMAG.COM (Jan. 1 2010), http://www.managedcaremag.com/archives/1001/1001.preterm.html.

50. Sofia Resnick, *Texas Proposed Law Could Jail Women for Taking Drugs During Pregnancy*, AM. INDEP. (Feb. 24, 2011, 3:30 PM), http://www.americanindependent.com/171004/texas-proposed-law-could-jail-women-for-taking-drugs-during-pregnancy (quoting Rep. Miller).

51. *Id.*

52. Graham W. Chance, *Neonatal Intensive Care and Cost Effectiveness*, 139 CMAJ 943, 943 (1988).

53. For example, Dr. Deborah Frank, Professor of Pediatrics at Boston University School of Medicine, characterized "crack baby syndrome" as "a grotesque media stereotype, not a scientific diagnosis." Shalini Bhargava, *Challenging Punishment and Privatization: A Response to the Conviction of Regina McKnight*, 39 HARV. C.R.-C.L. L. REV. 513, 524 (2004).

54. Laura A. Schieve et al., *Use of Assisted Reproductive Technology-United States, 1996 and 1998*, 51 MORBIDITY & MORTALITY WKLY. REP. 97 (2002), *available at* http://www.cdc.gov /mmwr/preview/mmwrhtml/mm5105a2.htm (noting that multiple births increase the risk of low-birth-weight babies).

55. *Id.*

56. Kornhauser & Schneiderman, *supra* note 49.

EPILOGUE

1. *See* Travis Andrews & Fred Barbash, *Father Who "Repeatedly Raped His 12-Year Old Daughter" Gets 60-Day Sentence. Fury Erupts.*, WASH. POST, Oct. 19, 2016, https://www .washingtonpost.com/news/morning-mix/wp/2016/10/19/father-who-repeatedly-raped-his -12-year-old-daughter-gets-60-day-sentence-fury-erupts/?utm_term=.0ac06dd7b493. *See* Michele Goodwin, *Marital Rape: The Long Arch of Sexual Violence Against Women and Girls*, 109 AJIL UNBOUND 326 (2016).

2. Press Release, Santa Clara County District Attorney's Office, Victim Impact Statement (June 2, 2016), https://www.sccgov.org/sites/da/newsroom/newsreleases/Documents/ B-Turner%20VIS.pdf.

3. Michael E. Miller, *"A Steep Price to Pay for 20 Minutes of Action": Dad Defends Stanford Sex Offender*, WASH. POST (June 6, 2016), https://www.washingtonpost.com/news/morn ing-mix/wp/2016/06/06/a-steep-price-to-pay-for-20-minutes-of-action-dad-defends- stanford-sex-offender/?utm_term=.ead51338bcd3.

4. Jacqueline Lee, *Woman Testifies Against Former Stanford All-Star Swimmer Accused of Sexually Assaulting Her*, MERCURY NEWS (Mar. 18, 2016, 2:48 PM), http://www .mercurynews.com/2016/03/18/woman-testifies-against-former-stanford-all-star-swimmer- accused-of-sexually-assaulting-her/.

5. Alex Zielinski, *The Stanford Rapist's Father Offers an Impossibly Offensive Defense of His Son*, THINKPROGRESS (June 5, 2016), https://thinkprogress.org/the-stanford-rapists-father- offers-an-impossibly-offensive-defense-of-his-son-b3a7a254d2ad#.6a97m0gwh.

6. Sam Levin, *Stanford Sexual Assault: Read the Full Text of the Judge's Controversial Decision*, GUARDIAN (June 14, 2016, 6:00 PM), https://www.theguardian.com/us-news /2016/jun/14/stanford-sexual-assault-read-sentence-judge-aaron-persky.

7. Forbes Corporate Communications, *Stanford University Ranks No. 1 on Forbes' 9th Annual Ranking Of America's Top Colleges*, FORBES (July 5, 2016, 10:58 AM), http://www .forbes.com/sites/forbespr/2016/07/05/stanford-university-ranks-no-1-on-forbes-9th-annual -ranking-of-americas-top-colleges/#47b8d0427655.

8. David Lisak & Paul M. Miller, *Repeat Rape and Multiple Offending Among Undetected Rapists*, 17 VIOLENCE AND VICTIMS 73 (2002).

9. Gene Abel et al., *Self-Reported Sex Crimes of Nonincarcerated Paraphiliacs*, 2 J. INTERPERSONAL VIOLENCE 3 (1987).

10. *Id.* at 11.

11. *Id.*

12. *Id.* at 12.

13. *Id.* at 11.
14. Donald Dripps et al., *Panel Discussion: Men, Women and Rape*, 63 FORDHAM L. REV. 125, 130 n.21 (1994); J.S. Feild, *Juror Background Characteristics and Attitudes Toward Rape: Correlates of Jurors' Decisions in Rape Trials*, 2 LAW & HUMAN BEHAV. 73 (1978) (Black offenders receive more severe punishment than white offenders); Ronald Mazzella & Alan Feingold, *The Effects of Physical Attractiveness, Race, Socioeconomic Status and Gender of Defendants and Victims on Judgments of Mock Jurors*, 24 J. APPLIED SOC. PSYCHOL. 1315, 1319, 1325, 1327 (1994) (wealth and attractiveness influence sentencing in rape); Cassia C. Spohn & Julie Horney, *The Impact of Rape Law Reform on the Processing of Simple and Aggravated Rape Cases*, 86 J. CRIM. L. & CRIMINOLOGY 861, 879–80 (1996) ("The data displayed in Table 6 also reveal that four extralegal variables influence the length of the sentence. Judges gave significantly shorter sentences to offenders who pled guilty (b=70.80), to offenders convicted of assaulting women who engaged in some type of risk-taking behavior at the time of the incident (b=31.78), and to offenders convicted of assaulting black women (b=46.54). They also imposed significantly longer sentences on black offenders than on white offenders (b=68.74)."); *Race Tilts the Scales of Justice. Study: Dallas Punishes Attacks on Whites More Harshly*, DALLAS TIMES HERALD, Aug. 19, 1990, at A1.
15. Oliphant v. Suquamish Indian Tribe, 435 U.S. 191, 208 (1978) ("But an examination of our earlier precedents satisfies us that . . . Indians do not have criminal jurisdiction over non-Indians absent affirmative delegation of such power by Congress.").
16. Sierra Crane-Murdoch, *On Indian Land, Criminals Can Get Away with Almost Anything*, ATLANTIC (Feb. 22, 2013), https://www.theatlantic.com/national/archive/2013/02/on-indian-land-criminals-can-get-away-with-almost-anything/273391/; Jessica Rizzo, *Native American Women Are Rape Targets Because of a Legislative Loophole*, VICE (Dec. 15, 2015), https://www.vice.com/en_ca/article/bnpb73/native-american-women-are-rape-targets-because-of-a-legislative-loophole-511.
17. Eugene Kanin, *Date Rape: Unofficial Victims and Criminals*, 9 VICTIMOLOGY 95 (1984).
18. Ray Sanchez & Amanda Watts, *Montana Judge Defends 60-day Sentence in Child Incest Case*, CNN (Oct. 25, 2016, 2:29 PM), http://www.cnn.com/2016/10/19/us/montana-judge-incest-case-trnd/index.html.
19. Ben Jacobs, Sabrina Siddiqui & Scott Bixby, *"You Can Do Anything": Trump Brags on Tape About Using Fame to Get Women*, GUARDIAN (Oct. 8, 2016, 1:23 pm), https://www.theguardian.com/us-news/2016/oct/07/donald-trump-leaked-recording-women.
20. Georgie Kulczyk, *Blake Receives Suspended Sentence for Sex Crime*, GLASGOW COURIER (Oct. 12, 2016), http://www.glasgowcourier.com/story/2016/10/12/news/blake-receives-suspended-sentence-for-sex-crime/4227.html.
21. Andrews & Barbash, *supra* note 1.
22. Mitchell Byars, *Former CU Student Convicted of Boulder Rape Spared Prison Sentence*, DAILYCAMERA (Aug. 10, 2016, 9:56 AM), http://www.dailycamera.com/news/boulder/ci_30226973/former-cu-student-convicted-boulder-rape-spared-prison; Sam Levin, *No Prison for Colorado College Student Who "Raped a Helpless Young Woman,"* GUARDIAN (Aug. 10, 2016, 5:29 PM), https://www.theguardian.com/us-news/2016/aug/10/university-of-colorado-sexual-assault-austin-wilkerson.
23. Madeline Buckley, *Former IU Student Charged With Raping 2 Women During Parties*, INDYSTAR (Sept. 16, 2015, 1:04 PM), http://www.indystar.com/story/news/crime/2015/09/16/former-iu-student-charged-raping-two-women-parties/32502933/; Elizabeth Koh, *He Was Charged with Two Rapes and Spent One Day in Jail*, CHARLOTTE OBSERVER

(June 27, 2016, 2:08 PM), http://www.charlotteobserver.com/news/nation-world/national/article86225412.html.

24. Zack Peterson, *Former Hamilton County Bus Driver Won't Serve Jail Time After Pleading Guilty to Raping Student*, TIMES FREE PRESS (July 22, 2016), http://www.timesfreepress.com/news/local/story/2016/jul/22/bus-driver-serve-no-time-student-rape/377310/.

25. Christine Hauser, *Judge's Sentencing in Massachusetts Sexual Assault Case Reignites Debate on Privilege*, N.Y. TIMES (Aug. 24, 2016), http://www.nytimes.com/2016/08/25/us/david-becker-massachusetts-sexual-assault.html.

26. *Ex-Nantucket Man Gets Year in Jail for Raping Child*, WCVB (last updated Sept. 21, 2016, 9:11 AM), http://www.wcvb.com/article/ex-nantucket-man-gets-year-in-jail-for-raping-child/8248068.

27. Peter Holley, *Judge Admits His Decision in Domestic-Abuse Case Had "the Most Tragic Result Possible*," WASH. POST (Oct. 20, 2016), https://www.washingtonpost.com/news/post-nation/wp/2016/10/20/i-made-a-decision-that-had-the-most-tragic-result-possible-indiana-judge-says-after-domestic-abuse-case-turns-fatal/?tid=a_inl&utm_term=.8772f8a73dc9; Renee Bruck, *Judge: Made Decision with Tragic Result*, MADISON COURIER (Oct. 18, 2016, 3:03 PM), http://www.madisoncourier.com/Content/News/News/Article/Judge-Made-decision-with-tragic-result/178/961/99821.

28. Sheila Weller, *How Author Timothy Tyson Found the Woman at the Center of the Emmett Till Case*, VANITY FAIR (Jan. 26, 2017, 11:00 AM), https://www.vanityfair.com/news/2017/01/how-author-timothy-tyson-found-the-woman-at-the-center-of-the-emmett-till-case.

29. William B. Huie, *The Shocking Story of Approved Killing in Mississippi*, LOOK, Jan. 24, 1956.

30. The killing of George Stinney remains a focal point for racial injustice in the law. It highlights the rush to judgment in rape cases where the alleged assailant is Black and the victim is white. Long after his death, a judge overturned his conviction. Campbell Robertson, *South Carolina Judge Vacates Conviction of George Stinney in 1944 Execution*, N.Y. TIMES (Dec. 17, 2014), http://www.nytimes.com/2014/12/18/us/judge-vacates-conviction-in-1944-execution.html.

31. *Id.*

32. Donald H. Partington, *The Incidence of the Death Penalty for Rape in Virginia*, 22 WASH. & LEE L. REV. 43, 43 (1965).

33. *Id.*

34. Dixon v. State, 596 S.E. 2d 147 (Ga. 2004); Humphrey v. Wilson, 652 S.E. 2d 501 (Ga. 2007).

35. Lee Hill, *Teens, Sex and the Law: Genarlow Wilson*, NPR (June 12, 2007, 12:00 PM), http://www.npr.org/templates/story/story.php?storyId=10972703; Angela Tuck, *Genarlow Wilson's Journey from Prison to Morehouse*, ATLANTA J.-CONST. (May 18, 2013, 9:00 AM), https://www.ajc.com/news/crime--law/genarlow-wilson-journey-from-prison-morehouse/BSmOzTV5gU4sjRvAgsuEBM/.

36. Mike Celizic, *Genarlow Wilson: "I'm Coming Out a Man*," TODAY NEWS (last updated Oct. 29, 2007, 9:35 AM), http://today.msnbc.msn.com/id/21520324/ns/today-today_news/t/genarlow-wilson-im-coming-out-man/#.UEehe41lRJY.

37. Partington, *supra* note 32.

38. Stephanos Bibas, *Prosecutorial Regulation Versus Prosecutorial Accountability*, 157 U. PA. L. REV. 959, 960 (2009).

39. *Id.* at 961 (quoting McCleskey v. Kemp, 481 U.S. 279, 312 (1987)).

40. *Id.* at 961 (quoting McCleskey v. Kemp, 481 U.S. 279, 312 (1987)). Moreover, it is well known and well documented that teenage males are more likely to be prosecuted for statutory rape than females. *See* Carolyn E. Cocca, *Prosecuting Mrs. Robinson? Gender, Sexuality, and Statutory Rape Laws,* 16 MICH. FEMINIST STUD. 61 (2002).

41. Implicit racial bias is a cognitive process "whereby, despite even the best intentions, people automatically classify information in racially biased ways." Robert J. Smith & Justin D. Levinson, *The Impact of Implicit Racial Bias on the Exercise of Prosecutorial Discretion,* 35 SEATTLE U. L. REV. 795, 797 (2012).

42. *Id.* at 805–06.

43. Catharine A. MacKinnon, *Feminism, Marxism, Method, and the State: Toward Feminist Jurisprudence,* 8 SIGNS 635, 643 (1983).

44. *Id.*

45. Canadian Judicial Council, In the Matter of an Inquiry Pursuant to S. 63(1) of the Judges Act Regarding the Honourable Justice Robin Camp, Notice to Justice Robin Camp 3 (2016) (Can.) https://www.cjc-ccm.gc.ca/cmslib/general/Camp_Docs/2016-05-02%20Notice%20Allegations.pdf.

46. *Id.*

47. Richard Hartley-Parkinson, *Two Rapists Jailed for Just 40 Months Each Because a Judge Said Their 11-Year-Old Victim Was "Willing,"* DAILY MAIL (last updated Feb. 22, 2012), http://www.dailymail.co.uk/news/article-2104287/Child-rapists-jailed-just-40-months–judge-said-11-year-old-victim-willing.html.

48. Abigail Hauslohner, *Afghanistan: When Women Set Themselves on Fire,* TIME (July 7, 2010), http://www.time.com/time/world/article/0,8599,2002340,00.html.

49. Quentin Sommerville, *Woman Stoned to Death in North Afghanistan,* RAWA NEWS (Jan. 27, 2011), http://www.rawa.org/temp/runews/2011/01/27/woman-stoned-to-death-in-north-afghanistan.html.

50. Camila Domonoske & Martha Ann Overland, *Across the Country, Crowds March in Protest Against Trump's Victory,* NPR (Nov. 9, 2016, 10:16 PM), https://www.npr.org/sections/thetwo-way/2016/11/09/501513889/anti-trump-protests-break-out-in-cities-across-the-country.

51. David A. Fahrenthold, *Trump Recorded Having Extremely Lewd Conversation About Women in 2005,* WASH. POST (Oct. 8, 2016), https://www.washingtonpost.com/politics/trump-recorded-having-extremely-lewd-conversation-about-women-in-2005/2016/10/07/3b9ce776-8cb4-11e6-bf8a-3d26847eced4_story.html?postshare=3561475870579757&tid=ss_tw&utm_term=.cbod84dd92dc.

52. *Id.*

53. Jose A. DelReal & Jenna Johnson, *Trump, Threatening Nearly a Dozen Sexual Assault Accusers, Vows to Sue,* WASH. POST (Oct. 22, 2016), https://www.washingtonpost.com/news/post-politics/wp/2016/10/22/trump-threatening-nearly-one-dozen-sexual-assault-accusers-vows-to-sue/?utm_term=.84b219f87992.

54. Michael C. Bender & Janet Hook, *Donald Trump's Lewd Comments About Women Spark Uproar,* WALL ST. J. (last updated Oct. 8, 2016, 12:43 AM), https://www.wsj.com/articles/donald-trumps-lewd-comments-about-women-spark-uproar-1475886118; N.Y. Times, *Donald Trump's Long Record of Degrading Women,* N.Y. TIMES (Oct. 8, 2016), https://www.nytimes.com/2016/10/09/us/politics/trump-women-history.html; Rachel Sklar, *Women Know Why Donald Trump's Accusers Stayed Silent for So Long,* WASH. POST (Oct. 18, 2016), https://www.washingtonpost.com/posteverything/wp/2016/10/18/women-know-why-donald-trumps-accusers-stayed-silent-for-so-long/?utm_term=.ffacd2dcc7df; Tribune News Services, *A Guide to the Allegations Made by Women Against Donald*

Trump, CHI. TRIBUNE (Oct. 15, 2016, 5:42 PM), https://www.chicagotribune.com/news/nationworld/politics/ct-allegations-made-by-women-against-trump-20161012-story.html; Melissa Batchelor Warnke, *It Takes a Village to Raise a Misogynistic Monster like Donald Trump*, L.A. TIMES (Oct. 8, 2016, 12:15 PM), https://www.latimes.com/opinion/op-ed/la-oe-warnke-trump-tape-misogyny-supporters-20161008-snap-story.html.

55. Alexandra Berzon, Joe Palazzolo & Charles Passy, *Video Puts Spotlight on Donald Trump's History of Lewd Comments*, WALL. ST. J. (last updated Oct. 9, 2016, 10:20 AM), https://www.wsj.com/articles/video-puts-spotlight-on-donald-trumps-history-of-lewd-comments-1475985718.

56. Madeline Farber, *Why White Women Voted for Donald Trump*, FORTUNE (Nov. 30, 2016), https://fortune.com/2016/11/30/why-white-women-voted-trump/.

57. Karen Tumulty, *Trump's History of Flippant Misogyny*, WASH. POST (Aug. 8, 2015), https://www.washingtonpost.com/politics/trumps-history-of-flippant-misogyny/2015/08/08/891f1bec-3de4-11e5-9c2d-ed991d848c48_story.html?utm_term=.e0397e1ec790.

58. *Id.*

59. Callum Borchers, *Donald Trump to Megyn Kelly: I'm Sorry Not Sorry*, WASH. POST (May 17, 2016), https://www.washingtonpost.com/news/the-fix/wp/2016/05/17/megyn-kelly-gets-donald-trump-to-admit-it-hes-sorry-not-sorry/?utm_term=.b1c4c84d513f.

60. Jennifer Senior, *Review: Megyn Kelly Tells Tales out of Fox News in Her Memoir, "Settle for More,"* N.Y. TIMES (Nov. 10, 2016), https://www.nytimes.com/2016/11/12/books/review-megyn-kelly-tells-tales-out-of-fox-news-in-her-memoir-settle-for-more.html?mtrref=www.google.com.

61. Philip Rucker, *Trump says Fox's Megyn Kelly Had "Blood Coming out of Her Wherever,"* WASH. POST (Aug. 8, 2015), https://www.washingtonpost.com/news/post-politics/wp/2015/08/07/trump-says-foxs-megyn-kelly-had-blood-coming-out-of-her-wherever/?utm_term=.0fa68c7efdac.

62. Gregory Krieg, *It's Official: Clinton Swamps Trump in Popular Vote*, CNN (last updated Dec. 22, 2016, 5:34 AM), https://edition.cnn.com/2016/12/21/politics/donald-trump-hillary-clinton-popular-vote-final-count/; Nick Wing, *Final Popular Vote Total Shows Hillary Clinton Won Almost 3 Million More Ballots than Donald Trump*, HUFFINGTON POST (Dec. 20, 2016, 5:31 PM), https://www.huffpost.com/entry/hillary-clinton-popular-vote_us_58599647e4b0eb58648446c6.

63. Editorial Board, *Time to End the Electoral College*, N.Y. TIMES (Dec. 19, 2016), https://www.nytimes.com/2016/12/19/opinion/time-to-end-the-electoral-college.html?mtrref=undefined&assetType=opinion; Kamala Kelkar, *Electoral College Is "Vestige" of Slavery, Say Some Constitutional Scholars*, PBS (Nov. 6, 2016, 3:57 PM), http://www.pbs.org/newshour/updates/electoral-college-slavery-constitution/; Akhil Reed Amar, *The Troubling Reason the Electoral College Exists*, TIME (Nov. 8, 2016), http://time.com/4558510/electoral-college-history-slavery/; Chauncey DeVega, *Born of Slavery, the Electoral College Could Stand Against Racism in 2016 – And Stop Donald Trump*, SALON (Dec. 15, 2016, 5:00 AM), http://www.salon.com/2016/12/15/the-electoral-college-born-of-slavery-could-stand-against-racism-in-2016/; Paul Finkelman, *Original Sin: The Electoral College as a Pro-Slavery Tool*, L.A. REV. BOOKS (Dec. 19, 2016), https://lareviewofbooks.org/article/original-sin-electoral-college-proslavery-tool/.

64. Matt Flegenheimer & Maggie Haberman, *Donald Trump, Abortion Foe, Eyes "Punishment" for Women, Then Recants*, N.Y. TIMES (Mar. 30, 2016), https://www.nytimes.com/2016/03/31/us/politics/donald-trump-abortion.html?mtrref=www.google.com.

65. Casey Quackenbush, *The Impact of President's Trump's "Global Gag Rule" on Women's Health Is Becoming Clear,* TIME (published Feb. 1, 2018; updated Feb. 4, 2018, 8:14 PM), http://time.com/5115887/donald-trump-global-gag-rule-women.html [http://perma.cc /5ZGJ-UTKX].

66. *See, e.g.,* Christine Grimaldi, *Trump Unveils "Vicious" Women's Health Restrictions During "Women's Health Week,"* REWIRE NEWS (May 18, 2017, 10:22 AM), https://rewire .news/article/2017/05/18/trump-unveils-vicious-women-s-health-restrictions-during-women-s-health-week [https://perma.cc/5B2S-EWEP].

67. Roe v. Wade, 410 U.S. 113 (1973).

68. Christopher Ingraham, *Toddlers Have Shot at Least 50 People This Year,* WASH. POST (Oct. 20, 2016), https://www.washingtonpost.com/news/wonk/wp/2016/10/20/toddlers-have-shot-at-least-50-people-this-year/?utm_term=.e2c57994a76a.

69. Danielle Kurtzleben, *1 More Woman Accuses Trump of Inappropriate Sexual Conduct. Here's the Full List,* NPR (Oct. 20, 2016, 1:00 PM), https://www.npr.org/2016/10/13/ 497799354/a-list-of-donald-trumps-accusers-of-inappropriate-sexual-conduct.

70. Steve Benen, *List of Trump's Women Accusers Continues to Grow,* MSNBC (Oct. 24, 2016, 10:40 AM), www.msnbc.com/rachel-maddow-show/list-trumps-women-accusers-continues-grow. A prior allegation of marital rape involving Mr. Trump's first wife, Ivana, resurfaced during his campaigning for the presidency. Ivana explained that when she filed court documents stating that Mr. Trump raped her, she was not speaking in the criminal sense. During the campaign, a "Jane Doe" filed a lawsuit alleging that Mr. Trump raped her many years ago when she was thirteen years old at a party held by New York financier Jeffrey Epstein. (Mr. Epstein was convicted in 2008 of sex crimes against a minor.) Mr. Trump adamantly denied the allegations, issuing a statement calling the case "basically a sham lawsuit brought by someone who desires to impact the presidential election." Jane Mayer, *Documenting Trump's Abuse of Women,* NEW YORKER (Oct. 24, 2016), https://www.newyorker.com/magazine/2016/10/24/document ing-trumps-abuse-of-women; Alan Yuhas, *Woman Who Accused Donald Trump of Raping Her at 13 Drops Lawsuit,* GUARDIAN (Nov. 5, 2016, 9:33 AM), https://www .theguardian.com/us-news/2016/nov/04/donald-trump-teenage-rape-accusations-lawsuit-dropped.

71. MacKinnon, *supra* note 43, at 643 (1983).

Select Bibliography

1 CASE MATERIALS

1.1 Cases

Allaire v. St. Luke's Hosp., 184 Ill. 359, 368 (1900).
Ambrosini v. Labarraque, 101 F.3d 129, 131–32 (1996).
Bang v. Charles T. Miller Hosp., 88 N.W.2d 186 (Minn. 1958).
Berry v. Moench, 331 P.2d 814 (Utah 1958).
Birmingham S. Ry. v. Lintner, 141 Ala. 420 (1904).
Bonbrest v. Kotz, 65 F.Supp. 138 (D.D.C. 1946).
Bosley v. McLaughlin, 236 U.S. 385 (1915).
Bradwell v. Illinois, 83 U.S. 130 (1872).
Brotherton v. Cleveland, 923 F.2d 477 (6th Cir. 1991).
Buck v. Bell, 274 U.S. 200 (1927).
Buel v. United Rys. Co., 248 Mo. 126, 132–33 (1913).
Burton v. State, 49 So. 3d 263 (Fla. Dist. Ct. App. 2010).
Caban v. Mohammed, 441 U.S. 380 (1979).
Califano v. Goldfarb, 430 U.S. 1999 (1977).
Canterbury v. Spence, 464 F.2d 772 (D.C. Cir. 1972).
Chambers v. Omaha Girls Club, Inc., 834 F.2d 697 (8th Cir. 1987).
City of Akron v. Akron Center for Reproductive Health, 462 U.S. 416 (1983).
Cooper v. Doyal, 205 So. 2d 59 (La. Ct. App. 1967), *writ refused*, 251 La. 755, 206 So. 2d 97 (1968).
Craig v. Boren, 429 US 190 (1976).
Crawford v. Cushman, 531 F.2d 1114 (1976).
Cunningham v. Yankton Clinic, P.A., 262 N.W.2d 508 (S.D. 1978).
Daubert v. Merrell, 509 U.S. 579 (1993).
Davis v. Hubbard, 506 F. Supp. 915 (N.D. Ohio 1980).
Dietrich v. Northampton, 138 Mass. 14 (1884).
Dixon v. State, 596 S.E.2d 147 (Ga. 2004).
Doe v. Delie, 257 F.3d 317 (3d. Cir. 2001).
Doe v. Roe, 400 N.Y.S.2d 668 (Sup. Ct. 1977).
Doe v. Southeastern Pennsylvania Trans. Auth., 72 F.3d 1133 (3d Cir.1995).
Dred Scott v. Sandford, 60 U.S. (19 How.) 393 (1857).

Eisenstadt v. Baird, 405 U.S. 438 (1972).
Enright v. Eli Lilly & Co., 570 N.E.2d 198 (1991).
Ex parte Ankrom, 2013 WL 135748 (Ala. Jan. 11, 2013).
Ferguson v. City of Charleston, 532 U.S. 67 (2001).
Food & Drug Admin. v. Brown & Williamson Tobacco Corp., 529 U.S. 120 (2000).
Forbush v. Wallace, 341 F. Supp. 217 (M.D. Ala. 1971), *aff'd*, 405 U.S. 970 (1972).
Garza v. Hargan, 874 F.3d 735 (2017).
Geduldig v. Aiello, 417 U.S. 484 (1974).
Gideon v. Wainwright, 372 U.S. 335 (1963).
Goesaert v. Cleary, 335 U.S. 464 (1948).
Gonzalez v. Carhart, 550 U.S. 124 (2007).
Gorman v. Budlong, 23 R.I. 169, 176–77 (1901).
Gruenke v. Seip, 225 F.3d 290 (3d. Cir. 2000).
Hammonds v. Aetna Cas. & Sur. Co. 243 F. Supp. 793 (N.D. Ohio 1965).
Harris v. McRae, 448 U.S. 297 (1980).
Hobby Lobby Stores, Inc. v. Sebelius, 723 F.3d 1114 (10th Cir. 2013).
Holbrook v. Flynn, 475 US 560 (1986).
Hoyt v. Florida, 368 U.S. 57 (1961).
Humphrey v. Wilson, 652 S.E.2d 501 (Ga. 2007).
Hundley v. St. Francis Hosp., 327 P.2d 131 (Cal. Dist. Ct. App. 1958).
Hyde v. Scyssor (1620) 79 Eng. Rep. 462.
In re A.C., 573 A.2d 1235 (D.C. Ct. App. 1990).
In re Brown, 478 So. 2d 1033 (Miss. 1985).
In re Gault, 387 U.S. 1 (1967).
In re Goodell, 39 Wis. 232 (1875).
In re Medley, 134 U.S. 160 (1890).
In re Paquet's Estate, 101 Or. 393, 200 P. 911 (1921).
In re Sudol, OIE No. 2009.5 (Dec. 9, 2009).
In re Unborn Child of Samantha Burton, No. 2009 CA 1167, 2009 WL 8628562 (Fla. Cir. Ct. Mar. 27, 2009).
International Union v. Johnson Controls, 499 U.S. 187 (1991).
Jaffee v. Redmond, 518 U.S. 1 (1996).
Kilmon v. State, 905 A.2d 306 (Md. 2006).
Kirchberg v. Feenstra, 450 U.S. 455 (1981).
Korematsu v. United States, 323 U.S. 214 (1944).
Lanigan v. Bartlett & Co. Grain, 466 F. Supp. 1388 (W.D. Mo. 1979).
Lassiter v. Dep't of Soc. Servs., 452 U.S. 18 (1981).
Lipps v. Milwaukee Elec. Ry. & Light Co., 164 Wis. 272 (1916).
Little Sisters of the Poor Home for the Aged v. Burwell, 794 F.3d 1151 (10th Cir. 2015).
Little Sisters of the Poor Home for the Aged, Denver, Co. v. Burwell, 799 F.3d 1315 (10th Cir. 2015).
Loertscher v. Anderson, 259 F. Supp. 3d 902 (W.D. Wis.), *stay granted*, 137 S. Ct. 2328 (2017).
MacDonald v. Clinger, 84 A.D.2d 482 (N.Y. App. Div. 1982).
Magnolia Coca Cola Bottling Co. v. Jordan, 124 Tex. 347, 359–60 (1935).
Maher v. Roe, 432 U.S. 468 (1977).
Mahon v. Pfizer, Inc., 2011 N.Y. Slip Op. 33121.
McCormick v. England, 494 S.E.2d 431 (S.C. Ct. App. 1994).
McKnight v. State, 661 S.E.2d 354, 361 (S.C. 2008).
Meinhard v. Salmon, 164 N.E. 545 (N.Y. 1928).

Miller v. Wilson, 236 U.S. 373 (1915).
Minor v. Happersett, 88 U.S. 162 (1874).
Miranda v. Arizona, 384 U.S. 436 (1966).
Mohr v. Williams, 104 N.W. 12 (Minn. 1905).
Moore v. Regents of the Univ. of Cal., 793 P.2d 479 (Cal. 1990).
Natanson v. Kline, 350 P.2d 1093 (Kan. 1960).
N.D. State Bd. of Med. Examiners v. Albertson (Nov. 22, 2013).
N.D. State Bd. of Med. Examiners v. Wynkoop, OAH File No. 20130085 (Nov. 22, 2013).
Nelson v. Corr. Med. Servs., 583 F.3d 522, 524–25 (8th Cir. 2009).
New Jersey v. TLO, 469 U.S. 325 (1984).
Newman v. City of Detroit, 281 Mich. 60, 62–63 (1937).
Newman v. Sathyavaglswaran, 287 F.3d 786 (9th Cir. 2002).
Norma Wons v. Public Health Tr. of Dade Cty, 500 So. 2d 679 (Fla. Dist. Ct. App. 1987).
Ohio & Miss. Ry. v. Cosby, 107 Ind. 32 (1886).
Oliphant v. Suquamish Indian Tribe, 435 U.S. 191 (1978).
Olmstead v. United States, 277 U.S. 438 (1928).
Ozawa v. United States, 260 U.S. 178 (1922).
Parker v. Elliott, 20 Va. (6 Munf.) 587 (1820).
People v. Belge, 372 N.Y.S.2d 798 (1975).
People v. Chavez, 176 P.2d 92, 94 (Cal. Dist. Ct. App. 1947)
Pers. Adm'r of Mass. v. Feeney, 442 U.S. 256 (1979).
Planned Parenthood v. Casey, 505 U.S. 833 (1992).
Planned Parenthood Association v. Herbert, 839 F.3d 1301 (10th Cir. 2016).
Planned Parenthood of Southeastern Pennsylvania v. Casey, 505 U.S. 833 (1992).
Plessy v. Ferguson, 163 U.S. 537 (1896).
Pratt v. Davis, 79 N.E. 562 (Ill. 1906).
Radice v. New York, 264 U.S. 292 (1924).
Regina v. Knight, 2 F. & F. 46 (1860).
Rex v. Izod, 20 Cox's Criminal Law Cases 690 (1904).
Robinson v. California, 370 U.S. 660 (1962).
Roe v. Wade, 410 U.S. 113 (1973).
Rostker v. Goldberg, 453 U.S. 57 (1981).
Salgo v. Leland Stanford Jr. Univ. Bd. of Trs., 317 P.2d 170 (Cal. Ct. App. 1957).
S.C. Bd. of Med. Examiners v. Hedgepath, 480 S.E.2d 724 (S.C. 1997).
Schloendorff v. Soc'y of N.Y. Hosp., 105 N.E. 92 (N.Y. 1914).
Shuai v. State, 966 N.E.2d 618 (Ind. Ct. App. 2012).
Skinner v. Oklahoma, 316 U.S. 535 (1942).
Stallman v. Youngquist, 531 N.E.2d 335 (Ill. 1988).
Stanford v. St. Louis-San Francisco Ry. Co., 214 Ala. 611 (1926).
State v. Buckhalter, 119 So. 3d 1015 (Miss. 2013).
State v. Mann, 13 N.C. 263 (1829).
State v. McKnight, 576 S.E.2d 168 (S.C. 2003).
State v. Osmus, 276 P.2d 469, 476 (Wyo. 1954).
State v. Paolella, 554 A.2d 702 (1989).
Steele v. St. Paul Fire & Marine Ins. Co., 371 So. 2d 843 (La. Ct. App. 1979).
Strauder v. West Virginia, 100 U.S. 303 (1880).
Struck v. Sec'y of Defense, 460 F.2d 1372 (9th Cir. 1971).
Taylor v. Louisiana, 419 U.S. 522 (1975).
Thimatariga v. Chambers, 416 A.2d 1326 (Md. Ct. Spec. App. 1980).

Thornburgh v. American College of Obstetricians and Gynecologists, 476 U.S. 747 (1986).
Thurman v. City of Torrington, 595 F. Supp. 1521 (1984).
Town of Castle Rock v. Gonzales, 543 U.S. 955 (2004).
United States v. Bhagat Singh Thind, 261 U.S. 204 (1923).
United States v. Virginia, 518 U.S. 515 (1996).
United States v. Westinghouse, 638 F.2d 570 (3d Cir. 1980).
Vorchheimer v. Sch. Dist. of Philadelphia, 532 F.2d 880 (3d Cir. 1976), aff'd, 430 U.S. 703 (1977).
Wengler v. Druggists Mutual Insurance Co., 446 U.S. 142 (1980).
Whalen v. Roe, 429 U.S. 589 (1977).
Whitner v. State, 492 S.E.2d 777 (S.C. 1997).
Whole Woman's Health v. Hellerstedt, 136 S. Ct. 2292 (2016).
Wons v. Public Health Trust of Dade Cnty., 500 So. 2d 679 (Fla. Dist. Ct. App. 1987).
Young v. United Parcel Serv., 135 S. Ct. 1338 (2015).

1.2 *Briefs*

Reply Brief of Appellant-Petitioner, Ferguson v. City of Charleston, 532 U.S. 67 (2001) (No. 99-936).
Brief of Respondents, Ferguson v. City of Charleston, 532 U.S. 67 (2001) (No. 99-936).
Brief of Appellant, Oral Argument Requested, Gibbs v. State, No. 2010-M-819-SCT (Miss. Nov. 12, 2010).
Brief for Appellants, Roe v. Wade, 410 U.S. 113 (1973) (No. 70-18), 1971 WL 128054.
Brief of Appellee, Shuai v. State, 966 N.E. 2d 619 (Ind. Ct. App. 2012), (No. 49A02-1106-CR-486).
Brief for the Petitioner, Struck v. Sec'y of Defense, 460 F.2d 1372 (9th Cir. 1971) (No. 72-178).

1.3 *Amicus Briefs*

Brief for ACLU et al. as Amici Curiae in Support of Appellant, Burton v. Florida, 49 So. 3d 263 (Fla. Dist. Ct. App. 2010).
Brief for the Am. Med. Ass'n as Amicus Curiae in Support of Neither Party, Ferguson v. City of Charleston, 532 U.S. 67 (2001) (No. 99-936).
Brief for Am. Pub. Health Ass'n et al. as Amici Curiae Supporting Petitioner, Ferguson v. City of Charleston, 532 U.S. 67 (2001) (No. 99-936), 2000 WL 33599645.
National Association of Social Workers et al. in Support of Petitioner, Brief of Amicus Curiae, Gibbs v. State, No. 2010-M-819 (Miss. May 19, 2010).
NOW Legal Defense and Education Fund, Amicus Brief, National Abortion Rights Action League et al., In re A.C., rehearing en banc, Sept. 6, 1988.

1.4 *Court Documents*

Canadian Judicial Council, In the Matter of an Inquiry Pursuant to S. 63(1) of the Judges Act Regarding the Honourable Justice Robin Camp, 3 (2016) (Can.).
Affidavit of Ms. Carder's Cancer Specialist at 6, dated Nov. 5, 1987, filed Nov. 10, 1987, In re A.C., Misc. No. 199-87 (D.C. Super. Ct. 1987).
Trials of War Criminals Before the Nuremberg Tribunals Under Control Council Law No. 10, (U.S. Gov't Printing Office, 1946–1949) [Nuremburg Code].

2 STATUTES AND LEGISLATIVE MATERIALS

2.1 *Statutes*

10 U.S.C. § 919(a) (2004).

18 U.S.C. § 1841 (2004).

20 U.S.C. § 1091(r)(1) (2012).

22 U.S.C. § 2151(b) (2012).

42 U.S.C. § 290dd-2(c).

42 U.S.C. § 300a-7.

42 U.S.C.A. § 675(5)(E) (West 2015).

42 U.S.C. § 1437d(q)(1)(A) (2012).

42 U.S.C. § 1983.

42 U.S.C. § 2000e-2(a).

75 Fed. Reg. at 15,599.

ALA. CODE § 26-15-3.2 (West 2006).

ALA. CODE § 26-23E-9 (West, Westlaw through 2016 Reg. Sess.) ARIZ. REV. STAT. ANN. §§ 13-604, 13-604.01, 13-703, 13-1102, 13-1103, 13-1104, 13-1105, 13-4062, 31-412, 41-1604.11, 41-1604.13.

ARIZ. REV. STAT. ANN. § 35-196.02 (2011) (West, Westlaw through 2d Reg. Sess. of 52d Leg. (2016)).

ARIZ. REV. STAT. ANN. § 36-2154 (2016) (West, Westlaw through 2d Reg. Sess. of 52d Leg. (2016)).

ARK. CODE ANN. § 20-16-1405 (West, Westlaw through end of 2016 3d Extraordinary Sess. of 90th Ark. Gen. Assemb.).

ARK. CODE ANN. § 20-16-1504 (West, Westlaw through 2016 3d Extraordinary Sess. of 90th Ark. Gen. Assemb.).

Comm'n on Prof'l Ethics of the New York State Bar Ass'n, Op. 479 (1978).

FLA. CONST.

FLA. STAT. ANN. § 39.201(2)(a) (West 2013).

FLA. STAT. ANN. § 316.192 (West 2010).

FLA. STAT. ANN. § 782.071 (West 2001).

GA. CODE ANN. §§ 19-8-40 to 19-8-43.

Health Insurance Portability and Accountability Act of 1996 ("HIPAA"), 45 C.F.R. pt. 164.

IOWA CODE ANN. § 707.7 (West 2011).

LA. REV. STAT. ANN. § 9:125 (2012).

MISS. CODE ANN. § 41-41-73 (West, Westlaw current through 2017 Reg. Sess.).

MISS. CODE ANN. § 41-41-107 (West, Westlaw through 2017 Reg. Sess.).

MISS. CODE ANN. § 97-3-19(B) (West 2013).

MISS. R. APP. PROC. 5(a) (2008).

MISS. CODE ANN. § 97-3-21(2) (West 2013).

MODEL CODE OF PROF'L RESPONSIBILITY r. 1.6 (A), (C) (AM. BAR ASS'N 2018).

N.D. CENT. CODE § 14-02.1–05.3 (West, Westlaw through 2017 Reg. Sess. of 65th Leg. Assemb.).

S. Con. Res. 4009, 63d Leg. Assemb. (N.D. 2013).

S.D. CODIFIED LAWS § 34-23A-56 (West, Westlaw current through 2016 Sess. Laws).

TEX. ADMIN. CODE, tit. 25, §§ 139.4, 139.5, 139.23, 139.31, 139.43, 139.46, 139.48, 139.49, 139.50, 139.55, 139.58, 139.59 (2009).

Tex. Health & Safety Code Ann. §§ 171.0031, 171.041–.048, 171.061–.064 (West 2013).
Tex. Health & Safety Code Ann. § 171.044 (West, Westlaw current through end of 2015 Reg. Sess. of 84th Leg.).
Tex. Health & Safety Code Ann. §§ 245.010–.011, 164.052, 164.055 (West 2015).
Tex. Penal Code Ann. §§ 1191–94, 1196 (1961) (historical).
Utah Code Ann. § 76-5-201(4) (2010).
Wisc. Stat. Ann. § 48,133 (West 2013).

2.2 *Legislation*

Act of July 18, 2013, Ch. 1 (H.B. 2), §§ 1–12, 2013 Tex. Sess. Law Serv. 4795-802 (West).
H.B. 462, 2010 Gen. Sess. (Utah 2010).
H.B. 1243, 2011 Leg., 82d Sess. (Tex. 2011).
H.B. 2, 2013 Leg., 2d Called Sess. (Tex. 2013).
Housing Opportunity Program Extension Act of 1996, Pub. L. No. 104-120, 110 Stat. 834.
International Protecting Girls by Preventing Child Marriage Act, S. 414, 112th Cong. (as passed by Senate, May 24, 2012).
Pub. L. No. 97-121, § 525, 95 Stat. 1657 (1981).
Pub. L. No. 99-500, § 101(f), 100 Stat. 1783-217 (1986)
Pub. L. No. 105-277, § 101, 112 Stat. 2681-154 (1998).
Pub. L. No. 111-117, § 508(d)(1), 123 Stat. 3034, 3280 (2009).
S.F. 446, 85th Gen. Assemb., Reg. Sess. (Iowa 2013).
S.F. 704, 90th Sess. (Minn. 2017).

2.3 *Legislative Reports*

Amendment No. 68, H.R. Rep. No. 94-1555, at 3 (1976) (Conf. Rep.).
Minn. Dep't. of Health, Ctr. for Health Statistics, Report to the Legislature: Induced Abortions in Minnesota, Jan.–Dec. 2015 (July 2016).
Nat'l. Conference State Leg., Fetal Homicide Laws (May 2018).
Nat'l. Conf. State Leg. 2011 Ballot Measures: Election Results (Nov. 9, 2011)

2.4 *Legislative Testimony*

119 Cong. Rec. 32,292, 32,293 (1973) (statement of Sen. Helms).
119 Cong. Rec. 39,619, 39,632 (1973) (statement of Rep. Abzug).
122 Cong. Rec. 20,410 (1976) (statement of Rep. Hyde).
Durban, Dick, *Opening Statement, Reassessing Solitary Confinement: The Human Rights, Fiscal and Public Safety Consequences: Hearing Before the Subcomm. on the Constitution, Civil Rights and Human Rights*, S. Judiciary Comm., June 19, 2012.
Haney, Craig, *Testimony of Craig Haney, Reassessing Solitary Confinement Hearing*, June 19, 2012.
Krauthammer, Charles, *Children of Cocaine*, Cong. Rec., Proceedings and Debates of 101st Cong., Aug. 1, 1989.
Leahy, Patrick, *Statement of The Honorable Patrick Leahy, Reassessing Solitary Confinement Hearing*, June 19, 2012.

3 CIVIL SOCIETY AND ADVOCACY ORGANIZATIONS

ADVOCATES FOR YOUTH, ABSTINENCE-ONLY-UNTIL-MARRIAGE PROGRAMS: INEFFECTIVE, UNETHICAL, AND POOR PUBLIC HEALTH, POLICY BRIEF (2007).

AM. COLL. OF NURSE MIDWIVES, POSITION STATEMENT: SHACKLING/RESTRAINT OF PREGNANT WOMEN WHO ARE INCARCERATED (approved June 2012).

AM. COLL. OF OBSTETRICIANS & GYNECOLOGISTS, HEALTH CARE FOR PREGNANT AND POSTPARTUM INCARCERATED WOMEN AND ADOLESCENT FEMALES, COMM. OP. 511 (2011).

AM. MED. ASS'N, AMA CODE OF ETHICS, OPINION 5.05: CONFIDENTIALITY (last updated June 2007).

AM. PUBLIC HEALTH ASS'N, REDUCING US MATERNAL MORTALITY AS A HUMAN RIGHT, Policy No. 201114 (Nov. 1, 2011).

AMNESTY INT'L, CRIMINALIZING PREGNANCY: POLICING PREGNANT WOMEN WHO USE DRUGS IN THE USA (2017).

Bush-Baskette, Stephanie & Vanessa Patino, *The National Council on Crime and Delinquency's Evaluation of the Project Development of National Institute of Corrections/Child Welfare League of America's Planning and Intervention Sites Funded to Address the Needs of Children of Incarcerated Parents*, NAT'L COUNCIL ON CRIME & DELINQUENCY (Oct. 2004).

BUTCHART, ALEXANDER & ALISON PHINNEY HARVEY, WORLD HEALTH ORG. & INT'L SOC'Y FOR PREVENTION OF CHILD ABUSE & NEGLECT, PREVENTING CHILD MALTREATMENT: A GUIDE TO TAKING ACTION AND GENERATING EVIDENCE (2006).

Cadoff, Becca, *States Aim to Make the Grade When it Comes to Shackling Pregnant Prisoners*, ACLU (Mar. 31, 2011, 7:35 PM), http://www.aclu.org/blog/prisoners-rights-reproductive-freedom-womens-rights/states-aim-make-grade-when-it-comes.

CTR. FOR HEALTH & GENDER EQUITY, *Global Gag Rule*, http://www.genderhealth.org/the_issues/us_foreign_policy/global_gag_rule.

CTR. FOR REPRODUCTIVE RIGHTS, PUNISHING WOMEN FOR THEIR BEHAVIOR DURING PREGNANCY (Sept. 2000).

CTR. FOR SUBSTANCE ABUSE RESEARCH, LONG TERM DRUG TREATMENT OUTCOMES IN MARYLAND: RESULTS OF THE TOPPS II PROJECT (2003).

Cool, Lisa Collier, *Could You Be Forced to Have a C-Section?*, ADVOCATES FOR PREGNANT WOMEN (May 2005).

Courtney, Mark E. et al., *Midwest Evaluation of the Adult Functioning of Former Foster Youth: Conditions of Youth Preparing to Leave State Care*, CHAPIN HALL CTR. FOR CHILD. (2004), https://www.chapinhall.org/research/midwest-evaluation-of-the-adult-functioning-of-former-foster-youth/.

DOLAN, KATE ET AL., BECKLEY FOUNDATION DRUG POLICY PROGRAMME, PRISONS AND DRUGS: A GLOBAL REVIEW OF INCARCERATION, DRUG USE AND DRUG SERVICES (2007).

ECON. POLICY INST., *The Cost of Child Care in Alabama* (Apr. 2016), https://www.epi.org/child-care-costs-in-the-united-states/#/AL.

FROST, NATASHA A., ET AL., INST. ON WOMEN & CRIMINAL JUSTICE, HARD HIT: THE GROWTH IN THE IMPRISONMENT OF WOMEN, 1977–2004 (2006).

Gayner, Jeffrey, B., *The Contract with America: Implementing New Ideas in the U.S.*, HERITAGE FOUND. (Oct. 12, 1995).

GLOBAL JUSTICE CTR., THE RIGHT TO AN ABORTION FOR GIRLS AND WOMEN RAPED IN ARMED CONFLICT (2011), http://globaljusticecenter.net/documents/LegalBrief.RightToAnAbortion.February2011.pdf.

GREENE, MEGAN & LESLIE R. WOLFE, CTR. FOR WOMEN POLICY STUDIES, PREGNANCY EXCLUSIONS IN STATE LIVING WILL AND MEDICAL PROXY STATUTES, (Aug. 2012).

GUTTMACHER INST., *Counseling and Waiting Periods for Abortion* (Mar. 1, 2017).

GUTTMACHER INST., *State Facts About Unintended Pregnancy: Texas* (Sept. 2016).

GUTTMACHER INST., *Substance Use During Pregnancy* (Oct. 1, 2018), https://www.guttmacher.org/state-policy/explore/substance-use-during-pregnancy.

GUTTMACHER INST., *Teen Pregnancy*, https://www.guttmacher.org/united-states/teens/teen-pregnancy?gclid=CjwKCAjwnrjrBRAMEiwAXsCc44JXs5qtl64ErzQ28pbSpZROcL_R30I2eZgFNoCtxZOlc3808BIZ8x0Com4QAvD_BwE.

GUTTMACHER INST., *Unintended Pregnancy in the United States* (Jan. 2019).

HARRISON, ELIZABETH ET AL., WOMEN'S & CHILDREN'S HEALTH POLICY CTR., JOHNS HOPKINS UNIVERSITY. ENVIRONMENTAL TOXICANTS AND MATERNAL AND CHILD HEALTH: AN EMERGING PUBLIC HEALTH CHALLENGE (2009).

HUMAN RIGHTS WATCH, "WE HAVE THE PROMISES OF THE WORLD" – WOMEN'S RIGHTS IN AFGHANISTAN (2009).

IEG WORLD BANK, DELIVERING THE MILLENNIUM DEVELOPMENT GOALS TO REDUCE MATERNAL AND CHILD MORTALITY: A SYSTEMATIC REVIEW OF IMPACT EVALUATION EVIDENCE (2016).

INT'L ASS'N OF POLICE CHIEFS, TRAINING KEY NO. 16, HANDLING DISTURBANCE CALLS (1968–69), *quoted in* Sue E. Eisenberg & Patricia L. Micklow, *The Assaulted Wife: "Catch 22" Revisited*, 3 WOMEN'S RTS. L. REP. 138 (1977).

INT'L HUMAN RIGHTS CLINIC ET AL., THE SHACKLING OF INCARCERATED PREGNANT WOMEN: A HUMAN RIGHTS VIOLATION COMMITTED REGULARLY IN THE UNITED STATES: AN ALTERNATIVE REPORT TO THE FOURTH PERIODIC REPORT OF THE UNITED STATES OF AMERICA SUBMITTED PURSUANT TO THE INTERNATIONAL COVENANT ON CIVIL AND POLITICAL RIGHTS (Aug. 2013).

JOHNSTON, LLOYD D. ET AL., MONITORING THE FUTURE: NATIONAL SURVEY RESULTS ON DRUG USE 1975–2014, VOL. 2 COLLEGE STUDENTS & ADULTS AGES 19–55 (2015).

JONES, KELLY M., INT'L FOOD POLICY RESEARCH INST., EVALUATING THE MEXICO CITY POLICY: HOW US FOREIGN POLICY AFFECTS FERTILITY OUTCOMES AND CHILD HEALTH IN GHANA (2011).

KAISER FAMILY FOUND., THE MEXICO CITY POLICY: AN EXPLAINER (2017).

KAISER FAMILY FOUND., THE U.S. GOVERNMENT AND GLOBAL HEALTH (2016).

KAISER FAMILY FOUND., THE U.S. GOVERNMENT AND INTERNATIONAL FAMILY PLANNING AND REPRODUCTIVE HEALTH: STATUTORY REQUIREMENTS AND POLICES (2017).

KOHLER, HANS-PETER, DO CHILDREN BRING HAPPINESS AND PURPOSE IN LIFE? (Dec. 10, 2010), http://www.ssc.upenn.edu/~hpkohler/working-papers/kohl11dw.pdf.

Kolbi-Molinas, Alexa, *Pregnant Women Need Support, Not Prison*, ACLU (Mar. 31, 2011, 3:36 PM), https://www.aclu.org/blog/reproductive-freedom/pregnant-women-need-support-not-prison.

MAI, CHRIS & RAM SUBRAMANIAN, VERA INST. OF JUSTICE, THE PRICE OF PRISONS, https://www.vera.org/publications/price-of-prisons-2015-state-spending-trends/price-of-prisons-2015-state-spending-trends/price-of-prisons-2015-state-spending-trends-prison-spending.

MINN. COAL. FOR BATTERED WOMEN, FEMICIDE REPORT (Jan. 31, 2017).

MIRON, JEFFREY A. & KATHERINE WALDCOCK, CATO INST., THE BUDGETARY IMPACT OF ENDING DRUG PROHIBITION (2010).

NARAL FOUND., CHOICES: WOMEN SPEAK OUT ABOUT ABORTION (1997).

Nash, Elizabeth et al., *Laws Affecting Reproductive Health and Rights: 2013 State Policy Review*, GUTTMACHER INST., http://www.guttmacher.org/statecenter/updates/2013/statetrends42013.html.

Nat'l Advocates for Pregnant Women, Media Advisory, Petition Filed Today Seeking U.S. Supreme Court Review of Unprecedented South Carolina Decision Treating a Woman Who

Suffered a Stillbirth as a Murderer (May 27, 2003), http://www.advocatesforpregnantwomen.org /issues/prmcknight.htm.

Nat'l Advocates for Pregnant Women, Press Release, Florida Doctor Threat of Arrest of Pregnant Woman Dangerous and Without Legal Authority (Mar. 6, 2013).

Nat'l Advocates for Pregnant Women, Press Release, Supreme Court of New Mexico Strikes Down State's Attempt to Convict Woman Struggling with Addiction During Pregnancy (May 11, 2007).

NAT'L CTR. FOR THE VICTIMS OF CRIME, *Child Sexual Abuse Statistics.*

NAT'L CHILD TRAUMATIC STRESS NETWORK, *Child Sexual Abuse Fact Sheet* (Apr. 2009).

NAT'L COAL. AGAINST DOMESTIC VIOLENCE, *National Statistics*, http://ncadv.org/learn-more /statistics.

NAT'L WOMEN'S LAW CTR., 2013 STATE LEVEL ABORTION RESTRICTIONS: AN EXTREME OVERREACH INTO WOMEN'S REPRODUCTIVE HEALTH CARE (Jan. 28, 2014).

PAI, NO EXCEPTIONS: HOW THE HELMS AMENDMENT HURTS WOMEN AND ENDANGERS LIVES (2015).

PALTROW, LYNN M., CRIMINAL PROSECUTIONS AGAINST PREGNANT WOMEN: NATIONAL UPDATE AND OVERVIEW (1992).

PAN AMERICAN HEALTH ORG., DOMESTIC PARTNER VIOLENCE DURING PREGNANCY (2011).

PEW RES. CTR., ISSUE RANKS LOWER ON THE AGENDA: SUPPORT FOR ABORTION SLIPS (2009).

POPULATION ACTION INT'L, THE GLOBAL GAG RULE & CONTRACEPTIVE SUPPLIES (2017).

PROJECT PREVENTION, *Objectives*, http://www.projectprevention.org/objectives/.

RAPE, ABUSE & INCEST NAT'L NETWORK, *Victims of Sexual Violence: Statistics.*

RAPE, ABUSE & INCEST NAT'L NETWORK, *Who Are the Victims?*

REPUBLICAN PARTY PLATFORM COMM., REPUBLICAN PLATFORM 2016 (2016).

S. POVERTY LAW CTR., *Sterilization Abuse*, http://www.splcenter.org/seeking-justice/case-docket/relf-v-weinberger.

JUSTICE POLICY INST., *Substance Abuse Treatment and Public Safety* (2008).

S.C. Advocates for Pregnant Women, *South Carolina: First in the Nation for Arresting African-American Pregnant Women – Last in the Nation for Funding Drug and Alcohol Treatment*, Briefing Paper to Democratic Presidential Candidates (Jan. 8, 2003).

TEXAS POLICY EVALUATION PROJECT, KNOWLEDGE, OPINION AND EXPERIENCE RELATED TO ABORTION SELF-INDUCTION IN TEXAS (Nov. 17, 2015).

TEXAS POLICY EVALUATION PROJECT, TEXAS WOMEN'S EXPERIENCES ATTEMPTING SELF-INDUCED ABORTION IN TEXAS (Nov. 17, 2015).

TRAVIS, JEREMY ET AL., URBAN INST., FROM PRISON TO HOME: THE DIMENSIONS AND CONSEQUENCES OF PRISONER REENTRY (June 2001).

UNCHAINED AT LAST, *About Arranged Forced Marriage.*

UNCHAINED AT LAST, *Shocking Statistics.*

WALMSLEY, ROY, INTERNATIONAL CTR. FOR PRISON STUDIES, WORLD PRISON POPULATION LIST (9th ed. 2011).

WARREN, JENIFER, PEW CTR. ON THE STATES, ONE IN 31: THE LONG REACH OF AMERICAN CORRECTIONS (2009).

POPULATION ACTION INT'L, *With a Stroke of the Pen – Trump's Global Gag Rule Dramatically Expands Harmful Health Impacts*, (last updated Jan. 26, 2017), http://pai.org/newsletters/ stroke-pen-trumps-global-gag-rule-dramatically-expands-harmful-health-impacts.

WOMEN'S PRISON ASS'N, QUICK FACTS: WOMEN & CRIMINAL JUSTICE – 2009 (2009).

WORLD HEALTH ORG., DOMESTIC PARTNER VIOLENCE DURING PREGNANCY (2011).

WORLD HEALTH ORG., SAFE ABORTION: TECHNICAL AND POLICY GUIDANCE FOR HEALTH SYSTEMS (2d ed. 2012).

WORLD HEALTH ORG., UNSAFE ABORTION: GLOBAL AND REGIONAL ESTIMATES OF THE INCIDENCE OF UNSAFE ABORTION AND ASSOCIATED MORTALITY IN 2008 (6th ed. 2011).

WORLD HEALTH ORG. ET AL., TRENDS IN MATERNAL MORTALITY: 1990 TO 2008 (2010).

4 GOVERNMENT REPORTS

18TH WORLD MEDICAL ASSOCIATION GENERAL ASSEMBLY, DECLARATION OF HELSINKI: ETHICAL PRINCIPLES FOR MEDICAL RESEARCH INVOLVING HUMAN SUBJECTS (1964).

BLANCHFIELD, LUISA, CONG. RESEARCH SERV., R40750, THE U.N. CONVENTION ON THE ELIMINATION OF ALL FORMS OF DISCRIMINATION AGAINST WOMEN (CEDAW): ISSUES IN THE U.S. RATIFICATION DEBATE (2011), https://fas.org/sgp/crs/row/R40750.pdf [https://perma.cc/3GBS-UARZ].

BLANC, JOHN & MATTHEW FRIEDMAN, U.S. AGENCY FOR INTERNATIONAL DEVELOPMENT., MEXICO CITY POLICY IMPLEMENTATION STUDY (1990).

BONCZAR, THOMAS P., BUREAU OF JUSTICE STATISTICS, U.S. DEP'T OF JUSTICE, PREVALENCE OF IMPRISONMENT IN THE U.S. POPULATION, 1974–2001, (2003).

BUREAU OF JUSTICE STATISTICS, U.S. DEP'T OF JUSTICE, NATIONAL CRIMINAL VICTIMIZATION SURVEY: CRIMINAL VICTIMIZATION, 2010 (Sept. 2011).

CARSON, ANN E., U.S. DEPARTMENT OF JUSTICE, PRISONERS IN 2013 (2009).

CARSON, ANN E. & WILLIAM J. SABOL, BUREAU OF JUSTICE STATISTICS, U.S. DEP'T OF JUSTICE, PRISONERS IN 2011 (2012).

CENT. INTELLIGENCE AGENCY, *World Factbook: Maternal Mortality Rate*.

CHILDREN'S BUREAU, U.S. DEP'T OF HEALTH & HUMAN SERVS., CHILD MALTREATMENT 2014 (2016).

CTR. FOR BEHAVIORAL HEALTH STATS. & QUALITY ET AL., RESULTS FROM THE 2010 NATIONAL SURVEY ON DRUG USE AND HEALTH: SUMMARY OF NATIONAL FINDINGS (Sept. 2011).

CTRS. FOR DISEASE CONTROL & PREVENTION, *About Teen Pregnancy* (May 9, 2017).

CTRS. FOR DISEASE CONTROL & PREVENTION, *Pregnancy Mortality Surveillance System*.

CTRS. FOR DISEASE CONTROL & PREVENTION, *Sexual Violence and Consequences*.

CTRS. FOR DISEASE CONTROL & PREVENTION, *Stats of the State of Minnesota* (2013–2014).

CTRS. FOR DISEASE CONTROL & PREVENTION, *Table 50. Use of Selected Substances in the Past Month Among Persons Aged 12 and Over, by Age, Sex, Race, and Hispanic Origin: United States, Selected Years 2002–2016* (2017), https://www.cdc.gov/nchs/data/hus/2017/050.pdf.

CTRS. FOR DISEASE CONTROL & PREVENTION, *Tobacco Use and Pregnancy* (last updated Sept. 23, 2013).

DEP'T OF DEF., *Fact Sheet on Department of Defense Annual Report on Sexual Assault in the Military for Fiscal 2011* (Apr. 13, 2012).

DIRECTORATE-GEN. FOR EXTERNAL POLICIES, EUR. PARLIAMENT, SEXUAL VIOLENCE AGAINST MINORS IN LATIN AMERICA (2016).

EXEC. OFFICE OF THE PRESIDENT OF THE U.S., FY 2012 BUDGET AND PERFORMANCE SUMMARY: COMPANION TO THE NATIONAL DRUG CONTROL STRATEGY 5 (2011).

EXEC. OFFICE OF THE PRESIDENT OF THE U.S., NATIONAL DRUG CONTROL STRATEGY: FY 2010 BUDGET SUMMARY (2009).

GLAZE, LAUREN E., & LAURA M. MARUSCHAK, BUREAU OF JUSTICE STATISTICS, U.S. DEP'T OF JUSTICE, PARENTS IN PRISON AND THEIR MINOR CHILDREN (2008).

INDEP. EVALUATION GRP., DELIVERING THE MILLENNIUM DEVELOPMENT GOALS TO REDUCE MATERNAL AND CHILD MORTALITY: A SYSTEMATIC REVIEW OF IMPACT EVALUATION EVIDENCE (2016).

KILPATRICK, DEAN G. ET AL., NAT'L INST. OF JUSTICE, YOUTH VICTIMIZATION: PREVALENCE AND IMPLICATIONS (Apr. 2003).

MCVAY, DOUG ET AL., JUSTICE POLICY INST., TREATMENT OR INCARCERATION?: NATIONAL AND STATE FINDINGS ON THE EFFICACY AND COST SAVINGS OF DRUG TREATMENT VERSUS IMPRISONMENT (2004).

MINN. DEP'T OF HEALTH, 2015 *Minnesota County Health Tables, Mortality Table 4: Minnesota's 10 Leading Causes of Death* (2015).

MINN. DEP'T OF HEALTH, THE HEALTH OF MINNESOTA, STATEWIDE HEALTH ASSESSMENT: PART TWO (May 2012).

NAT'L INST. OF CHILD HEALTH & HUMAN DEV., *What Is Prenatal Care and Why Is It Important?*, http://www.nichd.nih.gov/health/topics/pregnancy/conditioninfo/Pages/prenatal-care.aspx.

NAT'L INST. ON DRUG ABUSE, U.S. DEP'T OF HEALTH & HUMAN SERVS., DRUG ABUSE AMONG RACIAL/ETHNIC MINORITIES (rev. ed. 2003).

NOWELS, LARRY, CONG. RESEARCH SERV., RL30830, INTERNATIONAL FAMILY PLANNING: THE "MEXICO CITY" POLICY 4 n.7 (2001).

OFFICE OF NATIONAL DRUG CONTROL POLICY, A *Drug Policy for the 21st Century*, https://obamawhitehouse.archives.gov/ondcp/drugpolicyreform.

OLSON, MARSHA S. & SUSAN S. STUMPF, PREGNANCY IN THE NAVY: IMPACT ON ABSENTEEISM, ATTRITION, AND WORKGROUP MORALE (1978).

PLANTY, MICHAEL ET AL., BUREAU OF JUSTICE STATISTICS, U.S DEP'T OF JUSTICE, FEMALE VICTIMS OF SEXUAL VIOLENCE 1994–2010 (Mar. 2013).

SENTENCING PROJECT, REPORT OF THE SENTENCING PROJECT TO THE UNITED NATIONS HUMAN RIGHTS COMMITTEE REGARDING RACIAL DISPARITIES IN THE UNITED STATES CRIMINAL JUSTICE SYSTEM (2013).

STEWART, DONNA E. ET AL., TORONTO PUBLIC HEALTH, POSTPARTUM DEPRESSION: LITERATURE REVIEW OF RISK FACTORS AND INTERVENTIONS (2003).

Tadlock, John, Report of Officer John Tadlock, Blountstown Police Department, Dec. 21, 2015.

TEXAS POLICY EVALUATION PROJECT, *Access to Abortion Care in the Wake of HB2* (July 1, 2014).

U.N. Conference on Population (2d. Sess.), Policy Statement of the United States of America (Aug. 6–13, 1984).

U.N. POPULATION FUND, ADOLESCENT GIRLS IN DISASTER & CONFLICT: INTERVENTIONS FOR IMPROVING ACCESS TO SEXUAL AND REPRODUCTIVE HEALTH SERVICES (2016).

U.S. AGENCY FOR INT'L DEV., USAID GUIDANCE FOR IMPLEMENTING THE SILJANDER AMENDMENT (PROHIBITION ON LOBBYING FOR OR AGAINST ABORTION) (May 22, 2014).

U.S. AGENCY FOR INT'L DEV., STANDARD PROVISIONS FOR NON-U.S. NONGOVERNMENTAL ORGANIZATIONS 87 (Oct. 4, 2017).

U.S. DEP'T OF AGRIC (USDA), *The Cost of Raising a Child: $233,610* (Mar. 2017), https://www.usda.gov/media/blog/2017/01/13/cost-raising-child.

U.S. DEP'T OF AGRIC., *Supplemental Nutrition Assistance Program*, https://www.fns.usda.gov/snap/eligible-food-items.

U.S. DEP'T OF HEALTH & HUMAN SERVS., CHILD MALTREATMENT 1996: REPORTS FROM THE STATES TO THE NATIONAL CHILD ABUSE AND NEGLECT DATA SYSTEM (1998).

U.S. DEP'T OF HEALTH AND HUMAN SERVS., THE HEALTH CONSEQUENCES OF SMOKING – 50 YEARS OF PROGRESS: A REPORT OF THE SURGEON GENERAL (2014).

U.S. DEP'T OF HEALTH AND HUMAN SERVS., *Postpartum Depression Facts.*

U.S. Gov't Accountability Office, GAO/RCED-83-168, Siting of Hazardous Waste Landfills and Their Correlation with Racial and Economic Status of Surrounding Communities (1983).

U.S. Sentencing Comm'n, *Quick Facts: Mandatory Minimum Penalties* (2011).

5 BOOKS

Allen, James et al., Without Sanctuary (2000).

Baum, Dan, Smoke and Mirrors: The War on Drugs and the Politics of Failure (1996).

Bertrin, Joan, *Reproductive Hazards in the Workplace, in* Reproductive Laws for the 1990s 277 (Sherrill Cohen & Nadine Taub eds., 1989).

Boyd, Susan, Mothers and Illicit Drugs: Transcending the Myths (1999).

Burton, Sandra, Becoming Ms. Burton: From Prison to Recovery to Leading the Fight for Incarcerated Women (2017).

Cahn, Naomi & June Carbone, Red Families v. Blue Families: Legal Polarization and the Creation of Culture (2011).

Cohen, Adam, Imbeciles: The Supreme Court, American Eugenics, and the Sterilization of Carrie Buck (2016).

Coke, Edward, The Third Part of The Institutes of the Laws of England: Concerning High Treason, and Other Pleas of the Crown, and Criminal Causes (1680).

Comm. on Opportunities in Drug Abuse Res., Inst. of Med., Pathways of Addiction: Opportunities in Drug Abuse Research (1996).

Dayan, Colin, The Law Is a White Dog: How Legal Rituals Make and Unmake Persons (2013).

Entezar, Ehsan M., Afghanistan 101: Understanding Afghan Culture (2008).

Epstein, Deborah & Lisa A. Goodman, *Domestic Violence Victims' Experiences in the Legal System, in* Stress, Trauma, and Wellbeing in the Legal System 45 (Monica K. Miller & Brian H. Bornstein eds., 2013).

Epstein, Deborah & Lisa A. Goodman, *The Justice System Response to Domestic Violence, in* 2 Violence Against Women and Children 215 (Jacquelyn W. White et al. eds., 2010).

Feinberg, Joel, *The Expressive Function of Punishment, in* Doing & Deserving: Essays in the Theory of Responsibility (1970).

Finigan, Michael, Societal Outcomes and Cost Savings of Drug and Alcohol Treatment in the State of Oregon (1996).

Finkelhor, David, Child Sexual Abuse: New Theory and Research (1984).

Foucault, Michel, Discipline and Punish: The Birth of the Prison (Alan Sheridan trans., 1977).

Fraser, Gertrude Jacinta, African American Midwifery in the South (1998).

Gehshan, Shelly, A Step Toward Recovery: Improving Access to Substance Abuse Treatment for Pregnant and Parenting Women (1993)

Gómez, Laura, Misconceiving Mothers: Legislators, Prosecutors, and the Politics of Prenatal Drug Exposure (1997).

Gustafson, Kaaryn S., Cheating Welfare: Public Assistance and the Criminalization of Poverty (2011).

Hale, Matthew, The History of the Pleas of the Crown (1736).

Hallman, Nai, The Southern Regional Project on Infant Mortality: A 20-Year Retrospective (2005).

HILL COLLINS, PATRICIA, BLACK SEXUAL POLITICS: AFRICAN AMERICANS, GENDER, AND THE NEW RACISM (2005).

HOFFMAN, S.D., KIDS HAVING KIDS: ECONOMIC COSTS AND SOCIAL CONSEQUENCES OF TEEN PREGNANCY (2008).

JACOBS, JAMES B., THE ETERNAL CRIMINAL RECORD (2015).

JEFFERSON, THOMAS, NOTES ON THE STATE OF VIRGINIA (electronic ed., 2006), https://docsouth .unc.edu/southlit/jefferson/jefferson.html

Johnson, Rucker C., *Ever-Increasing Levels of Parental Incarceration and the Consequences for Children*, in DO PRISONS MAKE US SAFER?: THE BENEFITS AND COSTS OF THE PRISON BOOM 177 (Steven Raphael & Michael A. Stoll eds., 2009).

JOHNSON, SHERRY, FORGIVING THE UNFORGIVABLE (2013).

JORDAN, WINTHROP D., WHITE OVER BLACK: AMERICAN ATTITUDES TOWARD THE NEGRO 1550–1812 (1977).

MACKINNON, CATHARINE A., WOMEN'S LIVES, MEN'S LAWS (2005).

MCCAIN, JOHN & MARK SALTER, FAITH OF MY FATHERS (1999).

MURRAY, PAULI, THE AUTOBIOGRAPHY OF A BLACK ACTIVIST, FEMINIST, LAWYER, PRIEST, AND POET (1987).

Murray, Pauli, *The Liberation of Black Women*, in WOMEN: A FEMINIST PERSPECTIVE 351 (Jo Freeman ed., 1975).

MURRAY, PAULI, STATES' LAWS ON RACE AND COLOR (1951).

NARAL FOUNDATION, CHOICES: WOMEN SPEAK OUT ABOUT ABORTION (1997).

NAZI DOCTORS AND THE NUREMBERG CODE (George J. Annas et al. eds., 1992).

NUSSBAUM, MARTHA C., HIDING FROM HUMANITY: DISGUST, SHAME, AND THE LAW (2004).

PARENTS IN PRISON, THE SENTENCING PROJECT (2012).

REAGAN, LESLIE J., WHEN ABORTION WAS A CRIME: WOMEN, MEDICINE, AND LAW IN THE UNITED STATES, 1867–1973 (1997).

ROBERTS, DOROTHY, KILLING THE BLACK BODY (1997).

Rowland Hogue, Carol J., *Demographics & Exposures*, in STILLBIRTH: PREDICTION, PREVENTION AND MANAGEMENT 57 (Catherine Y. Spong ed., 2011).

ROYCE, JOSIAH, THE PHILOSOPHY OF LOYALTY (1930).

SCHOEN, JOHANNA, ABORTION AFTER ROE (2015).

Siegel, Reva, *Gender and the United States Constitution: Equal Protection, Privacy, and Federalism*, in THE GENDER OF CONSTITUTIONAL JURISPRUDENCE 306 (Beverley Baines & Ruth Rubio-Marin eds., 2005).

Sommerville, Diane Miller, *Rape, Race, and Castration in Slave Law in the Colonial and Early South*, in THE DEVIL'S LANE: SEX AND RACE IN THE EARLY SOUTH 74 (Catherine Clinton & Michele Gillespie eds., 1997).

STANFORD, SIR WILLIAM, LES PLEES DEL CORON (1557).

STATES' LAWS ON RACE AND COLOR (Pauli Murray ed., Univ. Ga. Press 1997) (1951).

STEPHEN, JAMES FITZJAMES, LIBERTY, EQUALITY, FRATERNITY (Stuart D. Warner, ed., Liberty Fund 1993) (1874).

STIEHM, JUDITH HICKS, ARMS AND THE ENLISTED WOMAN (1989).

STORER, HORATIO ROBINSON, ON CRIMINAL ABORTION IN AMERICA (1860).

STORER, HORATIO ROBINSON, WHY NOT? A BOOK FOR EVERY WOMAN (1868).

TALTY, STEPHAN, MULATTO AMERICA: AT THE CROSSROADS OF BLACK AND WHITE CULTURE; A SOCIAL HISTORY (2003).

TYSON, TIMOTHY, RADIO FREE DIXIE: ROBERT F. WILLIAMS AND THE ROOTS OF BLACK POWER (2001).

UNEQUAL TREATMENT: CONFRONTING RACIAL AND ETHNIC DISPARITIES IN HEALTH CARE (Brian D. Smedley et. al. eds., 2003).

Vijayakumar, Lakshmi et al., *Socio-Economic, Cultural and Religious Factors Affecting Suicide Prevention in Asia*, in SUICIDE AND SUICIDE PREVENTION IN ASIA 19 (Herbert Hendin et al. eds., 2008).

VILLANUEVA, CHANDRA KRING, INST. ON WOMEN & CRIMINAL JUSTICE, WOMEN'S PRISON ASSOCIATION, MOTHERS, INFANTS AND IMPRISONMENT: A NATIONAL LOOK AT PRISON NURSERIES AND COMMUNITY-BASED ALTERNATIVES (Sarah B. From & Georgia Lerner eds., 2009).

VUIC, KARA DIXON, OFFICER, NURSE, WOMAN: THE ARMY NURSE CORPS IN THE VIETNAM WAR (2010).

WALMSLEY, ROY, WORLD FEMALE IMPRISONMENT LIST (2d ed. 2013).

WYATT-BROWN, BERTRAM, SOUTHERN HONOR: ETHICS AND BEHAVIOR IN THE OLD SOUTH (1982).

6 ARTICLES

6.1 *Law Journals*

Albiston, Catherine & Laura Beth Nielson, *Welfare Queens and Other Fairy Tales: Welfare Reform and Unconstitutional Reproductive Controls*, 38 HOW. L.J. 473 (1995).

Alexander, Elizabeth, *Unshackling Shawanna: The Battle over Chaining Women Prisoners During Labor and Delivery*, 32 U. ARK. LITTLE ROCK L. REV. 435 (2010).

Appell, Annette, *"Bad Mothers" and Spanish Speaking Caregivers*, 7 NEVADA L.J 759 (2007).

Baio, Jo-Anne M., *Loss of Consortium: A Derivative Injury Giving Rise to a Separate Cause of Action*, 50 FORDHAM L. REV. 1344 (1982).

Banashek, Kathryn S., *Maternal Prenatal Negligence Does Not Give Rise to a Cause of Action*, *Stallman v. Youngquist*, 125 *Ill. 2d* 267, 531 N.E.2d 335 (1988), 68 WASH. U. L.Q. 189 (1990).

Bardaglio, Peter W., *Rape and the Law in the Old South: Calculated to Excite Indignation in Every Heart*, 60 J. S. HIST. 749 (1994).

Barot, Sneha, *Abortion Restrictions in U.S. Foreign Aid: The History and Harms of the Helms Amendment*, GUTTMACHER POL'Y REV., Summer 2013.

Bartlett, Katharine, *Pregnancy and the Constitution: The Uniqueness Trap*, 62 CAL. L. REV. 1532 (1974).

Bhargava, Shalini, *Challenging Punishment and Privatization: A Response to the Conviction of Regina McKnight*, 39 HARV. C.R.-C.L. L. REV. 513 (2004).

Bibas, Stephanos, *Prosecutorial Regulation Versus Prosecutorial Accountability*, 157 U. PA. L. REV. 959 (2009).

Boonstra, Heather D., & Elizabeth Nash, *A Surge of State Abortion Restrictions Puts Providers – and the Women They Serve – in the Crosshairs*, 17 GUTTMACHER POL'Y REV. 9 (2014).

Borgmann, Caitlin E., *The Meaning of "Life": Belief and Reason in the Abortion Debate*, 18 COLUM. J. GENDER & L. 551 (2009).

Boyle, Edward Patrick, *It's Not Easy Bein' Green: The Psychology of Racism, Environmental Discrimination, and the Argument for Modernizing Equal Protection Analysis*, 46 VAND. L. REV. 937 (1993).

Cantor, Julie D., *Court-Ordered Care: A Complication of Pregnancy to Avoid*, 366 NEW ENG. J. MED. 2237 (2012).

Chemerinsky, Erwin & Michele Goodwin, *Abortion: A Woman's Private Choice*, 95 TEX. L. REV. 1189 (2017).

Cherry, April, *The Detention, Confinement, and Incarceration of Pregnant Women for the Benefit of Fetal Health*, 16 COLUM. J. GENDER & L. 147 (2007).

Cockrell, Phillip, *Pregnancy Disability Benefits and Title VII: Pregnancy Does Not Involve Sex?*, 29 BAYLOR L. REV. 257 (1977).

Coleman, Harriet Hubacker, *Barefoot and Pregnant – Still: Equal Protection for Women in Light of* Geduldig v. Aiello, 16 S. TEX. L.J.211 (1975).

Crenshaw, Kimberlé, *Demarginalizing the Intersection of Race and Sex: A Black Feminist Critique of Antidiscrimination Doctrine, Feminist Theory and Antiracist Politics*, 1989 U. CHI. LEGAL F. 139.

Crenshaw, Kimberle, *From Private Violence to Mass Incarceration: Thinking Intersectionally About Women, Race, and Social Control* 59 UCLA L. REV. 1418 (2012).

Crimm, Nina J., *The Global Gag Rule: Undermining National Interests by Doing unto Foreign Women and NGOs What Cannot Be Done at Home*, 40 CORNELL INT'L L.J. 587 (2007)

De Ville, Kenneth A. & Loretta M. Kopelman, *Fetal Protection in Wisconsin's Revised Child Abuse Law: Right Goal, Wrong Remedy*, J.L. MED. & ETHICS 332(1999).

Doetzer, Geraldine, *Hard Labor: The Legal Implications of Shackling Female Inmates During Pregnancy and Childbirth*, 14 WM. & MARY J. WOMEN & L. 365 (2008).

Dripps, Donald et al., *Panel Discussion: Men, Women and Rape*, 63 FORDHAM L. REV. 125 (1994).

Fentiman, Linda, *The New "Fetal Protection": The Wrong Answer to the Crisis of Inadequate Health Care for Women and Children*, 84 DENV. U. L. REV. 537 (2006).

Fentiman, Linda, *Pursuing the Perfect Mother: Why America's Criminalization of Maternal Substance Abuse Is Not the Answer – A Comparative Legal Analysis*, 15 MICH. J. GENDER & L. 389 (2009).

Ferrell, Ruth, *The Equal Rights Amendment to the United States Constitution – Areas of Controversy*, 6 URB. L. 853 (1974).

Figdor, Emily & Lisa Kaeser, *Concerns Mount over Punitive Approaches to Substance Abuse Among Pregnant Women*, 1 GUTTMACHER POL'Y REV., Oct. 1998.

Fineman, Martha, *Images of Mothers in Poverty Discourses*, 1991 DUKE L.J. 274.

Fox, James W. Jr., *Doctrinal Myths and the Management of Cognitive Dissonance: Race, Law, and the Supreme Court's Doctrinal Support of Jim Crow*, 34 STETSON L. REV. 293 (2005).

Getman, Karen. A, *Sexual Control in the Slaveholding South: The Implementation and Maintenance of a Racial Caste System*, 7 HARV. WOMEN'S L.J. 115 (1984).

Ginsburg, Ruth Bader, *Gender and the Constitution*, 44 U. CIN. L. REV. 1 (1975).

Ginsburg, Ruth Bader, *Gender in the Supreme Court: the 1973 and 1974 Terms*, 1975 SUP. CT. REV. 1.

Ginsburg, Ruth Bader, *Some Thoughts on Autonomy and Equality in Relation to* Roe v. Wade, 63 N.C.L. REV. 375 (1985).

Godsil, Rachel D., *Remedying Environmental Racism*, 90 MICH. L. REV. 394 (1991).

Gold, Rachel Benson, *Lessons from Before* Roe: *Will Past Be Prologue?*, 6 GUTTMACHER POL'Y REV. 8 (2003).

Goldfarb, Phyllis, *Counting the Drug War's Female Casualties*, 6 J. GENDER RACE & JUST. 277 (2002).

Goodwin, Michele, *Fetal Protection Laws: Moral Panic and the New Constitutional Battlefront*, 102 CAL. L. REV. 781 (2014).

Goodwin, Michele, *Law's Limits: Regulating Statutory Rape Law*, 2013 WISC. L. REV. 481.

Goodwin, Michele, *Marital Rape: The Long Arch of Sexual Violence Against Women and Girls*, 109 AJIL UNBOUND 326 (2016).

Goodwin, Michele, *Prosecuting the Womb*, 76 GEO. WASH. L. REV. 1657 (2008).

Goodwin, Michele, *When Institutions Fail: The Case of Underage Marriage in India*, 62 DEPAUL L. REV. 357 (2013).

Goodwin, Michele & Allison Whelan, *Reproduction and the Rule of Law in Latin America*, 83 FORDHAM L. REV. 2577 (2015).

Graber, Mark A., *Rethinking Equal Protection in Dark Times*, 4 U. PA. J. CONST. L. 314 (2002).

Gray, Karen F.B., *An Establishment Clause Analysis of* Webster v. Reproductive Health Services, 24 GA. L. REV. 399, 418 (1990).

Griggs, Claire, *Birthing Barbarism: The Unconstitutionality of Shackling Pregnant Prisoners*, 20 AM U. J. GENDER SOC. POL'Y & L. 247 (2011).

Guttmacher, Alan F., *Law, Morality, and Abortion*, 22 RUTGERS L. REV. 415 (1967).

Haddad, Lisa B. & Nawal M. Nour, *Unsafe Abortion: Unnecessary Maternal Mortality*, 2 REV. OBSTETRICS & GYNECOLOGY 122 (2009).

Hamilton, Vivian E., *The Age of Marital Capacity: Reconsidering Civil Recognition of Adolescent Marriage*, 92 BOS. L. REV. 1817 (2012).

Hasday, Jill Elaine, *Contest and Consent: A Legal History of Marital Rape*, 88 CALIF. L. REV. 1373 (2000).

Healy, Michael P., *The Preemption of State Hazardous and Solid Waste Regulations: The Dormant Commerce Clause Awakens Once More*, 43 WASH. U. J. URB. & CONTEMP. L. 177 (1993).

Humphreys, Janice C. & William O. Humphreys, *Mandatory Arrest: A Means of Primary and Secondary Prevention of Abuse of Female Partners*, 10 VICTIMOLOGY 267 (1985).

Kanin, Eugene, *Date Rape: Unofficial Victims and Criminals*, 9 VICTIMOLOGY 95 (1984).

Larson, Jane. E, *"Even a Worm Will Turn at Last": Rape Reform in Late Nineteenth-Century America*, 9 YALE J.L. & HUMAN. 1 (1997).

Lavelle, Marianne & Marcia Coyle, *The Federal Government, in Its Cleanup of Hazardous Sites and Its Pursuit of Polluters, Favors White Communities Over Minority Communities Under Environmental Laws Meant to Provide Equal Protection for All Citizens, a National Law Journal Investigation Has Found*, 15 NAT'L. L.J., Sept. 21, 1992, at S2.

Law, Sylvia A., *Rethinking Sex and the Constitution*, 132 U. PA. L. REV. 955 (1984).

Lazarus, Richard, *Pursuing Environmental Justice: The Distributional Effects of Environmental Justice*, 87 NW. U. L. REV. 787 (1993).

Levi, Robin et al., *Creating the Bad Mother: How the US Approach to Pregnancy in Prisons Violates the Right to Be a Mother*, 18 UCLA WOMEN'S L.J. 1 (2010).

Loue, Sana, *Legal and Epidemiological Aspects of Child Maltreatment: Toward an Integrated Approach*, 19 J. LEGAL MED. 471 (1998).

MacKinnon, Catharine, *Reflections on Sex Equality Under Law*, 100 YALE L.J. 1281 (1991).

Murphy, Jane, *Legal Images of Motherhood: Conflicting Definitions from Welfare "Reform," Family, and Criminal Law*, 83 CORNELL L. REV. 688 (1998).

Murray, Pauli & Mary O. Eastwood, *Jane Crow and the Law: Sex Discrimination and Title VII*, 34 GEORGE WASH. L. REV. 232 (1965).

Nourse, Victoria & Gregory Shaffer, *Varieties of New Legal Realism: Can a New World Order Prompt a New Legal Theory*, 95 CORNELL L. REV. 61 (2009).

Oberman, Michelle, *Mothers and Doctors' Orders: Unmasking the Doctor's Fiduciary Role in Maternal-Fetal Conflicts*, 94 NW. U. L. REV. 453 (1999–2000).

Ocen, Priscilla A., *Punishing Pregnancy: Race, Incarceration and the Shackling of Pregnant Prisoners*, 100 CAL. L. REV. 1239 (2012).

Paltrow, Lynn M., *Pregnant Drug Users, Fetal Persons, and the Threat to* Roe v. Wade, 62 ALB. L. REV. 999 (1999).

Paltrow, Lynn M. & Jeanne Flavin, *Arrests of and Forced Interventions on Pregnant Women in the United States, 1973–2005: Implications for Women's Legal Status and Public Health*, 38 J. HEALTH POL. POL'Y & L. 299 (2013).

Partington, Donald H., *The Incidence of the Death Penalty for Rape in Virginia*, 22 WASH. & LEE L. REV. 43 (1965).

Peach, Lucinda J., *From Spiritual Descriptions to Legal Prescriptions: Religious Imagery of Woman as "Fetal Container" in the Law*, 10 J.L. & RELIGION 73 (1994).

Pleck, Elizabeth, *Criminal Approaches to Family Violence, 1640–1980*, 11 CRIME & JUST. 19 (1989).

Ratnayake, Ann, *The Confrontation Clause After* Ohio v. Clark: *The Path to Reinvigorating Evidence-Based Prosecution of Intimate Partner Violence Cases*, 84 GEORGE WASH. L. REV. ARGUENDO 18 (2016).

Roberts, Dorothy, *Prison, Foster Care, and the Systemic Punishment of Black Mothers*, 59 UCLA L. REV. 1474 (2012).

Roberts, Dorothy, *Punishing Drug Addicts Who Have Babies: Women of Color, Equality, and the Right of Privacy*, 104 HARV. L. REV. 1419 (1991).

Rosen, Kenneth M., *Fiduciaries*, 58 ALA. L. REV. 1041 (2005).

Rowan, Andrea, *Prosecuting Women for Self-Inducing Abortion: Counterproductive and Lacking Compassion*, 18 GUTTMACHER POL'Y REV. 70 (2015).

Saks, Stephen, *The "Constitution in Exile" as a Problem for Legal Theory* 89 NOTRE DAME L. REV. 2253 (2014).

Scott, Austin W., *The Fiduciary Principle*, 37 CAL. L. REV. 539 (1949).

Scott, Charity, *Why Law Pervades Medicine: An Essay on Ethics in Health Care*, 14 NOTRE DAME J. L. ETHICS & PUB. POL'Y 245 (2000).

Shaw, Jessica, Full-Spectrum Reproductive Justice: The Affinity of Abortion Rights and Birth Activism, 7 STUD. IN SOC. JUST. 143 (2013).

Siegel, Reva B., *Reasoning from the Body: A Historical Perspective on Abortion Regulation and Questions of Equal Protection*, 44 STAN. L. REV. 261 (1992).

Siegel, Reva B., *"The Rule of Love": Wife Beating as Prerogative and Privacy*, 105 YALE L.J. 2117 (1996).

Siegel, Reva, *Why Equal Protection No Longer Protects: The Evolving Forms of Status-Enforcing State Action*, 49 STAN. L. REV. 1111.

Siegel, Neil S. & Reva Siegel, *Equality Arguments for Abortion Rights*, 60 UCLA L. REV. DISC. 160 (2013).

Smith, Robert J. & Justin D. Levinson, *The Impact of Implicit Racial Bias on the Exercise of Prosecutorial Discretion*, 35 SEATTLE U. L. REV. 795 (2012).

Spohn, Cassia C. & Julie Horney, *The Impact of Rape Law Reform on the Processing of Simple and Aggravated Rape Cases*, 86 J. CRIM. L. & CRIMINOLOGY 861 (1996).

Suter, Sonia, *Bad Mothers or Struggling Mothers?*, 42 RUTGERS L. J. 695 (2011).

Torres, Gerald, *Race, Class, and Environmental Regulation*, 63 U. COLO. L. REV. 839 (1992).

Van Detta, Jeffrey A., *Constitutionalizing* Roe, Casey *and* Carhart: *A Legislative Due-Process Anti-Discrimination Principle that Gives Constitutional Content to the "Undue Burden" Standard of Review Applied to Abortion Control Legislation*, 10 S. CAL. REV. L. & WOMEN'S STUD. 211 (2001).

Walsh, Michael. G, Annotation, *Criminal Responsibility of Husband for Rape, or Assault to Commit Rape, on Wife*, 24 A.L.R. 4TH 105 (1983).

Welch, Donna M., *Mandatory Arrest of Domestic Abusers: Panacea or Perpetuation of the Problem of Abuse*, 43 DePaul L. Rev.1133 (1994).

West, Robin, *Equality Theory, Marital Rape, and the Promise of the Fourteenth Amendment*, 42 Fla. L. Rev. 45 (1990).

Zaher, Claudia, *When a Woman's Marital Status Determined Her Legal Status: A Research Guide on the Common Law Doctrine of Coverture*, 94 L. Libr. J. 459 (2002).

6.2 Medical and Health Journals

ACOG Committee on Obstetric Practice, *Management of Stillbirth*, 113 Obstetrics & Gynecology 749 (2009).

ACOG Committee on Obstetric Practice, *Committee Opinion: Cesarean Delivery on Maternal Request*, 121 Obstetrics & Gynecology 904 (2013).

Annas, George J., *The Legacy of the Nuremberg Doctors' Trial to American Bioethics and Human Rights*, 10 Minn. J. L. Sci. & Tech. 13 (2009).

Annas, George J., *Pregnant Women as Fetal Containers*, 16 Hastings Ctr. Rep. 13 (1986).

Annas, George J., *Protecting the Liberty of Pregnant Patients*, 316 New Eng. J. Med. 1213 (1987).

Arria. Amelia M. et al., *Drug Treatment Completion and Post-Discharge Employment in the TOPPS-II Interstate Cooperative Study Treatment*, 25 J. Substance Abuse Treatment 9 (2003).

Biggs, M.A., *Does Abortion Reduce Self-Esteem and Life Satisfaction?*, 23 Quality Life Res. 2505 (2014).

Bendavid, Eran, Patrick Avila & Grant Miller, *United States Aid Policy and Induced Abortion in Sub-Saharan Africa*, 89 Bull. World Health Org. 873 (2011).

Biggs, M. Antonia et al., *Women's Mental Health and Well-Being 5 Years After Receiving or Being Denied an Abortion: A Prospective, Longitudinal Cohort Study*, 74 JAMA Psychiatry 169 (2017).

Brender, Jean D. & John S. Griesenbeck, *Hazardous Waste Sites, Industrial Facilities, and Adverse Pregnancy Outcomes in Dallas, Denton, and Tarrant Counties, 1997–2000* Tex. A&M Sch. Rural Pub. Health 1 (2008).

Bullock, L.F. & J. McFarlane, *Higher Prevalence of Low Birthweight Infants Born to Battered Women*, 89 Am. J. Nursing 1153 (1989).

Carter, Carolyn S., *Perinatal Care for Women Who Are Addicted: Implications for Empowerment*, 27 Health & Soc. Work 166 (2002).

Campbell, Jacquelyn C., *Health Consequences of Intimate Partner Violence*, 359 Lancet 1331 (2002).

Centers for Disease Control & Prevention, *Infant Mortality Rates, by Race and Hispanic Ethnicity of Mother – United States, 2000, 2005, and 2009*, 62 MMWR 90 (2013).

Chance, Graham W., *Neonatal Intensive Care and Cost Effectiveness*, 139 Canadian Med. Ass'n J. 943 (1988).

Chasnoff, Ira J. et al., *The Prevalence of Illicit Drug or Alcohol Use During Pregnancy and Discrepancies in Mandatory Reporting in Pinellas Country, Florida*, 322 New Eng. J. Med. 1202 (1990).

Cheyney, Melissa et al., *Development and Validation of National Data Registry for Midwife-Led Births: The Midwives Alliance of North America Statistics Project 2.0*, 59 J. Midwifery & Women's Health 8 (2014).

Cheyney, Melissa et al., *Outcomes of Care for 16,484 Planned Home Births in the United States: The Midwives Alliance of North America Statistics Project, 2004–2009*, 59 J. MIDWIFERY & WOMEN'S HEALTH 17 (2014)

Coeytaux, Francine, et al., *Maternal Mortality in the United States: A Human Rights Failure*, 83 CONTRACEPTION 189 (2011).

Conner, Kenneth R. et al., *Low-Planned Suicides in China*, 35 PSYCHOLOGICAL MED. 1197 (2005).

Council on Scientific Affairs, American Medical Association, *Violence Against Women: Relevance for Medical Practitioners*, 267 JAMA 3184 (1992).

de Jonge, A. et al., *Perinatal Mortality and Morbidity in a Nationwide Cohort of 529,688 Low-Risk Planned Home and Hospital Births*, 116 BJOG 1177 (2009).

DeLee, Joseph B., *Progress Toward Ideal Obstetrics, Speech at Sixth Annual Meeting of the American Association for Study and Prevention of Infant Mortality (Nov. 11, 1915)*, in 73 AM. J. OF OBSTETRICS & DISEASES OF WOMEN & CHILDREN, 407 (1916).

DiFranza, Joseph R. et al., *Legislative Efforts to Protect Children from Tobacco*, 257 JAMA 3387 (1987).

Di Mauro, Diane & Carole Joffe, *The Religious Right and the Reshaping of Sexual Policy: An Examination of Reproductive Rights and Sexuality Education*, 4 SEXUALITY RES. AND SOC. POL'Y: J. NAT'L SEXUALITY RES. CTR. 67 (2007).

Duncan, Renae et al., *Childhood Physical Assault as a Risk Factor for PTSD, Depression, and Substance Abuse: Findings from a National Survey*, 66 AM. J. ORTHOPSYCHOL. 437 (1996).

Edwards, Marc, *Fetal Death and Reduced Birth Rates Associated with Exposure to Lead-Contaminated Drinking Water*, 48 ENVTL. SCI. & TECH. 730 (2014).

Ernhart, Claire B. et al., *Intrauterine Exposure to Low Levels of Lead: The Status of the Neonate*, 41 ARCHIVES ENVTL. HEALTH 287 (1986).

Ferszt, Ginette Gosselin, *Giving Birth in Shackles: It's Time to Stop Restraining Pregnant Inmates During Childbirth*, 110 AM. J. NURSING 11 (2010).

Finer, Lawrence B. et al., *Declines in Unintended Pregnancy in the United States, 2008–2011*, 374 NEW ENG. J. MED. 843 (2016).

Flanders-Stepans, Mary Beth, *Alarming Racial Differences in Maternal Mortality*, 9 J. PERINATAL EDUC. 50 (2000).

Flenady, Victoria et al., *Major Risk Factors for Stillbirth in High-Income Countries: A Systemic Review and Meta-Analysis*, 337 LANCET 1331 (2011).

Frank, Deborah A. et al., *Growth, Development, and Behavior in Early Childhood Following Prenatal Cocaine Exposure*, 285 JAMA 1613 (2001).

Fullerton, J.T. et al., *Outcomes of Planned Home Birth: An Integrative Review*, 52 J. MIDWIFERY & WOMEN'S HEALTH 323 (2007).

Gazmararian, J.A. et al., *Prevalence of Violence Against Pregnant Women: A Review of the Literature*, 275 JAMA 1915 (1996).

Gazmararian, J.A. et al., *Violence and Reproductive Health: Current Knowledge and Future Research Directions*, 4 MATERNAL CHILD HEALTH J. 79 (2000).

Geppert, Cynthia M.A. & Laura Weiss Roberts, *Protecting Patient Confidentiality in Primary Care*, 3 SEMINARS IN MED. PRAC. 7 (2000).

Greene, Tom & Claire B. Ernhart, *Prenatal and Preschool Age Lead Exposure: Relationship with Size*, 13 NEUROTOXICOLOGY & TERATOLOGY 417 (1991).

Grimes, D.A., *Estimation of Pregnancy-Related Mortality Risk by Pregnancy Outcome, United States, 1991 to 1999*, 194 AM. J. OBSTETRICS & GYNECOLOGY 92 (2006).

Goldenberg, R.L. et al., *Stillbirth: A Review*, 16 J. OF MATERNAL-FETAL & NEONATAL MED. 79 (2004).

Holmes, M.M. et al., *Rape-Related Pregnancy: Estimates and Descriptive Characteristics from a National Sample of Women*, 175 Am. J. Obstetrics & Gynecology 320 (1996).

Hurt, Hallam et al., *Children With and Without Gestational Cocaine Exposure: A Neurocognitive System Analysis*, 31 Neurotoxicology & Teratology 334 (2009).

Hurt, Hallam et al., *Children with In Utero Cocaine Exposure Do Not Differ from Control Subjects on Intelligence Testing*, 151 Archives Pediatric Adolescent Med., 1237 (1997).

Hurt, Hallam et al., *A Prospective Comparison of Developmental Outcome of Children with In Utero Cocaine Exposure and Controls Using the Battelle Developmental Inventory*, 22 J. Developmental & Behav. Pediatrics 21 (2001).

Hurt, Hallam et al., *School Performance of Children with Gestational Cocaine Exposure*, 27 Neurotoxicology & Teratology 203 (2011).

Hutton, E. et al., *Outcomes Associated with Planned Home and Hospital Births in Low-Risk Women Attended by Midwives in Ontario, Canada, 2003–2006: A Retrospective Cohort Study*, 36 Birth 180 (2009).

Janssen, P., *Outcomes of Planned Home Birth with Registered Midwife Versus Planned Hospital Birth with Midwife or Physician*, 181 Canadian Med. Ass'n J. 377 (2009).

Kindler, Kenneth, *Childhood Sexual Abuse and Adult Psychiatric and Substance Use Disorders in Women*, 57 Archives Gen. Psychiatry 953 (2000).

Kornhauser, Michael & Roy Schneiderman, *How Plans Can Improve Outcomes and Cut Costs for Preterm Infant Care*, ManagedCare (Jan. 1 2010), http://www.managedcaremag .com/archives/1001/1001.preterm.html.

Larson, Charles, *Poverty During Pregnancy: Its Effects on Child Health Outcomes*, 12 J. Pediatric Child Health 673 (2007).

LeBolt, S.A., D.A. Grimes & W. Cates, Jr., *Mortality from Abortion and Childbirth: Are the Populations Comparable?*, 248 JAMA 188 (1982).

Lombardo, Paul, *Phantom Tumors and Hysterical Women: Revising Our View of the Schloendorff Case*, J.L. Med. & Ethics 791 (2005).

Lyons, Peter & Barbara Rittner, *The Construction of the Crack Babies Phenomenon as a Social Problem*, 68 Am. J. Orthopsychiatry 313 (1998).

MacDorman, Marian F. et al, *Recent Increases in the U.S. Maternal Mortality Rate: Disentangling Trends from Measurement Issues*, 128 Obstetrics & Gynecology 447 (2016).

Malacrida, Claudia, *Complicated Mourning: The Social Economy of Perinatal Death*, 9 Qualitative Health Res. 504 (1999).

May, Philip A. & Phillip Goassage, *Maternal Risk Factors for Fetal Alcohol Spectrum Disorders*, 34 Alcohol Res. & Health 16 (2011).

Mitchell, Allen A. et al., *Medication Use During Pregnancy, with Particular Focus on Prescription Drugs: 1976–2008*, 250 Am. J. Obstetrics Gynecology 50 (2011).

Murphy, Claire C. et al., *Abuse: A Risk Factor for Low Birth Weight? A Systematic Review and Meta-Analysis*, 164 Canadian Med. Ass'n J. 1567 (2001).

Nagahawatte, N. Tanya & Robert. Goldenberg, *Poverty, Maternal Health, and Adverse Pregnancy Outcomes*, 1136 Annals N.Y. Acad. Sci. 80, 81 (2008).

Paley, Blair & Mary J. O'Connor, *Intervention for Individuals with Fetal Alcohol Spectrum Disorders: Treatment Approaches and Case Management*, 15 Developmental Disabilities Res. Revs. 258 (2009).

Paltrow, Lynn M., *Roe v. Wade and the New Jane Crow: Reproductive Rights in the Age of Mass Incarceration*, 103 Am. J. Pub. Health 17 (2013).

Paulson, Margaret & Anthony H. Dekker, *Healthcare Disparities in Pain Management*, 105 J. Am. Osteopathic Ass'n S14 (Supp. 3 2005).

Pearson, Veronica, *Goods on Which One Loses: Women and Mental Health in China*, 41 SOC. SCI. & MED. 1159 (1995).

Pearson, Veronica, *Ling's Death: An Ethnography of a Chinese Woman's Suicide*, 32 SUICIDE & LIFE-THREATENING BEHAV. 347 (2002).

Peretti, P.O., *Holiday Depression in Young Adults*, 23 PSYCHOLOGIA 251 (1980).

Phillips, Michael R. et al., *Risk Factors for Suicide in China: A National Case-Control Psychological Autopsy Study*, 360 LANCET 1728 (2002).

Putnam, Frank, *Ten-Year Research Update Review: Child Sexual Abuse*, 42 J. AM. ACAD. CHILD & ADOLESCENT PSYCHIATRY 269 (2003).

Raymond, Elizabeth G. & David Grimes, *The Comparative Safety of Legal Induced Abortion and Childbirth in the United States*, 119 J. OBSTETRICS & GYNECOLOGY 215 (2012).

Richardson, Chinué Turner & Elizabeth Nash, *Misinformed Consent: The Medical Accuracy of State-Developed Abortion Counseling Materials*, 9 GUTTMACHER POL'Y REV. 6 (2006).

Robinson, Sharon A., *A Historical Development of Midwifery in the Black Community: 1600–1940*, 29 J. NURSE-MIDWIFERY 247 (1984).

Rocca, Corinne H. et al., *Decision Rightness and Emotional Responses to Abortion in the United States: A Longitudinal Study*, 10 PLoS ONE (July 8, 2015).

Sandall, Jane et al., *Midwife-Led Continuity Models Versus Other Models of Care for Childbearing Women*, COCHRANE DATABASE SYSTEMIC REV., no. 4, 2016.

Sansone, Randy et al., *The Christmas Effect on Psychopathology*, 8 INNOVATIONS IN CLINICAL NEUROSCI. 10 (2011).

Sheppard, Vanessa B. et al., *Providing Health Care To Low-Income Women: A Matter Of Trust*, 21 FAMILY PRACTICE 484 (2004).

Silver, Robert M. et al., *Work-Up of Stillbirth: A Review of the Evidence*, 196 AM. J. OBSTETRICS & GYNECOLOGY 433 (2007).

Sims, Melissa A. & Kim A. Collins, *Fetal Death: A 10-Year Retrospective Study*, 22 AM. J. FORENSIC MED. & PATHOLOGY 261 (2001).

Smulian, John C. et al., *Fetal Deaths in the United States: Influence of High-Risk Conditions and Implications for Management*, 100 OBSTETRICS & GYNECOLOGY 1183 (2002).

Stanger-Hall, Kathrin F. & David W. Hall, *Abstinence-Only Education and Teen Pregnancy Rates: Why We Need Comprehensive Sex Education in the U.S.*, 6 PLoS ONE (2011).

Stevenson, Amanda J. et. al., *Effect of Removal of Planned Parenthood from the Texas Women's Health Program*, 374 NEW ENG. J. MED. 853 (2016).

Stillbirth Collaborative Research Network Writing Group, *Association Between Stillbirth and Risk Factors Known at Pregnancy Confirmation*, JAMA 2470 (2011).

Thornton, Terry E. & Lynn Paltrow, *The Rights of Pregnant Patients: Carder Case Brings Bold Policy Initiatives*, 8 HEALTHSPAN 10 (1991).

Turney, Kristin, *Stress Proliferation Across Generations? Examining the Relationship Between Parental Incarceration and Childhood Health*, 55 J. HEALTH & SOC. BEHAV. 302 (2014).

Velamoor, V. et al., *Feelings About Christmas, as Reported by Psychiatric Emergency Patients*, 27 SOC. BEHAV. & PERSONALITY 303 (1999).

Ventura, Stephanie J. et al., *Trends and Variations in Smoking During Pregnancy and Low Birth Weight: Evidence from the Birth Certificate, 1990–2000*, 111 PEDIATRICS 1176 (2003).

Wallace, John M., Jr., *The Social Ecology of Addiction: Race, Risk, and Resilience*, 103 PEDIATRICS 1122 (1999).

Warren, Kenneth R. et al. *Fetal Alcohol Spectrum Disorders: Research Challenges and Opportunities*, 34 ALCOHOL RES. & HEALTH 4 (2011).

Wisborg, K. et al., *Psychological Stress During Pregnancy and Stillbirth: Prospective Study*, 115 BRIT J. OBSTETRICS & GYNAECOLOGY 882 (2008).

Yip, Paul S.F.F. & Ka Y. Liu, *The Ecological Fallacy and the Gender Ratio of Suicide in China*, 189 BRIT. J. PSYCHIATRY 465 (2006).

6.3 *Other Periodicals*

Abel, Gene et al., *Self-Reported Sex Crimes of Nonincarcerated Paraphiliacs*, 2 J. INTERPERS. VIOLENCE 3 (1987).

Akrich, Madeleine et al., *Practising Childbirth Activism: A Politics of Evidence*, PAPIERS DE RECHERCHE DU CSI/CSI WORKING PAPER SERIES NO. 023 (2012).

Barr, Kellie E.M. et al., *Race, Class, and Gender Differences in Substance Abuse: Evidence of Middle Class/Underclass Polarization Among Black Males*, 40 SOC. PROBS. 314 (1993).

Becket, Katherine, *Choosing Cesarean: Feminism and the Politics of Childbirth in the United States*, 6 FEMINIST THEORY 251 (2005).

Bilchik, Shay, *Mentoring: A Promising Intervention for Children of Prisoners*, 10 RES. IN ACTION 1 (2007).

Cocca, Carolyn E., *Prosecuting Mrs. Robinson? Gender, Sexuality, and Statutory Rape Laws*, 16 MICH. FEMINIST STUD. 61 (2002).

Condon, Charles, *Clinton's Cocaine Babies*, 72 POL'Y REV. (Apr. 1, 1995).

Davis-Floyd, Robbie, *Anthropology and Birth Activism: What Do We Know?*, ANTHROPOLOGY NEWS 37 (May 2005).

Gellman, Lauren, *Female-Headed Households and the Welfare System*, POVERTY & PREJUDICE: SOCIAL SECURITY AT THE CROSSROADS, June 4, 1999.

Gilliam, Franklin D., Jr., *The "Welfare Queen" Experiment: How Viewers React to Images of African American Mothers on Welfare*, NIEMAN REP., Summer 1999.

Jones, Kelly M., *Contraceptive Supply and Fertility Outcomes: Evidence from Ghana*, 64 ECON. DEV. & CULTURAL CHANGE 31 (2015).

Karch, Debra L. et al., *Surveillance for Violent Deaths – National Violent Death Reporting System, 16 States, 2009*, MORBIDITY & MORTALITY WKLY. REP., SURVEILLANCE SUMMARIES 61 (6), Sept. 14, 2013.

Kong, Augustine et al., *Rate of De Novo Mutations and the Importance of Father's Age to Disease Risk*, 488 NATURE 471 (2012).

Lang, Ariel J., Murray B. Stein, Colleen M. Kennedy & David W. Foy, *Adult Psychopathology and Intimate Partner Violence Among Survivors of Childhood Maltreatment*, 19 J. INTERPERS. VIOLENCE 1102 (2004).

Lisak, David & Paul M. Miller, *Repeat Rape and Multiple Offending Among Undetected Rapists*, 17 VIOLENCE AND VICTIMS 73 (2002).

MacKinnon, Catharine A., *Feminism, Marxism, Method, and the State: Toward Feminist Jurisprudence*, 8 SIGNS 635 (1983).

Man, Coramae Richey & Lance H. Selva, *The Sexualization of Racism: The Black as Rapist and White Justice*, 3 W. J. BLACK STUD. 171 (1979).

Mazzella, Ronald & Alan Feingold, *The Effects of Physical Attractiveness, Race, Socioeconomic Status and Gender of Defendants and Victim's on-Judgments of Mock Jurors*, 24 J. APPLIED SOC. PSYCHOL. 1315 (1994).

McCabe, Sean Esteban et al., *Race/Ethnicity and Gender Differences in Drug Use and Abuse Among College Students*, 6 J. ETHNICITY SUBSTANCE ABUSE, no. 2 (2008).

Schieve, Laura A. et al., *Use of Assisted Reproductive Technology – United States, 1996 and 1998*, 51 MORBIDITY & MORTALITY WKLY. REP. 97 (2002).

7 NEWSPAPER ARTICLES AND MEDIA SOURCES

$5 M Settlement in Hysterectomy Trial, ABC NEWS, Sept. 17, 2009.

Aaronson, Becca, *House Approves Abortion Restrictions*, TEX. TRIB., July 10, 2013.

Abortion Access Under Attack in 2013, ACLU, http://www.aclu.org/maps/states-where-they-think-were-stupid-abortion-access-under-attack-2013.

About Us, WHOLE WOMAN'S HEALTH, https://wholewomanshealth.com/about-us/.

Aghajanian, Liana, *Los Angeles Midwives Aim to End Racial Disparities at Birth*, ALJAZEERA AM., Sept. 5, 2015.

A Guide to the Allegations Made by Women Against Donald Trump, CHI. TRIB., Oct. 15, 2016.

Aguilar, Rose, *Utah Governor Signs Controversial Law Charging Women and Girls with Murder for Miscarriages*, ALTERNET, Mar. 9, 2010.

Alesia, Mark, *Lawsuit: Former Marion County Jail Inmate Denied His Cancer Treatment*, INDYSTAR (Jun. 18, 2018), https://www.indystar.com/story/news/2018/06/18/prison-medical-care-marion-county-jail-correct-care-solutions/637068002/.

Allen, Ellen, *Breast Cancer Behind Bars: One Woman's Story*, REWIRE NEWS (Oct. 24, 2014, 4:25 PM), http://rhrealitycheck.org/article/2014/10/24/breast-cancer-behind-bars-one-womans-story/.

Amar, Akhil Reed, *The Troubling Reason the Electoral College Exists*, TIME, Nov. 8, 2016.

Am. Coll. of Obstetricians & Gynecologists, *FAQ: Cesarean Birth* (May 2018), https://www.acog.org/Patients/FAQs/Cesarean-Birth.

Am. Pregnancy Ass'n, *Abusing Prescription Drugs During Pregnancy*, http://www.americanpregnancy.org/pregnancyhealth/abusingprescriptiondrugs.html.

Andrews, Travis & Fred Barbash, *Father Who "Repeatedly Raped His 12-Year Old Daughter" Gets 60-Day Sentence. Fury Erupts.*, WASH. POST, Oct. 19, 2016.

Angell, Marcia & Michael Greene, Opinion, *Where Are the Doctors?*, USA TODAY (last updated May 15, 2012, 6:36 PM), http://www.usatoday.com/news/opinion/forum/story/2012-05-15/women-contraception-abortion-reproductive-rights-doctors/54979766/1.

Anthony, Kontji, *Police: Woman Earns DUI for Endangering Fetus*, WMCTV (June 30, 2013), http://www.wmcactionnews5.com/story/20525700/police-pregnant-woman-earns-dui-for-endangering-fetus/.

Ashley, Keith, *Voters in the Georgia GOP Primary Will Vote on Personhood*, PERSONHOOD USA (May 22, 2012), http://cm.personhoodusa.com/voters-georgia-gop-primary-will-vote-personhood.

Associated Press, *Court to Hear Case of Woman Accused in Stillbirth*, JACKSON FREE PRESS, Apr. 1, 2013.

Associated Press, *Kansas Law Maker Compares Abortion to Holocaust*, WICHITA EAGLE (Mar. 9, 2015), http://www.kansas.com/news/politics-government/article13112999.html.

Attiah, Karen, *Why Won't the U.S. Ratify the U.N.'s Child Rights Treaty?*, WASH. POST (Nov. 21, 2014), https://www.washingtonpost.com/blogs/post-partisan/wp/2014/11/21/why-wont-the-u-s-ratify-the-u-n-s-child-rights-treaty.

Bader, Eleanor J., *Criminalizing Pregnancy: How Feticide Laws Made Common Ground for Pro-and Anti-Choice Groups*, TRUTHOUT (Jun. 14, 2012), https://truthout.org/articles/criminalizing-pregnancy-how-feticide-laws-made-common-ground-for-pro-and-anti-choice-groups/.

Bassett, Laura, *More Abortion Laws Enacted in Past Three Years Than in Entire Previous Decade*, HUFFINGTON POST (Jan. 3, 2014, 12:21 PM), http://www.huffingtonpost.com/2014/01/03/states-abortion-laws_n_4536752.html.

Bassett, Laura, *North Dakota Personhood Measure Passes State Senate*, HUFFINGTON POST (Feb. 7, 2013, 5:24PM), http://www.huffingtonpost.com/2013/02/07/north-dakota-personhood_n_2640380.html.

Bassett, Laura, *Paul Ryan Cosponsors New Fetal Personhood Bill*, HUFFINGTON POST, Jan. 9, 2013.

Bassett, Laura, *Trent Franks: "The Incidence of Rape Resulting in Pregnancy Are Very Low,"* HUFFINGTON POST (June 12, 2013), http://www.huffingtonpost.com/2013/06/12/trent-franks-rape-pregnancy_n_3428846.html.

Bates, Eric, *What You Need to Know About Jesse Helms*, MOTHER JONES (May–June 1995) http://www.motherjones.com/politics/1995/05/what-you-need-know-about-jesse-helms.

Bauerlein, Valerie, *North Carolina to Compensate Sterilization Victims*, WALL ST. J. (July 26, 2013), http://www.wsj.com/articles/SB10001424127887323971204578629943220881914.

Bazelon, Emily, *Obama's Executive Order on Abortion*, SLATE, Mar. 21, 2010.

Becker, Daniel, *Georgia Legislature Passes Nation's First Embryo Adoption Law*, CHRISTIAN NEWS WIRE (Apr. 3, 2009), http://www.christiannewswire.com/news/630359951.html.

Belkin, Lisa, *Is Refusing Bed Rest a Crime?*, N.Y. TIMES (Jan. 12, 2010, 12:50 PM), http://parenting.blogs.nytimes.com/2010/01/12/is-refusing-bed-rest-a-crime/.

Bender, Michael C. & Janet Hook, *Donald Trump's Lewd Comments About Women Spark Uproar*, WALL ST. J. (last updated Oct. 8, 2016, 12:43 AM), https://www.wsj.com/articles/donald-trumps-lewd-comments-about-women-spark-uproar-1475886118.

Bendery, Jennifer, *Michael Burgess: I Oppose Abortion Because Male Fetuses Masturbate*, HUFFINGTON POST (May 18, 2013), http://www.huffingtonpost.com/2013/06/18/michael-burgess-abortion_n_3459108.html.

Benen, Steve, *List of Trump's Women Accusers Continues to Grow*, MSNBC, Oct. 24, 2016.

Berzon, Alexandra, Joe Palazzolo & Charles Passy, *Video Puts Spotlight on Donald Trump's History of Lewd Comments*, WALL ST. J., Oct. 9, 2016.

Besharov, Douglas, *Crack Babies: The Worst Threat Is Mom Herself*, WASH. POST, Aug. 6, 1989, *reprinted at* http://www.welfareacademy.org/pubs/childwelfare/crackbabies-0889.shtml.

Black Men Tragic Victims of White Milwaukee Man's Gruesome Murder Spree, JET MAG., Aug. 12, 1991.

Blackmon, Douglas A., *An Interview with Eric Holder on Mass Incarceration*, WASH. MONTHLY: TEN MILES SQUARE, Feb. 11, 2014.

Blakeslee, Sandra, *Crack's Toll Among Babies: A Joyless View, Even of Toys*, N.Y. TIMES, Sept. 17, 1989.

Blinder, Alan, *North Carolina House Passes New Restrictions on Abortion*, N.Y. TIMES, July 12 2013.

Block, Jennifer, *Jailed for a Suicide Attempt*, DAILY BEAST, Apr. 12, 2013.

Block, John, *Siljander Expresses Anger Over O'Connor Nomination*, TOLEDO BLADE, July 9, 1981.

Bluestein, Greg, *Pew Study: Prison Recidivism Rates Remain High*, CNS NEWS, Apr. 13, 2011.

Boonstra, Heather D., *The Heart of the Matter: Public Funding of Abortion for Poor Women in the United States*, GUTTMACHER INST. (Mar. 5, 2007), https://www.guttmacher.org/about/gpr/2007/03/heart-matter-public-funding-abortion-poor-women-united-states.

Borchers, Callum, *Donald Trump to Megyn Kelly: I'm Sorry Not Sorry*, WASH. POST, May 17, 2016.

Broder, David S., *Jesse Helms, White Racist*, WASH. POST, (July 7, 2008, 12:00 AM), http://www.washingtonpost.com/wp-dyn/content/article/2008/07/06/AR2008070602321.html.

Brody, Jane, *Coming a Long Way on Smoking with a Long Way to Go*, N.Y. TIMES BLOG, Jan. 20, 2014.

Brown, David, *"Crack Baby" Theory Doubted*, WASH. POST, Mar. 28, 2001.

Bruck, Renee, *Judge: Made Decision with Tragic Result*, MADISON COURIER, Oct. 18, 2016.

Buckley, Madeline, *Former IU Student Charged With Raping 2 Women During Parties*, INDYSTAR, Sept. 16, 2015.

Buffardi, Danielle, *Benefits of a Vaginal Birth*, PREGNANCY ASS'N PREGNANCY BLOG, Feb. 3, 2012.

Byars, Mitchell, *Former CU Student Convicted of Boulder Rape Spared Prison Sentence*, DAILYCAMERA, Aug. 10, 2016.

Cadoff, Becca, *States Aim to Make the Grade When It Comes to Shackling Pregnant Prisoners*, ACLU BLOG OF RIGHTS (Mar. 31, 2011, 7:35 PM), http://www.aclu.org/blog/prisoners-rights-reproductive-freedom-womens-rights/states-aim-make-grade-when-it-comes.

Calhoun, Ada, *The Criminalization of Bad Mothers*, N.Y. TIMES, Apr. 25, 2012.

Celis, William, *Family Sought New Life Only to Find New Pain*, N.Y. TIMES, July 31, 1991.

Celizic, Mike, *Genarlow Wilson: "I'm Coming out a Man,"* TODAY NEWS, Oct. 29, 2007.

Chemaly, Soraya, *"Personhood" and the Punishment of All American Women*, FEM2.0 (Jan. 15, 2013), http://www.fem2pto.com/?p=17737.

Chemerinsky, Erwin, *Chemerinsky: What Will the Presidential Election Mean for SCOTUS?*, ABA J. (Sept. 6, 2016), http://www.abajournal.com/news/article/chemerinsky_what_will_the_coming_election_mean_for_scotus.

Chinese Immigrant Pleads Guilty in Baby's Death, ABC NEWS (Aug. 2, 2013).

Chung, Andrew, *Supreme Court Lifts Ban on Wisconsin's "Cocaine Mom" Law During Appeal*, REUTERS (July 7, 2017, 5:10 PM), https://www.reuters.com/article/us-usa-court-cocaine/supreme-court-lifts-block-on-wisconsin-cocaine-mom-law-during-appeal-idUSKBN19S2YX [https://perma.cc/BSB6-HHRZ].

CNN Wire Staff, *Akin Bows out of CNN Appearance at the Last Minute*, CNN (Aug. 21, 2012, 9:33 AM), http://www.cnn.com/2012/08/20/politics/campaign-wrap/index.html.

Collins, Jeff, *$84,000 is Low-Income in O.C.*, ORANGE COUNTY REG. (May 3, 2017, updated Oct. 30, 2018), https://www.ocregister.com/2017/05/03/84000-a-year-now-qualifies-as-low-income-in-high-cost-orange-county/.

Corless, Damian, *When a Wife Was Her Man's Chattel*, INDEPENDENT, Jan. 4, 2015.

Coster, Helen, *Are Pregnant Women's Rights at Risk?*, MARIE CLAIRE (May 30, 2012), http://www.marieclaire.com/world-reports/news/bei-bei-shuai-pregnant-suicide-attempt.

Crane-Murdoch, Sierra, *On Indian Land, Criminals Can Get Away with Almost Anything*, ATLANTIC, Feb. 22, 2013.

Crouse, Julia, *Initiative Seeking to Keep Inmates, Children Together*, CHAPEL HILL HERALD, Jan. 16, 2008.

Culp-Ressler, Tara, *In the Past 3 Years, We've Enacted More Abortion Restrictions Than During the Entire Previous Decade*, THINKPROGRESS, Jan. 2, 2014.

Davidson, Curt, *Emelle, Alabama: Home of the Nation's Largest Hazardous Waste Landfill*, http://www.umich.edu/~snre492/Jones/emelle.htm.

DelReal, Jose A. & Jenna Johnson, *Trump, Threatening Nearly a Dozen Sexual Assault Accusers, Vows to Sue*, WASH. POST, Oct. 22, 2016.

Depres, Esme, *U.S. Abortion Rights Fights*, BLOOMBERG NEWS, July 7, 2016.

DeVega, Chauncey, *Born of Slavery, the Electoral College Could Stand Against Racism in 2016 – And Stop Donald Trump*, SALON, Dec. 15, 2016.

Dickerson, John, *Arpaio's Jail Staff Cost Ambrett Spencer Her Baby, and She's Not the Only One*, PHOENIX NEW TIMES, Oct. 30, 2008.

Domonoske, Camila & Martha Ann Overland, *Across the Country, Crowds March in Protest Against Trump's Victory*, NPR, Nov. 9, 2016.

Donald Trump's Long Record of Degrading Women, N.Y. TIMES, Oct. 8, 2016.

Drummond, Tammerlin, *Mothers in Prison*, TIME, Oct. 29, 2000.

Eckholm, Erik, *Case Explores Rights of Fetus Versus Mother*, N.Y. TIMES, Oct. 24, 2013.

Eckholm, Erik, *Voters in Mississippi to Weigh Amendment on Conception as the Start of Life*, N.Y. TIMES, Oct. 26, 2011.

Editorial, *Time to End the Electoral College*, N.Y. TIMES, Dec. 19, 2016.

Editorial, *Fitful Progress in the Antismoking Wars*, N.Y. TIMES, Jan. 9, 2014.

Einhorn, Bruce, *Suicide: China's Great Wall of Silence*, BLOOMBERG, Nov. 1, 2004.

Elstein, Aaron, *Not-So-Fine Moments in Accounting History*, WALL ST. J. ONLINE (last updated Jan. 23,2002, 12:01 AM), http://online.wsj.com/article/SB1011734437826162440.html.

Ertelt, Steven, *Texas Law Banning Abortions After 20 Weeks Still Intact Despite Supreme Court Decision*, LIFENEWS.COM, June 27, 2016.

Europe's Deadly Cold Snap Maintains Grip, BBC NEWS, Dec. 3, 2010.

Ex-Nantucket Man Gets Year in Jail for Raping Child, WCVB, Sept. 21, 2016.

Fahrenthold, David A., *Trump Recorded Having Extremely Lewd Conversation About Women in 2005*, WASH. POST, Oct. 8, 2016.

Farber, Madeline, *Why White Women Voted for Donald Trump*, FORTUNE (Nov. 30, 2016), https://fortune.com/2016/11/30/why-white-women-voted-trump/.

Fernandez, Manny, *Abortion Restrictions Become Law in Texas, but Opponents Will Press Fight*, N.Y. TIMES, July 18, 2013.

Fernandez, Manny, *Texas Woman Is Taken Off Life Support After Order*, N.Y. TIMES, Jan. 26, 2014.

Fernandez, Manny & Erik Eckholm, *Court Upholds Texas Limits on Abortions*, N.Y. TIMES, June 9, 2015.

Fernandez, Manny & Erik Eckholm, *Pregnant, and Forced to Stay on Life Support*, N.Y. TIMES, Jan. 8, 2014.

Fessler, Pam, *Report: Foster Kids Face Tough Times After Age 18*, NPR (Apr. 7, 2010, 12:01 AM), http://www.npr.org/templates/story/story.php?storyId=125594259.

Fewer Abortion Clinics in Texas, N.Y. TIMES, June 10, 2015.

Fingerhut, Hannah, *On Abortion, Persistent Divides Between – and Within – the Two Parties*, PEW RES. CTR., Apr. 8, 2016.

Finkelman, Paul, *Original Sin: The Electoral College as a Pro-Slavery Tool*, L.A. REV. OF BOOKS, Dec. 19, 2016.

FitzGerald, Susan, *"Crack Baby" Study Ends with Unexpected but Clear Result*, PHILA. INQUIRER, July 22, 2013.

Flegenheimer, Matt & Maggie Haberman, *Donald Trump, Abortion Foe, Eyes "Punishment" for Women, Then Recants*, N.Y. TIMES, Mar. 30, 2016.

Florida Officer Resigns Months After Handcuffed Woman at Hospital Dies, CBS NEWS, June 1, 2016.

French, Howard W., *Single Mothers in China Force a Difficult Path*, N.Y. TIMES, Apr. 6, 2008.

Frieden, Terry, *Study Finds Nearly 1 in 10 State Prisoners is Sexually Abused While Incarcerated*, CNN, May 17, 2012.

Friedersdorf, C., *Working Mom Arrested for Letting Her 9-Year-Old Play Alone at Park*, ATLANTIC (July 15, 2014), http://www.theatlantic.com/national/archive/2014/07/arrested-for-letting-a-9-year-old-play-at-the-park-alone/374436.

Friedman, Emily, *U.S. Hospitals and the Civil Rights Act of 1964*, HOSPS. & HEALTH NETWORKS DAILY (June 3, 2014), http://www.hhnmag.com/articles/4179-u-s-hospitals-and-the-civil-rights-act-of-1964.

Gaston, E., *Conway Homicide Case Sets Precedent*, SUN NEWS, May 18, 2001, at A1.

Georgia's "Defender of Life," GEORGIA RIGHT TO LIFE, http://www.grtl.org/?q=node/174.

Goldstein, Joseph, *U.S. Soldiers Told to Ignore Sexual Abuse of Boys by Afghan Allies*, N.Y. TIMES (Sep. 20, 2015), https://www.nytimes.com/2015/09/21/world/asia/us-soldiers-told-to-ignore-afghan-allies-abuse-of-boys.html.

Goodman, Ellen, *Just How Far Can the State Go in Protecting an "Unborn" Child?*, BOS. GLOBE, Sept. 10, 2000, at F7.

Goodnough, Abby, *Flint Weights Scope of Harm to Children Caused by Lead in Water*, N.Y. TIMES, Jan. 29, 2016.

Governor Cuomo Signs Legislation Ending Child Marriage in New York, N.Y. STATE (June 20, 2017).

Greene, Sharon, *Regina McKnight Released from Prison*, CAROLINALIVE.COM, June 19, 2008.

Greenhouse, Steven, *Capping the Cost of Atrocity: Survivor of Nazi Experiments Says $8,000 Isn't Enough*, N.Y. TIMES, Nov. 19, 2003.

Greenwood, Arin, *"One Strike" Public Housing Policy Hits Virginia Woman Who Needs Kidney Transplant*, HUFFINGTON POST, Dec. 22, 2011.

Grimaldi, Christine, *Trump Unveils "Vicious" Women's Health Restrictions During "Women's Health Week,"* REWIRE NEWS, May 18, 2017.

Hallett, Stephanie, *8 Stories That Show What Abortion Was Like Before* Roe v. Wade, Ms. MAGAZINE BLOG, Jan. 19, 2016.

Hauser, Christine, *Recordings Add Detail in Death of Woman Forced from Florida Hospital*, N.Y. TIMES, Jan. 7, 2016.

Hart, Carl, *The Real Opioid Emergency*, N.Y. TIMES (Aug. 18, 2017), https://www.nytimes.com/2017/08/18/opinion/sunday/opioids-drugs-race-treatment.html.

Hartley-Parkinson, Richard, *Two Rapists Jailed for Just 40 Months Each Because a Judge Said Their 11-Year-Old Victim Was "Willing,"* DAILY MAIL, Feb. 22, 2012.

Hauser, Christine, *Judge's Sentencing in Massachusetts Sexual Assault Case Reignites Debate on Privilege*, N.Y. TIMES, Aug. 24, 2016.

Hauslohner, Abigail, *Kabul, Afghanistan: When Women Set Themselves on Fire*, TIME, July 7, 2010.

Hawkins, Derek, *Tennessee Judge, Under Fire, Pulls Offer to Trade Shorter Jail Sentences for Vasectomies*, WASH. POST (Jul. 28, 2017), https://www.washingtonpost.com/news/morning-mix/wp/2017/07/28/tennessee-judge-under-fire-pulls-offer-to-trade-shorter-jail-sentences-for-vasectomies/?noredirect=on&utm_term=.c4782cfa4d21.

Hayes, Kevin, *Did Christine Taylor Take Abortion into Her Own Hands?*, CBS NEWS, Mar. 2, 2010.

Henderson, N.M., *Debra Harrell Back on Her Job at McDonald, Lawyer Says*, WASH. POST, July 24, 2014.

Herbert, Bob, *Poor Black and Dumped On*, N.Y. TIMES, Oct. 5, 2006.

Hill, Lee, *Teens, Sex and the Law: Genarlow Wilson*, NPR, June 12, 2007.

Hoffman, Jan, *When Men Hit Women*, N.Y. TIMES MAGAZINE, Feb. 16, 1992.

Holley, Peter, *Judge Admits His Decision in Domestic-Abuse Case had "the Most Tragic Result Possible,"* WASH. POST, Oct. 20, 2016.

Hopkins, Ellen, *Childhood's End: What Life Is Like for Crack Babies*, ROLLING STONE, Oct. 18, 1990.

Huie, William Bradford, *The Shocking Story of Approved Killing in Mississippi*, LOOK MAGAZINE, Jan. 24, 1956.

Ingraham, Christopher, *Toddlers Have Shot at Least 50 People This Year*, WASH. POST, Oct. 20, 2016.

"I Was Scared": Woman Accused of Killing her Unborn Baby by Drinking Rat Poison Speaks Out Ahead of Murder Trial as her Lawyer Insists it was a Suicide Attempt, DAILY MAIL ONLINE, Apr. 25, 2013.

Izadi, Elahe, *Denied an Abortion, 11-Year-Old Rape Victim in Paraguay Gives Birth*, WASH. POST (Aug. 14, 2015) https://www.washingtonpost.com/news/worldviews/wp/2015/08/14/denied-an-abortion-11-year-old-rape-victim-in-paraguay-gives-birth.

Jacobs, Ben, Sabrina Siddiqui & Scott Bixby, *"You Can Do Anything": Trump Brags on Tape About Using Fame to Get Women*, GUARDIAN, Oct. 8, 2016.

Jackson, Janine, *The Myth of the "Crack Baby," Despite Research, Media Won't Give Up Idea of "Bio-Underclass,"* FAIRNESS & ACCURACY IN REPORTING, Sept. 1, 1998.

James, Susan Donaldson, *Pregnant Woman Fights Court-Ordered Best Rest*, ABC NEWS (Jan. 14, 2010), http://abcnews.go.com/Health/florida-court-orders-pregnant-woman-bed-rest-medical/story?id=9561460.

Johnson, Corey G., *Female Prison Inmates Sterilized Illegally, California Audit Confirms*, Center for Investigative Reporting, REVEAL NEWS (Jun. 19, 2014), https://www.revealnews.org/article/female-prison-inmates-sterilized-illegally-california-audit-confirms/.

Kay, Jane & Cheryl Katz, *Pollution, Poverty, People of Color: The Factory on the Hill*, ENVTL. HEALTH NEWS, June 4, 2012.

Kelkar, Kamala, *Electoral College is "Vestige" of Slavery, Say Some Constitutional Scholars*, PBS, Nov. 6, 2016.

Kenney, Kara, *Inmates Sleeping on Floor at Marion County Jail*, RTV6, THEINDYCHANNEL (Oct. 17, 2017), https://www.theindychannel.com/news/call-6-investigators/inmates-sleeping-on-floor-at-marion-county-jail.

Kerby, Sophia, *The Top 10 Most Startling Facts About People of Color and Criminal Justice in the United States*, CTR. FOR AM. PROGRESS, Mar. 13, 2012.

Koh, Elizabeth, *He Was Charged with Two Rapes and Spent One Day in Jail*, CHARLOTTE OBSERVER, June 27, 2016.

Kolata, Gina, *Bias Seen Against Pregnant Addicts*, N.Y. TIMES, July 20, 1990.

Krauthammer, Charles, *Worse Than "Brave New World": Newborns Permanently Damaged by Cocaine*, PHILA. INQUIRER, Aug. 1, 1989.

Krieg, Gregory, *It's Official: Clinton Swamps Trump in Popular Vote*, CNN, Dec. 22, 2016.

Kristof, Nicholas, *11 Years Old, A Mom, and Forced to Marry Her Rapist*, N.Y. TIMES, May 26, 2017.

Kristof, Nicholas, *Women as a Force for Change*, N.Y. TIMES, July 31, 2013.

Kristof, Nicholas, *Women's Rights: Why Not?*, N.Y. TIMES (June 18, 2002), http://www.nytimes.com/2002/06/18/opinion/women-s-rights-why-not.html.

Kulczyk, Georgie, *Blake Receives Suspended Sentence for Sex Crime*, GLASGOW COURIER, Oct. 12, 2016.

Kurtz, Dayna M., *We Have a Child-Care Crisis in This Country. We Had the Solution 78 Years Ago*, WASH. POST (July 23, 2018), https://www.washingtonpost.com/news/posteverything/wp/2018/07/23/we-have-a-childcare-crisis-in-this-country-we-had-the-solution-78-years-ago/?noredirect=on&utm_term=.246e347185bf.

Kurtzleben, Danielle, *1 More Woman Accuses Trump of Inappropriate Sexual Conduct. Here's the Full List*, NPR, Oct. 20, 2016.

Lacayo, Richard, *Down on the Downtrodden*, TIME, Dec. 18, 1994.

La Ganga, Maria L., *Most Abortion Clinics in Texas Will Be Forced to Close Under Court Ruling*, L.A. TIMES (Oct. 2, 2014, 9:38 PM), http://www.latimes.com/nation/la-na-texas-abortion-20141002-story.html.

Law, Victoria, *How Many Women Are in Prison for Defending Themselves Against Domestic Violence*, BITCH MEDIA, Sept. 16, 2014.

Law, Victoria, *"You Go Through it Alone": New Bill Would Keep Incarcerated Pregnant Women from Being Put in Medical Isolation*, REWIRE NEWS, Mar. 22, 2019.

Le Coz, Emily, *Mississippi Stillborn Manslaughter Charge Raising Fears*, USA TODAY, May 29, 2013.

Lee, Jacqueline, *Woman Testifies Against Former Stanford All-Star Swimmer Accused of Sexually Assaulting Her*, MERCURY NEWS, Mar. 18, 2016.

Levin, Sam, *No Prison for Colorado College Student Who "Raped a Helpless Young Woman,"* GUARDIAN, Aug. 10, 2016.

Levin, Sam, *Stanford Sexual Assault: Read the Full Text of the Judge's Controversial Decision*, GUARDIAN, June 14, 2016.

Lilliston, Lynn, *Abortion Coalition Fighting for Right to Decide*, L.A. TIMES, June 19, 1974.

Liptak, Adam, *Prisons Often Shackle Pregnant Inmates in Labor*, N.Y. TIMES, Mar. 2, 2006.

Liss-Schultz, Nina, *A Judge Struck Down the "Cocaine Mom" Law That Put Pregnant Women in Jail*, MOTHER JONES (May 1, 2017), https://www.motherjones.com/politics/2017/05/tamara-loertscher-unborn-child-protection-wisconsin-pregnant-jail/3/.

Lopez, Elwyn, *Raped 11-Year-Old Stirs an Abortion Debate in Chile*, CNN NEWS, July 11, 2013.

Love, Lindsay, *A Dangerous Initiative: "Personhood" Measure Being Pushed in Montana*, WOMEN ARE WATCHING BLOG (June 5, 2012), http://www.womenarewatching.org/article/a-dangerous-initiative-personhood-measure-being-pushed-in-montana.

Luck, Melissa, *Born Behind Bars: Inmates Raising Children in Prison*, KXLY, Sept. 9, 2011.

Madera, Melissa, *6 Women Share Their Harrowing Stories of Illegal Abortion Before Roe v. Wade*, VICE NEWS (Jan. 22, 2018, 11:23 AM), https://broadly.vice.com/en_us/article/43qm5d/6-women-share-their-harrowing-stories-of-illegal-abortion-before-roe-v-wade.

Martin, Nina, *Black Mothers Keep Dying After Giving Birth: Shalon Irving's Story Explains Why*, NPR, Dec. 7, 2017.

Martin, Nina, *The State That Turns Pregnant Women into Felons*, ALTERNET (Sept. 23, 2015), https://www.alternet.org/drugs/when-womb-crime-scene.

Mayer, Jane, *Documenting Trump's Abuse of Women*, NEW YORKER, Oct. 24, 2016.

Mazelis, Joan Maya, *Punishing the Poor Isn't Just Bad Policy, It's Wasting Taxpayer Money*, THE HILL, Feb. 20, 2018.

McDonald, S.N., *Shanesha Taylor, Arrested for Leaving Children in Car During Job Interview, Speaks*, WASH. POST (June 23, 2014), http://www.washingtonpost.com/news/morning-mix/wp/2014/06/23/shanesha-taylor-arrested-for-leaving-children-in-car-during-job-interview-speaks/.

McMahon, Colin, *Race Kept Cry for Help from Being Heard, Some in Milwaukee Say*, CHI. TRIB., July 28, 1991.

Mehta, Sarah, *There's Only One Country That Hasn't Ratified the Convention on Children's Rights: U.S.*, ACLU (Nov. 20, 2015, 1:30 PM), https://www.aclu.org/blog/human-rights/treaty-ratification/theres-only-one-country-hasnt-ratified-convention-childrens.

Miller, Michael E., *"A Steep Price to Pay for 20 Minutes of Action": Dad Defends Stanford Sex Offender*, WASH. POST, June 6, 2016.

Mills, Shamane, *Opponents of Wisconsin's "Cocaine Mom" Law Continue Fight*, WIS. PUB. RADIO (Aug. 1, 2018), https://www.wpr.org/opponents-wisconsins-cocaine-mom-law-continue-fight.

Myers, Steven Lee, *A Paradox for Helms on an Abortion Issue*, N.Y. TIMES (Aug. 1, 1997), http://www.nytimes.com/1997/08/01/us/a-paradox-for-helms-on-an-abortion-issue.html.

Neil, Martha, *Pregnant Pro Se Mom Argued Treatment Case from Hospital Bed & Lost; Will Lawyer Win Appeal?*, ABA J,. Jan. 26, 2010.

Nelson, Paula, *Raised Behind Bars*, BOS. GLOBE, Dec. 14, 2012.

Netburn, Deborah, *After Texas Stopped Funding Planned Parenthood, Low-Income Women Had More Babies*, L.A. TIMES, Feb. 3, 2016.

Newman, Susan, *Mothers with One Child Are Happiest*, PSYCHOL. TODAY, Feb. 5, 2010.

Nichols, Bryan, *Burlington Woman Will Not Be Charged with Feticide*, RADIO IOWA, Feb. 10, 2010.

Nositer, Adam, *In Alabama, a Crackdown on Pregnant Drug Users*, N.Y. TIMES, Mar. 15, 2008.

Novack, Sophie, *Texas' Maternal Mortality Rate: Worst in Developed World, Shrugged Off by Lawmakers*, TEX. OBSERVER, June 5, 2017.

Ogletree, Charles J., Jr., Opinion, *Condemned to Die Because He's Black*, N.Y. TIMES, July 31, 2013.

Page, Clarence, *College Loans Are Casualties in Drug War*, CHI. TRIB., Apr. 29, 2001.

Paquette, Danielle, *Why Pregnant Women in Mississippi Keep Dying*, WASH. POST: WONKBLOG, Apr. 24, 2015.

Parker, Suzi, *Arkansas Senate Passes "Fetal Heartbeat" Law to Ban Most Abortions*, REUTERS, Jan. 31,2013.

Pear, Robert, *Birth Control Mandate to Apply to Self-Insuring Religious Groups*, N.Y. TIMES, Mar. 16, 2012, at A14.

Peterson, James Braxton, *America's Mass Incarceration System: Freedom's Next Frontier*, REUTERS: THE GREAT DEBATE, July 24, 2015.

Peterson, Zack, *Former Hamilton County Bus Driver Won't Serve Jail Time After Pleading Guilty to Raping Student*, TIMES FREE PRESS, July 22, 2016.

Pickler Memorial Library, *Harry H. Laughlin Papers*, TRUMAN STATE UNIV., http://library.truman.edu/manuscripts/laughlinindex.asp.

Pieklo, Jessica Mason, *Murder Charges Dismissed in Mississippi Stillbirth Case*, REWIRE NEWS (Apr. 4, 2014), https://rewire.news/article/2014/04/04/murder-charges-dismissed-mississippi-stillbirth-case/.

Pieklo, Jessica Mason, *Pregnant Wisconsin Woman Jailed Under State's "Personhood"-Like Law*, REWIRE NEWS (Dec. 12, 2014), https://rewire.news/article/2014/12/12/pregnant-wisconsin-woman-jailed-states-personhood-like-law/.

Pilane, Pontshoe, *Loophole Could Protect South African Organisations from US Gag Rule on Abortions*, BHEKISISA, Nov. 16, 2017.

Pilgrim, David, *What Was Jim Crow?*, FERRIS STATE UNIV. (last edited 2012), http://www.ferris.edu/jimcrow/what.htm.

Pilkington, Ed, *Alone in Alabama: Dispatches from an Inmate Jailed for Her Son's Stillbirth*, GUARDIAN (Oct. 7, 2015), https://www.theguardian.com/us-news/2015/oct/07/alabama-chemical-endangerment-pregnancy-amanda-kimbrough.

Pilkington, Ed, *Indiana Prosecuting Chinese Woman for Suicide Attempt That Killed Her Foetus*, GUARDIAN, May 30, 2012.

Pill, *Anthony Comstock's "Chastity" Laws*, PBS, http://www.pbs.org/wgbh/amex/pill/peopleevents/e_comstock.html.

Pollitt, Katha, *The Story Behind the Maternal Mortality Rate in Texas Is Even Sadder than We Realize*, NATION, Sept. 8, 2016.

Porter, Bekah, *Dubuquer Gives Birth Alone in Jail Cell*, TELEGRAPH HERALD, May 15, 2009.

Quackenbush, Casey, *The Impact of President's Trump's "Global Gag Rule" on Women's Health Is Becoming Clear*, TIME (Feb. 1, 2018, updated Feb. 4, 2018).

Race Tilts the Scales of Justice. Study: Dallas Punishes Attacks on Whites More Harshly, DALLAS TIMES HERALD, Aug. 19, 1990.

Ravitz, Jessica, *Maternal Deaths Fall Across Globe but Rise in US, Doubling in Texas*, CNN, Apr. 17, 2018.

Ravitz, Jessica, *Two States Passed Abortion Amendments to Their Constitutions in The Midterm: What Does That Mean*, CNN (Nov. 7, 2018, 5:25PM), https://www.cnn.com/2018/11/07/health/abortion-ballot-measures-amendments/index.html.

Re, Richard M., *The New Supreme Court and the Jurisprudence in Exile*, PrawfsBlawg, Feb. 17, 2016.

Reagan, Mark, *HB2 Increasing Wait Times for Women Seeking Abortion Services*, San Antonio Current, Oct. 6 2015.

Resnick, Sofia, *Texas Proposed Law Could Jail Women for Taking Drugs During Pregnancy*, Am. Indep. (Feb. 24, 2011, 3:30 PM), http://www.americanindependent.com/171004/texas-proposed-law-could-jail-women-for-taking-drugs-during-pregnancy.

Richardson, Robin Y., *Marion County Inmates Sue over Jail Conditions*, Longview News Journal (Oct. 1, 2016), https://www.news-journal.com/news/police/marion-county-inmates-sue-over-jail-conditions/article_8ead079c-60dc-5670-9e9b-bce899224238.html.

Ritchie, Carrie, *Murder Charge Raises Women's Rights Questions*, USA Today (Jan. 6, 2013, 12:18 AM), www.usatoday.com/story/news/nation/2013/01/05/infants-death-raises-womens-rights-questions/1566070/.

Rivas, Jorge, *California Prisons Caught Sterilizing Female Inmates Without Approval*, ABC News (Jul. 8, 2013), https://abcnews.go.com/ABC_Univision/doctors-california-prisons-sterilized-female-inmates-authorizations/story?id=19610110.

Rizzo, Jessica, *Native American Women Are Rape Targets Because of a Legislative Loophole*, Vice News, Dec. 15, 2015.

Roberts, Dan & Karen McVeigh, *Eric Holder Unveils New Reforms Aimed at Curbing US Prison Population*, Guardian, Aug. 12, 2013.

Robertson, Campbell, *South Carolina Judge Vacates Conviction of George Stinney in 1944 Execution*, N.Y. Times, Dec. 17, 2014.

Rogin, Josh, *Who Killed the Bill to Prevent Forced Marriages?*, Wash. Post, Dec. 22, 2010.

Rood, Lee, *"I Never Said I Didn't Want My Baby": Mom Won't Be Prosecuted*, Des Moines Reg., Feb. 10, 2010.

Rovner, Julie, *Abortion Foes Push to Redefine Personhood*, Nat'l. Pub. Radio (June 1, 2011) http://www.npr.org/2011/06/01/136850622/abortion-foes-push-to-redefine-personhood.

Rovner, Julie, *Woman Who Tried to Commit Suicide While Pregnant Gets Bail*, Nat'l Pub. Radio, May 18, 2012.

Rucker, Philip, *Trump says Fox's Megyn Kelly Had "Blood Coming out of Her Wherever,"* Wash. Post, Aug. 8, 2015.

Sanchez, Ray & Amanda Watts, *Montana Judge Defends 60-day Sentence in Child Incest Case*, CNN, Oct. 25, 2016.

Saul, Heather, *Afghan Woman Raped, Impregnated and Jailed for "Adultery by Force" Marries Her Attacker*, Independent (Apr. 8, 2015, 2:28 PM), https://www.independent.co.uk/news/world/middle-east/afghan-woman-raped-impregnated-and-jailed-for-adultery-by-force-mar ries-her-attacker-10162694.html.

Schneider, Keith, *Minorities Join to Fight Polluting Neighborhoods*, N.Y. Times, Oct. 25, 1991, at A20.

Schwab, Kyle, *Women Who Accused Fired Cop Daniel Holtzclaw of Sexual Assault Are a Long Way from Resolving Lawsuits*, NewsOK, Nov. 5, 2018.

Schwartz, John, *Texas Senate Approves Strict Abortion Measure*, N.Y. Times, July 13, 2013.

Senior, Jennifer, *Review: Megyn Kelly Tells Tales out of Fox News in Her Memoir, "Settle for More,"* N.Y. Times, Nov. 10, 2016.

Severson, Kim, *Thousands Sterilized, a State Weighs Restitution*, N.Y. Times, Dec. 9, 2011, at A1.

Share Our Wealth, Huey Long: The Man, His Mission, and Legacy, https://www.hueylong.com/programs/share-our-wealth.php.

Shea, Brie, *Here Are All the Anti-Abortion Laws Going into Effect Next Month*, Rewire News (June 28, 2019), https://rewire.news/article/2019/06/28/here-are-all-the-anti-abortion-laws-going-into-effect-next-month/.

Sher, Andy, *Tennessee Judge Ends Controversial Sentence Reduction Program for Inmates Choosing Birth Control*, Times Free Press (Jul. 28, 2017), https://www.timesfreepress.com/news/local/story/2017/jul/28/tennessee-judge-ends-sentence-reductiprogram/440713/.

Shirk, Martha, *Domestic Violence Is a Leading Hazard for Women*, St. Louis Post Dispatch, May 6, 1992, at 10A.

Silva, Daniella, *Shackled and Pregnant: Wis. Case Challenges "Fetal Protection" Law*, NBC News, Oct. 24, 2013.

Silver-Greenberg, Jessica & Natalie Kitroeff, *Miscarrying at Work: The Physical Toll of Pregnancy Discrimination*, N.Y. Times, Oct. 21, 2018.

Silver-Greenberg, Jessica & Natalie Kitroeff, *Pregnancy Discrimination Is Rampant Inside America's Biggest Companies*, N.Y. Times, June 15, 2018.

Sklar, Rachel, *Women Know Why Donald Trump's Accusers Stayed Silent for So Long*, Wash. Post, Oct. 18, 2016.

Smalley, Suzanne, *Should Female Inmates Raise Their Babies in Prison?*, Newsweek, May 13, 2009.

Smith, Chuck, *The Case Against Jesse Helms*, Wall St. J., Sept. 4, 2001.

Smith, Jordan, *Updated: Senate Passes House Bill 2: Rejected Amendments, Dramatic Speeches, and Finally a Vote*, Austin Chron., July 12, 2013.

Smith, Morgan et al., *Abortion Bill Finally Bound for Perry's Desk*, Tex. Trib., July 13, 2013.

Solis, Maria, *Here's What the Trump Administration's Proposed Title X Rule Would Do to Abortion Access in America*, Newsweek, May 2, 2018.

Sommerville, Quentin, *Woman Stoned to Death in North Afghanistan*, Rawa News, Jan. 27, 2011.

Stack, Liam, *Light Sentence for Brock Turner in Stanford Rape Case Draws Outrage*, N.Y. Times, June 6, 2016.

Stallings, Erika, *This Is How the American Healthcare System Is Failing Black Women*, Oprah Mag., Oct. 2018.

Stanford University Ranks No. 1 on Forbes' 9th Annual Ranking of America's Top Colleges, Forbes, July 5, 2016.

Stein, Letitia, *USF Obstetrician Threatens to Call Police if Patient Doesn't Report for C-Section*, Tampa Bay Times, Mar. 6, 2013.

Stingl, Jim, *Cleveland Tried to Stop Dahmer from Killing*, Milwaukee J. Sentinel, Jan. 4, 2011.

Stryker, Jeff, *Cracking Down*, Salon, July 10, 1998.

Tavernise, Sabrina, *List of Smoking-Related Illnesses Grows Significantly in U.S. Report*, N.Y. Times, Jan. 17, 2014.

Tennessee Sterilisations in Plea Deal for Women Evoke Dark Time in America, Guardian (Mar. 28, 2015), https://www.theguardian.com/us-news/2015/mar/28/tennessee-forced-sterilizations-plea-deals-women.

Texas Releases Abortion Booklet with Debunked Cancer Link, Suicide Risk Claim, CBS News, Dec. 6, 2016.

Thomas, Chanda R., *Why Is Genarlow Wilson in Prison?*, Atlanta, Jan. 2006.

Tuck, Angela, *Genarlow Wilson's Journey from Prison to Morehouse*, Atlanta J. Const., May 18, 2013.

Tuma, Mary, *Roe's End? Supreme Court Case Will Decide the Future of Abortion Access in the U.S.*, Austin Chron. (Jan. 29, 2016).

Tumulty, Karen, *Trump's History of Flippant Misogyny*, Wash. Post, Aug. 8, 2015.

Ura, Alexa & Jolie McCullogh, *Once Again, the Texas Legislature Is Mostly White, Male, Middle-Aged*, Tex. Trib., Jan. 9, 2017.

U.S. *"Most Dangerous" Place to Give Birth in Developed World, USA Today Investigation Finds*, CBS News, July 26, 2018.

Van Tassel, Priscilla, *Schools Trying to Cope with "Crack Babies,"* N.Y. Times, Jan. 5, 1992.

Villarosa, Linda, *Why America's Black Mothers and Babies Are in a Life-or-Death Crisis*, N.Y. Times, Apr. 11, 2018.

Warnke, Melissa Batchelor, *It Takes a Village to Raise a Misogynistic Monster like Donald Trump*, L.A. Times, Oct. 8, 2016.

Wedge, Dave, *Judge Confines Cult Mom to Secure Hospital*, Bos. Herald, Sept. 1, 2000, *available at* 2000 WLNR 22748.

Weisberg, Jessica, *This Woman's Little-Known 1972 Case Could Have Reframed Abortion History*, Elle Mag. (Oct. 21, 2014), https://www.elle.com/culture/career-politics/a14816/susans-choice/.

Weiss, David, *Court Delivers Controversy*, Times Leader (Wilkes-Barre, PA), Jan. 16, 2004.

Weller, Sheila, *How Author Timothy Tyson Found the Woman at the Center of the Emmett Till Case*, Vanity Fair, Jan. 26, 2017.

Why It Matters, Women's Prison Ass'n, http://www.wpaonline.org/about/why-it-matters.

Wilkinson, Tracy, *El Salvador Jails Women for Miscarriages and Stillbirths*, L.A. Times (Apr. 15, 2015), http://www.latimes.com/world/great-reads/la-fg-c1-el-salvador-women-20150415-story.html.

Wilson, Charles, *Bei Bei Shuai Trial: Rat Poison Link to Newborn's Death "Unreliable," Judge Rules*, Huffington Post, Jan. 23, 2013.

Wilson, Charles, *Ind. Woman Rejects Plea Deal in Death of Newborn*, CBS News, July 13, 2013.

Winerip, Michael, *Revisiting the "Crack Babies" Epidemic That Was Not*, N.Y. Times, May 20, 2013.

Wing, Nick, *Final Popular Vote Total Shows Hillary Clinton Won Almost 3 Million More Ballots Than Donald Trump*, Huffington Post, Dec. 20, 2016.

Witchel, Alex, *At Home With: Norma McCorvey; Of Roe, Dreams and Choices*, N.Y. Times, July 28, 1994, http://www.nytimes.com/1994/07/28/garden/at-home-with-norma-mccorvey-of-roe-dreams-and-choices.html. *Women & the Drug War*, Drug War Facts, https://drug warfacts.org/taxonomy/term/45.

Woods, Lisa, *9 Older Women Share Their Harrowing Back Alley Abortion Stories*, Thought Catalog, Dec. 30, 2015.

Worthington, Rogers, *Could Police Have Saved Young Victim? – 911 Tapes Show Officers Were in Dahmer's Place, Left Teen to Fate*, Seattle Times (June 3, 2017), http://community.seattletimes.nwsource.com/archive/?date=19.

Wyler, Grace, *Personhood Movement Continues to Divide Pro-Life Activists*, Time (July 24, 2013), http://nation.time.com/2013/07/24/personhood-movement-continues-to-divide-pro-life-activists/.

Yeoman, Barry, *Surgical Strike: Is a Group That Pays Addicts to Be Sterilized Defending Children or Exploiting the Vulnerable?*, Mother Jones, Nov./Dec. 2001.

Young, Stephen, *Texas Women Face Long Abortion Waits in HB2's Wake*, Dallas Observer, Oct. 6, 2015.

Yuhas, Alan, *Woman Who Accused Donald Trump of Raping Her at 13 Drops Lawsuit*, Guardian, Nov. 5, 2016.

Zielinski, Alex, *The Growing List of Anti-Abortion Bills Texas Conservative Lawmakers Hope to Pass This Year*, San Antonio Current (Jan. 25, 2017), https://www.sacurrent.com/the-daily

/archives/2017/01/25/the-growing-list-of-anti-abortion-bills-texas-conservative-lawmakers-hope-to-pass-this-year.

Zielinski, Alex, *The Stanford Rapist's Father Offers an Impossibly Offensive Defense of His Son*, THINKPROGRESS, June 5, 2016.

Zucchino, David, *Sterilized by North Carolina, She Felt Raped Once More*, L.A. TIMES (Jan. 25, 2012), http://articles.latimes.com/2012/jan/25/nation/la-na-forced-sterilization-20120126.

8 FILMS

CONCENTRIC MEDIA, *When Abortion Was Illegal: Untold Stories*.

HAIMOWITZ, REBECCA, *62 Days*

TAMARKIN, CIVIA, *Birthright*

9 VIDEOS

Terry Curry Discusses the Bei Bei Shuai Case, USA TODAY, http://usatoday30.usatoday.com/video/terry-curry-discusses-the-bei-bei-shuai-case/2119743594001.

10 OTHER SOURCES

Background Paper, "From Prison to Home" Conference (Jan. 30–31, 2002), http://www.urban.org/UploadedPDF/410632_HHSConferenceBackground.pdf.

Goode, Keisha La'Nesha, Birthing, Blackness, and the Body: Black Midwives and Experiential Continuities of Institutional Racism (Oct. 1, 2014) (unpublished Ph.D. dissertation, City University of New York) (on file with author).

Holder, Eric, Att'y Gen., U.S. Dep't of Justice, Remarks at the Annual Meeting of the American Bar Association's House of Delegates (Aug. 12, 2013), http://www.justice.gov/opa/speech/attorney-general-eric-holder-delivers-remarks-annual-meeting-american-bar-associations.

McLemore, Monica, 2019 Sadie T.M. Alexander Commemorative Symposium: What Could The Future of Reproductive Justice [Look] Like?, University of Pennsylvania Law School (Feb. 9, 2019).

Memorandum from President Barack Obama on Mex. City Policy and Assistance for Voluntary Population Planning to the Sec'y of State and the Adm'r of the U.S. Agency for Int'l Dev., 74 Fed. Reg. 4903 (Jan. 28, 2009).

Memorandum from President Donald Trump on the Mex. City Policy to the Sec'y of State, the Sec'y of Health and Human Services, and the Adm'r of the U.S. Agency for Int'l Dev., 82 Fed. Reg. 8495 (Jan. 25, 2017).

Memorandum from President William J. Clinton on the Mex. City Policy to the Acting Adm'r of the U.S. Agency for Int'l Dev. (Jan. 22, 1993).

Nomination of Ruth Bader Ginsburg, to Be Associate Justice of the Supreme Court of the United States, 103d Cong. 150 (1993).

Nourse, Victoria, *History, Pragmatism, and the New Legal Realism* (Nov. 2005) (on file with the author).

Obama, Barack, President, Remarks at the NAACP Conference (July 14, 2015).

Santa Clara County District Attorney's Office, Press Release, Victim Impact Statement (June 2, 2016).

Transcript of Oral Argument, Ferguson v. City of Charleston, 532 U.S. 67 (2001) (No. 99-936).

United States of America, Policy Statement, at the United Nations International Conference on Population, 2d Sess., Mexico City (Aug. 6–14, 1984), *reprinted in* 10 Pop. & Dev. Rev. 574 (1984).

Index

Printed in the United States
by Baker & Taylor Publisher Services